The Theory of the Accommodation Based Consumerist Economic System

4th Edition

By Michael Salaniuk

ISBN 978-1-999475826

Self Published through Lulu.com 2022.
Oakville, Ontario, Canada.

Paperback available for purchase online at : https://lulu.com/spotlight/salaniukmichael

Comment and follow the commentary on this economic system at Michael Salaniuk's blog here:
https://accommodationbasedconsumeristesystem.blogspot.com/

Distribution Inquiries may be made here, and please email questions, comments, criticism and suggestions regarding this Economic System to Michael Salaniuk and his marketing team at :
tTotABCES@gmail.com

Watch for more information and developments, as well as criticize, make comments, present questions and make suggestions on the website at :
https://sites.google.com/view/ttotabces

Cover art by **Paul Tomas**: http://www.lulu.com/spotlight/tomaspaul
Formatting by **David Foster** : https://sites.google.com/site/vid932008/

9 781999 475826

Dedications

This book is dedicated to Valdimort for inspiring me.

Acknowledgements

I would like to thank my parents, Anna and Andrzej for their support. I also value the encouragement of my brother Tom and sister Andrea. Thanks also go out to Paul Tomas for his wonderful artistic contributions. David Foster contributed his formatting expertise as well.

About the Author

Michael Salaniuk is a theoretical economic philosopher from Oakville, Ontario, Canada. He was born in Opole, Poland in 1982 but moved to Canada with his family in 1989. He graduated with a Bachelor of Science degree from the University of Toronto in 2012. Michael is also interested with Mathematics, Philosophy, Physics and Psychology. He also likes to learn foreign languages. As a hobby he plays the guitar, mandolin and harmonica.

Table of Contents

Preface to the 4th Edition

The 4th edition of this book has many changes. There are many ideas that weren't included in the 3rd edition. There are over 80 new chapter-sections in the 4th edition that didn't appear in the 3rd edition. Thus the 4th edition of this book has many more ideas that weren't discussed in the 3rd edition.

In writing this book I have sometimes took occasion to repeat myself. When an idea was worthy of repetition it was good to mention it more than once. Ideas that were worthy of repeating were the ones that I decided to mention more than once.

The ideas presented in this book are given in a step-motherly fashion. That is, the following ideas are based on ideas that have been presented earlier. The sequence of concepts in this book are developed in a step by step fashion.

I took some effort in making this book "readable". By this I mean that I want this book to be accessible and available to a large audience. Although the book is meant for economists and those interested in economics, I also wanted this book to be available to casual readers.

I have tried in this book to omit extraneous writing. Everything in this book is essential to the understanding of the economic system. I have tried to omit information that is not necessary. This book could easily have ballooned to a 1200 page monster. I deliberately decided to write to the point. I included in this book only the most important information for the comprehension of how accommodation based consumerism works. Thus I was able to present all the most important information in about 500 pages. In this book there are no "filler" sentences or paragraphs. I did not add unnecessary material for the sole purpose of making the book longer. Thus everything written in this book has value and is pertinent to grasping accommodation based consumerism.

Accommodation based consumerism retains all the useful and beneficial concepts of socialism and free market capitalism. Thus it makes absolutely no sense to write something about or talk about "capitalist consumerism". Accommodation based consumerism has already extracted everything advantages about capitalism in its structure.

This book is full of reason and math. The reasoning is not difficult to understand thus making this book accessible to a large audience. The math is not very complex either. There is no calculus or advanced algebra. The math here is limited to arithmetic and simple algebra.

May the reader have many pleasant moments reading what follows.

Introduction

Dear distinguished economists, Honorable statesman and interested readers:

This is the solution to human poverty. It is a grand third alternative to capitalism and communism.

Currently there are two general theories regarding economic systems. On one side there is the capitalist free-market system and on the other there is the socialist command system. The free-market system is designed to benefit the "capitalists"- those who own the means of production. The socialist command system is designed to benefit the state- the community as a whole. Many of the countries under the free-market system in Africa (Chad, Madagascar) are impoverished and getting poorer. This is the strongest argument against the free-market system- it doesn't always work and it doesn't work everywhere. Then there is the dreaded business cycle of booms and recessions which has produced the infamous Great Depression, one of the greatest non-violent man made misery we ever created for ourselves. Many of the countries under the command system around the world (i.e. the U.S.S.R.) have had their economies collapse and were forced to change their economic system. This is the main argument against the command system. It will eventually collapse due to a lack of incentives. Experience has taught us that neither of these systems is perfect and that they each have their own problems.

Can we do better? Right now the free enterprise system is the best we can muster. The only alternative to it is some kind of socialist or communist system. Thus we are caught between a rock and a hard place. But there is a third alternative- *accommodation based consumerism*. Accommodation Based Consumerism is a third alternative to free-market and communist systems. Thus it is incorrect to categorize it as a purely socialist system just because it is not completely free enterprise.

The consumerist system, as its name suggests, is designed to benefit the consumerists- the class of people who consume goods and services. Since everyone is a consumerist, the system benefits everyone. The whole system revolves directly or indirectly around the consumerist to promote his interests. Yet it also promotes the other economic actors, namely producers, employers and investors. It is not a utopic invention. It is firmly rooted in reality, having all the ingredients and incentives to make it function. There are incentives for workers to work, employers to employ and investors to invest.

It makes little or no sense to dissolve the free-enterprise system in countries where it is working well. These countries include the U.S., France, Canada, Germany and Great Britain among others. Right now these nations do not need another economic system. Yet it is unknown whether the free-market system will eventually collapse sometime in the future or not. It would be good to have something to hold onto in case everything falls to pieces and we can't put the pieces back together again. Consumerism is good to keep as a device of last resort. Yet even now there are many dozens of countries worldwide that would flourish and prosper if they were given the methodology to do so. The consumerist economic system would lift these countries into economic splendour.

Accommodation based consumerism is not a political system. Although it is not a system about justice, consumerism has some things to say about laws and punishment. The system could work alongside almost any type of political structure with the exception of communism. It works well under democracy, parliamentary monarchy and even autocracy. Democracy and the free-market system, although they usually go hand in hand, are not inseparable. Many officials and policy makers try to defend the free-market system by defending democracy. Yet one is an economic system and the other is a political system. This fallacy is similar to defending cats by providing the virtues of dogs or talking about apples by speaking about bananas.

This treatise explains what accommodation based consumerism is, how it works and how it is to be applied to society. Many of the numbers and variables are exemplary and need not be followed exactly as set out. Although this will not be mentioned all the time, it is implied that the numbers provided are done so as to have an example to talk about. Other parts must necessarily be followed as prescribed. They will be noted accordingly. If certain areas do not work as intended, it may be necessary to make some adjustments.

I must now iterate what this system offers. It offers the end of poverty, hunger, homelessness, misery and all the ills that go along with them. The business cycle and the depressions and recessions that are tied to it are no more. There is no inflation (for the most part) and unemployment is low or nonexistent. Not only is it impossible for the stock market to collapse but all investors are guaranteed to make a profit in one of the stock markets. There are no taxes in the sense that we generally think of them. Those who purchase items are able to purchase the finest things available. Yet rights like private property are protected. There are incentives for firms to do business in the consumerist nation, employing workers in the process. In short, consumerism is not about the pursuit of happiness but about the actual attainment of it.

Prelude to the System

In order to do anything we need a place to start. Therefore to develop our system we must begin somewhere. Our system must have some grand purpose to satisfy and the system should satisfy that purpose.

What is the purpose of our system? The purpose is to increase the material wealth and quality of life of the people under the system. Such a setup offers the highest level of happiness. A traffic system of lights, roads and signs is designed to benefit automobile drivers. Who else? A political system whether it is democracy, monarchy, communism or autocracy is designed to benefit someone or a group of people. Who it benefits is different for each system.

Why should we strive under the system to benefit all the people with a high quality of life? A high quality of life is what everyone universally wants. Those who have a high quality of life and an abundance of material wealth enjoy life much more than people who do not.

Now that we have a place to start, the first question is: how do we increase the material wealth and quality of life of people? This is done by giving people goods and services and giving them enough leisure time to enjoy these. We will use the term possessions to denote property, food and objects. By services we mean such things as the help of a mechanic and access to health care and the police. The more possessions and services, the greater is the material wealth of people and the better is their quality of life.

How do we give people lots of possessions and services? In order to give lots of potatoes to people, it is necessary to produce lots of potatoes and make them easy to obtain for people. How do we give a cat a lot of cat food? We make a lot of it available in a bowl and make it easy for the cat to obtain it. How do we give a horse a lot of water? We would provide him with a lot of water and make it easily available for him. Therefore if we provide a lot of possessions for people and make the possessions easily available for people to obtain them, the people will have a lot of possessions.

However, if we do not provide a lot of goods to people then there is a limit to the accumulation of goods of our people. In addition, if goods are not easily accessible then it is hard to get the people to obtain goods and increase their wealth.

How do we give people a lot of services such as teaching? People who want to be taught karate must have someone to teach them. The teacher must know what she is teaching. Suppose it is necessary for a dog to be taken on a walk. For this to transpire there must be someone willing to do this. He can't carry the dog or ride a car and let the dog run behind. In order for a cat to be spayed, there must be someone to do this, a veterinarian, or else the job will not be done properly or not at all. Therefore to obtain services, people must have someone to provide the services to them and that person must be someone who knows how to perform the service. If people have no one to provide the service, the service won't be done because a service can't be done by itself. If people have no one who knows how to perform that service that service won't be done well. To have services of the highest quality, he or she who performs the service must be very competent in performing it. The more trained a surgeon is and the more experience he has the better he will perform the surgery. A taxi driver who knows all parts of a city and has been driving for 15 years is better than one who does not have these qualities.

The next logical question is: what is the best way of producing lots of possessions, i.e. houses, cars, TV's? How do we produce a lot of potatoes? We would grow them in huge numbers on a farm. How would we produce a lot of trees? We would plant large quantities of seeds or saplings in a fertile area. How would we produce a lot of coal? We would do this by digging a lot of it out from a place where it is found, i.e. mine. The best way to produce lots of possessions is by creating, building, growing or manufacturing a particular kind of possession in an area suitable for its production. The possessions should be produced in special areas because certain areas will allow for the greatest production of possessions while others will allow for lesser production of possessions. For example, it is hard to grow corn in a plutonium mine because corn will not grow there and the conditions for growing it there are not suitable. Likewise for manufacturing chairs on a farm. The place is not suitable for the purpose. It's best to create chairs in a factory because it is easiest to produce them there. Likewise for growing tomatoes on a farm. It is easier to produce tomatoes on a farm than anywhere else. Some things are easy to produce in one area, location, building etc. while some things are hard to produce in other areas, locations, buildings etc.

To produce lots of possessions, the possessions should be created in vast numbers in the easiest way possible that can create a lot of a kind of a possession. Potatoes should be grown in such a manner that the most potatoes are produced. This implies that they have enough water, correct spacing and fertile soil. Trees should be produced in such a way that most trees grow. This implies enough sunlight and proper spacing. Coal should be mined such that the maximum amount of coal is mined. This implies using good equipment and working during optimal conditions. Possessions should be created such that the maximum amount of them is produced in a certain area, location or building. This will maximize the production of possessions.

What is the best way to make possessions easily available for people? What is the best way to make grass easily available to a cow? It would be to give the cow the ability to get it. We would put her into a situation where she can consume it. This is done by putting grass in front of her nose and letting her eat it. What is the best way to make water easily available for a horse? It would be to put the water near the horse and letting him drink it. The best way to make possessions easily available to people is to put the people into a position where they can take them and by giving people the ability to obtain them. This means giving the possessions directly to a person and allowing him to take it, just as we would put grass in front of a cow's nose. That is to give it to her or put it on the ground in front of her.

Let's return our focus back on services. What is the best way to obtain people who know how to perform the service they are supposed to perform? What is the best way to obtain someone who knows how to walk a dog? It would be to show him how to do it. What is the best way to obtain someone who can teach French? It would be to teach him French and show him how to teach it. What is the best way to obtain someone who is a veterinarian? It would be to teach him about animals and how to treat them. What is the best way to obtain someone who is a dentist? It would be to teach her about teeth and how to fix them when there is something wrong with them. Therefore, to obtain someone who can perform a service it must be the case that he or she is made competent in the area of his or her expertise by education, training and experience.

How do we obtain a lot of people who can perform a service? How do we obtain a lot of people who can fix teeth? We would do so by encouraging people to do this and making them interested in the art of fixing teeth. How do we obtain a lot of people who walk dogs? We would do so by making lots of people want to walk dogs. How do we obtain a lot of people who mow lawns? We would do so by making people want to mow lawns. Therefore, we would obtain a lot of people who can perform a service by making them want to perform the service or by encouraging them to do so thus making them interested in it.

People need a reason to do something and the fewer the number of people that want to do something the fewer there are that do it. If people have a reason to perform a service such as wanting to do the service then more people would be inclined to do the service. Therefore there will be a lot of people who perform a particular service.

Let's return to possessions. How do we make people produce, manufacture, create or grow a lot of possessions? How would we make people grow a lot of trees? We would give them a reason or purpose for doing so. How would we make people mine a lot of coal? We would give them a reason to dig and make their digging worth their while. How would we make people grow a lot of potatoes? We would give them a reason to want to do it. Therefore, we would make people produce a lot of possessions by giving them a reason to want to produce them or a purpose for doing so. Thus people will be encouraged to produce possessions.

What is the best reason that can be given to people to make them want to produce something? What is the best reason that we can give a person to plant trees? It would be to give the person something in return for his actions and to reward the person. If happiness is the only reason for productivity then the interest will soon fade as the worker looses motivation. Eventually indifference stalls progress. Happiness should be part of the reason for producing things and working but not the only one. What is the best reason that we can give a person to mine coal? It would be to reward him in return for his work with either possessions or services. What is the best reason we can give a person to grow wheat? It would be to give the person possessions or services in return. The best reason we can give people to make them want to produce something is to give them something in return for their actions. If this is the case then their material wealth and quality of life will be raised at the same time that they are raising the quality of life and material wealth of the people whom they are providing with possessions. This is the purpose of the system.

How should people be rewarded for their work? Their reward should be proportional to the work done. If a person who grows corn receives less of a reward or none of it if he grows four hectares of corn rather than three, he will lose his reason for working. If a person who mines coal receives less of a reward or none of it for digging for 8 hours rather than 6 he will also have no motive for working. The reward must be proportional to the work done because there must be a reason to do more work rather than less of it.

We need an economic system that will ensure that producers produce more goods, that workers will provide more services and that those who provide have an incentive to do so. The following is that system. It is called *accommodation based consumerism*. We will call the people who receive and utilize goods and services, "*consumerists*".

Why Do We Need a New Economic System?

The answer to this question depends on what is meant by "we". Free market nations are in need of accommodation based consumerism in a different sense than are third world countries.

At this point in time, early 2022, the majority of free market nations in the world do not really need this system. This includes countries like Canada, the U.S., France, England, Germany, Japan and even places like China. Although these countries may not need accommodation based consumerism now, they may desperately need it in the future. It is quite conceivable that the economic systems of these countries may collapse into a huge depression. The great depression of 1929 has demonstrated that a powerful economy can collapse leading to ruin and misery for all involved. Nevertheless in most leading free market nations there is a recession every 10 to 12 years. During a recession all the wrong entities and individuals are blamed for the recession. We blame the head of state, the central bank (the Federal Reserve), a greedy stock market, the banks, unscrupulous investors, etc. Those who understand the underlying problem recognize that the real culprit behind every recession is the free market system itself. A free market system provides us with a perpetual cycle of booms, recessions, booms, and even more recessions with the final result being a huge depression. These types of things do not exist in accommodation based consumerism. This is the reason why the leading economies of the world should look favourably to accommodation based consumerism when tragedy in an economic sense strikes.

The situation with third world countries is a bit different. The people of these countries (for example: Africa, South America, Asia) do not have enough to eat, they sleep on a pile of hay, they live in a small shack, they wear rags, and they drink filthy water. These countries do not have a reason at all not to try something new. Accommodation based consumerism will surely provide the people in these economies with a higher quality of life. The poorer countries of the world have nothing to lose in adopting accommodation based consumerism. For the above reasons, countries of the world do need accommodation based consumerism.

So when things are not right, take a chance on a complete system rather than patch up a failing system. Even free market systems today, as well as in the past, are patched up with social remedies that burden the free market dynamics, and fail to meet the social needs. This already existing patchwork will one day need at least an overhaul if not a rebuild or replacement, as any mechanical system in reality will need eventually. Accommodation based consumerism is ready.

Indeed, if third world countries are successful with accommodation base consumerism as their economic system, they may indeed exceed the success of first world nations in the very near future.

A Simple 4 Person Economy as a Demonstration of Pure Consumerism

We describe a simple four person economy. Actually, there is a fifth person but he doesn't contribute to the output and his role is purely administrative. This example will show how consumerism works in its purest form. Thus this example is useful in introducing the accommodation based consumerist economic system.

We suppose that we have four people; Joe, Bob, Emma and Paul. Joe is a rancher and produces beef. Bob is a producer of pork. Emma raises chickens and produces eggs. Paul grows potatoes. All these people just love what they do. Furthermore, they can produce the most of their product if they specialize in it and only produce that product than if they were to make two things at the same time.

In a single day Joe produces 20 kg of beef. Bob produces 20 kg of pork. Emma makes 20 kg of eggs and Paul grows (produces) 20 kg of potatoes. Now, if these people could only consume what they produce they would have too much of one good and none of the other three. To obtain each other's goods they choose the consumerist system.

We have Ed who doesn't produce anything and doesn't consume anything. What he does is that he sets prices for all four goods and keeps track (on a piece of paper) of all transactions. First of all, he divides the four person economy into two sectors – the *meat sector* and the *food sector*. In the meat sector we have pork and beef and in the food sector we have eggs and potatoes. He sets the prices of each good as follows:

Pork: 1$/kg

Beef: 1$/kg

Potatoes: 2£/kg

Eggs: 2£/kg

The meat sector output:

Pork- 20kg x 1$/kg = $ 20

Beef- 20kg x 1$/kg = $ 20

Total $20 +$20 = $40

Each person receives $40/4 = $10 to spend on the meat sector. When someone buys something with this money from Joe or Bob, it gets deducted from their records (which are run by Ed) and the equivalent number of £ are added to Joe's or Bob's records. Interestingly, if Joe or Bob want pork or beef they will have to buy it from themselves. However, they would receive revenue for doing so.

So, in day 1 Bob, Joe, Paul and Emma all receive $10 to buy things in the meat sector;

beef and pork. Note that this is not physical money like cash or coins but rather book entries that are managed by Ed. This is what they bought:

Bob- 5 kg of beef, 5 kg of pork

Joe- 4 kg of beef, 6 kg of pork

Emma- 5 kg of beef, 5 kg of pork

Paul- 6 kg of beef, 4 kg of pork

Since they all spent money, Bob and Joe have revenue for selling pork and beef. Bob sold 20 kg of pork and Joe sold 20 kg of beef. In Ed's records these become converted to £ so that Joe and Bob can buy things in the food sector. When $ are exchanged for things in the meat sector, the $ are deducted from the buyer and an equivalent number of £ are added the sellers. We assume that $1 = 1£ but these currencies cannot be exchanged directly for one another.

So Joe now has 20 £ to buy potatoes and eggs and Bob now has 20 £ to buy potatoes and eggs. Recall that there are 20 kg of eggs and they sell for 2£/kg and that there are 20 kg of potatoes and they sell for 2£/kg. Joe buys 5 kg of eggs and 5 kg of potatoes and Bob buys 5 kg of eggs and 5 kg of potatoes. Thus Paul earns 20 £ and Emma earns 20 £.

Now Emma and Paul buy things from the food sector. At this point Ed introduces the *food sector markdown*. It is set at 50%. This represents how much money is taken away from a transaction in the food sector. So Paul has 10£ and Emma has 10£. Emma buys 3 kg of eggs and 2 kg of potatoes and Paul buys 2 kg of eggs and 3 kg of potatoes. Thus Paul earned 10 £ (he keeps 5 £) and Emma earned 10 £ (she keeps 5 £)

With the 5 £ Paul buys 1 kg of eggs and 1 kg of potatoes (and has 1 £ left over) and with her 5 £ Emma buys 1 kg of eggs and 1 kg of potatoes (and has 1 £ left over). The next day both Paul and Emma earn 4 £ and keep 2 £. Paul buys a kg of potatoes and Emma buys a kg of eggs. So, there are 2 kg of potatoes left over and 2 kg of eggs left over and both Paul and Emma have 1 £ remaining. If the whole entire process is repeated the next day, Paul and Emma will start off with 1 £ each and Paul with 2 kg of Potatoes and Emma with 2 kg of eggs.

In general, the above process is continued until A) all the goods are bought and there is money left over or B) there is no more money to buy goods. In either case, the leftovers, either money or goods are carried over to another day's scenario where more goods are produced.

The consumerist paradigm we just described allows for the exchange of goods. It can, in general, be considered a form of trade. All our four individuals were able to benefit from consumerism.

The Benevolent Social Planner

We can start this treatise by introducing a hypothetical imaginary being we will call the *benevolent social planner* (BSP). The benevolent social planner is an imaginary figure who introduces the right variables, adjusts the correct values for the parameters, special mechanisms, programs and systems. His ultimate goal is to provide the highest level of well being for the consumerist nation while taking care of all the economic actors in the system like consumerists, employers, firms, investors and the government.

It is very crucial to note that all the numbers for the parameters in this treatise are exemplary, i.e. they need not be so in the actual system. They are created simply so that we have something to talk about. On the other hand, the actual existence of these parameters is an integral feature of this system.

The benevolent social planer is a made up figure. When we talk about a benevolent social planer we are really talking about the founding fathers of the consumerist nation. This transfers over to entities like the government, the central bank, firms and consumerists.

The benevolent social planner is there so as to maximize the material well being of consumerists and the consumerist nation in general. The benevolent social planner brings society the highest level of utility or happiness.

We imagine that there is a BSP who is in charge of creating, establishing and running our consumerist society. Although some parameters are to be adjusted by the central bank or the government we imagine that a benevolent social planner has a guiding hand in adjusting these parameters so that they work in everyone's well being.

Imagine Consumerism

Accommodation based consumerism is a wonderful economic system. It contains all that is good about capitalism and socialism without their problems. Seen from a different perspective, it is a new way to organize a society in the material sense.

In some sectors of consumerism there is what is called quality selection. Simply speaking, firms compete with each other not in terms of undercutting each other in price but in how their products and services are perceived in the eyes of consumerists. Thus consumerists drive sports cars and limousines, wear the best made suites and coats, and sleep on the most comfortable beds. Consumerists wear the best shoes, use the fastest and most productive computers and watch the most entertaining shows on the highest quality largest TVs. Producers compete with each other to make the largest, tastiest most nutritious pizza that consumerists will buy from them. When a consumerist wants to buy a beer, he can have the largest, tastiest beer he can possibly imagine. Consumerists play the most entertaining video and computer games. With the exception of several items that are in the laissez-faire sector, there is, in the consumerist system, competition among producers in terms of quality rather than price so as to please consumerists and give consumerists the highest quality life of any country.

A good thing about consumerism is that effort has been made not to allow for any "tax". First of all, there is absolutely no tax of any kind in the laissez-faire sector. In the other sectors, taxes are invoked only as a final, last resort if the government can't manage to earn enough revenue. There is however, the positive personal income tax if it is invoked. In this tax, tax payers make a profit in the long run while the government has revenue to pay for social services. After a set period, all tax payers receive all the money they paid with interest. Other taxes do not exist anywhere- that is property tax, corporate tax, sales tax and other taxes.

The "welfare system" in consumerism actually makes money. All people who cannot find a job after a multitude of "anti-unemployment measures" are given a job in the command partition – the one they would do best. The firms that provide work for these "welfare recipients" inevitably make a profit. This goes to the government as a source of revenue.

In consumerism, there is no (or very little) unemployment. There is a multitude of special "anti-unemployment measures" designed to create jobs. If there is still unemployed workers there are special unemployment-eradication measures like the command partition, the laissez-faire labour system and the disability work program.

No one in consumerism is homeless. The government provides absolutely everyone with some type of living arrangement. These could be condos, apartments or small bungalows. In the end the consumerists who took advantage of this have to pay for the accommodation.

Consumerism has two stock markets. Consumerism has a special stock market where every investor is guaranteed to make a profit. In this system, all stocks cost the same price per stock and investors make money through "post-reinvestment dividends". Since the price of the stock is fixed and the investor is always making dividend profits, he is guaranteed an overall profit in the long run. In the other stock market, there are mechanisms to prevent total collapse of the stock market.

The consumerist system has an ultra-universal healthcare system. In this system all medical procedures are covered by the government rather than through private enterprises. The health care system is totally publicly funded. Things like surgeries, medications, dentistry, walk-in visits, service of a psychiatrist, vision care, services of a chiropractor- they are all covered through the government by public funding.

The consumerist system also has free universal education. Elementary and secondary schools are paid for by the government. So are all universities and colleges. Also, all trade schools are funded by the government.

Inflation is controlled in consumerism. There are quite a few initiatives designed to control the money supply. In the end, whether there is an inflation, deflation or equilibrium is determined by the government and the central bank.

There is no poverty in consumerism. There are more than 22 special anti-poverty measures designed to do just that. Everyone has enough of the basic necessities and most people have a lot more.

There are measures designed to reduce or eliminate hunger. Several new ideas and concepts ensure that everyone (or almost everyone) does not go to bed hungry.

Consumerism introduces the new idea of "bankruptcy insurance". Any firm taking out a loan or issuing stocks or bonds must insure this so that there is no debt in the case the firm bankrupts or defaults on the interest repayment. This idea of bankruptcy insurance ensures all investors that they do not lose all their money on the speculative stock market if the firm that they invested in bankrupts.

It is very, very unlikely that accommodation based consumerism as a complete system will actually collapse. The reason is that there are over 140 special parameters that can be manipulated by either the government, the central bank or other entities. If the economy runs into problems, adjusting the correct parameter will surely correct the issue.

That's a glimpse into accommodation based consumerism. This system is an alternative system to free-market capitalism and socialism-communism. It has many unique features we will describe more fully in this book.

The Ideals of Accommodation Based Consumerism

The accommodation based consumerist economic system has a set of ideals that belong to it. By ideals we mean truths that we hold sacred due to the beauty of their meaning. These ideals are a testament of the goals of accommodation based consumerism. They are:

1) The quality of life of a human being is a nation's most important priority

2) There must not exist material poverty

3) No one should be homeless

4) No one should be hungry

5) Progress is a virtue

6) An economy must be both productive and efficient

7) The consumerist dream is to own a palace or a mansion

8) One should have the opportunity to be able to have any profession one wishes to have

9) One should have the opportunity to be able to become anyone they desire to become

10) One should have the opportunity to be able to have anything one wants to have

11) Hard work should be rewarded. The more one works the more one should earn

12) One should be able to keep all the money one earns to spend as one desires to spend it

13) One has the right to own private property

14) One has the right to do what one wishes with one's land possessions as long as it is within the law

15) All should have an equal opportunity to dream of, pursue and attain happiness

These are the ideals of accommodation based consumerism. They are the goals the system wants to accomplish. This treatise explains how we make these ideals real.

Axioms and Suppositions of General Economics

In order to make our theory logically sound we must list several fundamental axioms and suppositions. A supposition is something we take to be true without bothering to prove its validity. An axiom is a fact that we recognize as being obviously true simply by thinking about it. In this section we discuss the axioms and suppositions of economics in general and accommodation based consumerism in particular.

We suppose that the system applies to an actual country and is not a mere theoretical invention. All rules, parameters and ideals are applicable to a large group of people. The bigger the group, the better. Although the system can be adequately applied to smaller scenarios, it makes the most sense for it to be adopted by a country. For the greatest utility, the system ought to be adopted by a whole country or a group of nations.

We suppose that there are people in the country under the system. It is hard for a country not to be populated. There must be people in our country. A country is defined as an area where people live. Every country, including the one under our system, must have people living in it. It is the people of a nation whose best interests we are promoting.

The people would rather be happy than miserable. No one wants to live in misery, poverty and poor living conditions. Happiness gives meaning to life. The material happiness of our people is the ultimate goal of our system. Compared to misery, everyone would instead want to live a happy life. In developing this system, our main goal to keep in mind is to make our citizens as happy as possible.

The people are capable of doing work. By work we mean things like building, cleaning and managing. An able bodied person has tremendous potential if he or she applies himself or herself. The harder people work the better. With effort people have the power to do work. The ability to do work is a fine attribute of a human being.

People look favourably on progress. This implies that people would rather see things improve than worsen. It is almost universally held that there will be progress in the future. Countries that have a higher level of progress in some sense have a higher standard of living and better quality of life. People want progress to continue. Progress is a positive goal.

Now let's look at several important axioms. They are all general and apply to all economies not just accommodation based consumerism. They are universal in nature. These axioms must be preserved when creating an economic system. Usually most treatise begin with a logical set of axioms.

Everything must have a reason or else there must be a reason why it does not. This implies that everything in economics must have meaning and purpose. For everything we talk about in economics it must be clear why it is so. A reason has to belong to all the expositions we make. Where it doesn't it must be clear why not.

People always look to promote their own self interests. People do what benefits them. They seek to obtain or become what suits them the most. They would rather have something positive than not have it. In general, everyone wants as much of the economic pie as possible.

This is due to greed. Everyone thinks that they are entitled to the most. Whenever the economic pie is split among the members of society, each individual battles his counterparts for the most. This is the greed principle.

Many people are guided by a principle that I have arbitrarily named Bronson's Principle. This is an entirely arbitrary naming that does not reference any thing or any person, living or dead. This principle states that people are constantly comparing themselves to their neighbours. Suppose that there are two workers, both cashiers. One works 20 hours while the other works 80. The person working 20 hours earns $5 000.00 while the other who works 80 hours earns $ 1 000.00. The second person, instead of being happy that he earned a thousand dollars is infuriated that he made less than the other worker who worked less doing the same job. People sometimes care more about how much they earn in relation to another worker than about how much they actually earn themselves. This is Bronson's principle.

Another important principle is at the foundation of any economic system. It is that people do what is moral and legal. Of course, in particular cases it is violated and theft, bribery and exploitation appear. Yet most citizens are honest most of the time. If all people were dishonest, property rights would be violated and every economic system would fall apart. Most people expect others to act justly and legally and strive to do so themselves; at least in most situations. This is the honesty principle.

People need incentives to do anything. If people have a reason to do something they are more likely to do it. A reward of some kind motivates people to act. An incentive is a means for getting people to do things. The more of an incentive a person has to do something, the more likely he is of doing it. This is the incentive principle.

The greater the output of a society in terms of goods and services, the better off that country is. A country that produces more things is in better shape economically compared to one that produces less. It is very favourable to increase output as much as possible. In general, the total level of output of an economy is one of the measures of the nations standing among other nations. Thus it is clear that the output of a society should be as high as possible. This is a very important principle called the *output maximization principle*.

The amount of goods that can possibly be produced at any one time is limited. This is due to the scarcity of the resources used for production. Either the economy uses its resources to produce one thing or another or a limited combination of both. There is a maximum as to how much goods can be produced in a society. People always want more than there is available. Only in utopia, which is unattainable, is scarcity nonexistent.

The economy must be constructive. That is, it must benefit some people, some groups of people or the group itself. An economic system must have some positive rather than negative purpose. It must benefit someone or some entity.

An economic system is the means by which society produces and redistributes goods and services. There may be several ways to create an economic system and decide how people are to go about producing goods and services. The way goods and services are produced in a society depends on the economic system and how the system works. Likewise, the redistribution of goods and services in a society is a function of the efficacy of the economic system. These are the primary functions of an economic system.

Competition drives progress. Generally speaking competition refers to people or groups struggling with each other to excel in a particular parameter; for example lowest price. The more competition we have in a society, the better it functions. Through competition, technology growth and wealth increase. Progress is assured by competition. Competition can take several forms, including price, quality and quantity.

Trade is necessary to increase well being whether individually or collectively. Through trade, new goods can be acquired. Also something can be gained from selling goods as well. By trading, each person increases his material wealth. Furthermore, when nations trade with each other, both nations as well as their people prosper.

Exchange is the essence of an economy. Although direct exchange is possible, a medium of exchange facilitates the process. A medium of exchange can be coins, paper bills or precious metals like gold and silver. Exchange can also be in the form of bank entries. The ability to exchange one good or service for another spurs the growth of an economy. An economy works due to the people's ability to exchange goods.

In order to work, an economy must have some means of production. An economy must have a way of making goods and services. The production of goods is the way to gaining prosperity. There are many theories of the means of production each peculiar to an economic system. If an economy cannot produce goods and services, it cannot function. However, if an economy produces many goods and services, the better off it is in terms of functioning.

There are two fundamental principles that appear when formulating an economic system. These are the principles of ambiguity and rigidity. These two principles tear at each other. The principal of ambiguity states that ideas must be clear, well defined and well elaborated on as opposed to given in general and non specific terms. However the principal of rigidity states that if the ideas are too concrete and specific one has little room making adjustments that may arise when trying to put things into place. If too many details are dictated then there is little room to maneuver. One must strike a perfect balance between these two important principles.

Some key suppositions and axioms relate to economics. They apply to our system and to most other economic systems. Our discussions in the upcoming sections are hinged on these rules.

The Three Questions

There are three very important general economic questions that must be answered regarding an economic system. The first question is: "What goods and services should be produced?" The second question is: "How do we go about producing these goods and services?" The third question is: "How do we go about dividing the output of the economy, these goods and services, among ourselves?"

The answer to the first question is that we produce those goods and services that the consumerists in our economy want and need. We want to produce as much of these as possible. In cases where we cannot, we produce those goods and services that are most important and vital. That is, those that are most desired. The goal is to increase the material wealth of the consumerists. Sometimes we must produce things like factories that are necessary for material wealth. We produce things of the highest quality possible.

The answer to the second question is this. We produce things in a manner that will maximize productivity and efficiency. Workers will do the jobs that they are the best at or enjoy doing the most. Production is carried out in institutions that are best suited for producing that good or service. We call these firms.

The answer to the third question is this. As regards the third question, there is no single answer. Materially speaking, all non- institutionalized consumerists are granted a certain equivalent of money, with those who work getting more than those who do not. This the consumerists can spend on material goods and services. Those who contribute more to the economy earn more accommodational and laissez-faire money depending on their contribution to it. What this is will be further discussed in later sections. So in one sense there is no gap between the rich and the not so rich, yet in another sense there is an enormous gap between the rich and not so rich. The rich own palaces while the not so rich own apartments.

The answers to the three basic questions are very important. They give us a general idea of how this system works. The answers to these 3 questions guide the formulation of Accommodation Based Consumerism.

Wealth

In our system we want our citizens to be wealthy. First we must know what it means to be "wealthy". We have three hypotheses as to what wealth is: A) A large amount of money, B) A large amount of assets and access to services; and C) Assets and services of the highest quality. Let's compare two people; a rich person and a peasant to see what the real difference between them is.

While the rich man may have a large fancy car or sport car, the peasant may have a bike. They both have goods used for the same purpose – transportation- but the difference is in the quality of the asset. Although the rich man has better cars he does not necessarily have a large quantity of them (unless he collects them).

A rich man may have a well prepared fancy dinner with fine ingredients such as shark, steak and caviar. He may eat anything he wants. At the same time the peasant eats bread and potatoes. They both have food but the real difference is in the quality of the food. The rich man probably will not have 1000's of pounds of shark or fish. He has just enough to satisfy himself.

The rich man may have about a dozen tuxedos and outfits made by famous designers. The peasant on the other hand has two or three white shirts and a plain pair of pants. They both have clothes but again the difference is in the quality or prestige of the commodity. The rich man will probably not have more than 30 suites.

The rich man may have a very large television set, a home theatre and several stereos. The peasant may only have a newspaper and a simple ham radio. Each person has a form of entertainment but the difference is in the quality.

Finally, the rich man may have several sofas, some couches, some love-seats and several of the best built chairs and tables. The peasant may have a poorly built small table and a pair of chairs. Both people have furniture but the furniture differs in quality.

The question now is, would a rich man choose quantity or quality when choosing a good. If the rich man was offered 25 bicycles or a limousine, he would still want the limousine. If the rich man was offered 15 loaves of bread or a lobster and steak dinner, he would choose the later. If the rich man was offered 50 plain white shirts or a single tuxedo he would still prefer the tuxedo. If the rich man was offered 25 news papers or a wide screen TV, he would still choose to have the TV. Thus the difference between a rich and a poor person is not the quantity of goods that counts but the quality of these goods and services.

For clarity and concreteness, what is the difference between living in a prison camp and in a luxurious palace/mansion? The person in the prison camp has a deck of cards to entertain himself while the rich man swims in a pool or watches movies. Both have entertainment yet the difference is clearly in quality. The man in the prison camp has rags to clothe himself while the rich man has the most fashionable and comfortable clothes possible. Both have clothing yet the difference is again in quality. The man in the prison camp has to walk to wherever he wants to go while the rich man goes from place to place in a limousine. Both have transportation but the difference is in the quality of the transportation. We can extend this sort of argument to any area of the lifestyle of the man in the prison camp and the one in the mansion. Therefore, we are entitled to conclude that "true wealth" lies in the quality of the goods and services that a human being possesses.

Imagine the following thought experiment. We have a person, Philip, with a lot of money, $1, 000, 000. He goes to a supermarket that sells poor quality goods. Rotten apples cost $0.50/kg, stale bread costs $1.00 per loaf and the beef is rancid and costs $2.00/kg. The milk is sour and costs $2.00 per litre. If Philip spends the million dollars he would buy a very large quantity of goods. However no matter how much he buys he will still be poor because what he bought is poor quality. Despite his monetary wealth he lives in misery. A homeless person could have obtained the same items by rummaging through garbage cans.

Let's run another thought experiment. Suppose Gary walks into a store similar to the one above. He has $100.00. The only difference is that the second store has goods of better quality. The apples are fresh. The bread is crispy. The beef is tender and fresh. The pop is bubbly. The fish is good. The milk is tasty. If Gary spent all of the $100.00 in the store and bought similar types of things as Philip but of better quality, he would be better off than Philip since what he has is of higher value than what Philip has. The denominator is what is preferred. The second case is preferred to the first.

There is an interesting point in the meaning of wealth. If we are talking about a particular type of asset, it is better to have a larger quantity of it than less of it. Given a choice between two lobsters or four, a person would pick four lobsters. One would pick 8 tuxedos over five of them. A person would rather have two wide screen TV's than just one.

Sometimes wealth is measured in terms of money. Although this is good for quantitative purposes, it has several problems. Suppose someone has a million dollars. Is he rich or poor? If a hamburger costs $200, 000 and a car costs 100 million dollars, then he is poor. However when the inflation is small, the amount of money one has can be helpful in comparing the degree of wealth of an individual.

Suppose we ask a capitalist or capitalist professor, "What is 'Wealth'?" He may respond by saying that wealth is something like the financial assets one owns- how much money one has. But if we questioned him again we ought to ask him if the financial assets make one rich or is it the goods and services that these financial assets can be exchanged for. Most capitalists will concede the latter. Now, when it comes to what one may buy, is wealth more a function of "quality" or "quantity"? Clearly when considering goods and services of the same type- identical ice cream cones, identical T- shirt- the capitalist, using his common sense will say that more is better. However, when comparing items (goods and services) that differ in quality- a tuxedo vs. a poorly made blouse, a sports car vs. an economy car- it is very likely he will agree with us that it is better to own a higher quality good or have access to a higher quality service. It is also very, very likely that our capitalist friend will choose a limited amount of a higher quality item than a large supply of a very poor quality item. Thus his views will be consistent with what we have derived.

What conclusions can we draw from this analysis? We will call "true wealth" the possession of goods and services of high quality. Fundamentally, wealth is qualitative, subjective and relative as opposed to purely objective, absolute and quantitative. We can compare wealth between two individuals by how much of the same asset they have. That is, a person is said to be wealthier if he has more of the same asset as another person. However, measurement in terms of money is not completely useless. We will call the possession of a lot of money, "prosperity". Due to the way we defined wealth, our system must be designed such that the people who consume, the consumerists, obtain goods and services of the highest quality.

So, then "true wealth" refers to the possession of high quality goods and services of the highest quality. However, possession of a lot of a particular good or having access to a lot of a service is also a good thing. We will call this "abundance". Also, "prosperity" or "being rich" is something good. This refers to the possession of a lot of money, all other things being equal.

There is also another form of wealth that should be recognized. That is "spiritual wealth". Spiritual wealth refers to happiness from non-mundane reasons. Sometimes people who are genuinely happy can be considered wealthy. Spiritual wealth arises from things other than materialistic things. However, we will not talk at length about spiritual wealth in this book. This book is mostly interested in materialist wealth.

Knowing what true wealth is, we in this consumerist system will do everything to promote and preserve it. Consumerist theory is, in essence, a theory of how to maximize true wealth.

Economic Taxonomy

In this section we introduce the concept of economic taxonomy. Like almost anything else in this treatise it is an original idea regarding economics. We can proceed in one of two ways. Either we discuss the purpose of the concept first and discuss what it is later or vice versa. But then if we try to talk about the concept without defining it, we wouldn't know what we are talking about and proceeding in this fashion would be impossible. Therefore we will first talk about what economic taxonomy is and after doing so we will talk about its importance.

Economic taxonomy is a concept similar to biological taxonomy. Biologists try to organize all organisms on Earth into taxons or sets of hierarchical classifications. Economic taxonomy is the idea of organizing all goods, services and inputs produced by the economy into a hierarchical system of classification.

Biologists classify all organisms into categories that become smaller and more and more specific. Thus they organize all organisms into one of three domains. These are then divided into kingdoms and these are divided into phyla. Phyla are divided into classes and classes are divided into orders. Orders are divided into families which are divided into geneses. Finally geneses are divided into species. Species are the most specific. This system classifies all the organisms found on Earth. Once again, the ordering of classifications is:

Domain
Kingdom
Phylum
Class
Order
Family
Genus
Species

In economic taxonomy the idea is similar. The economy is divided into sectors. Each sector is divided into industries. Each industry is divided into classes. Each class is divided into categories. Each category is divided into families. Each family is divided into a product/service. Each product/service is given a designation. Each successive level of classification is called a taxon. Schematically, the hierarchy looks like this:

Economy
Sector
Industry
Class
Category
Family
Product/Service
Designation

As can be seen, there is considerable congruence between the two classification systems. There is one main difference. In the biological system, all classifications are in Latin. In economic taxonomy the classifications need not be so. They are in English (in English speaking countries)

The economy is divided into four sectors- the materialist sector, the accommodational sector, the laissez-faire sector and the governmental sector. The accommodational sector is, potentially, the biggest in terms of the number of products and services that are included in it. Let's first discuss the materialist sector. The most important industries found in the materialist sector are:

- Hospitality
- Transportation
- Entertainment
- Furniture
- Hygiene
- Information
- Apparel
- Health
- Education
- Synthetics
- Manufacturing

The most important industries found in the governmental sector are:

- Education
- Administrative
- Law enforcement and protection
- Infrastructure
- Community centres
- Public transportation
- Health care
- Gambling

The most important industries found in the accommodational sector are:

- Land
- Housing
- Utilities
- Appliances
- Home accessories
- Leisure
- Adult entertainment
- Alcohol and tobacco

The most important industries found in the laissez-faire sector are:

- Entertainment
- All auctions
- Apparel
- Gifts and gratuities
- Works of art

- Insurance
- Legal payments
- Gambling

A key point is that some industries can belong to several sectors so that some goods and services in one industry can belong to one sector while other goods and services in an industry may belong to a different sector.

The output of an economy can only belong to one of two classes. They are "good" and "service". A product can only belong to one of three designations. It can be called "retail". This means that it is a final good sold at stores that sell directly to consumerists. Examples include crackers and chips sold at a grocery store. It can also be a "final good". This means that it is a good made at a factory or production facility and is sold to vendors. Examples include cars made at a factory and chairs made at a factory. It can also be an "input". An input is a good used to make a final good. Examples include steel for making cars and flour for making cake. All services are designated "service".

Goods and services are classified in this system based on their similarity of usage. The highest taxons (sector, industry) are general in terms of the usages or purposes of the goods and services that they classify. Each successive taxon gets less and less general and products and services with increasingly more specific similarities of uses become grouped together. Thus goods and services in a family have a similarity of use that is more general than the similarity of use for outputs in the group "products/services".

We will use a particular example to illustrate this. Take the product bananas. They are in the materialist sector. They share this position with cars. They are in the hospitality industry. They share this position with an ice cream cake. They are in the goods class. They share this position with pots. They are in the food category. They are grouped along with steaks. They are in the tropical fruit family. They share this characterization with pineapples. Finally they are in the bananas product section along with other sizes of bananas.

Each taxon or level of organization must have a definition of its essence. That is it must be specified what is required for something to belong to a particular taxon. For example, the taxon of the category "drink" would be, "a liquid taken internally that is useful for the body". The taxon of the family "soft drink" would be, "a sweet carbonated liquid taken internally". The same idea applies to all other taxons at all levels of classification.

The classification of a product, input or service into its taxons is called a taxonomic structure. In what follows we give examples of many taxonomic structures. In doing so, we will develop a sub-discipline of economics. We cannot make taxonomic structures for all services and products here. Doing so will take a lot of time. It remains for inspired economists to finish this work that we have begun. Economists working for a branch of the government are given the task of completing this.

1) Product- binder
Economy
Sector- materialist
Industry- educational
Class- good
Category- learning utensils

Family- note taking aid
Product- binder
Designation- retail

2) Product- oranges
    Economy
    Sector- materialist
    Industry- hospitality
    Class- good
    Category- food
    Family- citrus fruits
    Product- oranges
    Designation- retail

3) Service – wheel alignment
    Economy
    Sector- materialist
    Industry- transportation
    Class- service
    Category- automotive
    Family- car repairment
    Service – wheel alignment
    Designation- service

4) Product – root beer
    Economy
    Sector- materialist
    Industry- hospitality
    Class- goods
    Category- drink
    Family- soft drink
    Product- root beer
    Designation- retail

5) Product- limousine
    Economy
    Sector- materialist
    Industry- transportation
    Class- good
    Category- automotive
    Family – automobile
    Product- limousine
    Designation –final

6) Product- wooden table
    Economy
    Sector- materialist
    Industry- furniture
    Class- good
    Category- dinning furniture
    Family- table

42

Product- wooden table
Designation- final

7)   Product- kitchen chair
Economy
Sector- materialist
Industry- furniture
Class- good
Category- dining furniture
Family- chair
Product- kitchen chair
Designation –final

8)   Product- blueberries
Economy
Sector- materialist
Industry- hospitality
Class- good
Category- food
Family- berries
Product- blueberries
Designation- retail

9)   Product- carrots
Economy
Sector- materialist
Industry- hospitality
Class- good
Category- food
Family- root vegetables
Product- carrots
Designation- retail

10)   Product- potatoes
Economy
Sector- materialist
Industry- hospitality
Class- good
Category- food
Family- root vegetables
Product- potatoes
Designation- retail

11)   Product- wide screen television set
Economy
Sector- materialist
Industry- entertainment
Class- good
Category- electronics
Family- TV's
Product- wide screen television set

Designation- retail

12)   Product – 64 bit video game console
        Economy
        Sector- materialist
        Industry- entertainment
        Class- good
        Category- electronics
        Family- video game system
        Product- 64 bit video game console
        Designation- retail

From what we have observed, some products were either "retail" or "final" as regards their designation. It is usually the case that most goods are both "final goods" and "retail". If a good is retail it must have also been a final good because it must have been produced somewhere. Similarly, all "final" goods must be sold and they must be sold to retailers like department stores or grocery stores.

All "inputs" are automatically in the accommodation sector. This is because material/governmental/laissez-faire goods are goods that are immediately available to consumers. If a good is used as an input than it is definitely one that belongs to the accommodation sector.

It is possible that the same good may have more than one use. An example is the computer. A computer may be a form of entertainment or a business tool. Thus it may have two taxonomic structures each being equally valid. Neither taxonomic structure is more valid than the other. This is similar to the idea of resonance structures in chemistry. Thus the two taxonomic structures are called "resonance taxonomic structures". The following is an example of resonance taxonomic structures:

13)   Product- PC computer
        Economy
        Sector- materialist
        Industry- entertainment
        Class- good
        Category- electronics
        Family- computer
        Product- PC computer
        Designation- retail

14)   Product- PC computer
        Economy
        Sector- materialist
        Industry- information
        Class- good
        Category- electronics
        Family- computer
        Product- PC computer
        Designation- input

The same idea applies to books. Books can be information or entertainment depending on

44

how they are used. So the following are another example of taxonomic resonance structures:

15) Product- book "**Drawn & Courted**" by R. David Foster
   Economy
   Sector- laissez-faire
   Industry- information
   Class- good
   Category- books
   Family- art instruction
   Product- book "**Drawn & Courted**" by R. David Foster
   Designation- retail

16) Product- book "**Drawn & Courted**" by R. David Foster
   Economy
   Sector- laissez-faire
   Industry- entertainment
   Class- good
   Category- books
   Family- art instruction
   Product- book "**Drawn & Courted**" by R. David Foster
   Designation- retail

17) Service- internet service
   Economy
   Sector- materialist
   Industry- information
   Class- service
   Category- media
   Family- computer service
   Service- internet service
   Designation- service

18) Product- modern tank
   Economy
   Sector- governmental
   Industry- defence
   Class- good
   Category- military
   Family- tank
   Product- modern tank
   Designation- final

19) Product- heavy duty dishwasher
   Economy
   Sector- accommodational
   Industry- appliances
   Class- goods
   Category- kitchen appliance
   Family- dishwasher
   Product- heavy duty dishwasher

Designation- retail

20) Product- microwave
Economy
Sector- accommodational
Industry- appliance
Class- good
Category-kitchen appliance
Family- cooking appliance
Product- microwave
Designation- retail

21) Service- optometrist appointment
Economy
Sector- governmental
Industry- health
Class- service
Category- medical
Family- doctor's appointment
Service- optometrist appointment
Designation- service

22) Service- family doctor's appointment
Economy
Sector- governmental
Industry- health
Class- service
Category- medical
Family- doctor's appointment
Service- family doctor's appointment
Designation- service

23) Service- heart operation
Economy
Sector- governmental
Industry- health
Class- service
Category- medical
Family- emergency internal surgery
Service- heart operation
Designation- service

24) Product- hammer
Economy
Sector- materialist
Industry- manufacturing
Class- good
Category- tools
Family- household tools

Product- hammer
Designation- retail

25) Product- ammonia
Economy
Sector- accommodational
Industry- synthetics
Class- good
Category- chemicals
Family- industry chemicals
Product- ammonia
Designation- input

26) Product- blue paint
Economy
Sector- accommodational
Industry- home improvement
Class- good
Category- decorational item
Family- wall covering
Product- blue paint
Designation- retail

27) Product- carpet
Economy
Sector- accommodational
Industry- home improvement
Class- good
Category- floor furnishings
Family- floor covering
Product- carpet
Designation- retail

28) Product- tiles
Economy
Sector- accomodational
Industry- home improvements
Class- good
Category- floor furnishings
Family- floor coverings
Product- tiles
Designation- retail

29) Product- tooth paste
Economy
Sector- materialist
Industry- hygiene
Class- good
Category- oral hygiene
Family- teeth cleaning cream

Product- tooth paste
Designation- retail

30) Service- lecture by biology professor
Economy
Sector- government
Industry- educational
Class- service
Category- instruction
Family- service of a university professor
Service- lecture by biology professor

31) Service- firefighting team ladder operation
Economy
Sector- governmental
Industry- defence and protection
Class- service
Category- internal protection
Family- firefighting
Service- firefighting team ladder operation
Designation- service

32) Product- hot water
Economy
Sector- accommodational
Industry- utilities
Class- good
Category- household utility
Family- hot water
Product- hot water
Designation- final

33) Service- Defence Legal representation by a private lawyer
Economy
Sector- Laissez-faire
Industry- Legal
Class- Service
Category- Legal representation
Family- Private representation
Service- Defence Legal representation by a private lawyer
Designation- Service

In addition to the economic taxonomy system we have just developed there is a corollary system of classifying goods and services. It is called the numerical economic taxonomy system. The taxons are replaced by numbers. Every good and service would have a sequence of numbers that correspond to its taxonomic structure. The first number designates the sector of the good or service. It can only be 1, 2, 3 or 4. The next sequence of numbers designates the industry. Two numbers indicate the industry the good or service is in. For example, 02 could mean hospitality and 31 could mean transportation. The third number in the sequence refers to the class. It is either 1, referring to goods or 2 referring to services. The next number is a three digit number describing the category. Each category in the industry has an original three number sequence.

Something similar applies to the next eight digit number which describes the family of the good or service in the particular category. The next taxon is product/service. It may have up to twelve digits. Each good or service has twelve digits describing what it is in the family. Finally the last number describes the good's or service's designation. 1 stands for retail, 2 for final product, 3 for input and 4 for service. An example illustrates the idea. Let's find the numerical economic taxonomy number for a hammer. First recall the taxonomic structure. It is the following:

Sector- materialist
Industry- manufacturing
Class- good
Category- tool
Family- household tool
Product- hammer
Designation- retail

It may have the following numerical economic taxonomy description:
1 – 17- 1 – 412- 00097774- 340001255513-1

We need to explain the above number. The 1 stands for the sector, in this case the materialist sector. 17 stands for the industry, in this case manufacturing. The next 1 stands for class, in this case goods. The 412 corresponds to the category, the category being "tools". 00097774 represents the family, which here is "household tools". The product is identified by the number 340001255513, which corresponds to "hammer". Finally, the last digit, 1, designates the hammer as being a retail commodity. Thus operates the numerical economic taxonomic system.

In this numbering system, a good or service can have the same number in its classification as long as the numbers before it are different. For example, 1- 17 …. and 2-17 refer to two different items. The "17" after "1" refers to a different industry than the "17" after the "2". The same reasoning applies to all classifications in the numerical taxonomy system.

Now that we know what economic taxonomy and numerical economic taxonomy are and have numerous examples of taxonomic structures, it would be good to discuss the importance of economic taxonomy. Economic taxonomy simplifies our understanding of the economy. We begin to grasp the relationships between various goods and services. By looking at taxonomic structures we can know what our economy produces and the services that people can do for each other. As we will see later on there is a particular price or wage/salary function for each family of products or services. This greatly simplifies shopping as the consumerist knows exactly how much everything costs. Classifying products and services informs us of their relationships. We might want to know the relationship between goods and services in order to know how various goods were invented and how innovations came about. Also these relationships might help inventors come up with newer and better goods and ways of doing things. Since this classification is based on similarity of usage, studying it will help us know how similar goods are in terms of use. An economic taxonomy book (or an App on a cell phone), similar to a phone book will be a useful tool for all, listing all products, services and the price. Such a book (or app) would greatly simplify shopping. This notion of taxonomic organization is very useful for the Accommodation Based Consumerist Economic System. We will see its many applications in the forthcoming sections. That is the reason why we began this treatise with it.

Economic taxonomy and numerical economic taxonomy are central to consumerism.

Many examples illustrate these concepts. There are reasons why these concepts are so important. The proceeding sections will fully incorporate what we have discussed here.

What is Accommodation Based Consumerism?

Accommodation based consumerism is a general economic system. It is neither completely a market economy nor a purely command economy. However, depending on the wishes of the people under the system, the system can have a quasi free-market or quasi socialist orientation. By itself, it is more general and has certain command and certain free-market elements. The means of production, although not completely, are in the hands of firms. The central bank sets certain parameters and is in charge of decisions as to prices and wages. The firms make most of the production decisions. That is, they decide what to produce, how to produce it and how to use resources such as labour. In this capacity the system resembles the free-market system. Free-market capitalism is actually a special limiting case of Accommodation Based Consumerism where the laissez-faire sector is very large, the governmental sector is smaller and the materialist and accomodational sectors are very small or non-existent. There are some differences like for example how to raise taxes for the governmental sector. Nevertheless, Accommodation based Consumerism collapses (to some degree) into free-market capitalism.

In a few ways the system standouts. First, there are four sectors. There are three currencies. There are three partitions. The society is cashless. The government does not have sweeping powers to tax everything. There are only three taxes and they are reserved for special circumstances. There is no inflation or business cycles of boom and recessions in three of the four sectors. Many workers own their jobs. There are also many other differences that we will discuss later.

Why is the system called "accommodation based ?" As mentioned before, and as we will see later, there are four sectors. One of them is the accommodational sector. By contributing to the economy in general, the consumerists earn profit to spend in the accommodational sector, on things like real estate, utility bills and leisure. The accommodational sector is the incentive for working.

Why is the system called "consumerism ?" The system is designed to benefit the consumerist. The consumerist is the person who acquires goods and services. Everything else works directly or indirectly to benefit the consumerist. This system revolves around consumerists. Of course, great lengths are taken to help producers, workers and investors. Their well being is also promoted but differently.

The system has the following form. The consumerist society functions like a soccer team. The team wins games as a team regardless of who scores goals, who assists on these goals and who saves goals. Thus if the team wins the world cup, everyone on the team wins the world cup. However there are also individualistic rewards for individual players on the team. Players who score more goals are usually played more. The more saves a goalie successfully makes the more likely he is to get some kind of bonus. There are other rewards too- most valuable player, highest scorer, best rookie, etc. - which individual players dream to win. In trying to benefit the team, they also benefit themselves and in trying to benefit themselves, they benefit the team. The accommodation based consumerist system works in a similar way. Consumerists strive for individual wealth and in doing so increase the prosperity of the entire society. At the same time, when society's prosperity is raised all consumerists reap the rewards. This causes a spiral of prosperity that we will talk about later in detail.

In general, consumerism strives for self-sufficiency. Free trade is desired and encouraged. However, it is preferable if as many goods and products are made in our consumerist nation.

Consumerism is a collective-individualistic system. That is, it has collective as well as individualistic characteristics. Consumerism tries its best to keep as many of the good free-market and socialist ideas as possible.

These are some of the characteristics of the accommodation based consumerist system. How it works precisely follows. The following is a very simplified model of the system.

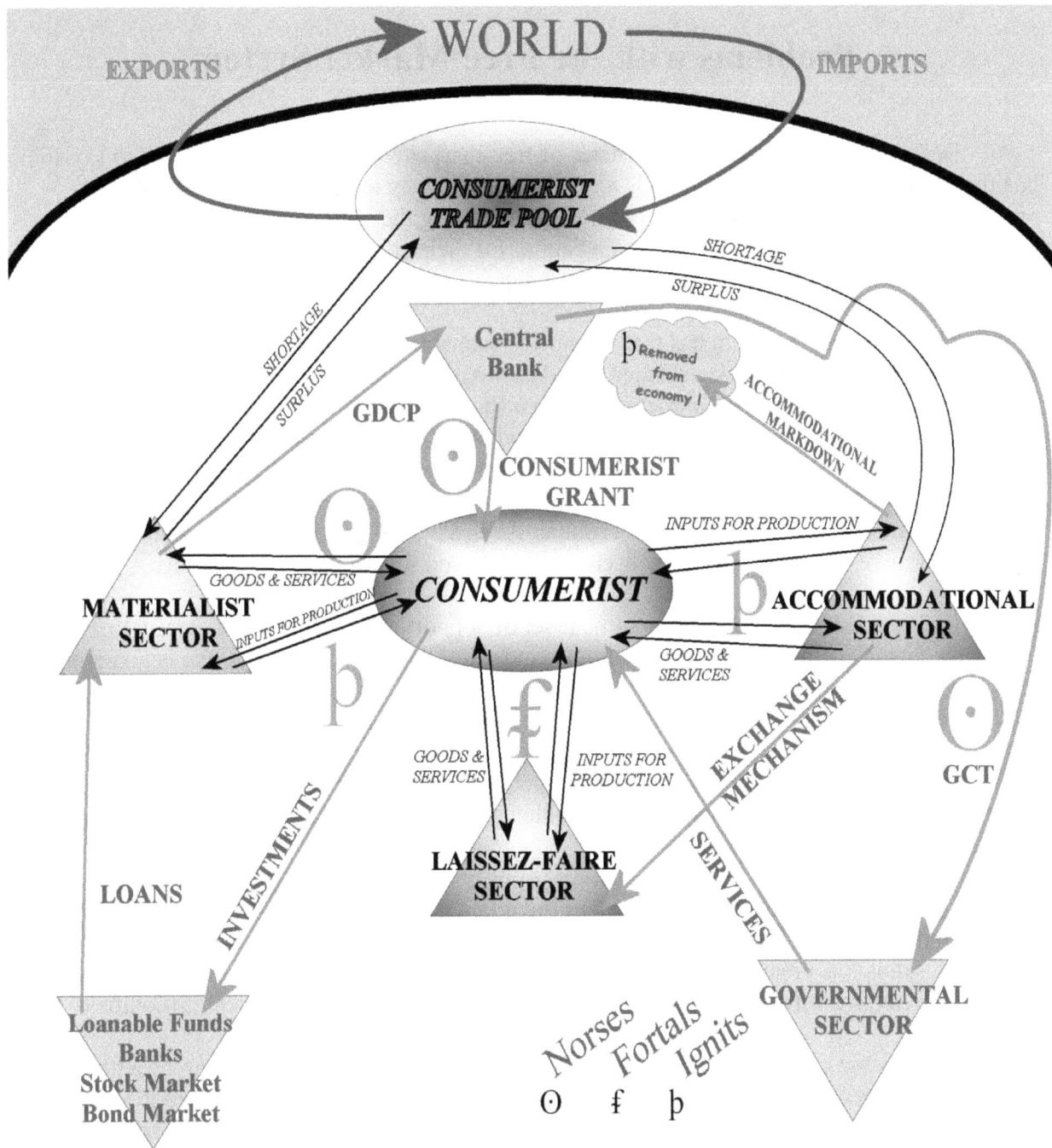

Accommodation Based Consumerism

Figure 1

Figure 1

Problems with the Free-Market System

Before we talk about the deficiencies of free-market capitalism, it is adequate to say some positive things about it. First of all, it is a relatively good way to organize a market. We can provide for the many needs and wants of households using the market system. As long as households contribute to society, they gain capital for their efforts. They can exchange this capital for goods and services that make them happy.

The free-market system has well designed mechanisms to fight certain kinds of shortages and surpluses. In the free-market system, "market forces" alleviate problems associated with shortages and surpluses. For example, if there is a shortage, the price of the good or service increases. If there is a surplus, the price of the good or service decreases.

Also, free-market capitalism has built in incentives to make it work. The profit motive that is the cornerstone of the free-market system gives a reason for employers to employ workers, for investors to invest, for households to buy and for banks to lend money.

In free-market nations there is some level of "opportunity". If one finds a way to contribute to society, then he can have a high standard of living. Although no one is guaranteed a high quality, happy life, there remains the possibility that one may achieve one if he finds a way how. So there is at least the hope of becoming rich and famous.

The free-market system is far from perfect, however. The majority of economists agree that there are several fundamental internal problems with the free-market system. Here we will have a look at them.

The economic philosopher Karl Marx did a fantastic job critiquing capitalism more than a century and a half ago. A lot of his points show the problems and inadequacies of pure capitalism. Thus it is rather hard to improve on his work. In this section we will briefly talk about the major areas where free market capitalism runs into practical and theoretical difficulties.

Perhaps the most profound difficulty is the business cycle. There seems to be a never ending cycle of recessions and booms. A recession is an economic downturn where the G.D.P., that is the general output of the economy, decreases over two quarters. A boom is a period where the economy gains momentum over two quarters. Recessions are bad for everyone; workers, capitalists, consumers and the government. The recessions are periodic and unavoidable. All we know is that they will happen sometime. No one has yet found a way to stop the business cycle in a free-market society.

A major argument against free-market capitalism is that, on its own, it is an unjust system. The distribution of income isn't fairly established. Some people have much more than they need while others do not have enough to even get by.

The scariest part of the free-market is the existence of depressions. A depression is a period of time in which the economy falls into severe trouble. Besides war, a depression is one of the greatest forms of man-made misery. Unemployment skyrockets. The output of the economy crashes greatly. Stock prices drop tremendously. Businesses close or lose a lot of money and many banks go under. Real G.D.P. fell by around 30% in most countries between 1929 and 1933.

In Canada, unemployment rose by 25 %. Price levels decreased by 15% and stock prices dropped 90%. Many people who lost everything committed suicide. Usually depressions last quite a while. The Great Depression of the 1930's lasted almost 10 years. There is no natural mechanism to get out of a severe depression. In systems other than the free-market, depressions and business cycles do not occur, indicating that these are free-market phenomenon. The frightening thing about the modern free-market system is that we do not know when the next depression will hit and whether or not it will be more severe than the one in the 1930's.

The free-market system, left to its own devices, quite often fails to give an equitable distribution of well being. The free-market system promotes those that have the ability to provide goods and services that other people will compensate for these things. The free-market system does not assure that all people's quality of life is equal. For example, the managers of companies have a higher standard of living than artists like musicians and writers who are not well known (Kneebone, R.D. 2002).

The free-market has a stock market with several problems. It is guided by the forces of supply and demand and the prices of stock can increase or decrease. This leads to the possibility of a crash or a sudden drop in prices. If this happens, stocks loose all their value and investors loose all their money. Something similar happened during the great depression. A tremendous stock market crash can wreck havoc on an economy.

All economists agree that monopolies in a free-market system are a problem. A monopoly is a firm or organization that doesn't have much competition in terms of providing a good or service. A monopoly provides an inefficient amount of a good or a service than it would if the market were more competitive. We say that there is "dead weight loss". That is, the economy looses production compared to what is otherwise achievable. Also a monopoly confers tremendous profit to the owner. There is a debate as to how this profit should be distributed. Monopolies produce difficulties in the free-market system.

Some contend that the free-market system contributed to the start of the Second World War. The war was about more than power. It was about money and economic domination. Each of the nations that fought wanted more money and going to war was a method for attaining that purpose. The Second World War was brought about at least in part by economic factors.

Sometimes the forces of supply and demand lead to economic absurdity. In Brazil, some coffee growers have destroyed their crops so as to raise the price of their coffee. Yet there are 100's of millions of people in third world countries that can only dream of coffee. In general, in the free-market, producers often restrict the supply of the product to raise its price, often by destroying the product. The people who lose out are those who do not get the good.

Few people who pay taxes actually like doing so yet the existence of taxes is a necessary part of the free-market system. Many people think that they are unavoidable. Hard working people pay a lot of their earnings in the form of taxes. There are several dozens of ways that the government has cleverly devised to steal people's money. Taxes also hurt the economy as they cause *dead-weight losses*. Dead weight loss refer to a decrease in production and output from levels that are possible in other circumstances. Although it is impossible to avoid paying taxes in a free-market system, it is not impossible to get rid of them in another economic system.

Under the free-market system, only those things that can be marketed are produced. There is a general loss of philosophy, art, poetry, music and culture. Many public things are not provided without aid from the government. We lose the priceless things that give society its beauty.

Exchange rate crises are possible under the free-market system. In an exchange rate crisis, due to speculation, a currency is forced to be devalued or the interest rate drastically increased, thus destroying the economy. Exchange rate crisis have destroyed many currencies and have broken up many unions including the European Monetary Fund. This is a serious problem of the free-market system.

We now point out the Communist objection to the free-market system. Communists argue that workers are exploited. This applies especially to workers in the third world. Some workers earn only enough to subsist. Communists point out that workers work extremely hard, under inhuman conditions and get next to nothing for it. Meanwhile the capitalists keep all the profit. This was certainly true during the birth of the industrial revolution. Yet there are still sweat shops in poor countries where little children are forced to work.

Poverty exists in all free-market countries. There is a group, the poor, who lead miserable lives and cannot enjoy the same goods and services as their neighbours. Although the suffering is bad in itself, these people sometimes resort to crimes like robbery and drug trafficking to provide for themselves. The free-market economy always has an impoverished group.

There is also a lot of hunger in free-market nations. Even in very well off countries in North America and Europe there are many people who do not have enough food to eat. These people rely on charity to get by.

Unemployment plagues most free-market systems. People have no work and fall into poverty. In most economies, unemployment is possible but not that dangerous if it is small. If the unemployment rises over 20%, then the economy is in bad shape. Unemployment can ruin the lives of the unemployed in particular and society in general. The unemployed lose their self worth in addition to their income. Certainly, the existence of unemployment is a failure of the free-market system.

A very important problem of the free-market economic system is that there is market failure. In some cases these appear as externalities and market power. Externalities are of the positive and negative type. A good example of a positive externality is a researcher producing a new model of a disease that helps many people. An example of a negative externality is a production facility that produces many cars and car parts but also gives off green house gases. These two examples are troublesome from an effectivity and efficiency perspective (Kneebone R.D. 2002).

Inflation exists in the free-market system. In some cases inflation can be excessively great as has occurred in the German economy in the early 1920's, where the Mark decreased in value millions of percent. The well known Phillips curve tells us that there exists a trade-off in the short run between unemployment and inflation. Clearly, under capitalism, in the short run, we must choose between inflation and high unemployment. Clearly this is a fault of the free-market system.

A free-market system can be destroyed or crippled by bank runs. A bank run is the occurrence when people want their money from the bank and the bank doesn't have it, resulting in the collapse of all firms the bank lent to. If a bank run happens, everyone loses. The possibility of a bank run is a critical fault of the free-market system.

A free-market economy can experience stagflation. Stagflation is the occurrence of both high unemployment and high inflation. It brings only misery to all those involved. Stagflation sometimes persists for quite a while before it is fixed. It exists specifically in the free-market system.

The free-market system has problems. The reasons these issues are problematic are clear. In designing our system, we must not have these problems in our economy.

Problems with the Command System

Before talking about the faults of the command system it is good to point out some positive attributes of the command system. This system allows the central planners to focus on the production of any good it sees necessary to make. If the central planners want to make more cars, they can use workers to make them. If they want to make more farms, they can use workers to make them.

A positive attribute of the command system is the strong social net. Although the odds are high against you being extremely rich, the command system is designed so you do not become overwhelmingly in need of goods and services. Almost everyone has enough to subsist. The command system is designed so that no one is impoverished.

The command system does not have a business cycle like the one in the free-market system. There does not exist a perpetual cycle of booms, downturns, recessions and expansions. Thus it appears that the economy is always growing. In fact of all major nations, the USSR was among the only ones to avoid the economic collapse of the 1920's and 1930's..

Clearly most households organize themselves under some kind of mutual general command system. Someone does the dishes, someone vacuums, someone cooks dinner, and someone walks the dog while someone else does the grocery shopping. The household works for the greater common good of the family and benefit of everyone and everyone works together. It would be problematic if everyone in the family charged for their contribution to the household. Someone would not make lunch unless they were paid $6.00 a plate. The kids would not make their beds unless they were paid $4.00 for making their beds. And whoever walks the dog would not do so until he was paid $5.00 for doing so. Clearly, most households are organized under a mutual command system. The main problem occurs when the command system generalizes to too many people; i.e. it gets too big. In such a case, problems of greed make it less effective than it is in theory.

Now it is time to make a critique of the command system. The point here is to expose the weaknesses of the command system. We will examine the problems of the command system one by one.

About a century ago in some places people thought the command system was a brilliant idea. There was constant talk of revolution. Some proclaimed that once the capitalists were gotten rid of and workers were given power, everything would be better. Yet they did not know how everything would be better. There wasn't a coherent, well thought out plan of an economic system. All there was, was rhetoric.

It was as if the communists were expecting a baby. They thought that as soon as the baby was born everything would all of a sudden change and life would be better. But having a baby requires having responsibility and work and things weren't all that rosy.

Communism may have worked on paper but not in reality. It wasn't practical. Most of the countries that have experimented with it have seen its folly. Most of them have collapsed. Among these were the Soviet Union and the Eastern European countries.

Communism puts the community before the individual. If one has the greatest, strongest, most powerful and influential ship on the sea, it is of little good if the crew is miserable, hungry and sick. The needs of the individual are the most important. A community with happy, well off people is happy and well off because then the people have something to defend and the will to defend it.

Communism has another fault. People do not succeed due to merit or hard work. They succeed due to political shrewdness. An uncreative, uneducated, lazy man can become the owner of a factory just because he has friends in important political positions. People advance for the wrong reason.

One very important element is missing in the command system. This is incentive. People need an incentive to work and be efficient. This the command system lacks. It assumes that people will operate unselfishly.

Communism is both inefficient and ineffective at a grand level. The central planners are not able to effectively deal with shortages and surpluses. The central planners are unable to respond to the demands of the people. Things are produced that no one needs and things that people need are not produced. The resources and inputs are mismanaged. They are not used to the maximum potential or are overused.

Coordinating all production in a large country under the command system is extremely hard or even impossible. The literally millions upon millions of production decisions cannot be practically made by a central government. The management of all economic decisions under a command system is inefficient and impractical.

Another problem with the command system is that it is hard to be too rich. Personal profit is discouraged. In the command system, there is encoragement for everyone to be equally wealthy.

Some issues make the command system in general and communism specifically, troublesome. In designing our system we must be careful that we do not run into any of these problems. However it is a good idea to borrow some of the positive ideas of the command system.

Benefits of Consumerism

There are several benefits that consumerism has over the free-market and command systems. Here we give a brief description of them. The rest of the treatise is dedicated to explaining the consumerist system.

In consumerism we incorporate the positive attributes of free-market and socialist paradigms. Meanwhile, we discard all the problems and discrepancies these two economic systems have. Of course, as we shall see, there is a lot more to accommodation based consumerism than free-market and socialist ideas. The majority of this system is founded on new concepts.

In accommodation based consumerism there is no material poverty. The central bank grants money (Norses) to all members of society regardless of their occupation. Those not working or not in the work force are granted less money to give them an incentive to find work. Those in institutions are not granted money as they are taken care of directly by transfers from the government. The working all receive the same amount if they contribute over a certain threshold to the economy. There is no gap between the rich and the poor (materially speaking) as long as they are working.

In addition to an absence of poverty, in consumerism there are also no homelessness and hunger. Certain parameters ensure absolutely everyone has a place to live. Other parameters ensure absolutely everyone has something to eat when they are hungry. No one in consumerism starves or freezes on the streets.

There is no inflation or deflation and price functions in 3 of the 4 sectors cannot increase or decrease. They are fixed permanently by the central bank. The central bank cannot print money at random like in the free-market system. All prices functions and wage functions remain fixed.

There is no business cycle. The free-market experiences business cycles because at the boom demand outstrips the supply and inflation starts rising rapidly. To combat this, the free-market central bank raises interest rates and the bank rate to offset the rising inflation and a recession starts. With no inflation possible, the possibility of a recession evaporates. The free-market business cycle of recession and expansion does not exist. The business cycle is replaced by the consumerist spiral of prosperity. At the point where the demand begins to outstrip the supply, instead of their being inflation, there is a surge in the supply side. The economy works like a tornado, constantly perpetuating itself. The more people buy, the more people sell, the more people make money and more people receive goods and services. The economy grows exponentially. First it grows quite slowly. As soon as it picks up momentum, it grows at a faster and faster rate. This effect will be discussed in detail later.

In the free-market economy, a lot of students are infuriated about ever increasing tuition costs for their education. In consumerism tuition is paid by the government. The government of a consumerist nation, whether federal or provincial, pays for a student's education. Education at all levels is free.

There are only 3 taxes in consumerism which are made use of as a last resort. The money the government earns does not come out of anyone's pockets for the most part. There are no corporate, alcohol, tobacco, property or sales taxes. The government does need money but it receives it not from consumerists but from the central bank. The average person makes money paying personal income taxes to the government.

There are two general types of stock markets. The consumerist stock market, due to the way it is set up, cannot collapse. All stocks in the "market" are of the same price regardless of the firm they are from and how many shares the firm issued. Prices do not fluctuate. If they do not fluctuate, they cannot depreciate in value and hence the stock market cannot crash.

It is impossible to lose money while investing in the consumerist stock market. All investors earn a profit from stocks via dividends based on the profit of the firm and how much of the total shares an investor has. In a free-market society, if a firm bankrupts the investor who had the company's stock loses all his money. However in the consumerist society if a firm bankrupts it has to pay the investors the value of the shares they own, essentially buying them back. If it doesn't have the money after selling off its assets, a bankruptcy insurance firm steps in to pay the investors.

There can be no depression. An essential part of a depression is a decrease in prices and wages. Since wage functions and price functions are fixed, there cannot be a depression. Depressions are impossible.

The goods and services are of the highest quality. There is an incentive for producers to produce goods of the finest quality. Since all prices for a type of good are fixed the net effect is that most people have luxurious goods and top quality professional services. This is called *quality selection*.

The consumerists are granted money from the central bank. They are granted this money for being citizens. They can spend it on goods and services they desire in the materialist sector. This includes things like TV's, cars, clothes and pets. Why do they receive this? So they can have the best life possible.

Consumerism does not resort to the rhetoric of a revolution. This treatise is a rather complete description of a consumerist society, omitting only specific details. It does not promote revolution but suggests an alternative economic system which intelligent people will judge to be better than anything before it. Consumerism appeals to reason whereas the communist system appeals to rhetoric and emotion.

The individual is put ahead of the state. The most important maxim of the system is that the quality of life and well being of the consumerist should be increased. Everything is done to help the consumerist. The state is only as valuable as its people. Merits are rewarded. Those that put effort into life and help society are those that get ahead. Political shrewdness isn't much of an asset as this system is workable with democracy. The right qualities of a person are rewarded.

The idea of an incentive to motivate people to work and be efficient and productive is present in consumerism. The incentive is the profit motive. The higher one's contribution to society, the more profit one earns for the accommodational sector and laissez-faire sectors to buy things like houses or vacations. The more someone contributes to society, the more prosperous he is in terms of the accommodational and laissez-faire sectors.

The problems that result from grand central planning like shortages and misallocation of resources do not exist. Firms are the means of production. Firms will ensure that resources are used as best as possible. The means of production are used more effectively when in the hands of firms as opposed to the hands of central planners. However the benefits of central planning are extracted when we put normally idle workers to work to counteract unemployment.

A monopoly is not that much of a problem in consumerism. The reason being that the prices charged by monopolists are, like all other prices, fixed. The monopolist cannot charge any price he wants. Thus there is less dead-weight loss. In consumerism a monopoly is just like any other firm except that it has no competitors. Usually problems regarding monopolies are overcome as monopoly firms are restricted to the command partition.

The laws of supply and demand do not apply to consumerism in 3 of the 4 sectors the same way they do in capitalism. The absurdities relating to them do not exist. The case of Brazilian coffee growers would be resolved differently in consumerism. The prices of the coffee beans would be the same regardless of supply and demand and thus none of the crops would be destroyed. If there are too many coffee beans, they would be exported to countries that need them.

The fine things in life are kept alive by the government. The government sponsors art, philosophy and poetry through the command partition. In a free-market economy they would not exist yet we would be at a loss to lose them.

Workers are not exploited. Firms cannot pay their workers whatever the firm wishes. The central bank determines each worker's wage. These wages are designed such that at the least each worker gets by. In other jobs workers can make a handsome profit. This is the communist objection to the free-market system and here it disappears.

There is no disparity between the wages of women and men. All wage functions are set by the central bank. A worker, whether a woman or a man, receives the same pay for doing the same job. There is no economic discrimination by sex in consumerism.

Unemployment is minimized. Employers have an added incentive to hire new workers. Workers buy jobs from their employers and are guaranteed a certain salary in the accommodational sector of the natural partition. Firms are paid a bonus from the government for making a profit thus attracting more firms to the consumerist nation and providing more work. The government reimburses a portion of a worker's wages so that firms have a greater incentive to hire more people. Due to these measures and several more that will be discussed in detail later, unemployment should be drastically reduced.

Bank runs are impossible. In order for there to be a bank run, people must want their money from a bank. But consumerism is a cashless society. There is no money in cash (paper bills) or coins. All currency is in bank accounts and saving accounts. Therefore there cannot be bank runs.

Consumerism has benefits. They stand opposed to the problems of the communist and free-market systems. In the rest of this exposition we will explore these benefits in greater detail.

Axis I: The Consumerist Quatrotomy

A key feature of this system is that it is divided into four major sectors-accommodational, materialist, laissez-faire and governmental. Although there is only one economy, there are four separate semi-independent sectors. It is this setup that makes this system unique.

The communist system has one sector. Everything is run by the government. Communism and the variations of socialism subscribe to such an arrangement. This type of system is characterized by central planning.

The free-market system has two sectors. These are the private and public sectors. The private sector consists of all firms and enterprises owned by persons or shareholders trying to make a profit. In contrast, the public sector is there to provide services that the private sector could not. The public sector functions to promote the well being of society rather than a single person. Things like the army and schools are in the public sector. A two sector economy is the cornerstone for all modern free-market and mixed economies.

If society could produce everything how would it produce it? In order for there to be goods and services in an economy, someone must produce them. But in a Utopia people can have everything without working. If no one works nothing could be produced and therefore a Utopia is impossible.

Now the question is how to give people as many goods and services as possible? People must work and they must have an incentive to work in order to produce these goods and services. The solution is accomplished by dividing the economy into sectors. One sector, the materialist sector provides materialist goods and services to consumerists as much as possible. The governmental sector provides government services and goods to consumerists. These goods and services in the governmental sector are such that they are provided best publicly. The accommodational sector as well as the laissez-faire sector give consumerists the incentive to contribute to society through either the materialist, governmental, accommodational or laissez-faire sectors. The difference between the laissez-faire and accommodational sector is that in the laissez-faire sector there is competition in terms of price whereas in the accommodational sector there is competition in terms of quality. This is the consumerist quatrotomy.

When the system is being applied in an actual setting, that is a country adopts the system, it is important to understand the relative sizes of the four sectors. The most efficient and productive possibility is where:

accommodational sector > materialist sector > governmental sector > laissez faire sector

Ideally, either the materialist sector or accommodational sectors should be the largest. The governmental sector should be third in relative size while the laissez-faire sector should be the smallest. Such an arrangement will allow us to make do with only three taxes – the Grand Consumerist Tax, the positive income tax and the wealth tax. And these are made use of only in special circumstances. If we have a smaller materialist sector and a proportionally larger laissez-faire sector, then it is necessary to create "creative taxes" (for example property tax and corporate tax) on the accommodational and laissez-faire sectors and complicate the system.

63

Nevertheless, the relative sizes of the four sectors can be manipulated to whatever the benevolent social planner (i.e. the founding fathers and the government) - desire. Although, ideally, either the materialist or accommodational sectors should be the biggest, it is quite possible that the laissez-faire sector could be the largest. The laissez-faire sector could compromise anywhere from 5 % to 95 % of the economy. Clearly, if the government finds a system organized by the laws of supply and demand favourable, they will opt for a very large laissez faire sector and keep the other 3 sectors much smaller.

Although the (benevolent social planer) founding fathers of the system have the final say as to the relative sizes of the four sectors, we can make several good suggestions. The laissez-faire sector should be 5 to 20 percent of the overall economy. The governmental sector should be about 10 to 25 percent of the economy. The materialist sector should be about 25 to 55 percent of the economy whereas the accomodational sector should be about 25 to 55 percent of the economy.

Of the four sectors we can group three together as they are of a somewhat different nature than the fourth. We will call the governmental, accommodational and materialist sectors the *GAM sectors* in distinction from the Laissez-faire sector. In the GAM sectors prices and wages are set by the central bank while in the laissez-faire sector they are set by the interaction of firms and consumerists. Also inflation is a possible problem in the laissez-faire sector as opposed to the GAM sectors.

Accommodation based consumerism must allow the possibility for extreme "richness" and be seen as a land of opportunity. All consumerists that contribute to the economy, regardless of what sector of the economy, earn Ignits that have the potential of being converted into Fortals. Those that find a way to contribute, earn more and more of these types of money. So some people have the opportunity of living in enormous mansions (palaces), taking extremely pleasant and lengthy vacations and wear the most expansive jewellery.

The accommodation based consumerist system is divided into four sectors. This division is very important. In the following sections we will see what we mean by materialist goods and services, governmental goods and services, accommodational goods and services and laissez-faire goods and services.

Axis II: The Consumerist Trichotomy

Besides dividing the economy into four sectors, we can divide it into three partitions. The three partitions of the accommodation based consumerist economic system are the governmental partition, the natural partition and the command partition. All three are equally important for a properly functioning accommodation based consumerist economic system.

The governmental sector and governmental partition are one. The idea behind the governmental partition/sector is to provide services that are best provided by a general public entity rather than a private firm or enterprise. Good examples include health care; that is medical services for all consumerists and the police service that protects all consumerists. There are many others. These types of services are better provided publicly; that is by a centralized system rather than a profit maximizing entity.

The natural partition is by far the largest part of the consumerist economic system. The natural partition involves firms trying to earn a profit in the materialist, accommodational and laissez-faire sectors. The essence of the natural partition is that the means of production is organized in the hands of firms. These firms have constraints that are set by the central bank and government; for example wage functions, input functions and price functions (in the materialist and accommodational sectors) but in the end they want to earn a profit.

The command partition is a special part of the accommodation based consumerist system. It involves the same sectors and industries under the direction of the natural partition. The main difference is that these businesses are under the control of a centralized government entity called the *Human Resource Management Commission (HRMC)*. The main purpose of this partition is to give employment to individuals that cannot find a job under the natural partition and the governmental partition, and who would otherwise be unemployed and not doing anything productive. The profits from the command partition go directly to the government as an alternative source of revenue and this helps fund social programs like health care, defence and education. Furthermore if organizations run by the command partition function in the materialist sector, this is good because it increases the consumerist grant given to working and non working consumerists as well as adding to the Grand Consumerist Tax. More on this later.

All three partitions are important. The governmental partition functions to provide services that are best provided publicly. The other two partitions do not differentiate as to what goods and services are provided to consumerists. Rather the difference between these two partitions is how goods and services are provided to consumerists. In the natural partition goods and services are provided by profit maximizing firms. In the command partition goods and services are provided by organizations whose goal is to provide employment for consumerists as well as making a profit.

Of all these partitions, the natural one should be the largest and the governmental and command partitions should be smaller. The natural partition should be about 55% - 75 % of the economy. The command partition should be about 5 % to 20 % of the economy. The government partition should be about 10 % - 25 % of the economy.

The laissez-faire, materialist and accommodational sectors can be either in the natural or command partition. Thus there is a natural-laissez faire sector, a natural-accommodational sector, a natural-materialist sector, a command-laissez-faire sector, a command-accommodational sector and a command-materialist sector.

There are three partitions in accommodation based consumerism. Each gives a means of providing goods and services. Dividing accommodation based consumerism into partitions is, as we will soon see, a good way to organize it.

The Materialist Sector

The materialist sector is one of the four sectors of the consumerist economy. It is identified as everything non-governmental that does not belong to the accommodational/laissez-faire sectors. This sector has the distinguishing feature that consumerists receive the goods and services in this sector just for being consumerists. Each working consumerist regardless of age, sex or profession receives Norses (Θ), one of the currencies, from the central bank to exchange for anything they desire in this sector. The non working non institutionalized consumerists also receive Norses from the central bank but a little bit less. They must be granted less in order to maintain an incentive to work. Every working consumerist – that contributes to society above a threshold- is granted an equal amount of Norses and all non-working non-institutionalized consumerists are also granted an equal amount of Norses relative to one another. No one is left with an absence of money.

In this section we attempt to analyze the materialist sector. However due to the enormous multitude of goods and services in this sector in existence, this analysis will not be exhaustive. First let's list the industries in the materialist sector. They are:

Transportation
Apparel
Hospitality
Entertainment
Information
Synthetics
Hygiene
Educational
Furniture

Now let's list some of the categories in each industry. Note that this is neither complete nor exhaustive.

1) Transportation- automobile, passenger movement
2) Apparel- clothes, foot wear, swim wear, winter wear, costume
3) Hospitality- restaurant food, grocery food
4) Entertainment- electronic entertainment, social entertainment
5) Information- electronic, written, media
6) Synthetics- cleaning, building
7) Hygiene- oral, facial, internal
8) Educational- scientific, literary, school, personal knowledge
9) Furniture- dining, sleeping, studying, relaxation

Here is a list of goods and services that could be found in the materialist sector. Once again this list is neither exhaustive nor is it of necessity.

- running shoes
- widescreen TV
- CD player
- radio

- PC computer
- lab top computer
- a bed
- dishwashing liquid
- insect repellent
- a sports car
- a jet
- a dog
- a winter jacket
- a T-shirt
- a piece of paper
- a spoon
- a desk
- a pair of jeans
- plates
- a map
- a cup of coffee
- a bowl of spaghetti
- a pizza
- a bowl of soup
- a cat
- a guitar
- a pair of skis
- a tape
- a doughnut
- a carton of eggs
- a jug of milk

The materialist sector is an important section of the economy. We gave some examples of industries, categories and products and services in this sector. It is important to note that these lists were neither complete nor total. What is important is that the division of industries and categories among sectors is not fixed. It is up to the government of a consumerist nation to define the division between the materialist, accommodational, laissez-faire and governmental sectors. We have just provided a workable yet effective setup.

The Accommodational Sector

The next sector of the consumerist economy is the accommodational sector. To give people an incentive to work and produce goods and services they must earn something that is proportional to their contributions to the economy. We must come up with certain goods and services that people would be willing to work for as a reward for their contribution to society. As consumerists exchange the Norses they obtained from the central bank for goods and services in the materialist sector, those that produce these goods and services or helped to do so earn Ignits, one of the other currencies. The same concept applies to the governmental sector. For working for the government and serving the public, people earn Ignits. Likewise for the accommodational sector- those that contribute to it earn Ignits. With these Ignits consumerists purchase goods and services made available in the accommodational sector.

What are the goods and services in the accommodational sector? The most important is land. Almost every war in history was fought over land. World War II saw the Germans taking over land by attacking their neighbours. WWI was also about land as hundreds of thousands of soldiers died for only several miles in the western front. The Napoleonic wars and the crusades were focused on the acquisition of land from others. Even in ancient times, wars were raged over land. The Romans expanded their vast empire by subduing their neighbours. It seems like land is highly valued and it would be reasonable to include it as one of the rewards for contributing to society.

Another important part of the accommodation sector is accommodation (hence the name). In any system, accommodation, the place one lives in, is one of the most expensive possession one owns and it should be something to work for. Those who work hard and produce a lot for society live in large mansions while those who do not have to settle for apartment buildings. Accommodation is the essence of the accommodational sector and is the reason for the name of the system itself.

To make sure that everyone participates in contributing to the economy, it would be good to include the utility industry in the accommodational sector. Since the utility industry is so essential, including it under the accommodational sector will surely motivate even the least hard working consumerist into action.

The leisure industry is also included in the accommodational sector. This means that the more productive workers have the better vacations. All consumerists want some enjoyment in life and some time to relax; not just work all the time. To have a chance to "get away from it all", the consumerist must contribute to society.

The appliance and home accessory industries are affiliated with the accommodation sector. This means that in order to have a stove, microwave or a washing machine one must contribute to society. To improve the accommodation one lives in- by buying paint, carpet or wall paper- one must contribute to society. The appliance and home accessory industries are good motivators for working unless someone doesn't mind living without vital possessions like an oven and a dishwasher.

Most business interactions are considered part of the accommodational sector. This includes paying workers, purchasing firms, factories or stores as well as buying consumerist stock. All of the financial industry, with several notable exceptions, is affiliated with the accommodational sector. However, a good part of the financial industry also takes place within the laissez-faire sector

Since adult entertainment is strictly pleasure it would make more sense to include it in the accommodational rather than materialist sectors. Adults who enjoy this type of entertainment should be given it the more they contribute to society. People who desire this commodity should work for it. In order to obtain adult entertainment some people would work very hard. Thus they will contribute to society.

Finally we have alcohol and tobacco. This is also something few people really need but some enjoy it once in a while or a little more often. It would also make more sense to put this under the accommodational rather than the materialist sector. If a heavy smoker doesn't have cigarettes he will work very hard to buy them. Thus to buy them he works and contributes to society.

The exact definition of the "accommodation sector" is hard to find as the industries in the sector are quite varied. Initially it was meant to be a sector having to do with "accommodation". That is, the things having to do with living arrangements. Eventually other industries like the leisure industries were added in order to strike a balance between the accommodational and materialist sectors. Now the only thing that the industries under the accommodational sector have in common is the fact that Ignits as a currency are used. This will have to suffice as a definition.

The main industries in the accommodational sector are:
* Land
* Accommodation
* Utility
* Appliances
* Home accessories
* Leisure
* Financial
* Adult entertainment
* Alcohol and tobacco

Here is a list of some of the categories under some of the industries. This list is not exhaustive as there could be more categories that are not mentioned.

* Land- agricultural, residential, industrial, commercial, recreational
* Accommodation- house, apartment, condominium, mansion
* Utility- household utility, entertainment utility
* Appliances- laundry appliance, kitchen appliance, household appliance
* Home accessory- floor furnishings, decorative items, lights, wall furnishings
* Leisure- domestic vacation, international vacation
* Financial- stock market, bond market, banking, wages, salaries, corporate
* Adult entertainment- video, magazine
* Alcohol & Tobacco- tobacco, alcohol

Here is a list of a number of goods and services found in the accommodational sector. This list does not include everything and could be slightly altered depending on how the government wants to manage the economy.

- a bungalow
- a palace
- a mansion
- a condominium
- an apartment building
- industrial land
- residential land
- commercial land
- rural land
- electricity
- hot water
- heating
- a dishwasher
- an oven
- a washing machine
- a drier
- a carpet
- a rug
- lamps
- yellow paint
- wall paper
- tiles
- floor
- windows
- plumbing service
- hot tub
- cable setup
- shower head
- new faucet
- drapes
- a trip to Jamaica
- a trip to France
- stay at a hotel
- visit to a spa
- visit to an amusement park
- visit to a circus
- visit to a movie theatre
- visit to a rock concert
- purchase of consumerist stock
- purchase of a consumerist bond

The accommodational sector is another major sector of consumerism. There are reasons why certain industries should belong to this sector rather than the materialist one. We listed the categories in each industry. Finally we listed a number of goods and services that might be found in this sector.

The Governmental Sector/Partition

The governmental sector is one of the four sectors of the accommodation based consumerist economy. With a number of important differences, it is similar to the free-market public sector. The governmental sector can also be conceptualized as the governmental partition.

There are three levels of government- federal/central, provincial/state and municipal. There are several revenue streams for the various levels of government. One way the government makes money is by taking a percentage of the Gross Domestic Consumerist Product- what this is will be explained shortly. The percentage that is taxed is spread equally among the three levels of government. The government can be of any political alignment. It could be very socialist or it could be very right wing (conservative). The percentage of the Gross Domestic Consumerist Product (GDCP) that is taxed is reflective of the political ideology. A socialist government would tax a higher percentage and provide many social services for its people. A right wing government would tax very little of the GDCP and let the various firms in the economy provide goods and services. There are also governments in between. The government that is elected (assuming we have a democracy) decides how socialist or right wing the government is. This depends upon the wishes of the people.

There are many services that the government is supposed to provide. As consumerists, everyone deserves access to 1) free health care, 2) free education and 3) free clean drinking water 4) free transit. Of course there are a lot more that could be added to this short list. However these are among the most basic.

The governmental sector provides certain goods and services for consumerists. We will talk about them shortly. First we must discuss the source of revenue of the three levels of the government. One source of revenue depends on the output of the materialist sector called the GDCP. The government puts a tax on this called the Grand Consumerist Tax (GCT). We will talk about the determination of the Grand Consumerist Tax in another section. Suppose that the GDCP is 15, 000 ☉ and the GCT is 30% Therefore 4, 500 ☉ go to the government. The federal government receives 1/3 of this. The provincial/state governments receive 1/3 of this based on their populations. The municipal governments also receive 1/3 of this based on their populations. Thus in our example the federal government receives 1, 500 ☉. There are five provinces. They have populations of 10 000, 20 000, 30 000, 40 000 and 50 000. The 1, 500 ☉ is spent among the provinces in a ratio of 1:2:3:4:5. The provinces with the greatest populations receive the most and the provinces with the least people receive the least. The same applies to the municipalities but is a bit more complicated. The 1, 500 ☉ is split according to population. Each municipality receives a percentage of the 1, 500 ☉ equal to the percentage of the population of the whole country that the municipality has. For example there are, for simplicity, ten municipalities. They have populations in terms of percentage of the whole country equal to 10%, 20%, 5%, 5%, 10%, 30%, 5%, 5%, 5%, 5%. The municipality with 30 % of the country's population receives 30 % of the revenue for the municipalities or 450 ☉. The municipality with 5% of the country's population receives 5 % of the tax for municipalities.

The 3 levels of government function with all three types of currency. They function with Norses and Ignits and when there is a source of revenue in the form of Fortals, these are converted to Ignits. So the government can pay for services in different ways. Here's an example: If the federal government has 10 000 000.00 ☉ and wants to pay for a hospital, the Norses are converted to Ignits to pay those who build the hospital and those who operate it. So the 10 000 000.00 Θ are deducted from the governments bank entry and the equivalent of Ignits is added to the bank accounts of those who built the hospital. In the case when the government has 10 000 000.00 þ, they can pay directly as the 10 000 000.00 þ are deducted from the government's Ignit account and the equivalent in the form of Ignits is added to the bank accounts of those who created the hospital. If the government has Fortals to spend, these are first exchanged to Ignits and with these the government pays for services.

There is something called the *Inter-Governmental Transfer*. This means that one level of government can give money to another level of government. If the federal government made an abundance of money it can give some of it to a province that is running into debt. Also, the provincial government can transfer some money to municipalities within the province if they are short in money.

Now we present the industries that are found in the governmental sector. They are
- education
- health
- protection/defence
- parks and recreation
- water/sanitation
- support services
- infrastructure
- public transport
- research
- community centres
- land marks
- bureaucracy

We try to list some categories of goods and services that belong to the governmental sector. However trying to list all categories would be too tedious. A word of note: The industries and categories presented here as being under the governmental sector need not necessarily be so. This is a proposition. In a real application, the governmental sector would be relatively bigger under a quasi-socialist society and relatively smaller under a quasi-free-market society. So it is possible that some of the industries or categories of goods and services will be found under the accommodational, laissez-faire or materialist sector. Also some industries may have goods and services that are in different sectors. For example, an elementary education would be found under the governmental sector while a karate school would be under the materialist sector

- Education- elementary, secondary, post secondary
- Health- treatment facilities, medical procedures, information
- Protection/Defence- internal defence, external defence
- Parks and Recreation- parks, nature trails
- Water/ Sanitation- water purification, water recycling, solid waste management
- Support services- youth programs, transfer payments to needy
- Infrastructure-public transportation infrastructure, pedestrian transportation infrastructure
- Public Transport- public human transport
- Research- medical research, scientific research, military research
- Community Centres- information centres, sports centres
- Land Marks- statues, buildings, sights which attract tourists

- Bureaucracy- parliament members, government officials, social servants

Here is a list of several goods and services that belong to the governmental sector:

- sidewalks
- roads
- hospitals
- a fountain
- a statue of a famous person
- a library
- a swimming pool
- a heart transplant
- physical rehabilitation services
- kidney transplant operation and nursing
- bus transportation
- trains
- AIDS research institute
- payment to mayor
- payment to members of government
- research into more accurate theories of the universe
- courthouse
- judges salary
- medium security correctional facility
- garbage pickup
- recycling services
- water purification
- operation of an elementary school
- operation of a secondary school
- national defence
- police officers
- fire fighting officers
- benches
- street lights
- pension plan
- welfare payments
- parks

This is not an exhaustive list nor is it a list of necessity. There are many goods and services not mentioned here. Also there are many goods and services here that the government in power could move to one of the other three sectors.

Each level of government has different responsibilities. The services provided are peculiar to a level of government. However we will not mention which industries or categories are under the jurisdiction of which hierarchy of government. This is more of a matter for politics than economics.

Some services provided through the governmental sector could be classified as "government assisted" services. These include public transit (buses, trains, and underground railway), passes to the skating rink or swimming pool, access to public galleries and museums, application for driver's license or passport and several others. The government has two options. It can give access to these without payment. In that case, consumerists do not have to pay to board a bus or train or visit the museum. Also the government can charge consumerists for access to these services. However the government provides government assisted services depends on the wishes of the government and the people.

The governmental sector of the accommodation based consumerist economic system is important. There are several sources of revenue for the levels of government. Certain categories belong to various industries in this sector. We ended with a short list of several goods and services that could belong to this sector.

The Laissez-Faire Sector

The laissez-faire sector is one of the key sectors of the accommodation based consumerist economy. Among other things, it is distinguished because it has a separate currency and prices are dictated by supply and demand vs. price, thus leaving the possibility of inflation. However, there are mechanisms in place to control inflation. The means of production in the laissez-faire sector are in the hands of profit maximizing firms.

In the laissez faire sector we have things that it does not make sense to fix price functions. Quality selection- this term will be discussed shortly- is not feasible and it is simply better to price goods and services using the laws of supply and demand vs. price. Instead of having prices determined by the central bank, prices are set by free-market forces.

Under this sector we have things like paintings, precious metals, gold, silver, antiques and jewellery. These are part of the laissez-faire sector. The same goes for tips for waitresses, donations for charities, gifts, books, collector's items and memorabilia like hockey cards. How do we fix a price function for art (paintings)? Can we compare a 3rd graders picture (or an art students) to a Leonardo da Vinci or a Picasso? It is better to use the market forces of supply and demand. Speculative stocks and speculative bonds are also in the laissez-faire sector.

The prices of antiques, paintings, etc... are determined by the interaction of consumerists and producers via the laws of supply and demand. The higher the price, the lower the quantity demanded but the higher the supply. The lower the price the higher the demand and lower supply.

Bankruptcy insurance is part of the laissez-faire sector. Firms compete to insure companies so more "risky" firms have to pay more to be insured. As stated in other sections, when a company bankrupts, first all of its assets are liquidated and then the bankruptcy insurance firm steps in. This puts the default risk in the hands of the insurance company not the investor.

In the laissez-faire sector, goods should be only final goods not inputs for other goods, like for example wheat or oil. If they were inputs this would affect (fixed) price functions in other sectors. Laissez-faire goods should only be the final goods that are directly provided to consumerists.

The laissez-faire sector should not involve markets that are monopolies or oligopolies. This would result in a monopoly with market power. Accommodation based consumerism is so arranged that all monopolies and oligopolies are in the GAM sectors where price/wage and input functions are fixed. This kills a monopoly's market power.

Generally, laissez- faire firms are those where it makes more sense for them to compete through price rather than quality. Sometimes it is hard to tell if they compete in quality (sports watches, books, and works of art). If it is possible for things to compete both in price and quality, these things are not in the laissez-faire sector but rather in the GAM sectors. However, when in doubt about fixing price functions, it is advisable to put the good or service in the Laissez-faire sector.

Another basic rule is that whatever good or service is not put into either the accomodational, materialist or governmental sector can potentially be considered as being in the laissez faire sector. Thus the government must be very careful in how it establishes the consumerist quatrotomy.

Merchant capitalists and those that thrive in the free-market capitalist system will really enjoy the laissez-faire sector of Accommodation Based Consumerism. The laissez-faire sector is capitalism in its purest form, where goods and services are exchanged using a pricing system based on supply and demand vs. price. However, the main advantage this sector has over capitalism in free-market countries is that in the laissez-faire sector there is no tax – no sales tax, no income tax and no corporate tax. Perhaps the only drawback is that the whole system isn't organized this way.

Some of the families of goods and services found in the laissez-faire sector include:

- actor in a TV commercial
- goalie in a professional hockey team
- gold necklace
- stock in the speculative stock market
- bonds in the speculative bond market
- baseball card
- tips to a waitress in a French restaurant
- a monetary gift to another consumerist
- a donation to a charity that saves abused dogs
- a painting by a well known artist
- anything sold at an auction
- movie star
- silver earrings
- musician
- books
- antiques
- services of artist
- antique repair and restoration
- service of a private attorney
- comic books
- credit unions
- mortgages
- service of paralegal
- private school
- souvenirs
- mowing of neighbour's lawn
- lemonade stand
- selling chocolate bars door to door

There are also six special types of goods and services that ought to be included in the laissez-faire sector. They are,

1) Things that have different value in different time periods. For example pumpkins for Jackolanterns, Christmas ornaments and chocolate Easter bunnies

2) Things not having to do with quality but which price can be negotiated. For example negotiating to have a ride in a car when stranded in a forest or wagering on a hockey game.

3) Things which price should go down considerably in the near future. For example, new techno gadgets whose price goes down from $ 2000 to $40 in 3 years. Also, a trip to the moon or to outer space.

4) Whatever is not officially in the accommodational, materialist or governmental sectors

5) Goods and services sold through the method of auctioning

6) Tips and gratuities

7) Things for which there is a ridiculous price difference between the highest and lowest quality good. For example pens. A plastic pen can cost $1.50 for a pack of 20 or $200 for a fancy one. However, this should not apply to cars.

Two types of goods and services that must necessarily not be in the laissez-faire sector are:

1) Those in monopoly markets

2) Inputs for final goods in the materialist and accommodational sectors

The above list is not exhaustive. There could be many, many more families of goods and services depending on how quasi-free-market or how quasi-socialist the government is. Furthermore, some of the goods and services in the above list could be moved to another sector while other goods and services in the other 3 sectors could be brought to the laissez-faire sector.

The laissez-faire sector functions to provide balance in a consumerist economy. It has certain key attributes. Together with the other 3 sectors, the laissez-faire sector ensures that the consumerist economy works productively and efficiently.

The Natural Partition

As mentioned previously, there are three partitions in accommodation based consumerism. These are the governmental partition, the command partition and the natural partition. The natural partition is perhaps the largest partition in terms of how many economic transactions take place in that partition.

We define the natural partition as "all firms in the materialist, accommodational, and laissez-faire sectors trying to make a large profit, run by entrepreneurs and corporations under the stipulations of fixed price, wage and input functions in the accommodational and materialist sectors and the laws of supply and demand vs price in the laissez faire sector."

Firms in the natural partition are run by "merchant capitalists". These are individuals whose goal is to make a profit. Although there are capitalists in the free-market system, these same capitalists would find the accommodation based consumerist system, and its natural partition, preferable as there are no "disincentives" like those in the free-market system. For example, in accommodation based consumerism there does not exist corporate, sales, property tax or other tax. The GCT, the wealth tax and the positive personal income tax are implemented as a last resort.

By definition, the natural partition does not involve the governmental sector/partition. Thus things in this partition cannot include things like hospital visits, protection from police or elementary school education. The natural partition does not involve things that would better be provided collectively by the government.

The natural partition does, however, involve things in the materialist, accommodational and laissez-faire sectors. Clearly, this involves a wide variety of industries and families of goods and services. It includes things like houses, cars, restaurants, grocery stores, clothes, toys, beer, newspapers etc. Almost everything not provided by the governmental partition can be provided via the natural partition.

The key idea behind the natural partition is that goods and services provided to consumerists are done so through profit-maximizing firms. These firms are entities that offer goods and services to consumerists while trying to maximize the difference between revenue and cost (profit) in doing so. If a firm can earn a profit while providing goods and services to consumerists it is more likely to flourish in the natural partition specifically and accommodation based consumerism in general.

All three currencies are involved in the natural partition. The natural partition can operate within the materialist, accommodational or laissez-faire sectors. Thus in the natural partition there can be Norses, Ignits or Fortals.

The natural partition of accommodation based consumerism is vital for a well functioning economic system. Of the three partitions it is the largest and most important. Most of the businesses in consumerism are part of the natural partition.

The Command Partition

The Command partition is an important section of the economy. It is essentially a branch of government that decides how to employ workers that would not normally be hired through the natural or governmental partitions. A branch of the government, we will call the Human Resource Management Commission (HRMC), has an obligation to put people to use that would otherwise be unemployed. This is similar to free-market concept of "work-fare" but taken to a much, much higher level.

The Command partition is linked to the Socialist Labour Pool, an important entity that will be fully described in another section. The workers that work in the Command partition are called *auxiliary workers*. These workers can work in the Materialist, Accommodational or Laissez-faire sectors but they cannot work in the governmental sector. In some sense, this has similarities to Chinese state capitalism, but it is at a much grander scale.

We previously didn't have too many positive things to say about a centrally run economic system such as the one in communist countries. True, a command economy is hard to manage on a grand scale. However, when small, it can be beneficial. Firms run through a command system can be made to produce anything that the government wants them to produce. So, if statistics show that there is a housing shortage, these firms can be used to build more apartment buildings. If it seems that people have not enough food to eat, they can set up several farms or grocery stores. Furthermore on a scale as small as a single household it actually works very well. In most families, chores and duties like vacuuming, doing the dishes and walking the dog are organized without any money being exchanged. These actions are performed through a system of mutual cooperation.

Of note is the fact that of all industrialized countries, the Soviet Union was one of the only ones that avoided a Depression in the 1920's and 1930's. Thus a command economy is incapable of having a stock market crash like other countries had.

As stated, the HRMC cannot create jobs in the government sector. Otherwise the government would cut government jobs and fill them with auxiliary workers. For example, the government would fire teachers and police officers and replace these with auxiliary workers because they get paid less.

No matter how inefficiently a government puts people to work, it is better than if these people did nothing. It is better if a 100 people dug a hole and another 100 filled it up than to have 200 people sit around and do nothing. Even if a HRMC run firm makes a profit of only 1000 þ per month, this adds up with a large number of these firms.

It is important that the HRMC enterprises are efficiently and productively run. It is common opinion that government operated institutions are very inefficient- but is this because they are run by the government or because they have poor management? It is possible that people with business knowledge may be unemployed. This refers to people with a business degree or experience in management. These people should be put in charge of running the firms we are referring to.

The HRMC creates subsidiary firms that hire auxiliary workers. These HRMC firms compete with firms in the accommodational, materialist and laissez-faire sectors that belong to the natural partition. The prices in the materialist and accommodational sectors are fixed while those in the laissez-faire sector are determined by the interaction of consumerists and firms- which in this case are HRMC firms operated in the command partition.

The Human Resource Management Commission would build factories, farms, foundries, mines, stores and use auxiliary workers as human input. If auxiliary workers would get a payment for doing nothing anyways, it is better if they did something. The profits from these HRMC enterprises go to the government budget as a profit. Thus in our system, the "welfare" system actually makes money. Also if the HRMC enterprises contribute to the output of the materialist sector, the GDCP increases, which increase the General Consumerist Grant, the NWCG as well as the GCT, increasing government revenue even further. We will talk more about this later.

The HRMC can create several firms that act as bankruptcy insurance firms. Thus they can affect how much businesses pay for bankruptcy insurance. So the government, in an indirect way, has some control over the bankruptcy insurance rate premium.

The HRMC represents firms that are run by an organization whose goal is to find employment for people while still making a profit. It ensures that there are no unemployed. It is a program designed to give all consumerists some kind of shelter and everyone is guaranteed a job. The mandate of the Human Resource Management Commission is to:

1) Find employment for all who seek it
2) Make a profit
3) Resolve pure shortages and surpluses
4) Create healthy competition for firms in the natural partition
5) Discourage people from belonging to the Socialist Labour Pool
6) Control money supply
7) Eliminate hunger
8) Fight global shortage
9) Reduce market power of monopolies

No person, no matter how lazy, slow, irrational, uneducated, inexperienced or mentally ill or undeveloped shall be turned down from a job by the HRMC. The only question is what job he will be given

It is hard to coordinate an entire economy using the command system due to the many decisions that have to be made. It is more practical if we are dealing with a small portion of the population – those who cannot find jobs. If we have a country like Canada with 30, 000, 000 people and 4% are unemployed after all unemployment reducing measures, this is only 1, 200, 000 people.

One of the goals of the Command partition is to create Wonders of the World. There is prestige in having the largest (tallest) building in the world, having a stadium so big that it can seat a million people, a restaurant so big that it can accommodate 100, 000 people or perhaps putting a human on Mars. There is value in some things beyond the need to satisfy the consumerists.

Those that run the Command partition have the power to assign work for a large number of workers. For example, auxiliary workers can be assigned to clean a 100 m section of a street.

Their job would be to keep it totally clean and a supervisor would be assigned to make sure of that.

There are 3 levels of workers in the command partition. Level 1 workers perform jobs. Level 2 workers make sure level 1 workers do their job properly and level 3 workers make sure that level 2 workers do their job properly.

Auxiliary workers are paid by how much they work. vs. how much they should work. If the Human Resource Management Commission sets for a worker to work 35 hours for 600 þ and 300 ƒ and the worker works that much he gets 600 þ and 300 ƒ. However if he works 17.5 hours (50% of what he should) he gets 300 þ and 150 ƒ. Another way of restating this is that if an auxiliary worker works, he earns 17.14 þ per hour and 8.57 ƒ per hour. So if the worker works 17.5 hours he earns 300 þ and 150 ƒ per week. Auxiliary workers are still entitled to a vacation.

Another use of the command partition is to support the arts like poetry, philosophy, music etc. In a purely free-market economy, it is very difficult for anyone to make a profit writing poetry. One has to be extremely, exceptionally good at what he does. A lot of culture is lost as brilliant philosophers, poets and musicians are forced to find work where they will make more money. Fortunately, accommodation based consumerism preserves things like poetry and philosophy. If the human resource commission comes to the conclusion that someone has the ability or aspiration for the arts then that person should spend his time in that endeavour. The alternative is that he would be receiving welfare checks for not doing anything. The only outstanding issue is how these people would be paid. Instead of paying them for the hour, it is better if they were paid weekly.

The command partition is very useful in eliminating pure shortages and surpluses. When there is a surplus in a firm in the natural partition, a command partition buys that good to relieve the surplus. Also, when there is a shortage of a good in a natural partition firm, a command partition firm sells that good to the natural partition firm to relieve the shortage. This will be discussed more fully in an upcoming section.

Global shortages can be overcome with the help of the command partition. When a good is in a state of global shortage, the HRMC creates special firms to produce that good.

The command partition is useful in beating hunger. If the hospitality industry firms of the command partition have a surplus either normally or through the pure surplus resolution measure, they donate that food so it is accessible to hungry consumerists. Also, the no-food wasted initiative ensures that perfectly good food is not thrown out at the end of the day but given to hungry people.

Command partition firms also give "healthy" competition to natural partition firms. If a command partition café sells a really good donut, this will encourage a café in the natural partition to sell even better donuts.

It may be necessary to bring in production quotas for work in the command partition. For example, a wheat farm may have to produce a certain amount of wheat in a year and a comic book artist may have to come up with a certain amount of comic books in a month. This is done to stimulate production and reduce idleness.

To ensure that those workers that are working in the command partition are doing their job effectively, the HRMC may impose certain production quotas on these workers. For example, a comic book artist may need to create 4 comic books a month and a wheat farmer may need to produce a certain amount of wheat per year. This will ensure that command partition workers are productive. If they fail to meet these quotas, they may have their payment (extra work transfers) reduced.

The HRMC makes money by selling its goods and services to consumerists. The profit goes to pay for workers as well as to have a source of government revenue.

Sometimes the consumerist economy may be doing very well. In that case, it may be a good idea to decrease the scope of the command partition. In such a case the HRMC privatizes a certain firm. That is it sells it to investors who function in the natural partition. Then the firm operates like a firm whose main goal is to maximize profits. The money made from selling a command partition goes to pay for social services.

Imagine if a car factory is built in the command partition. This will provide jobs for tens of thousands of workers. The factory will likely make a huge profit and this can be used to pay for social services. It is also good competition for other car manufacturers and consumerists have access to high quality cars.

The command partition anti-inflationary deduction is another important use of the command partition. What this parameter does is that it takes some of the profit command partition firms make and destroys it. This is meant to lower the money supply.

It is a good idea if we stipulate that all monopoly markets must by necessity belong to the command partition. This will destroy the market power that arises when a firm is a monopoly.

The command partition is one of the three partitions of accommodation based consumerism. Its primary goal is to find employment for workers who would otherwise be idle. It should also make some profit. Together with the natural and governmental partitions, it allows the consumerist economy to work smoothly.

Interaction of the Sectors and Partitions

The four sectors interact with the three partitions in a special way. The governmental sector and governmental partition refer to the same thing. The laissez-faire sector, the materialist sector and the accommodational sector can be in either in the command partition or the natural partition. The following diagram illustrates the concept:

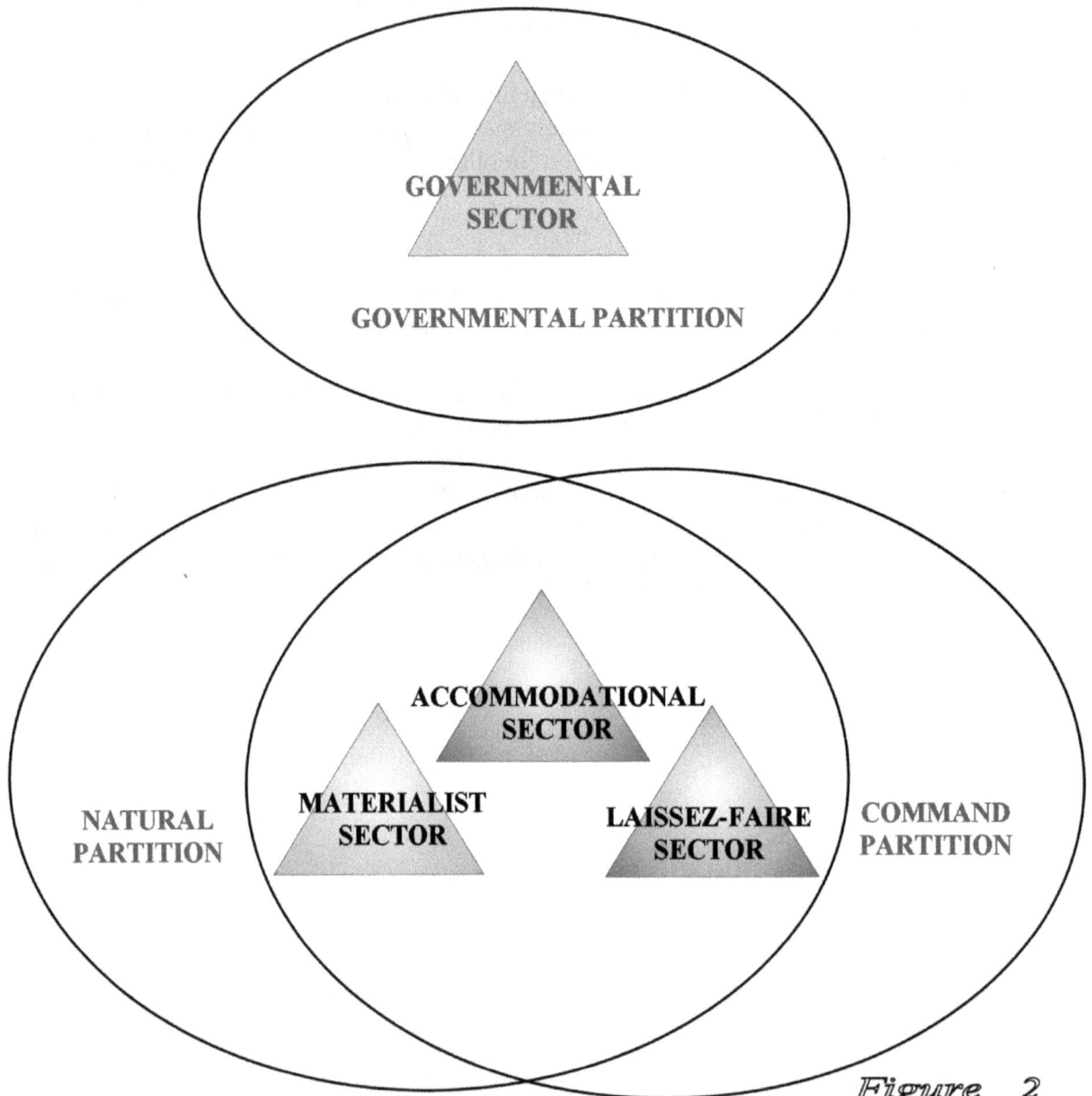

Figure 2

Parameters of the System

In this section we introduce the different parameters that come into play in accommodation based consumerism. By parameter we mean a variable that is determined by an individual or a group that effects the functioning of the system. In addition to parameters we include terms and determinants that are unique to this system. We will not describe these parameters and terms in detail here. We will simply define them and state who is in charge of that parameter or term. It is to the great advantage of the system that it has many rather than few parameters. A cook with a large selection of spices can make a tastier meal than one who only has salt and pepper. The free-market system is severely limited in its number of parameters. It only has fiscal policy and monetary policy. Besides interest rates, the money supply, taxes and spending there aren't too many options for manipulating the economy. The consumerist system has a lot of parameters that can be used to promote the well being of the system. The following are the parameters and unique terms of the accommodation based consumerist economic system. Included is what body or individual manipulates it.

Firm- an organization that transforms inputs into goods and services that people want

FR- firm revenue- the income, in Ignits or Fortals, a firm earns through its transactions

Population- the growth or decline of the number of people in the nation. Determined by how many immigrants are permitted into the country- government

Materialist Demand- the desire for more goods and services. The want for things made in the materialist sector like TV's and cars- consumerists in the materialist sector

Accommodational Demand- the desire for more goods and services produced in the accommodational sector. The want for such things as houses and vacations- consumerists

Materialist Supply- the ability to provide consumerists with goods and services in the materialist sector. The willingness to impart consumerists with goods and services in the materialist sector- materialist producers directly, consumers indirectly

Accommodational Supply- The ability to provide consumerists with goods and services in the accommodational sector. The willingness to impart consumerists with goods and services in the accommodational sector- accommodational producers directly, consumers indirectly

Norses- one of the three currencies in the system. Used in the materialist and the governmental sectors. Have the symbol Ɵ

Ignits- one of the three currencies in the system. Used in the accommodational and governmental sectors. Have the symbol þ

Fortals- one of the three currencies in the system. Used in the laissez-faire sector. Have the symbol ₤

Gross Domestic Consumerist Product (GDCP) - the total value of all goods and services sold or put into a position to be sold in the materialist sector during a period of time. Expressed in the form of Norses- firms in the materialist sector.

Individual Domestic Consumerist Product- the total value a specific firm in the materialist sector contributes to the Gross Domestic Consumerist Product total in a period of time. Expressed in Norses- particular firm in the materialist sector

Benevolent Social Planner- a being we hypothetically assume makes decisions of how the economy is arranged. Sets values for all the parameters of the system. In actuality it is the government, central bank or interaction of economic actors

Financial Punishment- A second layer of punishment on top of a justice punishment. Allows for governmental revenue - government

Profit Vacuum- The existence of an opportunity for economic actors in consumerism to make a profit. Encourages output and productivity in consumerism.

Grand Consumerist Tax (GCT) - a portion of the GDCP that is given to various levels of government. Used to provide governmental goods and services- the three levels of government

Accommodational Markdown- during certain transactions in the accommodational sector, a percentage of the transaction that is taken away from the seller and destroyed. Controls the over accumulation of Ignits in the accommodational sector- central bank

Retail Markup- a percentage increase in the price of retail goods in the materialist and accommodational sectors that the retailer can charge above the original price of the good. Allows retailers to make a profit- central bank

Price Functions- the cost of buying a good or service in the economy. Can be expressed in terms of Norses or Ignits per a certain quantity of good- central bank

Wage/ Salary Function- a function describing the amount a worker is paid for a service. Expressed in Ignits- central bank

Consumerist Universal Stock Price (CUSP) - the cost of buying a unit of consumerist stock. Expressed in Ignits- central bank

Extra Work Transfer- the amount of accommodational goods and services – like housing and utilities- that an unemployed person receives in order to subsist. It also involves money in the form of Ignits and Fortals that the welfare recipient can use to promote his interests- the government

Employment Reimbursement Transfer (ERT) - the money paid to firms as a reward for hiring more employees. Used to combat unemployment. Expressed as a percentage. - The government

Capital Investment Transfer (CIT) - the money paid to firms to cover the costs of purchasing capital to encourage investment. Used to combat unemployment. Expressed as a percentage- the government

Profit Reward Transfer (PRT) - a reward a firm makes for making a profit. Used to encourage investment and combat unemployment. Expressed as a percentage- the government

Interest Rate Stimulus (IRS) - a percentage of a loan that is paid to creditors by the government to encourage investment and decrease unemployment – the government

Quality Selection- the occurrence where firms compete with one another to provide the most desirable goods and services in a market where price functions of goods and services are fixed

Price Selection- the occurrence where firms compete with one another to provide consumerists with goods and services of the lowest price

Occupational Complexity Rating- a measure of how difficult a job is to perform- government

Governmental Bank- an entity that makes loans to businesses and the government

Exportation-Importation Companies- Firms who make a profit through buying items and either exporting or importing these items to foreign nations

Government Bank Chairman- the head of the government bank responsible for making many of the decisions the government bank makes

Deputy Government Bank Chairman- replaces the government bank chairman in times of a crisis

Governmental Business Loan Assistance Program- an initiative where the government loans businesses money to help them thrive -government

Governmental Business Loan Assistance Interest Rate- the interest rate levied on the loans the government makes to businesses – central bank

Pure Shortage and Surplus- the resolution of shortages and surpluses through the trading of goods between firms in the natural and command partitions

Consumerist Trade Pool Commission- A governing body that oversees transactions in the consumerist trade pool

Speculative Stock Protection Mechanism- A device that ensures that those who invest in speculative stock do not lose all of their money

Wealth Tax- a special tax levied on the richest people of the consumerist society
.
Governmental Employment Incentive Program- A system where the government gives money to businesses to increase employment -government

Command Partition Anti-Inflationary Deduction- A portion of the profits of the command partition that are deducted from the economy and destroyed so as to overcome inflation – central bank

Governmental Inflationary Markdown- a portion of the government revenue that is deducted and destroyed so as to overcome inflation - government

Laissez-Faire Markdown- Money taken away from the laissez-faire sector so as to reduce inflation – government

Gold Investment Certificates and Silver Investment Certificates- the ability to have in one's hand a certificate worth a certain amount of gold or silver

International Bonds – the government buys bonds from a foreign government and the foreign government eventually pays the government a higher amount- the government

International Bond Interest Rate- the interest rate a foreign nation has to pay us on the international bonds they bought- government

International Bond Maturity Period- the time when an international bond must be repaid - government

Speculative Mutual Fund- the owning of several stocks in various companies in the speculative stock market

Original issuing price of speculative stock- the price at which a stock in the speculative market is originally sold at. Factors in bankruptcy resolution- firms

Bankruptcy Insurance Anti-Inflationary Deduction- Money taken away from the profits of bankruptcy insurance firms that is destroyed so as to reduce inflation - government

GDCP Anti-Inflationary Mechanism- A system to reduce inflation whereby the money entering the GDCP is controlled – 3 levels of government

Partial Ownership of Firms by the Government- A mechanism where the government invests in firms so as to have a partial ownership of the firm - government

Government Revenue Stock- the occurrence where the levels of government issue stock in themselves to raise money for social spending - government

Premium Savings Bonds- the occurrence where the levels of government sell bonds in themselves. The money raised is invested and the interest is used to pay for social services- government

Premium Savings Bond Interest Rate- the amount of money consumerists are paid for buying premium savings bonds -government

International Loan Program- an initiative where the government loans money to foreign countries. The interest on the loan is used to pay for social services - government

Income Reimbursement Initiative (a positive income tax) – a program where the government raises money from consumerist's income while allowing consumerists to make a profit -government

Income Reimbursement Initiative Interest Rate- the interest rate paid on the positive income tax -government

Income Reimbursement Initiative Maturity Period- the amount of time at which income tax payers can expect to receive profit for paying their income tax – government

Income Tax Brackets- a schedule of how consumerists pay the income tax based on their earnings - government

Increase or decrease in scope of materialist sector- the procedure where industries are added or taken away from the materialist sector

Foreign Currency Exchange Adjustment- used to control the money supply when two currencies are being exchanged for one another- central bank

Proof of Foreign Visitor Status- the position where a tourist or someone visiting our nation has the right to buy things in the materialist sector with Ignits- government

Avoidance of Debt- the preposition that government revenue can be increased if spending on debt servicing is decreased or eliminated

Governmental Loan to Business Inflationary Deduction- Money taken away and destroyed when the government gives loans to businesses - government

Selective Occupation Promotion System- a program that ensures the most important and most valued jobs are supported in consumerism - government

Government Ownership of Stocks Inflationary Deduction- money that is taken away and destroyed when the government engages in initiatives of owning stocks in businesses – central bank

Laissez-Faire Business Limit- the threshold where goods and services can be traded in the laissez-faire sector as opposed to other sectors - government

International Credit Rating- A scale where countries are judged as to how reputable they are in terms of paying back loans – central bank

Accommodational Award Threshold- the minimum of amount of hours worked by a consumerist in a given time to be eligible for the accommodational award- government

Accommodational Award Deduction Incentive- a percentage deducted from a consumerist's NWCG to encourage him to work - government

Governmental Market Adjusted Price- A change in price to eliminate shortages and surpluses - government

Governmental Market Shortage/Surplus Resolution System- a system designed to eliminate shortages and surpluses by adjusting subsidies and money gained by firms -government

International Bankruptcy Insurance Firm- A firm that insures countries in case they default on their loan or can't make interest payments on their loans.

The WC grant- A payment from the government to a firm for providing toilet facilities for people entering the place of business - government

Disability Work Program- A system that tries to find employment for all people that are considered disabled

Consumerist Spending Reimbursement (CSR) - a reward from the government to consumerists for buying goods and services and spending more. Used to stimulate the economy and reduce unemployment. Expressed as a percentage. Exists as Accommodational Consumerist Spending Reimbursement and Governmental Consumerist Spending Reimbursement- the government and firms in accommodational sector

Accommodational Consumerist Spending Reimbursement- a reward from firms for shopping at a particular establishment- firms

Government Consumerist Spending Reimbursement- a reward from the government for shopping at a particular establishment- government

Public Veto- a political measure where if a significant portion of a population do not want a law, the law has to be reexamined- the people

Actual Exchange Rate- the value of our nations currency in terms of the currency of another country - interaction of firms in laissez faire sector and international firms

Working Grant Threshold- the threshold that differentiates between a "working" and "non-working" consumerist. In terms of hours worked as well as Ignits/Fortals earned. Those above the threshold earn the general consumerist grant while those below it earn the non working consumerist grant- the government

Real Estate Profit Percentage (REPP) - the percentage of the transaction a real estate firm earns during a transaction involving real estate property. Expressed as a percentage- central bank

Adjusted Revenue Price Duration (ARPD) - the price of purchasing a business from a former owner. Based on the revenue it earns in a certain length of time- central bank

Political Ideology- whether the society is left wing/quasi-socialist or right wing/quasi-free-market. Whether the GCT is small or large. How big the governmental sector is compared to the materialist, laissez-faire and accommodational sectors- the government indirectly, the consumerists directly

Rental Equivalence Duration (RED) - how long it will take a renter to pay the cost of the building he rents. A calculation of how much rent a consumerist must pay for his accommodation when renting- central bank

Insurance Premium Rate- A monthly payment to an insurance company – life, car, house- in return for coverage in that area- interaction of firms and those wishing to be insured

Input Price Function- a function describing the cost of buying an input for a product. How much the producer must pay for certain factors of production- central bank

Delivery Price Function- a function describing the cost of delivering certain goods over a distance calculated by a base time in addition to a price per kilometre. It is of the form $w\text{þ} + y\text{þ}$ where w is a base fee and y is a fee per kilometre- central bank

Bank Rate- the interest charged when private banks borrow from the central bank – central bank

Yearly Vacation Duration Period (YVDP) - the amount of paid free time from work a worker is

90

entitled to. Expressed as hours/days per year- government

Timing of Vacation- When a worker can take his vacation and leave work for several days or weeks- interaction of firms and workers

Yearly Sick Leave Exemption Period (YSLEP) - the number of days a worker is allowed to skip from work due to illness. Expressed in days per year- government

Maternity Leave Duration Period- How long a pregnant woman can take time off from her work to take care of her baby- government

Injury Severance Payment- How much a worker or his family receives from a firm in case of an injury that disables him from working. Expressed in Ignits and fortals-central bank

Economic Taxonomy- the organization of all goods and services and things produced into coherent groups. Similar to biological taxonomy- government

Externality Regulations-the set of rules about how to deal with positive and negative externalities. Designed to eliminate externalities- government

Means of Production- the method used to produce things. The determination of what inputs are used- firms

Interest Rates- the cost of borrowing or lending a number of Ignits. (central bank). Applicable to business and private loans as well as mortgages. If Fortals (laws of supply and demand)

Job Contract Price (JCP) - the amount of money required to buy a contract for work. This contract gives the worker the right to work at a particular job and a sense of job security– central bank

Adjusted Monthly Income Percentage (AMIP) - how much more a worker will earn in income than he originally had to pay for his JCP. Represented in terms of percent per month- central bank

Adjusted Yearly Income Percentage (AYIP) - how much more money a worker will earn than he had to pay for his job contract. Represented in terms of percent per year- central bank

Adjusted Income Earnings (AIE) - the amount of money a worker earns at the end of his contract minus the cost of the JCP and the interest to the bank for buying the JCP. Expressed in Ignits-central bank

Part –Time Character- how much work a particular worker does relative to the full time. Expressed in terms of a percentage- worker and firm

Rental Repayment Value (RRV) - the cost of renting a good or service in the accommodational or materialist sectors of the economy. Set as a percentage. - The central bank

Consumerist Trade Pool- a trading fund where excess profits from exporting and importing are used to subsidize the importing and exporting of other goods. Allows us to export things we don't need and import things we do without affecting prices- central bank

Nominal Exchange Rate- the price of one Ignit in terms of another foreign currency calculated using exports, imports and real exchange rates- central bank

The Consumerist Quatrotomy- how goods and services are divided among the four sectors- accommodational, materialist, laissez-faire and governmental. A reflection of the political ideology of the country- government

Defence Team Promotion Initiative- an extra incentive for the team representing a defendant to ensure he has a fair trial - government

Command Partition Compensation Adjustment- a mechanism to ensure all workers in the command partition are paid a fair wage/salary - government

Supply of Norses Issued- the amount of Norses put into the economy is always equal to the GDCP. It goes directly to the government or is distributed among the consumerists- central bank

Distribution of Land- how land should be divided. Land can be divided into residential, industrial, commercial, agricultural, recreational, conservational, protected etc- government

Work Schedule- the minimum amount of hours a worker is entitled to work as a consequence of owning a job contract. Calculated using the JCP, the wage function, the length of a worker's contract and the AMIP- central bank

Industry Hybrid-Patent Period- how long a person or firm has the right to be the sole producer of a product or service. Understood in terms of length of time, earning of revenue or profit. Different patent period for each industry- patent office (central bank)

Minimum Retirement Age- the minimum age at which a worker can retire. At this age a worker is entitled a pension- government

Retirement Pension Allowance- the amount of money granted to a retiree by the government. Expressed in Ignits. – The government

WC- number of working non institutionalized consumerists

NWC- number of not working non- institutionalized consumerists that are still in the labour force

General Consumerist Grant- the amount of money –in Norses – employed non-institutionalized consumerists are granted each period by the central bank. Expressed in Norses- central bank

Non-Working Consumerist Grant Markdown- how much less non-working non-institutionalized consumerists are granted relative to working consumerists. Expressed as a percentage- government

Non-Working Consumerist Grant- the amount of money, in Norses, unemployed, non-working non-institutionalized consumerists are granted by the central bank as well as those not in the labour force and those working below a certain threshold, expressed in Norses- central bank

GDCP per capita- the GDCP divided by the number of people in the society- a statistic

Gross National Product (GNP) - the value of the final output of the accommodational sector expressed in Ignits- a statistic

General Bond- a form of investment where there is a promise to payback a certain amount of money after a length of time called a maturity. Exist as consumerist and speculative general bonds

Profit Bond- a form of investment that takes into account a firm's profit and revenue. Exist as consumerist and speculative profit bonds

Stock-Bond – A form of investment that has characteristics of both a bond and a stock. Exist as consumerist and speculative stock-bonds- Central bank and interaction of firms and investors

Consumerist Stock-Bond Interest Rate- the interest rate the central bank puts on a consumerist stock-bond – central bank

Speculative Stock-Bond Interest Rate- the interest rate that applies to a speculative stock-bond- interaction of firms and investors

%OOS (% Ownership of Stock)- how much stock an investor has of a firm relative to the total issued

Consumerist General Bond Interest Rate (CGeBIR) - the interest rate on a consumerist general bond. Expressed as a percentage- central bank

Consumerist General Bond Interest Repayment Frequency (CGeBIRF) - how often an investor is paid his interest from owning a consumerist general bond – central bank

Consumerist Profit Bond Interest Rate (CPBIR) - the interest rate on a consumerist profit bond. Expressed as a percentage- central bank

Consumerist Profit Bond Interest Repayment Frequency (CPBIRF) – how often an investor is paid his interest from owning a consumerist profit bond – central bank

Consumerist Governmental Bond Interest Rate (CGoBIR) - the interest rate on a consumerist government bond. Expressed as a percentage – government

Consumerist Government Bond Interest Repayment Frequency (CGoBIRF) - how often an investor is paid his interest from owning a consumerist government bond – government

Speculative General Bond Interest Rate (SGeBIR) - how much interest rate an investor receives on a speculative general bond. Expressed as a percentage – interaction of investors and firms

Speculative Profit Bond Interest Rate (SPBIR) – the interest rate an investor earns from owning a speculative profit bond- interaction of investors and firms

Speculative Government Bond Interest Rate (SGoBIR) - the interest rate an investor earns from owning a speculative government bond- government

Profit Bond Investment (PBI) - the size of a profit bond- the interaction of firms and consumerists

Speculative Bond Interest Repayment Frequency (SBIRF) - how often an investor is paid his interest from owning a bond. Applies to speculative general bonds, speculative profit bonds but not speculative government bonds. May fluctuate – interaction of bond sellers and consumerists

Speculative Government Bond Interest Repayment Frequency (SGoBIRF) - how often an investor is paid his interest from owning a speculative government bond. May fluctuate- government

Length of Bond Maturity- the length of time in days, months or years until a bond has to be repaid to an investor by a firm- interaction of investors and firms

BV – (Bond Value or Size of Bond)- the value of a bond. How much money, in Ignits, an investor lends to a firm in exchange for interest payments- interaction of investors and firms

Consumerist Central Bank Stock- A special type of stock issued by the central bank to decrease the number of Ignits in circulation in the accommodational sector. Used as an anti-inflationary measure- central bank

Consumerist Central Bank Stock Interest Rate (CCBSIR) - How much profit one earns from owning Consumerist Central Bank Stock- central bank

Speculative Central Bank Stock – A special type of stock issued by the central bank to control the money supply by limiting the number or Fortals in circulation in the laissez-faire sector. Used as an anti-inflationary measure- central bank

Supreme Firm Director- the owner of a corporation. In charge of most of the decisions made by a corporation- picked by shareholders in the natural partition and by the human resource management commission in the command partition

Grand Chairman- an important member of the central bank. Responsible for many key decisions in the economy

Deputy Grand Chairman- person who replaces the Grand Chairman in case of a crisis.

Bankruptcy Insurance Premium Rate (BIRP) - how much an insurance company earns monthly from insuring a company by bailing it out in the case of a bankruptcy. The insurance company pays the bankrupting firm's debts to shareholders, bond holders, creditors and workers if the firm can't do so. The premium rate is expressed in terms of the money insured- firms

Post- Reinvestment Profit (PRIP)- The profit a firm makes minus its reinvestment in itself (to expand production). Used to calculate earnings from owning stock.

Command Partition- one of the three partitions of the system characterized by firms trying to make a profit while hiring as many unemployed workers as possible using central planning

Natural Partition- one of the three partitions of the system characterized by firms guided by the profit motive

Human Resource Management Commission- a body created by the government whose goal is to oversee the functioning of the command partition- command partition

Socialist Labour Pool- the collection of workers who are unemployed but are put to work in the command partition

Auxiliary Workers- workers in the socialist labour pool and the laissez-faire labour system

Auxiliary Worker Reimbursement Deduction (AWRD) - how much less a person in the socialist labour pool receives per month for being in the socialist labour pool. Expressed as a percentage- government

Unemployment Assistance Repayment (UAR) – how much money a worker has to repay the government when he finds a job in either the natural or government partition. Expressed as a percentage- government

Government Bond Pool- A special fund for collecting Fortals and Ignits from selling government bonds, either speculative or consumerist. Used as an anti-inflationary measure to control the money supply – the government

Consumerist Anti- Inflationary Pool- An anti-inflationary (money supply controlling) tool used to limit the number of Ignits circulating in the accommodational sector- central bank and government

Speculative Anti- Inflationary Pool- An anti-inflationary (money supply controlling) tool used to limit the number of Fortals circulating in the laissez-faire sector- central bank and government

Nominal Fortal- Ignit Exchange Mechanism – an arrangement for converting Fortals into Ignits and Ignits into Fortals. An anti-inflationary measure used to control the money supply – private bank

Reciprocal Fortal- Ignit Exchange Mechanism- an arrangement for converting Fortals into Ignits and Ignits into Fortals. Allows conversion of currency -private bank

Employment Agency- a firm that works to find workers for firms (in exchange for a fee) and also work for the unemployed

Inter- Governmental Transfer- The movement of money from one level of government to another or to another jurisdiction at the same level where one level of government has more funds than another jurisdiction that needs money - government

Work for Freedom Program- An arrangement where an inmate does supervised work in exchange for time off his sentence - government

Work/Freedom Incentive Ratio (WFIR) - How much time off his total sentence an inmate receives in exchange for doing productive work- interaction of firms, judge, attorneys and inmate

Recycle for Pay Program- A system where consumerists bring useless items (paper, cans, glass) in exchange for a payment. This the government then sells this to input processing firms – government

Recycle for Pay Percentage (RFPP) – How much a consumerist is paid for bringing useless items to be recycled and converted to inputs. Expressed as a percentage of the value of the raw material- government

Employment Assistance Program- A system where the government pays a firm for hiring workers. Later this worker must pay the government (with interest) for the service – government

Employment Assistance Program Interest Rate (EAPIR) - the profit in terms of interest the government receives from workers in exchange for helping them find employment – government

Laissez – Faire Labour System- An anti-unemployment measure where worker's wages are partially paid by firms in the Laissez-faire sector and partially by the government- government and firms in laissez- faire sector

Accommodational Award- the granting of some kind of accommodation to all consumerists (who need it) so as to eliminate homelessness- government

Accommodation Award Repayment Percentage (AARP) – how much a person receiving the accommodation award has to repay the government when he finds another form of accommodation (or continues to live there), expressed as a percentage- the government

Materialist Overdraft – the grant of extra Norses to consumerists during a set period when the consumerist is drastically short of Norses to pay for essential items- the government

Materialist Overdraft Limit- the maximum amount of Norses a consumerist can be granted during a set period when he is short of money for essential items- the government

Materialist Overdraft Interest – How much (in terms of a percentage) a consumerist has to pay the government for providing him with the materialist overdraft- the government

Consumerist Grant Distribution Schedule – At what point in time consumerists receive their General and Non-Working Consumerist Grants- the Government

Universal Consumerist Card- a card that all consumerists are given which they can use to purchase items in the materialist, accommodational and laissez-faire sectors- all consumerists

Industry Specific Chairman- A member of the central bank in charge of some decisions regarding wages and prices for a specific industry

Industry Specific Deputy Chairman- A central banker whose role is to replace the industry specific chairman if he is unable to fulfill his duties

Industry Specific Commissioners- A group of central bankers in charge of some decisions regarding wages and prices for a specific industry

Resonance Price Functions – Description of price functions in different terms.

Principal of Maximum Utility – the idea that an employment position should match the abilities of the individual seeking the employment

Accommodational Overflow Calamity – the occurrence where more and more Ignits enter the accommodational sector and are unable to leave

Consumerist Savings Bond- Special bonds issued to raise money for governmental services when the government is experiencing a deficit- the three levels of government

Consumerist Savings Bond Interest Rate- the interest paid on consumerist savings bonds – the three levels of government

Consumerist Savings Bond Interest Repayment Frequency- how often investors are paid their interest on consumerist savings bonds – the three levels of government

Consumerist Grant Minimum Allowance Age- the earliest age that a consumerist is eligible for a consumerist grant either general or non-working – government

Dynamic Gambling- a form of gambling where the profits are deducted as an anti-inflationary measure- governmental and laissez-faire sectors

Standard Gambling- a form of gambling where the profits go to pay for social services- governmental and laissez-faire sectors

Production Quotas- a stipulation that workers in the command partition must produce a certain amount of good in order to be paid their extra work transfer- government

Command Partition Productivity Incentive Deduction System- a setup where auxiliary workers have an incentive to work hard, work properly or produce high quality goods- central bank and government

Norse- Command Partition Productivity Incentive Deduction – a deduction from an auxiliary worker's Norse earnings when doing little work or poor quality work- central bank

Ignit- Command Partition Productivity Incentive Deduction – a deduction from an auxiliary worker's Ignit earnings due to doing little work or poor quality work- government

Fortal- Command Partition Productivity Incentive Deduction – a deduction from an auxiliary worker's Fortal earnings when doing little work or poor quality work- government

No Food Wasted Initiative – a program that encourages firms in the hospitality industry to give their surplus food to hungry people when closing for the day instead of throwing it out

Food Geared to Income Program (FGIP)- a setup made to ensure that all hungry receive food if they want it

Consumerist Food Center (CFC) - a place where the hungry can buy food using the Food Geared to Income Program

Universal Food Card- a card allowing hungry consumerist to obtain food at CFCs

Food Geared to Income Percentage- how much a hungry consumerist must pay in proportion to his materialist income to take advantage of the Food Geared to Income Program

Food Geared to Income Limit- the monetary value for the limit a consumerist has on taking things from the Consumerist Food Center

Global Shortage Stimulus- money given to natural partition firms to produce a good that is in a state of global shortage- government

These are the various parameters of Accommodation Based Consumerism. We made a thorough list of many ideas and concepts that are prominent in this system. We gave a brief description of each parameter. Additionally, we mentioned which group or identity has control over that parameter.

Money

The accommodation based consumerist economic system works differently at a very basic level than its free-market counterpart. The free-market system economy uses one currency whereas the consumerist system uses three types of currencies. Like the free-market system, money is used to buy things and as a means of exchange. However, in consumerism there is a schism as to what each currency can purchase.

Accommodation based consumerism is a cashless society. There are no coins or bank notes. All money is in private bank accounts and is transferred between individuals and firms using checks, debit cards and a special card called the *Universal Consumerist Card* (UC Card). There are many advantages to a cashless society. One is convenience. A check or card that is lost or damaged does not present a loss. A check can be stopped and a card replaced. For these reasons and many others the consumerist society is cashless.

There are three currencies in consumerism. There are Ignits, there are Norses and there are Fortals. The symbol for an Ignit is (þ). The symbol for a Norse is (Θ). The symbol for a Fortal is (f). The symbol follows the number in an expression of money. The reason that there are three different currencies is that they are used to buy things in different sectors. Norses are used to buy final goods and services in the materialist sector. Also the government uses Norses and Ignits to pay for its expenditures. The rest of the transactions are in Ignits or Fortals. Ignits are used to pay salaries and wages in the accommodational sector and to pay for the inputs to any sector. Consumerist stocks and bonds are purchased in Ignits. All products in the accommodational sector are bought with Ignits. The separation between Ignits and Norses is based on what they can purchase. Fortals are prominent in the laissez-faire sector.

Money in the GAM sectors of consumerism, unlike most free-market economies, is not fiat money- this means that it is more than paper that we agree to have value. It is exactly equal to the GDCP. The supply of Norses is pegged to materialist goods and services, giving the money actual value. Whatever the materialist sector produces in the span of one month is granted to the consumerists and the government. This is in Norses. Every two weeks, the central bank grants all working non-institutionalized and non-working non-institutionalized consumerists a sum of money in Norses. This grant is in either the form of a check or direct deposit in the private bank account which all consumerist are assumed to have. Thus the central bank grants Norses to consumerists to spend on anything they wish in the materialist sector and it grants the government Norses to pay for goods and services it provides.

Private bank accounts are of three basic forms. They can be either Norse accounts, Ignit accounts or Fortal accounts. Even though one Norse is worth exactly one Ignit, no one can directly exchange an Ignit for a Norse or a Norse for an Ignit. This stipulation is crucial. Firms that provide material goods and services can provide accommodational goods and services although it must use different currency for goods and services in different sectors. These two sectors must be separate. Thus a department store can sell TV's, computers and ovens at the same time but use different currencies in specific situations since the first two items are in the materialist sector while the third is in the accommodational sector.

To purchase materialist things like clothes, TV's or computers, the consumerist spends the Norses the central bank granted him and that are now in his bank account. At the moment of purchase, a consumerist receives a good or service and the materialist producer provides the good or service. At the same time, the price of that good or service is deducted from the consumerist's Norse bank account and the equivalent number of Ignits is added to the producer's bank account. This is the idea behind the conversion of Norses to Ignits during a transaction of goods and services.

An example will illustrate the process. A consumerist, let's call him Lucas, wants to buy a hat from Ultra-Z-Supermarket. The hat costs 5.00 Ο. Lucas writes a check for 5.00 Ο to Ultra-Z-Supermarket and Ultra-Z-Supermarket gives Lucas the hat. Ultra-Z-Supermarket takes the check to a private bank where, for simplicity, both Lucas and Ultra-Z-Supermarket have accounts. Lucas had a balance of 790.00 Ο on his Norse account. Ultra-Z-Supermarket had a balance of 20 500 þ on its Ignits account. Upon getting the check the bank subtracts 5.00 Ο from Lucas account leaving him with 785.00 Ο and adds 5.00 þ to Ultra-Z-Supermarket's account leaving them with 20 505 þ. Lucas could have also used a debit card. This is accomplished when Lucas swipes a card through a machine and enters a password (maybe more identification needs to be required for security reasons). This way the bank directly credits Ultra-Z-Supermarket with 5.00 þ and deducts 5.00 Ο from Lucas. When a buyer buys something in the materialist sector money is deducted from his Norse account while there is an increase in the producer's (seller's) Ignit account. This is an example of a simple purchase in the materialist sector.

Let's look at a transaction in the accommodational sector. In this example the consumerist Lucas, has earned 500.00 þ. With this he can make a purchase in the accommodational sector. He wants to buy tickets to a basketball game costing 50.00 þ. The ticket company gives Lucas the ticket and Lucas swipes his UC card. When the information is received at the bank, the bank deducts 50.00 þ from Lucas's Ignit account leaving him with 450.00 þ. The ticket company receives 50.00 þ which are added to their Ignit bank account. This is an example of a simple purchase in the accommodational sector.

An interesting phenomenon in consumerism is that of an intermediate purchase. John buys 100 Ο worth of groceries for Greg. John gives the grocery store 100 Ο. Subsequently John gives Greg the groceries while Greg gives John 100 Ο. All the time the transactions are in the form of bank book entries so John and Greg are exchanging money among each other using checks.

Let's entertain another example. The government is granted Norses as part of the GCT. Suppose that the federal government is granted 100 000.00 Ο. It wants to pay for a heart operation for a consumerist. Doctors must perform this operation. The price of an operation of this type is 2 500 þ. The doctor receives 2 500.00 þ when he performs this operation. The 2 500.00 Ο are deducted from the government's Norse bank account and 2 500.00 þ are added to this doctor's account. This is an example of a simple transaction in the governmental sector.

The exchange of money in the laissez-faire sector is similar to that in the accommodational sector. John wants to buy a book worth 10.00 f from a bookstore. He has 450.00 f in his Fortal account while the bookstore has 800 000.00 f in its Fortal account. John swipes his special debit card, the UC Card, entering a code, and the cashier gives him the book to take home and read. At that time 10 f are deducted from his account leaving him with 440.00 f and 10 f are credited to the bookstore leaving them with 800 010.00 f.

As mentioned, the currency in the laissez-faire sector is Fortals. To combat inflation, which the laissez-faire sector is prone to, we have the Ignit- Fortal exchange mechanism. Normally 1f = 1þ and 1þ = 1f. However, if we want to decrease the money supply, these exchange rates can be different so that one loses money when converting back and forth between Fortals and Ignits. For example the exchange rate could be 10 ƒ = 1þ and 6 þ = 1ƒ. So if we started with 600 þ, this converts to 100 ƒ and if we convert this 100 ƒ again we get 10 þ. Note that these exchange rates are not necessarily inverses of each other. Trading Fortals into Ignits and back again is the surest way to lose money. However it may be necessary to exchange currencies to buy goods and services in another sector. It is crucial to understand that one cannot trade Norses to Fortals or Fortals into Norses.

The consumerist economy is cashless and functions with three types of currencies. These are needed to service a quatro-sectoral economy. This is a major difference from any economic system in existence or any that has ever been thought up.

The Retail Mark-Up

We define retail as the selling of final goods directly to consumerists. It would be impractical if all factories or farms sold directly to its customers. Problems such as those relating to transportation would result. An economy would function more smoothly if retailers bought goods from a producer and sold them to consumerists in convenient locations.

A retail outlet buys goods from a manufacturer or factory and in selling these must make a profit. This profit is called the *retail mark-up*. The retail mark-up is a percentage increase in the price of a good sold at a retail store. The price functions for families of goods and services set by the central bank only apply to manufactured goods; not the ones sold to the public. The price the public pays for a good is affected by the retail mark-up.

We have a store that sells shoes. A pair of shoes costs 80.00 Ɵ/pair. The retailer must pay 80.00 þ to the shoe factory to acquire these shoes (although the final price is in Norses the retailer must pay in Ignits because they are at this stage considered inputs for retail purposes). The central bank sets a retail mark-up in terms of a percentage. Let's assume that it is 20% in our economy. Therefore the shoe salesman can sell the shoes at 80.00 Ɵ x 0.2 + 80.00 Ɵ = 96.00 Ɵ. The shoe salesman must sell the shoes at this price; no lower and no higher. The 16.00 Ɵ represent profit. It must cover all of the operating costs of the store such as shipping of the shoes, the wages of the shoe store employees and other costs. It is essential that when the central bank sets the retail mark-up it is high enough to cover the operating costs of the retail establishment. In this example, let's suppose that the consumerist spending reimbursement (CSR) is 0.4 %. In this case this is the Government Spending Reimbursement. So when the consumer buys the 96.00 Ɵ worth pair of shoes, the government reimburses him (96.00 Ɵ x 0.004) = 0.384 þ. The reimbursement is in Ignits while the shoes at the retail store are in Norses. This reimbursement encourages the consumerist to do more shopping and thus stimulate the economy.

Let's elicit two more examples for clarity. Take the case of a hardware store which sells paint. Paint from the factory costs 0.50 Ɵ /litre and comes in 4 L cans. The retail mark-up is 25%. Therefore the store must sell the cans of paint for (0.50 Ɵ x 4) x 0.25 + (0.50 Ɵ x 4) = 2.50 Ɵ. This should cover operating expenses like the shipping costs and wages and rent. If the CSR is 0.4% (government spending reimbursement), then the consumerist buying the paint receives 2.50 Ɵ x 0.004 = 0.01 þ.

Now take the case of a car dealer. Cars from the car factory cost 10 000.00 Ɵ and the retail mark-up is 25 %. The car dealership can sell each car for 10 000.00 Ɵ x 0.25 + 10 000.00 Ɵ = 12 500.00 Ɵ. This should cover operating costs. If the CSR (governmental spending reimbursement) is 1 %, the consumerist buying the car receives 12 500.00 Ɵ x 0.01 = 125.00 þ.

The retail mark-up can be manipulated by the central bank. It can be lowered to decrease retail profit and increase the amount of sales or it can be raised to help retailers and decrease sales. It does not have to remain fixed but can fluctuate from time to time. Its value is determined by the Grand Chairman of the central bank.

It is possible that factories, farms and manufacturing facilities may sell directly to the public if they wish. They then don't earn the amount set in a price function but are entitled to a retail mark-up. If they didn't we would have a problem as factories would sell for a lower price than the retailer and there would be competition in price. But this cannot be. Price functions must be fixed and producers must compete in quality (in the GAM sectors). Let's look at an example of this. A shoe factory makes shoes. A pair of shoes costs 80.00 ☉. Instead of charging this much to a shoe store which would charge a retail mark-up on this, the shoe factory has another option. They can sell directly to consumerists. The shoe factory builds a huge warehouse right next door to its factory. Let's assume that the retail mark-up is 25%. The shoe factory could charge each consumerist 80.00 ☉ x 0.25 + 80.00 ☉ = 100.00 ☉ for a pair of shoes.

The question now arises: if a factory can sell its products at a higher price by selling directly to the public, why would it bother to sell at the price set by the price function to retailers? There are a few reasons. Not everyone is willing to travel all the way to a factory to buy a good. Secondly, there are also costs associated with selling the good at the factory as there are in any retail store with the exception of transportation costs. A factory selling to the public would still have to pay its utility fees, worker's wages and for space. Also, retailers order goods from a factory in bulk whereas individual consumerists buy in much smaller quantities. In the shoe case, a consumerist may buy a pair of shoes from the factory at 100.00 ☉, but a shoe retailer would probably order several hundred at 80.00 þ per pair.

The retail mark-up must be included in the price of a good. A price tag on a good cannot say, for example, (1.00 ☉ + 25% retail mark-up). This may lead consumerists to believe that they are paying some kind of tax on the good. The retail mark-up is simply how much the retailer makes extra for retailing a final good. The price tag from before should say "1.25 ☉" not "1.00 ☉ + 25%".

The retail markup in general only applies to firms in the materialist and accommodational sectors. In the governmental sector, the purchases are essentially done by the government so there is no need for a retail markup. In the laissez-faire sector, final sale prices, including at the retail level are determined by the forces of supply and demand. Thus the retail markup is not necessary in the laissez-faire sector.

There is no double retail markup. A retail markup cannot be applied on another retail markup. The original retail markup is the limit to how much a price can increase over the fixed price set by the central bank.

The retail mark-up is the incentive for retailers to serve consumerists. Profit in the form of a retail mark-up ensures that consumerists will always have close access to quality goods. People with quality goods are in some ways happier people. At least, they are not worse from it.

The Gross Domestic Consumerist Product

We begin by talking about what the Gross Domestic Consumerist Product (GDCP) is. The official definition is: "the value of all final goods sold or in a position to be sold at the set price in the materialist sector plus the value of all final services in the materialist sector purchased by consumerists at the set price in a given period of time". The meaning of this definition will be made clear shortly.

Next we give examples of what would be counted in the GDCP. It would include a loaf of bread bought by Matthew in a grocery store. It would not include the cost of wheat, flour or water used to make bread or the purchase of the bread by the grocery store from a bakery. It would include the price of a car at a dealership. It would include the price of a chair at a furniture store. But not the wood or how much the furniture cost at the factory. The final good sold to the consumerists is included in the GDCP but the means of how it was produced is not.

Included in the GDCP are all products in the materialist sector which have the potential to be sold to consumerists. However they can only be counted once- not in several periods. If a convenience store does not sell 10 bags of chips, these are still counted towards the GDCP. If a car is not sold, it will nevertheless be counted towards the GDCP. It doesn't matter whether goods are actually sold. The crucial point is that they be available to consumerists. It is also crucial that they be only counted once, not every time they are not sold.

Services in the materialist sector are also counted towards the GDCP. The main distinction between the contribution of goods and services to the GDCP is that services must actually be bought by consumerists. Services such as teaching, cleaning, fixing cars or painting are included because they are final services. Non-final services like the work of a janitor, waitress, cashier, cook or baker are not included.

Final goods and services must originate from the materialist sector- not the accommodational, laissez-faire or governmental sectors. A house or a bottle of beer would not be included because they are items from the accommodational sector. Goods and services in the accommodational sector are discluded from the GDCP.

Business investments are not included because they are in the accommodational and laissez-faire sectors. Exports and imports only factor in as much as they affect the ability of consumerists to purchase goods from the materialist sector. Thus an export would not be added since consumerists can't purchase it. Imports may be added if a consumerist has the ability to purchase it. For example if a car dealership imports a car, that car would be added to the GDCP. Whether an item is added depends on the consumerist's ability to purchase it.

The time period in which the GDCP is counted is one month. Every month firms and retailers must report their contribution to the GDCP to the central bank. This is called the Individual Consumerist Product. In a way this is similar to reporting one's taxes every year in the free-market system. The important difference is that the firms and individuals do not actually give any money to the central bank. They just mention how much they contributed to the economy. As was mentioned, goods that were not sold but had the potential to be so, can only be reported for one period. Let's do a simple example. John's convenience store sold 10 bags of chips, 5 bottles of pop and 3 boxes of cookies. He had in stock 2 more boxes of cookies but couldn't sell them. This example is very simplified but it will serve its purposes. The chips cost 1.00 Ⲟ each bag. A bottle of pop costs 2.00 Ⲟ and a box of cookies cost 3.00 Ⲟ. There is a retail mark-up of 50 %. Let's see what John's convenience store's Individual Consumerist Product is:

$$10 \times 1.00\ Ⲟ + 10 \times (1.00\ Ⲟ \times 0.5) = 15.00\ Ⲟ$$
$$5 \times 2.00\ Ⲟ + 5 \times (2.00\ Ⲟ \times 0.5) = 15.00\ Ⲟ$$
$$3 \times 3.00\ Ⲟ + 3 \times (3.00\ Ⲟ \times 0.5) = 13.50\ Ⲟ$$
$$2 \times 3.00\ Ⲟ + 2 \times (3.00\ Ⲟ \times 0.5) = 9.00\ Ⲟ$$

Total = 52.50 Ⲟ

Thus John must fill out a form stating exactly all his transactions (with records and receipts) and tell the central bank that he contributed 52.50 Ⲟ to the GDCP. Once again, he doesn't actually give any money to the central bank. All other firms that contribute to the GDCP do something similar to what John did. If the central bank thinks he stated that he contributed more than he actually did, he can be audited. That is, he has to meet with a representative from the central bank to talk about his statement.

That is how the central bank arrives at a particular month's GDCP. With this figure the central bank grants money to consumerists and to the government. The central bank does not tax to earn money so as to redistribute it. It grants the equivalent of the GDCP to the government and the consumerists. For example let's suppose the GDCP for the month of January was 1 000 000 000.00 Ⲟ. The government sets a tax called the Grand Consumerist Tax. Let's suppose that it is 30%. Therefore the central bank will grant the government 300 000 000.00 Ⲟ to spend on social services. There are, theoretically speaking, two other taxes but they are implied as a last resort. We will give more detail on these taxes later on in other sections on taxes.

Now we have 700 000 000.00 Ⲟ to give to consumerists. The population is 15 000 000 people. The non-institutionalized population is 10 000 000. Of these 9 000 000 work and 1 000 000 are unemployed or not in the labour force and are non-institutionalized. If everyone was working the 700 000 000 Ⲟ would be divided equally between the 10 000 000 people. However those that do not work must receive a smaller percentage of the money so that they will have a reason to work. The government sets the Non-Working Consumerist Grant Reduction. This is how much money the unemployed and those not in the labour force are granted by the central bank relative to working consumerists. Let's say it is 20%. To find how much the working consumerist and non-working non-institutionalized consumerists are granted we must calculate the amount:

$$X = 700\ 000\ 000.00\ Ⲟ\ /\ [9\ 000\ 000 + 0.2(1\ 000\ 000)]$$

$$X = 76.09\ Ⲟ$$

Therefore the 9 000 000 working non-institutionalized consumerists would receive 76.09 Ⲟ. The 1 000 000 non-working non-institutionalized consumerists would receive $0.2 \times 76.09\ Ⲟ = 15.22\ Ⲟ$. These grants seem small but our population in this example is exceptionally large.

The difference between a working and non-working consumerist is defined by the government. If a worker only works an hour a month, this shouldn't qualify him as a "working consumerist." The definition would probably be based on how many hours he contributes to society a week as well as how much revenue (in Ignits or Fortals) he earns if he makes money through commission. The distinction between a working and non-working consumerist is determined by the government using a parameter called the Working Grant Threshold (WGT). It is how much a consumerist must contribute to society in hours worked or Ignits earned in order to be designated a working consumerist. So suppose that the government sets the WGT at 50.00 þ per week or 35 hours worked a week. A consumerist who earns 45.00 þ per week would earn the non-working consumerist grant and a worker who earns 89.00 þ would earn the general consumerist grant. A consumerist who works 43 hours a week would earn the general consumerist grant while one who worked 32 would earn the non working consumerist grant.

We need a formula for determining the consumerist grant. To determine the General Consumerist Grant (that is received by working non-institutionalized consumerists).We use:

$$GCG = [GDCP - GCT]/[WC + NWCGR(NWC)]$$

Where GCG is the General Consumerist Grant. GDCP is the Gross Domestic Consumerist Product. GCT is the Grand Consumerist Tax. WC is the number of working non-institutionalized consumerists. NWCGR is the Non-Working Consumerist Grant Reduction in decimal form; NWC is the number of not working, in the labour force non-institutionalized consumerists or those not in the labour force..

The formula for the Non Working Consumerist Grant (the amount of money the non-working consumerists are granted by the central bank) is:

$$NWCG = GCG \times NWCGR$$

Where NWCG stands for Non Working Consumerist Grant. The other two variables have been defined above.

Now the consumerists can buy whatever they want with the Norses in the materialist sector and they can spend as much of it as they desire as long as they still have it. Rather than being granted once a month, the grants are made every two weeks or twice a month. Thus in our calculations above we simply divide the GCG by two to determine how much working consumerists receive from the central bank bi-monthly. The NWCG also needs to be divided by two to come up with the value the non-working consumerists are granted from the central bank twice a month. Every two weeks almost every consumerist is granted some money to spend as see fit. The reason for the grant stems from the beginning of this treaty. It benefits the consumerists.

Although the two types of consumerist grants are given once every two weeks, not all consumerists are given their grant on the same day. If this was the case there would be a sudden rush to buy things the day the grant was given and consumerists would be fighting each other to buy various goods and services. Rather, the government enacts a *Consumerist Grant Distribution Schedule*. If we divide a 2 week period into 14 days, some people would be given their grant, either General or Non-Working, on day 1, others on day 2, others on day 3... and so on. People would be given their grant on different days of a 2 week cycle. One way to accomplish this is to differentiate people based on the first letter of their last name. So, people whose last name begins with A or B would be given their grants on day 1, people with last names beginning in C or D would be given their grant on day 2, people with last names beginning in E would be given their grant on day 3 and so on.

The money the consumerists are granted cannot be used in the accommodational or laissez-faire sectors. That requires other currencies and to obtain those currencies consumerists must somehow contribute to society. More about this will be mentioned later on.

The General Consumerist Grant as well as the Non Working Consumerist Grant are like gift certificates to be spent on the materialist sector. The government gives money to all non-institutionalized consumerists to spend as they will on goods and services in the materialist sector. This is clearly a wonderful way to support the consumerist economy.

The process of calculating the GDCP is repeated every month. Therefore the central bank is able to grant money to consumerists about every half a month. Every month the consumerists have money to spend on materialist goods and services. Each month they should earn more money as the process of granting money greatly stimulates the economy.

We have mentioned that the government receives money. How much it earns and how it spends it will be discussed in other sections.

A good question is how does the GDCP increase? The best and most productive way is if the actual output increases. That is, firms sell more goods and consumerists take advantage of more services. The GDCP can also increase if the retail markup increases. However that way consumerists have to pay more for the goods they buy. Another way to make the GDCP larger is to shift the consumerist quatrotomy and make more industries and families of goods and services part of the materialist sector.

Another important parameter having to do with the GDCP and consumerist grants is the *Consumerist Grant Minimum Allowance Age.* This is basically the age at which a consumerist is first entitled to receive either the General Consumerist Grant or Non-Working Consumerist Grant. It is set by the government. It can be birth, 10 years of age, 16 years of age or 18 years of age or something different. If it is at birth, the household has an incentive to procreate as another member of the family will raise the collective consumerist grant of the whole household. Throughout the rest of this book we will assume that this parameter is valued at birth.

The GDCP and the Individual Consumerist Product are at the basis of consumerism. Consumerists and the government are granted money from the central bank based on the GDCP. The concept of GDCP is at the heart of the consumerist economic system.

The Central Bank

The central bank is one of the cornerstones of the accommodation based consumerist economic system. It has tremendous power and influence. Many jurisdictions are directly under the control of the central bank.

The central bank is an institution with many purposes that works with the government but is separate from it. It is designed to aid the economy. Strictly speaking it is not a for-profit institution.

The central bank is a body of economists called central bankers. There are two types of central bankers- prime central bankers and industry specific central bankers. Thus there are hospitality industry central bankers, apparel industry central bankers, transportation industry central bankers. Each type has 102 members. For the prime central bankers, one is called the Grand Chairman. There is a Deputy Grand Chairman. The other 100 members are called Consumerist Commissioners. For hospitality industry central bankers we will have a hospitality industry chairman, a hospitality industry deputy chairman and 100 hospitality industry commissioners. The same reasoning applies for the other industry specific central bankers. It is a good idea if they are all appointed by the government (president, king, prime minister, finance minister); and are not elected. Each member is appointed for 15 years although this is not fixed; i.e. the length of being a member may be 10 or 20 years. However, as a suggestion, if the benevolent social planner (i.e. the government, founding founders, people) desire it, the members of the central bank can be elected. This would ensure accountability to all the decisions the central bank makes. However, this may have negative political externalities. The Grand Chairman, Deputy Grand Chairman and the Consumerist Commissioners have different jobs.

Certain parameters of consumerism are under the jurisdiction of the central bank. They are:

- Accommodational Markdown
- Retail Mark-Up
- Price Functions
- Wages and Salary Functions
- Consumerist Universal Stock Price
- Real Estate Profit Percentage
- Adjusted Revenue Price Duration
- Rental Equivalence Duration
- Input Price Functions
- Delivery Price Functions
- Injury Severance Payment
- Interest Rate (accommodational sector)
- Job Contract Price
- Adjusted Monthly Income Percentage
- Adjusted Yearly Income Percentage
- Adjusted Income Earnings
- Consumerist Trade Pool
- Nominal Exchange Rate

- Supply of Norses
- Work Schedule
- Industry Hybrid-Patent Period
- General Consumerist Grant
- Consumerist General Bond Interest Rate
- Consumerist Profit Bond Interest Rate
- Consumerist Stock-Bond Interest Rate
- Consumerist General Bond Interest Repayment Frequency
- Consumerist Profit Bond Interest Repayment Frequency
- Non-Working Consumerist Grant
- Rental Repayment Value
- Nominal and Reciprocal Ignit-Fortal exchange mechanism
- Government Business Loan Assistance Interest Rate
- Government Partition Anti-inflationary deduction
- Government Ownership of Stocks Inflationary Deduction
- International Credit Rating
- Foreign Currency Exchange Adjustment
- Command Partition Anti-Inflationary Deduction
- Bank rate
- Norse- Command Partition Productivity Incentive Deduction

Some of the above parameters are under the control of the Grand Chairman, others under the control of the Consumerist Commissioners and others both groups have a voice in the determinination of that parameter. Yet for others, the industry specific central bankers play a roll. The following are directly under the control of the Grand Chairman:

- Accommodational Markdown
- Retail Mark-up
- Real Estate Profit Percentage
- Adjusted Revenue Price Duration
- Interest Rate (accommodational sector)
- Adjusted Monthly Income Percentage
- Adjusted Yearly Income Percentage
- Nominal Exchange Rate
- Rental Equivalence Duration
- Consumerist General Bond Interest Rate
- Consumerist Profit Bond Interest Rate
- Consumerist Stock-Bond Interest Rate
- Consumerist General Bond Interest Repayment Frequency
- Consumerist Profit Bond Interest Repayment Frequency
- Rental Repayment Value
- Nominal and Reciprocal Ignit-Fortal exchange mechanism
- Government Business Loan Assistance Interest Rate
- Government Partition Anti-inflationary deduction
- Government Ownership of Stocks Inflationary Deduction
- International Credit Rating
- Foreign Currency Exchange Adjustment

- Command Partition Anti-Inflationary Deduction
- Bank rate
- Norse- Command Partition Productivity Incentive Deduction

For some parameters the Consumerist Commissioners and the Grand Chairman interact. They are:

- Delivery Price
- Adjusted Income Earnings
- Supply of Norses
- Work Schedule
- General Consumerist Grant
- Non-Working Consumerist Grant

For other parameters only the Consumerist Commissioners have influence. These are:

- Consumerist Universal Stock Price
- Industry Hybrid-Patent Period
- Injury Severance Payment

For still other parameters, both the industry specific Chairman and the industry specific commissioners have influence. They are:

- Price Functions
- Wage/Salary Functions
- Input Functions

Lastly, only the industry specific commissioners have affect on:

- Job Contract Price

We have already mentioned the Retail Mark-up and the Accommodational Markdown. They are both set by the Grand Chairman. The Grand Chairman has the power to adjust either the Retail Mark-up or the Accommodational Markdown, which are set as a percentage, when he sees fit. Every once in a while, the Grand Chairman announces a new Retail Mark-up or a new Accommodational Markdown. All industries in the sectors to which these changes apply must comply with the proclamation.

The Grand Chairman has power over the Real Estate Profit Percentage. He or she simply states the percentage of the transaction a real estate firm will earn in the process of a sale. The Grand Chairman can change this whenever he wants to. Whatever the Grand Chairman sets this parameter at, all individuals must comply with it in the transactions that this parameter applies to.

The Grand Chairman has control over the Adjusted Revenue Price Duration. He or she simply dictates the price of buying or selling a firm based on the length of time it takes the firm to make a certain amount of revenue. The Grand Chairman can also change this whenever he wants to. When the Grand Chairman sets the parameter, all firms that the parameter pertains to must abide with it.

The bank rate is determined by the Grand Chairman. He sets it every few weeks. This affects how much private banks have to pay the central bank in order to borrow money. When it is high it is useful for controlling inflation. However, if it is low, it stimulates the economy.

The Interest Rate is under the direct influence of the Grand Chairman. He has the power to change the cost of borrowing and lending a set amount of Ignits. Changes to the Interest Rate can be made at any time and the Interest Rate applies to the whole economy with the exception of the laissez-faire sector..

The Consumerist General Bond Interest Rate is also under the direct influence of the Grand Chairman. He has the power to change the cost of borrowing and lending money, in Ignits, through general consumerist bonds. Changes to this can be made at any time and this applies to all consumerist bonds.

The Consumerist Profit Bond Interest Rate is under the control of the Grand Chairman. The Grand Chairman can dictate this variable that is important in the payments of consumerist profit bonds

The Consumerist Stock-Bond Interest Rate is set by the Grand Chairman. He has an influence on how consumerist stock-bonds are created and has a say on how investors earn money by investing in these kinds of bonds.

The Consumerist General Bond Interest Repayment Frequency can be manipulated by the Grand Chairman. He sets how often an investor is paid interest on the general consumerist bonds he holds. This can be changed at any time.

The Consumerist Profit Bond Interest Repayment Frequency is under the control of the Grand Chairman. He can decide how frequently an investor is paid his interest on the consumerist profit bonds he holds. This can also be manipulated at any time by the chairman under his discretion.

The Rental Equivalence Duration is set by the Grand Chairman. He determines how long it will take a person to pay the price of the accommodation that he rents. He has the discretion to manipulate this variable every so often to adjust the economy, either to help renters or to help landlords.

Similar to the Rental Equivalence Duration is the Rental Repayment Value. Whereas the Rental Equivalence Duration deals with accommodation, the Rental Repayment Value deals with all goods and services other than accommodation. The Grand Chairman determines how much it will cost to borrow and lend a certain good or service. This is set as a percentage. If this parameter is high, this helps those that lend the good or service. On the other hand if this is low, this would favour those who borrow.

The Adjusted Monthly and Yearly Income Percentage are under the control of the Grand Chairman. He sets how much more a worker will earn from buying his job. This can be changed at any time and this applies to all of the economy.

The nominal and reciprocal Ignit-Fortal exchange mechanisms are set by the Grand chairman. He decides how much an Ignit is worth in terms of Fortals and how much a fortal is worth in terms of Ignits. When dealing with the nominal fortal-ignit exchange rate he has the power to manipulate the money supply as people loose money by continuously trading one currency for another. The grand Chairman decides in which situations and circumstances the reciprocal Ignit -Fortal exchange mechanism applies and in which the nominal Ignit-Fortal exchange mechanism applies.

The Grand Chairman can also manipulate the money supply by effecting the foreign currency exchange adjustment. In doing so, he sets how much money is taken out of circulation when a person trades Fortals for a foreign currency.

Also, to control the money supply, the Grand Chairman has jurisdiction over the Command Partition anti-inflationary deduction and the government ownership of stocks inflationary deduction. Here he controls the amount of money deducted from bank records (i.e. destroyed) when, in the first case, the command partition makes a profit and in the second, when the government makes profit from owning stocks.

The Grand Chairman has power over the Government Business Loan Assistance Interest Rate. He sets the interest rate on the loans the government (any level) offers to businesses to help them grow.

The Grand Chairman controls the Norse- Command Partition Productivity Incentive Deduction. This is a deduction from an auxiliary worker's GCG or NWCG when doing little work or poor quality work.

The International Credit Rating is under the influence of the Grand Chairman. He decides and ranks how trustworthy a foreign nation is in paying back its loan. This rating affects what kinds of loans we make to foreign nations.

For all of the above jurisdictions, the Grand Chairman has supreme control. He can change any of them at any time. He does so through press releases. All the entities to which these parameters apply must use the Chairman's edicts. There is veto power however. If the minister of finance or head of state disagrees with any of the Grand Chairman's policies, they can veto them. At that point if ¾ of the Commissioners (75) overrule the veto, the Grand Chairman's declaration still holds. However if they do not the Grand Chairman must change the policies so that they are not vetoed by the head of state or the minister of finance.

Most of the time, the Deputy Grand Chairman doesn't do anything. His function is to replace the Grand Chairman in case of an emergency. If the Grand Chairman becomes ill or something tragic happens to him, the Deputy Grand Chairman takes his post and becomes the Grand Chairman until the original Chairman comes back or a new central bank is appointed by the government.

For the following parameters both the industry specific Chairman and the industry specific Commissioners have a say: Prices, Wages and Salaries and Prices of Inputs. These are expressed as functions. The industry specific Chairman sets the form of the function while the industry specific Commissioners determine the monetary variable of the function. One such function could be a price function for the family of milk products. All things in the same family (taxon) and their substitutes have the same price/wage/input function. The industry specific Chairman, in this case the hospitality industry chairman, may decide to set the price in terms of price per 100 ml. Then, the price function might look like, x/100 ml. The hospitality industry commissioners vote on the value of x. The top 25 and bottom 25 votes are discarded and the middle 50 are averaged. This ensures that there won't any ridiculous votes like

112

500 million ☉ /100 ml or 0.01 ☉/100 ml. This is the democratic method of determining prices. It applies similarly to wages and salaries as well as to input price functions. The form of the function can be more complicated (this is up to the industry specific Chairman). The price functions are defined so that the consumerists will buy the products of the highest quality since prices for similar goods are the same.

The central bank works closely with the patent office to give prices to new goods and services that are completely original or have no known substitutes. After someone is granted a hybrid-patent for inventing a completely new family of products he is given a price function for his product by the central bank and he gains a monopoly on the production of his product for some time. This hybrid-patent is expressed in the form of length of time, earning of revenue or profit- whichever one comes first. The patent period for each industry in a sector is created by the patent office. The patent office sets how long a firm has to be the sole producer of an innovation or invention. The Industry Patent Period is also set democratically (i.e. through voting) by the Consumerist Commissioners. They determine how long a firm or person can hold a patent in a particular industry in terms of years, profit earned or revenue earned.

The wage functions and input functions are also set by the central bank through the democratic process described above. Wage functions are designed so that the worker is more productive and efficient; i.e. a janitor is paid by the hour (this would be determined by the industry specific chairman). He could be paid 10.00 þ/hour (this would be determined by the industry specific commissioners)

The following is a demonstration of the democratic method of price/wage/salary/input function determination. To make things simple, we have 20 Commissioners in this example and this is how they voted on the price of a light bulb family of products:

1) 5.00 ☉
1) 4.00 ☉
2) 0.01 ☉ x
3) 200.00 ☉ x
4) 7.00 ☉ x
5) 2.00 ☉
6) 1.00 ☉ x
7) 1.50 ☉
8) 0.50 ☉ x
9) 8.00 ☉ x
10) 9.00 ☉ x
11) 3.00 ☉
12) 2.00 ☉
13) 1.00 ☉ x
14) 3.00 ☉
15) 4.00 ☉
16) 5.00 ☉ x
17) 2.00 ☉
18) 1.00 ☉ x
19) 4.00 ☉

The votes with an (x) are discarded and the middle 10 are averaged to give us a price of 3.05 ☉ .

When deciding on these functions, the central bank's mandate is this: "To form a coherent system of prices for goods, services, wages, salaries and inputs by setting functions that are fair. Fair meaning that which is acceptable to both consumerists and producers". The finance minister and head of state also have veto power over price/wage/input functions. If either of these thinks that the resulting function is unfair, they may veto a function forcing the commissioners to re-vote their function. The consumerists also have veto power. If a considerable portion of the population signs a petition against a price/wage/input function, the function is vetoed and the commissioners must vote again. Also, as mentioned previously, producers can appeal a price function if they can demonstrate to the central bank, using business documents, that it is unprofitable to do business under the current price/wage/input function.

Why exactly do we have various types of central bankers, each particular to a different industry? The reasoning is that there are a lot of goods, services, wages, inputs to price even if we price things at the family taxon level. Having industry specific central bankers speeds up the process of finding prices for families of goods, services and wages.

The Consumerist Universal Stock Price is solely in the hands of the 100 Consumerist Commissioners. The reason that the Chairman has no influence is that there is no function to form. It is understood that the Consumerist Commissioners are voting on the price of a single stock. The cost to an investor, that is the price for one unit of stock, is determined by the democratic method of voting, discarding votes and averaging the remainder as described above. It is determined by the voting of Commissioners. The major difference between this and the above functions is that once set, the Universal Stock Price can never be changed or vetoed. Extreme havoc would result if the Consumerist Universal Stock Price were allowed to change.

The delivery price is set democratically by both the Consumerist Commissioners and the Grand Chairman. This concerns the cost of delivering certain goods over a certain distance. The form of the function is set by the Grand Chairman and the variables are determined by the Consumerist Commissioners by voting.

The Injury Severance Payment is determined by the Consumerist Commissioners. They use the democratic method to determine how much money a worker is entitled to receive in case of a debilitating injury. This is in the form of a function that takes into account his income and the extent of his injury; i.e. how career ending it is.

The Job Contract Price is set by the Industry specific Commissioners. Through the democratic method, the industry specific Commissioners find a price function for all families of jobs.

The Adjusted Income Earnings are determined by both the Grand Chairman and the Consumerist Commissioners. This is determined by the value of the Adjusted Monthly Income Percentage and the Job Contract Price. The Work Schedule is also derived by the interplay of other variables.

The supply of Norses is set by both the Consumerist Commissioners and the Grand Chairman. They must simply ensure that the amount of Norses granted each month is exactly equal to the Gross Domestic Consumerist Product.

The General Consumerist Grant and the Non-Working Consumerist Grant are also set by both groups of prime central bankers. The central bank functions in granting money (Norses). After the value of the GDCP is compiled each month from individual consumerist producers the central bank grants a sum of Norses to the government to spend on social services, based on the tax rate. What's left goes to the consumerists. Those that work earn more than those that are unemployed. Those working receive the General Consumerist Grant while the non-working or those working below a certain threshold, receive the Non-Working Consumerist Grant. This money the consumerists can spend on goods and services in the materialist sector.

The central bank has many powers and responsibilities. It is indeed a powerful entity. Almost everything that happens in the economy is in some way influenced by the central bank.

Consumerism and the Government

The theory of the accommodation based consumerist system is not a theory of politics or a functioning of the government. This theory stays as far as possible from the government. Politics is one subject where everyone and no one is an expert. However we give some suggestions that may be of some use in this area.

The economic system could work alongside any political system. The only exceptions are communism and anarchy. There cannot be a communist government and a consumerist economic system at the same time.

This economic system works well under democracy regardless who is leader. The leader could be a president, prime minister or a chancellor. This system could also work under a constitutional monarchy.

We now introduce a new concept into the theory of government. This is the concept of the *public veto*. Suppose that the government passes a law or act or any form of legislation. If 50% + 1 of the population sign a petition against this, the law is repelled or vetoed. This framework gives power back to the people. It ensures a more equitable system of checks and balances. A public veto strengthens the democratic system.

The government should promote trade as much as possible. Generally speaking, the more goods imported or exported the better. The reason behind this is that the more goods consumerists import the more choice they have in purchasing. Also they will have the ability to purchase goods of better quality. Trade is discussed later on.

An important function of the government is to regulate some industries. Some regulation, as long as it is not excessive, is necessary so that products are up to standard. For example, water for drinking must meet certain requirements before it can be sent to consumerists. Also meat must be inspected to insure that it is disease free. To this end the government must establish certain agencies to regulate firms for the well being of consumerists.

The government is responsible for issuing licenses and permits. These include fishing licenses, building permits and business or vendors licenses. This is done to regulate certain areas and ensure quality.

The government is responsible for the following parameters. All are discussed more fully later on.

- Population
- Grand Consumerist Tax
- Yearly Vacation Duration Period
- Sick Leave Exemption Period
- Maternity Leave Duration Period
- Extra-Work Transfer Payments
- Political Ideology
- Externality Regulations
- The Consumerist Quatrotomy

116

- The Distribution of Land
- Government Inflationary Markdown
- Accommodational Award Deductive Incentive
- Selective Occupation Promotion System
- Laissez-Faire Business Limit
- Minimum Retirement Age
- Retirement Pension Allowance
- Non-Working Consumerist Grant Markdown
- Economic Taxonomy
- Employment Reimbursement Transfer
- Capital Investment Transfer
- Profit Reward Transfer
- Consumerist Spending Reimbursement
- Interest Rate Stimulus
- Working Grant Threshold
- Government Bond Pool
- Laissez-Faire Markdown
- Bankruptcy Insurance Anti-Inflationary Deduction
- Consumerist and Speculative Government Bonds
- Auxiliary Worker Reimbursement Deduction
- Consumerist Grant Minimum Allowance Age
- Unemployment Assistance Repayment
- Work for Freedom Program
- Recycle for Pay Program
- Recycle for Pay Percentage (RFPP)
- Employment Assistance Program
- Employment Assistance Program Interest Rate (EAPIR)
- Laissez-Faire Labour System
- Occupational Complexity Rating
- Defence Team Promotion Initiative
- Financial Punishment
- Command Partition Compensation Adjustment
- Government Business Loan Assistance Program (GBLAP)
- Government-market shortage Surplus Resolution system
- Government Market Adjusted Price
- International Bond
- International Bond maturity Period
- International Bond Interest Rate
- GDCP anti-inflationary mechanism
- Partial Ownership of Firms By the Government Program
- Government Consumerist Spending Reimbursement
- International Loan Program
- Government Revenue Stock
- Income Reimbursement Initiative: Interest Rate, maturity Period and 5 brackets
- Government Loan to Business Inflationary Deduction
- Proof of Foreign Visitor Status
- Accommodation Award

- Accommodation Award Repayment Percentage (AARP)
- Materialist Overdraft
- Government Employee Incentive Program
- Materialist Overdraft Limit
- Materialist Overdraft Interest
- Consumerist Grant Distribution Schedule
- Consumerist Savings Bonds
- Consumerist Savings Bond Interest Rate
- Consumerist Savings Bond Interest Repayment Frequency
- Premium Savings Bonds
- Ignit- Command Partition Productivity Incentive Deduction
- Fortal- Command Partition Productivity Incentive Deduction
- No Food Wasted Initiative
- Food Geared to Income Program (FGIP)
- Consumerist Food Center(CFC)
- Universal Food Card
- Food Geared to Income Limit
- Food Geared to Income Percentage
- Global Shortage Stimulus

The government takes care of retirees. It sets the minimum retirement age; i.e. the minimum age at which a worker can retire. It also fixes a retirement pension allowance. This is how much money, in Ignits, a retired person receives from the government.

The government takes concrete steps to limit or eliminate unemployment. It creates and manages the Laissez-Faire labour system. It works in conjunction with firms in the laissez-faire labor system to create jobs that would not normally exist as they would be outsourced to another country. The government also runs the Employment Assistance Program to help workers buy jobs. The Employment Assistance Program Interest Rate (EAPIR) is dictated by the government. This is the extra income in terms of interest that the government receives from helping workers through the Employment Assistance Program.

The government takes care of those not working. The government makes Extra-Work Transfer payments. There is money involved and also the government provides minimal accommodation and the provision of utilities for those who do not contribute to society but are able to. The government also sets a non-working consumerist grant markdown. This is how much less those who are not working receive in the form of grants of Norses from the central bank. If it is set at 100% all non-institutionalized consumerists are granted an equal amount of Norses. The government may make this lower in order to provide an incentive to work or it may keep it high to fight poverty. In addition the government creates the Working Grant Threshold. This is essentially a definition of what it means to be a "working" consumerist. Let's say it is 200.00 þ per week or 40 hours per week. If a consumerist makes 550.00 þ per week then he is entitled to the General Consumerist Grant. If a consumerist earns 80.00 þ per week, he will get the Non-Working Consumerist Grant. If a consumerist works 45 hours per week then he is entitled to the General Consumerist Grant.

The government plays a role in making sure auxiliary workers are doing an effective job so it sets the Ignit- Command Partition Productivity Incentive Deduction and the Fortal- Command Partition Productivity Incentive Deduction. These parameters ensure command partition workers are doing a good job.

The government takes care of those not working in another way too. It sets the Auxiliary Worker Reimbursement Deduction (AWRD). This concerns how much less someone on welfare is given for being on welfare. This is set as a percentage. The government also creates the Unemployment Assistance Repayment (UAR). This indicates how much income a worker must repay the government after he finds employment in a partition other than the command partition. This is also set as a percentage. If these are set at zero, this will help fight poverty.

The government provides help for those who are homeless. It gives all homeless and those with low Ignit income a place to live- for example a condominium or small apartment. This we call the Accommodation Award. However, after making use of this program, the consumerist is subject to the Accommodation Award Repayment Percentage (AARP). This means, basically how much of the value of the accommodation the consumerist must pay the government. This parameter could also be set at zero to overcome poverty.

The levels of government pay for all consumerist's education. Every consumerist is entitled to a primary, secondary as well as a university/college education. However, as we will soon discuss, it is necessary to buy a job in the accommodational sector of the natural partition. This stands as the opposite of free-market capitalism where, essentially, a human being has to pay for their post secondary education but it is not necessary to purchase employment.

The Consumerist Grant Distribution Schedule is in the hands of the government. The government decides what day of a 2 week cycle –we are assuming that the Consumerist Grants are granted every 2 weeks- each consumerist is granted either the General or Non Working Consumerist Grant. This helps us avoid problems caused by everyone getting money on the same day and rushing into malls to be the first to buy goods.

The government is in charge of the consumerist grant minimum allowance age. It decides the earliest age someone has to be in order to be eligible for a consumerist grant.

The government has influence on the occupation complexity rating. It ranks occupations on how difficult they are. This affects how workers are compensated.

The Selective Occupation Promotion System is in the hands of the government. Through this system, the government makes sure that much needed occupations are preserved in consumerism. The government makes sure that talented, hard working individuals stay in our country to work here.

The Governmental Employee Incentive Program is run by the government. The government pays employees a little more for hiring certain workers. This encourages employment.

To aid consumerists, the government sets the Government Consumerist Spending Reimbursement. Essentially, when a consumerist shops in certain places, the government pays him for making purchases. This stimulates the economy greatly.

The International Loan Program is in the hands of the government. It decides how to make loans to other countries. The interest on the loan is used to pay for social services.

The government is also in charge of Government Revenue Stock. The government issues stock in itself. The profit for doing so is a source of government revenue.

The government plays a role in the income reimbursement initiative. This is at once a form of revenue for the government as well as for the tax payers. The government sets the interest rate which is how much taxpayers have to pay and have to pay back. The maturity period is the time at which the "tax" is repaid to tax payers. There are five brackets which determine how much the tax payer has to pay the government initially.

The government is in charge of fighting hunger. It instigates the No Food Wasted Initiative and the Food Geared to Income Program. It builds consumerist food centers to make sure people have access to food. It manipulates several parameters designed to curb hunger. These include the food geared to income limit and food geared to income percentage. It issues the universal food card to needy hungry consumerists.

The government is actively involved in controlling the money supply, i.e. inflation. The Government Inflationary markdown is a percentage of the government's income that is taken away and destroyed. The laissez-faire markdown is a percentage of a transaction in the laissez-faire sector that is taken away and destroyed.

In addition to these, the government sometimes makes special deductions from various transactions in the system so as to control the money supply. In the bankruptcy insurance anti-inflationary deduction, a portion of the profit a bankruptcy insurance earns is taken away from circulation. In the GDCP anti inflationary mechanism, a portion of the money in the GDCP is removed before it goes to consumerists and the government. In the governmental loan to business inflationary deduction, a portion of the money that the government loans to business is taken away and destroyed. These are the ways the government helps to fight inflation and balance the money supply.

The government controls the partial ownership of firms by the government program. The government has partial ownership of certain firms which it invests in. Later on, when these firms make a profit, the government earns some of the profit.

The government is in charge of issuing proof of foreign visitor status to interested tourists. This ensures that foreign visitors can buy things in the materialist sector when they visit our country. With this document, a tourist can buy things in the materialist sector with Ignits.

The Command Partition Compensation Adjustment is set by the government. This affects how those with difficult jobs are compensated when working in the command partition. Those people with jobs that have a high occupational complexity rating are compensated more than other workers if they are employed in the command partition.

The government has some control over the Government Business Loan Assistance Program (GBLAP). It plays a role in how the government bank makes loans to business.

The Government-Market Surplus Shortage Resolution System is operated by the government. It subsidizes some markets while earning money from other markets. This is a tool designed to eliminate surpluses and shortages. This system works when the government adjusts the Government Market Adjusted Price, another parameter, to achieve equilibrium in problematic markets.

The government can make a nice revenue by manipulating international bonds. It sets the

120

international bond maturity period which is when the value of the bond has to be paid back in full. It also effects the international bond interest rate which is the interest that is paid for buying these bonds.

The government dictates the Accommodational Award Deduction Incentive. This is a percentage deducted from a consumerist's NWCG to encourage him to work. While consumerism ensures everyone has housing, this particular parameter ensures that people do not take advantage of the system.

The laissez-faire business limit is also affected by the government. This refers to the threshold when a business can operate in the laissez-faire sector as opposed to the accomodational or materialist sectors.

The government takes care of the population. It determines how many immigrants are allowed to settle in the nation. How many people to let in depends on how well the economy is doing. If the economy is growing then it is a good idea to let in some immigrants.

The government has some influences in the justice system. It oversees the financial punishment applied in courts. Thus it has a say in how much a criminal must pay the government if he or she is convicted and how much the government pays them if they are acquitted. It also has influence on the defence team promotion initiative. It decides how much of a bonus the accused's defence team gets so that the accused has a fair trial.

Also under the government's control is the Yearly Vacation Duration Period. It sets the amount of paid time off a worker is entitled to in days. This can be altered at any time and all firms and individuals must comply with this parameter.

The Yearly Sick Leave Exemption Period is dictated by the government. The government can influence and change the number of days a worker is allowed to miss from work due to sickness. All workers and employers must abide with this proclamation.

The government has influence over both the Yearly Vacation Duration Period and the Sick Leave Exemption Period. It sets how many days in a year a worker can take time off for purposes of vacation or illness.

The government can potentially alleviate a global shortage. It creates the global shortage stimulus. It gives firms in the natural partition a financial incentive to produce more of a good that is globally in low supply.

The government also sets the Maternity Leave Duration Period. That is it dictates how long a person can take time off work to care for a newborn child.

All three levels of the government contribute to the creation of the Grand Consumerist Tax. This is the percentage of the GDCP that the levels of government receive to provide governmental services. Each level of government receives 1/3 of the total and among the different levels it is spread out by population; i.e. the states/provinces with more people are granted more of the tax.

Political ideology is determined through the government by the people. The government picks whether it is quasi-left wing or quasi-right wing. This effects spending and taxation.

The government is in charge of distributing land. It determines how land should be used. Whether land is designated as rural, residential, industrial, recreational, commercial etc depends on the policies of the government.

The government sets out how to regulate externalities. These include procedures on how to handle positive and negative externalities. The goal is to eliminate the externality as much as possible without hurting the economy.

One of the government's main responsibilities is the consumerist quatrotomy and the economic taxonomy. The government decides which industries and which families of goods and services go to each sector. Also a branch of the government is assigned the specific task of compiling the consumerist economic taxonomy. That means that it classifies all goods, services, inputs and wages into the appropriate classifications.

The government has control of several measures used to fight unemployment that will be discussed fully later on. These are the Employment Reimbursement Transfer (ERT), the Capital Investment Transfer (CIT), the Interest Rate Stimulus (IRS), the Profit Reward Transfer (PRT) and the Consumerist Spending Reimbursement (CSR). These are set in terms of a percentage. The money for these transfers is taken from the government budget. As these measures are directly used to combat unemployment, they are some of the best things the government can spend its money on.

Another one of the roles of the government is to regulate the Governmental Bond Pool. This is an anti-inflationary measure regarding both consumerist and speculative government bonds.

The government works with government bonds; both of the speculative and consumerist kind. It decides how much to sell of these. To do so it manipulates certain parameters. These include: Consumerist Government Bond Interest Rate (CGoBIR), Consumerist Government Bond Interest Repayment Frequency (CGoBIRF), Speculative Government Bond Interest Rate (SGoBIR), and the Speculative Government Bond Interest Repayment Frequency (SGoBIRF).

During government budget deficits, the government may issue Consumerist Savings Bonds. These may be issued by either the Federal, Provincial or Municipal governments. Thus there are Federal Savings Bonds, Provincial Savings Bonds and Municipal Savings Bonds. The governments sell these at a particular interest rate to raise revenues for social services. The interest paid on savings bonds is dictated by a parameter called the Consumerist Savings Bond Interest Rate and this is set by the various levels of government. How often investors are paid on their savings bond is determined by the Consumerist Savings Bond Interest Repayment Frequency. This parameter is also set by the various levels of government.

In addition to issuing Consumerist Savings Bonds the three levels of government can issue Premium Savings Bonds. The money gained through selling these savings bonds is invested into a high interest savings account or high interest paying bond. The value of these savings bonds is eventually repaid to those who bought the savings bonds. However the interest-profit the government earns from reinvesting the savings bonds goes to pay for social services. Thus these types of savings bonds do not contribute to a budget deficit.

The government has control over the work for freedom program. It works with judges, attorneys, inmates and firms to find suitable work for those convicted of crimes. Firms pay the government for the work of the inmate so this program is a source of revenue for the

122

government. The inmate gains as he has a reduced sentence. Also society gains as production (total output) is increased. The work for freedom program will be discussed more fully in another section.

The government has jurisdiction over the recycle for pay program. This is also a source of governmental revenue as the government buys material that would otherwise be thrown out and sells it to firms that use it to make material for input for other products. The consumerists also benefit as they get money for ordinarily useless things like cardboard, cans, newspapers, glass bottles etc. Thus it has the side effect that it can provide some income to some consumerists. Furthermore, the government sets the Recycle for Pay Percentage (RFPP). This basically refers to the amount of money that consumerists are paid to bring useless items to "recycling stores".

The government provides help to those consumerists that ran short of money given to them through either the Non Working Grant or General Consumerist Grant. This may be due to some unforeseen emergency or other reason. The government provides these consumerists with the Materialist Overdraft. This is extra money (in Norses) to help out a desperate consumerist. The Materialist Overdraft is subject to the Materialist Overdraft Limit. This parameter, set by the government, indicates the maximum in terms of a percentage of the General or Non Working Grant that the consumerist can be granted at any period of time. For providing the Materialist Overdraft, the government makes money, in terms of interest on the Materialist Overdraft. This is set by the government and is called the Materialist Overdraft Interest.

The government functions to make the consumerist economy work smoothly and efficiently. There are many parameters that the government has control over. From this it can be gathered that the government has strong influence on how the economy progresses.

Sources of Government Revenue

To fund all its expenses, the government needs sources of revenue. We should briefly mention the various sources of revenue that the levels of government have. We mentioned some previously, we discussed some in this section and we will encounter more in other sections. There are two types of sources of government revenue; primary sources of revenue and secondary sources of revenue. The primary sources of revenue are:

- Financial Punishment- criminals have to pay the government a monetary penalty in addition to their regular sentence
- Interest from governmental business loan assistance program- when the government makes loans to businesses, the interest is considered government revenue
- Positive balance in the consumerist trade pool- when the government manipulates the consumerist trade pool such that it is positive, the profit goes to the government
- Partial Ownership of Firms by the Government- when the government buys stock of a firm and thus becomes a partial owner of that firm, the dividends from that firm are considered government revenue
- Government revenue stock- the government issues stock in itself. The money from selling the stock is government revenue
- Premium Savings Bonds- the government issues savings bonds and puts that money in bonds with an even higher interest rate (or a high interest savings account). The interest return is government revenue
- International loan program- the government loans money to a foreign nation. The interest profit can be used by the government for spending
- Avoidance of Debt- by not allowing the nation to descend into debt, the government can save money that is paid on debt financing and use it to pay for social services instead
- Selling of land – when the government sells land for various uses to consumerists it makes money
- Gambling profits- the government makes money operating casinos and selling lottery tickets
- Work for freedom program- firms pay the government for work done by prison inmates
- Recycle for pay program- the government makes money buying waste and recyclable items and selling them to firms that process inputs
- Employment Assistance Program- the government charges prospective workers an interest for helping them find a job
- Unemployment Assistance Repayment (UAR) – those working for the command partition or Laissez-faire labour system pay a portion of the money granted to them as part of their extra-work transfer
- Accommodation Award Repayment – those receiving the accommodation award pay the government for taking advantage of the accommodation award once they find a job in the natural or governmental partitions or while living in that accommodation
- The command partition- a division of the economy where most of the profits go directly to the government
- Revenue from government assisted programs – consumerists pay a fee to board a train or to visit a museum or for processing of a passport
- Monopoly over selling things like marijuana; assuming these are made legal
- Advertising on public property- firms pay the government to put ads on things like buses,

trains or bus stop shelters

- Interest payments from consumerists for taking advantage of the materialist overdraft.
- Positive balance in the Governmental Market Surplus/Shortage Resolution Program- when the government makes more money from resolving surpluses than it does from subsidies shortages, the profit goes to the government
- Interest from investing in International bonds
- Food Geared to Income Percentage- how much a hungry consumerist must pay in proportion to his materialist income to take advantage of the Food Geared to Income Program

The secondary sources of government revenue are:

- The GCT- a general tax on the GDCP based on the output of the materialist sector
- The Wealth Tax- the profoundly rich in a society pay a very small portion of their prosperity for the functioning of the government
- The Income Reimbursement Initiative (Positive Personal Income Tax)- the government makes a profit on people's income while still allowing tax payers to make a profit on their tax payments

Of all these sources of revenue, the GCT, wealth tax and positive income tax should be used least and they should contribute the least as a source of revenue. This is because money taken through the GCT could otherwise be given to the consumerist grant, either working or not working and money taken from the other two taxes has to come from, initially, hard working consumerists.

The Funding of Public Programs in Accommodation Based Consumerism

Most politicians and economists would agree that some services are best provided publicly. However, experts disagree just how much to spend on social services and which services are best provided by the government.

One of the main differences of opinion between quasi- right wing/capitalist and quasi-left wing/socialist is the extent of the government involvement in the economic system. Free market proponents (right wingers) argue that only the most basic things should be provided by the government- among these are education (at least primary and secondary), clean water and spending on defence and law enforcement. On the other hand, socialists encourage more government involvement. They support things like universal health care and programs for the needy.

Where does accommodation based consumerism stand in this question? In fact it is very general and can be adjusted to be quasi-right wing or quasi-left wing. It all depends on the desires of the benevolent social planner who organizes and sets up our nation. Whether consumerism supports more or less social spending is not fixed. Whether the people of consumerism want more or less government spending depends on the consumerist people.

That being said, several programs are strongly encouraged for a well functioning accommodation based consumerism. These include, among others, free ultra-universal health care, free universal education and free services like bus and subway transportation. In accommodation based consumerism we have several programs that are better provided publicly – through the government- than through profit seeking firms. The major programs provided publicly in consumerism are healthcare, education and transit. Consumerism prides itself in the fact that all consumerists have unlimited access to these services.

In accommodation based consumerism everyone has access to all health services. This includes surgery, dental care, chiropractic, medical walk in clinic visits, psychiatric care, psychological care, etc. Everyone can take advantage of these services.

In consumerism there is also free education. All schools are free. This includes elementary, secondary, college, university and trade and vocational schools. A well educated population has a much greater potential than a non-educated one.

There is free transit in consumerism. All consumerists can travel on the bus all the time and wherever they want. The same applies to subway trains. However it costs a fee to take the train. Free public transit helps consumerists get to wherever they are going at no cost with the side effect of reducing the carbon foot print as it is better for the environment for people to take buses instead of cars.

People who work for the governmental sector/partition are paid directly from the government but indirectly from governmental revenue. They are paid in Ignits (þ). They can use this money to buy things in the accommodational and laissez-faire sectors (after the nominal Ignit-Fortal exchange mechanism)

Those who provide healthcare (doctors, dentists, chiropractors, psychologists) all have a wage/salary function that is set by the central bank. These people do not have to buy job contracts (i.e. pay for their jobs) as the government already has an incentive to hire workers. The wage set by the central bank is fixed.

The same logic applies to those who work in the education industry of the governmental sector. The central bank sets a wage function for all those in this industry and it is fixed. Those workers who do a similar job get paid a comparable wage/salary.

People who drive buses and subway trains, including all those who play a role in the transit system also earn a wage/salary in the form of Ignits. Those who do a comparable job earn a comparable pay.

So where does the funding for the healthcare system, the education system and transit system (including all wages and salaries) come from? There are many sources of revenue in consumerism that are not based on unnecessary, harmful taxes that disrupt the economy and hurt everyone.

There are other things that should also be considered best provided publicly. One is defence. A well protected nation can give peace of mind to those that are protected. We need strong law enforcement so that crimes are not committed and so that contracts are enforced and fraud is not committed. Also, our water should be clean and our meat should be inspected so it is free from disease. There should be special inspectors to make sure our meat and water is safe There should be some kind of food and drug administration that makes sure that the food and medicine consumerists consume is safe. The government should provide licenses for various activities like fishing, hunting and being a vendor of an establishment.. A patent office should ensure inventors and innovators come up with new ideas. Emergency services like the fire fighting team and paramedics should be provided by the government. Also services like a poison control centre or a crisis line should likely be funded by the government. The government should create infrastructure like roads and bridges. There are also quite a few other services that should be on this list.

However, there are other services that may or may not be provided publicly. Whether the country wants these services depends on the wishes of the people who live in that country.

The ideas just described allow us to finance the social services that we desire in consumerism. There are quite a few of them. They should allow the governments in consumerism to pay for free universal healthcare, free education and many other things that make our consumerist system truly great. One wonderful thing that stands out from these potential sources of revenue is that we were able to avoid hurtful taxes which distort the economy and reduce the incentive of workers to work and in general to contribute to society. The taxes, (the GCT, the wealth tax and positive income tax) should be reserved as a revenue stream of last resort.

Some services are better publicly funded. Some like universal health care and universal education are strongly encouraged in consumerism. The people of our nation decide whether other services are publicly funded or not.

The Profit Vacuum

Let's talk about the profit vacuum. The profit vacuum is an important idea that pervades the entire consumerist economic system. It is a primary incentive for people to work, invest and contribute to society.

In basic terms the profit vacuum is about the notion that there is a potential for a profit if a consumerist investor wishes to contribute to a particular part of the economy. The profit vacuum pertains to jobs, investment opportunities, business opportunities as well as any other type of money transaction.

The creation of jobs in consumerism represents a profit vacuum. If there is a position as a waiter in a restaurant in consumerism this represents a profit vacuum. If an individual chooses to be a waiter at that restaurant he will gain a profit.

Any incidence of an open job position is considered a profit vacuum. If a consumerist fills that job he is guaranteed a profit. Filling a job opportunity satisfies a profit vacuum in that whoever takes that job is guaranteed a certain profit.

Profit vacuums also apply to producers. If a real estate firm produces 500 homes they fulfill a profit vacuum in that whenever they build those homes they will be confident in making a profit. That is, they satisfy a certain profit vacuum.

So then, the profit vacuum is a vital catalyst for the consumerist economy. The profit vacuum gives reason for all types of consumerist economic actors to contribute to the system.

Political Ideology

The politics of economics can be put on a spectrum. Originally this spectrum was just a line. On the far right was free-market capitalism- where there is free enterprise and minimum government involvement. On the far left there was communism with its supreme command system and total government control of all aspects of the economy. Near the centre are forms of socialism and less extreme capitalism.

The 20th century saw the emergence of Nazi Germany and Stalinist Soviet Union. These two systems had more similarities than differences so the economic spectrum was changed. It was turned into the shape of a horse shoe, where the extreme left is near the extreme right.

Where does accommodation based consumerism fit in? This system is very general and could be either quasi-free-market or quasi-socialist. We are now forced to re-modify the politico-economic spectrum once again. We add a second dimension. It still has a horse-shoe shape but now it has depth. It looks like a rainbow. In the centre are unattainable and attainable systems. The bottom represents ideal- realistic systems while the top represents unattainable systems which include utopias.

The closer one gets to the outer perimeter, the unattainable one, the more one is dealing with utopic conditions. These are characterized by people having to do no work and everyone having plenty of everything. The closer one gets to the inner attainable perimeter, the more one is dealing with barter conditions, where things are exchanged for other goods or for a currency. These are characterized by the exchange of goods for other things and work. These two conditions are essentially opposites. In essence, attainability measures whether a system will fall apart due to lack of incentives (or other things) or whether it will last. The accommodational based consumerist economic system can be closer to the attainable line or closer to the unattainable line. This depends on the consumerist quatrotomy. The larger is the materialist sector, the closer the system reaches unatainability. The larger the accommodational sector, the closer the system reaches attainability. If there was no accommodational sector and there were only the materialist and governmental sectors the system would be an unattainable utopia. However if there was no materialist sector and there was only an accommodational, laissez-faire and governmental sectors, the system would be capitalist or communist depending on the relative sizes of the accommodational, laissez-faire and governmental sectors.

This system can be more or less socialist or free-market. This depends on how big the governmental sector is and how much tax the government levies. Under a quasi- free-market structure there is a relatively small government sector and the tax is small. The government spends only on the most essential, most basic services. Under a quasi-socialist structure there is a high tax and a relatively large governmental sector.

The attainability does have an impact on the type of government or economy. All Communist systems are equally far to the left. However they differ in how unattainable or attainable they are. Chinese communism is more attainable than Cuban communism which is more attainable than Soviet communism

There are many political ideologies that relate to this system. The accommodation based consumerism system, being general, can be anywhere on the revised econo-political spectrum.

Where it ends up in practice depends on the people and the government they choose. The following is the New Econo-Political Spectrum .

The New Econo-Political Spectrum

UTOPIA IDEAL

unattainable

Centre 4

5

UNATTAINABLE

unattainable

6

Right Wing

Left Wing 10 16 11 .9

12   8

ATTAINABLE

14   13   15

IDEAL

ATTAINABLE

PERFECTION

7

Socialism 1
2
3

Conservatism

17

TYRANNY

18

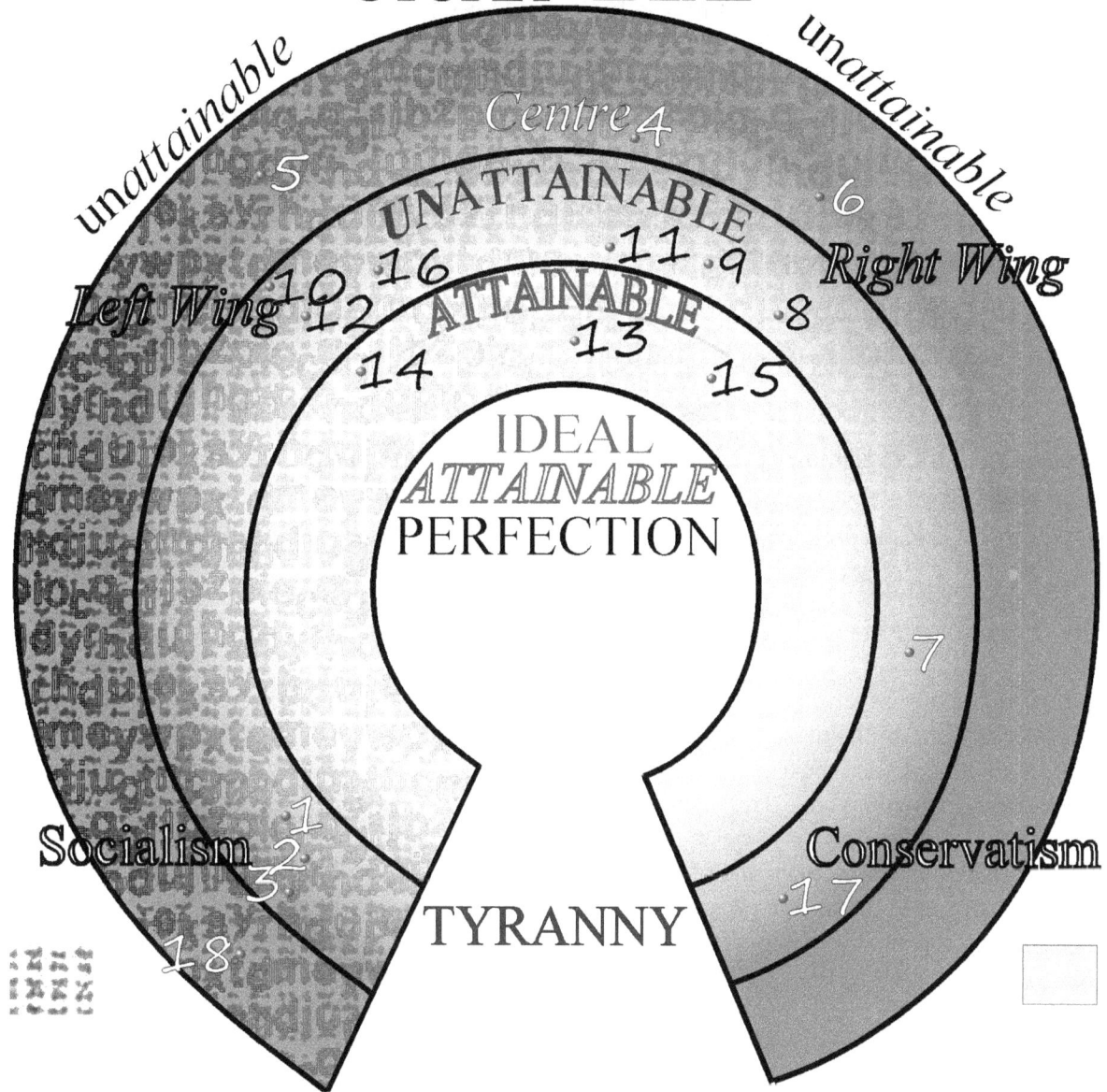

1	Chinese Communism	10	Government of Bill Clinton
2	Cuban Communism	11	Government of Paul Martin
3	Soviet Communism	12	Government of Tony Blair
4	Central Consumerism	13	Central Consumerism
	(Large materialist sector)		(Large accommodational sector)
5	Quasi-left wing Consumerism	14	Quasi left-wing Consumerism
	(Large materialist sector)		(Large accommodational sector)
6	Quasi-right wing Consumerism	15	Quasi right-wing Consumerism
	(Large materialist sector)		(Large accommodational sector)
7	Benito Mussolini's Government	16	Government of Juan Peron
8	Government of George Bush	17	Hitler's Nazism
9	Government of Steven Harper	18	Anarchy

Figure 3

Figure 3

Prices

No economic system would exist if there were no prices. Prices indicate the value of goods and services. It is almost universally agreed that it is impossible to set prices without a market system. Yet it is possible to create a coherent system of prices in the consumerist system. This is called the *democratic* or *consumerist* method of setting prices. First we discuss pricing under the free-market system and then we talk about pricing under accommodation based consumerism.

In the free-market, prices fluctuate. There is competition among firms in terms of price. A key maxim is to buy at a low price and sell at a high price. The market system uses prices to determine the equilibrium cost and the equilibrium quantity sold of a certain good. Certain factors can cause the equilibrium price and equilibrium quantity to fluctuate. These fluctuations are governed by the laws of supply and demand.

The consumerist system, for the most part, does not rely on a fluctuating-price market system, with the exception of the laissez-faire sector where it is encouraged. Prices in consumerism (in the GAM sectors) are permanently fixed. They are fixed by a panel of economists working at the central bank. Once a price has been fixed it must not be changed lest an absolute emergency or producers can demonstrate to the central bank that it is impossible to make a profit under the fixed price function. If prices do fluctuate, unnecessarily or too much, the consumerist system will surely collapse.

There are several benefits to fixing a price function. It eliminates the possibility of a depression. One of the reasons for the depression of the 1930's was that the prices of commodities such as wheat fell substantially. They fell so low that it was impossible to make a profit from growing wheat. The result was that people became unemployed and very poor.

One of the greatest faults of the free-market system is the business cycle. It is an inherent part of the system. There are periods of recessions, booms, expansions and downturns. This is bad. It can be completely avoided by fixing prices. Recessions are characterized by a relatively low level of prices. Booms are associated with inflation.

Inflation is a problem of the free-market system. However it does not exist in consumerism (with the exception of the laissez-faire sector). The essence of inflation is that prices of goods gradually increase over the years. Inflation has the effect that things today have a higher price than they did in the 1910's. The phenomenon of inflation will be discussed in detail later. Since prices are fixed in consumerism (in the GAM sectors) there can be no inflation.

Deflation is another possible problem of the free-market economy. The essence of deflation is that prices of goods fall over time. Deflation will be discussed in detail later. Although it is not as common as inflation, it could still hurt the economy. In consumerism, for the most part, there can be no deflation because price functions are permanently fixed in the GAM sectors.

A fixed price function system eliminates the idea of predatory pricing. That is firms do not excessively undercut their competitors in terms of price only to greatly increase their prices after eliminating their rivals.

Having fixed prices confers another advantage. It adds simplicity to the economy. Consumerists know exactly how much they must pay for a good or service. Also producers know exactly how much to charge for their goods and services. Thus fixed prices make the economy work more smoothly.

Yet another advantage of a fixed price system is the tremendous simplicity in terms of purchasing. It is conceivable that a shopper will know most if not all of the prices of goods and services in an economy. Imagine walking to a supermarket and being confronted not with tens of thousands of prices for items but just several hundred of them. This makes budgeting and smart shopping more possible.

It is kind of a mistake to say prices are fixed by the central bank. What the central bank does is that it sets *price functions* on families of goods and services. Goods and services that are in the same family (see the section on taxonomy) have the same price function. In consumerism goods and services that are substitutes or are very similar to each other are given the same price per quantity regardless of their quality. Here are some examples. Note that all prices in this section and throughout this treatise are simply examples and need not be the same in an actual economy. Cola/lemonade/iced tea (soft drinks) could be 0.50 Ⓞ /100 mL. All T-shirts could be 10.00 Ⓞ/unit. All wines could be 0.80 þ /litre. All C.D.'s could be 10.00 Ⓞ/unit. All computer games could be 25.00 Ⓞ /unit. All vine fruit (i.e. tomatoes) could be 0.50 Ⓞ /kg. All tropical fruits (i.e. bananas) could be 0.25 Ⓞ /kg. Some things have more complicated price functions. Agricultural land => 100.00 þ/m². Housing => 200.00 þ/m² + x200.00 þ + y2500.00 þ + z10000.00 þ. Where x = # of washrooms, y= # of bedrooms, z = # of floors. The price of a dwelling / house/ mansion/ apartment is very hard to arrive at because dwellings are the main incentives for consumerists to produce for society.

How are price functions set? The central bank has 102 officials for every particular industry. There is an industry specific chairman, an industry specific deputy chairman and 100 industry specific commissioners. For example in the entertainment industry there is an entertainment industry chairman, an entertainment industry deputy chairman and 100 entertainment industry commissioners. These people are appointed not elected. For every family of goods or services that exists in the economy (with the exception of those in the laissez-faire sector) the industry specific chairman sets the form of the price function. For example he may set the form of the price function for automobiles as αx. The x stands for money and the α stands for units. He may set the form of price functions for chocolate bars as x/100 grams. The x stands for money. Thus the price of cars would be set in terms of numbers of units (how many cars). The price of chocolate bars is set in terms of its weight (how many grams)

Now the industry specific commissioners vote on the value of the monetary variable (x). The 25 highest and 25 lowest votes are discarded and the middle 50 are averaged. This is done so that the industry specific commissioners set a reasonable price and do not make extreme prices (i.e. 0.01 Ⓞ for a car or 1 000 000 000.00 Ⓞ for a gram of chocolate). In our case let's suppose that the industry specific commissioners set a price of 12 129.00 Ⓞ for a unit of car and 0.25 Ⓞ for a 100 g of chocolate. Thus the price function for a chocolate bar is 0.25 Ⓞ/100 g and that of automobiles is 12 129.00 Ⓞ/car. So if a producer of chocolate makes chocolate bars in 500 g sizes it would seem he should charge the retailer 1.25 Ⓞ for each bar. It would also seem that the automobile producer would charge a car dealer 12 129.00 Ⓞ for a car. But this is not true. Only consumerists pay Norses for products and they can only do so at the retail level. Producers charge retailers in Ignits. The chocolate producer would actually charge 1.25 þ for the 500 g chocolate bar from a convenience store owner. The car manufacturer would actually charge 12 129 þ for the car from the car dealer.

If one person were to pick a price that would be good for both consumerists and producers, he would surely overvalue or undervalue the good or service. However with 100 economists voting on a price of a good or service, the price being determined democratically, there is more confidence that these prices are reasonable.

Fixing of price functions is similar to the way athletes are scored in diving and figure skating in the Olympics. In that case, several judges score a figure skating performance such that the lowest and highest scores are discarded and the middle ones are averaged. Something analogous happens when price functions are set in accommodation based consumerism.

In some cases it may be necessary to introduce *resonance price functions*. These are prices that are fixed with respect to a different parameter. For example pizzas can be priced per units of pie or per slices. There may be price functions like 8.00 Θ/unit pizza or 1.00 Θ per pizza slice. So when pizza producers compete with each other they can sell their pizza per whole pizza or per individual slice.

Fixing price functions also confers two more important advantages to members of the consumerist economy. Producers gain the security that the price of their product will never drop to levels where they cannot make a profit. For example, say the price of a bushel of wheat is usually $5.00. In the free-market system, there could arise a tragedy like a stock market crash, a terrorist attack or violent catastrophe where the price drops to $0.25 per bushel. No matter how much wheat the farmer sells, he cannot make a living and he will be forced to close his business. In consumerism, farmers and all other producers gain the valuable security that the price of their product will never drop.

Also, consumerists themselves gain stability and security from the fixing of prices. In the free-market system a cup of coffee that cost $0.60 fifteen years ago now costs $2.00. The coffee didn't become any better. However, in consumerism, the consumerist will benefit from the fact that if a medium cup of coffee cost 1.00 Θ today, it will cost the same tomorrow, next week, next year and fifteen years from now. This peace of mind is very valuable.

Remember from biology the concept of natural selection. Species that are adapted best to their environment are those that survive and produce offspring. In consumerism we have *quality selection*. All goods and services in a family (similar or close substitutes) have the same price function. The way that producers compete is through quality. The best made products are sold. Those goods that consumerists think are best are bought and produced. If all automobiles cost 10 000.00 Θ, then wouldn't everyone want to own a limousine or a fancy sports car? Of all cars limousines would be made most of all. Other car makers must make their cars better in the eyes of consumerists. They may do this by adding new features like more powerful car engines or they may make their cars roomier, faster and safer. Manufacturers will strive to invent things that will please consumerists and make a consumerist buy that car. The net effect of this quality selection is that whoever owns a car not only has a car, but has the finest, most luxurious one made.

If all shoes are 45.00 Θ then only the most comfortable, most durable, best made shoes are bought. The net result is that every consumerist who has a pair of shoes not only owns a pair of shoes but has the best shoes available.

In the free-market economy(as a rough estimate) only about 0.01 % or 1 in 10 000 people own a limousine (in most jurisdictions). Most people own average cars. These cars work but

134

there are finer ones on the market. There are also quite a number of people in the free-market economy who own extremely mediocre cars that are either old or poorly made. In consumerism the picture looks different. In the case where the price of a good or service exceeds a consumerist's budget (for example an automobile or a jet) the firm that sells such an expensive product may wish to charge by instalment. However the total price may not exceed the price set by the central bank. Example: Suppose an automobile costs 15 000.00 Θ. This is set by the central bank. Suppose a consumerist has a budget of 8 000 Θ/ month. This is how much he is granted by the central bank. The car dealer can charge a payment plan of 750.00 Θ a month for 20 months. However there can be no interest on the payment.

The fixing of price functions also helps producers and sellers in that they no longer have to find an optimal price for their product or service. The price for their product that the central bank provides may be better than one they could come up with on their own. Producers no longer have to adjust their prices to maximize profit by balancing price and quantity sold.

The set of price functions set by the central bank compromise part of what is called the consumerist constitution. If it turns out that the price of something in practice is incredibly unreasonable (i.e. the steel required to make a car costs more than the car itself) the central bank can vote again on the price function of goods in question. The central bank must be presented with a petition from a large number of unhappy producers. However this must not happen too often.

Sometimes fixed prices can be a problem for producers. This happens if the cost of producing a good is more than the revenue for that product. For example, suppose that a litre of milk is 2.00 þ, a bucket of ice cream contains a litre of milk and the bucket of ice cream sells for 1.00 Θ. Clearly, the ice cream maker is losing money. However they can appeal to the central bank with a form describing their financial situation. If the central bank accepts this appeal they simply vote again on the price of the ice cream. For this to happen there must be appeals from several ice cream producers. When the central bank votes on the new price function, they must make sure the new price function is greater than the original.

The way this concept of fixing price functions (for GAM sectors) means that there can be no "discounts". There can be no "sales" or "special events" where the price of a good is a certain percentage lower than before. So if running shoes are set by the bank to cost 60.00 Θ, there cannot be a special reduction to attract more consumerists.

The whole concept of budgeting in consumerism is the opposite of that of capitalism. In capitalism one walks into a store knowing roughly what to buy and tries to find the best price for these items. In consumerism one walks into a store knowing roughly how much he has to spend and tries to find the best goods he can get for that price.

Prices are an integral part of any economic system. There is a difference as to how they are set in the free-market and consumerist systems. In what follows we will see how prices make the consumerist system work.

Quality Selection

We started discussing the concept of quality selection in the last section. Here we will elaborate a little bit on it. Quality selection refers to the idea that producers compete with one another not by undercutting each other in price and producing products and services of the cheapest kind but rather by making products and services that have the most value in the eyes of consumerists. It is one of the most wonderful results of the theory of accommodation based consumerism.

Let's take the family of frozen desserts. To this family would belong various kinds of ice creams and frozen yogourts. In the free-market system, competition pertaining to this market would involve the firms trying to sell cheaper and cheaper frozen desserts. Every brand would have a different price and buyers would usually buy the ice cream that costs the least. In consumerism the idea is different. All products in this family cost the same. Suppose the central bank set the cost of all frozen desserts at 1.00 Ө/1 L and the retail markup at 25%. Thus when a consumerist goes to a grocery store he would have to pay 1.25 Ө for every litre of frozen dessert. Since all frozen desserts cost the same, the various frozen desserts producers compete with each other in terms of quality. They try to make their product the most desirable in the eyes of consumerists. So, some would try to make their desserts as healthy as possible (least fat and calories) and others would try to make original flavors. The different producers would make flavors of frozen desserts that would attract consumerists. Instead of being able to choose from 6-8 flavors in a grocery store operating under the free-market system, there would be maybe 25-30 flavors to choose from in the consumerist system. Thus the consumerists have access to the best quality frozen desserts.

As another example of quality selection let's take a look at the computer family of products. All computers would cost the same. Suppose that the central bank sets this at 600.00 Ө and the retail markup at 30%. So if someone wants a computer they would go to an electronics store and pay (600.00 Ө x 0.3) + 600.00 Ө = 780.00 Ө. Now, the computer producers compete with one another to make the best computer in the opinion of consumerists. So they would make their computers faster, with more space and with more improvements. They would also employ their research to find new ideas for making their computers better than before with fresh original ideas. The consumerists benefit from this type of competition because they have access to better computers.

Quality selection can also be applied to services. Let's examine the music teacher family. Every music teacher would be paid the same for the equivalent service he or she provides, with the compensation determined by the central bank. So if all music teachers cost the same to hire to teach music, students would be able to pick the best one to teach them. Music teachers would compete with each other, each trying to seem of the best value in the eyes of consumerists. This makes sure that the teachers that get hired are those that are best suited for the position. For example they may have gone to a better music school or have had more experience teaching. Here quality selection works once again in favour of consumerists.

Pizza producers would compete in accordance with quality selection. Assume that the central bank sets the price function of pizzas in terms of a unit of pizza; let's say at 6.00 Ө/per pizza. Then pizza makers would try to make better and better pizzas so that consumerists bought pizzas from them. This would mean that some pizzas are unbelievably huge or have a wide variety of toppings or are low in fat. Pizza makers would try to make their pizzas taste better than the other pizza makers. So the consumerists win by having access to well made pizza.

Grocery stores would also compete with each other in terms of quality rather than price. Thus they would have the most friendly cashiers and most knowledgeable clerks. Also they may be open 24hours a day so that if someone wants to buy a sandwich at 2 am (because they are working the night shift perhaps) they are able to do so. This really only requires one or two more extra cashiers for the night but the reputation that the store is open 24 hours a day will more than compensate for the cashier's wages.

In a consumerist society meat will probably be priced either in terms of kilograms per animal or meat from all animals may have the same price per kilogram. Suppose all meat cost the same per quantity. Let's say it is 10.00 ☉ per kilogram. All types of meat would cost the same whether it is chicken, pork, beef or veal. In that case a consumerist would be able to buy the type of meat that they truly desire. If someone wants ribs, he is entitled to it. If he wants a steak, he is entitled to it. If someone wants stewing meat, he is entitled to it… All that really matters is that the price of the meat from the animal is more than the animal itself. If meat from one type of animal is more preferred relative to other types of meat, meat producers should try to raise a different type of livestock.

Quality selection can be applied to land too. Even though land of the same type costs the same, some land is of better quality than other land. For example, developed land; that is land with crops growing on it or some building on it, is more desired than land with only grass and weeds growing on it. The location of land also affects how desired it is with regards to quality selection. So, those who compete in terms of selling land ought to factor in the quality of their land when attempting to sell it.

Finally let's take a look at the potato chip family of goods. Assume that the central bank sets the price of all chips at 1.00 ☉/100 g and the retail markup at 30%. So in a convenience store or grocery store, a consumerist would find bags of chips with different prices; a 250 g bag of chips for 2.50 ☉ + (2.50 ☉ x 0.3) = 3.25 ☉ and a 100 g bag for 1.00 ☉ + (1.00 ☉ x 0.3) = 1.30 ☉. The different chip manufacturers would compete with one another in terms of quality. That is they try to make their product most highly valued by consumerists. There are different ways they can compete. For example, some may be reduced in calories and fat while other potato chip manufacturers may make new and interesting flavors. A typical snack section in a free-market grocery store usually has maybe 6-10 different kinds of potato chips. In the consumerist system, to attain quality selection, a grocery store may have 30 – 40 different kinds of potato chips. Again, quality selection gives consumerists better and more improved products.

Some may have noticed that the opposite of quality selection occurs in free-market nations that are ruled by price selection. In some fast food establishments, the producer sells their french fries with less and less fries per portion. So, the medium french fries may have four fewer fries than before. This is beneficial for the restaurant as, in the long run, that is over several months, they may save (and thus earn) tens of thousands of dollars. This would be resolved quite differently in consumerism. In consumerism, the various fast food outlets will be competing in quality against one another. Thus there will actually be more fries in a portion than before.

In the free-market system there already is quality selection in the movie industry. The price of a ticket to the cinema costs the same regardless of the quality of the movie. That is, how much money it took to film the movie, how good the actors are, how good the sound effects or music are, how long it took to make the movie, how good the special effects are, etc... Movie goers see the movie they really want to watch and therefore the best one. The movie of the highest quality makes the most revenue as all tickets cost the same. This is an example of the concept of quality selection in the free-market system.

Furthermore there is some degree of quality selection in the employment market of the free enterprise system. Employers already have in mind how much they will pay their worker in terms of a salary or wage. They offer interviews to possible candidates to pick the most qualified one. Thus the worker of the highest quality is the one who is employed. For example, an accounting firm has a position for an accountant that pays $ 60,000 per year. They interview applicants and the one best suited for the job is the one that is hired and gets the job. Employer's hire a new employee, say a janitor, based on how good he would be at the job. The employer already knows how much to pay him. He hires the most capable worker that will fulfill the position. This is another example of quality selection in the free-market system.

There is quality selection in capitalism, in some sense, in the market for certain goods. When one goes to a grocery store, all tomatoes of the same type cost the same. Rotten tomatoes cost as much as fresh ones which cost the same as semi-ripe ones. Since they all cost the same per kilogram, a smart shopper chooses the fresher ones over the rotten ones.

As a very simple example, quality selection can be grasped with the market for hot beverages to which coffee, tea and hot chocolate belong to. The cup of coffee can cost a price per 100 ml or the price can be based on a single cup. This ensures that people have the best coffee (and any hot beverage for that matter) or if they want to they can buy the coffee per cup. In this case, coffee places will be competing with each other to give consumerists the biggest size cup possible.

In my younger days when I worked at a grocery store I was appalled by what happened when there was too much bread to be sold. The delivery truck came to the store and there was more bread than could be put on the shelves. Loaf after loaf was put directly into the dumpster. In the meantime there are people in third world countries who are starving. In consumerism, instead of throwing the bread out, the solution would be to sell it to an importation-exportation company all while keeping price functions constant or it could be sold to the command partition so the command partition can feed the hungry. This is discussed later.

The concept of quality selection is directly derived from our definition of what it means to be "wealthy". Remember we defined being wealthy as having access to goods and services of the highest quality. Quality selection achieves that goal. The idea of quality selection ensures that consumerists have goods and services of the highest standard available to them. Quality selection guarantees us that we have the biggest, tastiest hamburger possible, the most entertaining video game, the best made bicycle and the best set of tires on our car. Consumerists are guaranteed to drive limousines and the fastest sports cars. They wear the warmest, most insulated coats and their gloves are the best that can possibly be made. They have the largest TV's and the fastest, top of the line computer. Their beds are the most comfortable to sleep on and their coaches are the most comfortable to sit on.

Quality selection does not apply to the laissez-faire sector. It only pertains to the GAM sectors. The laissez-faire sector functions based on the laws of supply and demand and therefore there is competition in price.

Some theorists may argue that it is very hard to create a fixed price function for a good or service. Let's compare a sports car and an economy car. In a capitalist nation these would have

138

vastly different prices. The economy car may cost $ 10 000.00 while the sports car can cost up to $ 90 000.00. However these two probably cost a similar amount to produce. They both have about the same amount of steel, aluminum, copper wire, glass, plastic, upholstery, electronics, etc... Although the sports car probably costs more to produce than the economy car, the difference is not as great as the price tag would have you believe. If one adds up all the production costs, the economy car most likely costs about $ 4 000.00 to make while the sports car costs about $ 8 500.00 to make. In fact the majority of the price in the capitalist scenario is due to a markup. In that case, if we in our consumerist nation, price our automobiles at a higher price than their production costs then the whole concepts of price fixing and quality selection work. So, if we price the economy car and sports car at $12 000.00, then car dealers and manufacturers can sell both cars at a profit. Of course, for most people the sports car is of a higher quality so most people will buy the sports car relative to the economy car. However, since the economy car cost less to produce, car manufacturers would make more profit per car if they sold more economy cars.

In pure capitalism there is in some instances an inflationary death spiral. We have a pub that sells, among other things, a nacho platter. The platter sells for $10.00. However, business is bad and less people come to the pub. To raise revenue, the pub increases the price of the dish to $ 14.00. Since the price went up, even less customers come. In desperation, to compensate for the loss of customers and revenue, the pub increases the price of the platter to $ 20.00. At this price, no one comes to the pub except for the loyal patrons. With no revenue, the pub is forced to close its doors.

How would the above situation resolve itself in consumerism? Let's say the central bank sets the price of the nacho platter, like all platters, at 12.00 Ө. Now the restaurant owner needs to solely concentrate on making the best nacho platter in the eyes of consumerists. He totally need not worry about the price of the nacho platter. Originally, it costs 5.00 þ to make a platter in the kitchen. To improve the quality of the platter, the pub adds three kinds of cheeses, a large side of guacamole and chipotle sauce as well as ground pork and jerk chicken. So now it costs the pub 8.00 þ to make each platter. If the pub makes the best nacho platter in town they will have a large proportion of the nacho platter market, i.e. they will have a lot of customers. In this case, the pub makes 4.00 þ from every platter.

Quality selection can be applied to vacation resorts. We will use dollars in this example. We have a 4 star resort that charges vacationers $500.00 per week and a 1 star resort that charges $100.00 per week. In capitalism a lot of people would go to the 1 star resort as it would save them money. However, in consumerism we allow the resorts to compete in terms of quality. The total cost to operate the 4 star resort is $200 per week and $60 per week for the 1 stat resort. If we (the central bank) set the general price for a vacation at $300 per week, than we can be assured that both resorts make money. However, consumerists will go to the better resort. In this situation, the 1 star resort should compete with the 4 star resort to make it more appealing to consumerists. It creates 5 drinks bars, it offers scuba diving lessons, it opens up 7 different kinds of restaurants, it makes its rooms larger and it offers guided tours to nearby sites. Thus it will be more competitive in the eyes of consumerists. Now consumerists, when they go on vacation, know that they will have vacation resorts doing everything they can to make the consumerists happy.

This is the concept of quality selection. Several examples from different industries in the consumerist economic system help illustrate it. It can clearly be seen that quality selection works in favour of consumerists as well as producers who make a profit.

Price Selection

We discussed quality selection in a previous section. Here we will talk about a related concept called *price selection*. Both quality selection and price selection refer to the orientation in which producers compete with each other to sell their goods and services. In quality selection firms compete with each other with regards to quality. On the other hand, in price selection firms compete in price.

Quality selection belongs to the GAM (governmental, accommodational, materialist) sectors. In these sectors firms battle against one another to produce products and services that will impress consumerists. Those firms that make products and services that consumerists really want, assuming a fixed price function that is set by the central bank, are those that thrive and have a larger share of the market. This paradigm has been discussed extensively in the previous section.

In price selection firms try to undercut each other in price so that of two products and services that are similar in make, the one with the lower price tag is the one that is bought, sold and produced. If for example, we have two identical products and one costs 1.00 ₤ and the other costs 2.00 ₤, it is very certain that the one with the lower price will be bought and sold.

Price selection is restricted to the laissez-faire sector. In fact it is not permitted at all in the GAM sectors since in these we have quality section. In the laissez-faire sector prices of goods and services are determined not by the central bank but by a market. We will discuss this market in detail in another section. Since price selection is in the laissez-faire sector, fortals (₤) are used.

Let's use books in our discussion. It is hard to price books using quality selection. For how would we go about pricing them? If we put books in general in the laissez-faire sector, authors will compete with each other in making their books the most readable and interesting and they would cost the least. Let's also assume that all the books we talk about are in a certain bookstore. This bookstore sets the price of all the books in the store and it has the potential to price every book at any price it wants to. A particular book store on the other side of town sells a particular children's bedtime book. Our store also sells the same book. Our store sells it at 10.00 ₤ while the other store sells it for 9.00 ₤. We lower our price to 8.00 ₤. This competition ends in the situation where the store that has the lower price sells more copies of the book. The most competitive store in terms of competing for price has a greater share of the market.

The concept of an auction is a good example of an application of price selection. We have an abandoned locker with items in it. A group of people get together to "outbid" each other and purchase the locker. The person or group of people that offers the highest price for the locker are the ones that have the right to buy it. Isaac bids 10.00 ₤, Paul bids 15.00 ₤ while Kevin outbids them both by offering 25.00 ₤ for the locker. Isaac offers 30.00 ₤. No one offers more than 30.00 ₤ for the locker and so Isaac owns the locker as soon as he pays 30.00 ₤ for the abandoned locker to the auctioneer.

In consumerism there is both price selection and quality selection. Both are useful. However, they function in different sectors so that they are rather distinct from each other.

Price Selection Versus Quality Selection in Consumerism and Capitalism

In consumerism we have two major ways of marketing items (goods and services). Things can be sold and bought per price (price selection) and via quality (quality selection). A similar but limited form of this idea functions in free market capitalism.

First we will talk about the capitalist case. In price selection an item is marketed based on how much it costs to buy and sell it. Producers of two similar items, for example two identical t-shirts, will compete with each other to sell their item. Price is determined by supply and demand. Since the t-shirts are totally identical, it is likely that the less costly t-shirt will be more sold and more bought. Most things are sold (and bought) in this way in capitalism as this paradigm applies to a wide variety of goods and services.

Price selection, the concept of selling things through price based on supply and demand also appears in consumerism. However it is restricted to the laissez-faire sector, one of the four sectors in consumerism. The laissez-faire sector contains all things that are better sold and bought based on price not quality. This includes things like books, jewellery, art, service of a lawyer, antiques, private school, tips, etc..It is up to the government of a nation to divide the economy into sectors. This means that if it is desired for many things to be under price selection, the laissez-faire sector should be large. Also if a small amount of goods and services are to be under price selection, the laissez-faire sector should be small.

Quality selection is very important in accommodation based consumerism. The idea behind this is that goods and services are bought and sold based on how they are valued by consumerists while a price function is fixed for a family of goods and services. For example, if all cars cost the same – limousines cost the same as sports cars- cost the same as utility cars- cost the same as import cars, the consumerists will buy (and producers will sell) the car that they really want and the higher quality (value in the eye of the consumerist) cars are more sold.

In consumerism, quality selection applies in the governmental, accommodational and materialist sectors (GAM sectors). Here goods and services are marketed based on quality not price although it is up to the government to decide what comprises each of the GAM sectors. The GAM sectors should be ideally much larger than the laissez-faire sector where price selection dominates.

Here is an example of quality selection in the materialist sector. All ice cream (and frozen desserts) cost the same per quantity. Let's say it is 1.00 Θ per 100 mL. The various ice cream makers compete with one another to make original new flavors as well as to make their ice cream more healthy (less calories and less fat). Thus when frozen desserts are bought, the ones of the highest quality (highest value in the eyes of consumerists) are the ones that are bought. Thus goods and services are under quality selection for which it makes sense for them to compete in quality rather than price.

In capitalism goods and services are priced under both price selection and quality selection. In consumerism there are also quality selection and price selection. However the key difference between these two systems is that in capitalism price selection dominates while in consumerism quality selection is the more common paradigm.

Occupational Complexity Rating

Some occupations are more difficult than others. It is more difficult to be a dental surgeon than a janitor and it is more difficult to be a physics professor than a sandwich maker. We need a system to compare jobs based on how difficult they are.

The occupational complexity rating system rates jobs based on how complex they are by ranking them on a scale from one to ten. A job that is very easy will be rated 1 and a job that is very hard would be rated 10. This rating system is instituted by the government.

Overall, it is sort of subjective. A job that is hard to do, requiring a lot of skill and a lot of education to perform would be ranked high. A job that is easy, requiring very little skill or education would be rated low.

For example, a janitor's job would be rated 1, a cashier's job would be rated 2.5, a high school teacher's job would be rated 4, a physicist's job would be rated 7 and a neurosurgeon's job would be rated 9.

Overall, jobs with a high occupational complexity rating would be paid higher than jobs with a lower occupational complexity rating. So, a heart surgeon would be paid more per hour than a window washer.

The occupational complexity rating tells us how difficult a job is in skill, education and required training. The wages and salaries paid to workers for their jobs reflect their job's occupational complexity rating.

The Principals of Merit and Maximum Worker Utility

The principals of merit and maximum worker utility help us find the best jobs for our workers. When applied properly they promote economic efficiency and productivity. They are general principals regarding employment.

The principal of maximum worker utility states that essentially a worker does a job that A) he likes, B) he wants to do, C) he is most suited for, or a combination of these. One would not force a doctor to be a janitor because it is more productive if this educated person is a doctor and someone less educated is a janitor. One of the goals of employment is to find work for employees so that the job fits the worker and the work arrangements are such that society extracts the most productivity from workers.

Here is an example of the application of the principal of maximum worker utility using 4 people and 4 employment positions:

1) A man with a PhD in physics
2) A women with a high school education and a pharmacy technician diploma
3) A high school dropout
4) A developmentally challenged man with an IQ of 65 on a wheelchair

We have 4 positions:

1) A research and lecturing position at a university
2) A position as a helper at a pharmacy
3) A sandwich maker position at a fast food place
4) A job counting screws

The man with the PhD should work at the university. The women with the pharmacy technician diploma should work at the pharmacy. The high school dropout should work as a sandwich maker. The developmentally challenged man should sort screws. This is the most productive use of human resources because if the man with the PhD made sandwiches the high school dropout could not teach at university

When two people are competing for a position at a firm the employer must choose between the two potential employees. The one that has the most merit should be the one that is hired. This means that the candidate has a good education, is experienced and possesses other skills like being punctual, hardworking and trustworthy. This is the principal of merit. However, the principal of maximum worker utility should be observed. So one would probably not hire a man with a post-secondary education to be a cashier as there are other workers that could work well as cashiers with only, say, a high school diploma. A potential employee may have so much merit that he could work at a job where those skills and knowledge have applications.

In consumerism we should have as many people as possible contributing to society as this raises the total output. To find employment for everyone there are special anti-unemployment measures. We might make exceptions for people recovering from heart surgery and similar problems. But even a blind man can help society. For example, he can sing, play the flute or pack groceries. A person on a wheelchair can still do many things. The more people helping society, the better.

The principals of merit and maximum worker utility, theoretically, guide employment decisions. They ensure that an employment position fits an employee's skill. If properly applied, these principals ensure that we obtain the most value out of our workers in consumerism.

Unemployment, Wages and Salaries

In this section we will discuss unemployment, wages and salaries; what they are and what are their natures. As important determinants of an economy, not just the consumerist economy, it is paramount that they be understood. A full knowledge of these will help us understand how the consumerist system works. By wages and salaries we mean the way a worker is compensated for his work. By unemployment we mean the inability to find jobs for workers who desire them.

In the absence of a market system it is hard to calculate wages. A major argument against the communist system is that there is no sensible way of determining wages. However the consumerist system has an alternative non market based method for determining wages and salaries. This method is carried out in the central bank. The central bank doesn't simply determine wages; rather it creates wage functions per family of occupation. Once these functions are set they are permanently fixed. We now turn to the method the central bank has for setting wage and salary functions. The central bank has industry specific Chairmen and their deputies and 100 industry specific commissioners. We have industry specific Chairman and Commissioners since it would take too much time and work for a general set of Chairman and Commissioners to determine wage and salary functions. The industry specific Chairman sets the form of the wage function. By this we mean the criteria by which a worker will get paid. For example a teacher may have one like x/hour and a car salesman may have one such as z/hour + y/car. The industry specific Chairman, in this case the educational industry chairman, decides that the teacher gets paid by the hour and the transportation industry chairman decides that the car salesman is paid both per hour and per car sold. The education industry commissioners determine the value of x and the transportation industry commissioners determine the value of z and y. They put the variable to the vote among themselves. The 25 highest and 25 lowest votes are rejected and the middle 50 are averaged. The process ensures that the industry specific commissioners with a bias are excluded. As an example, suppose the education industry commissioners voted on the teacher wage function. One votes 3.00 þ/hour and another voted 40.00 þ/hour. In the process these votes were counted and the 25 highest and 25 lowest were rejected. Out of the remaining 50 votes an average mean of 29.50 þ/hour was obtained. Thus a teacher would work for 29.50 þ/hour in our example. The figures and numbers proceeding and following are examples and need not be as written in the real system.

The wages and salary functions are designed to maximize productivity and efficiency among workers so that workers contribute to society as much as possible. A policeman would not be paid by how many people he arrested. That would lead him to arrest too many innocent people. It would be better if the policeman were paid by the hour. A painter would not be solely by the hour as that way he would deliberately take a long time to finish painting. It would be better if he were paid by how many square meters he painted. A doctor would not be paid by how many pills he prescribed to his patients as this would result in patients taking drugs when they don't really need them. It would be better if a doctor were paid by how many patients he sees or how many hours she spends with her patients. A teacher would not be paid by how much chalk she used to write her lessons as that way she would write excessively to waste chalk. It would be better if she were paid by how many hours she teaches. Finally a cook would not be paid by how many spices he adds to his meals as that would make food that is undesirably salty or spicy. It would be better if he were paid by how many hours he works

Although the industry specific Chairmen ultimately create the format of the wage function, we can suggest some reasonable ones for the jobs listed above. Wage functions are not set for each profession but rather per *family of services*. Recall the section on consumerist taxonomy. The wage function forms could be:

Policeman-x/hr
Painter-x/m^2 painted
Doctor- x/hr + y/patient
Cook- x/hr

The values of x and y in each case are determined by the voting of the industry specific Commissioners.

Let's turn to the phenomenon of unemployment. Unemployment is the situation where there are more people looking for a job than there are jobs available. Thus there are people who do not work. Let's ask the question: "Is unemployment desirable or should we eliminate it altogether (or at least greatly reduce it)?" If everyone is employed, then the maximum amount of output can be produced given the technology level. However as less and less people are employed, less and less goods and services are produced. But a society that creates many goods and services is better off than one that produces less, economically speaking. This would suggest that the lowest possible unemployment level is most desirable.

Here is a thought experiment. Let's compare two island societies with the same amount of people, the same kind of people and the same conditions of regarding everything else. The only variable is the percentage of people unemployed. On island 1 there are 20 people and everyone has a job. 5 people reap coconuts, 5 people hunt fish, 5 people cook the coconut and fish and 5 people make houses. At the end of the day, each of the coconut finders reaped 4 coconuts, each house builder made 4 houses, each fisherman caught 4 fish and each cook cooked a combination of coconut and fish. The output is 20 coconuts, 20 fish and 20 huts. The coconuts and fish are all cooked. How they divide this output is irrelevant for this thought experiment. Now let's imagine an almost identical island. Here however 25 % of the people are unemployed. Otherwise the two islands are the same. 4 people reap coconuts, 4 catch fish, 4 build houses and 4 cook the food. Let's assume that each working islander has the same output. The difference is that 25 % of the people – the unemployed – do nothing. They bathe in the sun or try to look for a job. The output of the island economy is 16 coconuts, 16 fish and 16 houses. The output is clearly less than in the other island with 0% unemployment. If the output is equally divided per person, each person has less than on the other island. In fact any way one divides the output here the society is worse off. People have more if a greater percentage is producing more. This is an argument in favour of eliminating unemployment.

Now that we know what unemployment is and that it is better to reduce or eliminate it, we need a way of doing so. Suppose that there are more chairs to seat people than there is room around the table. How do we make these extra chairs useful? We make or obtain a bigger table. Suppose that there are more carrot seeds then there is soil to plant them in. How do we make these extra seeds useful? We obtain a larger piece of land. Suppose that there is more apple juice than can fit in a container. How do we make this extra juice useful? We get more containers. Therefore if there are more people than there are jobs for them, we create more jobs. How do we create more jobs for unemployed people?

How do we obtain a bigger table if we have a smaller one? We get it from someone who has a bigger table. How do we get a larger piece of land? We obtain it from someone who has it. How do we obtain more containers for apple juice? We get them from someone who has these containers. Therefore we create more jobs for unemployed people by getting jobs from someone who has them.

Who has a bigger table? A table maker or owner. Who has a large piece of land? The owner of a large piece of land. Who do we get containers for apple juice from? The owner or maker of containers. Therefore we would obtain more jobs for unemployed people from those who own or make jobs. But who is it that makes or owns jobs? It is the employer.

How do we get a bigger table from a table maker or owner? We give him something for which he will give us a bigger table. How do we get a larger piece of land from the owner of a large piece of land? We give him something for which he will give us this land. How do we get a large container from he who makes or owns a container? We give him something for which he will give us this container. How do we get more jobs from an employer? We give him something for which he will give us the job. In all cases we give money.

If there are many chairs what do we do to use them all? We get more tables. Therefore we need to increase the amount of table owners or makers. If there are more seeds than land what do we do to use them all? We obtain more land. Therefore we need to increase the amount of land owners and amount of land that can be sold. What do we do if there is more juice than there are containers? We get more containers and therefore we need to increase the amount of container makers or owners. If there are a lot more people than jobs what do we do to employ them all? We create more jobs. Therefore we need to increase the amount of employers.

How do we increase the amount of table makers or owners? We give them an incentive to produce more. How do we increase the amount of land owners who are willing to sell land? We give them a greater incentive to sell land. How do we increase the amount of container makers or owners? We give them an incentive to make them. Therefore to increase the amount of employers we need to give them an incentive to hire people.

What is the best incentive to give table makers to make more tables? The more tables a table maker makes the more money he earns. What is the best incentive to give to land owners to sell more land? The more land a land owner sells the more money he makes. What is the best incentive to give a container maker so that he makes more containers? The more containers he makes the more money he earns. Therefore the best incentive an employer can receive for employing people is also money. The more people an employer employs the more money he should earn.

The big question now is: "Who pays the employer for hiring people?" The person who buys the container for excess juice from the container maker is he who needs it. The person who buys the land for excess carrot seeds from the previous owner is the person planting the seeds. The person who buys the table for excess chairs from the table maker is the person who needs the place for all his chairs. Therefore it seems logical that the person who receives a job should be the one who needs it. That is the employee. To decrease or even eliminate unemployment each employee buys a job from an employer unless he is self employed. This gives an incentive for the employer to hire more employees.

In consumerism employment is maximized because workers buy *job contracts* from their employers. Essentially they purchase a job, thus having a right to work at it and receive a wage or salary that is ultimately higher than the price of the job contract. Once again these do not apply to owners or the self employed.

We mentioned previously that wage functions are applicable at the family taxon level of organization. The same holds for job contracts. A job contract is set for a family of services. We now show some examples of families that wage functions and job contracts apply to. A family wage function/ job contract is the same for professions that are essentially similar; i.e. in the family "school teachers" we have "high school calculus teacher", "grade 7 science teacher", "high school French teacher" and "grade 8 gym teacher". In the family "building property cleaners" we have "janitor", "maid" and "window cleaner". In the family "fast food preparation work" we have "hamburger cook", "hot dog vendor" – unless he is self employed- "French fryer" and "taco wrapper". In the family "cashiers" we have "grocery cashier", "fast food cashier", "department store cashier" and "convenience store cashier". These are all examples of families with similar job contracts/ wage functions. There are many, many others and there are many more jobs under each family. The point here is to give an example.

Central to the consumerist employment system is the idea of job contracts. It is a contract for work between an employee and an employer under which the employee pays a certain price, the job contract price, to an employer in exchange for employment for a certain length of time. If an employee does not have enough money for a contract but still requires a job, he or she may borrow a certain amount of money from a private bank- with certain interest or alternatively seek assistance through the employment assistance program. The job contract is bought with Ignits as it is in the accommodational sector - consumerists need not buy job contracts if they work in the governmental or laissez-faire sectors. Also, those working in the command partition need not buy job contracts. The job contract is determined by the central bank in a manner similar to a wage function. That is through the voting of 100 industry specific commissioners and the rejecting of the top 25 and lowest 25 votes and averaging the middle 50. The only difference is that there is only one variable, the price of the job, meaning that there is no role for industry specific Chairman. Each industry in the accommodational sector has 100 commissioners who decide the value of the job contract for each family of service. This is so there is less work to do if there was just one set of general commissioners. The job contract is based on productivity. This means that usually jobs that pay high wages cost a bit more to buy. The job contract price is fixed for a family of jobs. It cannot change.

Let's look at some examples. A fast food cashier pays 1 000.00 þ for a year contract. Her wage is 9.00 þ/hr. Both of these are determined by the central bank. Let's assume that there is no income tax. In this case she would need to work 112 hours in the year in order to get back the original 1 000.00 þ. Obviously the employer must employ the cashier for more than 112 hours in a year for the cashier to have any benefit.

A cook makes 15.00 þ/hr and her job contract costs 2000.00 þ for half a year. She must work a minimum of 133 hours in half a year. A job contract must give at a minimum 100% return on the job cost.

A high school teacher makes 20.00 þ/hr and her contract costs 5 000.00 þ per year. 5 000.00 þ/20.00 þ/hr = 250 hours for 100 % return. She must work at least 250 hours per year.

A raspberry picker earns 2.00 þ/hr. A 6 month contract costs 600.00 þ per 6 months. The raspberry picker must work at least 300 hours in 6 months.

The percentage earned from buying a contract is called the *adjusted income percentage*. Some contracts are set for different time periods – some are for 6 months while others are for 3 years. Thus the adjusted income percentage must be set for a certain time frame. The most common types of adjusted income percentages are Adjusted Monthly Income Percentage (AMIP) and Adjusted Yearly Income Percentage (AYIP). They are equivalent except that they are expressed in different time frames. If the AMIP is 100 % then the AYIP is 1200%. This is set by the central bank although unlike the wage and salary functions, the AMIP is not fixed. The higher the AMIP is the more money a worker earns and the more willing he is to work. The AMIP that applies to a job contract is the one that was present at the time of the signing of the contract between the worker and the employer. Once a worker signs a contract with an employer, the current AMIP or AYIP is locked in and doesn't fluctuate.

The central bank sets the AMIP and AYIP as it sees fit. The Grand Chairman is in charge of setting it and he can vary it when he sees it is necessary to do so. Suppose the central bank sets the AMIP at 500 %. This means that the worker must earn 5 times the job contract cost during a month of work. An AMIP of less than 100% for a one month contract is bad because the worker will pay more in buying the contract than he will earn in final income from his wage/salary. In order to increase employment the central bank should lower the AIP. In order to help workers and stimulate the economy it should increase the AIP. The AYIP/AMIP may fluctuate.

Once the AMIP/AYIP is set and the central bank has fixed the wage function and job contract price, the minimum number of hours required from the worker can be found out. We will look at some specific examples.

Let's do some calculations. A teacher has a 5 month contract. She is paid 10.00 þ/hour. The job contract price is 500.00 þ for a 5 month contract. The AMIP is 500%

# of hours to work to attain 100 % profit = 500.00 þ hour/10.00 þ = 50 hours
500 %/ month x 5 months = 2500 % AIP
50 hours x 2500% = 1, 250 hours

Thus the teacher works 1, 250 hours in 5 months. Now we calculate her earnings. 1,250 hours x 10.00 þ/ hour = 12 500.00 þ

Thus she earns 12, 500.00 þ in 5 months. However she happened to borrow the 500.00 þ from a private bank to purchase the job contract. The interest rate was 5% simple interest- in the actual economy this could be compounded. Here we will simplify and use simple interest. Therefore she must pay back 500.00 þ x 0.05 + 500.00 þ = 525.00 þ. She is allowed to keep 12 500.00 þ - 525.00 þ = 11 975.00 þ. She doesn't have to pay property tax or unemployment insurance- these do not exist in our system and we assume that the government does not need to introduce income tax.

Let's do another calculation. A cashier buys a job contract for 6 months. She earns 5.00 þ/hour and the job contact price is 500.00 þ for a 6 month contract. The AYIP is 2000 %. We assume that she doesn't borrow money to buy the job contract but simply has the money saved up.
500.00 þ hour/ 5.00 þ = 100 hours
AIP in 6 months (X) => 2000%/12 months = X/6 months
X = 1000%

She must work 100 hours to obtain 100 % profit. To get 1000% profit she must work 10 x 100 hours = 1000 hours in 6 months. Since she earns 5.00 þ/hour, she earns 1000 hours x 5.00 þ/hour or 5000.00 þ.

Let's look at the case of a car salesman. His wage function is 1000.00 þ/car commission and 5.00 þ/ hour. The central bank sets the AMIP at 200%. There is a JCP in this case. It is 5000.00 þ. His contract is for 5 months. How many cars must he sell or how many hours must he work? In 5 months he makes 5 x 200% = 1000% profit on his JCP. Thus he can sell 50 cars in 5 months or 49 cars and 1000.00 þ/5.00 þ/hour = 200 hours or 48 cars and 2000.00 þ / 5.00 þ /hour = 400 hours. Either way, the car salesman earns a profit of 50 000.00 þ – 5000.00 þ = 45 000.00þ.

The *Adjusted Income Earnings* (AIE) is the amount of money a person earns at the end of a contract minus what he pays to buy the contract. A worker is entitled to earn a percentage increase over his JCP at the end of his contract. This is the minimum the worker will receive at the termination of his contract. Workers are not paid once at the end of their contracts but every two weeks. The AIE can be more than the minimum guaranteed by the AIP but not less unless the worker decides voluntarily to work less. If our car salesman sells 20 cars and works 1000 hours he will make more than he had to pay for his job contract. At the same time his employer will also make a profit. The worker earns 1000.00 þ commission per car sold but the owner of the car dealership (the employer) earns profit from selling the car at the retail level.

The AIP need not be equivalent to that set out by the central bank as in the case of jobs paid by commission. However it should hold for jobs that are paid by the hour. The AIP is determined differently depending on whether a worker is paid by the hour or commission.

A police man's wage function is 20.00 þ /hour and his JCP is 2 000.00 þ for a 6 month contract. His AMIP is 200%

To find hours => 2 000.00 þ/ 20.00þ/hour = 100 hours (for 100% profit)
100 hours x 6 months x 200%/month = 1 200 hours

Thus he works 1 200 hours in 6 months and his AIE is (1 200 hours x 20.00 þ /hour) – 2000.00 þ = 22 000.00 þ If he works 6 months and is paid every 2 weeks he receives 24 000.00þ /13 = 1 846.00 þ every 2 weeks. The 2 000.00 þ are sunk costs in buying the job.

Now we focus our attention on movie actors and hockey players. Simply put, these workers are employed in the laissez-faire sector. They do not have a wage function particular to them. How they are paid is determined by the laws of supply and demand vs. price. Furthermore, they are paid with Fortals not Ignits.

Finally let's look at the predicament of a janitor. His wage function is 20.00þ/hour. The JCP is 3 000.00 þ for 9 months. The AMIP is 150 % so he must work:
- 3 000.00 þ /20.00 þ /hour => 150 hours for 100% return on investment
- 150 % x 9 = 1 350 %
- 150 hours x 13.5 = 2 025 hours in 9 months
- 2 025 hours x 20.00 þ / hour = 40 500.00þ

He gets paid every two weeks, so 40 500.00þ/39/2 = 2 076.92 þ

To sum things up, the janitor works 2 025 hours in 9 months and every 2 weeks he receives a paycheck for 2 076.92 þ .

Sometimes a worker may want to work for less for some reason. He or she may be studying or caring for a child or have several jobs. Thus he or she may not want to work full time but may want to instead work part time. We need to find a way to calculate the number of hours

150

worked and the AIE of a part time worker. Here we will characterize *part time* as a percentage of full time. Full time is what we calculated before. A person with a Part Time Character (PTC) of 50% works half as much as a full time worker. Part Time Character is defined as how much work a part time worker has relative to a full time worker expressed in terms of a percentage or decimal.

We can gain insight by performing calculations. We have a job where the worker earns a wage of 15.00 þ/hour. The job contract costs 1 000.00þ for a 6 month period. The AMIP is 200%

- Hours worked for 100% profit => 1000.00 þ/15.00 þ/hour = 67 hours
- Increase => 6 months x 200 %/ month = 1200 %
- With the income adjustment => 67 hours x 12 = 800 hours
  Amount of pay: 800 hours x 15.00 þ /hour = 12 000.00 þ

Suppose the worker can't work 800 hours in 6 months. The worker wants to work about half as much as a full time worker. Therefore his Part Time Character is 0.5 or 50% of full time. We multiply the AMIP by 0.5. Thus 200% x 0.5 = 100 %. In 6 months the worker will earn 100% x 6 = 600% profit. To find out how many hours he works in 6 months we multiply 67 hours by 6. This equals 400 hours. The worker works for 400 hours in this setup. His pay is 400 hours x 15.00 þ/hour = 6 000.00 þ. He gets paid 6 000.00 þ /13 = 461.54 þ every two weeks. Since he had to pay 1000.00 þ for the job contract the AIE is 6000.00 þ – 1000.00 þ = 5 000.00 þ.

Up to this point we have had to calculate the variables in an intuitive fashion. It would be helpful if we derive a formula for calculating these parameters. To calculate the number of hours worked during a contract period we use the formula:

Work Hours = PTC[JCP x hours/wage x AMIP x (n)]

Where PTC is Part Time Character with the values between 0 and 1. JCP is the price of a contract per n months. Hours/wage is the inverse of the wage function –the inverse of the number of Ignits paid for each hour of work. The AMIP is the profit made during a month of a contract. (n) is the length of the contract in months.

The AIE (Adjusted Income Earnings) is the money a worker earns from working minus the initial investment to obtain the job. It is paid in regular intervals rather than as a lump sum.

The formula is:
AIE = {PTC[JCP x AMIP x (n)]} – JCP

Where PTC is Part Time Character, JCP is job contract price, AMIP is the adjusted income percentage in one month and (n) is the length of the contract in months.

We would like to know how much a worker is paid when he receives his paychecks. Usually checks are issued every two weeks but this is not fixed- it is up to the central bank to decide this variable. However we will use the 2 week length of time in our examples. To find the income earned on a regular paycheck we use the following formula:

Pay check Value = PTC[JCP x AMIP(/(52/12)(1/2)]

The variables were defined before. Let's give an example. For a PTC= 0.8, a JCP of 1000.00 þ and AMIP of 200% and a contract length of 9 months, a bi-weekly paycheck will have this much value:

$$0.8\{1000.00 \text{þ} \times 2 / [(52/12) \times (1/2)] \} = 738.00\text{þ} \text{ per 2 weeks}$$

The hours we have calculated that a worker is entitled to for buying a contract are simply the minimum that a worker is guaranteed for that length of time. However, if the employer wants to, he can offer the employee more than this. This can be due to any reason. Perhaps he likes the work ethic of the employee. However he cannot choose to give a worker less unless of course the worker desires herself to work less and have a part time character. Once a worker buys a job contract she owns the job. Although not very tangible, it is just as much of a possession as a house or car. Through working, one is entitled to reap the profits of this investment. There is the important caveat that the worker can't sell his job to someone else. The job must belong to the person to whom the firm sold it to.

A worker cannot be laid off. The only way a worker can lose his job is if he is fired. The reasons for being fired must be very serious. The employer cannot fire a worker simply because he doesn't like the worker. In order to get fired, the worker must demonstrate gross incompetence or cause serious damage to the firm. The details for being fired will not be discussed here. Rather it will be the job of the human resources in the consumerist system (not to be confused with the human resource management commission) to come up with a list of the reasons one can be fired for. It suffices to say that being fired deserves just cause.

The employee does have the option of quitting their job. When this happens, he does not recover any money and this includes the JCP. It is disadvantageous to quit a job too soon after being hired since the worker could have made more money if he or she stays with the current employer.

Job contracts have their advantage. They aid employers in several ways. First they give employers money that can be invested in their firm. Secondly they ensure the employer that the employee won't quit the job too quickly. Job contracts also aid employees. They ensure the employee that he will make a handsome profit from working. Also the employee gains protection from downsizing and layoffs. A firm cannot downsize or lay off workers that own job contracts. Employees gain self esteem and self respect by being a valuable part of society. Job contracts are one of the best ways to fight unemployment.

From all this talk about job contracts it may seem that firms would hire anyone. Although job contracts do combat unemployment and give profit to the firm that sells them, this is not necessarily the case. A firm would still benefit from hiring the best employees and consequently selling job contracts to them. Given a choice between selling a job contract to a high school dropout and a university graduate the firm would do to its advantage if it sold the job contract to the university graduate assuming he is best suited for the position and there are other jobs for less skilled workers available. The consumerist system shares with the free-market system the idea that the best employees are the ones that should be hired.

We mentioned before that one of the major Communist objections to the free-market system is that workers are exploited. That is, workers are paid less than they should be, working in sweat shops for just enough to get buy. This objection disappears in consumerism. Employers cannot pay their workers what the employers like. They are constrained by the parameters set by the central bank and the government, namely wage functions, job contract prices and Adjusted Income Earnings. Also of note is that the idea of fixed wages relieves the problem of discrimination between sexes and between minority groups. All workers of the same profession have the same wage function regardless of their gender, ethnicity, religion or background.

Having discussed that it is advantageous to lower or eliminate unemployment we now turn to several other ideas that should work towards this end. First of all, there are none of the taxes that are pervasive in the free-market system. There is no corporate, sales, goods or property taxes. Unless the wealth tax or positive income tax are invoked there are no taxes other than the GCT. The absence of these taxes makes it more attractive to do business in a nation under consumerism than one under the free-market or communist orientations.

In consumerism a certain sense of stability is sought after. There are patents to ensure that inventors have rights to their new ideas. The prices of all goods and services, in the GAM sectors, are fixed. The costs of all inputs are fixed. Also all wages and salaries are fixed. This means that these values will not get out of hand due to unmanageable inflation. Also security must be ensured so that business can proceed and there is no danger from rebels or unrest from criminals and thieves.

There is a parameter that directly gives an incentive to firms to hire more employees. It is called the *employment reimbursement transfer* (ERT). In essence the government pays a firm or business a portion of an employee's wage/salary. The ERT is set in the form of a percentage. Let's say, for example, it is 1.5 %. A firm employs 22 workers who each make 2000.00 þ per week. So then each week the government pays the particular firm 22 x 2000.00 þ x 0.015 = 660.00 þ. It is clear that if a firm is paid for having workers and the more workers they have the more they will be paid then the firm will want to hire more workers. This should lower unemployment. The disadvantage of the ERT is that it increases government spending and contributes to the government debt.

A useful way to decrease the unemployment is to increase the size of the army. This is the quickest way to lower the unemployment rate. This may contribute to an increasing debt and deficit. However the main disadvantage of hiring more soldiers is the reputation that it creates in your neighbours and in the international community. Some countries may see this as a form of aggression and hostility and your relations with your neighbours may deteriorate. On the other hand this can be overcome if you make your large army seen not as a threat to world peace but as some kind of "global force of good". By this I mean that instead of using the army to invade your neighbours you use it to help disadvantaged nations when for example they are afflicted by a tsunami or earthquake.

Another parameter designed to lower unemployment is the *capital investment transfer* (CIT). In essence, the government pays a portion of the costs to set up or expand a firm. The CIT is a percentage that involves Ignits. Let's say for example that the CIT is 2%. A winery firm buys a factory for 500 000.00 þ and machines for 200 000.00 þ. The government would give this firm (500 000.00 þ + 200 000.00 þ) x 0.02 = 14 000.00 þ. A year later they buy 50 000.00 þ more worth of equipment. The government would give them 1 000.00 þ. If a firm has some of its start up or expansion costs decreased, it is more likely to start operating in our consumerist nation than in one where it has to pay for all its start up costs by itself. When a firm chooses to do business in our country, it will hire workers, thus lowering unemployment. The main disadvantage to this parameter is that it increases the deficit and may contribute to a greater debt.

The *profit reward transfer* (PRT) also lowers unemployment but in a different way. It is clear that if a firm makes a larger profit it is more inclined to locate itself in the place where it made that profit. The profit reward transfer can be conceptualized as a negative corporate tax. The government pays a firm for making a profit. The PRT is a percentage and has to do with

Ignits. So let's say that the PRT is 3%. We have a tire producing firm that has a revenue of 1 000 000.00 þ and running costs of 800 000.00 þ. So its profit is 200 000.00 þ. In this case, on top of this profit the government would give the firm an extra (200 000.00 þ x 0.03) = 6 000.00 þ. A firm that makes money on top of profit will surely want to locate its production/business centre in a consumerist nation that in a free-market nation where it has to pay a corporate tax just for the privilege of doing business in that country. Any investor/entrepreneur/company owner will clearly see the advantage of the PRT as opposed to paying a corporate tax elsewhere. Therefore more firms/business will be found in our nation. The presence of a firm brings a requirement of workers and thus the decrease of the unemployment rate. Again the disadvantage of the PRT is that it increases spending and may lead to a higher debt or deficit.

In Accommodation Based Consumerism we also have a parameter called the Interest Rate Stimulus (IRS). Essentially the government pays a portion of an investor/borrower's debts to a creditor. The IRS is set as a percentage and deals with Ignits. It can be applied on interest rates in general or certain interest rates (mortgage rate). So suppose the government sets the IRS at 0.02 % and suppose that the central bank sets the interest rate at 3.00 %. Now a firm making calculators and simple electronics borrows 1 000 000.00 þ from a creditor to start their business and expand. Now when it comes time to pay back the loan the firm would have to pay back 1 000 000.00 þ + (1 000 000.00 þ x 0.0028) = 1 002 800.00 þ and the government would pay (1 000 000.00 þ x 0.00020) = 200.00 þ. The creditor would earn a return equal to 3.00 % of the loan but the money comes from both the government and the investor. If the borrower pays less to borrow, he is more likely to invest in the economy. This stimulates the economy as the investment helps firms which hire more workers. In the long run the investment may indirectly increase the materialist output and thus the GDCP. So, ceteris paribus (that is, keeping taxes constant), this may lead to an increase in government revenue through the GCT. On the down side, the IRS directly increases the deficit and government debt. However it is probably the best, or one of the best, things the government can spend its money. In the end the stimulus the IRS provides for the Consumerist economy may be worth the government spending on this parameter.

The last parameter we have for decreasing the unemployment rate works rather indirectly. It is called the *consumerist spending reimbursement* (CSR). The main idea is to bring more firms to our consumerist nation so that they do business here and employ consumerists. If we increase consumerist spending on goods and services in the consumerist nation, the firms will make more revenue and thus more profit and will be more favourable to doing business in this nation. What the CSR does is that it pays consumerists for spending money on goods and services. We will go into detail about this parameter in a future section.

Unemployment, wages and salaries exist in the consumerist system. Certain variables and parameters are peculiar to consumerism. There are different parameters and ideas designed to lower unemployment.

154

Anti-Unemployment Measures

Unemployment is the occurrence when there isn't enough work for our workers. As a consequence, some people are without a job. We came to the conclusion that unemployment is very undesirable. In this section we will discuss several anti-unemployment measures; that is special programs designed to combat and eliminate unemployment.

We list anti-unemployment measures. The name of the measure is followed by a very brief description of it. These are designed to reduce the level of unemployment. Some of these have been discussed before while others will be talked about in detail in future sections.

- The non-existence of taxes unless they are specially invoked, This includes the GCT, the wealth tax and positive income tax- a lack of corporate, sale and property tax helps the economy while decreasing unemployment
- Consumerist Spending Reimbursement (CSR)- money is given to consumerists for buying things, thus increasing spending and attracting firms
- Interest Rate Stimulus (IRS)- the government pays a portion of a firm's loan; thus increasing firm's investment and increasing employment
- Profit Reward Transfer (PRT)- a firm earns money from the government for making a profit – a negative corporate tax- thus increasing the likelihood that the firm will do business in our nation and hire workers here
- Selective Occupation Promotion System- provides good compensation for work that is highly valued in Consumerism
- Capital Investment Transfer (CIT) – a firm earns money from the government for expanding operation; thus increasing the likelihood that the firm will do business in our nation and hire workers here
- Employment Reimbursement Transfer (ERT)- the government pays a portion of a worker's wage making it more likely that a firm will hire a worker
- Increase the size of army- by hiring soldiers, the government directly decreases the unemployment rate; may have negative externalities
- The existence of purchasable Job Contracts- an employer is paid to hire more workers; giving him an incentive to hire more workers
- The Work for Freedom Program- prison inmates are given an occupation in exchange for time off their sentence
- The recycle for pay program- consumerists are paid by the government when they bring in their recyclable items
- Employment agency – employers pay a firm to hire more workers
- Employment Assistance Program – the government pays employers to hire more workers in exchange for an interest on the price of the job
- Governmental Employment Incentive Program- the government pays employers directly to hire more workers
- Partial Ownership of firms by the government – investment from the government promotes the economy thus creating more jobs
- Command Partition Compensation Adjustment- extra pay to certain workers in the command partition to reflect the fact that they have more difficult jobs
- Governmental Business Loan Assistance Program- ensures that businesses have money to operate while employing workers

The above anti-unemployment measures can be considered ways to reduce the level of unemployment. The next three anti-unemployment measures are designed to completely eradicate unemployment:

- The Command Partition- the command partition employs virtually anyone that is unable to find a job in the natural or governmental partition
- The Laissez-Faire Labour System- also hires anyone that cannot find work
- The Disability Work Program – hires all workers that are considered "disabled"

Consumerism, clearly, has a lot of ways to reduce or eliminate unemployment. Having a society with an absence of unemployment is one of the merits of consumerism.

Anti-Inflation Measures

Inflation is defined as the steady increase in general prices from one period of time to another. Most economists agree that when it is extremely low, < 2%, it shouldn't be a problem for any economy. However it is universally recognized that an economy can be virtually destroyed with a huge inflation. Such was the case in Germany in the 1920's when their currency devalued about a billion percent over a span of three years.

For the most part, inflation shouldn't be much of a problem for our system since the price/wage/input functions in the GAM sectors are fixed by the central bank. There may be difficulties in the laissez-faire sector as in that sector prices are not fixed and the prices of goods/services/wages are determined by the forces of supply and demand. Nevertheless there is still some problem as the money supply in the four sectors increases due to the consumerist grant (both general and non-working) and the GCT. This is caused by the GDCP which every once in a while creates a greater money supply.

So the state of affairs is such: there are constantly more and more money, Norses, in the materialist and governmental sectors due to the GCT and working and nonworking consumerist grants. After transactions for goods and services, the money turns into Ignits in the accommodational sector. From there it either circulates indefinitely or is turned into Fortals and it circulates in the laissez-faire sector indefinitely. This, of course, does not cause major problems if there isn't too much circulating money. In fact such a setup actually indicates a healthy growing economy.

The problem occurs when there are too many Ignits and Fortals circulating in the accommodational and laissez- faire sectors due to the fact that, in the accommodational sector there is pressure on fixed price functions and in the laissez-faire sector demand starts to outstrip supply causing inflation. We need some kind of mechanism or mechanisms to slow the rate of money supply growth in the accommodational sector. For the laissez-faire sector we need something to prevent hyperinflation and keep the inflation at as low a level as possible. In this section we describe seventeen such mechanisms

There are seventeen anti-inflationary measures in the accommodation based consumerist economic system. Although they refer to controlling inflation, these parameters actually control the money supply. They are 1) the accommodational markdown, 2) the nominal Ignit/Fortal exchange rate mechanism, 3) the consumerist central bank stock, 4) the speculative central bank stock, 5) the consumerist governmental bond, 6) the speculative governmental bond, 7) command partition anti-inflationary deduction, 8) governmental anti-inflationary markdown, 9) laissez-faire markdown, 10) bankruptcy insurance anti-inflationary deduction, 11) GDCP anti-inflationary mechanism, 12) increase or decrease in scope of materialist sector, 13) governmental loan to business inflationary deduction, 14) governmental ownership of stocks inflationary deduction, 15) foreign currency exchange mechanism, 16) dynamic gambling, 17) high bank rate. They will be discussed in detail in later sections but for now let's examine each of them briefly in turn.

The anti-inflationary measures are grouped into two groups; primary anti-inflationary measures and secondary anti-inflationary measures. The primary anti-inflationary measures should be employed first. The secondary anti-inflationary measures should be invoked only as a last resort if the other anti-inflationary measures are not working and we really need to control the money supply.

The primary anti-inflationary measures are:

- the nominal Ignit/Fortal exchange rate mechanism
- the consumerist central bank stock
- the speculative central bank stock
- the consumerist governmental bond
- the speculative governmental bond
- command partition anti-inflationary deduction
- governmental anti-inflationary markdown
- bankruptcy insurance anti-inflationary deduction
- GDCP anti-inflationary mechanism
- increase or decrease in scope of materialist sector
- governmental loan to business inflationary deduction
- governmental ownership of stocks inflationary deduction
- foreign currency exchange mechanism
- dynamic gambling

The secondary anti-inflationary measures are:

- the accommodational markdown (AMD)
- laissez-faire markdown
- high bank rate

The first anti-inflation measure we talk about is called the nominal Ignit-Fortal exchange mechanism. The nominal Ignit/Fortal exchange rate mechanism is a special program that decreases money in circulation- both Ignits and Fortals- in a quite roundabout way. Essentially it costs money to exchange Ignits to Fortals back and forth. The exchange rate mechanism refers to how much it costs to trade one Fortal for an Ignit and one Ignit for a Fortal. The key idea is that the two are not necessarily inverses. For example, it is possible that $5\,\text{þ} = 1\text{f}$ and $7\text{f} = 1\,\text{þ}$. So for every 5 Ignits one gets 1 Fortal, and for every 7 Fortals one gets 1 Ignit. Clearly, if one were to continuously exchange the two currencies back and forth, he would lose a lot of money. The Ignit-Fortal exchange mechanism is a very subtle way to decrease the money supply and take Ignits and Fortals out of circulation.

The consumerist central bank stock represents stock that the central bank sells to investors for a fixed price. Investors make a profit on these stocks based on an interest rate. The money (in Ignits) received from selling these stocks goes to a special pool called the Consumerist Anti-Inflationary Pool and is thus taken out of circulation from the accommodational sector. Investors can sell these stocks to other investors or the central bank as long as it is at the price set by the central bank. When an investor makes an interest profit or wants to sell his consumerist central bank stock to the central bank, the central bank repays him through the money still in the Consumerist Anti-Inflationary Pool. The fact that this pool is always larger than an investor's single investment ensures us that the central bank can always repay investors their gains and the value of the stock through the Consumerist Anti-Inflationary Pool. As a final consequence, investors are guaranteed to earn a profit by buying Consumerist Central Bank Stock.

The speculative central bank stock is similar to other speculative stocks and stocks in free-market capitalism in general. The central bank sells speculative central bank stock to interested investors. The money (in the form of Fortals) from selling this stock is taken out of circulation in the Laissez-faire sector. It is not spent on anything but taken out of circulation and put into the *speculative anti-inflationary pool.* Traders and investors trade the speculative central bank stock on a speculative stock market. The price of the stock is not fixed and can fluctuate up or down in value. Investors/traders loose or gain money depending on how they sell or buy the stock as the price of the stock goes up or down.

The consumerist governmental bond is very important in controlling the money supply-particularly in the accommodational sector. The government sells bonds to investors. It sets an interest rate and an interest repayment frequency. When the government sells a consumerist governmental bond, the revenue from the purchase is placed inside the consumerist anti-inflationary pool. When it is time to repay the investor his maturity or pay him his interest rate profit, the money in the consumerist anti-inflationary pool is used for that purpose. Usually the money in the consumerist anti-inflationary pool is much greater than what is needed to pay an investor what he is owed from his bond maturity or interest payments. In this way the government reduces the amount of Ignits circulating (in bank book entries) in the accommodational sector.

The speculative governmental bond functions to reduce the money supply (in the form of Fortals) in the Laissez-faire sector. The government sells speculative governmental bonds to investors. However, unlike in the case with consumerist governmental bonds, the parameters regarding these bonds are not set by the government. The interest rate, repayment frequency, size of bond as well as the maturity are determined through the interaction of the government and investors. The money (in Fortals) from selling speculative governmental bonds is put into the speculative anti-inflationary pool. When it is time for the government to pay an investor his maturity and interest payments, the payments are taken directly out of the speculative anti-inflationary pool.

The last two ways to decrease the money supply and fight inflation involve governmental bonds, both consumerist and speculative. Consumerist governmental bonds decrease the amount of Ignits in circulation (in bank book entries) while speculative governmental bonds decrease the amount of Fortals in circulation (in bank book entries). Essentially, the government sells one of the two types of bonds. Instead of investing this money into infrastructure, schools, defence, health care, it puts it aside into a governmental bond pool made of both the consumerist and speculative anti-inflationary pools. The governmental bond pool contains both large sums of Fortals and Ignits. The investor is paid from the governmental bond pool every set amount of time that is dictated by the repayment frequency. When it is time to pay the whole value of the bond upon the maturity of the bond then either 1) the government subsidizes the bond repayment from the government budget. Or 2) there may still be money in the governmental bond pool from selling government bonds previously that have a maturation date a long time in the future.

The command partition anti-inflationary deduction is also useful in controlling the money supply. In this case the revenue generated from firms in the command partition is destroyed and taken out of circulation. This should represent a large amount of money. Suppose the Command Partition Anti-Inflationary Markdown is 5 % and firms in the command partition make 10 000 000 000 þ. In this case, 500 000 000 þ are taken out of circulation.

The money supply can also be limited trough the Governmental Inflationary Markdown. This represents the percentage of the government's (all 3 levels) operating budget that is taken out of circulation. So suppose that the federal government has a budget of 100 000 000 000 þ and the Governmental Inflationary Markdown is 0.1 %. Here, 100 000 000 þ are taken out of circulation so as to lower the amount of money circulating in the economy.

The Bankruptcy Insurance Anti-inflationary Deduction can also control inflation. If the Bankruptcy Insurance Anti-Inflationary Markdown is 1 % and there are 50 bankruptcy insurance firms in our economy and in total they make 50 000 000 000 þ per year, quite a bit of money can be taken out of circulation. In fact 500 000 000 þ can be destroyed.

The GDCP Anti-Inflationary mechanism can also help in combating inflation. With this parameter, money is taken out directly out of the GDCP. This helps to limit the Norses entering the economy. This will have the overall effect of decreasing the Ignits and Fortals circulating in the economic system.

The money supply can be manipulated by increasing or decreasing the scope of the materialist sector. If we increase the scope of the materialist sector this will raise the money supply as it will directly increase the GDCP. However if we decrease the scope of the materialist sector, this should lower the money supply as it will decrease the GDCP.

Also in our arsenal for fighting inflation is the Governmental Loan to Business Inflationary Deduction. When the government loans money to businesses, a portion of that money is deducted and destroyed. This controls the money supply. So, if the central bank sets the Governmental Loan to Business Inflationary Markdown at 1 % and in a year the government makes loans to 5 000 firms with the value of the loans being 50 000 000 000 þ, 500 000 000 þ are taken out of circulation.

There is also the Governmental Ownership of Stocks Inflationary Deduction. When the government invests in stocks of other firms, a portion of the revenue from the dividends of the stock gets taken away as an anti-inflationary measure. So if the central bank sets the Governmental Ownership of Stocks Inflationary Markdown at 1% and, through investing in firms in the natural partition, the government makes a profit of 20 000 000 000 þ, 200 000 000 þ are removed from the money supply.

The foreign currency exchange mechanism can also influence the money supply. When an investor or tourist exchanges foreign currency (Canadian dollars or Euros for example) into Fortals (and vice versa) a percentage of the transaction is deducted. This amount of Fortals is destroyed; i.e. taken out of the bank records and out of circulation.

The accommodational markdown is a special parameter that controls the removal of Ignits from the accommodational sector. This parameter does not affect either the governmental, laissez-faire or materialistic sectors. Essentially, a portion of the revenue from sales for certain goods and services in certain industries and classes is deducted from the seller in the accommodational sector. This money does not go to the government as revenue for social services. It is completely destroyed. That is, it is removed from bank book entries. In a way it appears as a strange sales tax but the difference is that no money goes to the government. The accommodation markdown is set by the central bank. Suppose it is set at 20%. If John sells a 1 000 000 þ piece of land to Kevin, Kevin pays John 1 000 000 þ but John only keeps 800 000 þ. The 200 000 þ (20 % of 1 000 000 þ) are taken away from the bank records. To help the economy grow, the accommodational markdown could be very small or even zero. We will discuss in future sections more details regarding this parameter and what goods and services could potentially be under the influence of this parameter although decisions regarding the accommodational markdown are ultimately under the control of the central bank. There are quite a few goods and services under the accommodation markdown. Those that are not are usually those affected by the retail markup. But certainly, things like land, accommodation and utilities are.

The laissez-faire markdown works similarly to the accommodational markdown. It takes money out of circulation in the laissez-faire sector. It is a goal of the laissez-faire sector to have the least governmental involvement as possible and to allow the laissez-faire sector to be run by the interaction of consumerists and producers. Thus the laissez-faire markdown should only be used as a tool of last resort. It is the least preferable anti-inflationary mechanism that we discussed.

Dynamic gambling can be used to reduce the money supply and control inflation. In this case, the profits from gambling, i.e. lotteries, casinos, etc are deducted from bank records and destroyed. So instead of the government making money in the gambling industry, these profits are taken out of circulation to curb inflation.

A high bank rate can potentially lower inflation. The bank rate refers to the interest rate the private banks have to pay the central bank when they borrow from the central bank. The problem with this parameter is that a high bank rate usually causes a recession. Therefore, it is a secondary anti-inflationary measure.

The GDCP and the seventeen anti-inflationary measures can, very generally, be used to manipulate the money supply in accommodation based consumerism with regards to 2 currencies; Fortals and Ignits. If the GDCP is higher than the anti-inflationary measures than there will be a greater amount of Ignits and Fortals in the accommodational and laissez-faire sectors. However, if the seventeen measures remove more money than the GDCP puts in, the total money supply should steadily decrease

Of the seventeen anti-inflationary measures the AMD, high bank rate and the Laissez-faire markdown are least favourable. When trying to reduce the money supply it is preferable to make use of the other anti-inflationary measures first. This is due to the fact that the AMD, high bank rate and laissez-faire markdown have a negative effect on the economy more so than the other anti-inflationary measures. The AMD, high bank rate and laissez-faire should be used as a last resort to combat increases in the money supply.

These are the 17 anti-inflationary measures. This is how we fight inflation and decrease the money supply. There are seventeen main measures to combat inflation that we saw. These are the accommodational markdown, the Fortal-Ignit exchange mechanism and the Speculative/Consumerist governmental bond and stock markets, command partition anti-inflationary deduction, governmental anti-inflationary markdown, laissez-faire markdown, bankruptcy insurance anti-inflationary deduction, GDCP anti-inflationary mechanism, increase or decrease in scope of materialist sector, governmental loan to business inflationary deduction, governmental ownership of stocks inflationary deduction, foreign currency exchange mechanism. Some are under the influence of the government while others are under the influence of the central bank. They are meant to reduce and control the money supply in the accommodational as well as Laissez-faire sectors. They are designed to restrict the quantity of Fortals (f) and Ignits (þ) in two very important sectors of the accommodation based consumerist economy. With a managed inflation/money supply we can avoid many of the problems that have plagued other economies.

The Employment Assistance Program

In the employment assistance program the government pays the employer to hire a worker. The worker then later pays the government for helping him find an employer. He pays back with a considerable interest.

This program is primarily intended for those job-seekers that can't afford to pay or don't want to pay for the job contract for employment. Recall that for jobs in the accommodational sector of the natural partition, a consumerist must buy a "job contract". This entitles him to work for a job for a certain length of time and ensures him a considerable profit. It also protects him from being laid-off through downsizing. This gives the employer an incentive to hire more employees as the more workers he hires and more job contracts he sells, the more income he earns from that.

A worker interested in a particular job in the accommodational sector of the natural partition has two options. He can either buy the job contract from the employer directly, thus earning the right to work at that job. Alternatively, he can have help from the employment assistance program. In that way, the government buys the job contract from the employer and the money goes to the employer. Eventually, the employee has to pay the government the value of the job contract but with a considerable interest. This special interest is called the *Employment Assistance Program Interest Rate* (EAPIR). It is set by the government.

Let's do some calculations. Someone wants to be a cashier. The job contract to be a cashier costs 500.00 þ for a 6 month contract. The AMIP is 100 %. The EAPIR is 20 %. So in 6 months this cashier would make 6 x 500.00 þ = 3000.00 þ. The cashier needs to pay the government with interest for helping him find a job. He pays (500.00 þ x 0.2) + 500.00 þ = 600.00 þ. He can pay in instalments (every month or every 2 weeks) or as a lump sum at the end of the contract.

In the above example, several groups greatly benefited. First, the cashier obtained a job and made a considerable profit. The employer earned 500.00 þ upfront as a reward for hiring the worker. Furthermore the government made money through the EAPIR. In fact it made 100.00 þ.

The employment assistance program is a win-win-win system. It helps job seekers find a job more smoothly and efficiently. It ensures that employers are more likely to find an employee to hire and make a profit for doing so. It acts as a source of revenue for the government. Thus it functions as both an anti-unemployment measure and a source of governmental revenue.

Last point to mention is that in this discussion of the employment assistance program we have used the term "government" very vaguely. The profit from this program, i.e. the EAPIR, actually goes to all levels of government. All three levels of government receive 1/3 of the profit and at each level the distribution is based on relative population.

The employment assistance program functions to help both the employee as well as the employer. It also helps the three levels of government by making interest-profit on job contracts.

The Government Bank

There are three main types of banks in accommodation based consumerism. There is the central bank, the private bank and finally there is the government bank. We discussed or will discuss the central and private banks in other sections. Here we will talk about the government bank.

The government bank is essentially different from the private bank and central bank. We will talk about the private bank in an upcoming section. It is distinct from these types of banks and works in a different sense then they do. All three are important for the smooth functioning of our consumerist system.

The central bank is a separate entity than the government but it works in conjunction with it to coordinate the economy. There are two types of private banks – those run by natural partition firms and those run by command partition firms; although both are primarily in the laissez faire sector. The natural partition private banks are totally private and run to promote the interests of those who own and run the banks. The command partition private banks are designed to run efficiently but in the end the proceeds go to the 3 levels of government.

In contrast to these two we have a government bank. The government bank is purely owned, run and operated by the government (3 levels). Furthermore, it runs in a different sense than the other two types of banks.

The governmental bank makes loans to businesses and firms (this will be discussed in another section). For this it makes profits or interest payments from these loans. Although the two types of banks also make loans to firms, the government bank actually tries to charge a lower interest rate.

The government bank makes loans to the government (3 levels) in particular. In order for the many firms in the command partition to get started or expand they can receive money to do so from the government bank.

Since the consumerist society is a cashless one, the government bank does not really need a cash reserve ratio to protect its loans.

The government bank works together with bankruptcy insurance firms- both the domestic and international ones- to protect the loan made by the government bank.

In order for a firm to borrow, let's say 1 000 000 þ from the governmental bank, it must insure the loan with a domestic bankruptcy insurance (DBI) firm in case the firm defaults on its loan or it can't make interest payments on its loan.

The interest rate on loans made by the government bank is different than that for the central bank. The main interest rate and the interest rate of the government bank need not be identical. This is so that firms have an incentive to borrow from the government bank.

We mentioned that the government bank functions to make loans for businesses and command partition firms. So, what do the two types of private banks do? The private banks are mostly there for consumerists to make mortgage loans on their homes. Also they aid in making personal loans. For example, if a consumerist needs 5 000 þ to buy a stove, the private bank will loan him that money to make that purchase (with interest of course).

The government bank system works to coordinate the consumerist economy. It is a useful entity in the consumerist system. As we will soon see, the existence of the government bank greatly stimulates the economy.

A New Way of Lending Money

When businesses, whether large or small, wish to expand or start up, they need money. They can obtain this money in the form of a business loan from a private bank. In accommodation based consumerism, businesses have an alternative when they do not want to deal with private banks.

In accommodation based consumerism there exists the Governmental Business Loan Assistance Program (GBLAP). Essentially, the government rather than a private bank provides firms with a business loan. The government earns money by lending funds to various firms in consumerism. This profit is used to pay for social services like health care, education, defence and infrastructure.

Suppose that the Grand Chairman of the central bank sets the official interest rate at 2.0 %. Thus to borrow money from a private bank, a private a firm would have to pay 2.0% interest on a loan provided by a private bank. Under the GBLAP, the government sets a rate of borrowing and lending called the Governmental Business Loan Assistance Interest Rate (GBLAIR) that is lower than that set by the central bank. Suppose it is 1 %. So to borrow from the government a firm pays a lower interest rate than if it borrowed from a private bank.

The GBLAP is run by a branch of the government called the Government Bank. This is not the same as the Central Bank that has many other functions. Care must be taken not to confuse the central bank and the Government Bank.

The Government bank is operated by a Government Bank Chairman and there is also a deputy government bank chairman to replace the government bank chairman in case the government bank chairman can't perform his duties. These individuals' salaries are paid based on the parameters set by the industry specific commissioners in the central bank.

The only real variable parameter that the Government Bank Chairman has control over is the government business loan assistance interest rate (GBLAIR). This represents how much it costs firms to borrow money from the government bank. It is expressed as a percentage. So if the government bank lent a particular firm 1 000 000 þ at 1%, the government bank will eventually earn 10 000 þ when the loan is repaid.

The government business loan normally applies to the accommodational sector and Ignits are involved. The government bank does not lend Norses in the materialist sector. Loans in terms of Norses are provided to consumerists through the materialist overdraft program which is explained thoroughly in another section. If a business is in the laissez- faire sector a loan in terms of Ignits is simply turned into a loan of Fortals through the Fortal-Ignit exchange mechanism. The government bank can lend Ignits to firms in the materialist sector.

The profits (interest) earned though the GBLAP go directly to pay for social services. Instead of the profit from lending money going to private bank CEO's and board members as it does in capitalism (who already have millions of dollars), the profit is distributed to the 3 levels of government for the purpose of paying for social services similar to the way the Grand Consumerist Tax (GCT) is distributed. The profits from the GBLAP go to the 3 levels of government based on population. Thus the federal government earns 1/3, the provincial government earns 1/3 depending on population and the municipal governments earn 1/3 depending on population. Of course, the inter-governmental transfer factors in. This means that the various levels of government can give money to each other if one level has an abundance of money and another has a deficit.

The advantage of the GBLAP is that it allows the governments to raise money for social services in ways other than through taxes. Taxes distort the economy and are bad for both consumerists and producers. We say they have deadweight loss. The GBLAP is a more efficient way of raising money than through taxes.

As with any loan, there is the possibility of a risk of default. To overcome this, we invoke the idea of bankruptcy insurance. When a firm borrows money from the government bank, it must purchase bankruptcy insurance. So suppose a firm borrows 1 000 000 þ from the governmental bank at a rate of 1 %. A bankruptcy insurance firm insures the loan for 0.1 % per month. So the firm that is borrowing money receives 1 000 000 þ to expand operation. It must eventually pay back this amount plus 10 000 þ (the interest). However, every month the firm must pay 0.1 % of the loan (1000 þ) to the bankruptcy insurance firm. If the firm bankrupts, it must liquidate (sell off all of its assets) to pay for the loan. If it is short, the bankruptcy insurance firm steps in and pays the remaining part of the debt for the borrowing firm.

The governmental business loan has the same or similar effect as a business bailout. With an extra influx of money a firm can restructure its financial situation. So if we have a truck manufacturing company on the brink of bankruptcy, the government, through the government bank, can save the firm and keep its workers employed. A loan of say 1 000 000 000 þ can help the firm restructure its finances, modernize its facilities and survive for at least several more decades. The loan accomplishes four things. It allows workers to remain employed as a company expands and avoids complete shutdown. This is an anti-unemployment measure. It keeps a firm producing a good or service so that society's general level of output is maximized. It protects firms in our nation vital to our security. For example, a firm that makes submarines for our military. Finally, the interest on the loan is a form revenue for the three levels of government, which ensures that the three levels of government have an alternative source of revenue in addition to the Grand Consumerist Tax (GCT), the command partition and gambling profits.

The interest rate offered through the government bank is usually much lower than that of private banks. Therefore businesses are most likely to borrow money from the government bank than a private one. However loans from the government bank are restricted to those to businesses so private banks can still make a profit by providing loans in the form of mortgages for houses for consumerists, among other things.

The money for the governmental business loan essentially comes from the three levels of government. To simplify things, suppose that there is only one province and one municipality. If the government bank loans 1 000 000 000 þ to a struggling airline company at an interest rate of 1%, this money comes from the three levels of government. The federal government gives the airline company 333 333 333 þ. The provincial and municipal governments also give this amount of money so that the airline company receives in total 1 000 000 000 þ in order to restructure its enterprise. The airline company must eventually repay the loan. When it does so, it gives the government bank 1 000 000 000 þ plus the interest. The interest on the loan is 10 000 000 þ. All this money is given to the three levels of government such that the federal, provincial and municipal governments each receive 1/3 of the principal plus the interest. If we are dealing with several provinces and municipalities, each would receive money based on its population.

The Governmental Business Loan Assistance Program is another way for businesses in accommodation based consumerism to acquire a loan. This helps them when they are in a desperate financial situation so that they can avoid closing their doors and ending the employment of their workers. The interest payment on this loan goes to the three levels of government to pay for social services like health care, education and defence.

Governmental Loan to Business Inflationary Deduction

The consumerist system has an alternative method for combating inflation. It is clear that the money supply should be balanced. That is the rate of inflation should be controlled.

One useful way to manage the money supply (i.e. control inflation) is to manipulate the governmental loan to business. In consumerism the government loans money to businesses to help them grow and flourish. This loan helps businesses overcome bankruptcies and issues having to do with financial difficulties.

We have the Governmental Loan to Business Inflationary Deduction (GLBID). It is set as a percentage. This represents the amount of money that is deducted from a government loan to business. In consumerism when the government (all levels) loan money to a business that is struggling, a percentage of the money is taken out of circulation and destroyed.

So suppose we have a business that produces steel. Steel is essential for the well being of our economy. The business has financial problems and is on the verge of collapse. The provincial government steps in and helps out. It loans the business 1 000 000 þ at 10% interest. At the same time a portion of the money is deducted as an anti-inflationary measure. Let's say it is 5 %. This is 200 000 þ. Thus 200 000 þ are deducted from the bank book records and 200 000 þ (1 000 000 x (10% -5%)) are given to the government as revenue.

It is essential that the inflationary deduction is less than the profit the government makes by giving loans. Otherwise there really is no point for the government to offer loans to businesses.

When the government (all 3 levels) loan a certain amount of money to a firm that is struggling, a portion of that money is deducted and taken out of circulation. This deduction is meant to control inflation, i.e. an unchecked increase in the money supply. Among the other anti-inflationary measures, this is a way of keeping the economy from experiencing runaway inflation.

It may be a good idea to keep this parameter at zero. If it is set high, this fights inflation. However, if it s set low it increases government revenue.

The governmental loan to business inflationary deduction (GLBID) takes money away from transactions where the government offers a loan to enterprises. This is an important parameter in keeping the money supply in balance. Whenever the government (all levels) loan money to a firm the GLBID is deducted and destroyed, i.e. removed from book records.

The Employment Agency

The employment agency is a crucial type of firm in the accommodation based consumerist economic system. Its main role is to find workers for other businesses. Whenever a firm needs workers but is simply unable to find them on its own, it can hire workers through the employment agency.

If a firm has a shortage of workers, it turns to the employment agency. In exchange for a payment, the employment agency tries to find the best workers for the firm. At the same time, people without work approach the employment agency so that it can help them find work. The job-seekers do not have to pay the employment agency for the service of helping find work. The employment agency makes money when firms looking for workers ask their help.

One of the reasons that a firm may have for not being able to find workers is that their wages/salaries are just too low. In the free-market system this would be remedied by increasing the wage. In consumerism what we do is introduce the existence of an employment agency. Although a firm may have a hard time finding workers with its current salary, there is, with quite certainty, a lot of people- for example those on welfare- that would definitely take the job if they only knew about it. The concept of the employment agency accomplishes in consumerism what wage manipulation achieves in the free-market system.

We mentioned earlier that for most jobs the employing firm makes money by selling jobs to workers. They can find these workers on their own or enlist the help of an employment agency. To hire workers that would otherwise be unavailable, the firm pays the employment agency. How much it costs to hire a worker is not set by the central bank. The employment agency actually functions in the laissez-faire sector. This is because there really isn't any quality selection involved in this case. It makes the most sense for employment agencies to compete for money as opposed to anything to do with quality.

The employment agency operates both in the natural partition and command partition. However it does not operate in the governmental partition. Thus profit-maximizing firms in the natural partition compete with each other to give firms the best workers for the best price and as many of them as possible. Meanwhile, firms in the command partition ensure that there are employment agencies to begin with and also that they provide worker-seeking firms with high quality workers for a good price and an adequate amount of them.

It is good to have as many of these firms as possible. There should be as many employment agency firms in the various partitions as necessary.

Employment agencies play a key role in accommodation based consumerism. Their existence is necessary to ensure that worker-seeking firms have access to workers without having to manipulate wage functions set by the central bank. Employment agencies help maximize employment for those that seek it.

Governmental Employment Incentive Program

The consumerist economic system strives to find ways to drastically reduce or perhaps eliminate unemployment. The lower the unemployment, the better off society is as it has (usually) higher general output and more goods and services to share among its people. There should be programs designed to reduce/eliminate unemployment in accommodation based consumerism.

One such anti-unemployment program we will discuss next is called the Governmental Employment Incentive Program (GEIP). It is designed, for the most part, to fight unemployment. In basic terms the government (all 3 levels) pay certain employers in order to hire an unemployed consumerist seeking employment.

In the GEIP, the 3 levels of government pay a portion of a worker's JCP (the price of a contract to start a job) so that the employer receives even more money for hiring an employee. The logic is that if an employer is paid to hire workers he will be more likely to hire more of them (as long as they are needed). This should reduce unemployment and maximize employment.

As an example, let's look at the case of a cashier. For a 6 month contract, it costs the cashier 1000.00 þ. This money goes to the employer – usually the owner of a store, perhaps a grocery or convenience store. The central bank sets the other parameters regarding her employment such as how much she gets paid per hour and how many hours she gets per contract period.

In this case, to give an extra layer of incentive for the employer to hire the cashier, the government sets the GEIP at 5 %. So that on top of the money the worker gives to the employer, the government gives the employer 5 % x 1000.00 þ = 50.00 þ. Thus for hiring the cashier the employer receives a total of 1000 þ + 50.00 þ =1050.00 þ. The more money the employer receives for hiring a worker, the more incentive he has for doing so. However this has to be balanced with the fact that the GEIP has to come from a source of revenue. Therefore, it can't be too high. It should be just high enough to persuade a potential employer to hire another worker.

Workers employed through this program can't be terminated too easily. Otherwise the employer would take money from the GEIP and the money paid by the worker for the job contract and get rid of him as soon as he is hired. The reasons for termination have to be severe- the employee must cause substantial damage to the firm. Also, the employer can't "downsize". As soon as a worker is hired he is entitled to work the full length of his contract.

The Governmental Employment Incentive Program works to help the economy and it aids workers. It reduces/eliminates unemployment by encouraging employers to hire more workers. However, it must be carefully used and balanced as if it is too high the government budget will be easily drained.

Increase or Decrease in Scope of Materialist Sector

As we have seen, the materialist sector is an important section of the economy. The GDCP which turns into the general consumerist grant, non-working consumerist grant and the GCT is all derived from the materialist sector. Controlling and manipulating what compromises the materialist sector is clearly an integral part of manipulating these key parameters.

If we want to increase the GDCP (ceteris paribus) as well as increasing the general consumerist grant, the non-working consumerist grant and the GCT we could broadly increase the scope of what it means for something to be in the materialist sector. Likewise, if we want to decrease the GDCP, the general consumerist grant, the non-working consumerist grant and the GCT, we could decrease the scope of what it means to be in the materialist sector.

Thus it is clear that to manipulate the GDCP and along with it the money supply, it is good to manipulate the scope of the materialist sector. To increase the GDCP we ought to add industries and families and goods and services to the materialist sector and to lower the GDCP we ought to reduce the amount of industries, families and goods and services in the materialist sector.

The government can increase the scope of the materialist sector and increase the GDCP by including the hospitality industry in the materialist sector. Things like pancakes, pizzas, restaurant buffets and pineapples would be in the materialist sector. To buy these things it would require money but if these things are produced, the equivalent monetary value is given to the consumerists.

On the other hand, the government can decrease the scope of the materialist sector by taking the transportation industry out of the materialist sector. Things like cars, vans and motorcycles would no longer be part of the GDCP and they would no longer be purchasable using Norses. The GDCP would decrease.

By increasing or decreasing the scope of the materialist sector, the government can manipulate the GDCP, the general consumerist grant, the non-working consumerist grant and the GCT. This is a very powerful way of controlling the money supply.

The International Loan Program

The international loan program is an interesting way for the government (3 levels) to make a profit to use to pay for social services. On the side, it helps support our friends and strengthens our relationships with foreign nations. Of the many methods for the government to raise government revenue this one should be used as among the first.

In basic terms, in the international loan program the government (3 levels) borrow money from the governmental bank at a set interest rate. They then loan this money to a nation that needs money to start up and expand. For example, it needs money to build roads, schools, hospitals, police stations. We charge the nation that we lent the money to a higher interest rate than our government bank charged our government. We take in the interest payments on the loan from the foreign country and we pay the interest on the loan the government took out. Since the interest on the loan to the country we lent to is larger than the one our country borrowed from the governmental bank, we clearly have profit in the end. This profit is used to pay for social services like healthcare, education and infrastructure. In the end our country repays the loan from the governmental bank as soon as our debtor nation pays us. Alternatively, we can make interest payments on our loan indefinitely. As long the interest rate the debtor nation has with us is higher than the government's interest with the governmental bank, we will always be in good standing. That is, we will always be making profit on the difference between interest rate x value of loan. And that is what is used to pay for social services.

We will look at two mathematical examples for clarity. First, the federal government borrows 10 000 000 000 £ from the governmental bank. The interest rate on this loan is 0.8 % per year. A poor country somewhere in Africa needs money as its people are hungry and without homes and it needs to boost their economy. Let's assume that 1£ = 1$. The federal government gives the 10 000 000 000 £ = $ 10 000 000 000 to that country. The country has an interest rate to pay us of 2.0 % per year. So it must pay us 200 000 000 £ every year or 200 000 000 £/12 = 16 670 000 £ every month.

Usually, the nations that are impoverished get loans from the world bank. However, in order to compete, our country undercuts the interest rate set by the world bank and charges the debtor nation an interest rate less than that set by the world bank. So as to revisit our previous example, the world bank would charge the poor African nation 2.7 % on their loan. In order to be competitive, we will only charge them 2.0 %. Thus we will get the profits from the interest paid by the debtor nation.

So, in the previous example all that is necessary for good standing is that we make interest payments to the governmental bank – we do not have to pay back the loan in full. However, we could if we wanted to. We get money for the payments when the debtor nation pays us the interest on their loan. Clearly, we will always be making money on this proposition.

There is another setup that is somewhat similar. Instead of the government lending money to a debtor nation, one could have the governmental bank make the loan directly thus avoiding the middle man. Suppose that a very poor African nation needs money to develop and grow. Let's assume again that 1£ = $1. The governmental bank loans 1 000 000 000 £ = $ 1 000 000 000 to that nation. It sets the interest rate on the loan to that country at 1.5 % per year whereas the world bank would make loans for 2.0 %. Clearly, the poor nation would rather borrow from us. Thus the country must pay the governmental bank 1.5% x $ 1 000 000 000 = 15 000 000 £ =

$15 000 000. It makes monthly payments of 15 000 000 £/12 = 1 250 000 £. This is given directly to the 3 levels of government to pay for social services.

The international loan has similar essence to a grand mortgage. Instead of giving money to a home buyer we are giving it to a nation and instead of dealing with houses the foreign nation uses the money to build infrastructure. It is clear that in the long run the people providing a mortgage, usually a bank, have a tremendous profit over their initial investment. In the case of international loans, each month (or other set time) the debtor nation pays a percentage of the actual loan, that is, the principal. Eventually, after some time, the debtor nation is expected to pay back the value of the loan and a substantial interest rate. This profit goes to pay for social services.

One interesting quality in this paradigm is what happens when a debtor nation can't pay its interest payments. This is discussed fully in another section. But basically, the International Bankruptcy Insurance Firm steps in to help out. Also when a country can't make the required payments its international credit rating goes down, making it harder for them to get a future loan and raising their interest on loans.

Since the proceeds from the governmental bank go to the government (3 levels) all the money that comes from paying the loan by the debtor nation goes to the 3 levels of government.

On the side what the international loan program accomplishes is that it allows our nation to create friends among other nations. If lent several billions of fortals to a poor nation, that poor nation will remember it in the future and help us out when we need it. Lending money to a nation creates friends and allies.

It is always better to be a creditor than a debtor nation. Debtor nations have a debt from a loan that they must eventually pay back and the longer they take to pay it back, the more havoc it causes on their economic system. The only problem with being a creditor nation is that some other nation will default on the loan. However, this does not happen in consumerism as we have international bankruptcy insurance firms. Thus there are no risks to lending – only rewards.

The international loan program works to simulate the economy. It is a good way to raise money easily and quickly. It also strengthens international relationships.

Selective Occupation Promotion System

There are quite a few distinguished professions we would like to have more of in our consumerist society. We may be short of people performing some occupations and we must do everything we can to have them working for us. We ensure we have people with jobs having a complexity rating greater than 7 by making use of the selective occupation promotion system (SOPS).

In the SOPS the government (it is immaterial which level at this point) pays people to come to our consumerist nation to work here. Recall that jobs in the accommodational sector of the natural partition and those in the government partition are paid a certain wage or salary for performing a certain job. This wage function may be comparatively low so that workers with a job with a complexity rating greater than 7 will want to be and work in another country. To encourage workers to migrate to our nation we (the government) pay these workers a payment on top of their original wage/salary function.

In consumerism we want the best doctors, psychiatrists, cancer researchers, physics professors and those with similar jobs. These jobs usually have a complexity rating greater than 7. To make sure that these people come to our country we make sure that they are well compensated for their services.

Let's see some concrete examples. We have a shortage of good doctors and we desperately need more. The wage/salary function for a doctor is 80 000 þ per year. In other countries a doctor is paid $ 170 000. Assume that 1 þ = $1. To ensure that the doctor comes to our country the government will pay him an additional 100 000 þ on top of the 80 000 þ he is already getting. If a prestigious, educated, experienced doctor were to decide between 170 000 þ in one country and 180 000 þ in our country (assuming 1 þ =$1), then Ceteris Paribus he will more likely come to our country to practice.

We need the best psychiatrists and cancer researchers. Let's suppose that a psychiatrist is paid 100.00 þ for every patient that he sees. In another country he will be paid 250.00 þ = $ 250.00 per patient. So the government pays him an additional 160.00 þ for every patient that he sees. Usually, this psychiatrist if given the choice and everything else is comparable will want to help people in our country.

It would be good to have the finest professors in our universities that are publicly provided. We need to pay them more for teaching in our consumerist nation than in another country. Suppose a professor is paid $ 300 000.00 to teach in a university in Canada. Assuming $1 = 1 þ, if we pay him 350 000.00 þ he is more likely to want to teach in our nation.

The logic (and math) we came up with for the last three examples applies to all types of professions. In particular it applies to professions that a) have a complexity rating of >7 and b) we have a desperate shortage of and c) we want the finest professionals in the world to work for us in our country.

The major drawback to the SOPS is that it can be quite expensive to maintain. On the positive side we gain a multitude of the finest professionals from all over the world who will come to our consumerist nation. On the other hand, it clearly costs money. However consumerism has come up with a multitude of ways to accumulate revenue in the absence of a tax. Look back to that section for a thorough discussion of how the government raises money. All in all though, this program is easily one of the best things that the government can spend its money on.

There are also jobs in the laissez-faire sector. For example, actors, film directors, athletes and entertainers. We also want the best hockey and soccer players playing for a team in our consumerist nation. However, in these cases, the government does not step in. We rely on the market forces of supply and demand to find the best people who will work in the laissez-faire sector. Thus, if we have a hockey team that earns 200 000 000 f every year in profit, to make sure that they acquire more fans and sell more tickets they hire (pay for) the best hockey players in the league. If a movie making firm earns about 150 000 000 f per movie they can attract the world's best actors to star in their films. So they can afford to pay the actor 15 000 000 f per movie. Note that in the laissez-faire sector there are no wage/salary functions. The government promotes the acquisition of the best professionals indirectly. What it does is that it does not impose a business tax or corporate tax on any transactions in the laissez-faire sector. Money that would otherwise be spent on a corporate tax can be uses by firms to acquire the best workers from around the world.

The SOPS works from a different angle as well. There may be jobs that very few people want to do; for example being a garbageman or toilet cleaner. In order to ensure that we have people working at these jobs, the government pays these workers a little extra. Thus people have an incentive to work at unpleasant jobs.

The Selective Occupation Promotion System is a key feature of accommodation based consumerism. It does a great job of ensuring the best and brightest remain in or come to our consumerist nation. Thus the most intelligent, hard working and most productive people live and work in our country. It also ensures we have workers for jobs that not too many people want to work at.

Partial Ownership of Firms by the Government: Another Source of Revenue for the Government

It would be useful if we could find a way for the levels of government to raise money for social services without levying a tax, whether that tax is on income, sales, property or corporate profits. In accommodation based consumerism this is accomplished through a program that invokes partial ownership of firms by the government. What happens, essentially, under this setup is that the government, whether federal, provincial or municipal, buys shares of a firm in the natural partition and earns dividends based on the post-reinvestment profit the firm makes.

Under the partial ownership of firms by the government program (POFG), essentially the government (all levels) act as investors in a firm (in the natural partition) and earn profit (dividends) based on how well the firm is doing.

Suppose a firm that makes computers- let's call it ABCD computers- issues 1 000 000 shares and that the central bank sets the consumerist universal stock price at 10.00 þ per share. Now the federal government buys 400 000 of these shares and another consumerist, Daniel, buys 10 000 shares. Other investors buy the rest of the shares. So the government gives the firm 400 000 x 10.00 þ/share = 4 000 000 þ and Daniel pays 10 000 x 10.00 þ/share = 100 000 þ. The federal government owns 40 % of the company and Daniel owns 1 % of the company. In this example, ABCD computers earns 50 000 000 þ in one year. It reinvests 30 000 000 þ back into itself. For example, it expands its factory, hires more workers, buys more capital to increase production, improve its products, etc. So now it has 20 000 000 þ profit left over. This is paid to the various investors. This includes, in our example, the federal government and Daniel. The federal government earns 20 000 000 þ x 40 % = 8 000 000 þ and Daniel earns 20 000 000 þ x 1% = 200 000 þ. Thus, in the end, the federal government earns 8 000 000 þ – 4 000 000 þ = 4 000 000 þ and Daniel earns 200 000 þ – 100 000 þ = 100 000 þ. In one year the federal government made a profit of 4 000 000 þ and Daniel made a profit of 100 000 þ. Other investors who bought shares also earned profit but we are only interested (for the purpose of this example) in the case of the federal government and Daniel. Daniel uses his earnings to enhance his quality of life. That is, he buys a bigger house, goes on vacation and buys many things in the accommodational sector. The federal government uses the 4 000 000 þ it earned to pay for social services that are provided through the federal government.

The POFG program can be compared to a subsidy or bailout. Instead of a firm that is having financial troubles being bailed out by a government (let's say the provincial government) it can sell consumerist stock at the price set by the central bank. Now, instead of the provincial government just giving money to the troubled firm, it can "invest" in the firm and earn some money (through dividends) for helping the firm in need.

Clearly, the government (all levels) can't buy shares of every firm. They ought to buy shares from firms that would normally be subsidized or bailed out if they were under the socialist or capitalist system. For example, a firm in a vital industry or one that employs a huge number of workers or needs to be protected for various reasons, can be helped through the partial ownership of firm by the government program. Thus the government helps the firms that are crucial to society. However, the levels of government can also invest in firms that are doing well in anticipation of large dividend profits.

Of course, there exists the possibility of the firm that is being helped simply bankrupting. To that end we invoke the bankruptcy insurance firm to aid in this situation. A firm that issues shares must insure their shares in case the firm bankrupts and the shares become worthless. If a firm issues 1 000 000 shares for 10.00 þ per share, these shares must be insured. Let's say the firm finds a bankruptcy insurance firm that offers to insure the stock for 0.01 % per month. The stock issuing firm must pay the bankruptcy insurance firm 1 000 000 shares x 10.00 þ/share x 0.01%/month = 10 000 þ/month. If the stock issuing firm bankrupts for any reason it must sell off all its assets to buy back its worthless shares. If it doesn't have enough, the bankruptcy insurance firm comes to help. If the government buys 100 000 shares for 10.00 þ/share, the bankruptcy insurance firm would give the government 1 000 000 þ. This is how much it had to pay to obtain stock from the stock issuing firm. However, if a stock issuing firm made any profit during its existence, the federal government would have made a considerable profit through dividends.

The POFG program does not apply to either the command partition or governmental partition. It does factor in the natural partition. Firms in the materialist and accommodational sectors of the natural partition can be helped through the POFG program. If the firm in question is in the laissez-faire sector of the natural partition the nominal Ignit-Fortal exchange mechanism must be made use of. That is, the government (all levels) must exchange Ignits for Fortals and vice versa.

This program functions in the consumerist stock market rather than the speculative stock market. Thus Ignits are involved. All stocks cost the same price per unit. This is set by the central bank and is called the Universal Consumerist Stock price.

Besides the fact that the POFG setup helps firms that are vital for the country's well being or employ a large number of workers, the major benefit of the program is that it is a useful source of revenue for the federal, provincial, and municipal governments. Dividend profits from the POFG program, that is from investing in firms, go directly to pay for important, vital social services in conjunction with the other sources of revenue, to make life higher quality for consumerists. Thus it pays for our ultra universal health care system so everyone is entitled to care from a doctor, surgeon, dentist or optometrist. It pays for both elementary, secondary, and college, university and trade schools. It pays for the defence of our country. It also pays for clean drinking water and infrastructure. It pays for other things as well.

In a socialist or capitalist system it is usually the case that the social services consumerists enjoy are paid for by taxes. In accommodation based consumerism we try to minimize taxes or eliminate taxes altogether. Although there is the GCT (Grand Consumerist Tax) it is small and minimal. Accommodation based consumerism succeeds in the fact that there are no property tax, sales tax, corporate tax, gasoline tax, tobacco tax or other taxes that are predominant under socialist and capitalist systems.

The Partial Ownership of Firms by Government program functions to stimulate the economy. It helps the firms that the government invests in. The profit earned by the government allows us to pay for needed social services without invoking common taxes like sales, income, property, or corporate tax.

Government Revenue Stock

The accommodation based consumerist system supports several programs that are best provided publicly. These are ultra-universal health care, universal education and free transit. We need several ways other than taxes, which hurt people, to raise funds for these services. One useful source of governmental revenue is the governmental revenue stock.

The idea behind governmental revenue stock is rather simple. Either of the levels of government issue certain stocks in the governmental at a special issuing price. These stocks are then traded by speculators in the speculative stock market. They can be thus considered common stock. The money accrued from selling these stocks goes directly to that level of government to pay for social services like health care and defence.

So then, suppose the federal government issues 10 000 stocks for 500 f each. If an investor, Nathan, buys the stock and sells it for 600 f he would make a profit of 100 f per share. However if Theodore buys the stock at 600 f and sells it for 300 f, he would have lost 300 f. Clearly, money in the form of Fortals can be made (or lost) by selling Governmental revenue stock.

In the above example, the government issued 10 000 shares for 500 f. This is 5 000 000 f. All this goes to the government that issues the stock. It goes to pay for social services.

The government does not really need to take out bankruptcy insurance like all other firms that issue shares have to. This is due to the fact that the government can't really go bankrupt. Investors have peace of mind that their shares will never become worthless.

Government revenue shares are a little bit different than other shares we have talked about. There is no dividend profit to be made in these shares. Furthermore, ownership of shares does not represent in any terms ownership of the government. The only use for investors that these shares have is to have something to trade. Money is lost when shares are bought high and sold low and money is gained when shares are bought low and sold high.

The government can quickly and easily raise income for services just by issuing more stocks. Every time it wants money it issues stocks. This is preferable to just printing money or raising taxes.

Clearly, government revenue shares are a good way to raise funds for the government. They provide investors with an item to trade while providing the levels of government with a steady source of revenue.

Management of Premium Savings Bonds

In consumerism we try to find as many alternative sources of government revenue as possible. Alternative governmental sources of revenue have two main goals. First, they allow us to have capital to finance the social services we desire. For example, ultra universal health care and universal education. They allow us to fund other types of services that we may provide if the benevolent social planner chooses to have them. Also they allow us to avoid relying on taxes that no one likes to pay and that reduce the incentive for working- such as property tax.

Thus here we introduce the management of premium savings bonds as a source of government (3 levels) revenue. This is a way for the various governments to raise funds. Premium savings bonds are special bonds that the levels of government sell to consumerists to get money. By managing and manipulating these premium savings bonds we will see how the levels of government can extract revenue for social services.

Let's work with the federal government for the purpose of this example. The federal government issues federal premium savings bonds. We would assume that the federal government uses this money to pay for social services. But it doesn't. What happens is something totally different. The government takes this money (that they obtained by selling federal premium savings bonds) and uses it to purchase high interest bonds in the speculative bond market or puts the money in a high interest savings account. It then uses the interest profit from this investment to pay for social services. When the consumerists want to sell the federal premium savings bonds back, the government takes it out of the high interest savings account or sells its high profit speculative bonds and it gives it back to investors.

Here's a numerical example using a provincial government. The provincial government sells provincial premium savings bonds and it sells them for 10.00 f per unit (it sets the price). It manages to sell 10 000 000 of these bonds. Thus it earns 100 000 000.00 f. However it doesn't use this money to pay for spending on services. The interest rate on these bonds is 0.5 %. The provincial government puts the 100 000 000.00 f in a high interest savings account. Here the interest rate is 3.5 % per year. The provincial government makes profit on this transaction. It earns (3.5 % - 0.5 %) x 100 000 000.00 f = 3 000 000.00 f. This is what is used to pay for social services. The consumerists who buy savings bonds also make money. They make 0.5 % x 10.00 f = 0.05 f per bond/per year. Thus when they sell their bond to the provincial government they will get 10.05 f per bond x the number of bonds they bought.

Now, how does the private bank that allows us to have high interest rates make money? They raise money by issuing private loans and mortgages. So if the high interest rate that the government took advantage of is 3.5 %, the 5 year fixed mortgage could be perhaps 4.5 %.

Alternatively, the government can put the money gained from selling premium savings bonds into a special stock or bond that also works to lower inflation. This includes the consumerist central bank stock, the speculative central bank stock, the consumerist governmental bond or the speculative governmental bond. If these special stocks and bonds have a high interest rate, the government can also make a lot of money (by investing the earnings from selling premium bonds). At the same time it will be combating inflation.

Usually in capitalism when a government issues savings bonds it gets into debt. It has a debt to pay to those that bought the bonds from the government. In consumerism the government, in the end, does not acquire a debt selling savings bonds. It is also able to pay back investors in full without going into debt and still making revenue to pay for needed social programs.

This is how the 3 levels of government manage premium savings bonds. Those who buy the bonds make a profit on their investment, the government has revenue for services and it does not fall into debt.

Consumerist Spending Reimbursement

The consumerist spending reimbursement is a useful anti-unemployment measure. It is designed to stimulate the economy. The general idea is that consumerists are "paid to shop" at certain stores and organizations.

There are two types of consumerist spending reimbursements. There is the government consumerist spending reimbursement and there is the accommodational consumerist spending reimbursement. The consumerist spending reimbursement does not apply to firms in the governmental or laissez-faire sectors. The government spending reimbursement applies to retail firms in the materialist sector of both the natural and command partitions. Both the governmental and accommodational spending reimbursements apply to retail outlets in the accommodational sector of both the natural and command partitions.

In the accommodational sector the consumerist spending reimbursement works when the government works together with a store to reimburse the shopper so that he is more likely to come back and has more money to spend. The shopper is paid jointly through the store itself and partially through one of the levels of government. The accommodational sector retail firm sets an accommodational spending reimbursement and this is given as a store credit for the next time the consumerist shops at that store. On top of that the government sets a governmental spending reimbursement as a small percentage to encourage consumerists to spend more.

As an example we have an appliance store where Lou wants to purchase an oven worth 250.00 þ. The store offers an accommodational consumerist spending reimbursement (ACSR) at 2 % and the government sets its governmental consumerist spending reimbursement at 0.4 %. Thus the government will pay an additional 0.4% on top of the 2 % that the store will reimburse the shopper. In other words this is 2.4 %. So Lou pays 250.00 þ to the store. However, he is reimbursed 250.00 þ x 2.4 % = 6 þ. With this money Lou can buy even more goods at the same store thus stimulating the economy.

In the materialist sector there is only the governmental consumerist spending reimbursement. If we create a "materialist consumerist spending reimbursement" this would cause problems as it would create price selection where we would like pure quality selection. In the materialist sector the government through the governmental consumerist spending reimbursement, pays shoppers so that they have more money and can make more purchases in the future thus stimulating the economy.

Carol wants to buy a car. The car costs 10 000.00 Θ at the dealership. Since all cars cost the same, she buys a sports car. The governmental consumerist spending reimbursement is made at 1 %.Thus, Carol will be reimbursed 10 000 þ x 1.0 %. = 100 þ. Carol can use this money to buy things in the accommodational sector.

It is quite likely that the governmental spending reimbursement could be 0. The major problem with this parameter is that it greatly increases the budget deficit. On the other hand, it is an excellent tool to stimulate the economy when we want the economy to do better.

The consumerist spending reimbursement stimulates the economy. It ensures that consumerists have money for other things in the future.

The Ignit –Fortal Exchange Mechanism

The Ignit fortal exchange mechanism is a key component of the accommodation based consumerist economic system. Essentially it refers to the ability of consumerists, investors, producers and other actors to trade Ignits for Fortals and Fortals for Ignits.

Recall that accommodation based consumerism has three currencies. There are Norses, Ignits and Fortals. Norses are restricted to the materialist sector (although they are sometimes used in the governmental sector). Ignits are used in the accommodational sector and Fortals are used in the laissez-faire sector.

It would be useful if those who contributed to the accommodational sector could convert their money and buy things in the laissez-faire sector. Also it would be useful if those who contributed to the laissez-faire sector could exchange their money so as to buy things in the accommodational sector. The Ignit-Fortal exchange mechanism allows just that.

There are actually two types of Ignit-Fortal exchange mechanisms. They are the reciprocal Fortal-Ignit exchange mechanism and the nominal Fortal-Ignit exchange mechanism. They are both vital to the workings of the consumerist economy.

The reciprocal Ignit-Fortal exchange mechanism is easy to understand. Essentially, the price to exchange a unit of Fortals into Ignits is the same as the price to exchange one unit of Ignits into Fortals. Now, this does not mean that they are exchanged at par. What it does mean is that $\alpha f = \beta \text{\th} \rightarrow \beta \text{\th} = \alpha f$

Sometimes it is necessary for exchanges between Ignits and Fortals and vice versa to be at the reciprocal rate. This usually has to do with circumstances regarding stocks, bonds, and bankruptcy insurance firms.

However the vast majority of the time exchanges between Fortals and Ignits (and vice versa) are under the jurisdiction of the nominal Ignit-Fortal exchange mechanism. There the price to exchange Fortals into Ignits is not the same as to exchange Ignits into Fortals. So, if $\alpha f = \beta \text{\th}$ where $\alpha > \beta \rightarrow \alpha \text{\th} = \beta f$ where $\alpha > \beta$

The nominal Ignit- Fortal exchange mechanism is in fact a very useful and potent anti-inflationary-mechanism. That is, it helps to control the money supply. The money in circulation (both Ignits and Fortals) are eliminated when people exchange money using the nominal Ignit – Fortal exchange mechanism. Whether the reciprocal or nominal is required in a situation is set by the Grand Chairman of the central bank.

It should be clear that the nominal Ignit-Fortal exchange mechanism is a good way to loose money in the long run. By continuously converting Ignits into Fortals, Fortals into Ignits and back again, an investor or consumerist losses money. So, if $5f = 1\text{\th}$ and $2\text{\th} = 1f$ and someone has 50 f, if he trades his fortals for Ignits he will get 10 $\text{\th}$ and if he trades this back again into Fortals he will get 5 f. Clearly, he lost a lot of money in this arrangement.

The nominal Ignit-Fortal exchange mechanism should be applied instead of the reciprocal Ignit-Fortal exchange mechanism the vast majority of times. The reciprocal Ignit-Fortal exchange mechanism should only be used in special cases where the value of Ignits and Fortals must be preserved. Otherwise, the nominal Ignit-Fortal exchange mechanism should be applied. This will work profoundly in controlling inflation.

Command Partition Compensation Adjustment

Recall that all non institutionalized people receive the consumerist grant either in the form of the general consumerist grant or the non working consumerist grant. This money can be spent in the materialist sector. However, all consumerists also need Ignits to spend in the accommodational sector. Here we will discuss how workers in the command partition earn money in the form of Ignits and Fortals for the accommodational and laissez-faire sector.

People in the command partition do various jobs that are comparable to jobs in the natural partition. They can be security guards, bakers, comic book artists, store clerks or mechanics. They are paid through the extra work transfer which exists in five forms. The EWT can be either hourly, daily, weekly, monthly or yearly. The EWT rewards those working in the command partition who are ambitious and hard working. So if a grocery clerk works 35 hours a week he will earn more money than another worker with the same job who only works 7 hours a week.

All five types of EWT are set by the government and are expressed in both Fortals and Ignits. So a command partition worker is paid in two currencies – Ignits and Fortals. As an example, the hourly EWT may be 10.00 þ and 10.00 f and the daily EWT may be 60.00 þ and 60.00 f .These EWT are designed to maximize productivity.

It may seem unfair that all workers in the command partition are paid exactly the same compensation. Should a janitor working one hour make the same amount of money as an engineer working one hour? To recognize that certain jobs are more demanding and difficult and have a higher occupational complexity rating we introduce the command partition compensation adjustment (CPCA),

Under this mechanism people with various jobs earn more than those in others. Thus the EWT is just a minimum of what one can earn in the command partition. The CPCA is set as a percentage and it represents how less the worker receives relative to if the occupation was found in the natural partition where there are fixed wage/salary functions set by the central bank. It is influenced by the occupational complexity rating.

Let's do some examples using certain occupations. We will assume for simplicity that 1þ = 1f and 1 f =1 þ although this isn't always the case. We have a security guard who works by the hour and she works 12 hours a day. The EWT is (15.00 þ + 6.00 f)per hour. In the natural partition security guards are paid 40.00 þ per hour. The government sets the CPCA at 30%. Thus she would earn, hourly, 40.00 þ – 30 % = 28.00 þ. Since this is more than the hourly EWT, she will receive this amount per hour. The more hours that she works the more income she has.

We have a janitor. He also works hourly and his EWT is (15.00 þ + 2.00 f)per hour. In the natural partition the janitor will get paid 18.00 þ per hour. The government sets the CPCA at 40 %. so the janitor will receive 18.00 þ – 40 % = 10.2 þ. Since this is less than the hourly EWT, he will get the hourly EWT which is 15.00 þ + 2.00 f.

We have a comic book artist who is compensated weekly. The EWT in terms of weeks is 300.00 þ + 200.00 f. In the natural partition comic book artists are paid 650.00 þ per week. The CPCA is 50 %. So he might get 650.00 þ – 50 % = 325 þ. Since this is less than the EWT he earns the EWT which is 300.00 þ + 200.00 f.

As a last example we have an actor. Acting is in the laissez-faire sector and there are no actual EWT in the laissez-faire sector of the command partition. The actor is paid (and keeps) however the firm that hires him to act decides to pay him, his pay rate being determined by the forces of supply and demand.

The command partition compensation adjustment can be specific to industries or it can be universal in terms of a percentage. If it is universal than all occupations in the command partition have the same adjustment. Thus the adjustment of a cashier would be equal to that of a chef. However it can also be particular to industry. So all workers in the hospitality industry will have the same parameter.

Due to the existence of command partition compensation adjustments, the five types of extra work transfers are reduced to a sort of minimum wage. That is all workers in the command partition are guaranteed to earn at least the value of an extra work transfers. Usually though, the command partition compensation adjustments ensure workers earn quite a bit more.

The command partition compensation adjustment makes sure that workers in the command partition are highly rewarded. Those with more complex jobs are paid slightly more than their counterparts who do simpler jobs. So in this way we fight unemployment, reduce poverty and maximize output.

Command Partition Productivity Incentive Deduction System

We need to talk a little bit about how the command partition is organized. We need the workers in the command partition to be productive in terms of quality and quantity. That is, we need the command partition workers (i.e. auxiliary workers) to produce high quality goods and services and a lot of them.

First recall that auxiliary workers are paid the non-working consumerist grant (NWCG). That is, they are paid less than most workers in the natural and governmental partitions. This is so that they (paradoxically) have a reason to find work in the other two partitions. With the money gained through the NWCG, auxiliary workers can buy things in the materialist sector, i.e. cars, food, clothing, etc.

In addition to money earned through the NWCG, auxiliary workers are paid one of five extra work transfers (EWT). They can be paid hourly, by the day, by the week, by the month or by the year. How they get paid is set by the benevolent social planner (central bank) and is designed so that auxiliary workers are the most productive and efficient. The 5 EWT are both in terms of Ignits and Fortals. With this money auxiliary workers can buy things in the accommodational and laissez-faire sectors. There are many goods and services that this applies to.

Let's for the sake of argument introduce numbers for the EWT. Please remember that all these values are purely exemplary. A person could be paid (5.00 þ + 5.00 f) per hour. Another person could be paid (20.00 þ + 20.00 f)per day. Someone else could be paid (90.00 þ + 90.00 f) per week. Another individual could earn (250.00 þ + 250.00 f)per month. Another person could be paid (2000.00 þ + 2000.00 f) per year. As a suggestion, a cashier could be paid by the hour, a janitor could be paid by the day, a comic book artist could be paid by the week, a novelist could be paid by the month and a farm hand could be paid by the year. Note that auxiliary workers are paid in such a manner that they are most productive. That is, a worker can have his EWT level transferred to another if he is ambitious. So if the EWT is (20.00 þ + 20.00 f) per hour and (70.00 þ+ 70.00 f) per day and a clerk works 6 hours a day he will probably want to be paid by the hour rather than by the day.

The more a previously unemployed (auxiliary) worker works the more money he will be paid through the EWTs. This is his incentive to contribute to society and be productive. How much an auxiliary worker gets paid is in his hands.

We need to ensure that auxiliary workers are doing top quality work and producing what they need to. To solve this problem we introduce the *command partition productivity incentive deduction system*. Basically, if a worker works less or works poorly he will have either have his NWCG decreased or have his EWT decreased. That is if a worker does a poor job, he will receive less Norses, Ignits and or Fortals to spend.

There are three forms of command partition productivity incentive deduction (CPPID); Norse - CPPID, Ignit- CPPID and Fortal- CPPID. Each parameter is designed to motivate auxiliary workers to do a good job.

186

Let's start with the Norse- CPPID. Clearly, it involves Norses and pertains to the materialist sector. It is set as a percentage. Let's say it is 10 %. If someone does a poor job or does less work than he was supposed to, the central bank deducts 10 % of the worker's NWCG each pay period. So, if the NWCG is 1000 Θ, the lazy auxiliary worker will receive 900 Θ. If this continues, there will be another deduction from the NWCG next period.

The Ignit- CPPID works with Ignits and is set as a percentage. Let's say it is 15%. If a worker earns 100 þ per day, the next pay period he will get 85.00 þ. To avoid this, the worker is encouraged to be more productive and efficient.

The Fortal- CPPID works similarly to the Ignit- CPPID but here fortals are used instead of Ignits. Let's say that this parameter is set at 20 % . So if a worker is paid 10.00 ₣ per hour if he does a poor job (or not at all) he will get 8.00 ₣ per hour.

Another of the aims of CPPID system is to create quotas on what workers need to produce. For example we have a comic book artist who earns (40.00 þ and 40.00 ₣) per week drawing comic books. The HRMC sets as a goal that the comic book artist produces one (good quality) comic book every 3 weeks. If he doesn't produce a comic book that often or his comic book is of poor quality, the HRMC may 1) introduce to the worker one, two or all three of the CPPID (in the form of Norses, Ignits or Fortals) or 2) move him to an occupation where he would be more effective (i.e. making french fries). The prospect of these two outcomes will likely encourage our comic book artist to create comic books of high quality and as many of them as required.

How is the command partition productivity incentive deduction system handled? Recall that there are 3 levels of workers in the command partition- level 1, level 2 and level 3. Level 2 workers make sure that level 1 workers do a good job and level 3 workers make sure level 2 workers do a good job. So if a level 2 worker suspects a level 1 worker is doing a job poorly or improperly, he must report it to the HRMC auditors. They will interview the level 1 worker and assess the situation. If necessary, they will apply one or several of the CPPID parameters.

An interesting side outcome of the CPPID system is that the money not given to workers in the command partition is given to other workers (i.e. in the natural partition) through the GCG and the NWCG. Also, having to pay less through the EWT leaves a bit more money for the government to spend on social services.

What happens if an auxiliary worker chooses not to work too much. First of all, he won't be paid too much through the EWT. Furthermore, there is the *accommodation award incentive deduction*. We will discuss this more thoroughly in another section. But briefly, if an auxiliary worker works below a certain threshold that is set by the central bank, he will have a portion of his NWCG reduced by a certain percentage. So let's say the Accommodation Award Deduction Incentive Threshold is 5 hours a week. The worker must work this amount of hours to be paid the full amount of the NWCG. Let's say the NWCG is 1000 Θ and the Accommodation Award Incentive Deduction is 10 %. Thus if he works below the threshold every two week period the worker gets paid 10 % less through the NWCG than the previous pay period. The Accommodation Award Incentive Deduction is similar to and works with the Norse- CPPID.

The command partition productivity deduction system gives incentive to workers in the command partition to be productive and efficient. This system extracts from these workers as much output as possible.

Avoidance of Debt

One of the most important yet somewhat subtle ways for the government (3 levels) to have more money for spending is to balance the budget. The 3 levels of government can avoid paying huge amounts of money needlessly by avoiding getting into debt. By simply avoiding the acquisition of debt the country can save a lot of money in the long run.

First of all, it is probably necessary for a country that is just developing to get into some debt. If our country is still in its developmental stage, money is necessary to boost the economy, create infrastructure and build society. However, absolutely all effort should be made to pay back this debt as soon as possible – preferably in 2-3 years.

It is usually the case that ordinary people get into some kind of debt. This may be due to, for example, taking out a mortgage. However, it doesn't make much sense to get into a debt (through mortgage) if one doesn't think he will ever possibly repay it. So, if someone has a yearly revenue of $40 000, he has no right buying a house (and taking a mortgage for) that costs $ 5 000 000. He can never hope to repay it. Actual governments should follow this logic. They should never get into debt such that they will never be able to repay it.

The main reason why getting into debt is so terrible is because it gets the nation into a "debt spiral". When a country is in debt a considerable portion of its GDP (or GDCP if it's in consumerism) goes to servicing the debt. That is, a huge amount of money is dedicated to just paying the interest on the debt. The longer the country is in debt, the greater the country's debt interest financing is.

Another major problem with getting into debt is that the debt grows and grows to the point that it is almost impossible for the country to pay the debt in full. All a country can do is pay off the interest payments on the debt. A country would be ruined and plunged into havoc if it actually tries to pay off its debt. It would have to drastically raise taxes and other measures that cause problems.

A good portion of the government's spending goes, unfortunately, to pay off the interest on the debt. If this was avoided the government would have a tremendous amount of money to pay for social services. For example health care, defence, education, free transit. Thus in a sense avoiding getting into debt is one of the most efficient and productive ways for the government to raise revenue.

We can see the logic of avoiding debt when we examine the predicament of the United States. As of August 21, 2020 the U.S. Federal debt held by the public was 20.22 trillion dollars and that held by intergovernmental holders was 5.26 trillion dollars. Thus the total debt was 26.7 trillion dollars. This is 99.3 % of the GDP of the United States. (Source: Wikipedia)

Now, the United States makes huge payments just trying to pay the interest on their debt. Recently the interest on the loan was about 450 billion dollars a year. The average interest rate from 1966- 2015 was 2.0 % of GDP. However, it is estimated that this interest will be 799 billion dollars in 2024 or 3.0 % of GDP. (Source: Wikipedia)

Now imagine if the US didn't have this debt and it didn't have to service the debt. They could easily afford a Canadian style healthcare system and still have more than enough to feed every men, women and child breakfast, lunch and dinner for the whole year.

Getting into debt should be avoided unless it is absolutely necessary for a developing nation. Avoiding debt lowers the interest debt payments to service the debt. The money not spent on financing the debt can be better used to pay for needed social services.

How Unemployment is Eliminated in Accommodation Based Consumerism

Unemployment is the occurrence where there are not enough jobs for workers who desire them. It is a major problem in both capitalist and socialist societies. Policy makers throughout the world have tried for more than a century to find ways to eliminate unemployment or greatly reduce the incidence of unemployment. Nevertheless, even in very wealthy countries like Canada, the United States, France, England and Germany, there is a substantial part of the population who do not have work but want to work and would work if given the opportunity. Solving the problem of unemployment would be a tremendous step forward for the global society.

Things are brighter in consumerism. In consumerism, there are programs designed to completely eliminate unemployment. Unemployment doesn't exist in consumerism.

The solution to the problem of eliminating unemployment in accommodation based consumerism lies in the existence of the socialist labour pool. In this section, we will discuss the essence of how unemployment is eliminated in the consumerist system.

As discussed earlier in the book, there are three partitions in consumerism; the natural partition, the command partition and the governmental partition. Most jobs are either in the natural or governmental partitions. The command partition is designed for people who lost their jobs in the natural or governmental partitions. The command partition is run by an agency called the Human Resource Management Commission (HRMC) and these workers in the command partition are those we call being in the socialist labour pool.

Whenever a worker looses his job, for any reason, he can apply to the Human Resource Management Commission for a job. The Human Resource Management commission is like a huge hiring organization. The unemployed worker fills out an application and submits a resume and the HRMC helps him find a job in the command partition. The worker is guaranteed a job, no matter how lazy, slow, careless, irrational or unmotivated the worker is. All that is in question is what job he gets.

The HRMC creates firms. It establishes gas stations, doughnut shops, grocery stores, farms, mines, restaurants, pet stores, clothing stores, etc. Some readers may know that in some capitalist countries there are firms created by the government. These include TV stations, gas companies and liquor stores. The consumerist system takes this idea to a much higher level.

The HRMC uses the previously unemployed workers in the socialist labour pool and uses these workers to staff the newly created firm. So a donut shop in the command partition would hire bakers who were previously unemployed and cashiers who were previously unemployed. The donut shop would be cleaned by janitors who were previously unemployed and it would be managed by a person with a management degree who can't find work else where. Furthermore, the donut shop would be built by construction workers who can't find work elsewhere.

The profits from a firm in the command partition go to the three levels of government to pay for social services. So in our example of the donut shop, we created jobs for several previously unemployed individuals (bakers, cashiers, janitors) and still managed to make a profit (as long as the donut shop has higher revenue than costs). Therefore we managed to make money while employing people.

The HRMC has nine mandates:

1) Make a profit
2) Employ everyone that applies for a job
3) Discourage workers from working in the command partition
   Although somewhat paradoxical, the HRMC encourages workers to find a job in the natural or governmental partitions.
4) Resolve pure shortages and surpluses
5) Create healthy competition for firms in the natural partition
6) Control the money supply
7) Fight hunger
8) Fight global shortage
9) Reduce or eliminate the market power of monopolies

In free market capitalism, at least in some instances, there is something called workfare. The idea is to put workers to work rather than to give them a welfare check for doing nothing. The Command Partition is somewhat similar but it works on a much grander level; employing all individuals who would otherwise remain idle. In addition, the firms these workers are employed in generate revenue that pays for needed social services.

The workers that work in the command partition are paid proportionally to how much they work although there is a common hourly wage set by the government. Let's say the government stipulates that a previously unemployed worker earns 10.00 þ and 8.00 ƒ per hour and a janitor works 20 hours per week. He would be given 200.00 þ and 160.00 ƒ. This he can spend on either the accommodational or laissez faire sectors as these sectors involve Ignits and Fortals. Other workers would be paid on a weekly basis; for example poets. However those working in the command partition need not worry about the materialist sector. They are given the Non-Working Consumerist Grant. They are given a little less Norses for the materialist sector so as to encourage them to find work in the natural or governmental partitions.

The experience a worker earns while working in the command partition is helpful for finding a job in the other two partitions. This experience can be put on a resume and enhance the workers jobs prospects in other partitions.

The command partition should not be too large. It should not be more than 15% of the population. It is preferable that a worker works in the natural or governmental partitions than in the command partition.

The HRMC gives a job to absolutely everyone. It is similar to the concept of Chinese state capitalism. Everyone does a job that they are either good at, or want to do. It is better if a previously unemployed person were paid for writing poetry than if he got a welfare check for doing absolutely nothing.

The problem of unemployment, that is putting people to work so they contribute to society, is essentially solved in accommodation based consumerism. All individuals, regardless of their characteristics, talents and skills are absolutely guaranteed work in the command partition. All that matters is what employment these people are given. In addition, the firms in this partition have the potential to make a profit that helps fund social services.

The Accommodational Markdown

We now come upon one of the more important parameters in the Accommodation Based Consumerist economy. This is the accommodational markdown. The accommodational markdown is a deduction of money in the form of Ignits from certain industries in the accommodational sector upon a transaction between two agents. This money is not given to the government or back to the central bank. It is completely destroyed- erased from the bank records .

The reason for the accommodational markdown (AMD) is to have something to combat the problem of the *accommodational overflow calamity*. This occurs when the amount of money in the accommodational sector keeps growing out of control like a pool. The logic for the presence of this calamity is this. The central bank grants Norses to consumerists. These turn into Ignits during a transaction. Ignits are used to purchase accommodational goods and services because they cannot be used to purchase materialist goods nor can they be exchanged for Norses. Thus everything turns into Ignits in the end; which circulate in the accommodational sector. The problem is not that they end up there but that they cannot leave. Since more and more Norses are granted, the amount of Ignits becomes bigger and bigger, in a sense overflowing. This makes it hard to keep the prices of goods and services fixed and to maintain the steadiness of wages and salaries. Thus the forces of inflation and the steadiness of prices rip at each other. The excess of Ignits tries to raise inflation in the same way that more money in a free- market causes the prices of goods to increase. So what are we to do? Either we let prices fluctuate or dispose of this excess of Ignits and keep prices constant. The solution is the Accommodational Markdown. During many transactions in the accommodational sector a percentage of the trade is taken out of the sector. The value of this percentage is set by the central bank.

The AMD affects the sellers much more so than the buyers. In many circumstances, which we will soon discuss, when someone sells something in the accommodational sector, a percentage of the trade is deducted from the seller and destroyed. It is taken permanently out of bank account records. This money does not go to the government as a tax but is completely eliminated. To be cynical, this could be called a "tax". However unlike a usual tax none of the money goes to the government.

Let's work through some examples, Gregory works in a doughnut shop and he is paid 20 000.00 þ a year for his services. He can spend this on the accommodational sector. He finds a house costing 20 000.00 þ and wants to buy it. Paul owns the house. Gregory gives Paul the 20 000.00 þ and he receives the house. Now Paul has 20 000.00 þ. However he must give a percentage of this to be taken out of the economy in accordance with the AMD. If the AMD is 20 % then Paul keeps 16 000.00 þ for his profit to spend as he sees fit. 4 000.00 þ are erased from his account. In this example we have omitted a parameter that we will discuss more fully later. This is the Real Estate Profit Percentage. This factors in if real estate agents are used to buy or sell the house in the above example.

Mike works at a car dealership. In a year he accumulates 30 000.00 þ. He wants to own land. Residential land costs 500.00 þ per square meter. He can therefore buy 60 square meters of land. Mrs. Sue owns such land. She sells 60 square meters of land to Mike and she earns 30 000.00 þ minus the AMD. If the AMD is 20 %, she earns 24 000.00 þ and 6 000.00 þ are destroyed (erased from bank records). The AMD factors in cases where land is exchanged.

Patrick works as a dentist. He makes 50 000.00 þ per year. He has to pay 400.00 þ for electricity to his electricity provider. During payment the 400.00 þ are deducted from his bank account and the utility company takes this minus the AMD. If the AMD is 20% the utility company has 320.00 þ added to its bank account and 80.00 þ are destroyed. The AMD factors in cases where utility services are provided.

An interesting question arises. Why would anyone sell a house or land or anything at a loss? In the first case Paul sold a house for 20 000.00 þ but received only 16 000.00 þ. Why would he be willing to incur such losses? The reason is that now he needs only 4 000.00 þ to buy a better house than the one he sold to Gregory. So suppose he finds a job as a grocery clerk. He earns 15 000.00 þ more. (For simplicity we forget about other purchases in the accommodational sector such as utilities, appliances and vacations). With the new money he can now buy a better house and earn 24 800.00 þ (assuming 20% AMD). He can earn some more money and repeat the process. This way he can go from a better to a better house every time.

Now let's look at the case of buying and selling land. Why would Mrs. Sue want to sell land at a loss? She has 60 m^2 of land worth 30 000.00 þ which Mike buys from her. She only keeps 24 000.00 þ. If she only finds a job and makes more than 6 000.00 þ she can earn enough to buy more land than she originally started off with. Suppose she becomes a cashier and makes 20 000.00 þ in a year. In this case we are also assuming that all her expenditures are on land (not utilities, appliances or accommodation etc). Thus she now has 44 000.00 þ (24 000.00 þ + 20 000.00 þ). She can buy 44 000.00 þ worth of the same type of land. She buys residential land with the money. She can buy 88 square meters of residential land (44 000.00 þ /500.00 þ/m^2). She can repeat the process. She can sell the land earning 35 200.00 þ (assuming the AMD is 20%) and continue working as a cashier. The following year she would have 55 200.00 þ. With this she can buy a plot of residential land the size of 110 square meters. Mrs. Sue gradually becomes better and better off.

Let's see how the AMD operates in the other industries of the accommodational sector. Let's look at the utility industry. Let's suppose that electricity costs 10.00 þ /kWh. Alex is a doctor and earns 100 000.00 þ a year. We assume that the AMD is 20 % and he only spends his income on electricity (just to isolate the case). In a year he uses 500 kWh. Thus he must pay 500 kWh x 10.00 þ /kWh = 5 000.00 þ per year for electricity. The electricity provider earns 5 000.00 þ x 0.8 = 4 000.00 þ and 1 000.00 þ are destroyed. This would not affect the electric company much because it is probably operating at economies of scale and is a monopoly. This is how the AMD would apply to the utility industry.

The AMD doesn't apply to the appliance and home accessories industries. Suppose a stove costs 800.00 þ from a factory and that the retail mark up is 25 % and the accommodational markdown is 30 %. If this were the case then the retailers that are selling the stove must necessarily lose money. Now suppose a rug costs 2.00 þ/m^2 and the retail mark-up is 25 %. Now if the AMD is anything higher than 25 %, the retailer would be losing money. Yet it is sometimes necessary to set a high AMD. There is no AMD on stocks, bonds, salaries, wages, loans and investment profit. The financial, appliance and home accessories industries are the main industries to which the AMD does not apply.

Regarding the leisure industry of the accommodational sector, the AMD does apply. It applies because there is no retail mark-up to worry about. In the appliance and home accessories industries the sellers obtained all their income from the retail mark-up. Therefore any accommodational markdown greater than the retail mark-up would result in negative profit. The leisure industry is mostly a service industry. If a vacationer pays for a vacation in a Caribbean resort, those that provide the vacation package will receive what the consumerist paid minus the AMD. Suppose Kurt makes 100 000.00 þ a year as a lawyer. He is interested in a 2 week vacation to Jamaica. The all-inclusive package costs 5 000.00 þ. This is how much Kurt pays. If the AMD is 20 %, the vacation company earns 0.8 x 5 000.00 þ = 4 000.00 þ. The 1 000 þ is simply destroyed (deducted from the bank accounts). Here's one more example. Joanne makes 15 000.00 þ as a waitress per year and loves a local rock group (let's assume that she only spends on tickets). Tickets cost 100.00 þ. She pays this to get in. The rock group earns (assuming 20% AMD) 80.00 þ from every ticket sold. This is how the AMD affects the leisure industry.

So which industries in the accommodational sector does the AMD apply to? As a principle, it does *not* apply to those that are affected by the retail mark-up. We have mentioned the appliance, home accessory and financial industries. We can add to this the "alcohol and tobacco" industry. The AMD does not apply to inputs to products, i.e. cotton for a t-shirt.

A very important point about the AMD is this. It necessarily shrinks the economy, lowering the GNP. Therefore when the economy is just developing it would make more sense to just leave it at 0%. An economy may be better off without it. It should only be invoked if the economy has certain growth and the accommodational overflow calamity is perceived to be a problem.

The accommodational markdown is important in confronting the accommodational overflow calamity.. It works to control the money supply. It's application to the consumerist economy is thus very useful.

Laissez-Faire Markdown

One of the aims of accommodation based consumerism is to control the money supply. We must guard against inflation. It is beneficial for the economy if the money injected into the economy by way of the GDCP were counter balanced by several measures we will call anti-inflationary measures. One of these measures is the laissez-faire markdown.

The laissez-faire markdown is an anti-inflationary measure used to control the money supply. Essentially what it does is that it takes some of the money in the form of Fortals out of certain transactions in the laissez-faire sector. Not all transactions in the laissez-faire sector are under the laissez-faire markdown.

As an example, let's say the laissez-faire markdown is 10 %. A golden ring is 10 000 ₤. So, 0.1 x 10 000 ₤ of the transaction is removed from circulation = 1 000 ₤. The sellers and buyers of the good (the golden ring) decide who pays the laissez-faire markdown. Perhaps the buyer pays 10 500 ₤ and the seller receives 9 500 ₤ and the laissez-faire markdown is 1 000 ₤.

The laissez-faire markdown is restricted to the laissez-faire sector. The government decides which industries, families of goods and services are subjected to the laissez-faire markdown.

Along with the accommodational markdown, the laissez-faire markdown should be instigated as a last resort when the country simply cannot manage the money supply using the other Anti-Inflationary Measures. That is, the other anti-inflationary measures take precedence over the laissez-faire markdown.

To put things in perspective, the laissez-faire markdown takes away from the laissez-faire sector a portion of the money (fortals) that enter that sector. Thus, in a way, what is removed in terms of money is counterbalanced with what comes in to the sector.

Ideally the laissez-faire markdown should be zero. This promotes efficiency, effectivity and general output in the laissez-faire sector. However, it may have to be invoked to take out of the sector that comes in as an excess- i.e. through the ignit-fortal exchange mechanism.

The laissez-faire markdown is a useful tool in controlling the money supply. It reduces the money circulating in the laissez-faire sector. However, it should only be invoked as a last resort.

Governmental Inflationary Markdown

The government in a consumerist system has an operating budget. It has many sources of revenue to pay for things and it uses this money to pay for things it deems worthy of spending the money on. One of the things it may spend its money on is the *Governmental Inflationary Markdown*. We will discuss this idea right here.

Essentially, the governmental inflationary markdown represents spending money to reduce inflation, that is to reduce the amount of money in circulation. The government (all 3 levels) can reduce the money supply by investing in the governmental inflationary markdown. This is paramount to destroying money and thus taking it out of circulation permanently.

So then, suppose that the federal government accrues 10 000 000 þ. To reduce the money in circulation, i.e. to lower the money supply, it can set the governmental inflationary markdown at 10 %. In this case, 1 000 000 þ are destroyed and taken out of circulation.

The governmental inflationary markdown, along with the other anti-inflationary measures, helps bring the GDCP in equilibrium with the money supply, that is, $GDCP = \Sigma\, AIM$.

The governmental inflationary markdown takes away from the economy what the GDCP adds to it. That is, it is an anti-inflationary measure equal to the input of the GDCP. It appears that the consumerist grant, the non-working consumerist grant and the GCT are paid for by the anti-inflationary measures.

The governmental inflationary markdown is essential in controlling the money supply. Along with the other anti-inflationary measures, it equilibrates the GDCP and the AIMs. In fact, the governmental partition markdown is one of most powerful ways in controlling the money supply.

GDCP Anti-Inflationary Mechanism

Throughout this book we have stressed the importance of controlling inflation (the money supply). In consumerism inflation takes the form of an abundance of money (Ignits, Fortals) circulating in the system. If we do not control the money supply, i.e. balance the anti-inflationary measures with the increase of the GDCP we will have serious problems.

In this section we introduce yet another anti-inflationary mechanism. It is simply called the *GDCP Anti-Inflationary Mechanism.* Whereas other anti-inflationary mechanisms took money out of circulation from various sources, this mechanism takes money out of the GDCP itself. Thus it is, in essence, a little bit different than the other AIM. Whereas they focused on controlling the amount of Fortals and Ignits in circulation, the GDCP anti-inflationary mechanism focuses on Norses.

The 3 levels of government determine the GDCP anti-inflationary markdown. This is set similarly to the way the GCT is formed where the federal, provincial and municipal governments have 1/3 of the vote based on population. Let's say it is 2 %. When the central bank determines the GCT, the general consumerist grant and the non-working consumerist grant, it deducts the GDCP anti-inflationary markdown and divides the rest 3 other ways depending on the wishes of the government.

As a concrete example, let's again assume that the GDCP AIM is 2 %. The GDCP (the output of the materialist sector) is 10 000 000.00 Θ. 200 000.00 Θ are deducted from the economy and destroyed as they are not in the form of cash. The other 9 800 000.00 Θ are granted to consumerists and the government in the form of the Grand Consumerist Tax, the General Consumerist Grant and the Non-Working Consumerist Grant.

Clearly, the GDCP AIM can be helpful in reducing inflation (overabundance of money supply). The main problem with this is that it lowers the GCT as well as the general and nonworking consumerist grants.

Government Ownership of Stocks Inflationary Deduction

It is clear that inflation must be kept in check. In this part of the book we introduce another method for controlling inflation (that is, the money supply). This method should decrease the growth of inflation.

As mentioned in another section of this book, the consumerist governments (all 3 levels) are entitled to own stocks of a particular business. By owning shares of a business the government is entitled to dividend profits from this business. So if a provincial government owns 20 % of the shares of a business and the business it invested in earns 1 000 000 þ, after re-investment, it is entitled to 200 000 þ.

The present discussion is centred on the idea of reducing inflation of the government ownership of stocks. The central bank sets the Government ownership of Stocks inflationary Deduction (GOSID). It is a percentage. This represents the amount of money that is deducted from the government for owning stocks of a firm in the laissez-faire, accommodational or materialist sectors.

Suppose the federal government buys 10 % of the stock of a company (ABCD). The GOSID is set at 1 %. The value of this stock is 1 000 000 þ. Thus 1 % is deducted from the economy. So, 10 000 þ are deducted from the economy and destroyed. This contributes to overcoming inflation.

The governmental ownership of stocks inflationary deduction must be less than the profits the government makes through buying stock. Otherwise there would be no point for the government to own stocks in the first place.

It is perhaps, a good idea to keep the GOSID near zero. If it is high it helps to decrease the money supply. However, if it is desired to raise the government revenue, it should be low.

The GOSID is used to combat inflation. If it is set high it contributes to fighting increases in the money supply.

Bankruptcy Insurance Anti-Inflationary Deduction

In accommodation based consumerism there is a strong need to control the money supply. To reduce the amount of money (Ignits, Fortals) circulating in the system as book entry accounts, we need mechanisms to take money out of circulation and simply destroy it.

A prominent anti-inflationary mechanism is the bankruptcy insurance anti-inflationary deduction (bankruptcy insurance AID). Essentially, what it does is that it takes money that a bankruptcy insurance firm made for insuring a) loans, b) stocks, c) bonds, d) job contracts and takes it out of circulation.

For example, a convenience store issues 10 000 þ worth of stocks. It must insure this stock in case the convenience store bankrupts and these shares become worthless resulting in investors loosing all their investment. After some searching, the convenience store finds a bankruptcy insurance firm that would insure the stock for a premium of 0.5 %. We assume that 1 þ= 1£. So every month the convenience store pays the bankruptcy insurance firm 10 000 þ x 0.5 % = 50 £ = 50 þ. If the store were to bankrupt the convenience store must liquidate all of its assets to buy back the 10 000 þ worth of stocks. If it can't the bankruptcy insurance firm pays for them (buys out worthless shares).

However, in the above scenario we must now include the bankruptcy insurance AID. Suppose that it is 0.1 %. 10 000 þ x 0.1 % = 10 þ = 10 £. Thus the bankruptcy insurance firm keeps 50 þ – 10 þ = 40 þ while 10 þ are deducted as an anti-inflationary measure. The 10 þ are totally destroyed- taken out of circulation in book entries.

Let's look at another scenario. A gas station borrows 500 000 þ to expand operations. It finds a bankruptcy insurance firm that covers their investment/loan for 0.8 % per month. In case they default the gas station sells off its assets to pay back the loan. To simplify things, we avoid consideration of interest payments on this loan. In case the gas station comes short, the bankruptcy insurance firm pays the total of the loan. However the bankruptcy insurance firm earns 500 000 þ x 0.8 %/ month = 4 000 þ per month. The government sets the bankruptcy insurance AID at 0.2 %. 500 000 þ x 0.2% per month = 1000 þ per month. Thus in this case every month 1000 þ are destroyed (taken out of circulation) and 4000 þ – 1000 þ = 3000 þ are given to the bankruptcy insurance firm.

This is how the bankruptcy insurance AID works in a general sense. It is a key mechanism for reducing inflation. Along with the other anti-inflationary mechanisms, the money supply in consumerism can be balanced.

Command Partition Anti-Inflationary Deduction

The command partition is an important part of the accommodation based consumerist economic system. Not only does it provide jobs for those that are unemployed but it also provides a source of income for the three levels of government. Although the command partition is small relative to the natural and governmental partitions it should still make money. This is then given to the three levels of government. The command partition should ideally compromise 4-15 % of the overall economy.

There are literally 10's of thousands of firms that could function in the command partition. Many countries have command partition firms already, in the alcohol industry, gasoline industry and hydro-electric industries. There could be potentially many, many more. For example in the hospitality, agricultural, banking and entertainment industries. A command partition firm could spring up in any area where a natural partition firm does business. So there could be command partition gas stations, donut shops, hair salons, pet shops, ice cream parlours, clothing stores, shoe stores, sports stores, book stores, etc..

If these firms are run well, that is they are managed properly, they will make a profit. This profit goes for the most part to the 3 levels of government. However a portion goes to the *command partition anti-inflationary deduction* (command partition AID). Thus money is simply deducted and destroyed. So then suppose that the command partition AID is 10 % and that a security guard in the command partition makes 20 000 þ per month. In this case, 2 000 þ would be deducted from the firm's profit and this wouldn't be given to the government. Also suppose that the command partition AID is 15 % and a shoe store makes 20 000 þ per month. In this case 4, 500 þ would be deducted and destroyed and would not be given to the three levels of government.

The command partition AID does not go to any special entity or person. It is merely deducted from bank account records, i.e. it is destroyed. So if 10 000 þ were deducted from a shoe store's profit and the store made 40 000 þ, the government (3 levels) would be given 30 000 þ.

The command partition AID is a measure to reduce the inflation and adjust the money supply. Money is taken from firms in the command partition and destroyed –taken out of circulation- so as to reduce the amount of money circulating in the economy.

Foreign Currency Exchange System

In consumerism we must allow for the exchange of the currencies of consumerism with the currencies of other countries. Although people in our nation can only use our currency (Norses, Ignits and Fortals) we must make allowance for people coming to our country as visitors as well as in cases where people from our country visit other countries and need to use foreign currencies.

Private banks in consumerism have three primary bank accounts; those with Fortals, those with Ignits and those with Norses. Private banks can also have bank accounts with any other currency on Earth. So a private bank can have an account for an investor/person in Euros or Canadian Dollars.

The private banks can exchange foreign currency for the currency used in consumerism. We spoke earlier about the Ignit-Fortal exchange mechanism. In that setup Ignits are exchanged for Fortals and Fortals are exchanged for Ignits. In consumerist private bank foreign currency (i.e. Canadian dollars as well as Euros and Australian dollars) can be exchanged directly for Fortals and Fortals can be exchanged for foreign currency.

There are restrictions regarding foreign currency exchange. Ignits can be exchanged for foreign currency when it is necessary to make trades (import and export) involving the accommodational sector. In this case the nominal exchange rate factors in. However Ignits can be exchanged for Fortals and these can be exchanged for foreign currency. Furthermore, Norses, the currency involved in the materialist sector, can never, ever be exchanged for foreign currency or vice versa.

The exchange of foreign currency for Fortals is based on the Actual Exchange rate. The actual exchange rate is (or should be) a function of the nominal exchange rate that was devised by accountants in the consumerist trade pool exchange commission. The nominal exchange rate is the exchange rate that best facilitates exportation and importation between two countries. The actual exchange rate that is how much a currency is exchanged for another is based on other factors besides the nominal exchange rate.

When in a real situation two currencies are exchanged directly for one another, we apply the Foreign Currency Exchange Adjustment (FCEA). This special parameter is useful for controlling the money supply. It is set as a percentage. In this adjustment, a certain amount of the exchange is taken out of circulation and destroyed. Let's suppose that it is 1 % and we have an investor exchanging 1000 Fortals for Canadian dollars. Let's assume for simplicity that the actual exchange rate is$ 1 CDN = 1 £. If someone exchanges 1000 Fortals for Canadian dollars, he will get $1000 CDN because we can't destroy foreign currency. However, if someone wants to exchange $1000 CDN for Fortals and $1 CDN = 1 £.; then he will get 990 £. The 10 £ are deducted from bank account records.

We now introduce a new parameter/ concept called the proof of foreign visitor status. If a visitor or tourist from a foreign nation comes to our country and wants to buy things in the materialist sector, he must have a means of doing so. He exchanges foreign currency for Fortals and Fortals for Ignits using the Fortal-Ignit exchange mechanism. The foreign visitor status allows the person to buy things with Ignits in the materialist sector.

The foreign visitor status is mutually exclusive with the consumerist grant, either the general or non-working types. If someone is earning a grant than he or she is not eligible for the foreign visitor status and if someone has foreign visitor status then he or she can not get a consumerist grant. The foreign visitor status doesn't give anyone any money. It just allows someone to exchange Ignits directly for materialist goods and services in the materialist sector.

It is imperative that consumerism remains a cashless society. This allows us to avoid bank runs and to manipulate the money supply with ease. There are many other benefits to having a cashless society. So then, what if someone wants to use foreign cash in our consumerist country? We have a tourist in Canada with $1000 CDN in cash. He puts this in his bank. We will call the bank in Canada Supreme Secure Bank and the bank in our country Premium Secure Bank. They are both private banks. Upon leaving to our country the Canadian tourist transfers $1000 CDN from Supreme Secure Bank to Premium Secure Bank. When he buys the plane ticket he must apply for a foreign visitor status card (or certificate). This should (hopefully), be processed in less than a week. Also Premium Secure Bank gives him a blank check book of 200-500 checks to use in our country. The tourist arrives in our country and the first thing he does is to exchange his $1000 CDN for Fortals. The exchange rate is 1 $ = 1 f and the FECA is 1 %. Therefore he is given 990 f. He exchanges 600 fortals into Ignits. The Ignit-Fortal exchange mechanism is also 1 f = 1þ. So he gets 600 þ. He can spend the 390 f in the laissez-faire sector and the 600 þ in the materialist and accommodational sectors. He is entitled to buy things in the materialist sector with Ignits as he has received the foreign visitor status. When he is done his vacation he still has 100 f left over. He exchanges this for Canadian dollars and gets $ 100 CDN. He transfers this money to the bank account he had in Canada and from this bank account he can take out $ 100 CDN in cash.

The foreign currency exchange system allows for converting money in the form of one currency to another. It makes tourism possible. The concept of foreign visitor status allows people visiting our country to buy things in the materialist sector like food and clothing.

The Work for Freedom Program

The work for freedom program is a special economic arrangement whereby prison inmates can work in exchange for time off their sentences. A prisoner is able to contribute to society by increasing the output of goods while being rewarded with slightly less prison time. This program is beneficial not only for the prisoner but also for the government and certain profit maximizing firms.

In the work for freedom program a judge or a panel of judges creates a special parameter called the *work/freedom incentive ratio*. Essentially this sets how much time off a sentence an inmate receives in exchange for work. For example, if it is 1hr W/2hr F, for every 1 hour of work an inmate performs, he receives 2 hr off their sentence. So if a shoplifter receives a sentence of 6 weeks or 42 days = 1008 hours, for every hour of work he does, he has 2 hours less of time to serve. If in week one he works 40 hours, he has to spend 80 hours less in the remaining 5 weeks.

When a person is convicted in court the judge gives him a sentence and offers him the opportunity to work in the work for freedom program. If he agrees, the inmate together with his lawyer, the judge (or panel of judges) and the prosecution determine what kind of work will be done. Finally the judge or panel of judges set the work/freedom incentive ratio. It is quite clear that a prison inmate would rather be compensated for his services with time off his sentence rather than with money he can't really spend.

Clearly the jobs the inmate can do are quite limited. Generally speaking, the inmate can't do anything that will help him escape or that is dangerous and can aid in the making of weapons. Some suggestions include adhering stamps to envelops, checking the address on letters, ensuring that the labels on packages are properly attached, putting letters into envelopes, counting papers and other jobs that are similar. The jobs the inmates perform should have an occupational complexity rating < 3.

In this program, a firm in the natural partition approaches the judicial committee in charge of the program and asks them to find inmate workers for their positions. They pay a payment that goes directly to the government to pay for social services. In exchange this committee assigns workers to that occupation. The inmates work not for money but for a reduced prison sentence. For example, a telemarketing company goes to this committee looking for people to fill letters into envelopes. Instead of giving this work to someone with a commerce degree it is more economical to give it to a prison inmate while the university graduate does more demanding work in line with the principal of maximum worker utility. The judicial committee assigns workers to this position and gives them a proper work/freedom incentive ratio. The firm pays, for example, 2.00þ /hour for the service of the inmate. This goes to the government as revenue. The worker, that is the inmate, in the meantime, works to have a shorter sentence. If the work/freedom incentive ratio is 1 hr W/ 3hr F the worker will get three hours off his sentence for every 1 hour that he works.

The prisons in a consumerist nation will have a special section set aside for inmates to do productive work through the work for freedom program. This is similar to having a factory inside the prison where inmates can do things like weighing letters on a scale or making sure that there is a stamp on every envelope they inspect. In that case there must be special correction officers whose job it is, besides making sure the inmates are safe, to ensure that the inmates are doing their job and doing it properly.

There may be problems when inmates deliberately try to sabotage the work they are doing. In that case they get three warnings and after each warning the inmate is penalized. Suppose the work for freedom incentive ratio is 1W/1F and for every hour of work the inmate does, he has one hour deducted off his sentence. If he is caught sabotaging for example putting labels on jars improperly, he is penalized by having his work for freedom incentive ratio increased to say 2W/1F. Now he has to work 2 hours for every hour of freedom he earns. The second time the inmate causes problems he has the work for freedom incentive ratio increased even further and he receives more time on his sentence. So now that parameter becomes 2.5W/1F and he has 3 weeks added to his sentence. The third time the inmate causes problems he is simply expelled from the program all together. In addition, his sentence is severely prolonged. If it was originally 52 weeks it now becomes 104 weeks.

What about the cases where people have life sentences? If such inmates do a lot of work it may be possible for them to have their sentences slightly reduced or enhance their likelihood of being let out on parole. However in this case the work for freedom incentive ratio should be steeper than for other inmates. Now, if these inmates cause problems they will be penalized by being removed from the program, losing their ability for parole and if the problems reoccur two or three times, they may be moved to solitary confinement.

On the other hand if inmates are consistently doing a great job for a very long time, they may be entitled to a "raise". This raise is not in terms of money but with regards to a decreased work for freedom ratio incentive. Suppose a shoplifter is sentenced to prison for 150 weeks and the judge along with the attorneys present determine the work for freedom ratio at 1W/2F. If, for 50 weeks the inmate does an exemplary job at say, putting letters into envelopes, he may have his work for freedom ratio incentive improved to 1W/3F. Now he earns three hours of freedom for every hour of work.

This program is probably incompatible with violent offenders. So if someone committed a very severe crime like serial murder he will most likely not be able to take advantage of the work for freedom program.

Clearly it is better from the standpoint of society as a whole if inmates are doing something productive rather than simply wasting time in a cell staring at the wall. Any time more goods or services are produced, it is better for society. This program allows inmates to pay their debt to society in a much better way. It is also evident that the inmates benefit because they serve a shorter sentence. The firms that participate in this program clearly benefit as they get very cheap labour- much below what they would normally pay if the wage for these jobs was dictated by a central bank or a market. Also, the government benefits since the money firms pay for this work goes directly to three levels of government as revenue. Thus this program is a win-win-win-win proposition.

In essence, that is how the work for freedom program works. Clearly, it is good for several individuals or entities. Through this program, the inmate, the government, participating firms and society as a whole gain.

The Recycle-For-Pay Program

The recycle for pay program is a setup where things that would otherwise be considered waste are exchanged for money. Things like cardboard, plastic, glass, paper, etc are exchanged for money.

In the recycle-for-pay program the government, whether federal, provincial or municipal assigns a monetary value for things that are normally considered waste. A consumerist takes the item to a special store run by the government. We will call such a store simply, "recycling store". The government pays the individual a certain amount of money for the items. Afterwards the government sells the item to an input receiving firm for profit.

Initially, the government sets a special parameter called the *recycle for pay percentage* (RFPP). This dictates how much a consumerist is paid when selling his useless things. Suppose that an aluminum making factory makes usable aluminum for 1.50 þ per kilogram and that they pay 1.00 þ per kilogram for raw materials. Let's suppose that the RFPP is 50%. In that case for every kilogram of aluminum that a consumerist brings to a recycling store, he will receive 50 % of the basic value of the raw aluminum. In this case it is 0.50 þ. The other 0.50 þ goes to the government to pay for social services.

The RFPP can be universal or it can be specific to an item for recycling. There could be RFPP's for paper, RFPP's for glass and RFPP's for plastic. Alternatively, there can be one RFPP for everything.

Suppose that a paper mill buys raw material for creating paper for 2.00 þ and sells it later as paper to other firms. If the RFPP is 40%, the consumerist who brings various forms of paper to a government recycling store would get 0.80 þ for every kilogram of useless paper he brings in. The government receives 1.20 þ for every kilogram of paper brought in.

Many things other than obvious "waste" can be bought by the government through this program. The government can buy (and set RFPP's for) things like the rubber from bicycle tires or wheels, the steel from old utensils and the cotton and polyester from t-shirts.

What the recycle for pay program accomplishes is that it gives value to things that in other economic systems would be considered "garbage". Our landfills should be considerably smaller than those in other economic systems. The problem we will have won't be what to do with useless garbage, but how does one protect one's garbage so that one can get paid for selling it.

It is true that people in free-market economies already recycle to some degree. However they don't have any real monetary incentive to do so. Furthermore, the range of things that can be "recycled" is far greater in consumerism than in other systems. Many of the things that go directly to the landfill- for example, apple cores, banana peels, and tea bags can be purchased by recycling stores. The government buys these things and sells them to companies that make compost – for soil, for example. If we have too much soil from compost we can export this to other nations where they would be grateful to buy it from us.

There will probably still be people who do not have the initiative to take their garbage to a recycling store, even if they gain money for doing so. We have to make use of waste management trucks and waste management workers in this case. They pick up the garbage on the edge of the driveway; whether it is paper, pop cans, and plastic or apple cores. At that point the government sells the recyclable and garbage material to various firms where they transform it to useful inputs- paper, steel, aluminum, soil, etc... The RFPP in this case is 0%. The government makes all the profit for selling recyclables to input processing firms and uses this to pay for social services. Its costs are the waste management workers and equipment used to collect the garbage and bring it to recycling stores. If people do not want to make use of this program, then waste management workers will have to segregate garbage to separate steel, glass, paper and cardboard from waste.

Clearly, the recycle for pay program succeeds in four areas. We already mentioned that it decreases the amount of garbage that goes into our landfills. It also acts as a source of revenue for the three levels of government. It decreases the amount of spending by the government on waste management so that the government can spend that money on things like defence, education and health care. Of course some money will still have to be spent on waste management but considerably less than if the recycle for pay program wasn't in place. Finally, it works as an anti-unemployment measure. If an individual has a hard time finding employment, he can start collecting pop cans or cardboard.

These are the ways the recycle-for-pay program works. It helps our economy in various ways. Both the government, the unemployed as well as the environment benefit from the recycle for pay program.

Gambling

It should be possible to gamble in a consumerist society. We look at two types of gambling; dynamic vs. standard gambling. Furthermore, gambling can take place through lotteries and in casinos. By lotteries we mean opportunities to win a large sum of money by buying a lottery ticket and picking the right numbers. By casinos we mean institutions where consumerists get together and play games in which they can make money or lose money. Games played at casinos include poker, black jack, roulette and slot machines among others. Gambling is in the laissez-faire sector and involves Fortals. However the proceeds from standard gambling go to the three levels of government to pay for social services, although some lotteries are operated by particular government jurisdictions. The proceeds from dynamic gambling are destroyed as it is an anti-inflationary measure. The laissez-faire markdown does not apply to gambling.

First let's look at lotteries. Scratch-and-Win cards are sold for a markup in the laissez-faire sector but the proceeds go to the government or are deducted from circulation. Suppose the government sets the price of a lottery ticket at 2.00 f. It sells these tickets to firms in the laissez-faire sector who charge gamblers a higher price in terms of Fortals. Let's suppose here it is 3.00 f. If a gambler, John, buys a lottery ticket for 3.00 f, he has a chance to win the lottery. All lottery gaming is owned and operated by the government but works in conjunction with the laissez-faire sector. In this case 1.00 f goes to the firm in the Laissez-faire sector that sold John the ticket. Assume for simplicity that 1f = 1þ. Then 2.00 f = 2.00 þ go to the government to pay for social services if the lottery is of the standard type or it is deducted from circulation if it is of the dynamic type.

Not all tickets cost 2.00 f. Some may be 1.00 f and others may be 15.00 f. The rewards of winning are set by the lottery company run by the government. The higher the grand prize or the greater the chances of winning smaller prizes, the more it can charge per ticket, the more tickets the lottery company sells and thus the more profit it earns. If John wins the lottery and the jackpot is 1 000 000.00 f, he keeps 1 000 000.00 f (because there are no taxes or laissez-faire markdown to worry about). If the government run lottery company earns a profit of 10 000 000.00 þ (after giving out prizes), it keeps 10 000 000.00 þ if it is of the standard type or it destroys 10 000 000 if it is of the dynamic type.

As stated, lottery tickets are operated by the levels of government but they are sold directly to consumerists in the laissez-faire sector. Firms in the gambling industry of the laissez-faire sector could be either of the command partition or natural partition type. If they are from the natural partition the profit from selling the lottery ticket (price minus what goes to the government) goes to profit maximizing firms. If firms selling lottery tickets are from the command partition, then there is even more revenue going to the government for social services or as an anti-inflationary measure. For example, if the government sells a lottery ticket for 2.00 f to a command partition-laissez faire firm and this firm sells the ticket for 3.00 f, then 3.00 f total go to the government to pay for social services (2.00 f + (3.00 f – 2.00 f)) = 3.00 f or 3.00 f are taken out of circulation.

Also, laissez-faire firms in the command partition dictate, somewhat, the price of the lottery ticket. If a command partition-laissez faire firm charges 4.00 f for a ticket and another natural partition-laissez faire firm charges 5.00 f for the same ticket, most consumerists would buy the 4.00 ₤ ticket.

Now let's look at casinos. Casinos are owned, managed and operated by the government. Gambling in a casino closely resembles gambling in a free-market economy in that gamblers can wage any amount of money on games and machines. The laissez-faire markdown does not apply to the winnings of the casino. Suppose Bob plays poker and wins 10 000.00 ₤. He gets a check from the casino for this amount and keeps 10 000.00 ₤. If a casino earns 100 000 000.00 ₤ in a year, it keeps 100 000 000.00 ₤. After being exchanged to Ignits through the Ignit- Fortal exchange mechanism, this also goes to the government to help pay for social services if the gambling is of the standard type or it is deducted from circulation if it is of the dynamic type.

The laissez-faire markdown, even if it is invoked in general, probably won't apply to the various forms of gambling. Dynamic gambling accomplishes the same thing that the laissez-faire markdown is designed to do. Thus it is not necessary.

The idea of gambling has a negative side, however. Excessive gambling can lead to gambling addiction. Lives can be hurt and personal savings can be ruined if a person's gambling leads to addiction. Gambling addiction hurts lives personally and it hurts society. Thus the consumerist government should embark on programs designed to help those with gambling issues. Support groups, counselling and help lines should be made available for those struggling with gambling addiction

Gambling is a part of the consumerist system. In this system a gambler could play the lottery or enjoy the casino. Gambling exists as a method of entertainment or as a way to become instantly rich. It is also beneficial as the proceeds from gambling go to the government to pay for needed social services. Also, gambling helps to control the money supply.

Output Maximization Measures

It is an important goal of accommodation based consumerism to raise the general output of the whole economy. An economy with a higher output is better off compared to other countries that have a lower output. Raising output increases the size of the economic pie so to speak.

There are quite a few measures designed to increase general economic output. Now we list them. They will be explained in full in other sections. They are:

- the non existence of many taxes. There is no corporate tax or bussiness income tax
- the existence of the profit vacuum – firms have the opportunity to make a profit by investing and creating jobs
- Retail Markup- a percentage increase in the prices of final goods at the retail level in the accommodational and materialist sectors. Ensures retailers sell more products while making a profit
- Partial Ownership of Firms by the Government- investment from the government stimulates the economy and raises general output
- Employment Reimbursement Transfer- the money paid to firms as a reward for hiring more employees. Used to combat unemployment and stimulate the economy
- Capital Investment Transfer- the money paid to firms to cover the costs of purchasing capital. Encourages investment and reduces unemployment
- Profit Reward Transfer- A reward a firm is given for making profit- Encourages investment and combats unemployment
- Interest Rate Stimulus- A percentage of a loan that is paid to creditors by the government- Encourages investment and fights unemployment
- Quality Selection- the situation where firms compete with each other to give the most desirable goods and services in a market with fixed price functions- ensures the output of the economy is of the highest quality
- Price Selection- the occurrence where firms compete with each other to give the best prices for goods and services in the laissez-faire sector- ensures the output of the laissez-faire sector is most effective and efficient
- Government Business Loan Assistance Program- the government loans money to certain firms to stimulate production and help the economy
- Consumerist Spending Reimbursement- a reward from the government to consumerists for buying goods and services- used to stimulate the economy and reduce unemployment
- the WC grant- a payment from the government to certain firms for maintaining washing commodes- ensures all consumerists have access to use washrooms when they need them
- Industry Hybrid-Patent period- how long a firm or person has the right to be the only producer of a good or service. Expressed in terms of length of time, profit earned or revenue accumulated-promotes the creation of new products and services
- There are no real wage/salary functions for running or owning a business. Running a sucessful bussiness is encouraged
- Profit motive- for contributing to the economy, people are given money to spend on goods and ervices
- Work for Freedom Program- an agreement where an inmate does supervised work in exchange for time off his sentence- stimulates production of goods

- Recycle for Pay Program- a setup where consumerists take useless items and give them to the government for a payment. The government then takes this and sells it to input processing firms- reduces garbage while making the most of items that would otherwise be thrown away
- Employment Assistance Program- a setup where the government pays a firm for hiring workers. Later the worker must pay the government (with interest) for the service- creates more jobs and helps workers find jobs
- The stipulation that children and minors are encouraged to work at least 3-4 hours a week
- Laissez-Faire Labour System- a setup where workers wages are partially paid by firms in the laissez-faire sector and partially the government- promotes the creation of work and encourages firms to return to our country if they previously outsourced
- Governmental Employment Incentive Program- A system where the government gives money to businesses to increase employment- stimulates the economy and decreases unemployment
- Selective Occupation Promotion System- ensures that the brightest, best and hard working are employed in Consumerism
- Disability Work Program- A system that tries to find employment for all people that are considered disabled- ensures that those who identify themselves as "disabled" are provided with employment. The more people working, ceteris paribus, the greater the general output of the whole economy
- Governmental- Market Surplus Shortage Resolution System- helps the economy by overcoming surpluses and shortages
- Imposition of production quotas on workers in the command partition- ensures that workers in the command partition are most productive
- Low Bank Rate- when this parameter is low, firms are more likely to borrow and invest thus encouraging the growth of the economy
- there is no cash reserve ratio for banks- this makes it easier for banks to make loans thus stimulating the economy
- Command Partition Compensation Adjustment- ensures workers in the command partition have an incentive to do more difficult and demanding jobs
- Bankruptcy Insurance- certain firms provide insurance to other firms for buying stocks and bonds. Lowers the risk dealing with investment thus encouraging more people to invest
- Existence of brand names- firms have a certain reputation to uphold and ensure consumerists that there products are of the highest quality
- Command Partition Productivity Incentive Deduction System– a mechanism that encourages workers in the command partition to do work of high quality
- Low Accommodational Markdown- money not spent on fighting inflation can be spent on goods and services in the accommodational sector
- Low Laissez-Faire Markdown- money not spent on fighting inflation can be spent on goods and services in the laissez-faire sector
- Fixed price functions for inputs- ensures all goods are made of the highest quality materials

These are the tools we have to raise output. We said it before and we will reiterate it again: a population with a high output is generally speaking better off than one where the output is low. The measures we described above ensure us that the output of a consumerist nation will be as high as it can be.

Anti-Poverty Measures

A key goal of the accommodation based consumerist economic system is to eliminate poverty. Although attempts to accomplish this have been made throughout history, this system offers meaningful suggestions and ideas to get rid of poverty. If we can accomplish the task of creating an economic system where poverty is non existent or ridiculously low this would mean consumerism has succeeded in what it sets out to accomplish.

Poverty can be conceptualized in several forms. One type of poverty, the opposite of true wealth, is the occurrence where a consumerist has goods and services of low quality. By low quality we mean things that are less desirable in the eyes of consumerists.

Another type of poverty is in the form of quantity of goods owned or access to services available. This is the opposite of "abundant wealth". For example, a person with 1 t-shirt is poorer relative to a person who has 2 of the same identical t-shirt.

Yet another type of poverty is in terms of money possessed. This is the opposite of "being prosperous". For most people this is how poverty is usually thought of. A person with 20 ₤ is poorer than a person with 80 ₤.

Also, poverty may refer to the consumerist's ability or inability to enjoy their possessions and having free time to do so. Having some time off is just as important as money as long as we have money to enjoy that time off.

We have many anti-poverty measures in accommodation based consumerism. We can categorize these anti-poverty measures into two groups. One will be called "general anti-poverty measures". The other one will be called "variable anti-poverty measures". General anti-poverty measures can be manipulated by the central bank, the government or firms to directly reduce poverty. On the other hand, with the variable anti-poverty measures, there is a trade off. For example, with incentive to work or governmental spending. Thus to reduce a variable anti-poverty measure, there is an associated cost.

The General Anti-Poverty measures are:

- Quality selection
- Accommodational Award
- Materialist overdraft
- Materialist overdraft interest
- Disability work program
- Ultra-universal healthcare
- Universal education
- Free transit
- Retirement pension allowance
- Command Partition Compensation Adjustment
- Food Geared to Income Program
- No Food Wasted Initiative
- Consumerist Food Center
- Food Geared to Income Limit

- Food Geared to Income Percentage

The Variable Anti-Poverty measures are:

- General Consumerist grant
- Non-working consumerist grant
- Non-working consumerist grant markdown
- 5 types of extra work transfers
- Working grant threshold
- Minimum retirement age
- Positive personal income tax
- Yearly vacation duration period
- Yearly sick leave exemption period
- Maternity leave duration period
- Injury severance payment
- Auxiliary worker reimbursement deduction
- Unemployment assistance repayment
- Accommodation award repayment percentage
- Increase scope of materialist sector
- Adjusted Income Percentage

These measures have been discussed before or will be discussed more fully in a future section. What follows is a short characterization of what these measures actually mean.

Quality selection is the idea that consumerists buy goods and services of the highest quality with price functions being fixed. This occurs in the GAM sectors. With access to high quality possessions and services, consumerists have a high quality life and economic well being.

The accommodation award is the situation where the government provides housing for all consumerists who cannot afford their own accommodation – house, apartment, condo. Eventually, the consumerists repay the value of the accommodation. Nevertheless, it has the effect that no one, absolutely no one is homeless – unless they chose to be so of their own free will.

The materialist overdraft gives consumerists extra money (in the form of Norses) to spend on materialist goods should they run out or have severe budgeting problems. This ensures that all consumerists always have enough food to eat and clothes to wear. Eventually, that money is deducted from the next consumerist grant.

The materialist overdraft interest is the cost of taking advantage of the materialist overdraft. If the government lowers it, it will lower poverty as consumerists can borrow more money through the materialist overdraft. The lower the materialist overdraft interest, the more it helps consumerists.

The disability work program is a special setup where people who identify themselves as "disabled" are provided special jobs. The government works hard to find jobs for these people and pays these people a certain amount of Ignits and Fortals (2 different currencies) equal to a certain wage.

Ultra-universal healthcare gives all consumerists access to high level healthcare should they need it. The consumerists do not pay for health care services out of their pockets as health care is provided publicly. No one in consumerism suffers a disease that may impact them from working as all types of health care services are universally provided to everyone.

Universal education ensures everyone in our consumerist system is educated if they want to be. This enables them to find high paying jobs. People in consumerism do not remain in a vicious cycle of poverty caused by a lack of education.

Free transit in the form of free transportation for bus and subway commuters allows all consumerists get to where they're going in their city. This fights poverty in that people taking public transit do not have to pay for their transportation out of pocket. Public transit is funded publicly.

Retirement pension allowance ensures that those who worked their lives and contributed to the economy are, in the end, paid some money. Those individuals who choose to retire (after a certain age) receive Ignits and Fortals to spend on items in the accommodational and laissez-faire sectors.

The command partition compensation adjustment helps to overcome poverty. Certain workers in the command partition are paid more than other command partition workers to reflect the fact that they have more difficult and more demanding jobs.

Some anti-poverty measures actually work to fight poverty in the form of hunger. The No Food Wasted Initiative promotes and encourages firms in the natural partition and command partition to give their excess food at the end of the day instead of just throwing it out.

The Food Geared to Income Program provides food for hungry consumerists based on a percentage of their materialist income (NWCG). Those who are having a hard time making ends meet can get their food from special Consumerist Food Centers.

Consumerist Food Centers provide food for those in need of food. The food in these places comes from surpluses command partition firms have if they operate in the hospitality industry. Also some food comes from generous consumerists.

Food Geared to Income Percentage refers to how much of the NWCG or GCG a consumerist needs to pay in order to take advantage of the Food Geared to Income Program. The lower this is, the better it fights poverty in the form of hunger.

The Food Geared to Income Limit refers to how much food a hungry consumerist can take from a consumerist food center each week. It is expressed in Norses. A consumerist can take from a CFC this much worth of food or less. The higher this is, the more it fights poverty in the form of hunger.

By increasing the scope of the materialist sector, the government puts more families of goods and services in the materialist sector. This increases the various consumerist grants as well as possibly, the GCT. However this may increase the accommodational overflow calamity.

The general consumerist grant can be used to lower poverty. The more money (Norses) an individual earns from the central bank, the more money he has to spend on things in the materialist sector. Thus a person who has received a high general consumerist grant can spend his money on things like clothes, cars, food and entertainment. In doing so, he is less poor.

The same logic as for the general consumerist grant also applies to the non-working consumerist grant. People who receive the non-working consumerist grant earn money for the materialist sector to buy things like cars, clothes and food. The non-working consumerist grant should be lower than the general consumerist grant so as to give workers an incentive to work.

A key variable anti-poverty measure is the non-working consumerist markdown. This parameter refers to how much more a "working" consumerist earns than a "non-working" consumerist. The higher it is, i.e. the smaller the gap between the general and non-working consumerist grants, the more the government fights poverty. However, the lower it is, i.e. the larger the gap between the general and non-working consumerist grants, the higher is the incentive to work and produce for the economy.

The Extra Work Transfers (EWT) refer to a special type of payment. The EWT is how much people in the command partition, laissez-faire labour system and the disability work program are compensated for their contribution to society. The higher the EWT, the more we fight poverty as these workers have more money to spend on goods in the accommodational and laissez-faire sectors. The lower the EWT, the more incentive we give to those who work as the same worker will have to work more to earn a certain amount of money.

The working grant threshold determines the point at which a "non-working" consumerist becomes a "working" consumerist. Working consumerists are paid more than their non-working counterparts. The lower the working grant threshold, the lower the poverty rate in consumerism as there are more working consumerists. However if we increase the working grant threshold we increase the incentive for work for consumerists as they need to work more hours to earn the working consumerist grant.

The minimum retirement age can be manipulated to lower poverty or to increase output. The lower the minimum retirement age, the lower the poverty incidence while the higher it is, the more work consumerists have to do before they can take advantage of retirement pension.

The positive personal income tax is an interesting way to fight poverty. Recall that in consumerism tax payers earn a nice profit on their income tax payments in the long run. The higher the interest rate paid on the income tax, the more tax payers earn and the more poverty is reduced as tax payers have more money than before. However, the initial income tax interest rate effects poverty. By lowering the income tax rate, the more we eliminate poverty in the short run.

The yearly vacation duration period fights poverty but not in terms of money or material things. This parameter refers to the amount of time a consumerist has to take off from work and enjoy – and possibly going on a vacation. If this parameter is high, people are less poor as they have more time to enjoy life. However if it is too high, consumerists are not working at their jobs.

The yearly sick leave Exemption Period (YSLEP) refers to the amount of days a consumerist can take off work if he is sick. Clearly, the more is better from the eyes of a consumerist as long as he is really sick. However, this has to be juggled with the fact that if a worker is sick, he isn't working. Thus this parameter has to be carefully balanced.

The maternity leave duration period (MLDP) is also a parameter that needs to be balanced. The MLDP refers to how much time a mother can take off to take care of her new born

214

child or if she is pregnant. It is better for the woman (as long as she's paid) but worse for the employer if this parameter is high.

The injury severance payment refers to the amount of money a worker receives after losing his job. It is better for the worker if it is higher and worse for the employer if it is higher.

The auxiliary worker reimbursement deduction (AWRD) is how much less a person in the socialist labour pool receives per month for being in the socialist labour pool. The lower this is, the more we fight poverty as some workers will earn more money. However if it is higher, it gives workers more of an incentive to work.

The unemployment assistance repayment is how much money a worker has to repay the government when he finds a job in either the natural or governmental partitions. If this is low, we lower poverty as certain workers will have more money. However, if it is higher, we give these workers an incentive to leave the socialist labour pool.

The Adjusted Income Percentage reflects how much money workers are paid in the end by their employers. Thus, if we keep this low, we help employers. However, if we keep it high, we help workers and fight poverty.

Finally, there is the accommodational award repayment percentage. This is how much a person receiving the accommodational award has to repay the government when he finds another form of accommodation or pays for the one he currently lives in. The lower this is, the more we fight poverty as we allow consumerists to keep their money. On the other hand, by allowing this parameter to be high, we discourage people from abusing the accommodational award program and find a home else where.

Not too long ago I saw a physically disabled man begging outside a large store. He had a sign that said he has starving children, that he has a debilitating medical condition and that he needs money. This is a depressing circumstance and it won't happen under consumerism. First of all, this man and his family would be granted the non working consumerist grant so they would have enough for food and clothes. Furthermore, this man would find work in the disability work program. He can be made to rate movies or songs and write a report about them. He could become a food critic. There are hundreds of other occupations this man could have in consumerism. In consumerism no one is forced to begging.

These are, specifically, how consumerism fights poverty. Some of these parameters are clearly seen as ways to reduce poverty. Others, however, must be weighed as they have "side effects" usually in the form of lowering the incentive to work or decreasing the output of the economy. Nevertheless, poverty in consumerism should be extremely small at worst and non-existent at best.

Consumerist Opportunity

Those that contribute to the accommodation based consumerist economy should be rewarded greatly for their contributions. If someone helps the consumerist economy by providing consumerists with needs and wants and produces goods and provides services, he should definitely be recognized. Those that make consumerism great should be rewarded by having a wonderful lifestyle.

A consumerist nation should be a nation of opportunity. It should be possible to "get ahead" if one knows how. There should be a way to thrive in a consumerist economy.

We stressed throughout this book the importance of reducing or even eliminating poverty. That is wonderful. However, just reducing poverty is not enough. It should be possible to become wealthy, prosperous and abundant. It should be possible to have a luxurious life.

Many of the North American and European nations have the fine attribute that it is possible to be prosperous, wealthy and abundant in their nations. Consumerism borrows this idea. Consumerism should also be considered a place of opportunity.

In consumerism we need to reward entrepreneurs, moguls and tycoons. These people provide jobs and produce goods in vast quantities and provide services in great amounts. If we reward entrepreneurs, tycoons and moguls we will greatly stimulate the economy, reducing unemployment and increasing general output.

There are several ways consumerism helps moguls, tycoons and moguls. First of all, there is no wage/salary function for running a business. If one runs a business or enterprise well, he can amass an almost limitless amount of money. All the business owner earns by contributing to consumerism, he keeps for himself.

Also, there are no real taxes. There is no corporate or sales tax. The positive personal income tax and the wealth tax do exist as a possibility but they should only be invoked if the government can't raise enough revenue through the other methods.

We need consumerism to be a land of opportunity for workers as well. This is provided by the profit motive. The harder workers work and the more productive they are, the more money they will amass (as Ignits and Fortals) and they can spend it on whatever they wish in the accommodational and laissez-faire sectors.

In consumerism everything should be done for moguls, entrepreneurs and tycoons to make a profit. There must be opportunity. This ideal of economic opportunity will definitely inspire a lot of people to come to our country to do business here and live a wonderful life.

Physical Inputs

To produce goods, an economy needs inputs. A physical input is a material item used to produce another good. Steel and plastic are required to make cars. Plastic is used to make certain toys. Glass and wood are used to make windows. Cotton and polyester are used to make clothes. Rubber is used to make shoes. Synthetics are used to make paint. In this section we will talk about the relationship physical inputs have with the economy.

Recall from the section on economic taxonomy that a physical input is one that has the title "input" in its designation taxon. We group inputs into families. Two inputs that can be used to make the same product are relatively similar and can be exchanged one for the other are grouped in the same family. This grouping of inputs into families is very important.

All physical inputs of the same family have the same *input function*. This is how much it costs to use such an input. An input function is created similarly to a price function or a wage function. The industry specific Chairman sets the form of the input function. The 100 industry specific Commissioners vote on the parameters of the input function. The top 25 and bottom 25 votes are discarded while the middle 50 votes are averaged. This system of setting prices for inputs is more efficient than if a single person were to pick the price of the input and is much less time consuming than if it were done by a single Grand Chairman and 100 Consumerist Commissioners.

Let's see some examples of input function families. Pine and oak are used to make tables and chairs so they would be in the same family. Cotton and polyester are used interchangeably to make clothing so they would be in one family. Duck feathers and goose feathers are both used to make pillow stuffing so they would be in one family. Suppose that in the "bird feathers" family, to which duck and goose feathers belong, the industry specific Chairman sets the form of the input function as x/kg. This means that the 100 industry specific Commissioners must vote on the value of x. Suppose that they vote a value of 2.50 þ for x. Therefore a kilogram of goose or duck feather would cost 2.50 þ. Prices are in Ignits as inputs are not sold directly to consumerists and are therefore in the accommodational sector.

The point of making input families with inputs of the same cost is to instigate quality selection. Since all production choices cost the same, producers pick the input of the highest quality. French fry makers pick the tastier, healthier potatoes rather than the inferior ones. Cars brake down less frequently since their components are superior. The steak at a restaurant is always of the highest grade. Bridges collapse less often because what they are made of is longer lasting. In general all the products made by producers are top of the line. Overall, this enhances true wealth.

Physical inputs, as we have seen, are necessary for the production of any and all goods. In our system we group the various inputs into families. Each family has a different input function. This ultimately leads to a situation where only the best inputs are utilized.

Ultra Universal Healthcare

Accommodation based consumerism prides itself with its grand health care system. A country's healthcare system is a direct reflection of the well being of a nation. The more universal the health care system, the better. We, in consumerism, want the highest level of healthcare possible as the country gains prestige by having a robust health care system.

In accommodation based consumerism, all consumerists, without discrimination, receive a government issued "health card". They present this card when seeking help from a member of the medical community. The health care provider then directly bills the government, either at the federal or provincial/state level. Free universal health care is provided entirely by the government through the sources of revenue the levels of government have; including the GCT, gambling profits, and profits from the socialist trade pool.

The accommodation based consumerist economic system encapsulates a grand inclusive healthcare system. Almost all aspects of the healthcare system are publicly funded in accommodation based consumerism. The ultra universal healthcare system of accommodation based consumerism is many steps ahead of the current healthcare system found in Canada today. More aspects of healthcare are covered in accommodation based consumerism than at any time in the Canadian system.

There are two types of ultra universal healthcare systems in accommodation based consumerism – Type A and Type B. The difference is that in type B healthcare system the pharmacological industry is covered in the system while in type A it is not. However in both ultra universal health care systems in accommodation based consumerism, almost all aspects of the health care system are run by public funding. This universal health care coverage includes all hospital stays, all medication, vision care, dentistry, chiropractic, naturopathic treatment, trips to the local walk-inn clinic, psychologist and psychiatrist, blood work at the blood clinic and many other things. Everything that has to do with medicine is covered by the government; i.e. it is part of the governmental sector. Each medical service; i.e. heart operation, the filling of a cavity, psychologist appointment, etc... has a price/ wage function set by the central bank. How much each medical practitioner is paid is determined by the members of the central bank as they vote on wage/price functions for medical services. Fortunately the only things not covered by the ultra universal health care system of accommodation based consumerism are treatments for dogs and cats at veterinary clinics- because they are not human.

In accommodation based consumerism all autistic children will be completely cared for their condition. All forms of funding for treatment for this disease are provided.

All forms of cancer therapy are provided publicly in consumerism. Chemotherapy, surgery as well radiation therapy are given to cancer patients in consumerism without the individual having to pay for it out of pocket.

To a large extent, a universal health care system helps everyone regardless whether they are helped directly by it. For example, if a police officer has a broken leg, he can't serve the community. However, if we help heal his leg then we can get him back to his job so he can continue helping people. Providing medical services to one person invariably provides benefits to all other people that can now benefit from his services.

218

One might wonder where the funding for this treatment comes from. There are over 22 sources of revenue for the government in accommodation based consumerism. The achievement of accommodation based consumerism is that it allows for government programs like universal health care without resorting to taxes.

There are no special premiums for healthcare services. No consumerist who receives a healthcare service will ever have to pay any money for the services he receives. The healthcare services in consumerism are 100 % totally paid by the government through the many governmental revenue sources we discussed in this book.

Accommodation based consumerism has a very high standard health care system. All medical services, from trips to the doctor, the hospital or the eye doctor are financed by the government, either the federal or provincial. A healthy, well cared for population is a more productive one.

Gross National Product

The Gross National Product (GNP) is the main way to compare the consumerist economy relative to other nations in terms of productivity/prosperity. The GNP is to the accommodational sector what the GDCP is to the materialist sector. Basically the GNP refers to the final output of goods and services in the accommodational sector.

The GNP measures the output of the accommodational sector. It is therefore expressed in Ignits. Let's talk about what is and what isn't included in the GNP. All land bought and sold is part of the GNP. This includes residential, commercial and recreational land. All accommodation is also included. This means all houses, apartments, office buildings and palaces. But it would not include the cost of building materials or construction workers salaries that were needed to construct buildings. All utilities are also included. This means the price of electricity, hot water and cable. Thus if a consumerist owes 200.00 þ to his electricity provider, this would count towards the GNP. Appliances and home accessories are included. Their value is after the retail markup and the accommodational markup. It would thus pertain to things like a refrigerator at a department store but not the price the department store had to pay to the factory to purchase the refrigerator. Also all leisure factors in. So the price of vacations and tickets to events are involved. For example a ticket to an opera concert worth 100.00 þ would be included.

The GNP does not tell us anything about the output of either the materialist, governmental or laissez-faire sectors. Thus it clearly underestimates the actual value (output) of our economy. However since all Norses eventually, at some point, become turned into Ignits, the GNP has some usefulness in categorizing the prosperity of a consumerist nation.

The main purpose of the GNP is as a statistic. It has no real effect on other aspects of the economy but tells us where we stand relative to other nations. A large GNP may indicate a prosperous economy or as we will see in another section one with an overabundance of Ignits in circulation.

This is the idea behind the term gross national product (GNP). There are many examples of what would be counted towards the GNP. The main value of this parameter is as some abstract measure of prosperity between nations.

The Consumerist Trade Market

In the Consumerist market we analyze how the consumerist economy works. The Consumerist market explains at the microeconomic level the functioning of the accommodation based consumerist economic system. By studying it we gain valuable insight. Note that this discussion does not apply to the laissez-faire sector where economic decisions are based on the law of supply and demand vs. price.

We construct quality-demand graphs. Quality is plotted on the y-axis. Output is plotted on the x-axis. We define quality as a rating of superiority in make, usefulness or consumerist satisfaction. The higher the quality rating the more valued is the good or service; i.e. the more people would prefer it to other substitutes. Quality is a relative term. When a good or service is chosen over another by a consumerist, we say it is of better quality. Output refers to how much of a product or service is produced, used or made available to consumerists.

In quality-demand graphs we look at the production of a family of goods or services. Recall from our discussion on economic taxonomy the following taxonomic hierarchy:

- Economy
- Sector
- Industry
- Class
- Category
- Family
- Service/Product
- Designation

Therefore we study not just potatoes but all root vegetables which could include carrots. Wines of all makes and from all places are studied regardless of their alcohol content. We look not just at strawberries but all berries including raspberries, blueberries and gooseberries. Likewise for all families of goods and services.

How do we go about constructing quality-output graphs (we use this term interchangeably with "quality-demand" graphs and "consumerist demand graphs")? We poll a set number of consumerists regarding a particular family of goods or services that we are interested in. We ask them to pick three goods or services out of that family. If they wish they may pick the same product/service more than once. Usually the higher the number of people we poll the better the graph.

We make a quality demand graph for automobiles. We give the consumerists 5 choices to choose from:

1) A 1980 Foreign Economy Car
2) A 1990 Domestic Economy Car
3) A new Foreign Compact Car
4) A new European Sports Car
5) A new limousine

They were given 3 votes. Here is how the votes came in:

1) 1980 Foreign Economy Car -   1
2) 1990 Domestic Economy Car -   2
3) New Foreign Compact Car-   2
4) New European Sports Car-   5
5) New limousine-   5

Now we graph the results. Let the number represent the different choices for automobiles instead of writing the name of the automobile

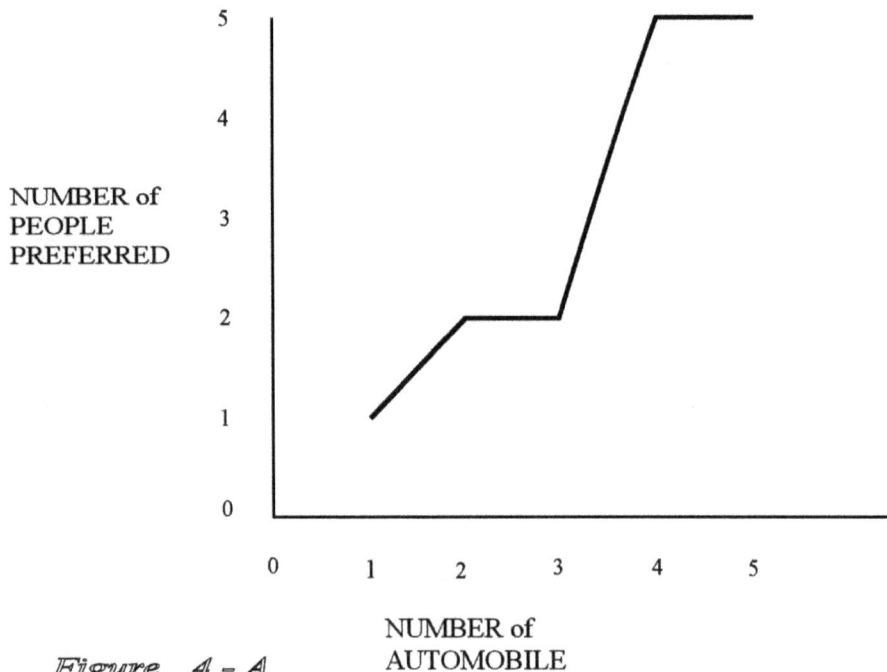

Figure 4-A

NUMBER of
PEOPLE
PREFERRED

NUMBER of
AUTOMOBILE

Figure 4-A

The above is a quality demand curve. What the above graph means is that more people will buy a limousine or a European Sports Car rather than a 1980 Foreign Compact Car, Foreign Economy Car or Domestic Economy Car since the price is the same for each.

Let's repeat the procedure for another family of goods- root vegetables. Again we have 5 consumerists and they have to make 3 choices. Their choices are:

1) Golden Potatoes
2) Yams
3) White Flesh Potatoes
4) Carrots
5) Onions
6) Radishes

Technically a potato is not a root but it is easier to classify it with these others because the part of the potato we eat grows underground. There are many more root vegetables than in the above list. We omit them for simplicity as we are only interested in constructing consumerist demand tables and graphs. If we had more people to poll we would add to our list.

This is how the votes came in:

1) Golden Potatoes- 2
2) Yams- 1
3) White Flesh Potatoes-2
4) Carrots- 4
5) Beets- 1
6) Onions- 3
7) Radishes- 2

If we now make a graph with the root vegetables on the y-axis in the order we arranged them our graph would look something like this:

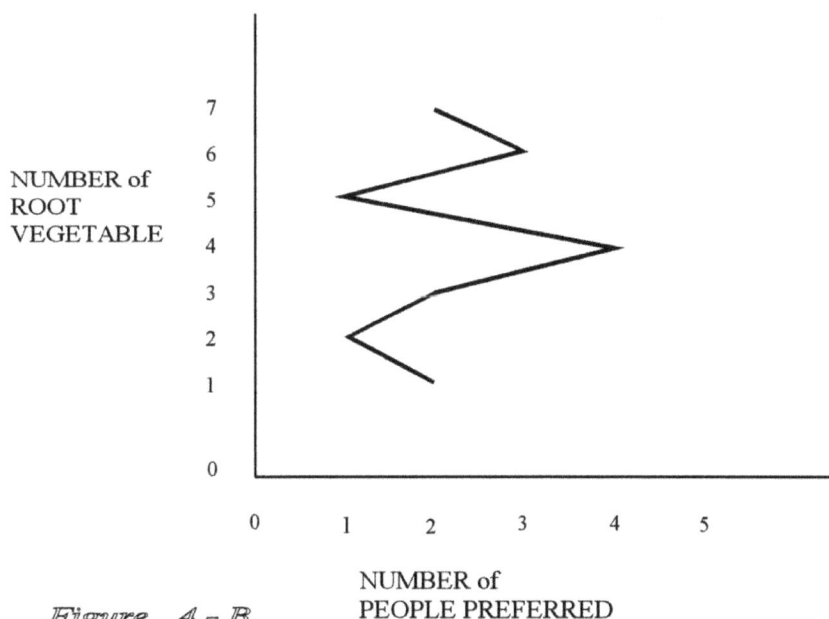

Figure 4 - B

NUMBER of
PEOPLE PREFERRED

Figure 4-B

This graph looks different than the one for automobiles and is confusing. Instead of a number corresponding directly to a good or service arbitrarily, in this case to vegetables, in our new quality demand graphs, the number will correspond to a "quality rating"; the higher the better.

To revisit our previous root vegetable demand table we have the following:

1) Beets- 1 vote
2) Yams- 1 votes
3) Radishes- 2 votes
4) White Flesh Potatoes – 2 votes
5) Golden Potatoes- 2 votes
6) Onions- 3 votes
7) Carrots- 4 votes

The consumerist demand graph now looks like the following:

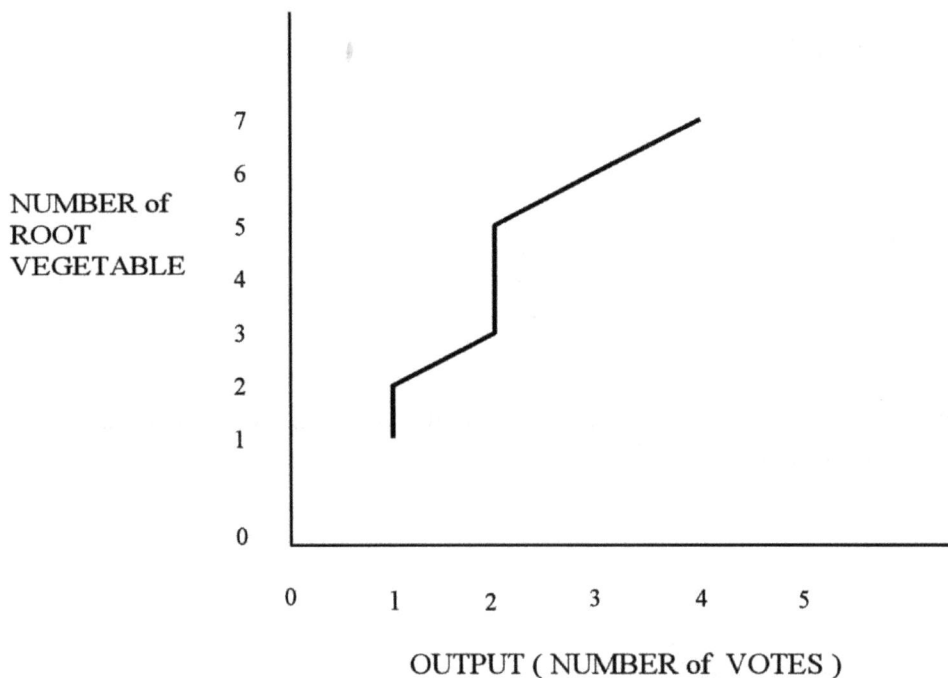

Figure 4 - C

Figure 4-C

How about if we add another product to our consumerist demand table; let's say celery root. Let's also add more consumerists. Our new table could look like this:

- Beets 1
- Yam 1
- White Flesh Potatoes 2
- Radish 2
- Golden Potatoes 2
- Onions 3
- Celery root 3
- Carrots 4

If we compare these two tables we see that the only differences are that celery root received 3 votes. Everything is the same as before. How does our consumerist demand graph change? Notice that celery root has 3 votes –the same as onion but less than carrots. What we do is give it a quality rating of 6.5. Our new graph looks like this. (We label each point: A- Carrots, B- Celery Root, C- Onions, D- Golden Potatoes, E- Radishes, F- White Flesh Potatoes, G- Yams, H-Beets)

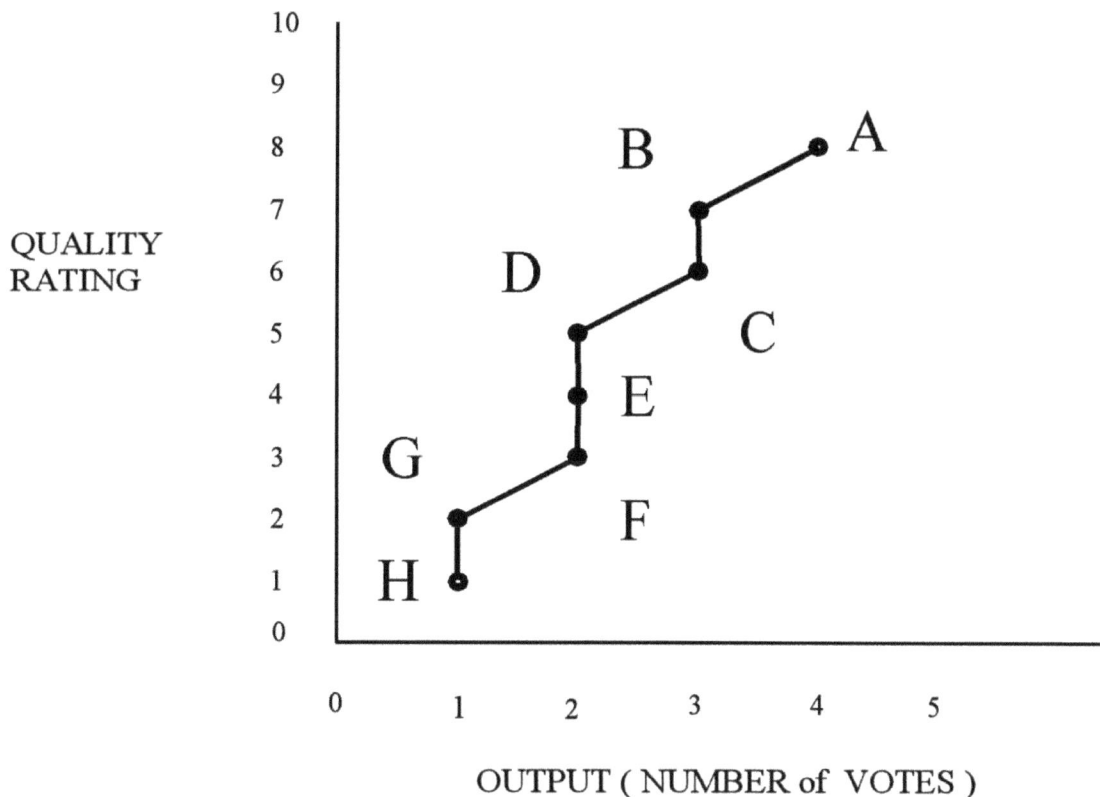

Figure 4 - D

Figure 4-D

We would use the same procedure for any additional new product or service we add into our analysis. We simply give it a quality rating in between those products it has a greater or lesser output (vote) than.

Let's look back at our root vegetables analysis. This time there are 10 consumerists who each have 3 votes. This is how they could respond to a poll:

225

-	Yam	2 votes
-	Beets	2 votes
-	Radish	3 votes
-	Golden Potatoes	3 votes
-	White Flesh Potatoes-	3 votes
-	Celery root	4 votes
-	Carrots	7 votes
-	Onions	8 votes

A demand graph can drastically change the more people are polled or if different people are polled. The demand graph would look like this: We label each point: A- Onions, B- Carrots, C- Celery Root, D-White flesh potatoes, E- Golden Potatoes, F- Radishes, G- Beets, H-Yams)

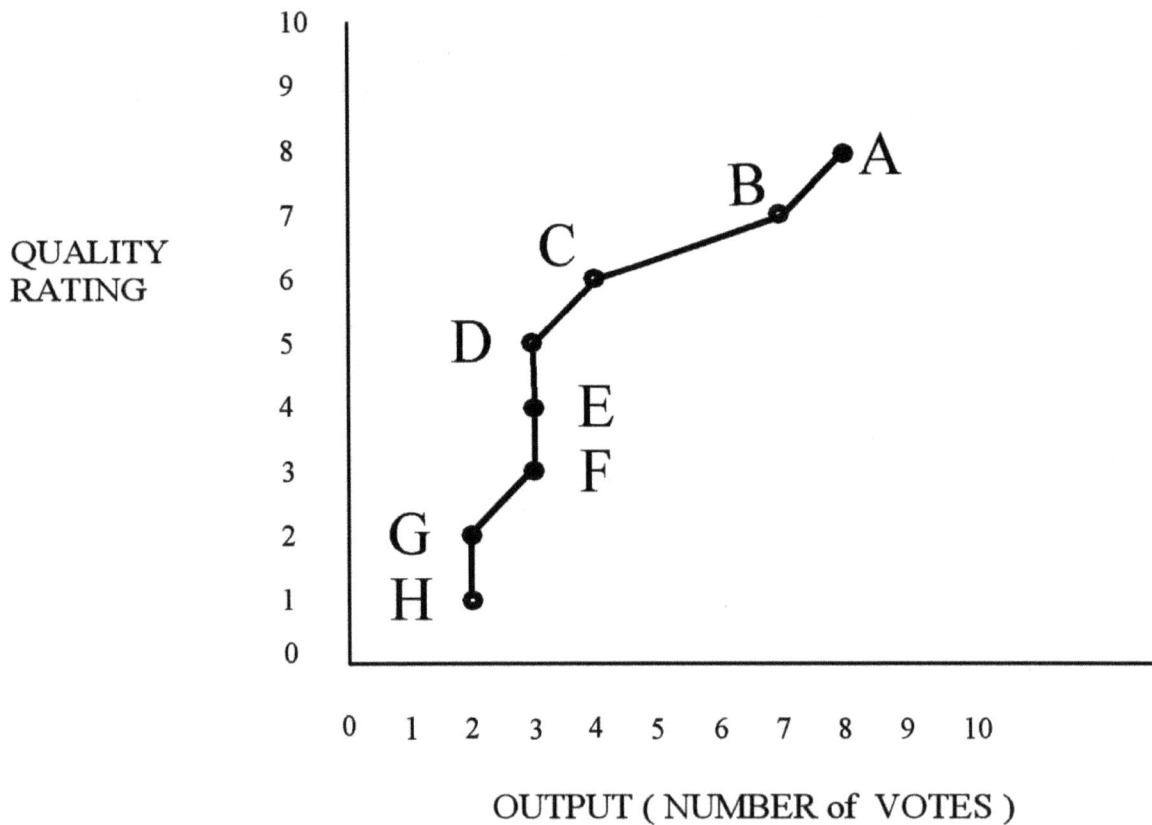

Figure 4 - E

Figure 4-E

These two graphs and tables are very different even though the same root vegetables are being analyzed. However if a large number of people are polled, say 1000, than the graph and tables would be more accurate.

Now let's analyze consumerist supply tables and graphs. Let's take our first root vegetables demand table. Here each vote equals one kilogram

- Onions- 3 kg
- Golden Potatoes- 2 kg
- White Flesh Potatoes- 2 kg
- Radishes- 2 kg
- Yams- 1 kg
- Beets- 1 kg

A farmer grows root vegetables in order to make a profit; i.e. to spend on the accommodational and laissez-faire sectors. All root vegetables in our example are 0.35 ⊙ /kg regardless of which vegetable. It would make the most sense if our farmer grows the root vegetables that are desired. 4 kg of carrots are demanded but just 1 kg of beets is demanded. If the farmer grew 4 kg of carrots he would sell them all. If he grows 1 kg of beets he would also sell them all. How about if he plants 6 kg of carrots and 0.5 kg of beets? He would have too many carrots and the possibility of selling 0.5 kg more of beets. It would make the most sense if the farmer planted root vegetables in the exact same ratio as they are demanded. That is, carrots, onions, golden potatoes in a 4:3:2 ratio. So it seems that the supply curve coincides with the demand curve. The producer will make the most money when he makes goods or offers services in the way that they are demanded.

Let's go back to our automobile graph from the beginning.

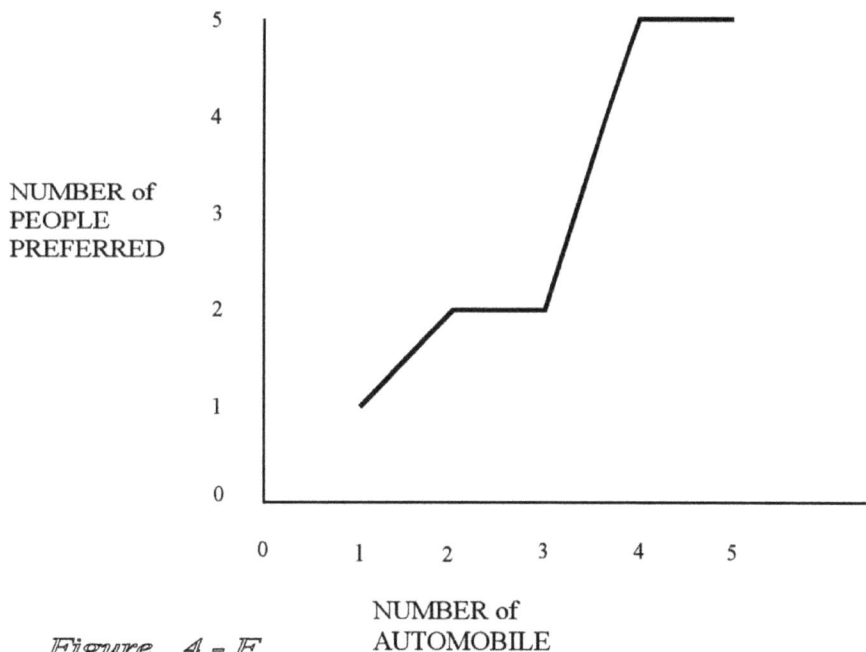

Figure 4 - F

Figure 4-F

In this case producers will produce more limousines than European Sports Cars, more European Sports Cars than Foreign Compact Cars and more Foreign Compact Cars than Domestic Economy Cars. All automobiles have the same price. Since more consumerists prefer limousines than Foreign Compact Cars, more limousines will be sold than Foreign Compact Cars. Thus producers have an incentive to produce limousines over Foreign Compact Cars. Therefore the shape of the consumerist supply curve should have the same shape as the consumerist demand curve.

We construct a graph for wine. There are four wines to choose from: a South American wine, a Californian wine, a French wine and an Australian wine. We poll 1000 people. Each person has 3 choices and each choice represents a litre of wine. The results of the poll are:

- South American-   1500 L
- Californian-   750 L
- French-   500 L
- Australian-   250 L

The graph looks like this: (We label each point: A- South American, B- Californian. C- French, D- Australian)

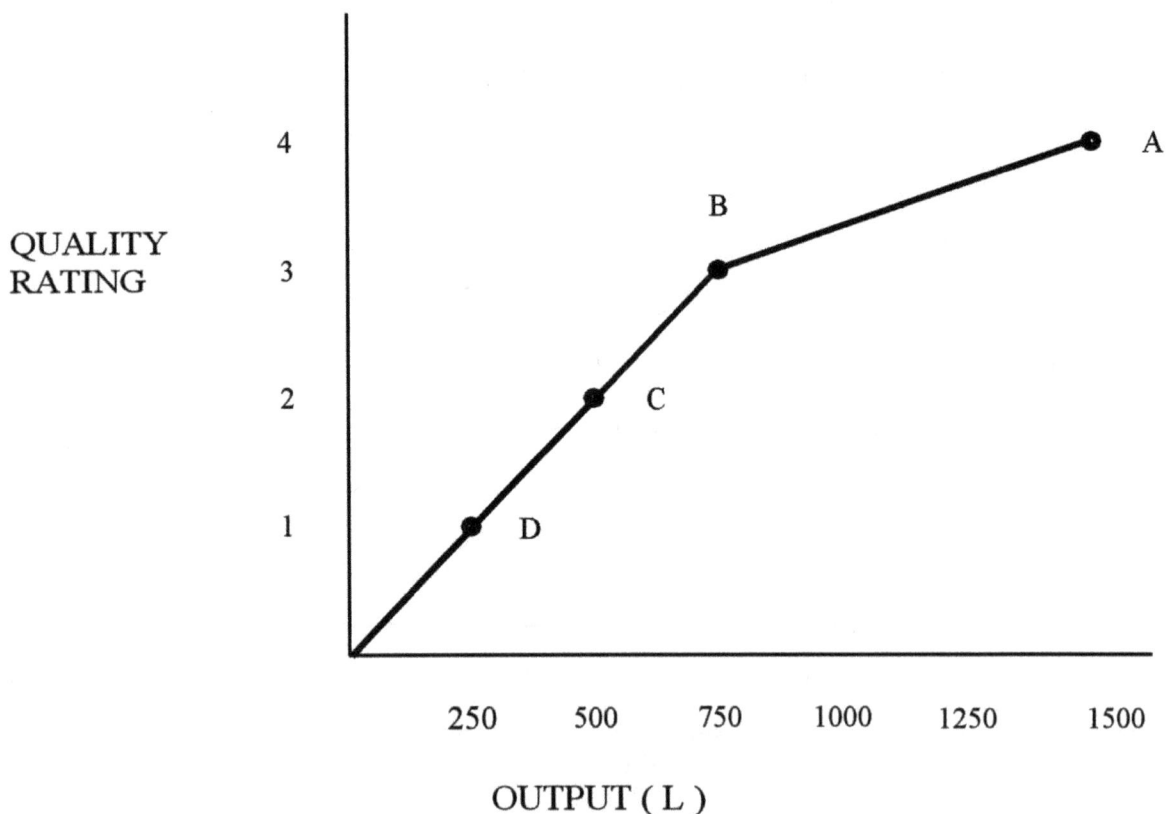

Figure 4 - G

Figure 4-G

228

Now we find out how much each wine maker is able to bring to the market. The supply table looks like this:

- South American 1000 L
- French 1000 L
- Californian 1000 L
- Australian 1000 L

The consumerist supply curve would then look like this (The points are: A- South American, B- French, C- Californian, D- Australian)

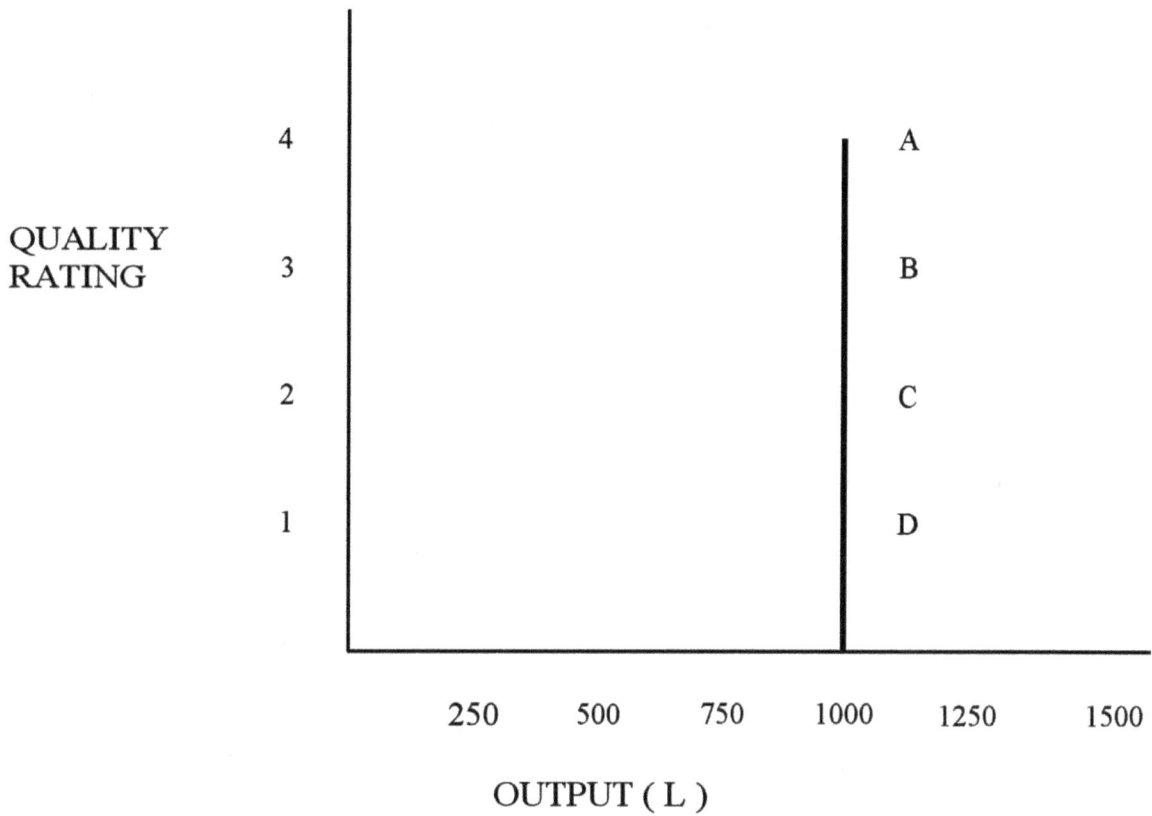

Figure 4 - H

Figure 4-H

If we put both the supply and demand curves together we get: (The labelled points are: A- South American, B- Californian, C- French, D- Australian)

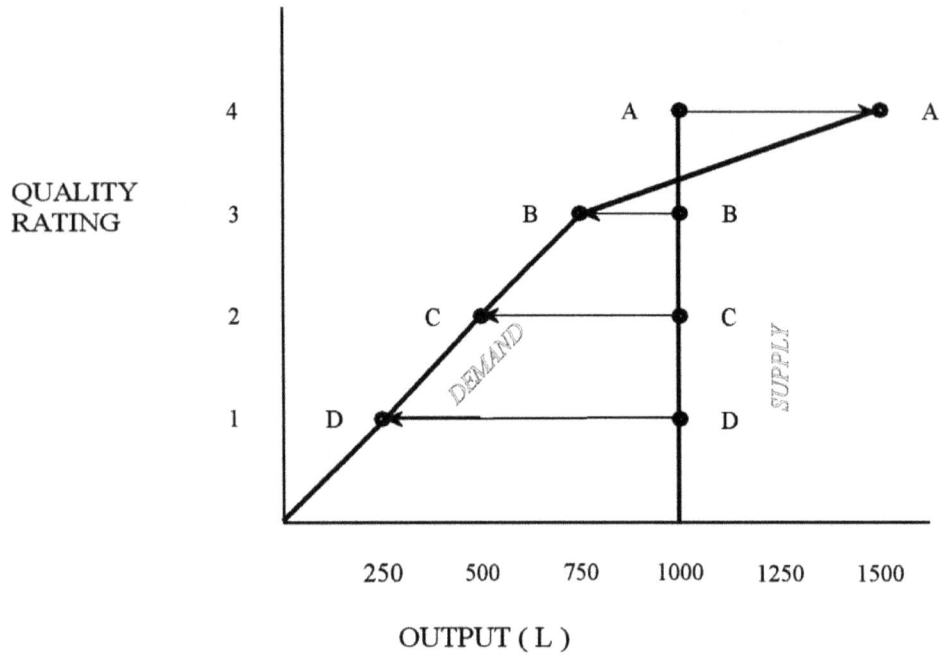

Figure 4 - I

Figure 4-I

The supply curve shifts to fall on the demand curve. If this is so then the Consumerist market is said to be at its optimal.

Here is an imaginary graph:

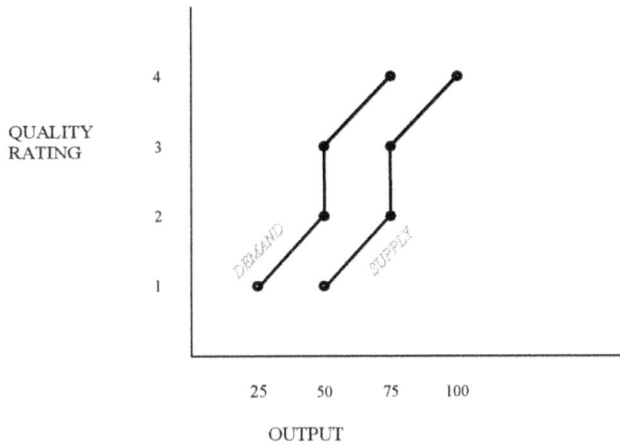

Figure 4 - J

Figure 4-J

When for a given product the supply curve is to the right of the demand curve, the market is said to be in surplus for that good. Likewise if the demand curve is to the right of the supply curve there is a shortage. Both situations fix themselves as both curves try to coincide with one another,

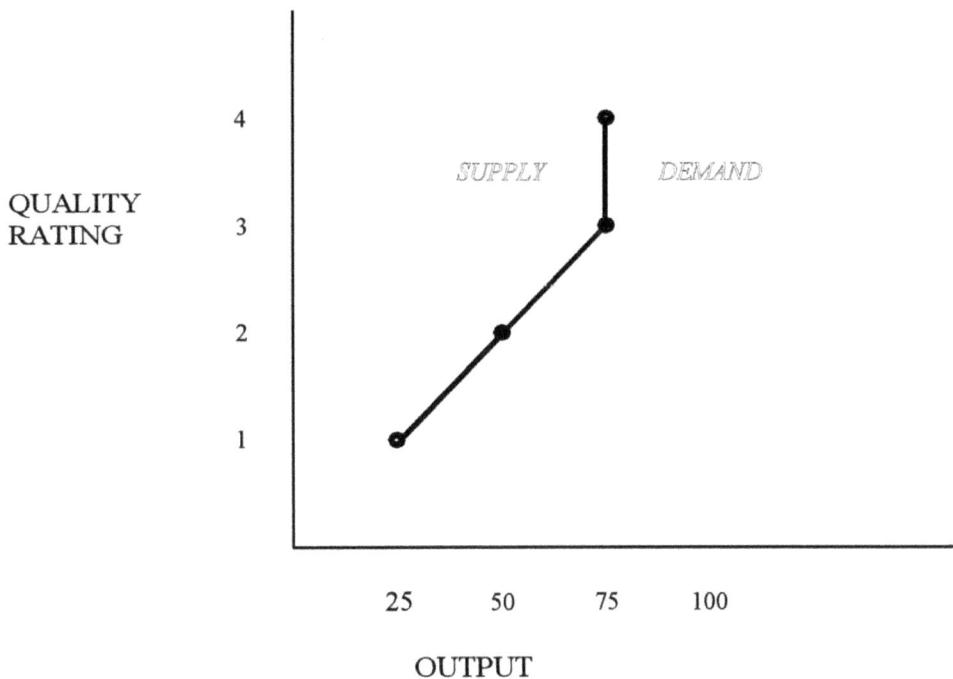

Figure 4 - K

Figure 4-K

The most interesting and informative demand graphs are those where the goods or services are given a quality rating from 1 to 10. The products or services in a market are given a quality rating based on how much of them are demanded.

Assume that there are 30 000 consumerists. We are interested in a limited time frame. Let's say it is a month and this is how often the central bank grants money to consumerists. The price of wine is 0.50 þ /litre. We omit the retail mark-up for the time being. 100 000 litres of wine are bought in the market. The demand schedule is:

- Australian-   40 000 L
- Californian-   30 000 L
- South American-   20 000 L
- French-   10 000 L
-

The consumerist demand curve looks like this: We label the points: A- Australian, B- Californian, C- South American- D- French.

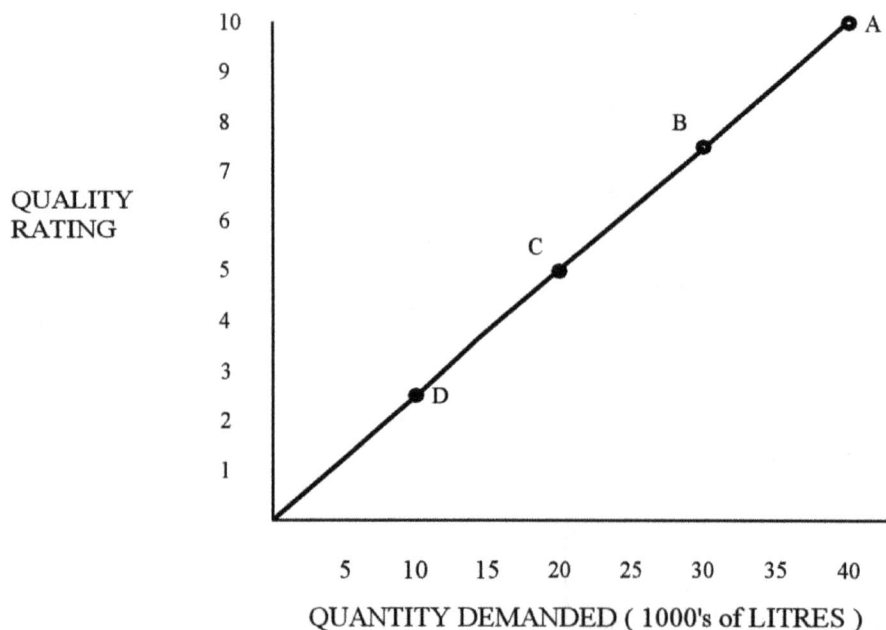

Figure   4 - L

Figure 4-L

French wine has a quality rating of 2.5. South American wine has a quality rating of 5. Californian wine has a quality rating of 7.5 and Australian wine has a quality rating of 10. We will soon see how these quality ratings were calculated.

What could change this graph? There are four main causes. They are:

1) The introduction of a newer and better product of a particular family in this case wine. An example is the introduction of Polish wine.
2) A change of taste. People may prefer South American to Australian wine
3) The number of consumerists who want to buy wine changes or there is a change in how much wine existing consumerists buy.
4) There is an increase in income (or there is a decrease). If consumerists are granted more (or less) money they can buy more (or less) wine.

Let's analyze the effects of these adjustments to our wine market (as an example). First let's see what happens when there is another new product. Suppose that there is a new wine on the market- Polish wine. Everything else is the same (ceteris paribus). All other factors are kept constant. *Ceteris Paribus* is a Latin expression meaning "all things remaining equal."

232

So our new consumerist demand schedule looks like this. There are 100 000 L of wine bought and wine costs 0.50 þ /litre regardless of type. We ignore the retail mark-up

- Polish wine-   40 000 L
- Australian wine-   30 000 L
- Californian wine-   15 000 L
- South American wine   10 000 L
- French wine-   5 000 L

Our new graph is: (The labelled points are; A- Polish, B- Australian, C- Californian, D- South American, E- French)

Figure 4-M

Figure 4-M

To determine quality ratings we do the following. We set the family leader's quality rating equal to 10. Polish wine automatically receives a quality rating of 10 as it is demanded the most. We use a formula that uses ratios to determine the quality ratings of the other wines. The formula has the form

$10/A = x/B$

Where A is equal to the family leader's demand. B is equal to the demand of the wine being sought and x is the particular wine's quality rating. Let's do the calculations for the four other types of wines.

We know Polish wine has a quality rating of 10.

Australian wine- $10/40\ 000 = x/30\ 000$
x= 7.5

Therefore Australian wine has a quality rating of 7.5

Californian wine- $10/40\ 000 = x/15\ 000$
x = 3.75

233

South American wine- $10/40\,000 = x/10\,000$
$x = 2.5$

French wine- $10/40\,000 = x/5\,000$
$x = 1.25$

So to summarize, Polish wine has a quality rating of 10. Australian wine has a quality rating of 7.5. Californian wine has a quality rating of 3.75. South American wine has a quality rating of 2.5. French wine has a quality rating of 1.25. This is shown in the graph we drew above
.

Let's analyze what happens when people change their tastes. They for some reason like the taste of one wine over another. This may be caused by aggressive advertising or by a study that indicates that one type of wine is better for one's health than another. We will stay with our original four wines.

A new consumerist demand schedule could look like this (still 100 000 L of wine is bought and the price is 0.50 þ/L)

- South American   50 000 L
- Australian   25 000 L
- French   20 000 L
- Californian   5 000 L

We now determine the quality ratings

South American	10 (it is the family leader)
Australian	$10/50\,000 = x/25\,000$
$X = 5$	
French	$10/50\,000 = x/20\,000$
$X = 4$	
Californian	$10/50\,000 = x/5\,000$
$X = 1$	

Our graph looks like this

Figure 4-N

Figure 4-N

We could label points corresponding to the wines. Let A represent South American wine, B represent Australian wine, C French wine, and let D represent Californian wine. It appears that our graph is a straight line.

Now we will see what happens when there are more consumerists in the market than before. This could happen if more people immigrate to our society. This would naturally increase the number of litres of wine bought. Instead of 100 000 L of wine bought, 200 000 L of wine are bought. The price of wine is 0.50þ /L. We will use the same few types of wines. Everything else is ceteris paribus. Our new consumerist demand schedule could look like this:

- South American wine   90 000 L
- Californian wine   60 000 L
- Australian wine   40 000 L
- French wine   10 000 L
-

Our quality ratings are:

South American wine-   10

Californian wine $10/90\ 000 = x/60\ 000$
$X = 6.7$

Australian wine $10/90\ 000 = x/40\ 000$
$X = 4.4$

French wine $10/90\ 000 = x/10\ 000$
$X = 1.1$

Our graph is

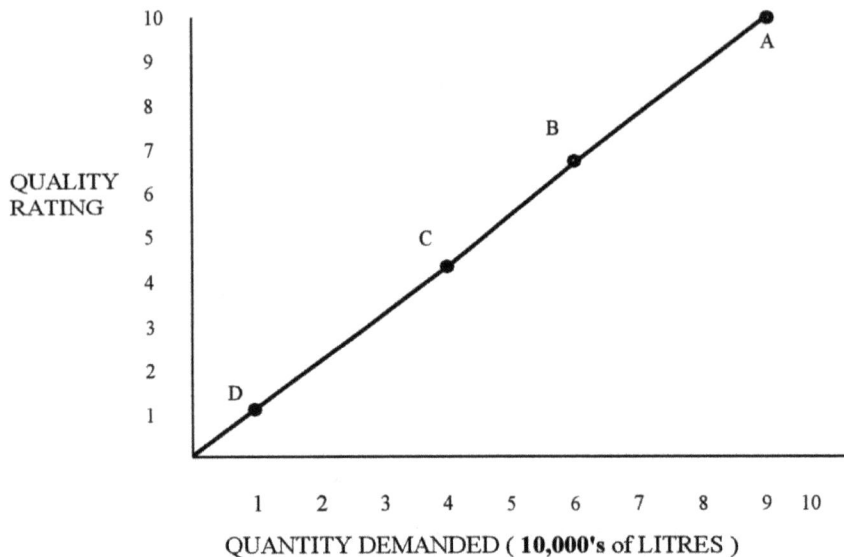

QUALITY RATING (y-axis, 1–10)
QUANTITY DEMANDED (**10,000's** of LITRES) (x-axis, 1–10)

Figure 4 - O

Figure 4-O

Where: A stands for South American wine
          B stands for Californian wine
          C stands for Australian wine
          D stands for French wine

Now let's see what happens when consumerist's income increases. This occurs when there is growth in the materialist sector or there is a cut in taxes or there is a birth in the household. With a higher income consumerists are able to buy more. Almost the same thing happens in this case as when there are more consumerists because the net effect is more wine bought.

Now let's analyze the supply of goods and services. Suppose we have four makers of wine and that one maker of wine cannot make another type of wine. So we have an Australian wine maker, a French wine maker, a Californian wine maker and a South American wine maker.

Each wine maker wants to make money. This is his incentive for working. The more money he earns the more he can spend on the accommodational and laissez-faire sectors; i.e. he can buy land, a house or pay bills. It is also true that each producer wants to make as much money as possible. If a producer makes less wine than is demanded he can increase his profit by making more of that type of wine. If a producer makes more wine than is demanded than he has extra wine on his hands. When a wine maker makes as much wine as is demanded than we have a situation we will call equilibrium.

Let's analyze a particular consumerist supply schedule

- French wine   50 000 L
- Australian wine   50 000 L
- Californian wine   50 000 L
- South American wine 50 000 L

We can superimpose both the demand and supply curves on one graph as follows:

236

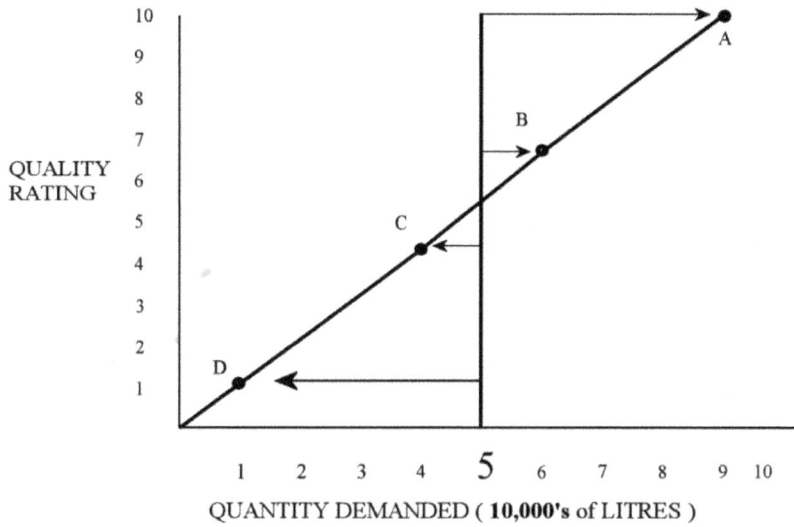

Figure 4-P

Figure 4-P

The point of intersection does not have any real significance. The quality ratings are the same as for the demand schedule. If a product is in greater supply then it does not necessarily have a greater quality rating. Quality ratings are determined by the demand schedule. The supply curve has a tendency to coincide exactly with the demand curve. In this condition consumerists are buying all they want and suppliers are selling all they have.

If there is a shortage for a product then either

1) Producers will make more of it, or
2) It will be imported from another country

If there is a surplus than either:

1) Producers will make less of the product
2) The product will be exported to another country

It is a good thing if the supply curve is a bit more to the right than the demand curve. This indicates an expanding economy. Both the demand and the supply curves slope in the same direction.

Let's go back to our automobile example. The consumerist demand schedule looks like this. (Each car costs 1000.00 Θ). 10 000 automobiles are demanded.

- Limousine-   5 000
- European Sports Car-   3 000
- Foreign Compact Car-   1 000
- Domestic Economy Car-   500
- Foreign Economy Car-   500

A retail mark-up of 20% means that the automobiles cost 1200.00 Θ at the dealership.

The quality ratings are as follows:

A) Limousine-
   10
A) European Sports Car $10/5\ 000 = x/3000$
        X = 6
B) Foreign Compact Car $10/5\ 000 = x/1\ 000$
        X = 2
C) Domestic Economy Car $10/5\ 000 = x/500$
        X = 1
D) Foreign Economy Car $10/5\ 000 = x/500$
        X = 1

The demand curve looks like this:

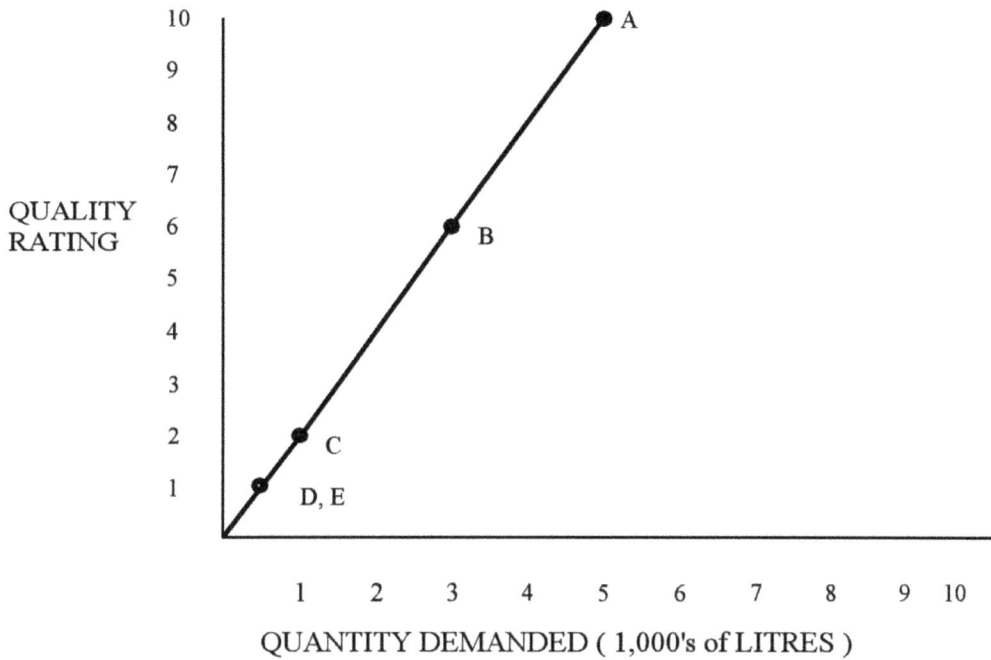

Figure 4-Q

Figure 4-Q

The consumerist supply schedule looks like this:

A) Limousine-   5000
B) European Sports Car-   4000
C) Foreign Compact Car-   1000
D) Domestic Economy Car-   2000
E) Foreign Economy Car-   250

Each automobile sells for 1 000.00 Θ. It is sold to car dealerships who make a 20% profit (retail mark-up) of 200.00 þ/car. The cars the dealership buys depend on the cars consumerists buy from the dealership. The same quality ratings used for demand curves are used for supply curves; i.e. we do not calculate new ratings based on how much of a good is sold or produced. For example, if a product has a quality rating of 4 calculated by how much it was demanded, it will have a quality rating of 4 on its supply curve regardless of how much it was supplied. The supply curve looks like this. In general it is not a straight line.

Figure 4-R

We now put the two together:

Figure 4-S

Here A represents limousines, B represents European Sports Cars, C represents Foreign Compact Cars, D represents Domestic Economy Cars and E represents Foreign Economy Cars. In the above graph, 5000 limousines were purchased and 5000 were demanded so they are in equilibrium. The same is for Foreign Compact Cars; 1000 were made and 1000 were demanded. Thus Foreign Compact Cars are also in equilibrium. In the case of Foreign Economy Cars only 250 were made but 500 were supposed to be bought. 250 Foreign Economy Cars could have been bought/sold. The makers of Foreign Economy Cars step up their production of Foreign

240

Economy Cars or else car dealers import Foreign Economy Cars from a foreign country. From the curves we can see that the number of European Sports Cars and Domestic Economy Cars made and sold to car dealers is higher than the amount bought. Although this would lead to a surplus of both European Sports Cars and Domestic Economy Cars at a car dealership, this actually spurs on the economy. The reason being that for every Domestic Economy Car and European Sports Car at a car dealership (it is directly available to consumerists) the equivalent of their value (number of automobiles x price) is counted towards the GDCP which is tabulated by the central bank and given to consumerists. As more consumerists have more income they will be able to buy more automobiles. The economy is driven by surplus.

Now let's analyze the consumerist supply curve and schedule. There are 3 main factors that affect quantity supplied.

1) Technology- if a firm creates a machine for making its products more efficiently it can produce more of that product.
2) Number of sellers- if a firm makes the same product as another, the original can't sell or produce as much
3) Invention or innovation- if a firm makes a product which is more preferable than any others in its family, it will sell more of this product and other firms will produce and sell less of theirs

Suppose that in our example the Foreign Compact Car makers find a robot for every part of the manufacturing process. This saves money otherwise spent on human workers. The firm now earns more money on each automobile (1000 þ minus manufacturing costs) and makes more automobiles for the same cost. A schedule could look like this

	Original	After technological change
Limousine	5 000	5 000
European Sports Car-	4 000	4 000
Foreign Compact Car-	1 000	3 000
Domestic Economy Car-	2 000	2 000
Foreign Economy Car-	250	250

The only difference (ceteris paribus) here is that Foreign Compact Car has made technology that makes its production more efficient; i.e. replacing human labourers with robots. The curve is:

Figure 4 - T

Figure 4-T

Let's see what happens to our graph and schedule when the numbers of sellers increases. Suppose another company starts making limousines

	Original	With a new limousine company
Limousine	5 000	10 000
European Sports Car-	4 000	4 000
Foreign Compact Car-	1 000	1 000
Domestic Economy Car-	2 000	2 000
Foreign Economy Car-	250	250

In this case there are now more limousines made.

A graph of both schedules looks like this

OUTPUT (1,000's of CARS SUPPLIED)

Figure   4 - U

Figure 4-U

Another factor that can change our consumerist supply schedule or graph is (ceteris paribus) if a new firm produces an original invention that improves the products in a family. For example a firm invents a flying automobile. We first need to give it a quality rating. We go back to the demand schedule. Originally the demand schedule looked like this. There were 10 000 cars demanded.

Limousine	5000
European Sports Car	3 000
Foreign Compact Car	1 000
Domestic Economy Car	500
Foreign Economy Car	500

The quality ratings were:

Limousine	10
European Sports Car	6
Foreign Compact Car	2
Domestic Economy Car	1
Foreign Economy Car	1

With the addition of a new product (flying car) the schedule could look like this:

Flying car-	5000
Limousine	3000
European Sports Car	1 000
Foreign Compact Car	500

| Domestic Economy Car | 400 |
| Foreign Economy Car | 100 |

The new quality ratings would then be:

Flying car   10
Limousine $10/5000 = x/3000$
X= 6
European Sports Car $10/5000 = x/1000$
X =2
Foreign Compact Car $10/5000 = x/500$
X = 1
Domestic Economy Car $10/5000 = x/400$
X = 0.8
Foreign Economy Car $10/5000 = x/100$
X = 0.2

Our flying car has a quality rating of 10. More people buy it and less of the other automobiles. Now let's see a consumerist supply schedule

			Quality rating
A-	Flying car-	6 000	10
B-	Limousine	5 000	6
C-	European Sports Car	4 000	2
D-	Foreign Compact Car	1 000	1
E-	Domestic Economy Car	2 000	0.8
F-	Foreign Economy Car	250	0.2

Our new consumerist supply graph is:

QUALITY RATING

OUTPUT (1,000's of CARS SUPPLIED)

Figure 4 - V

Figure 4-V

245

Now let's put both the supply and demand curves together:

Figure 4 - W

Figure 4-W

We mentioned almost everything we could about these graphs. Our analysis of the Consumerist Trade market is over. The general conclusion we get from the analysis of the Consumerist Trade market is that the good of the highest quality rating, that is the one most favoured in its family, is the one bought, produced and sold most. With the knowledge gained here we will be able to understand how everything else works in this system.

The Laissez-Faire Trade Market

We talked in the previous section about the consumerist trade market. The consumerist trade market pertains to the accomodational and materialist sectors. Now, let's discuss the laissez-faire trade market. This pertains to how the market in the laissez-faire sector is organized.
.

The laissez-faire sector is pure capitalism. It is what the economic philosopher Adam Smith would want in an economic system. It is ruled by the laws of supply and demand vs. price.

The laissez-faire trade market represents the purest of pure capitalism. It is organized along the lines of a true free market economy. There are no taxes (at all) and unemployment and inflation are reduced. There is also no minimum wage. All economic transactions are left alone to the actors in the laissez-faire sector.

We will use two different types of goods as examples for this section of the book. One is a gold ring. The other is a book called "Guide to Wild Birds".

In the upcoming discussion we will use several imaginary people as examples. Our buyers are Michael and Chris. Our producers are John and Carol.

The laissez-faire trade market is peculiar to the laissez-faire sector. Thus Fortals are used. In this sector all business decisions (with perhaps a few exceptions to control inflation) are determined by the interaction of buyers and sellers.

Most of the information that we discuss in this section is already common knowledge. Most economists, business people and economy students and professors know how a free market is organized. However, for those unfamiliar with the functioning of the free market system, the upcoming discussion will be quite useful.

The laissez-faire trade market is predicated on the laws of supply and demand vs. price. Let's talk about demand first.

We will make the assumption that the laissez-faire trade market is a perfectly competitive market. Although this is not always true in reality, it is nevertheless a useful assumption. By the proposition that the laissez-faire trade market is perfectly competitive we mean that A) the goods being offered are all the same or are very, very similar and B) there are so many consumerists and producers that the price determined by our market is not influenced by any single one of them.

We define "quantity demanded" of a product as the total of that produced that consumerists in the laissez-faire sector are comfortable of exchanging for Fortals. Quantity demanded is influenced by several factors including: price, future prospects, economic revenue, price of associated goods and personal preferences.

If we only allow for changes in price and control all the other variables we can begin to understand how quantity demanded and price interact. Generally speaking, the higher the price of a product or service the less people want to buy it (keeping all other variables fixed) and the lower the price of a product or service, the more people want to buy that product. This is known as the *law of demand*. (Kneebone, R.D. et al, 2002)

Let's take the case of Michael buying a golden ring. At different prices Michael would buy different amounts of gold rings. We can display this on a "demand schedule".

Price of Gold Ring	Quantity Demanded of Golden Rings
0.00 ₤	20
50.00 ₤	18
100.00 ₤	16
150.00 ₤	14
200.00 ₤	12
250.00 ₤	10

A different consumerist, Chris, may have a different demand schedule. It may be,

Price of Gold Ring	Quantity Demanded of Golden Rings
0.00 ₤	15
50.00 ₤	12
100.00 ₤	9
150.00 ₤	6
200.00 ₤	3
250.00 ₤	0

They can be combined into one *market demand schedule*.

Price of Gold Ring	Quantity Demanded of Golden Rings		
	Michael	Chris	Market
0.00 ₤	20	15	35
50.00 ₤	18	12	30
100.00 ₤	16	9	25
150.00 ₤	14	6	20
200.00 ₤	12	3	15
250.00 ₤	10	0	10

These can be displayed graphically in a *market demand curve*.

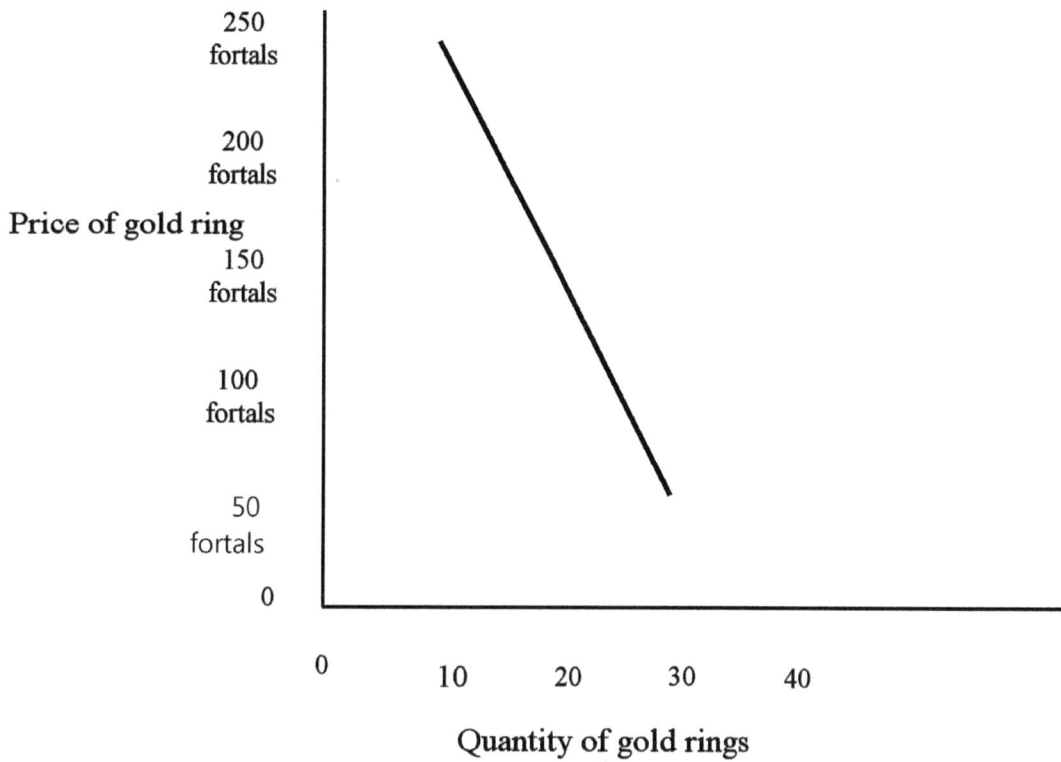

Figure 5 - A

Figure 5A

The demand curve itself can shift. The demand curve adjusts to the right if there is a change that increases the amount consumerists want to buy at a fixed price. The demand curve shifts to the left if there is a change that decreases the amount consumerists want to buy at a fixed price. We can understand these ideas graphically as:

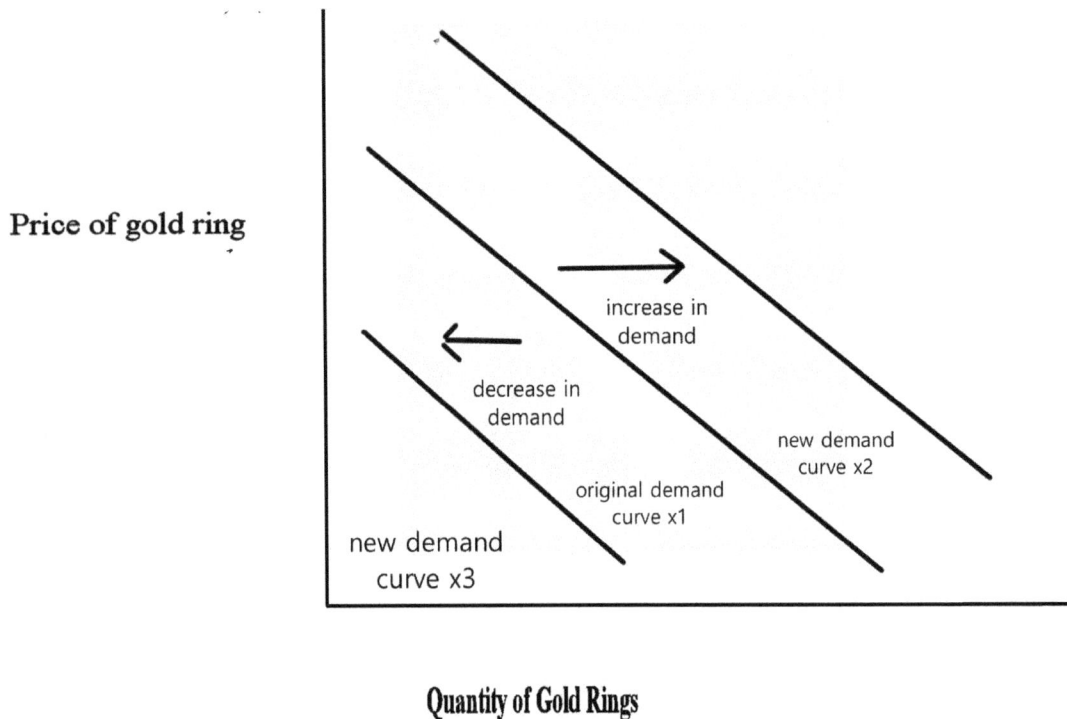

Price of gold ring

increase in demand

decrease in demand

new demand curve x2

original demand curve x1

new demand curve x3

Quantity of Gold Rings

Figure 5 - B

Figure 5 B

Now let's turn to supply. *Quantity supplied* of a product is the quantity that producers are happy to sell their products in exchange for Fortals. Like demand, supply is influenced by several factors. They are price, input costs, level of technological sophistication and future considerations.

Generally speaking, when the price of a good or service increases, the quantity of that good or service put on the market increases (other things being equal). Conversely, if the price of a product or service decreases the quantity of that good put on the market also decreases. This is known as the *law of supply*. Quantity supplied and price rise in the same direction. (Kneebone, R.D. et al, 2002)

Like we did for quantity demanded we can construct supply schedules for certain consumerists. A supply schedule is an illustration that displays how changes in price respond to changes in quantity supplied. We will use golden rings as an example. We have two producers that supply golden rings: John and Carol. Their supply schedules might look like this:

John's Supply Schedule

Price of Golden Ring	Quantity of Gold Ring Supplied
0 £	8
50.00 £	9
100.00 £	10

250

150.00 £	11
200.00 £	12
250.00 £	13

Carrol's Supply Schedule

Price of Golden Ring	Quantity of Gold Ring Supplied
0 £	0
50.00 £	3
100.00 £	6
150.00 £	9
200.00 £	12
250.00 £	15

Now we can construct a market supply schedule. The market supply schedule is the sum of the individual supply schedules of all producers in our market for that product or service. The market supply schedule is influenced by several factors: They are price, input costs, level of technological sophistication and future considerations.

Price of Golden Ring	Quantity of Gold Ring Supplied		
	John	Carrol	Market
0 £	8	0	8
50.00 £	9	3	12
100.00 £	10	6	16
150.00 £	11	9	20
200.00 £	12	12	24
250.0 £	13	15	28

From the market supply schedule we can create the market supply curve. The market supply curve tells us the relationship between the market price of a golden ring in fortals and the market quantity of golden rings put on the market.

Figure 5 - C   Quantity of Gold Rings

Figure 5 C

Like the demand curve, the supply curve can also shift. If something increases the amount of products that sellers want to put on the market at a certain price this moves the supply curve to the right. Also, if something decreases the amount of products that sellers want to put on the market at a certain price, this moves the supply curve to the left.

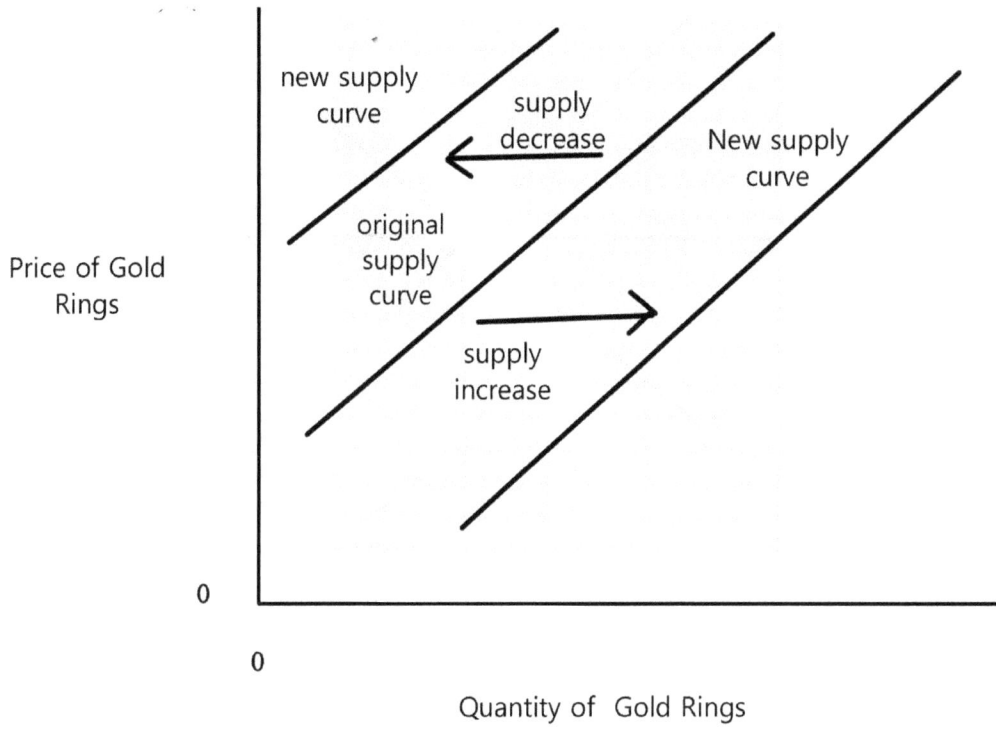

new supply
curve

supply
decrease

New supply
curve

Price of Gold
Rings

original
supply
curve

supply
increase

0

0

Quantity of Gold Rings

Figure 5 - D

Figure 5 D

Now we put the supply and demand curves together. So,

Figure 5 - E

Price of Gold Rings (Fortals)

Quantity of Gold Rings

Figure 5E

In the above figure there are three important things. The equilibrium is the condition where supply and demand balance themselves out. The special equilibrium price is the amount in Fortals at which demand and supply are balanced. Lastly, the special equilibrium quantity is the amount demanded and amount supplied at the point where price has been able to balance demand and supply.

The *law of supply and demand* states that the price (in Fortals) of a product or service balances to make supply and demand in equilibrium. However, there are sometimes surpluses and shortages.

A surplus is the circumstance where quantity demanded is less than quantity supplied. In a surplus of a product, let's say books, producers are incapable of selling all they wish to at the price. The laissez-faire response to a surplus is to cut prices. Prices are forced to decrease to the point where the market reaches equilibrium again. Here is a picture of a surplus of books.

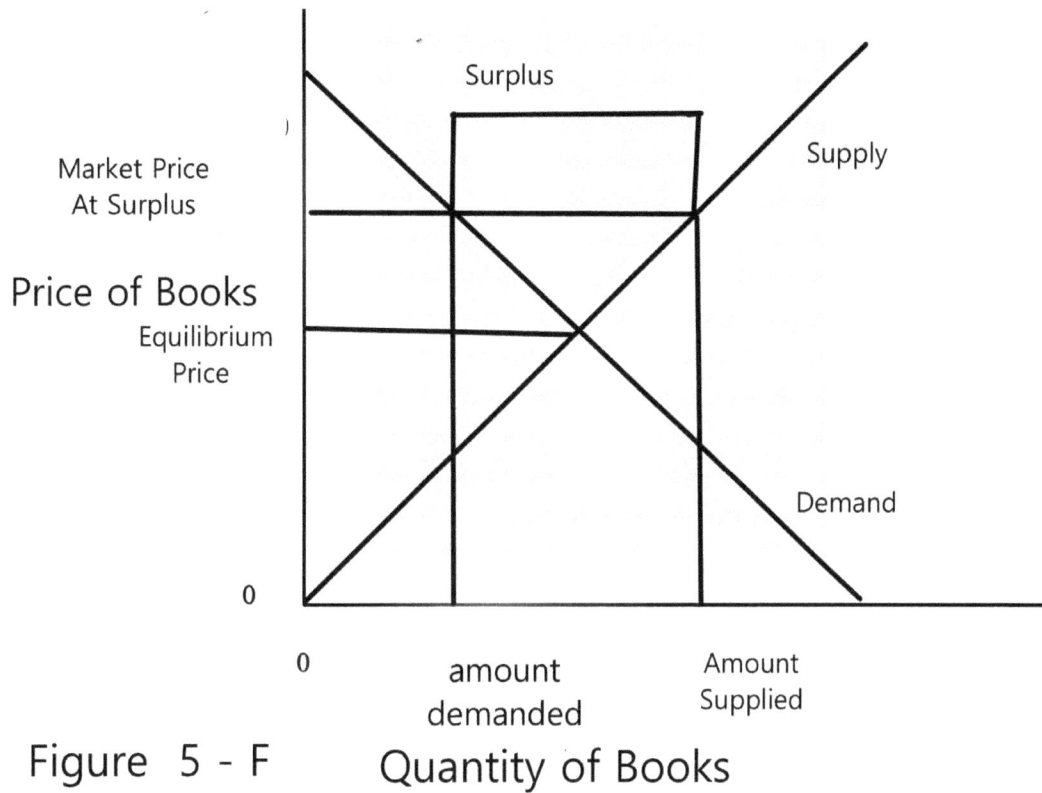

Figure 5 - F

Figure 5F

A shortage is the circumstance where quantity supplied is less than quantity demanded. This occurs when the market price is less than the equilibrium price. Consumerists are incapable of purchasing all they wish at the market price. The solution to this in the laissez-faire trade market is to raise prices. Prices rise until the market price reaches a balance with the equilibrium price. Here is the case of a shortage of books in graphical form:

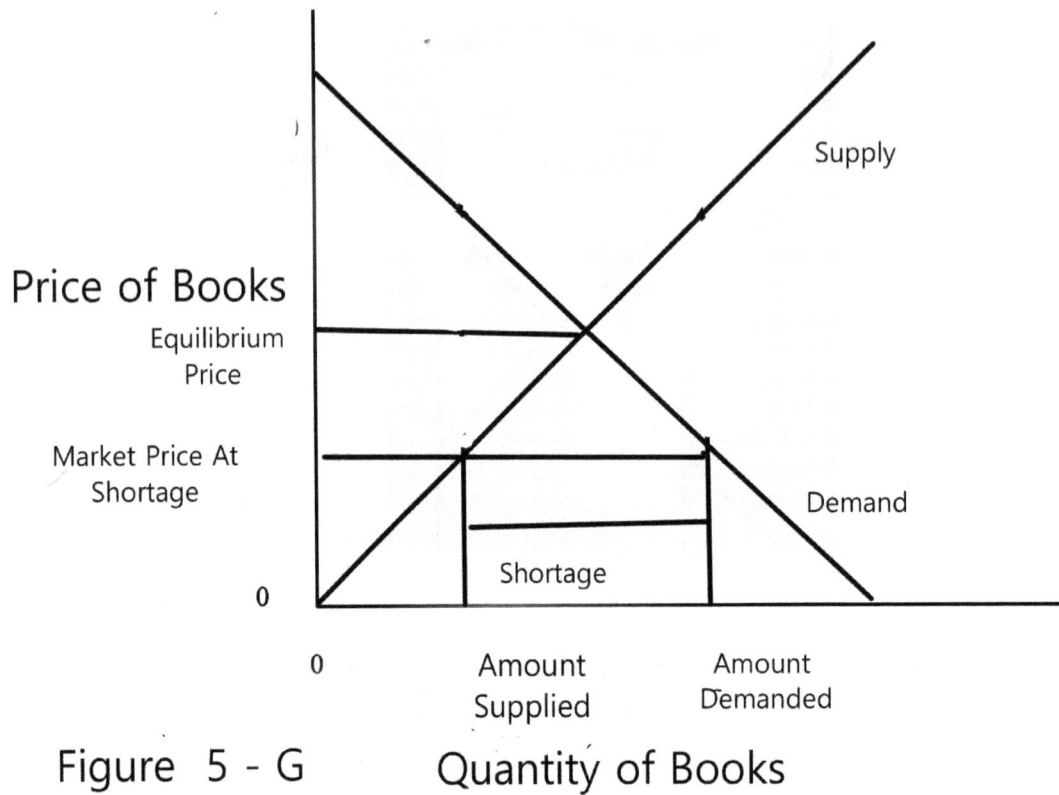

Figure 5 - G

Figure 5G

The laissez-faire market works quite similarly to a market in the free enterprise system. The laws of supply and demand work to determine the equilibrium price. The equilibrium price and equilibrium quantity put on the market prevent the occurrence of shortages and surpluses.

Interest Rates

Interest rates are the profit earned from lending money. They are also the cost incurred from borrowing money. People who lend money want to earn interest for lending their money. People who want to borrow money must pay interest on what they borrow.

Interest rates can apply either to the accomodational sector or the laissez-faire sector. In the laissez-faire sector they are set by supply and demand vs/ price. Interest rates in the accommodational sector are determined by the central bank. The Grand Chairman sets the interest rate. He does so once a week and without the input of the Consumerist Commissioners. Thus the interest rate is not fixed but can fluctuate freely. Whatever the Grand Chairman sets the interest rate at, all private banks and lending institutions must charge the same interest rate. The central bank is in charge of setting the interest rate that all private banks charge their clients for borrowing money in the accommodational sector.

The interest rate does not apply to all money. It only applies to Ignits and Fortals. No one can borrow Norses from the private bank, the reason being that it will distort the GDCP. For the same reason there cannot exist credit cards (in the materialist sector). A borrower can borrow Ignits to buy things in the accommodational sector but cannot borrow Norses to buy things in the materialist sector. A person can borrow money to purchase a firm or finance a mortgage. Nevertheless there remains the possibility to buy things in instalments so someone can burrow to buy a car.

There are several cases of interest rates in the laissez-faire sector. This may apply to, perhaps, mortgages. In this instance, all these interest rates are determined by the interaction of investors and firms. That is, they are governed by the forces of supply and demand. The Grand Chairman has no influence on interest rates in the laissez-faire sector.

Interest rates have a strong impact on the economy. High interest rates are good for lending and bad for borrowing. Low interest rates are bad for lenders and good for borrowers. The central bank through the Grand Chairman can manipulate the economy by adjusting the interest rate in the accommodational sector.

The interest rate at the time of borrowing/lending is the one that is in place until the debt is repaid even if the interest rate goes up or down during that time. Interest rates are compounded continuously. For example a shoe factory borrows 1000.00þ at 5%. The shoe company must pay the principle plus the interest in 3 years. This is given by the equation:

$$A = A_o e^{rt}$$

Thus in our example:

$$A = 1000.00 \text{ þ } e^{(0.05)3}$$
$$A = 1000.00 \text{ þ } e^{(0.15)} = 1\ 161.83\text{þ}$$

The shoe factory must pay this amount even though the central bank may decrease the interest rate to 4.5 % the next day.

To increase investment, stimulate the economy and lower the unemployment, the government can set an Interest Rate Stimulus (IRS). Thus the government pays a portion of the loan giving the effect that the interest rate is actually a bit lower than that set by the central bank. So suppose that the government sets the IRS at 0.5 % in the above example.
The government would pay:

$A = 1000.00$ þ $e^{(0.005)3}$
$A = 1000.00$ þ $e^{(0.015)} = 1\ 015.11$ þ.
$1\ 015.11$þ $- 1000.00$ þ $= 15.11$þ
The creditor earns $1\ 161.83$ þ
And the shoe factory pays $(1\ 161.83$ þ $- 15.11$ þ$) = 1146.72$ þ

It doesn't matter whether the interest rate is higher or lower than the accommodational markdown. The things that interest rates apply to are different than what the accommodational markdown applies to. Whereas the interest rate raises the supply of Ignits in the accommodational sector, the accommodational markdown serves to lower it.

Interest rates are the mechanism by which lenders and borrowers come together to exchange money. The interest rate is set by the Grand Chairman of the central bank when dealing with the accommodational sector. Unlike some of the other parameters set by the central bank, interest rates have the potential to fluctuate.

The Bank Rate

The concept of the bank rate is very, very important in free market capitalism. In free-market capitalism, the bank rate influences the money supply as well as the output of the economy as a whole in the short run. Theoretically, as well as practically, when the bank rate is high it can lessen the severity of an inflation or reduce it and if it is low it can spur the growth of the economy.

Like in capitalism, in consumerism the central bank is a sort of banker to private banks. If these banks need to borrow money from the central bank, they do so at the bank rate. Private banks may need money when transferring money (in the form of bank book entries) from one bank to another.

The bank rate is set as a percentage minus half a percent. This is called the "operating band". This interest rate is very, very important since private banks never need to pay a greater amount for a loan of money. Also they never need to accept less than the bank rate.

The Grand Chairman of the central bank sets the bank rate every several weeks. He can set it low to promote growth or he can set it high to curb inflation., i.e., decrease the money supply.

The raising of the bank rate to high levels is one of the least preferable ways to fight inflation as it is known that in capitalism setting a high bank rate sometimes leads to a recession. Thus when deciding on the bank rate the Grand Chairman needs to use other output maximization measures when he is setting it high to decrease inflation. Technically, any of the other anti-inflation measures are better than raising the bank rate to high levels. Any of the other 16 anti-inflationary measures would work better than raising the bank rate. The raising of the bank rate is a last resort anti-inflationary measure.

However, a very low bank rate can be considered a very useful output maximization measure. By keeping the bank rate very low, the central bank promotes investment, employment and helps the economy.

The bank rate effects the money supply. It can have an impact on output and inflation. In consumerism the bank rate is set by the Grand Chairman of the central bank. As a useful suggestion, the bank rate should be as low as possible to encourage growth and one of the other 16 anti-inflationary measures should be implemented to control inflation if an increasing money supply becomes an issue.

Surplus-Shortage Resolution Measures

It is integral to accommodation based consumerism to reduce or even eliminate surpluses and shortages. The less shortages and surpluses the better. We define a shortage as a situation where more of a group of people want something that is unavailable. We define a surplus as a situation where there are more of something than people can buy. In this section we will restrict our discussion to goods and services.

There are several shortage/surplus resolution measures in consumerism. Each is designed to reduce or eliminate a shortage or surplus in a certain market. First we will list them and then we will briefly discus them. These measures are discussed and well elaborated on in further sections of this book.

The main surplus/shortage resolution measures are:

- pure shortage and surplus resolution
- command and natural domestic shortage/surplus resolution measures
- the governmental–market shortage/surplus resolution system
- increase of scope of laissez-faire sector as a shortage/surplus resolution measure
- consumerist trade market
- equilibration of forces of supply and demand in laissez-faire sector
- international shortage/surplus resolution
- exportation and importation of goods
- global shortage resolution

In the pure shortage and surplus resolution system, firms in the command partition and natural partition work together to alleviate shortages and surpluses. When a natural partition firm is experiencing a surplus, it sells some goods to a command partition firm. When a natural partition firm is experiencing a shortage, it buys some goods from a command partition firm.

In the command and natural domestic shortage/surplus resolution system firms, whether in the command or natural partition, alter the amount of goods they put on the market. During a surplus, they scale down the production of goods or produce less of a service. During a shortage, they increase the amount of goods they bring to the market.

The Governmental-market shortage/surplus resolution system also acts to control shortages and surpluses. During a shortage, the government subsidizes a purchase so that producers have more of an incentive to sell more of a good and provide more services. During a surplus, the government takes some money from a trade so as to reduce the price of a good or service and bring supply and demand in equilibrium while preserving quality selection.

The government can also increase the scope of the laissez-faire sector so as to reduce shortages and surpluses. When the government moves an industry or a family of goods from one sector to the laissez-faire sector, it puts the goods in that industry under the control of the laws of supply and demand that are part of the laissez-faire sector. This will ensure that the shortage or surplus will be resolved.

The consumerist trade market can offset shortages and surpluses. In this market, producers try to match the amount of goods they put on the market to the amount that is desired. Also, the services providers tries to parallel the quantity of services desired.

We know from the free market system that left on their own the forces of supply and demand work to eliminate shortages and surpluses. The laissez-faire sector works along these lines. So it follows that all goods and services provided through the laissez-faire sector should be in a state of equilibrium (unless they have market power). That is, they should not be in a shortage or surplus.

Global shortage resolution works to alleviate the shortage of a good in the world economy. A command partition firm may be made to produce a certain good. Also, the government can give a monetary subsidy to natural partition firms so they have an incentive to produce a good in short supply.

Finally, we have the notion of international shortage/surplus resolution. This involves importing and exporting. When we have a surplus of a good that we don't really need, we simply export it to another country that may want it. When we have a shortage of a particular good that we need we import it from another country. If the good is in the accommodational sector, there is an entity called the consumerist trade pool commission that ensures that regardless whether we export or import, quality selection is preserved.

There are several methods at our disposal to counteract shortages and surpluses. Having less shortages and surpluses will make our system run more effectively and ensure that our resources are utilized to the fullest advantage.

Surplus, Shortage and International Trade

It is appropriate to discuss shortages and surpluses; how they arise and how to be rid of them. We begin with a definition. A surplus occurs when there is more of a good than there are people who want to buy the good. The result is that goods are not sold. In contrast a shortage occurs when there is less of a good than there are people who want to buy the good. The result is that not enough of a good is available.

The traditional free-market response to surpluses is to lower the price of the good. The traditional free-market response to a shortage is to raise the price of the good. The consumerist response to these situations is different. In most cases a surplus is remedied by the exportation of the good to a country that wants to buy the good. The remedy to a shortage is to import more of the good from countries that are willing to sell the good. Through international trade consumerist nations eliminate their surpluses and shortages.

The logic behind consumerist trade is straightforward. We export what we have an abundance of and import what we lack. So if we have too much wheat we export it to countries that want it and if we do not have enough oil we import it from countries that have an abundance of it. Furthermore we export low quality goods we don't want and import high quality goods we like. So we export used cars to countries that would love to buy them and we import sports cars.

Price is not the only factor when considering international trade. We should not import things we do not need regardless of the price. If there is too much bread and we cannot eat any more bread then there is no point in importing more. Inuit would not import snow and people in the dessert would not import sand regardless of the price of these items. We also shouldn't export things that are needed by people regardless of price. If a person walking the dessert only has a canteen of water, he would be wise not to sell it. If he sells it for a lot of money he would die of thirst and be unable to spend his money. Also, a person travelling the Arctic would not sell his clothes. Even if he sold them for a lot of money, he would freeze to death along with his money. Necessity is just as important as price when considering whether or not to buy or sell.

At the outset we must point out an important rule regarding shortages and surpluses. It is best if a shortage or surplus is at a minimum. It is better to have 3 % shortage than 5 % surplus and it is better to have 2 % surplus than 4 % shortage. The closer something is to the equilibrium, generally it is better that way. This idea universally applies to shortages and surpluses of goods, services and jobs.

We must now make a distinction between 3 fundamental types of surpluses/shortages. We will call one International, one Domestic and the third Absolute. An international surplus or shortage can be elevated simply by exporting or importing the good in question. An example is oil. If there are not enough we simply import it. Domestic shortages and surpluses cannot be gotten rid of by international trade. An example of a domestic shortage is parking space. The third surplus/shortage will be discussed at the end. There are also several special shortages/surpluses we will encounter shortly. We will first deal with international shortages/surpluses.

We now introduce the concept of the *consumerist trade pool*. The consumerist trade pool is a trading fund operated by the central bank where excess profits from exporting and importing are used to subsidize the importing and exporting of other goods. There are four possible scenarios. We deal with each of them in turn.

In the first case there are 1000 too many chairs in the economy. For the purpose of this section let's assume that the retail mark-up is 25%. The price of a chair from the factory is 20.00 þ. If the chair were sold to a retailer it would cost a consumerist 20.00 Θ + 0.25 x 20.00 Θ = 25.00 Θ. A quality market graph could look like this where sofas (D) have a rating of 2, stools (C) have a rating of 3, chairs (B) have a rating of 5 and rocking chairs (A) have a rating of 10.

Figure 6-A

Figure 6-A

Since there are 1000 excess chairs, they should be exported. We assume that the exchange rate is 1$ = 1þ.We will deal with exchange rates in detail later on. Keep in mind that 1.00 Θ = 1.00 þ but that they cannot be exchanged directly for one another. The international market equilibrium price for a chair is $ 30.00 and the factory exports the 1000 chairs to a foreign country, let's say the U.S. We will use the U.S. as our trading partner throughout this section. During exporting the chair factory earns 30.00 þ per chair since 1$ =1 þ in this example. The chair factory earns profit in Ignits not in Norses. The chair factory's international trade profit is (30.00 þ– 20.00 þ) x 1000 = 10 000.00 þ. However the chair factory does not keep this extra profit. Rather it earns as much as it would earn if it sold those chairs to retailers in the consumerist nation at 20.00 þ per chair. They would earn 20.00 þ x 1000 = 20 000.00 þ. The 10 000 þ from the international trade goes to the trade pool. The reason that this factory must not earn a higher profit from exporting is that it would then choose to export rather than sell internally. This is how the consumerist trade pool factors in when a firm is exporting to a nation where the price of the good in the foreign nation is higher than in ours.

We now move onto a different case. Unless the consumerist nation has a natural source of oil, it is likely that the nation will require to import oil. Suppose that the nation needs 1000 L of oil. The price of oil in the consumerist nation is 0.50Ө/L and since the retail mark-up is 25%, the gas station charges 0.50 Ө + (0.25 x 0.50 Ө) = 0.625 Ө /L. A quality market graph might look like this:

Flammable Gas

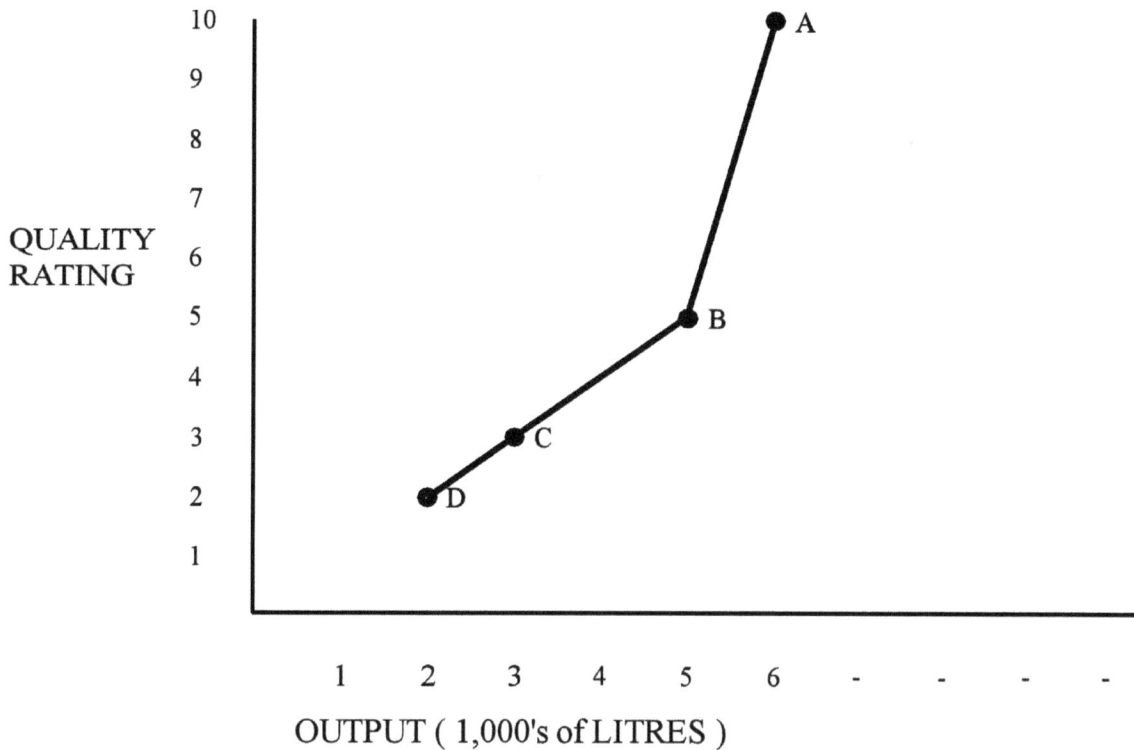

Figure 6-B

Figure 6-B

Where oil (A) has a quality rating of 10, propane (B) has a quality rating of 5, natural gas (C) has a quality rating of 3 and kerosene (D) has a quality rating of 2.

The international price of oil is $0.30 per litre and the consumerist nation imports the 1000 L of oil. Since in our example 1$ = 1þ our nation pays 0.30 þ per litre thus paying the foreign nation a total of 1000 L x 0.30 þ /L = 300.00 þ. The oil is directly imported by gas retailers which bear the cost of transportation. During the trade they create 1000 L x 0.625 þ /L = 625.00 þ. The gas retailers earn 125.00 þ (625.00 þ – 500.00 þ). Actually they make a bit less than this due to transportation, advertising and other costs. The trade pool profits 500.00 þ – 300.00 þ = 200.00 þ. This helps to offset the subsidies in cases we will see next.

Let's move onto another case. Here exporting takes place when the international market equilibrium price (say the price in the U.S.) is higher than the consumerist price. Suppose we have too much ketchup. We have an excess of 5000 bottles of ketchup. The consumerist price is 2.00 þ and the product at the retail level costs 2.50 Θ. A quality market graph might look like this. Where D stands for mustard, C stands for ketchup, B stands for relish and A stands for mayonnaise.

Condiments

Figure 6-C

Figure 6-C

The international market price is $1.50. The trade is subsidized. The trade pool gives each bottle an extra 0.50 þ. So the trade deficit in the trade pool is 5000 x 0.50 þ = 2 500.00 þ. The domestic ketchup makers and exporters earn 2.00 þ x 5000 = 10 000.00 þ. This is one case where the trade pool has to subsidize.

Another case involves imports. Suppose that we have few automobiles and we need another 50 cars. The consumerist factory price is 10 000.00 þ and the retail price is 12 500.00 Θ per car. The international market equilibrium price is $20 000.00 per car. A quality market graph might look like this:

Automobiles

Figure 6-D

Figure 6-D

Where A is limousines, B is S.U.V.'s, C is minivans and D is sports cars. Here the trade pool pays a subsidy of $10 000.00 = 10 000.00 þ per car and the retailers are the importers so the retail profit is 50 x (12 500.00 þ – 10 000.00 þ) = 50 x 2 500 þ = 125 000.00 þ. Although retailers make a profit the trade pool is decreased.

The trade pool is designed to balance the profits from the first and second cases and the losses from the third and fourth cases. We calculate the trade pool balance from the above examples:

Case 1	+ 10 000.00 þ
Case 2	+ 200.00 þ
Case 3	- 2 500.00 þ
Case 4	-500 000.00 þ
Balance=	-492 300.00 þ

The trade pool has a negative balance. This is not a good thing. The central bank should manipulate the things that are exported and imported in order to achieve a favourable trade pool balance. More on this later.

The consumerist economy thrives on trade. It would be to the consumerist's advantage that the goods of the highest quality are bought. If the products are made cheaply in other countries and are imported to the consumerist nation then we would have a scenario like case 3.

This hurts the trade pool.

Suppose that the U.S. is making a car, car A, and the final price of the car is $5 000.00. The exchange rate is $1 = 1þ. In our country the price of cars is 8 000.00 þ from the factory and 10 000.00 Θ at the dealer. In this case the car dealer will buy the American car for $5000.00 and sell it for 10 000.00 Θ. At the moment of purchase of Norses are deducted from the consumerist buying the car and Ignits are added to the retailer. Thus of the 10 000.00 þ the dealer keeps 2 000.00þ and 3 000 þ (8000.00 þ – 5000.00 þ) goes to the trade pool to subsidize other trades. As we can see, this is a win-win-win-win situation for several groups. First the Americans managed to sell their cars. The consumerist retailer made a profit of 2 000.00 þ. The consumerists have the choice of buying an American car in addition to the ones already available. Finally the trade pool increased by 3000.00 þ, allowing the subsidization of other trades. This is one way in which the consumerist trade pool assists open trade.

Now let's examine a situation where the exporting country has a product that is costly. Let's use cars as an example. Once again the factory price is 8 000.00 þ and the price at the car dealership is 10 000.00 Θ. We are importing goods from the U.S. Their cars cost $15 000.00 and $1 = 1þ. Here, the importation of cars must be subsidized. The trade pool must pay 15 000.00 þ – 8 000.00 þ = 7 000.00 þ per car to import the cars. The car retailer sells them for 10 000.00 Θ and earns 2 000.00 þ per car. This is a loose-win-win-win situation. The main looser is the trade pool. It is not very wise to keep subsidizing everything. The consumerists win because they have the opportunity to buy an American car. The car dealership gains 2 000.00þ for every car they sell. The Americans earn $15 000.00 per car. Some trades would not be possible without the existence of the consumerist trade pool.

Ideally the trade pool should be balanced. However the situation may occur where there may be more trade expenditures than income (i.e. more subsidizing than profit). It is the central bank's duty to make sure that the trade pool is positive most of the time or that trades involved give the least difference between subsidies and earnings. To do this it has the right to restrict certain subsidies if it deems that they are too expensive. Thus the economy does not have 100% complete free trade although it strives for it. The balance of the trade pool is the foremost concern as long as consumerists are able to export and import as much as they need.

We will now talk about exchange rates. A real exchange rate is the relative price of foreign goods in terms of domestic goods. A nominal exchange rate is the price of foreign currency in terms of domestic currency. Norses (Θ) cannot be exchanged for any other type of currency; not $; not þ; not £. They can only be used by consumerists to purchase goods and services in the materialist sector. However Ignits can be traded for any other foreign currency.

Let's look directly at exchange rates. Suppose a chair in a consumerist factory costs 20.00 þ. The same chair in the U.S. costs $40.00. We drop the supposition that $1 = 1þ. The real exchange rate is now $40.00/20.00 þ= $2/1þ. Although this is the real exchange rate, the nominal exchange rate can be a lot different. Suppose that the nominal exchange rate is (again) $1 = 1 þ and we are selling 20 chairs. The U.S. must pay $800.00 and we earn 400.00 þ The U.S. pays us $800.00 x 1 þ/$1 = 800.00 þ. The 800.00 þ - 400.00 þ = 400.00 þ is kept by the trading pool.

Now suppose that the nominal exchange rate is $3/1þ. We are again selling 20 chairs to the U.S. The U.S. must pay $800.00 and we earn 400.00 þ. The U.S. pays us $800.00 x 1 þ/$3 = 267/00 þ. The 400.00 þ - 267.00 þ = 133.00 þ must be given to the trade pool.

We have seen what happens when, during exporting, the nominal exchange rate is higher and lower than the real exchange rate. Now let's see what happens during importing. We will use chairs as our product and our trading partner will once again be the U.S. The price of a chair in a factory is 20.00 þ and 25.00 Θ at the retail level. It is $40.00 in the U.S. The real exchange rate is again $2.00/1.00 þ. The retailer imports 20 chairs when the nominal exchange rate is $1.00/1.00 þ. The retailer has to pay 400.00 þ for the chairs and the U.S. manufacturer receives $800.00. The retailer must pay $800.00 x 1.00 þ/$1.00 = 800.00 þ. The 400.00 þ (800.00 þ – 400.00 þ) is subsidized by the trading pool. The retailer earns (25.00 þ x 20) - 400.00 þ = 100.00 þ on the trade. Only one more scenario follows.

Again an importer imports 20 chairs from the U.S. The prices are the same as above but the nominal exchange rate is $3.00/1.00 þ. The retailer has to pay 400.00 þ and the manufacturer must receive $800.00. The retailer must pay $800.00 x 1.00þ /$3.00 = 266.00 þ. The retailer pays 400.00 þ and (400.00 þ– 266.00 þ) = 133.00 þ are gained by the trade pool. Thus appear all possible scenarios.

The next question is this. How is the (nominal) exchange rate determined? The closer the exchange rate is to the real, the less is the need for a trade pool. It is hard to apply a fixed exchange rate because the prices of foreign goods are constantly fluctuating. In some countries the exchange rate is fluctuating. In others it is fixed. Still in others it is pegged to some other currency. In accommodation based consumerism the nominal exchange rate is dictated by the central bank and it is usually calculated. The nominal exchange rate is calculated using real exchange rates of imports or exports and their weights in the process of trade on world markets. Finally all of this is averaged to arrive at a nominal exchange rate. An example follows.

Quantity	Product	U.S. Price	Consumerist Nation Price
200	Chairs	$1.00/Chair	0.50 þ /chair
300	Automobiles	$1000.00/car	1000.00 þ/car
400 L	Oil	$0.50/litre	1.00 þ /litre
500	Hamburgers	$2.00/burger	5.00 þ /burger
100	Pillows	$3.00/pillow	4.00 þ/pillow
800	Windows	$10.00/window	5.00 þ/window
1000	Books	$8.00/book	10.00 þ/ book
500	Jars of Pickles	$1.00/pickle jar	2.00 þ / pickle jar

Real Exchange Rates

- Chairs $2/þ
- Automobiles $1/þ
- Oil $0.5/þ
- Hamburgers $0.4/þ
- Pillows $0.75/þ
- Windows $2/þ
- Books $0.8/þ
- Pickle Jars $0.5/þ

Nominal exchange rate=
# of units = 200 + 300 + 400 + 500 + 100 + 800 +1000 + 500 = 3 800 units

Units x real exchange rate = (200 x $2/þ) + (300 x $1/þ) + (400 x $0.5/þ) + (500 x $0.4/þ) + (100 x $0.75/þ) + (800 x $2/þ) + (1000 x $0.8/þ) + (500 x $0.5/þ) = 3 825 $/þ

Nominal exchange rate = (3 825$/þ)/(3 800) = $1.0066/þ

This exchange rate is not definitely the one that gives the most positive balance, but one that will give the smallest differences between subsidies and profits for the trade pool. We may try to find a better formula that gives a more favourable trade balance.

Now that we know how to calculate the nominal exchange rate, let's observe some generalizations:

1) During importing, a nominal exchange rate higher than the real exchange rate means that there will be a positive trade pool balance
2) During importing, a nominal exchange rate lower than the real exchange rate means there will be a negative trade pool balance
3) During exporting, a nominal exchange rate higher than the real exchange rate means that there will be a negative trade pool balance
4) During exporting, a nominal exchange rate lower than the real exchange rate means that there will be a positive trade pool balance
5) Whether the exchange rate is high or low is indifferent to the exporter and importer

The exchange rate must be adjusted to ensure a favourable trade balance. During cases when there is more importing than there is exporting, the central bank strives for a low foreign nominal exchange rate. During times when exports exceed imports, the central bank strives for a high foreign nominal exchange rate. The central bank has no effect on real exchange rates. Therefore it must manipulate the nominal exchange rate by restricting the trade of certain goods.

There is another type of exportation in accommodation based consumerism. There exists something called *exportation-importation companies*. These can be run either privately or through the government. That is, they exist in all three partitions- the governmental, the natural and the command partitions. The purpose of these companies is to buy products from consumerists and firms in consumerism and sell them to other countries or give them as gifts.

We have previously discussed Type 1 trade. This involves the consumerist trade pool. Now we can discuss Type 2 trade. This involves exportation-importation companies although the trade pool is made use of in type 2 trade too. To preserve quality selection (in 3 of the 4 sectors), we must not allow consumerists to compete for goods and services in terms of price so as to make sure that only the highest quality goods are bought. However, we still have the option of selling lower quality goods to foreign countries as this does not interfere with quality selection. This is where exportation-importation firms enter into the arena. What they do is that they buy lower quality good from consumerists or producers in consumerism and sell them to another country or perhaps even give them as gifts to improve international relations. Whether they are sold or given to another country, the other country will be more than happy to receive these goods.

This is how Type 2 trade functions: An importation-exporting company buys a good from someone in consumerism for less than the fixed price of the good and sells it to another nation for the price set by the bank. Whatever the difference is, this the exporting-importation company gets in terms of profit. How much the consumerist or producer sells his good for depends on the interaction of exporting firms and producers/consumerists. The main stipulation is that the agreed upon price must definitely be lower than that fixed by the bank. The consumerist trade pool is involved. Usually this is a win-win-win situation. The consumerist/producer got money for something that he didn't want more of anymore. The foreign nation received a good they can use

270

in their economy. Finally, the exportation-importation firm made a profit.

Let's work out a concrete example. The central bank sets the price of a car at 10 000.00 þ. Our exporting company is called ACEBS and we are exporting to Nicaragua. We are making the unrealistic assumption (to simplify calculation) that the Nicaraguans are using the same currency. A consumerist, Joseph, has a 5 year old car but he doesn't need it anymore as he is planning to buy a limousine with the money he saved up. He sells his car to ACEBS for 8 000.00 þ. The firm ACEBS sells the car to someone in Nicaragua for 12 000.00 þ. The trade pool earns 2 000.00 þ (12 000.00 þ – 10 000.00 þ) while ACEBS earns 2 000.00 þ (10 000.00 þ- 8 000.00 þ). Joseph earns 8 000.00 þ. All parties benefit and this is a win-win-win-win situation. Joseph got money for a car he did not need. ACEBS made a profit from exporting vs. buying the used car from Joseph. The Nicaraguans now have a car to drive in. We did not value that car that much, but they probably would. Lastly, the consumerist trade pool made a profit from the trade that allows it to subsidize other trades.

There is another situation where the price of the car in Nicaragua is lower than our fixed price, perhaps 7 000.00 þ. Assuming all other variables are the same, this is a loose-win-win-win situation. The Nicaraguans, firm ACEBS and Joseph all make a profit while the consumerist trade pool must lose some money.

The Importation-Exportation (I-E) firm is instrumental in helping us sell low quality goods and purchase high quality goods. Suppose that a firm in our country makes cars and for simplicity some are sports cars and others are mediocre ones. The cost to buy a car from the factory is 10 000 þ. The firm sells the sports cars at this price to car dealerships. Let's say that the total cost of making the worse car is 5 000 þ. The car company sells that car to an importation-exportation firm for a mutually agreeable price in between 5000 þ and 10000 þ. Let's say it is 7 0000 þ. The car manufacturer makes 2 000 þ selling the inferior car and the importation-exportation firm sells the car for 10000 þ to a foreign nation. It makes 3 000 þ per car. In some cases to facilitate trade the trade pool commission will be needed.

Let's entertain another example where I-E firms would play a role. John has a used 7 year old mattress. All mattresses of all sizes, cost 400 þ and with a 25 % retail markup, 500 þ. Instead of throwing out the mattress and making the landfill bigger, John sells the used mattress for 200 þ to an I-E firm. Now he only needs 300 þ more to buy a new one. The I-E firm sells the used mattress to a third world nation for 400 þ. They are pleased to have bought it.

The I-E firm can also help the consumerist society by importing high quality items. A foreign European nation makes well sought after limousines. Limousines, like all cars in our system cost 10 000 þ and at the dealership for 12 500 Ⓞ (assuming 25 % retail markup). The I-E firm buys a limousine for 8000 þ and we assume that 1$ = 1 þ. It sells it to a car dealership for 10 000 þ and the dealership sells it to a consumerist for 12 500 Ⓞ. Thus the I-E firm and the dealership both made money. A consumerist buys the limousine for 12 500 Ⓞ and has a great quality product.

A grocery store can also sell to an I-E firm. A bag of chips costs 2.00 þ and 2.50 Ⓞ with the retail markup. The grocery store can't sell some of its low quality chips. It sells them to the I-E firm for a price in between 2.00 þ and 2.50 þ, let's say 2.20 þ. It makes 0.20 þ on every bag of chips that it sells. The I-E firm makes money. The consumerist trade pool may be made use of in these types of situations.

The exportation-importation firm can exist in either the natural, governmental or command partitions. It primarily involves Ignits. However the consumerists can still get rid of goods they no longer need by selling goods to the exportation-importation firm that are in the materialist sector and involve Norses. For example, a consumerist can sell that old suit that he doesn't need to an exportation-importation firm. He must sell it, however, for less than the price set by the central bank. He would like to sell it for as close to the fixed price as possible. So if the suit cost 100.00 Θ, he can sell it for 90.00 þ to the exportation-importation company. Upon selling the suit to another country, with the help of the consumerist trade pool, the exportation-importation firm will earn 10.00 þ

We will now discuss domestic shortages and surpluses. The free-market response to a shortage is to raise the price of the good. If there is a surplus one would lower the price. In consumerist domestic shortages we expand the operation. In consumerist domestic surpluses we decrease the scope of the operation or get rid of it entirely. Let's look at some examples.

First we will look at domestic shortages. Suppose that we have a university parking lot and that there are more students needing to park than there is space for them to do so. Instead of raising prices, we buy the land around the parking lot and turn it into a parking lot. Since there are already students willing to use the parking lot we have a "profit vacuum". That is, we are sure to make a profit. Our only constraint however is that the price of the nearby land is less than the profit from renting the parking space to students. A diagram that follows on the next page illustrates the idea.

Before

Parking Space
Room for 100 vehicles
Pay 10.00 Norses per day

- shortage of space
- not enough space
  for 100's of students

empty space
(undeveloped grassland)
cost = 35,000.00 þ

Convenience Store
(Failing)
Revenue = 40,000.00 þ (year)
ARPD = 3 years

Playground
  - Owned by municipal government
  - Cost of land = 160,000.00 þ

Figure 6-E

After

Parking Space
(After buying surrounding land)

950 Students pay 10.00 Norses/day
Total maintenance per day = 15.00 þ
Result = no shortage

Figure 6-F

Calculations: in one year => 950 x 10.00 þ x 365 = 3 467 500.00 þ

Costs: Maintenance per year=> 15.00 þ x 365 = 5 475.00 þ

Land Purchases: 35 000.00 þ + 160 000.00 þ + (3 x 40 000.00 þ) = 315 000.00 þ

Balance = 3 467 500.00 þ – 315 000.00 þ – 5 475.00 þ = + 3 147 025.00 þ/year

Now let's look at another example; let's say a lemonade stand. Suppose someone selling lemonade experiences a shortage of lemonade. Instead of raising the price, the owner should buy more lemons and make more juice. For our third example we will examine a chair shortage in a school classroom. The sensible thing to do is to take chairs from a classroom that has too many of them. The consumerist response to shortages has the advantage that it doesn't discriminate in favour of the prosperous but rather it tries to give as many people as possible a particular good. By raising prices the effect is that only a select group, the prosperous group, receives a good while the others still need it. Try this thought experiment. There are 10 people starving for food. 1 of them is extremely rich and the other nine are not. There is not enough food to go around. Due to the shortage in this free-market example the price of food goes up. Now only the rich one can eat. The shortage is alleviated but there are still 9 desperately hungry people with nothing to eat since they cannot afford the food. Wouldn't the sensible thing to do be to increase the production of food, raise more cows, and grow more apples etc. (without raising prices)? That way every one has enough to eat.

Now we look at domestic consumerist surpluses. If we have a factory that makes widgets and nobody at all wants to buy them then such a factory shouldn't even exist. The factory should bankrupt and close down. Suppose a pop company comes up with a soft drink that just tastes awful. If people don't want the drink the pop company should halt production and try to come up with something more flavorful. Lastly, let's look at a fashion company that makes ugly clothes. Instead of lowering the price of the clothes and making some people look very unfashionable, they should change the clothes they sell or fire their fashion designers. These would be the best responses to a consumerist domestic surplus.

There is also a third type of shortage called an absolute shortage which cannot be dealt with by importing or rising prices or expanding the operation. Here there is a limited amount of a good and there can only be less of it. Examples of this type of shortage include food in a submarine, air in outer space and perishables in a winter cabin.

The counterpart of absolute shortage is absolute surplus. Here one cannot get rid of the surplus by exporting, price lowering or decreasing the scope of the enterprise. Examples of this include pollution and garbage accumulation.

This is a good time to discuss a major problem that could arise with regards to free trade. It is absolutely mandatory that Norses not be exchanged directly for Ignits. If they are, the incentive for work is lost as consumerists trade the Norses they were granted by the central bank for Ignits they could then use to improve their accommodational standing. A problem arises when the following happens. A consumerist purchases a limousine with Norses, drives it to another country, sells it, trades it for Ignits and now has Ignits for spending. This is known as the *export-smuggling calamity*. It must be guarded against. We have made it illegal to trade Norses for a foreign currency. If this were not the case, a clever consumerist would trade Norses for dollars and dollars for Ignits. So to stop the calamity we need controls at the borders so that consumerists don't cross the border with something valuable just to sell it. This would not include things like food, clothes, shoes, blankets or presents. It would concern things like TV's, stereos, watches and jewellery. Some things it would be completely illegal to smuggle while other things must be noted by the officer in charge of border crossings. It may be required that some travellers pay a deposit upon leaving the country. Upon returning if they come back with everything they brought over the border, their deposit is given back. Further discussion on this calamity is not required here as it is for the most part a matter for law.

There are several types of shortages and surpluses that appear in consumerism. We have found the solution to the more common two using mathematics as our tool. Now we know how the trade and exchange of goods and money happens in accommodation based consumerism.

Consumerist Trade Pool Commission

We talked at length about the consumerist trade pool. The consumerist trade pool is vital to our ability to trade (import/export) while keeping price functions fixed for a family of goods.

We now introduce into the equation the consumerist trade pool commission. The consumerist trade pool commission is in charge of coordinating the operations of the consumerist trade pool. Although it is somewhat affiliated with the central bank of a consumerist nation it is solely in charge of the consumerist trade pool.

The consumerist trade pool commission has several duties. First and foremost it ensures that all consumerists have access to goods by allowing importation of necessary goods. If a consumerist nation is short in wheat, cars, gasoline, or milk, it is the duty of the consumerist trade pool commission to make sure these are imported.

Secondly, the consumerist trade pool commission ensures that all surpluses are exported to countries that actually need that good. For example, if we have too many cars or if we have an abundance of steel or wheat, the consumerist trade pool commission ensures that these items are exchanged for to a foreign nation. Although we have more wheat than we can possibly eat there are other countries that have a starving population. The consumerist trade pool commission ensures that what we have too much of is given to another country (in exchange for money of course).

We mentioned in the previous section that there are four situations that can occur during importing and exporting. In two of them the trade pool makes money and in the other two it must subsidize. One other, yet very important function of the consumerist trade pool commission is to have a favourable balance. That is, the profits from two scenarios are greater than the losses in the scenarios involving subsidization. Of course, the primary role of the consumerist trade pool commission is to satisfy the needs and wants of the consumerists. So, the balance is of secondary importance.

The consumerist trade pool commission is occupied with accountants who are good at book keeping. Thus they must find 1) an optimal nominal exchange rate between our countries currency and a foreign nations currency, 2) optimal number of things to export, 3) optimal number of things to import.

If the consumerist trade pool commission is successful there will be a positive balance between the scenarios involving importing and exporting. This is good news. This money can be considered a form of government revenue. That is, it helps to pay for government spending like health care, education, and infrastructure. This is clearly much better than raising revenue through the imposition of taxes.

However, it is possible that the trade pool will have a negative balance after satisfying the 4 scenarios of importation and exportation. In this case, the extra money comes out of the government's budget. That is, it is paid for by using other sources of revenue like the GCT.

The consumerist trade pool commission has several vital roles. Its role in coordinating the function of consumerism should not be underestimated.

Pure Shortage and Surplus

We talked about several ways to eliminate surpluses and shortages. It is vital for an economy's well being to eliminate surpluses and shortages. One outstanding attribute of free market capitalism is its ability to quickly, easily and effectively, resolve surpluses and shortages.

In consumerism there are a number of ways to eliminate shortages and surpluses. Some examples include exporting surpluses and importing shortages as well as increasing or decreasing the scope of business operations. Now we present another useful mechanism to alleviate surpluses and shortages. It is called pure surplus and shortage resolution. It borrows from capitalism the concept that adjusting prices may function to overcome surpluses and shortages.

The current surplus/shortage resolution system works with the command partition. Essentially, when there is a surplus of goods in the natural partition, the command partition firm buys these goods and then sells them to consumerists at a later time or simply exports them. Also to overcome a shortage, the command partition firm sells goods to a natural partition firm while increasing production of that good in the command partition.

Let's look at the simple market for t-shirts. The central bank has set the price of all t-shirts at 10.00 ϴ. They are in the materialist sector. The total cost for producing another t-shirt (in this example) is 5.00 þ. Notice that there are different currencies since to produce the t-shirt using inputs is actually in the accommodational sector. However, 1 þ = 1ϴ (although the two currencies cannot be exchanged one for another). Now suppose that there are 1000 t-shirts but only 800 were bought in a single month. What happens now is that the makers of the t-shirts sell the extra 200 shirts to a firm in the command partition. The firm selling the t-shirts and the command partition firm negotiate the price in a free market sense. The price must be between the central bank price (10.00 þ) and the price to make the t-shirts (5.00 þ). The two firms bargain until they find a mutually agreeable price. Let's say it is 8.00 þ. Thus the t-shirt selling firm would sell 200 shirts for 8.00 þ to a command partition firm. This gets rid of the surplus in the natural partition. With the extra 200 shirts the command partition firm can sell them to consumerists at a later time (for 10.00 ϴ, the fixed price) or alternatively the command partition firm can export the t-shirts.

Now what if the t-shirt selling firm has a shortage of t-shirts? It makes 1000 t-shirts but they were all sold out and another 100 more could have been sold. Again it works with a command partition firm but this time it buys from the command partition firm. The command partition firm and the t-shirt firm bargain to find a price between the cost to make the shirt and the fixed price. Let's say it is 9.00 þ. Now the t-shirt firm sells the 100 t-shirts to consumerists for 10.00 ϴ and it makes a profit of 10.00 þ – 9.00 þ = 1.00 þ per t-shirt.

It is important to note that it is better for the natural partition firm not to bargain with the command partition firm to get rid of shortages and surpluses as they can make more money selling directly to consumerists.

Now let's look at a retail store. A grocery store has a surplus of 100 bottles of pop. The price of a bottle of pop is 2.00 ϴ and the retail markup is 25%. The store sells the 100 bottles of pop to another grocery store in the command partition for a mutually agreeable price in between 2.00 þ and 2.50 þ (the price after the retail markup). Let's say it is 2.30 ϴ = 2.30 þ. Thus the grocery store sells 100 bottles of pop for 2.30 þ to the command partition store and it sells them at the command partition store for 2.50 þ. They both win. The natural partition firm reduces a surplus and it makes 2.30 þ – 2.00þ = 0.30 þ profit per bottle. The command partition store wins as it can sell the pop for   2.50 Ө – 2.30 Ө = 0.20 Ө per bottle to consumerists.

Now the case of shortage. We will use the case of pop bottles as an example. A natural partition grocery store is running out of pop bottles to sell. It buys 100 bottles for a mutually agreeable price in between the price of the product and the price of the product with the retail markup. Let's say it is 2.20 þ. So the natural partition grocery store sells 100 bottles of pop for 2.50 þ and earns 2.50 þ – 2.20 þ = 0.30 þ per bottle. The command partition grocery store earns 2.20 þ – 2.00 þ = 0.20 þ per bottle.

Suppose a natural partition firm is experiencing a shortage. Let's say it is short on wheat. It can buy wheat at a mutually agreeable price from the command partition. At that point, this is a signal for the command partition to expand production for the good in shortage (wheat in this case). So the HRMC should try to build a wheat farm or convert another farm (one making barley for example) to one that makes wheat.

Clearly the command partition has an additional use besides creating jobs, goods, services and generating government revenue. The command partition drastically reduces or eliminates shortages and surpluses. However, it must be mentioned that it is not obligated to trade with natural partition firms experiencing surpluses and shortages. It has discretion with regards to this. For example, if a natural partition firm has a surplus of "widgets" the command partition firm need not necessarily buy them. It has to take into consideration whether anyone will buy anything from the command partition firm.

Pure surplus resolution can combat hunger when it occurs in the hospitality industry. Suppose a natural partition firm has an excess of 1000 kg of hamburgers and the price is 1 þ per kg and there is a retail markup of 25%. Here a command partition grocery buys the hamburgers for 1.20 þ per kg. Thus the natural partition firm makes 0.20 per kg of hamburgers. Now the command partition grocery store gives the surplus hamburgers it bought to the Food Geared to Income Program so as to feed hungry consumerists. The command partition (government) makes money through the Food Geared to Income Percentage. Thus this measure can fight poverty in the form of hunger.

There are several ways of counteracting surpluses and shortages. Shortages and surpluses can be beat by exporting/importing, increasing/decreasing scope of operation and by trading with a command partition firm. Thus it is possible to overcome shortages and surpluses in the absence of a market economy.

Command and Natural Domestic Shortage/Surplus Resolution

It is very, very important to control surpluses and shortages in consumerism. There are several ways of doing so in our system. We described several before and we will talk about others later. Now we will discuss command and natural domestic shortage/surplus resolution.

To reiterate, a surplus occurs in a market when there are more people trying to sell a good than there are people buying it. There are excess goods that no one wants to buy. In a shortage, there is more people willing to buy a good than there are of that good on the market. Thus there is not enough of that good for everyone to buy.

We touched a little bit about the domestic shortage/surplus resolution system a while ago. Here we will talk about it in full. First we will talk about the natural partition case and later we will talk about the command partition case. It should be clear that in this section we are solely referring to the accommodational and materialist sectors. The command and natural domestic shortage/surplus resolution system does not apply to the governmental or laissez-faire sectors.

In the natural partition firms compete with each other so that the profits go to business owners, entrepreneurs, moguls, CEO's and stock and bond holders. When there is a shortage of a good, firms in the natural partition step up production of that good. That is, they fill a "profit vacuum". So, if there are 1000 cars produced in a factory and a car dealership has zero inventory because all its cars are selling so fast the car factory in the natural partition builds more cars. It does so by hiring more workers, buying more steel, glass, rubber and making its current workers work overtime. When there is a situation of a shortage of bottles of pop in a grocery store (because everyone wants to buy them) the grocery store buys more pop bottles from the manufacturer. To fill this, the pop manufacturer increases production of pop. It buys more plastic, water, sugar, flavourings and makes its workers work longer hours. In both cases both groups win. When a car factory makes more cars they have more cars to sell to car dealerships. Also, with more cars the car dealership makes more money selling cars to consumerists.

A surplus can also occur. Let's revisit the same two cases of firms selling cars and bottles of pop. If a car dealership can't sell its cars, i.e. there are 200 cars in its lot that were there for over three years, it stops ordering cars from the factory. So if the factory usually sells 12 cars to a particular dealership per month, in this case it may have to sell none because no one is buying them. Now to the case of selling bottles of pop. If the grocery store can't sell pop, it has to order less bottles of pop from the factory that makes them. In both cases these remedies overcome surplus in the natural partition.

Now let's move to the command partition. To be concrete we will use the markets for wheat and chocolate bars. During a surplus a firm in the command partition decreases the amount of goods it puts on the market and sells to consumerists. So if a firm in the command partition creates 1 000 000 bushels of wheat and only 800 000 bushels of wheat are bought the wheat making firm makes less wheat in the future. They will plant less wheat and scale down the production of wheat. They will transfer the resources used for making wheat to another crop. So a wheat making firm will grow oats instead of wheat. This remedies a surplus in the command partition. A surplus can occur in the market for chocolate bars. There are more chocolate bars than there are people who want to buy them. The solution to this is to decrease the number of chocolate bars made. The resources put into making chocolate bars should be put into making something that is more needed like cakes and candy or a different type of chocolate bar. When there is too much of a particular good, the domestic resolution is to decrease the amount of that good brought to market. This solves the problem of surpluses in some markets.

Finally, let's look at shortages in the command partition. There is not enough wheat for all consumerists to enjoy. A firm (or many firms) expand production of wheat. That is, they buy more land and devote more land to growing wheat. There is a profit vacuum. If a firm grows more wheat by using more land or devoting resources for other goods (barley, oats) into making wheat, there will be more wheat and the shortage will be resolved.

The same logic applies to a shortage of chocolate bars. There are 4 firms that make chocolate bars of various varieties and they make 100 000 chocolate bars. However, people want 200 000 of them. The Human Resource Management Commission creates more factories that make chocolate bars. In the process it hires workers and helps the economy by buying inputs like sugar, plastic and peanuts. There is a profit vacuum and it is satisfied. However, the shortage was resolved.

As we have seen, various goods can be in a state of shortage or surplus. The domestic resolution to these problems, which applies to both the command and natural partitions, is useful in resolving surpluses and shortages. Being able to overcome surpluses and shortages makes consumerism a more comprehensive system.

The Governmental-Market Surplus/Shortage Resolution System

There are several ways to overcome surpluses and shortages in consumerism. We discussed several previously. Now we will talk about another- the *Governmental-Market Surplus/Shortage Resolution System* or GMSSRS.

This system is special in that it is used as a last resort. It is preferable to use the other ways to eliminate surpluses and shortages. That is, it is better to resolve surpluses and shortages through exportation/importation, the domestic system, the consumerist trade system and the pure surplus/shortage resolution system.

Furthermore, this system is not for all markets or all firms competing against one another. There are problems if firms in the market artificially or wilfully restrict supply to create a situation of shortage. However, surpluses are not much of a problem in this system. The government has a right to determine which markets, industries and firms can be helped using GMSSRS to reduce surpluses and shortages in their situation.

This system works by adding or decreasing a payment above the fixed price function. In times of shortage, the government gives money (sort of like a subsidy) to firms to increase supply and offset the shortage. In times of surplus, the government takes money away from firms so as to reduce the quantity supplied and thus reduce the surplus. What this system accomplishes is the stability of price functions regardless of a shortage or surplus. That is, consumerists pay the same amount for a good regardless if there is a shortage, surplus or there is a balance. Therefore we preserve quality selection.

We will look at the application of the GMSSRS to two markets- the market for bread and the market for apartment units. If there is a surplus of bread the government tries to reduce supply while preserving the price consumerists pay. Let's say the price of bread is 10.00 þ per loaf. There are 10 000 loaves of bread on the market but only 8 000 are sold. The government takes a portion of the price and uses it as a source of revenue. So the consumerists pay 10.00 þ per loaf but the producers only keep 8.00 þ per loaf. The 2.00 þ per loaf goes to the government. The supply of bread, due to the lower price, decreases to 8 000 loaves, which is equal to quantity demanded. Thus consumerists pay 10.00 þ/loaf x 8000 loaf = 80 000 þ. The bread makers make 80 000 x (10 þ -2 þ) = 64 000 þ and the government makes 80 000 þ – 64 000 þ = 16 000 þ

Now let's see a bread market with a shortage. Again, the price of bread is 10.00 þ per loaf. There are 8000 loaves of bread demanded and 6 000 loaves brought to market. In this case, the government gives money to firms to raise supply. It adds 2.00 þ per loaf for every transaction. So the fact that the price per loaf is now 12.00 þ/loaf raises the amount supplied to 8 000 loaves. In this scenario the consumerists pay 10.00 þ per loaf x 8000 loaves = 8 000þ and the bread makers make 8 0000 loaves x (10 þ+ 2 þ) = 96 000 þ. 96 000 þ – 80 000 þ= 16 000 þ are deducted from the government's operational budget.

In this case we can see that the money from subsidizing shortages is equal to the money gained from adjusting surpluses. Although this is not always the case, a balance is sought after. However, if the money gained from helping in cases of surpluses is greater than that for helping shortages then the government has a useful source of governmental revenue for social services.

As another example, let's look at the particular market for apartment units. In this example,we look at things in the long run. This implies that producers can build apartment units or take some off the market.

First the surplus. There are 1000 apartment units in a given area. 800 consumerists demand these units. The price function (simplified) is 1000 þ per unit. To reduce the supply in the long run the government tries to lower the supply. The government sets a new Governmental-Market Price for each unit at 800 þ. So each would-be tenant pays 1000 þ per unit but the landlords only receive 800 þ of that payment. Since the selling of each apartment units gives landlords less money less apartment buildings will be built in the future and some apartment buildings will be converted to other purposes like office space. Thus the supply of apartment units goes from 1000 units to 800 units and the demand for units is equal to the supply for units. The tenants pay 800 x 1000 þ = 800000 þ and the landlords receive 800 x 800þ = 64 000þ. Thus the government pockets 800 000 þ – 640 000 þ = 160 000 þ. This is used for social services.

Now let's examine the case of shortages. We have a shortage in the market for apartment units. 800 people would like to buy an apartment unit but only 600 units are available. Again the price per unit is 1000 þ. The government subsidizes the purchase of apartment units giving the money to landlords so as to raise the supply (build more buildings) and thus decrease the shortage. The government sets a Government Market Adjusted price at 1200 þ. So now landlords are paid 1200 þ instead of 1000 þ to make (offer) more apartment units. With this monetary incentive, they should offer more units and increase supply until theoretically supply = demand and 800 units are demanded and supplied. So in our example, the consumerists pay the fixed price function price while the landlords receive the governmental-market adjusted price (GMAP). This preserves quality selection. The consumerists pay 800 x 1000 þ = 800 000 þ while the landlords receive 800 x 1200 þ = 960 000 þ. The government pays 960 000 þ – 800 000 þ = 160 000 þ from its operating budget.

In the above example the government subsidized the equivalent of what it made. Thus it was able to reduce a case of shortage and a surplus without incurring any problems.

This method for the resolution of shortages and surpluses is very useful. It allows us to preserve quality selection meaning the consumerists try to buy things of the highest quality. Also, if the amount earned through surpluses is greater than the subsidy of shortages, the government can make money for revenue to spend on social services.

Increase of Scope of Laissez-Faire Sector As a Surplus/Shortage Resolution Measure

As we have seen, there are quite a few programs designed to eliminate shortages and surpluses. Here we present yet another one. It is special in that it is used when the other ones do not do the job of overcoming shortages and surpluses.

In this method of surplus/shortage resolution we manipulate the sizes of the various sectors. Recall that accommodation based consumerism has 4 distinct sectors: the accomodational sector, the materialist sector, the governmental sector and the laissez-faire sector. In general we eliminate a shortage/surplus by moving a market to the laissez-faire sector.

The laissez-faire sector deals nicely with shortages and surpluses. It uses the market system found in capitalism to eliminate shortages and surpluses. The price mechanism of the laissez-faire sector works to make sure that the laws of supply and demand cause an equilibrium quantity of goods and an equilibrium price for these goods where there no longer remains a shortage or surplus.

Suppose in the market for cars there is a surplus of 1000 cars each month. We are assuming that cars originate in the materialist sector. If we can't eliminate the surplus through the other measures we discussed earlier, one course of action is to move the car industry to the laissez-faire sector. In that case, as long as there is no monopolist with market power the market forces of supply and demand will work to destroy the car shortage. By relegating cars from one sector, the material sector, to the laissez-faire sector, we accomplish the goal of eliminating a surplus. We did so without major problems. The only problem is that now consumerists can't buy cars based on quality and cars are under the effects of price selection.

Now suppose we have a shortage of oil (gasoline). There are 100 000 barrels supplied but 120 000 barrels are needed by consumerists. Originally, the gasoline is in the accommodational sector. If we move the gasoline market to the laissez-faire we can be quite confident that at least theoretically the shortage will be overcome. The price will adjust so that supply will balance demand and the market is in equilibrium and thus not in a state of shortage. This has the cost of taking the gasoline market out of the accommodational sector where consumerists would be competing in quality for various fuels and there would be fixed price functions.

This is how this program works. It is simple and straightforward. It allows the economy to overcome a shortage or surplus by changing the scope of the laissez-faire sector. In doing so, we can be assured that the market forces will usually eliminate shortages and surpluses by adjusting supply, demand, price and quantity until there is a state of neither surplus or shortage.

Solutions to Global Shortage

A global shortage represents a major world wide economic problem. By global shortage we mean that there is not enough of a good produced to meet demand in a global sense. A global shortage can create a great economic problem for a global society.

First we will examine the situation of a global shortage of central processing units (CPUs). These are needed to make cell phones, tablets, computers and gaming console systems. If there are not enough of CPUs made, a command partition firm will make more of them. Suppose a command partition normally makes microphones, batteries or cables. Since a command partition firm operates through central planning, it allocates production resources from microphones and batteries to the production of CPUs. If there is a shortage of CPUs globally, a command partition firm will make more CPUs than other goods. This should alleviate the global shortage of central processing units.

A global shortage of CPUs can be alleviated if we encourage CPUs to be made in the natural partition of consumerism. In this case the government gives a certain incentive called the Global Shortage Stimulus to a firm so as to produce more CPUs. If a natural partition firm normally makes 100 000 CPUs and the Global Shortage Stimulus is 100%, a natural partition firm will make 200 000 units of CPUs. The government, as an example, can give natural partition firms a certain amount of money for additional CPUs made. The monetary incentive should entice natural partition firms to create more CPUs.

Another solution to global shortage is to shift from one product to a substitute. So if there is a global shortage of gasoline, firms and consumerists are encouraged to start relying on alcohol based fuels.

Global shortage can be reduced when command partition firms are made to create a product that is in a global state of shortage. Also the global shortage stimulus encourages firms in the natural partition to make more of a good that is in a global state of shortage.

Solutions to Hunger

Hunger is a very common misery throughout the world. In many places around the globe people do not have enough to eat. In consumerism we talk about measures to eliminate hunger.

One of the best ways to beat hunger is to raise the ability of consumerists to buy food. Keep in mind that food refers to things in the hospitality industry of the materialist sector. If consumerists have more money to spend on the hospitality industry they will have more food and less people will be hungry. To do this it is good to keep the General Consumerist Grant (GCG) and Non Working Consumerist Grant (NWCG) high. The GCT should be minimal so that more money (used to buy food) is given to consumerists. To fight hunger we ought to keep the non working consumerist markdown low so that there is less of a gap between working and non working consumerists. However this has to be put into perspective with the fact that if the difference between working and non working consumerists is small, this discourages people to be productive.

To raise the GCG and NWCG we ought to increase the general output of the materialist sector where the hospitality industry is found. The greater the output of the materialist sector, ceteris paribus, the higher the GDCP, the GCG and the NWCG. A higher GCG and NWCG give more money for consumerists to buy hospitality items.

The best way to raise the materialist output (i.e. GDCP) is to increase the number of firms in the materialist sector. When dealing with the natural partition there are, in addition to the profit motive, several output maximization measures that the central bank and government can manipulate to increase production and raise the GDCP. These are discussed thoroughly in other sections of this book. In the command partition, the best thing to do is to let the HRMC create more firms in the materialist sector and staff them with auxiliary workers that were previously unemployed.

To produce more food directly we need firms in the materialist sector of both the natural and command partition to create a greater amount of things to eat. Again the profit motive as well as other output maximization measures (IRS, PRT, ERT) can increase the likelihood of hospitality industry firms to spring up or expand operations in the natural partition. In the command partition the HRMC simply creates farms, grocery stores, cafes, restaurants and fast food establishments.

There is also the materialist overdraft for those who are unable to obtain all the food they need with the money they were granted by the central bank (GCG, NWCG). Suppose the NWCG is 1000 Θ and a consumerist can't buy enough food with that. If the central bank sets the materialist overdraft limit at 10% and the materialist overdraft interest at 50% the consumerist is granted an additional 100 Θ to buy things in the hospitality sector. However next grant period he is granted less. He is granted 1000 Θ – 100 Θ – (100 Θ x 0.5) = 850 Θ next grant period. To offset hunger and poverty, it is best if the materialist overdraft interest is close to zero so that a consumerist is not punished for being short for food from time to time. It is also good to set the materialist overdraft limit high.

In accommodation based consumerism we have the No Food Wasted Initiative (NFWI) Basically under this program hospitality firms give the food they have in surplus that day (i.e. they couldn't sell all their food) and they give it to hungry people instead of just wasting it. We have a cafe that sells about 300 donuts, 150 muffins and 400 cups of coffee a day. However, at closing time (12 am.) they still have 6 donuts, 3 muffins, and enough coffee for 4 cups. Normally under capitalism this would be dumped outside. However, in consumerism the cafe gives the left overs to hungry needy people.

We have a fast food restaurant that sells hamburgers, french fries and chicken nuggets. At the end of the day they have 8 hamburgers, 5 portions of french fries and 30 chicken nuggets. Under a free-market system these would be thrown out. However, we allow the restaurant to give these food items to people who are hungry.

This NFW initiative has the positive side effect that if a hungry person receives a free donut and he really likes it, he may come back later (when he has more money) and buy that same donut for the regular price. So this acts something like a "free sample".

Under this paradigm both firms in the natural and command partition are encouraged to cooperate. All the command partition food places (restaurants, cafes, donut shops) comply with the NFW initiative. The natural partition firms are encouraged to work in this program. It makes them "look generous".

Another program that works to beat hunger is the Food Geared to Income (FGI) program. The government creates special places called Consumerist Food Centers (CFC) in several parts of a city. For a city the size of 100 000 people there should be about 25 such centers. These places give food to hungry consumerists.

The CFCs get their supply of food from command partition firms that function in the hospitality industry of the materialist sector. Whenever a command partition firm has too much of a food related good it gives that good to the FGI program.

The transfers from the command partition to the FGI program can come about if the command partition firm normally has too much of a good. So suppose a command partition grocery store has too much fish sticks that they can't sell. Instead of throwing these out to the dumpster it gives it to the FGI program to curb hunger.

This program also works also with the pure surplus resolution system we discussed before. A natural partition convenience store has too many bottles of pop. It sells them to a command partition run convenience store to resolve the surplus. Now the command partition store can either try to sell the pop at the set price, export it or give it to the FGI program.

Sometimes in the free market a delivery truck comes to a grocery store with a shipment of cookies. There are so many cookies that there is no room for them on the shelves. The cookies are taken out to the dumpster to be destroyed. This is a waste. In consumerism if there are too many cookies to fit on the shelves, the natural partition grocery store sells them to a grocery store in the command partition. Now the command partition grocery store can export them (via the I-E firms) or give them to hungry people through the FGI program.

Essentially, how much a hungry person pays for food depends on his materialist income (GCG or NWCG). Suppose the NWCG is 1000 ☉ and the *FGI Program Percentage* is 10 %. Thus a hungry consumerist who can't afford food (he is hungry) has to pay 100 ☉ to the government to have access to the CFC.

Most of the food in the CFC comes from surpluses from command partition firms.

However, generous consumerists can donate food items to CFC as well. This idea is reminiscent of food banks in well off free-market nations.

Now, a hungry consumerist does not have unlimited access to a CFC. That would encourage abuse of the system as a person would take too many food items of the shelves. There is the Food Geared to Income Limit (FGIL). Suppose that it is 200 ☉ per week. Thus every week a hungry, needy consumerist can take 200 ☉ worth of food items from a CFC.

The FGIL and the Food Geared to Income Percentage are not fixed but are manipulated by the government. To help the poor and hungry the government ought to keep the Food Geared to Income Percentage low and keep the FGIL high.

Every consumerist that desires it can apply for a Universal Food Card (UFC). This card allows them to buy anything he wants at a CFC. Care must be taken to make sure that individuals do not have several cards (this would constitute fraud). These cards would be issued at a certain minimum age, perhaps 12 years of age.

With the UFC a hungry consumerist can buy anything at a CFC up to the FGIL. If the limit is 200 ☉ per week and he spends 170 ☉ in week 1 he will have 200 ☉ not 230 ☉ in week 2. The balance does not carry over. The prices of goods at the CFC are after the retail markup.

Those needing food can obtain as much as they need up the limit. However, if they still need food they can buy food from either a natural partition or command partition firm with the money that they have from the NWCG or GCG.

The parameter we have called the food geared to income percentage can be considered a form of government revenue. However, the government should not rely on it too much. The lower it is the more the government fights poverty and hunger. However, if it is higher the government has more revenue.

Since the food items in this program are in the materialist sector, they are affected by quality selection. That is, hungry consumerists have access to high quality food items.

No one in consumerism should be hungry. Feeding the hungry is a grand goal of consumerism. Attaining this goal makes consumerism a wonderful society.

Volunteers

Volunteers are people who donate their free time to various causes. They offer their services for what they think is a worthy cause. What sets them apart from regular workers is that they do not want money for their time and effort.

Volunteers work in many areas of the economy. Some work in hospitals, some work at retirement homes while still others work to build playgrounds in the local park. Their contributions are wonderful and accommodation based consumerism wholly encourages their activities. The more volunteers the better.

Volunteers are clearly very useful. Our economy is better for their contributions. Their contributions in terms of time and effort make a consumerist society a more pleasant one for the lives that they touch.

Those who volunteer increase the output of society in general. Whatever service they provide or good they produce the more society gains. If a volunteer spends time at a hospital, the doctors and nurses benefit. But so do the patients and their families. And what is more, the volunteers gain a profound satisfaction for the work that they do.

Volunteers do many things. They function to help others. Clearly they make accommodation based consumerism better.

Population

People are one of the most important resources in a society. We need to have a coherent policy as to the size and fluctuation of a population. There are essentially 3 possibilities. 1) To decrease the size of the existing population, 2) To let the population stay roughly the same size or 3) To increase the size of the existing population. What is the wisest policy- a society with a large population or a society with a small population?

The consumerist grant depends on the population and how much of it is employed. If the GDCP, the GCT and the amount of employed people stay the same and the population increases, then each consumerist is granted less Norses to spend on the materialist sector. Conversely, if the GDCP, the GCT and the amount of employed people stay the same and the population decreases, then each consumerist is granted more Norses to spend on the materialist sector. These are the ways in which a change in the size of a population (ceteris paribus) affects the amount of Norses that are granted to consumerists.

There are two ways for the population to increase- through an increase in the number of immigrants and an increase in the number of births. In this case there is a decrease in the General as well as the Non-Working consumerist grants. We will call the sum of the general and non-working consumerist grants, the "GDCP per capita", even though it doesn't apply to those that are institutionalized. For those households where a birth occurs there is an increase in the amount of Norses granted to the whole house hold even though each member of the house hold earns less Norses. This is because all non-institutionalized members of society are issued Norses including new-borns. We are assuming a minimum grant allowance of birth. The newborn would be granted the non-working consumerist grant as he is without a job. Consequently, the household into which the child was born has a higher amount of Norses collectively. They can use the money (Norses) issued to the newborn to buy materialist goods and services. The same cannot be said of a single new immigrant. Although the GDCP grant decreases (assuming the same GDCP) only a new household becomes created in the society. This becomes different if a family member immigrated to someone who is already a citizen. In this case the household is also granted more Norses collectively. It is clear that there are incentives to procreating as well as to bringing over relatives if one is an immigrant.

What happens when the population decreases or stays the same? Suppose that a population decreases. The amount of workers would decrease and so would the amount of entrepreneurs. Clearly, the GDCP would decrease. With less consumerists, the GDCP is divided among less people. Now suppose that the population stays the same. New births and new immigrants have to balance deaths and emigrants. As the GDCP increases so would the GDCP per capita. However the GDCP would increase less for a population that stayed the same size than for one where the population grew due to an increase in workers and entrepreneurs.

What conclusion can we draw from the above for a society with a decreasing population? There is a decreasing GDCP. Also the GDCP increases less quickly in a society where the population stays the same than in one where there is a growing population. However in a society where the population is growing (assuming that most of the people are used to contribute to society) there is an increasing GDCP. On the other hand, in a steady or decreasing population there is an increase in the GDCP per capita. Yet it is not impossible for an increase in the GDCP per capita in the increasing population case if the GDCP grows faster than the population for a particular level of GDCP per capita. Thus the best choice is to have an increasing population, as long as the GDCP is increasing as well.

The population should steadily increase. However it should increase such that the GDCP per capita also increases from period to period. Although the government cannot influence deaths and births directly it can influence migration. The government should be in charge of controlling the population since the population size is a matter of public policy. From an economic point of view, however the government must only allow as many immigrants such that the GDCP per capita is increasing. Also which immigrants to let in should be at least partially based on the skills and education that the immigrants have. Thus it makes the most sense to allow immigrants to our country who are well educated in a trade or have advanced degrees. It appears that it is better to allow into our country a doctor who specializes in open heart surgery or a chemical engineer than a potential immigrant that was on social assistance in his original country. The movement of people across borders is in the hands of the government.

Here is an observation. All animals strive to multiply. Nature prohibits their populations from exploding. When there is plenty of food and there are good living conditions, rabbits will increase the size of their population. When the amount of food is limited and the living conditions are poor, rabbit populations decrease. Here is another observation. The population of bacteria increases if the bacteria have good growing conditions and plenty of food and space. Their populations decrease as food and space become limited. From these observations it appears that we should increase the population as long as the GDCP per capita is increasing for the last several periods. When the GDCP per capita repeatedly decreases for a few periods, the government should take measures to decrease the rate of immigration. The government's decision to allow more or less immigrants depends on the magnitude of the increase or decrease of the GDCP per capita.

Let's do some calculations. In January (period 1) suppose the population is 10 000 people of which 9 000 are working. The non-working grant reduction (NWGR) is 20%. The GDCP is 4 000 000.00 Ө. We assume a GCT of 10%. Thus the GDCP per capita is:
(4 000 000.00 Ө – 400 000 Ө)/10 000 = 360.00 Ө
(4 000 000.00 Ө – 400 000.00 Ө)/(9 000 + (0.2 x 1000)) = 391.30 Ө
391.30 Ө x 0.2 = 78.26 Ө

The GDCP per capita in period 1 is 360.00 Ө. The general consumerist grant is 391.30 Ө and the non-working consumerist grant is 78.26 Ө

In our calculations 1 month is equal to 1 period. We are now in February. There were 500 deaths and 1 500 births. Our population is 10 000 - 500 + 1 500 = 1100. The GDCP is 4 500 000.00 Ө. The GCT is still 10%. The NWGR is still 20%. There are 7 500 workers and 3 500 people are unemployed. Actually the "unemployed" are working for the command partition.

The GDCP per capita is
(4 500 000.00 Ө – 450 000.00 Ө)/11 000 = 368.18 Ө
(4 500 000.00 Ө – 450 000.00 Ө)/(7500 + (0.2 x 3 500)) = 489.02 Ө
489.02 Ө x 0.2 = 97.80 Ө

The GDCP per capita increases by (368 Ө– 360 Ө) = 8 Ө in one month. Also the general consumerist grant increases by (489 Ө – 391 Ө) = 98 Ө and the non-working consumerist grant rose by (97.8 Ө – 78.28 Ө) = 19.52 Ө

The government opts to allow new immigrants in March. 1800 new immigrants enter our country and 200 emigrants leave. There are 800 births and 500 deaths. Thus our population is now 11 000 – 500 – 200 + 1800 + 800 = 12900. The GDCP increases sharply to 6 000 000.00 Θ. The GCT is still 10% and the NWGR is 20%. There are 8 000 workers. The GDCP per capita is
(6 000 000.00 Θ– 600 000.00 Θ)/12 900 = 418.60 Θ
(6 000 000.00 Θ – 600 000.00 Θ)/(8 000 + (0.2 x 4 900)) = 601.34 Θ
601.34 Θ x 0.2 = 120.27 Θ

In one month the GDCP per capita grew by (418.60 Θ – 368.18 Θ) = 50.42 Θ. The general consumerist grant rose by (601.34 Θ– 489.02 Θ) = 112.32 Θ. The non working consumerist grant rose by (120.27 Θ -97.80 Θ) = 22.47 Θ

In April the government realizes how prosperous the economy is and how dramatically the grant to each consumerist is increasing. They do two things. First they raise the Grand Consumerist Tax to 25 % and allow 2000 new immigrants in. At the same time 200 emigrants leave the country. There are 200 births and 100 deaths. Thus our population is now, 12 900 + 2000 + 200 -100 – 200 = 14 800. The GDCP increases but not as sharply as before to 6 800 000.00 Θ. The amount of workers is 9 500 and the NWGR is 20%. The GDCP per capita is
(6 800 000.00 Θ – 1 700 000.00 Θ)/14 800 = 344.60 Θ
 (6 800 000.00 Θ – 1 700 000.00 Θ)/(9 500 + (0.2 x 5 300)) = 482.95 Θ
482.95 Θ x 0.2 = 96.59 Θ

This is a tremendous decrease in the GDCP per capita (344.60 Θ – 418.60 Θ) = 74.00 Θ
The general consumerist grant drops by (482.95 Θ – 601.34 Θ) = 118.39 Θ. The Non-Working consumerist grant drops by (96.59 Θ – 120.27 Θ) = 23.68 Θ

The government needs to do some changes in May. First, it lowers the GCT to 5% and then it closes its borders to new immigrants. In May there are 500 deaths, 1500 births and 200 emigrants. The population in May is 14 800 – 200 -500 + 1500 = 15600. The GDCP grew to 7 500 000.00 Θ. The NWGR is 20%. There are 7 300 workers. The GDCP per capita is equal to
(7 500 000.00 Θ – 375 000.00 Θ)/15 600 = 456.73 Θ
(7 500 000.00 Θ – 375 000.00 Θ)/(7 300 + (0.2 x 8 300)) = 795.20 Θ
795.20 Θ x 0.2 = 159.04 Θ

This is a tremendous increase in the 3 parameters. The GDCP per capita rose by (456.73 Θ– 344.60 Θ) = 112.13 Θ. The general consumerist grant rose by (795.20 Θ – 482.95 Θ) = 312.25 Θ. The non-working consumerist grant rose by (159.04 Θ– 96.59 Θ) = 62.45 Θ

In June the government could perhaps slightly increase the tax and let some (very few) immigrants in. However we have seen all that can happen in these possible circumstances. Therefore we will end our calculations with those of May's.

The government must be selective as to who is allowed to immigrate into our society. Priority must be given to people who will directly or indirectly contribute to the output of the materialist sector. Given the choice of letting a person who wants to open a convenience store and one who is a janitor by trade, the government should let in the former. If we let in people who will contribute to the materialist sector, the GDCP should increase from one time period to the next.

It is best to have a society with a growing population. It is essential for both the GDCP and the GDCP per capita to grow in a thriving economy. Finally the government can manipulate the number of immigrants it allows in in order to achieve these ends.

The Consumerist Stock Market

The consumerist system has its own stock market. In general, a stock is a claim of partial ownership of a firm. The purpose of this stock market is to allow firms to raise money to start and expand their operations. The consumerist and free-market stock markets are drastically different.

The consumerist stock market is not really a "market" in the free enterprise sense. It is more of a great exposition. In a giant multi-storied building, investors and firm representatives come together to buy and sell shares. Each firm has its own kiosk where it presents investors with the firm's business plan and answers any questions the investors may have about the firm.

The most important feature of the consumerist stock market is this. All shares, regardless of the company or firm that issues them and regardless of the number of shares issued, cost the same amount per share. This price is set by the central bank. It is called the *Consumerist Universal Stock Price* (CUSP). The consumerist stock market falls under the accommodational sector. We will assume for the purpose of this section that the CUSP is 10.00 þ, although this need not be. Investors do not make money by buying and selling stock as they would in a free-enterprise stock market system or the speculative stock market (which we will discuss shortly). Investors earn dividends on their stock which are paid on a per month basis. Shares represent a right to a firm's profit. The greater the percentage of shares of a company an investor has, the more dividends he earns. The firm's profit in this case is not total profit but *post-reinvestment profit*. That is the profit a firm has left over after re-investing back in itself. It is = (price of goods x quantity sold) – running cost – money used to build another outlet or buy more things that will improve the functioning of the firm (such as machinery). Whatever is left over goes to the investor. If an investor has 25 % of a firm's shares and the firm makes 1500.00 þ and reinvests 500.00 þ, then the investor earns (this month) 0.25 x (1 500.00 þ – 500.00 þ) = 250.00 þ. The firm has a right to issue an amount of shares once a month but it must announce that it is doing so. It is crucial that the CUSP remains fixed.

Firms must be careful about how many shares they issue. If a convenience store issues 10 million shares, few investors would buy the shares because the investor will not earn enough money to cover the cost of buying the shares. If someone buys 10 % of the convenience store shares, he would have 1 million shares and since in our example shares cost 10.00 þ, he would have to pay 10 million þ. Even if the convenience store earns 1 million þ post re-investment profit, the investor would only have 10% of the profit = 100 000.00 þ per month. In this example it would take the investor 100 months to earn any profit. Investors are not likely to invest in firms that do not have much potential to flourish.

Let's see an example. A firm that wants to start a car factory and make cars is more likely to sell a large amount of stock. It must convince investors, using its business plan, that the firm knows what it is doing and has good plans. A car factory is more likely to earn profit than other firms like a lawn mowing service. Let's suppose that a firm needs to buy inputs for its factory. It issues 10 000 000 shares. Each is worth 10.00 þ. Thus the company has 100 000 000 þ to start production. Within a year it makes a lot of profit. It earns 10 000 000.00 þ profit and reinvests 5 000 000.00 þ into research and building another plant. The 5 000 000.00 þ leftover is divided up by the investors. Someone who bought 100 shares for 1 000.00 þ will have 0.001 % of the profits which is 50.00 þ. The shareholder will earn what he invested in 20 months. Assuming the firm does not issue more shares, it will take less than 20 months to see a considerable return on investment because the firm is continuously reinvesting in itself, making it possible for even greater profit.

The owners of a firm face tradeoffs. Owning a firm is a kind of juggling act. Three important variables are the number of shares issued and how much money to reinvest and how much money to give to investors. The more shares a firm issues, the more money it has for starting and expanding if it sells all of its shares. However if it issues too much, the stock will be more diluted and the less dividends an investor will earn per share owned. The other variable to juggle is what to do with the profit. The more that is reinvested, the more the firm can earn in the future; i.e. two stores will earn more money than one, but the investors will earn less and less investors will want to own stock. However if more profits are given to investors as dividends, the more shares they will buy because each share has a greater return. But then the firm will not be able to expand as quickly as if it reinvested all of the profit back in itself.

Let's talk about "risky stock". This is stock that comes from a company that doesn't have a certain future, i.e. an oil drilling company. This type of company would issue fewer shares. Each investor would earn a higher percentage of profit the risky firm made. Suppose an oil drilling company formed. It issues 100 shares. If someone bought 80 of the shares or 80% he would receive 80% of the profit of the company. Thus if the company found oil and earned a million Ignits (post re-investment) the investor would earn 800 000.00 þ. However this is not usually the case as most drilling companies do not make much profit (hence the name "risky firm"). Therefore they would issue very few shares and the investors who find the profit making firm in the stock market are the ones that thrive.

It was said that dividends are paid based on post-reinvestment profit. But what if a firm does not have much profit? What if it loses money? Investors ought to be well advised not to invest in such a firm. A good investor does research first. If the firm wants to sell more shares it ought to remedy its financial situation first. If an investor has shares of a firm that is losing money, he doesn't receive any dividends. However he may want to hold onto such shares if in the future the firm does end up making a considerable profit.

The consumerist stock market system works as long as the price of a share traded is unchanged from that set by the central bank. The free-enterprise stock market can easily collapse if everyone starts panicking and starts selling shares at lower and lower prices. This collapse is impossible in the consumerist stock market as prices are frozen permanently. If they are frozen they cannot crash.

In the free-enterprise stock system the big crime is inside trading. The consumerist counterpart is overpricing or under-pricing. That is selling or buying stock at a price higher or lower than the consumerist universal stock price. Investors caught in this felony must be prosecuted as this ruins the system.

Although stocks can be bought directly from firms, they can also be bought from traders (as long as it is at the consumerist universal stock price). Investors who do not want a stock can sell it to another trader at the universal stock price. Also investors who want a stock can buy one from another investor at the universal stock price. If investors like the idea of trading stocks for fluctuating prices; that is buying at one price and selling at another- they are more than welcome to do so in the speculative stock market that we will discuss shortly. That stock market was specially created for those kinds of investors.

Stocks have another function besides being traded and raising funds for firms. The owner of 50 % of the stock of the firm is the owner of the firm. Owners of stock can vote for the leader of a corporation called the Supreme Firm Director based on how much stock they have. This will be discussed later.

The most wonderful thing about this consumerist stock market is that it is impossible to lose any money. In fact an investor is guaranteed to make money. Before a firm issues stock, it must purchase bankruptcy insurance. This is a form of insurance where the insurance firm will pay the bankrupting firm all its bankruptcy expenses. One of these bankruptcy expenses is stock dissolution. This means that if a firm bankrupts, it must buy all the stock it issued to investors. So if an investor bought 800 shares for 10.00 þ, he will be reimbursed the 8000.00 þ. However he probably made some dividend profit. Therefore he must have made some money. This applies to everyone. If a firm issues 100 000 shares worth 10.00 þ per share and bankrupts, it must buy back these stocks with whatever money they have left. If they do not have enough then the bankruptcy insurance firm helps in stock dissolution.

There is a special type of consumerist stock that is important to talk about. It is called *Consumerist Central Bank Stock*. It is actually a special anti-inflationary measure. That is, it is an instrument used to control the money supply. In order to remove money (particularly Ignits) from the economy, the central bank sells Consumerist Central Bank Stock to investors. When it does so, it takes money in the form of Ignits out of circulation (from bank entries). The money taken out of circulation is placed in the *Consumerist Anti-Inflationary Pool*. It is not spent by the central bank, the government or any other entity for any purpose.

There are two very important parameters regarding Consumerist Central Bank Stocks. One is the Consumerist Central Bank Stock Price. This is how much it costs to buy one unit of this stock. There is also the Consumerist Central Bank Stock Interest (CCBSI). This is how much profit one earns from owning Consumerist Central Bank Stock. Both parameters are set by the central bank. Whereas the Consumerist Central Bank Stock Price is fixed, the Consumerist Central Bank Stock Interest can fluctuate depending on the wishes of the central bank.

Let's discuss an example. John, an investor, buys 1000.00 þ worth of Consumerist Central Bank Stock from the central bank indirectly but through his local bank directly. The Consumerist Central Bank Interest is 0.5 %. Every month John owns this stock he earns 0.005 x 1000.00 þ = 5.00 þ. He will continue to make this amount as long as he owns the stock. Actually, he will earn more as the 5.00 þ profit he earns is reinvested. Thus in month #2, he will earn 1005.00 þ x 0.005 = 5.025 þ. At any time John can sell back this stock to the central bank. John can also sell these stocks to another interested investor under the stipulation that they are sold at the fixed price. If an investor wants to sell (or buy) stocks at fluctuating prices, he is entitled to do so in the speculative stock market. Clearly, an investor is guaranteed to make money on Consumerist Central Bank Stock since there is a positive interest rate, there are no barriers to reselling the stock to the central bank and the central bank can never possibly bankrupt.

The money (in Ignits) that the central bank receives from this stock is held in the Consumerist Anti-Inflationary Pool. It is kept there so that there is less money in the accommodational sector being exchanged by consumerists. When the investor wants to sell back his stock, the central bank uses the money in the Consumerist Anti-Inflationary Pool. Also the profit of owning the stock also comes out of the Consumerist Anti-Inflationary Pool. Here's an example: Suppose Kevin buys 5000.00 þ worth of Consumerist Central Bank Stock and the CCBSI is 0.1 %. 30 other investors also invested. In total they invested 1 000 000.00 þ. Thus the value of the Consumerist Anti-Inflationary Pool is 1 005 000.00 þ. Kevin keeps his stock for one month and then sells his stock back to the central bank. At that time the central bank gives Kevin 5000.00 þ + (5000.00 þ x 0.001) = 5005.00 þ. This is deducted from the Consumerist Anti-Inflationary Pool, leaving the pool with 1 005 000.00 þ – 5005.00 þ = 999995.00.þ

There is a possible situation where the amount of money in the form of stocks owned by a particular investor is large compared to the money in the pool. Like in the previous example, we have Kevin who bought 5000.00 þ worth of consumerist central bank stock with a CCBSI of 0.1%. He wants to sell back the stock to the central bank after one month. The central bank should pay him 5005.00 þ. However, in the extreme example where he is the only investor owning Consumerist Central Bank stock some of what he is entitled to after selling his stocks back to the central bank must come from the government. In this case, since Kevin is the only investor in this type of stock, the consumerist anti-inflationary pool is 5000.00 þ, that is, the value of the stock. After a month, after which point Kevin desires to sell his stock, he receives 5005.00 þ. 5000.00 þ comes from the consumerist anti-inflationary pool and 5.00 þ comes from the government. However, this is an extreme example as the consumerist anti-inflationary pool will most of the time be much larger than the gains from interest profit.

So this is how the consumerist stock market works. There are two different types of consumerist stocks. The consumerist stock market has advantages and important points. With a functioning stock market, the consumerist economy can prosper.

The Speculative Stock Market

The speculative stock market is an alternative to the Consumerist Stock Market. It is a little bit different than that system. The main difference is that the price of stocks can fluctuate up or down. The speculative stock market exists in the laissez-faire sector of accommodation based consumerism and Fortals are involved.

The company issuing stock has to insure its stock in case it bankrupts. If the company bankrupts the bankruptcy firm buys back the stock at the issuing price. If a firm bankrupts investors do not lose everything. The bankruptcy insurance firm buys back the value of the stock at the original issue price. Thus the issue price of a stock is very important.

There are two general types of speculative stock that a firm can issue. There are preferred speculative stock and there are common speculative stock. A firm can issue one or the other but not both at the same time.

Preferred stock, like common stock can be traded under a fluctuating price system. However, preferred speculative stock is special in that it allows the investor to have dividend profits based on how their firm is doing financially. The investor in this stock earns a percentage of a firm's post-reinvestment profits as a function of how much of the firm's preferred stock he has. This is understood by the formula:

PRIP x %OOS = payment to investor each pay period

Here PRIP means money the firm has left over after investing in itself. %OOS refers to percentage ownership of stock and is understood mathematically by:

%OOS = (number of preferred stock)/ (total stock issued) x 100%

As an example we have Mario who bought preferred stock in a computer company. The firm issued 100 000 shares each for 10 þ per share and Mario bought 20 of these shares. The firm made 1 000 000 f profit one month and reinvested 600 000 f back in itself . It thus has post reinvestment profit of 400 000 f. Thus each month Mario would earn:

400 000 f x 0.0000002 = 80 f per month

Since Mario initially paid 200 f for these shares, he will have a positive profit after 2.5 months.

The other speculative stock, the common speculative stock, works differently. Here the investor does not make any money through dividends. Rather investors make money by selling and buying common speculative stock at fluctuating prices in the laissez-faire sector.

Although there is potential for profit in the common speculative stock market, one can still lose money on this speculative stock market. If one buys a stock at 50 f and sells it for 30 f he will have lost 20 f in the process. However, if the price of the stock goes below the original issuing price one can still hold to the stock in case, 1) the price of the stock goes up or 2) the firm bankrupts. If a stock trades at 10 f and a firm issued these stocks at 20 f and the firm bankrupts, investors receive 20 ₤ per stock from the bankruptcy insurance firm.

Prices of a common speculative stock and preferred speculative stock can go up or down and people can lose or make money but there is protection from total crash if a firm issuing stock bankrupts. Investors are guaranteed to receive a payout equal to the original stock price. This is guaranteed by the bankruptcy insurance system. Upon bankruptcy, the stock issuing firm buys back the stock the investors bought at the original price. If they can't, the bankruptcy insurance agency steps in and pays the investors the original value of the stock.

The good thing about the bankruptcy insurance firm is that it takes some of the risk of investing off the hands of the investors. The result is that it is less risky to invest in companies. Therefore more investors are willing to invest, thus boosting the economy. More investors are likely to invest in the speculative stock market of accommodation based consumerism than a stock market in a free-market nation because the majority of the risk is in the hands of the bankruptcy insurance firm rather than the investors themselves.

A stock is a claim of partial ownership in a firm. Like in the consumerist stock market, the more shares one owns, the more ownership of that firm the investor has. If one has more than 50 % of the stock of a firm he is considered the owner of that firm.

A firm has choice as to what type of stock to issue. A firm can only issue consumerist stock, preferred speculative stock or common speculative stock but not all of them. This would cause problems in terms of the issue of partial ownership of the firm. For example if one investor has over 50 % of preferred speculative stock and another has over 50% of consumerist stock, who owns the firm? Furthermore, there are other issues regarding bankruptcy.

In our system there is also something called a speculative mutual fund. A mutual fund is an institution that sells shares to consumerists and uses that money to purchase a portfolio of various stocks and bonds. The size and value of the mutual fund can be anything. It is determined by the interaction of consumerists and investment firm. Like in other cases, the investing company selling mutual fund shares has to buy bankruptcy insurance for their financial product. In case the mutual stock issued losses its value due to firms bankrupting, the bankruptcy insurance firm steps in to buy the worthless mutual fund shares. The upside to this is that it decreases the risk associated with investment, thus encouraging investors to invest and benefiting our economy as a whole.

The speculative stock market has a built in anti-inflationary measure. It is called *speculative central bank stock*. These are special stocks the central bank issues so as to decrease the money supply (in Fortals) in the laissez-faire sector. This idea is similar to that of the Consumerist Central Bank Stock we discussed previously. However there are some important differences.

The central bank sells Speculative Central Bank Stocks to interested investors at an official offering price. There is no built in interest-earning or dividend system with these stocks. Rather, investors make money through pure speculation. The price of the Speculative Central Bank Stock is in no way fixed like the Consumerist Central Bank Stock. It is completely free to fluctuate. Money is made by anticipating whether the Speculative Central Bank Stock will go up or down in price.

The money (in Fortals) that is exchanged for Speculative Central Bank Stock is placed into the Speculative Anti-Inflationary Pool. This money is removed from circulation (in terms of bank book entries) and the money supply in the laissez-faire sector is decreased. That is, there are less Fortals being exchanged for laissez-faire sector goods and services. The money in the Speculative Anti-Inflationary Pool is not spent on anything at all. It is just there to be removed from circulation in the Laissez-faire sector.

Let's look at a particular example. Joseph buys 1000.00 ₤ worth of speculative central bank stock from the central bank (through a private bank). This goes into the Speculative Anti-Inflationary Pool. The stock is traded on a stock market and it goes up in value to 1050.00 ₤. Joseph sells this to another investor, Chris at that price. Now Joseph has made a profit of 1050.00₤ – 1000.00 ₤ = 50.00 ₤. This is clearly good for Joseph. Now, a week later the value of the stock goes down to 1030.00 ₤. Chris sells this to Matt. Chris has lost 1030.00 ₤ – 1050.00 ₤ = 20.00 ₤. Chris has lost money on the stock market. It is clear that through speculation, investors can make money or lose money on the speculative stock market where speculative central bank stocks are involved.

Essentially, it can be considered that the money (in Fortals) in the speculative anti-inflationary pool is kept there indefinitely. Unlike the case regarding consumerist central bank stocks, there is no need for the central bank to buy back the speculative central bank stocks. The more of these stocks are sold, the more the laissez-faire money supply is decreased. The stocks themselves circulate among investors in the speculative stock market.

There is really no need for the central bank to take bankruptcy insurance. The central bank cannot bankrupt. The central bank is not really a firm like the other firms in consumerism.

This is how the speculative stock market is designed to work. We examined the role of Speculative Central Bank Stocks. The speculative stock market is contrasted against the consumerist stock market. In some regards it is similar to the stock market in the free-market system. However the guarantee, through the bankruptcy insurance bailout mechanism, makes it in some ways better than that system. Another important advantage is that there is less risk on the shoulders of investors.

Speculative Stock Protection Mechanism

We talked about the essence of the speculative stock market. We noted that it is a lot like the stock market in many capitalist nations. In fact, the speculative stock market and the capitalistic stock market are quite similar.

There is one key distinguishing feature that sets our speculative stock market apart from the stock market of capitalist nations. That is the existence of a special mechanism that prevents a firm's stock from totally collapsing. Our speculative stock market cannot collapse.

In order for firms to sell their stocks on the speculative stock market they must insure their stock with a bankruptcy insurance firm. A firm cannot trade its stocks in the speculative stock market without being insured with a bankruptcy insurance firm.

A vital parameter is the original issuing price. A firm pays insurance premiums based on this amount. So if a firm issues 10 000 stocks at 100 ₣ the firm must pay a premium on this original amount. If it finds a bankruptcy insurance firm that offers a premium of 0.1 %/month it will have to pay 0.1% x 100 ₣ x 10 000 ▷/month to insure its stocks.

What the speculative stock protection mechanism accomplishes is that it makes sure that investors do not loose completely their investment if the firm they invested in bankrupts. If the firm they invested bankrupts, the bankruptcy insurance firm buys back the total of the worthless stock. However, the bankrupting firm must first liquidate all of its assets before the bankruptcy insurance firm steps in.

All speculative stocks are in the laissez-faire sector. Thus they are bought and sold using fortals (₣). The laws of supply and demand (vs. price) apply to the selling of stock. Even though it is impossible to lose everything in the speculative stock market it is still possible to loose in the speculative stock market. If an investor buys a stock for 500 ₣ and sells it for 400 ₣ he loses 100 ₣. However he did not lose everything. This mechanism applies to both preferred and common speculative stock.

As both the speculative stock and the bankruptcy insurance firm are in the laissez-faire sector, they are under the control of the pure free market system. So the more risky stock will probably cost more to insure than the ones that are more likely to thrive. What this does is that it takes away the risk of investment away from the investor and puts it in the hand of the bankruptcy insurance firm. This should increase investment, generally, in speculative stocks.

The Consumerist Bond Market

In general, a bond is a certificate of indebtedness. The consumerist bond market has two purposes. First it is an alternative market for loanable funds. It is designed to provide firms or the government with additional money to expand, start up or provide services. As a corollary, it benefits investors. It is part of the accommodational sector. Secondly, it has an anti-inflationary measure designed to take money out of circulation in the accommodational sector.

In accommodation based consumerism there are five basic types of consumerist bonds. There is a consumerist general bond, there is a consumerist profit bond, there is a consumerist government bond, a premium savings bond and then there is a consumerist savings bond. We will discuss all five but first we will take a look at consumerist general bonds. A consumerist general bond is a promise to pay back a certain amount of money (Ignits) after a length of time called a maturity. In the meantime the consumerist general bond holder receives interest on his bond. There is a bond market in the free-enterprise economy. However there also exists one in the accommodational based consumerist economy. Let's see how it works and how it differs from that of the free-market system.

In a free-enterprise bond market a company receiving money sells a certificate of indebtedness where the company promises to pay back the bond holder what he lent with interest. At the date of maturity, the company must pay back the bond holder. With bonds in the free-market economy there is a credit risk where the company may not be able to repay the bond holder everything. In the free enterprise system higher interests are paid to riskier investments and to bonds with longer dates of maturity.

Now let's turn to the consumerist general bond market. The interest paid on a consumerist general bond is determined by the central bank. The central bank sets an interest rate (per unit of time) called the Consumerist General Bond Interest Rate (CGeBIR). For example it could be 10% per year. Then a consumerist general bond with a 6 month maturity will give 5 % interest. A consumerist general bond with a maturity of 30 years will have an interest repayment rate of 300%. This interest rate could also be set in terms of days. For example it could be 0.01% per day. Then a two year maturity bond will give an interest of 7.3%

Another important variable is how often a consumerist general bond holder receives his interest profit. This is called the Consumerist General Bond Interest Repayment Frequency (CGeBIRF). This is set by the central bank. Let's suppose that it is one month. Then for a consumerist general bond with a maturity of 1 year, the bond holder receives interest earnings every month.

Let's look at an example. John buys 50.00 þ worth of general bonds from a telephone company. The CGeBIRF is 2 months. The date of maturity is 5 years. The central bank sets the yearly bond interest rate at 40%/year. Thus John's bond would give him 40% x 5 = 200 %. Since he invested 50.00 þ, he would make 50.00 þ x 200 % = 100.00 þ. Since there are 30 two month periods in five years, John will receive 100.00þ /30 = 3.33 þ every two months. At the end he will also get back the 50.00 þ that he invested.

What about firms that are risky; i.e. have a high credit risk? In the free-market system, such firms are likely to default and thus must pay higher interests on their bonds. But in the consumerist general bond market all firms have the same interest for a certain amount of time for their bonds. So what happens when a firm defaults on its general bond? The answer lies with the fact that every firm must purchase bankruptcy insurance in order to issue consumerist general bonds. We will discuss the details of the concept of bankruptcy insurance later on. We will say that if a firm is unable to pay its interest and the amount lent for any reason (i.e. bankruptcy) the bankruptcy insurance company does so for the firm. Suppose a firm, ABC, issues a consumerist general bond for 1000.00 þ and with a maturity of 5 years. The interest rate is set at 25% and the CGeBIRF is set at 6 months. These are set by the Central Bank. Suppose firm ABC defaults on its bond repayment. Then the bankruptcy insurance company that the firm ABC bought insurance from would have to pay the investors 1000.00 þ + (1000.00 þ x 0.25 x 5) = 2 250.00 þ

As for the parameters of the consumerist general bond market, the consumerist general bond interest rate (CGeBIR) and the CGeBIRF, these are not fixed. They can be manipulated by the central bank. The Grand Chairman can at any time decrease or increase (change) either the CGeBIR or the CGeBIRF. As soon as he announces it, all firms must follow these instructions.

What about trading bonds? Consumerist general bonds can be traded among investors on one condition. That is that the price of the general bond does not fluctuate. Suppose firm ABC issues a 1000.00 þ bond with a CGeBIR of 25 % and a CGeBIRF of 2 months. This general bond can be sold to another investor for 1000.00 þ.

So far we have given lengths of maturity as arbitrary examples. The length of maturity of a consumerist general bond is not determined by the central bank. The length of maturity can be any size. It can be a few days or many decades. The length of maturity of a consumerist general bond is determined by the interaction of investors and firms.

The same reasoning applies to the value of the consumerist general bond. The bond can be from 0.01þ to millions of Ignits. The central bank, to give flexibility, does not impose a particular size to the consumerist general bond. Here also, the size of the bond is determined by the interaction of investors and firms.

Now let's take a look at consumerist profit bonds. A consumerist profit bond works quite differently from a consumerist general bond. Suppose Andy buys a consumerist profit bond from company ABC worth 1000.00 þ. Company ABC has a revenue of 50 000.00 þ and running costs of 30 000.00 þ. It reinvests 10 000.00 þ back in itself, leaving a post-reinvestment profit of 10 000.00 þ. The central bank sets a parameter called the *Consumerist profit bond interest rate* (CPBIR). Let's say it is 25 %. To calculate the return on investment of this profit bond we divide the value of the profit bond by the firm's revenue and multiply by the CPBIR. This value is then multiplied by the firm's post reinvestment profit. This value is paid to the investor. To determine how often the investor is paid we use the same parameter as the CGeBIRF. For simplicity this can be called the BIRF.

Let's do the calculations for Joe's investment in company ABC. The formula we will use, as mentioned above, is the following:

(PBI/FR x CPBIR) x FPRIP = Payment to investor per period.

Here PBI stands for Profit Bond Investment, which is in our case 1000.00 þ. FR stands for firm revenue, which in our case is 50 000.00 þ. FPRIP stands for firm's post reinvestment profit, 10 000.00 þ.

$$(1000.00 \text{ þ}/50\ 000.00 \text{ þ}) \times 25\% \times 10\ 000.00 \text{ þ} = 50.00 \text{ þ}.$$

The central bank can raise the CPBIR if it wants investors to earn a higher investment profit and thus encourage investment in profit bonds. Or else, it can lower this parameter to help the firm that issued the profit bond.

There is another type of consumerist bond. It is called the Consumerist Governmental Bond. Unlike the other two bonds described above which are issued by firms to increase revenue to promote their business, the consumerist governmental bond is designed for the purpose of taking money out of circulation in the accommodational sector. What the government does is that it sells consumerist governmental bonds to consumerists in exchange for Ignits. One might assume that the government would use this money for government services. This is not the case. The government does not spend this money at all. It just takes it out of circulation (in bank entries).

The government sets an interest rate and repayment frequency for consumerist governmental bonds. These function quite similarly to consumerist general bonds. The interest rate for consumerist governmental bonds is called the Consumerist Governmental Bond Interest Rate (CGoBIR) and the repayment frequency is called the Consumerist Governmental Bond Interest Repayment Frequency (CGoBIRF). Officially they are under the influence of the federal government.

When the government sells a certain amount of consumerist governmental bonds it keeps them set aside in a "Consumerist Anti-Inflationary Pool". The government uses the money to pay the interest payments on these bonds. When it is time to pay the maturity of a consumerist governmental bond, the government uses the revenue in its budget to pay the value of the bond. The size of the bond and the length of maturity are determined by the interaction of consumerists and the government.

Here's an example. A consumerist, John, buys a 10 000 þ consumerist governmental bond with a maturity of ten years. The CGoBIR is 1% per year and the CGoBIRF is one year. So, since the maturity is ten years, John will make $0.01 \times 10\ 000 \text{ þ} \times 10 = 1000 \text{ þ}$ in total for his investment. Since the CGoBIRF is one year and there are ten one year periods in ten years, John will receive 100 þ every year for 10 years and after 10 years he will receive the original 10 000 þ investment. From the standpoint of the government, the original 10 000 þ are saved in the consumerist anti-inflationary pool. Every year the government takes 100 þ from this pool and uses it to pay John's interest payments. After 10 years, when the maturity is due, the government still has $10\ 000 \text{ þ} - 1000 \text{ þ} = 9\ 000 \text{ þ}$. To pay the full value of the maturity, the government takes money out of its operating budget. Thus the government transfers 1000 þ to John after 10 years in addition to the 9000 þ still left in the consumerist anti-inflationary pool. Although the government usually functions using Norses, it can directly convert 1 þ = 1 ⊖ for the purpose of this parameter.

Usually the consumerist anti-inflationary pool will be quite large as many, many individuals will want to buy consumerist governmental bonds. The government can set goals as to how many consumerist governmental bonds to sell and it can encourage more people to buy these bonds by increasing the interest rate i.e. CGoBIR.

The goal of selling this type of bond is to lower the amount of Ignits circulating in the accommodational sector in the form of bank book entries. After some thought, one can see that after the length of maturity is over, the government has actually increased the amount of Ignits in

304

circulation. However, what is actually happening is that the government is continuously selling bonds so that amount of bonds sold is greater than that has to be repaid. Here's an example. Suppose John bought 10000 þ worth of bonds with a maturity of ten years. Before the ten years are over, however, the government sells 15000 þ worth of bonds to two other individuals. Thus, when it comes to repay John's 10000 þ maturity, there is still a lot of money left in the consumerist anti-inflationary pool. The government can continue this indefinitely, always increasing the governmental bond pool to lower the Ignit money supply. If, by chance the government does want to pay back all bond holders in full, this would come from the consumerist anti-inflationary pool and the government operating budget.

Another bond or rather type of bond is the Consumerist Savings Bond. There are three categories of Consumerist Savings Bonds. They are Federal Consumerist Savings Bonds, Provincial Consumerist Savings Bonds and Municipal Consumerist Savings Bonds. The main purpose of these special bonds is to raise additional revenue for the 3 levels of government when the levels of government are short in revenue and need a source of income to finance social services. The basic idea is that the government exchanges a certain quantity of a particular variety of Consumerist Savings Bond in exchange for Ignits which it then uses to pay for social services. Every once in a while the particular government makes interest payments to bond holders and at the end of the maturity the government pays the total value of the bond. There are two important parameters regarding the 3 types of Consumerist Savings Bonds. They are the Consumerist Savings Bond Interest Rate (3 types- federal, provincial, municipal), CSBIR and the Consumerist Savings Bond Interest Repayment Frequency (3 types – federal, provincial, municipal), CSBIRF.

The size of the bond or the length can be anything the investor wishes it to be. So if an investor wants a Federal Consumerist Saving Bond worth 5 000.00 þ and a maturity of 10 years, he can purchase such from the private bank. Also there is no bankruptcy insurance involved in the issuing of the three kinds of consumerist saving bonds. The government can't default on a bond.

There is also something called a premium savings bond. We will go into a fuller discussion on these bonds in an another section. Premium savings bonds are sold directly to consumerists. The government does not keep this money or use it for the funding of social services. What it does is that it reinvests it (for example in a high interest bond or high interest savings account). The interest profits from reinvesting are used to finance social services. The consumerists that purchased the premium savings bonds earn interest on their bonds and eventually get their money back. A key parameter regarding premium savings bonds is the Premium Savings Bond Interest Rate. Suppose it is 0.5 %. If Andy buys 1000.00 þ worth of premium savings bonds he will get 1005 þ back at the end of the maturity.

These are the workings of the consumerist bond markets. The consumerist profit bond market, the consumerist government bond market, the consumerist savings bond market, the premium savings bond market and the consumerist general bond market differ on several major points from the free enterprise bond market. With a strong bond market comes a strong economy.

The Speculative Bond Market

The consumerist bond market has a counterpart. It is the speculative bond market. The speculative general bond market and the speculative profit bond market help firms earn money for expansion while also helping investors. The speculative government bond market has an anti-inflationary measure designed to control the amount of money. Whereas the consumerist bond market is in the accommodational sector, the speculative bond market is in the laissez-faire sector. Thus Fortals are involved.

Unlike in the consumerist bond market, the speculative bond market has three basic types of bonds. They are the speculative general bond, the speculative governmental bond and the speculative profit bond. We already discussed the consumerist bond market counterparts of the three types of speculative bonds and indeed the three types are somewhat similar. First we will talk about the speculative general bond. A speculative general bond is a promise to pay back a certain amount of money (Fortals) after a length of time called a maturity. In the meantime the speculative general bond holder receives interest on his bond.

The speculative general bond market is similar in some respects to the consumerist general bond market although in other ways it differs. The interest paid on a general bond is determined by the interaction of consumerists and those selling bonds rather than through a central bank. Together they arrive at an interest rate (per unit of time). For instance it could be 2% per month. So a speculative general bond with a 12 month maturity will give 24 % interest. A speculative general bond with a maturity of 10 years will have an interest repayment rate of 240 %..

How frequently a speculative general bond holder is given his interest profit is also a crucial variable. We call this the Speculative General Bond Interest Repayment Frequency (SGeBIRF). This is not set by the central bank but through the interaction of consumerists and bond sellers in a speculative general bond market. For our purposes, let's assume that it is two months. This means that for a speculative general bond with a maturity of 6 months, the bond holder obtains interest earnings every two months. Then for a speculative general bond with a maturity of 1 year, the bond holder receives interest earnings every two months.

Let's look at a numerical example. Peter buys 100.00 ƒ worth of speculative general bonds from a telephone company. The SGeBIRF is set at 1 month. The date of maturity is set at 2 years. The yearly bond interest rate is 50 %/year as determined by the action of buyers and sellers of bonds. Thus Peter's bond would give him 50% x 2 = 100 %. Since he invested 100.00 ƒ, he would make 100.00 ƒ x 100 % = 100.00 ƒ. Since there are 24 one month periods in two years, Peter will receive 100.00 ƒ /24 = 3.33 ƒ every two months. At the end he will also get back the 100.00ƒ that he invested.

Speculative general bonds, like consumerist general bonds, can be issued by firms that have a high credit risk. To circumvent this problem we do something similar to what we did for consumerist general bonds. That is we introduce the bankruptcy insurance firm into the equation. What do we do when a firm defaults on its speculative general bond? The solution to this problem lies with the idea that every firm must purchase bankruptcy insurance in order to issue speculative general bonds. If a firm cannot pay its interest and the amount lent for reasons like bankruptcy the bankruptcy insurance company helps the firm. Suppose a firm, let's call it ZZZ, issues a speculative general bond for 100.00 ₣ and with a maturity of 10 years. The interest rate is 10% per year and the SGeBIRF is 12 months. If firm ZZZ defaults on its bond repayment, then the bankruptcy insurance company that the firm ZZZ bought insurance from would have to pay the investors 100.00 ₣ + (100.00 ₣ x 0.25 x 5) = 225.00 ₣. However, the bankruptcy insurance firm only helps after the firm that is bankrupting liquidates all of its assets.

What is the policy regarding trading speculative general bonds? Speculative general bonds can be traded freely among investors. The price of the general bond can freely fluctuate. If a firm, ZZZ, issues a 5000.00 ₣ bond with a SGeBIR of 50 % and a SGeBIRF of 4 months this speculative general bond can be sold to another investor for any amount that is agreed upon.

The central bank does not set the length of maturity of a speculative general bond. The length of maturity can be any amount. It can be a few days or many decades. The length of maturity of a speculative general bond is determined by the interaction of investors and firms. The value of a speculative general bond is also not dictated by the central bank but is rather determined by the interaction of investors and firms. So it can be anything from 1.00 ₣ to 1 billion ₣.

The speculative profit bond is similar to its counterpart in the consumerist bond market but it works a little differently from a speculative general bond. Suppose Peter buys a profit bond from company ZZZ worth 5000.00 ₣. Company ZZZ has a revenue of 100 000.00 þ and running costs of 70 000.00 þ. It reinvests 20 000.00 þ back in itself, leaving a post-reinvestment profit of 10 000.00 þ. We assume that the exchange rate is 1₣ = 1þ and 1þ = 1₣. A parameter called the *Speculative profit bond interest rate* (SPBIR) is determined by the interaction of investors and firms. Let's say it is 15 %. To calculate the return on investment of this profit bond we divide the value of the profit bond by the firm's revenue and multiply by the SPBIR. This value is then multiplied by the firm's post reinvestment profit. The investor is paid this amount. The SBIRF previously set is used to determine how frequently the investor is paid.

We can do the calculations for Peter's investment in company ZZZ. We will use the following formula:

(PBI/FR x PBIR) x FPRIP = Payment to investor per period.

Here PBI represents Profit Bond Investment, which is in our case 5000.00 þ. FR stands for firm revenue, which in our case is 100 000.00 þ. FPRIP stands for firm's post reinvestment profit, 10 000.00 þ.

(5000.00 þ/100 000.00 þ) x 15% x 10 000.00 þ = 50.00 þ.

Lastly, let's talk about the Speculative Governmental Bond. It functions quite similarly to the Consumerist Governmental Bond that was discussed in the previous section. It is supposed to be a mechanism to decrease or manipulate the money supply. Whereas the consumerist governmental bond market involves Ignits, the speculative governmental bond market involves Fortals.

The government sells speculative governmental bonds in exchange for Fortals. The government does not use this money to pay for social services. Rather it takes it out of circulation to lower the money supply. The money goes to the Speculative Anti-Inflationary Pool. All the parameters, the interest rate and the repayment frequency are set by the interaction of the government and investors.

Suppose Mark buys 1000 f worth of speculative government bonds with a maturity of 10 years. The interest rate is 1% every year and the repayment frequency is every 2 years. Thus in total Mark will earn 1000 f x 10 x 0.01 = 100 f. Every 2 years he will receive 20 f.

To pay for Mark's interest payments, the government takes money out of the Speculative Anti-Inflationary pool and the rest is subsidized through the government transfers from the government budget. So if Mark is to be paid his original 1000 f investment plus a cumulative series of payments worth 100 f, he is entitled to 1100 f. The government pays the 1000 f it has put away in the Speculative Anti-Inflationary pool and the government pays 100 f. Since the government functions with Norses, it has to first exchange Norses to Ignits. These are at par, i.e. 1Θ = 1 þ. Then it has to convert Ignits to Fortals using the Ignit – Fortal exchange mechanism. So if 1f = 4 þ, the government has to give 400 Θ = 400 þ to give Mark the 100 f he is owed through this speculative government bond transaction.

Like in the consumerist governmental bond market, in this market the eventual money supply ought to be greater than at the beginning. However, the government is constantly selling speculative governmental bonds so that the Speculative Anti-Inflationary pool is always positive. So, in our above example, before Mark's maturity expires and he must be repaid 1000 f, the government could sell 2000 f worth of bonds with a maturity in the future.

These are the workings of the speculative bond markets. The speculative profit bond market, the speculative governmental bond market and the speculative general bond market differ on several major points from the free enterprise bond market and the consumerist bond markets although there are parallels. A strong bond market helps ensure a strong economy.

Speculative and Consumerist Stock-Bonds

In consumerism there is a special new entity called a *Stock-Bond*. This allows firms to raise money to start up and expand and it allows investors to make a profit. Stock-Bonds exist as consumerist stock-bonds and as speculative stock-bonds. Consumerist stock-bonds involve Ignits and are in the accommodational sector whereas speculative stock-bonds involve Fortals and are in the laissez-faire sector.

There are two types of stock-bonds; consumerist and speculative. A stock bond is something in between a stock and a bond. It is a hybrid of a stock and a bond. First we will talk about consumerist-stock bonds. Consumerist stock-bonds are understood by:

(BV x CSBIR)/2 + (PRIP x % OOS)/2 = payment to investor per period

Where BV is the bond value or the size of investment made. The CSBIR is the consumerist stock-bond interest rate. It is a percentage set by the central bank. The PRIP is the amount of money (profit) a firm has left over after re-investing in itself. The %OOS is the percentage of issued stock an investor has.

So, let's assume one buys an investment (bond) worth 1000 þ and the central bank sets the CSBIR at 5 %.per year. The company issues 10 000 000 in stocks. Since the investor bought 1000 of this, he owns 0.01 % of the firm. The firm makes 1 000 000 þ in a year and reinvests 500 000 þ back in itself. Thus it's post reinvestment profit is 500 000 þ. Thus the investor would earn:

(1000 þ x 0.05)/2   + (500 000 þ x 0.0001)/2 =250 þ + 250 þ = 500 þ per year

Now let's turn to the speculative stock-bond scenario. The formula is:

(BV x SBIR)/2 + (PRIP x %OOS)/2 = payment to investor per period

Here the investor chooses the size of the bond. The SBIR (the interest rate) is set by the forces of the free market rather than the central bank. The PRIP is the amount of money the firm has left over after investing money in itself. The % OOS is the percentage of the shares issued that the investor has.

As an example, an investor, George, invests 5000 f in a firm ABCD. The SBIR is 5 % as determined by the forces of supply and demand. The company ABCD takes the 5000 f and investments of other investors and makes money. It makes a profit of 10 000 f and reinvests 8 000 f. Thus it has a post-reinvestment profit of 2 000 f. The investor owns 3% of the firm. Thus he would make:

(5000 f x 0.05)/2 + (2 000 f x 0.03)/2= 155 f per month

Both consumerist as well as speculative stock-bonds can be traded freely among investors. An investor makes money when he sells his stock-bond for more than he bought it for. However he looses money if he sells it for less than he bought it for.

The only difference between the formula for consumerist stock-bonds and speculative stock-bonds is that in the consumerist case the bond interest rate (CSBIR) is set by the central bank and in the speculative (SBIR) case it is determined by the forces of supply and demand.

A firm that issues stock-bonds, whether of the consumerist or speculative kind, must take out bankruptcy insurance on the stock-bonds. Suppose a bankruptcy insurance firm offers to protect a stock-bond issuing firm for 0.5 %. Thus if an investor buys a stock-bond worth 1000 þ, the stock-bond issuing firm must pay the bankruptcy insurance firm 1000 þ x 0.005 = 50 þ per month.

Speculative and consumerist stock-bonds are great for firms if they want to raise money for start up or expansion. They are good for investors. Each pay period they give the investor a certain amount of money. Furthermore they can be traded among investors to allow for profit by speculation.

International Bonds

We spoke at length about two basic types of bonds- Consumerist bonds and Speculative bonds. There are various kinds of bonds that belong to these two categories. Here we introduce another category of bonds that deserve special attention- international bonds.

International bonds work in the opposite manner to consumerist savings bonds. In the case of savings bonds, a government sells bonds for a quick revenue stream. In the end, it acquires a debt that it needs to pay back. With consumerist savings bonds the government exchanges money in the short run for a debt in the long term.

The basic idea of international bonds is essentially the opposite. The government buys bonds from a foreign government and the foreign government pays the consumerist government a higher sum of money then the initial value of the bond since the foreign government must pay an interest on the bonds. Thus in the end our consumerist government makes a profit.

To talk intelligently about international bonds we need to introduce several terms and parameters. There is the International Bond Maturity Period (IBMP) and the International Bond Interest Rate. The value of the international bond is a variable; it can be 100 f = 100 þ= $100 CDN or 10 000 000 000 f = 10 000 000 000 þ = $ 10 000 000 000 CDN. As we discussed before regarding instances of default the International Bankruptcy Firm plays a role in the mater of international bonds.

Let's work out some examples. We buy an international bond (i.e. we give money to) from a nation in Africa. We give them 1 000 000 000 f. Using the foreign currency adjustment mechanism this amounts to $ 1 000 000 000. The interest rate is 3 % per year. The IBMP is 3 years.

Thus every year the foreign country will be giving us $1 000 000 000 x 0.03 = $ 30 000 000. At the end of the maturity the foreign country will give us the value of the bond, which is $ 1 000 000 000. Meanwhile our country will be making 3 % profit every year until the maturity. In the long run our country makes a decent profit.

It is a good idea if the IBMP is not much longer than 3 years. This ensures that we receive what we invested in a short amount of time.

Another thing to mention is the role of the International Bankruptcy Insurance firm. The IBIF helps a country out if they can't pay back the interest or value of a bond. So if a country sells bonds at a value of $ 1 000 000 and interest rate of 1 % for a year, the country will have to find an IBIF to protect the investment. Let's say that the country finds a firm that offers to protect the transaction for 0.1 % per month. In that case the country selling the bond will have to pay 0.1 % of the value of the bond and how much they have to pay back the creditor on a monthly basis.

International bonds are a good way to raise revenue for the government in the long run. This pays for social services so that taxes need not be implemented.

Gold Investment Certificates and Silver Investment Certificates

In addition to the consumerist stock market and speculative stock market there exists in consumerism another special market. This is the gold and silver market. Like the name implies, in this market investors and other consumerists trade Fortals for silver and gold. This market is in the laissez-faire sector.

In the gold market people trade gold for Fortals. The price of gold is dictated by the laws of supply and demand. Thus the price of gold can fluctuate based on the interaction of sellers of gold and buyers of gold.

The counterpart of the gold market is the silver market. Here Fortals are involved as the trading of silver is in the laissez-faire sector. When we talk about gold it is important to note that similar ideas apply to silver and the market for silver.

The central bank can buy gold in this market from other investors, individuals or entities. It then stores this gold in well guarded vaults. It then sells this gold to consumerists. The central bank issues special gold investment certificates which represent a certain amount of pure gold. So if a consumerist buys 50 g of gold he would get special gold investment certificates (GICs) that say that they are worth this amount of gold. At any time the consumerist can exchange the gold investment certificates for real gold at a bank. Instead of handling real gold the consumerists and banks deal with the gold investment certificates.

The gold investment certificates can be exchanged for Fortals but not Ignits or Norses. They can be given as gifts to other consumerists as long as they are not actually used to buy or sell anything.

The value of a gold investment certificate depends on the interaction of sellers and buyers of gold and can increase or decrease. It is dictated by the laws of supply and demand. So if a consumerist buys a certificate stating that he owns 100 g of gold for 300 f this 100 g of gold can increase or decrease in value of Fortals.

The gold investment certificates are a store of wealth but cannot be directly used to exchange for goods or services. They are like a painting by a famous artist or samurai armour. Although these two have value they cannot be used to buy things with. One cannot buy a meal at a restaurant with a work of art.

The gold investment certificates can be exchanged at a private bank for Fortals. Remember that Fortals are not in the form of cash but in the form of bank book entries. If someone has a certificate for 100 g of gold and let's suppose that the market price of gold is 1 g of gold = 10 Fortals, this person can bring the certificate into a bank and the bank will credit him with 1000 f. Now with the money the person can buy anything in the laissez-faire sector up to 1000 f or exchange this into Ignits using the Ignit Fortal exchange mechanism and buy things in the accommodational sector.

Gold investment certificates can be considered an alternative form of currency in addition to Fortals, Ignits and Norses. However they cannot be used to buy any good or service and can only be exchanged for Fortals. Gold investment certificates are a way to store money in a tangible form. They are in this way like a form of cash but they are not to be used to exchange for goods and services.

It is grossly illegal to try to use GICs as a medium of exchange. Using them as currency to buy goods and services is a type of fraud. If someone wants to buy something with their GICs they need to take them to their bank and the bank will credit them with money in their bank account.

Gold investment certificates are in a sense like pure capital. They have value. They are a way to put money into something that can be touched, held and felt. Gold investment certificates should be about the same size as Canadian dollar bills or Euros. They should be able to be stored conveniently in a person's wallet.

At any time a person wants to buy things with his gold investment certificates he will need to take them to a private bank and the bank adds the equivalent value of the certificates to the person's bank account. Now the person can buy anything in the laissez-faire sector and by extension the the accommodational sector. This is similar to the predicament in capitalism where a microwave, waffle iron or some lobster tails have some intrinsic value. However no one can buy anything with a microwave. First they need to sell the microwave and then use that money to buy things.

In capitalism we have John who has a $10 000 check. Clearly he cannot buy anything with it even though the check itself has tremendous value. John can't buy a computer with that check even though the check has more value than a computer. John must take his check to the bank and exchange it for money (cash) and use this to buy the computer he wants. The idea is similar with gold investment certificates. Although they have value, they need to be exchanged for Fortals (bank book entries) before anyone can buy anything with them.

Gold investment certificates can at anytime be exchanged for real pure gold. The value of a gold investment certificate is equal to a particular weight of gold. However it may make things a little bit easier if investors handle with gold investment certificates than actual gold. Since private banks may not always have a store of gold in their premise, the private bank needs to buy pure gold from the central bank (at the market price). This may take anywhere from 5-8 days.

GIC's are the opposite of a credit card. Whereas GIC's are a store of value they cannot be used to purchase things. On the other hand a credit card is just a piece of plastic. Yet a credit card can be used to buy almost any item.

Pretty much anything we have just said about gold and gold investment certificates can be transferred to silver and silver investment certificates. A consumerist can buy silver from the private bank using Fortals in the form of silver investment certificates. This is a way to store money in a tangible form. However these cannot be exchanged for goods and services, Ignits or Norses. They can only be exchanged for Fortals. Silver investment certificates can be exchanged for pure silver if the consumerist who owns them desires it. Silver investment certificates can increase or decrease in value depending on the supply and demand for silver.

Gold investment certificates and silver investment certificates are a strange kind of alternate currency to the other three we have already talked about. Though they are not exchangeable for goods and services they are nevertheless a great way to store value. In a sense, we were able to have (something like) a form of cash in a cashless society.

Taxes

Taxes are a payment to the government as a result of different situations and transactions. In order for the government to operate, providing services that can only be provided publicly, it needs revenue. There is a dramatic difference between the tax system of the free-enterprise economy and that of the consumerist economy.

Above a certain income, people under the free-enterprise system pay income tax. This income tax is designed so that the more one works, the more money he or she must pay to the government. Some people who earn a considerable amount of money can pay as much as 50% (or even more) of their income to the government.

There is also a property tax in capitalism. The people who own property have to pay the municipal government this tax. This tax pays for such things as schools, parks and waste pick-up. Even for a relatively modest amount of property, this tax can amount to tens of thousands of dollars per year.

Under the free-enterprise system we have sales tax. Many jurisdictions make people pay additional money for quite a few of the goods or services they buy. In some places this tax is small while in others it is over 20%. Usually it is around 15%.

Corporations have to pay corporate tax. This shrinks their profits. Money that could be reinvested back into the company goes to the government.

There are various other taxes on almost any good or service that the government decides to levy a tax on. These include alcohol, gasoline and cigarettes. There are also many other forms of luxury tax.

One of the greatest advantages of the accommodation based consumerist economic system is that there are only three special taxes. The government has different ways to raise funds.

Each month all final goods and services in the materialist sector are counted. They are counted whether they are sold to consumerists or have the potential to be so. A restaurant adds up all the meals they sold and multiplies this by their price. As for all retail stores, grocery stores, convenience stores, department stores, car dealerships etc., the amount of goods they have in stock is multiplied by their price. The value of all services purchased (mechanics, teachers, gardeners, taxi cab drivers) is added up. This calculation does not include intermediate services or goods like cashiers, cooks, janitors or flour, wheat, plastic, steal or coal. Once all of these are added up, the central bank has a value of the GDCP.

The government sets a tax called the GCT in terms of a percentage. The central bank grants the government a portion of the GDCP equal to the GCT. Thus no consumerist actually pays tax out of his own pocket.

How is the GCT determined? There are 3 levels of government; federal, state/provincial and municipal. Each of the 3 levels of government votes on the tax, with each level having exactly one third of the total representation. If there are several governments in a level (state, province or municipal) each has a weight for voting proportional to its population.

Thus if a province has twice as many people as another and there are only 2 provinces, one province will have a voting of 22% and the other 11%. An example illustrates this.

As an example, there is one federal government. There are four states. They have populations in the ratio 1:1:2:3 There are 6 municipalities with populations in the ratio1:2:3:3:4:4. They vote on the GCT as such

	Vote	Weight
Federal	25%	33%
State 1	40%	33%/7
State 2	10 %	33%/7
State 3	30 %	33% x 2/7
State 4	20 %	33% x 3/7
Municipality 1	20 %	33%/17
Municipality 2	30 %	33% x 2/17
Municipality 3	30 %	33 % x 3/17
Municipality 4	20 %	33 % x 3/17
Municipality 5	25 %	33 % x 4/17
Municipality 6	35 %	33% x 4/17

The GCT is (8.25 + 1.88 + 0.47 + 2.83 + 2.83 + 0.39 + 1.16 + 1.75 + 1.16 + 1.94 + 2.72) = 25.38 %. Thus the GCT is 25.38%

The GCT is divided similarly to how it is determined through voting. The federal government receives 33% of it and each of the state and municipal governments receive their share based on their ratio of populations. Now let's see the revenue. We will assume that the GDCP is 100 000 000.00 ☉

	Weight	Revenue (1000.00's)
Federal	33%	8 375.00 ☉
State 1	33 %/7	1 196.00 ☉
State 2	33%/7	1 196.00 ☉
State 3	33 % x 2/7	2 393.00 ☉
State 3	33% x 3/7	3 529.00 ☉
Municipality 1	33 % x 1/17	492.00 ☉
Municipality 2	33 % x 2/17	985.00 ☉
Municipality 3	33% x 3/17	1 478.00 ☉
Municipality 4	33% x 3/17	1 478.00 ☉
Municipality 5	33% x 4/17	1 976.00 ☉
Municipality 6	33 % x 4/17	1 976.00 ☉

For the vote weights of the municipal and state/province governments it may be simpler to use percentage weights as opposed to ratios. In our example the state/provinces had populations in the ratios of 1:1:2:3. These are equivalent to weights (respectively) of 14%, 14%, 28%, 42%. Thus each state has a vote weight corresponding to the percent of the whole population that is contained in that state.

Besides the GCT, the government has only right to two additional taxes. If a government votes a tax that is too high, it will probably not survive the next election. Thus the citizens have veto power over the government's (tax) voting powers.

In consumerism there is also the possibility of two other taxes- the positive personal income tax and the wealth tax. Through the positive personal income tax consumerists are guaranteed to make a profit and in the wealth tax only a very small percentage of the population pay. Furthermore, the wealth tax is so small, that those paying it can afford to do so.

It is possible that one level of government may transfer some of its tax revenue to another level of government. For example, if the federal government made 1 000 000 000.00 Θ and a municipal government earned only 50 000.00 Θ, then the federal government can transfer some of its revenue to the municipal government. So the federal government transfers 500 000.00 Θ to the municipal level government.

It is quite important to the workings of the system that there are only three taxes. This ensures that other groups are not discouraged from contributing to the economy. For example the lack of a corporate tax encourages more firms to do business in our nation and the lack of a usual income tax leads a worker to be more efficient as what he earns he can keep to spend as see fit. It is strongly discouraged to invent original taxes (property, income, sales, and luxury) even if it is to relieve the tax burden of the GCT.

The taxes may change from month to month. Every month when the GDCP is determined, the governments come together and vote on the GCT. They do so every month.

There are several other sources of revenue that a government has. It can sell land to consumerists. It can sell licenses or permits. It can issue savings bonds. The command partition can make a profit. It can make profit through the work for freedom program. It can also make profit through the recycling-for-pay program. There may be profits from gambling and casinos/lotteries.

The tax system in consumerism is different than that of free-market capitalism. We witnessed how the GCT is calculated. The consumerist tax system is an integral part of the system.

Wealth Tax

The wealth tax is a tax on the wealthy to pay for social services. The main argument in favour of the wealth tax is that it reduces inequality and boosts the economy. On the other hand those that are against it contend that it will not turn out in reality as it will in theory.

The wealth tax is a disincentive to working hard. People who have worked hard all their lives and have accumulated wealth are punished for doing so. The wealth tax is a punishment for hard work.

The wealth tax takes away money from those who earned and deserve the money and gives it to those who did not earn the money nor did anything to deserve it. Equality is a wonderful idea as long as people earn it. What's more important than equal income is equal opportunity to make a living, thrive and succeed. This is what consumerism supports to the highest degree.

The accommodation based consumerist economic system prides itself in the fact that there is no wealth tax, unless it is vitally needed. By this it is meant that there should be no wealth tax unless the government just can't raise revenue by other means. Those who earn money have the right to spend it as they see fit. In fact in Consumerism there are no property tax, corporate tax, luxury tax, alcohol tax or carbon tax. Those who earned their money are those who have the right the spend their money.

The wealth tax hurts those who contributed to society. Those who contribute to society have the right to spend their money as they chose. The wealth tax hurts the Canadian society and that of other nations as it forces the hard working to go to other countries to use their abilities.

However, after all the negative things that have been said about the wealth tax it is prudent to say something positive about it. Of all the taxes that can be enacted, the wealth tax is least hurtful to most people. Suppose the government enacts a tax where below an income of 100 million Ignits no one has to pay anything and afterwards the rich man pays 1% of his income. First of all, the vast majority of people would be totally unaffected by this tax and those that earned more than 100 million Ignits would only lose a tiny percentage of their money.

It is unlikely that the wealth tax will be invoked. However if the benevolent social planner does decide to introduce it, it is important to note that those paying the wealth tax do not pay the positive personal income tax. Furthermore, it will never, ever appear in the laissez-faire sector.

Also, ideally, the wealth tax effects a very minimal percentage of the consumerist population. It is hoped that less than 0.01 % of the population actually have to pay it. This amounts to, given a population of 10 million people, only 1 000 wealth tax payers. Those that pay the wealth tax have such an abundance of money that they will not be terribly hurt if they are asked to pay it.

Recall that there are absolutely no taxes in the laissez-faire sector. Thus, ambitious workers can't convert their income into Fortals (if they work in the accommodational sector) for the purpose of avoiding the wealth tax.

That being said, the wealth tax along with the Grand Consumerist Tax (GCT) and positive personal income tax should be governmental sources of revenue invoked as an absolute last resort. The government should receive revenue from the other sources that are well described in this book.

The Income Reimbursement Initiative- A Positive Personal Income Tax

There is yet another method for the (3 levels) of government to acquire revenue. Here we introduce the income reimbursement initiative. It can be thought of as a sort of "income tax" where the tax payer actually makes money in the long run.

In the free-market system taxes are a negative thing. Most people do not like paying them and they discourage progress, productivity, efficiency and the desire for work. What is the point of working if a vast amount of your prosperity goes to the government in the form of tax? In capitalism hard workers are punished for their contribution to society by a sometimes monstrous income tax that takes away most of what they earned and gives it to someone who didn't.

In consumerism most taxes do not exist- this includes property tax, corporate tax, luxury tax and tax on tobacco and alcohol and gasoline. In a sense there is a personal income tax but this tax has the wonderful quality that it is positive. This means that tax payers make money on the income tax system in the long run. Those that pay the income tax will have, after a certain period of time, more money than they originally paid. Thus this positive personal income tax is even better than if there were no income tax at all !

Before we talk about how the income reimbursement initiative works we need to introduce several useful parameters. There is the Income Reimbursement Initiative Interest Rate (IRIIR). There is the Income Reimbursement Initiative Maturity Period (IRIMP). Finally there are 5 tax brackets.

The functioning of the income reimbursement initiative is quite simple. The (3 levels) of the government tax those consumerists that make a certain amount of money where there are 5 income brackets and those who earn more pay more in taxes. The government takes this money and puts it in a high interest savings account or high interest paying speculative bond that has a higher interest rate than the IRIIR. The government makes profit from the interest on this account or bond and uses it for social programs. The tax payers are paid interest on the tax they paid. In the end after the IRIMP the tax payer is entitled to have all the money he paid reimbursed. Thus the tax payer gets back everything he paid but since he gets interest payments on what he paid as taxes, he comes out more prosperous than before he paid the tax. To reimburse the tax payer, the government periodically withdraws money from the savings account or bonds.

Let's work out a concrete example. All the numbers in this example are exemplary and need not be so in any actual system. So there are 5 tax brackets. Those who earn < 50 000.00 þ pay nothing. Those who make between 50 000 þ and 75 000 þ pay 5 % per year. Those who make between 75 000 þ and 100 000 þ pay 10 % per year. Those who make 100 000 þ to 150 000 þ pay 15 % per year and those who earn more than 150 000 pay 20 % tax. Those who earn 5 000 000 000 have to pay the wealth tax, assuming it is invoked.

Kyle earns 100 000 þ per year so he pays 10 % of this which is 10 000 þ. The IRIIR is 0.5 %. The IRIMP is 3 years. In the three years Kyle would receive a profit of 10 000 þ x 0.5 % x 3 = 10 150 þ. Every month 10 % of his paycheck is deducted from him and 0.5 % is added. After 3 years Kyle gets 10 000 þ x 3 = 30 000 þ from the government. But since he is paid interest on his taxes (of 0.5 % per year) he ends up with a lot more than he originally started off with.

It is important to mention again that the positive personal income tax and the wealth tax are mutually exclusive. If someone pays the positive income tax he need not pay the wealth tax. If someone pays the wealth tax he need not pay the positive income tax.

In this scenario the government, let's say the federal government, also wins. After collecting income tax from many people in the country they obtained 10 000 000 000 þ. In the capitalist system the federal government would use all this money to pay for social services and tax payers would be at a loss. However, in consumerism the federal government takes the 10 000 000 000 þ and puts it into a high interest paying savings account or in a high interest paying bond in the speculative bond market. Let's say that the interest rate is 3.5 % per year. So in a year the interest earned on this loan is 0.035 x 10 000 000 000 þ = 350 000 000 þ The IRIIR is 0.5 %. So in total 0.005 x 10 000 000 000 þ = 50 000 000 þ go to tax payers. Therefore the federal government made a total of 350 000 000 þ - 50 000 000 þ = 300 000 000 þ. This is money used to pay for ultra-universal health care, universal education, roads, hospitals, schools and for defence.

In consumerism there are no write-offs or deductions as to the positive personal income tax. Thus the individual can't find ways to pay less of this initiative. Actually, it is in his best interest to pay a lot. Although he will pay a certain amount of money initially, in the end he will get it all back with interest. What this tax actually does is that the government takes consumerist's money and invests it and gives the investor back all his money in totality. The interest profit from the investment is split between the tax payer and the government which uses the money to pay for social services.

Like in the case of the wealth tax, the income tax a person pays depends on which sector he made his income. If he earned his income in the laissez-faire sector, then he pays nothing. However, if he made income by working in the accommodational or governmental sectors he can't convert his money into Fortals to avoid paying the positive personal income tax. That is a form of fraud.

As we can see, this positive personal income tax is very useful and beneficial. Clearly, the income tax payers win in the long run. The government accrues quite a bit of money for social services. There is no clear loser as this positive tax is better than if there were absolutely no income tax.

The Welfare System and the Socialist Labour Pool

The welfare system can be defined as the system that takes care of those who are temporarily unable to provide for themselves. It is there so that the poorest do not live in abject misery and poverty. It is one of the government's duties to help the poorest of society at least as long as they can't help themselves.

In a free-market system the poor and those who do not have a job are assisted by the government. The government gives them a welfare check which they exchange for goods and services. However two problems arise from such a setup. First, people who still work may still be able to get a welfare check. There is welfare fraud. The second problem is that many unemployed lose their motivation for finding a job. Our welfare system must be able to help out the poor and avoid these problems.

In consumerism no one should have to worry about materialist things. Things like food, transportation, clothing and entertainment are provided to consumerists when the central bank grants Norses to them as part of the general and the non-working consumerist grants. Consumerists can exchange this money (Norses) for materialist goods and services. Governmental services like healthcare, sanitation and defence are provided by the three levels of government through the GCT and other sources. Many goods and services are within the easy reach of most consumerists.

The accommodational and laissez-faire sectors are the incentives for a consumerist's contribution to society. He who works harder receives a better house and a bigger property. But what if a consumerist is unemployed? He should not have to live on the street.

This is how the consumerist welfare system works. The government provides a decent sized apartment or condominium for the welfare recipient. It also provides him with running water, heat and electricity and some appliances and an additional check in Ignits and Fortals that the welfare recipient can exchange for goods and services in the accommodational and laissez-faire sectors. The government provides minimal living space and access to utilities to the welfare recipient in addition to money (£, þ) to do what they will.

The government issues welfare checks and provides housing. However, as soon as the welfare recipient finds a job, he will have to repay part of the cost of the apartment and appliances and all of the utilities that he took advantage of as well as the unemployment check. He will also have to pay with compound interest. The reasoning for this is this. If the welfare recipient knows that he is continuously getting into debt by living in a welfare apartment, he will have more of an incentive to look for a job. The longer the recipient spends in his welfare apartment, the bigger his welfare debt grows. The government actually makes money on the welfare system.

Suppose that in addition to the accommodation and appliances provided by the government, the welfare recipient receives 500 þ and 500 £ every month. This is to spend on goods and services in the accommodational and laissez faire sectors. To discourage fraud and encourage finding work in partitions other than the command partition, we have two parameters: Auxiliary Reimbursement Deduction (ARD) is how much less a welfare recipient receives per month for being in the socialist labour pool. This is expressed as a percentage. To fight poverty and help people, the ARD should be close to zero. So in our example if it is set at 1%, every month the auxiliary worker will receive 1% less than he did last month. The higher this parameter is, the more welfare recipients are encouraged to find a job in the natural or governmental partitions.

Another parameter is the Unemployment Assistance Repayment (UAR). This is how much money a worker has to repay the government when he finds a job in a partition other than the command partition. It is expressed as a percentage and set by the government. Like the ARD it is designed to discourage fraud. If a worker has to pay back for the assistance the government provided he is less likely to want to be on welfare. Let's suppose it is 20%. If an auxiliary worker receives 500 þ and 500 f every month, he will have to repay 20 % of this when he leaves the socialist labour pool. Here, if we want to support a welfare recipient's well being and fight poverty we would keep this parameter low, maybe even zero. However if we want to discourage people from being on welfare, we would make this value higher. Furthermore, people who go on welfare go find another job and then return to welfare have their welfare payments as they were when they were on welfare previously.

A natural question comes up. If the welfare recipient receives free living space and his utility bills are paid for and the longer he stays there the greater his welfare debt becomes, why wouldn't he just chose to live there indefinitely. The answer is that his living arrangements are very minimal; i.e. he will probably live in some kind of small apartment, and with several bedrooms. He may want to do better. He may want to own a house of his own one day. He will not want to live on welfare forever then and will start looking for a job. The quicker he does so the less he will have to pay back the government for providing him welfare and the sooner he can move onto bigger and better things.

There appears to be another problem. If everyone is granted Norses by the central bank for the materialist sector, why worry about the accommodational sector? Some people may see a positive trade off of not working and living in an apartment because the most important things are in the materialist sector (food, clothes, entertainment). The way out of this is that the non-working consumerists are granted much less Norses than their working counterparts. The government sets this. It is called the Non Working Grant Reduction. If this is 20% and each working consumerist is granted 1000.00 ʘ per month, the non-working consumerist is granted only 200.00 ʘ per month.

Back to the two problems we found in the free-enterprise system. People are unlikely to commit fraud as they will eventually have to pay the government back for what it provided them. Second we saw two ways to increase the motivation to find work. First, welfare recipients become indebted the longer they are on welfare. Secondly, consumerists on welfare receive drastically less Norses from the central bank to spend on the materialist sector than those that work.

People on welfare do not receive their welfare check for doing nothing. All unemployed, whether able or disabled- with a few exceptions- become part of the Socialist Labour Pool. The Socialist Labour Pool is a part of the Command partition and it is run by the Human Resource Management Commission. Whereas other measures reduced unemployment, the socialist labour pool completely eradicates unemployment. As stated in another section, this concept is similar to Chinese State Capitalism.

Both able bodied and disabled people can be made to contribute in the socialist labour pool. Whereas we find a suitable job for a skilled worker, we also try to find employment for a disabled or developmentally challenged individual. For example, in the disability work program, these people can be made to sort screw, lick envelopes or push shopping carts or be given jobs with an occupational complexity rating of < 2.5.

When a worker losses his job he can apply for extra-work transfer payments (similar to welfare). The individual fills out a form similar to an application or resume describing what he or she is good at, his education and experience. Jobs that match skills, knowledge or experience are assigned to that person. For example a person with martial arts training could be hired in an HRMC run martial arts training school while a developmentally disabled person could be put in an HRMC run grocery store packing shopping bags with groceries or pushing shopping carts. The Human Resource Management Commission is like a big hiring company that matches (currently unemployed) workers to jobs using the principle discussed before to find the most suitable jobs for people. For a person working in the socialist labour pool, the experience he receives is great on a resume after he leaves the socialist labour pool. Interestingly, workers in the socialist labour pool do not need to buy jobs (job contracts).

The extra-work transfers come in at least five forms. A formerly unemployed person can be paid by the hour, by the day, by the week, by the month or by the year. Which payment format is applied to a recipient of the extra-work transfer depends on how productive the individual is. So a cashier would be paid by the hour, a comic book artist would be paid weekly and a farmer would be paid yearly. The setup that maximizes output is the most ideal one.

This is the nature of the consumerist welfare system. This is how it operates. We found the solutions to the problems that appear in the free-enterprise welfare system while still helping those with limited income.

The Laissez-Faire Labour System

The laissez-faire labour system is designed to eliminate unemployment. It is a program created to put people to work that would otherwise be unemployed. It minimizes the cost of people on social assistance like "welfare".

Before we go into the details of this system let us show the logic of this program using dollars as our example. We have a welfare rate of $10.00 /hour. We recognize that many of our major manufacturing firms have outsourced their production to other third world nations like Bangladesh, Pakistan or Cambodia. Over there, the minimum wage is, for example, $2.00 /hour. We want those factories back so we provide an even lower minimum wage of $1.00/hour. So these major companies come back to our country. These companies pay our workers $1.00/hour and we subsidize this payment by $ 9.00/hour. So instead of idel workers doing nothing at all besides sleeping in and watching TV and getting paid $10.00/hour from the government, the government only pays $ 9.00/hour and the workers are doing something productive. In both cases the workers are paid $10.00/hour. Clearly this is better. But there is another benefit. Suppose a textile (clothing) company re-outsourced back into our nation. This company needs cotton and polyester thus giving business to our cotton and polyester manufacturers. The company needs machines to make clothing. This gives business to our manufacturers that make these machines. The company also needs to build a factory in our nation. This gives business to construction workers and contractors, and those that make building equipment like cement trucks.

Using the logic that was described above, the laissez-faire labour system strives to provide jobs for our workers that would otherwise be transferred to less well-off countries where workers are paid less. To accomplish this we completely redefine the notion of "minimum wage". The government sets aside several industries that participate in the laissez-faire labour system. For these industries there is no minimum wage. The manufacturing firm can pay their workers as little as it wants to. The workers working at these jobs are paid the equivalent of the extra-work transfer. The government pays these workers the equivalent of the extra-work transfer minus the wage given by the manufacturing firm. So, for example suppose the extra work transfer is 7.00 þ/hour + 3.00 f /hour and a company producing spoons pays 1.50 þ /hour. In this case, the government pays each worker 7.00 þ/hour – 1.50 þ /hour (+3.00 f/hour) = 5.50 þ /hour + 3.00 f /hour. Clearly this is better than if the government had to pay the total of the extra-work transfer directly to the worker.

Whenever we bring back a factory or manufacturing firm to our country, there are economic side-effects. If we entice a car manufacturing firm to come back to our country from say, Guatemala or Thailand, we are helping our economy in many other ways too. That car factory needs steel, glass, plastic and rubber. Our firms that produce steel, glass, plastic and rubber will have someone to sell their inputs to. A car factory needs a building to produce its cars. This represents jobs for construction workers and companies that make building supplies and equipment. Furthermore, the workers as well as the executives need food and accommodation. This also provides business to our firms.

The workers in the laissez-faire labour system should be entitled to union representation. The workers pay a small amount from their wages so as to be represented by a union. The union fights for the rights of the workers. They ensure that workers have proper working conditions and safe working standards. That is they ensure that the worker is not exploited and treated unfairly. One thing they can't interfere with, though, is the wages the firms pay to their workers. In fact it is counterproductive to do so. Ultimately, the workers are paid the equivalent of the extra-work transfer. How much the government pays for that depends on the wages the firms in the laissez-faire labour system give their workers.

Thus would work the laissez-faire labour system. It allows us to re-outsource firms from other countries while giving work to others in different industries. This system functions also to eliminate what is left of unemployment in our system.

The Disability Work Program

In Consumerism we need to take care of people who are 'disabled' as they represent a special portion of our society. By people who are disabled we mean people, for example, who are schizophrenic, blind, on a wheelchair, amputees or deaf, among others. In capitalism these people, unless they chose to work, would receive a small check from the government to pay for the things that they need. Unfortunately, this payment is so small that disabled people cannot buy too many things that they want. In Accommodation Based Consumerism we encourage these people to find work so they can contribute to society; increasing societies general level of output and they get paid for doing so.

The disability work program is very, very similar from a logical standpoint to the laissez-faire labour system. The government sets aside certain occupations that belong to this special program. The disabled person gets paid through the disabled work program the value of the extra work transfer. This payment is paid out jointly through the firm that hires him or her and partially through the levels of government.

Suppose the government normally pays $10.00 \, þ + 10.00 \, f$ per hour or $300.00 \, þ + 120.00 \, f$ per week to people who are unemployed. The government finds special jobs that suit disabled people, i.e. those that they can perform with quite proficiency. The firm pays a portion of the disabled worker's paycheck and the government pays the rest. So if we find a job for a disabled person, let's say a schizophrenic individual – like pushing shopping carts, the firm that employs the individual would pay him for example $2.00 \, þ$ per hour and the government would pay him $8.00 \, þ$ per hour $+ 10.00 \, f$ per hour. The government in this case would have to pay less to help the individual since it pays him only $8.00 \, þ + 10.00 \, f$ per hour rather than a full $10.00 \, þ + 10.00 \, f$ per hour. The schizophrenic individual can decide how much money he earns as he is paid by the hour. If he is ambitious and works hard he will make a lot of money to spend on the accommodational and laissez-faire sectors. Society in general wins since the output is increased. Furthermore, the firm that employs the disabled individual pays a lower wage for the labour.

Like the laissez-faire labour system, the major goal of the disability work program is to re-outsource simple jobs from other countries and bring them back to our country so that our disabled people have something to do. Let's recapitulate the logic. We have a simple job like putting stickers on buckets at a bucket factory. In a foreign country, somewhere in Asia, the factory pays their workers, for example, $2.50 \, þ$ per hour. We re-outsource the firm back to our nation. That is, in our country, the firm would pay only $1.75 \, þ$ for the same work. Thus it is likely, since the costs of doing business are lower, that the work will come back to our country. In that case we put disabled people to work at the bucket factory. Meanwhile we get more qualified people to do more sophisticated jobs like managing or running the factory. So the firm that runs the bucket factory pays $1.75 \, þ$ to each worker. The government sets the extra work transfer at $8.00 \, þ$ and $5.00 \, f$ per hour. This is how much each disabled person earns while working at the factory. However the government pays only $8.00 \, þ - 1.75 \, þ + 5.00 \, f$ per hour $= 6.25 \, þ + 5.00 \, f$ per hour. Thus this program lowers the cost of extra work transfers.

The disability work program, like the laissez-faire labour system is designed to eliminate unemployment, especially among the population who are disabled. Whereas the laissez-faire labour system is geared to the general population, the disability work program is specifically created for disabled people. It is a program made to put people to work who would otherwise be unemployed. Like the command partition and the laissez-faire labour system it decreases the cost of people on social assistance like "welfare".

The disability work transfer works primarily in the governmental and accommodational sectors. The disability work transfer provides money to disabled people based on how much hours they work (or weekly or monthly). With this money, the disabled people can buy things in the accommodational and laissez-faire sectors. However, the disabled have complete access to the services provided by the government (all 3 levels). So the blind, schizophrenics and those on wheelchairs have access to universal healthcare, free education, protection from police, help from the fire department and garbage pickup. The disabled are treated the same as those that are not disabled with regards to access to governmental services.

The disability work program does not directly affect the materialist sector. The central bank gives money (Norses) to all people including the disabled. However, the disabled are given the non-working consumerist grant rather than the general consumerist grant. This means that people who are disabled will receive a little less money than most working consumerists to spend on goods and services in the materialist sector like food, clothing, automobiles, etc..

An interesting part of the accommodation based consumerist economic system is that the disabled workers are not necessarily restricted to work at the disability work program. If a blind person, deaf person, retarded person on someone on a wheelchair can find a job in another part of the economy than he is more than welcome to do so. In that case he will earn more money than if he worked for the disability work program (as he is paid wages set by the central bank). Furthermore, if he works above a certain threshold, the disabled worker can earn the general consumerist grant, thus earning more money to spend on the materialist sector. (For example the disabled worker can find work at a more sophisticated job like lecturing, teaching, working at a call station, reception, etc...)

A positive benefit of the disability work program is that it gives disabled workers a higher self esteem and a sense of self satisfaction as they contribute to the economy. Instead of being a burden on society, they become valuable members of society. Clearly it is better if an individual is paid money for doing something useful, regardless of whether he or she is disabled or not.

The disability work program works to find employment for a portion of the consumerist society. It finds jobs for the disabled that have an occupational complexity rating < 3. It puts disabled people (schizophrenics, the blind, wheelchair persons) to work that suits them so that they do things instead of being idle and get money from the government for doing absolutely nothing. Thus the disabled earn an income while contributing to the output of society.

Minimum Wage

The concept of minimum wage is important in the free-enterprise system. Essentially the government sets a minimum wage a business can pay its employees in exchange for their services. Its necessity is evident when one considers that if a factory paid its workers a low wage, it may be impossible for the workers to earn enough to buy clothes or even food.

Countries with high minimum wages usually have high standards of living. Yet if the firms in a free-market system could pay their workers lower wages they would hire more workers. Under low minimum wage there is higher employment. There is a trade-off. Governments that set higher minimum wages have people that are well off but less are employed than if the minimum wage was lower.

Usually the minimum wage increases as time goes by. As minimum wage increases some firms raise the prices of their products to compensate for the loss they incur having to pay their employees more. Although this phenomenon is usually restricted to companies that give low wages it nevertheless contributes to an inflationary spiral.

With regards to accommodation based consumerism, the concept of minimum wage does not apply to the GAM sectors of the natural partition. Actually under accommodation based consumerism, minimum wage totally does not exist. All wages in the governmental, materialist and accommodational sectors of the natural partition are set by the central bank. They may be changed by veto; i.e. if a finance minister or head of state vetoes it or a considerable portion of the population signs a petition against a particular wage function.

In the laissez-faire sector, there must also be no minimum wage. The laissez-faire sector is such a pure capitalism that there is theoretically no minimum for firms to pay for workers. Prices and wages are set by the interaction of consumerists and producers. We must make sure that there is freedom for the forces of supply and demand to do their magic. There is no minimum wage dictated by the government.

The minimum wage that firms pay workers in the laissez-faire sector is influenced by the wages paid in the other sectors. The elimination of unemployment will raise the minimum wage paid to workers in the laissez-faire sector.

In the command partition, the workers are paid through one of the five extra work transfers. Actually, people with jobs with a high occupational complexity are paid a little bit more. Thus, due to the command partition compensation adjustment, it can be considered that the extra work transfers are a form of minimum wage.

Minimum wage, as we have discussed, is not necessary in the GAM sectors of accommodation based consumerism. It is managed in the laissez faire sector for the reasons we talked about.

The Accommodation Award

In many, if not most, of the leading economic superpowers there is a substantial portion of people who are homeless. These people either have no job or have a very low paying one and struggle for food, clothing and most of all, shelter. One just needs to walk down the busy streets of major cities like New York, Chicago, Toronto or Los Angeles to see people in desperate need of a place to live. The problem is even worse in third world nations. In consumerism, one homeless person is one too many. In a consumerist nation, everyone should have access to a shelter.

In major cities under capitalism the remedy is to provide emergency shelters for the homeless. Usually a well-meaning charity or the government will provide a bed for people who would otherwise freeze outside, especially in the winter. The problem is that the number of people who are homeless usually far exceeds the number of special beds in shelters. As a result, some people freeze and hope that their coat will keep them warm.

In consumerism, absolutely everyone is entitled to a place to live. First of all, we assume that most of those who work for the government sector/partition and accommodational sector of the natural partition, where wages are fixed by the central bank, all are able to buy a decent form of accommodation. The way that wages and price functions for accommodation are set (by the central bank) assures us of this with quite certainty.

Now, what about those people who don't have a job through either the accommodational sector or natural partition or government sectors? Remember that whoever is still "unemployed" is guaranteed a job through either the command partition or the laissez-faire labour system. All a homeless person has to do is sign up for work through either of these anti-unemployment systems and they are guaranteed a form of accommodation. Even if they don't work they are still entitled to shelter although they will not be receiving much in the form of the extra-work transfer in terms of money.

The accommodation that previously homeless people receive should be "minimal but not abysmal". That means it must be of sufficient quality but not so prestigious that other workers in the other sectors will have worse accommodation. That means that the previously-homeless should not have to live in shacks, one bed-room apartments or trailers. Yet they shouldn't either live in a luxurious mansion or 6 bedroom houses. Perhaps something like a condominium, a small bungalow or 3 bed-room apartment will be sufficient. The previously-homeless also receives utilities (hot water, electricity) and several appliances (fridge, oven, and microwave).

All those individuals eligible for the accommodation award are under the constraints of a parameter called the *accommodation award repayment percentage* (AARP). Essentially this means that a previously-homeless will have to pay a portion of the accommodation award that he was provided or he can pay for accommodation while living there.. The AARP could be 100 %, 0% or something in between. If it is 100 %, the individual must repay the value of the accommodation, the utilities and the appliances after he finds a job in either the governmental or accommodational sectors. If it is 0%, the individual doesn't pay anything, in the end, for what the government provided for the previously-homeless person. If it is for example, 70 %, the individual pays back 70% of the value of the accommodation award he was given. For example if someone got a condominium worth 1000 þ per month, 2000 þ worth of appliances and 400 þ worth of utilities per month and he lived there for 5 months he would have to pay the government 0.7(1000 þ x 5 + 2000 þ + 400 þ x 5) = 3500 þ. The higher the AARP, the more it discourages people from taking advantage of the accommodation award. The lower the AARP, the more it helps people in need- those that were previously homeless. If it is zero or close to zero, this will tremendously fight poverty. The main purpose of the AARP is to overcome fraud.

When the previously-homeless do decide to do work in the command partition or laissez-faire labour system, they will then be able to receive the extra-work transfer. This may offset the cost of the AARP, perhaps even neutralizing it. For example suppose that the extra-work transfer is 10 þ /hr (we ignore gains in Fortals for this example). If a previously-homeless person now gets a job in the command partition building houses and works 400 hours in 5 months, he can use this to offset his AARP payments. In the end he will still have (10 þ/hr x 400 hours) – 350 0þ = 500 þ .So he will have 500 þ left to buy things like a trip to a vacation destination or wine.

It is possible (although very unlikely) that individuals working for either the accomodational sector of the natural partition or governmental sectors could apply for the accommodational award if they are having a hard time making ends meet. They will be able to pay for their accommodation through their wages they receive in the accommodational or governmental sectors. For example, suppose a janitor makes 2500þ/month. He applies for accommodational award where the AARP is 60%. Over the time frame of a month the accommodation (including utilities and appliances) add up to 2000 þ. The janitor must pay 0.6 x 2000 þ = 1200 þ a month.

We want all our consumerists to have access to housing (accommodation) so that there is no homelessness in consumerism. That's what the accomodational award system accomplishes. It ensures that no one has to live on the street. However, we want to make sure that people do not abuse the system. We need to make sure consumerists contribute to society in exchange for their accommodation. There are a few measures and parameters designed to do just that.

First of all there is the NWCG (the Non working consumerist grant). It is how much people who receive the accommodational award from the government are granted to buy things in the materialist sector. Let's say it is 5 000 O per month in this example. Now those receiving the accommodational award have to work to get their housing. They can't say that they can't find work as consumerism has a multitude of measures to reduce and eliminate unemployment. So it is a lie if someone says that they can't find a job. Those that "can't" find a job are usually those who truly do not want to work. The command partition hires everyone who has a desire to work.

Now those receiving the accommodational award must work a certain amount of hours in order to get the full value of the NWCG. The central bank sets this threshold in either weeks or months. So let's say a person receiving the accommodational award must work 5 hours a week or earn 200 þ per week or work 20 hours a month or earn 800 þ per month to receive the full value of the NWCG which in our example is 5 000 þ.

If a worker works above these thresholds then he is in good standing. However, if he works less than he has a certain percentage of his NWCG deducted from his grant each 2 week period. This should motivate him to work as if he works less or not at all, he has less money for the materialist sector.

So now the government sets the accommodation award deduction incentive (AADI) at 5% per week. Every week the worker who gets the accommodational award and works less than the threshold has 5% of his NWCG deducted from him.

As an example, John has been provided with a free condo and the threshold is 5 hours a week and he doesn't work at all. The NWCG is 1000 þ. The AADI is 5% per week. Thus John only makes 950 þ. If he doesn't work the next week, he will receive 950 þ x 0.95. This whole system is designed to make sure that john contributes to society and doesn't take advantage of the accommodational award.

There may still be homeless people who are working in the laissez-faire sector. They are entitled to the accommodational award if they truly need it. The money they make in their laissez-faire sector job can be used to pay for the parameters of the accommodational award program (i.e. the AARP)

The accommodation award is provided to certain consumerists by the government. The government buys accommodation (houses, bungalows, apartments, condos) from other consumerists at the fixed price function. Or it hires previously unemployed construction workers to build the accommodation structure. This initial investment comes out of the government's running budget which is paid for by the many governmental sources of revenue we have in our system. By working in the command partition or the laissez-faire labour system, those who take advantage of the accommodational award can pay a portion of the accommodation award they are receiving.

The accommodational award program works to ensure homelessness does not exist in consumerism. It is designed to give accommodation as well as utilities and several appliances to those that have a hard time affording them. It ensures that no one in our consumerist society is homeless.

Bankruptcy

It is important to know the circumstances regarding a bankruptcy. By bankruptcy we mean the stoppage of production and functioning of a firm. Examples of firm bankruptcies include the following. A doughnut shop stops selling doughnuts and coffee and no longer services its customers. A farm no longer raises or sells its livestock or crops. A music teacher no longer teaches students at her facilities. A construction company no longer uses cement and trucks to put up buildings. A real estate company no longer engages in helping people find homes.

When a firm is losing money during operations, it may be better for it to close down and declare bankruptcy. When a firm bankrupts it ceases to exist. It must sell off all its assets. The bankrupting firm has four primary obligators. They are stockholders, bond holders, workers and creditors. When a firm bankrupts and sells its assets it must pay its obligators in this order: workers, stockholders, bondholders and finally creditors.

Before a firm can sell bonds or stocks or issue job contacts, it must buy bankruptcy insurance. This insurance helps pay off the obligators if there is not enough money after the firm has sold off its assets. The central bank does not set the *Bankruptcy Insurance Premium Rate.* This is how much a firm must pay an insurance company each month to protect it in the case of a bankruptcy. It is determined by the interaction of the bankruptcy insurance firm and the firm wishing to buy bankruptcy insurance.

Let's take the case of a convenience store, Steven's convenience. We examine how it bankrupts. The bankruptcy of other firms is similar to this case. The store has 3 workers. They buy job contracts for 500.00 þ and the Adjusted Yearly Income Percentage is 2000 %. They are given contracts for one year. The convenience store issues 100 stocks. The consumerist universal stock price is 10.00 þ per share. They issue 1000.00 þ worth of bonds with a maturity of one year at an interest rate of 10% per year compounded yearly. The convenience store borrows 5000.00 þ from a private bank at 10 % interest.

Steven must take out bankruptcy insurance in case his business fails. This is based on the total of his obligations to A) stockholders, B) bondholders,C) workers and D) other creditors like the bank. The bankruptcy insurance premium rate is 0.5% per month. So Steven has to pay:

Workers-	3 x 500.00 þ x 2000% = 30 000.00 þ
Stockholders-	1000 x 10.00 þ = 10 000.00 þ
Bondholders-	1000.00 þ + (10% x 1000.00 þ) = 1 100.00 þ
Loan from bank-	5 500.0
Total-	46 600.00 þ

So he pays 46 600 þ x 0.005 = 233.00 þ to the bankruptcy insurance firm every month,

The convenience store is in a bad neighbourhood. It is surrounded by 2 big grocery stores and other stores which compete with it. Sales are low and Steven decides to close his business.

Steven files for bankruptcy. He must first sell off all his assets. After selling all the inventory of goods in his store, the building and the land the building was on he accumulates

30 000.00 þ. The bankruptcy insurance also covers bank creditors or those who lent money to the firm. Steven must pay the creditors (bank) which lent him 5 000.00 þ at 10 % interest (5 500.00 þ). He owes the other 3 obligators 41 100.00 þ so his total debt is 46 600.00. Since he doesn't have enough, the bankruptcy insurance firm helps him. The bankruptcy insurance firm pays 46 600.00 þ - 30 000.00 þ = 16 600.00 þ. Now that all debts are settled, the bankruptcy process is complete.

Usually bankruptcy is unfortunate for the firm bankrupting. However, it may be beneficial for society as resources are transferred to another project. Suppose a firm that sells CD's bankrupts and the workers that worked there and lost their job find another job at an online firm. This is clearly beneficial from the standpoint of society.

Clearly the owner of a bankrupting firm is worried when his firm bankrupts. However, neither the workers, stock holders nor bond holders are particularly upset as the bankruptcy insurance firm pays either the value of their contract (how much they would earn if they worked the duration of their job contract) or the value of their bonds and stocks.

It may seem to some that the existence of bankruptcy insurance may cause those managing companies to want to bankrupt. However, this makes as much sense as saying that those who desire life insurance want to die or that those who desire car driver's insurance want to get into an accident. A firm that bankrupts must first pay its obligators from what it can accrue from selling all assets. Only then does the bankruptcy insurance firm play a role.

The term "bankruptcy insurance" was probably badly made. Unlike the name suggests, it doesn't really help the firm that is bankrupting. It actually helps those people or groups who would normally, under a free-market system, loose out. Thus it primarily helps the four types of obligators – stock holders, bond holders, creditors and workers.

The concept of bankruptcy applies specially to the consumerist system. We took the example of Steven's convenience. We looked at the payment of debts to obligators. This section explained what happens during a bankruptcy.

Inflation and Deflation

Inflation is the constant rise in prices, whether of products, services, inputs or wages. Deflation is the constant decline in prices whether of products, services, inputs or wages. Here we take a look at them.

It is usually believed that when inflation is quite low (1% to 4%), it is not a problem. In fact an equal inflation- when the prices of everything rise all at once – is considered neutral. Deflations are usually much rarer than inflations but when they are small they are also not much of a problem.

In free-market capitalism the inflation rate is measured by something called the *consumer price index.* This measures how the price of a fixed basket of goods changes from one year to year. In consumerism, since the price functions for all goods and services are fixed, the consumer price index or its equivalent will be a constant (i.e. it will not change from year to year).

There are some problems with inflation. One is called "shoe leather cost". This has to do with the constant trips to the bank an individual has to make. Inflations are bad for the creditor and good for the borrower. Inflations are also a key component of the wage-price spiral that hampers the economy.

A clear problem of inflation is that it can potentially destroy the savings someone has saved up over the years. If the inflation rate is higher than the interest rate on a savings account, the investor is actually losing money.

A hyper inflation can almost destroy an economy. In Germany in the 1920's the value of the Mark was inflated from 1 Mark per Dollar to 10 billion Marks per Dollar in the span of 3 years. If an economy is experiencing hyperinflation, we know it is falling apart.

Another problem of inflation that is often overlooked is that it is an integral component of the free-enterprise business cycle. (See figure 7). When there is a boom, eventually the demand outstrips the supply and prices rise. There is an inflation. At point (X) the bank raises interest rates to stop the inflation and the economy heads towards a recession. If we eliminate the possibility of inflations the central bank has no need of raising the interest rate and we thus put a stumbling block in any business cycle and possibly eliminate it altogether.

Yet another problem with inflation is more subtle. When people retire their income doesn't necessarily increase while the prices of goods and services increases. When someone retires with a certain amount of money, that money looses its value over time.

In consumerism there is no inflation or deflation in the GAM sectors. It is not possible as the prices of all goods are fixed with the exception of the laissez-faire sector. There may be one time increases in prices at the retail level due to manipulations with the retail mark-up; but this is not inflation because it is a onetime adjustment. The central bank doesn't just print money and issue money at random as it does in the free-market economy. Rather, the central bank only issues an amount of Norses equal to the production of the materialist sector. The AIMs control the money supply.

One problem is that this money eventually turns into Ignits when there is a transaction and it ends up in the accommodational sector. To combat the possibility of excess money, there are many anti-inflationary measures – for example the accommodational markdown - which suck the Ignits out of the accommodational sector and take them out of circulation in bank book entries. Yet there is no inflation or deflation as prices are fixed in the GAM sectors.

It is completely illegal for anyone to manipulate either the price of goods, services or wages (with the exception of the laissez-faire sector). Doing so would hurt the economy.

Inflation poses a special problem in the laissez-faire sector. In that sector, all decisions are carried out by the interaction of firms and consumerists under the guidance of supply and demand. Thus inflation is a real problem. There are several mechanisms designed to control it. One is the nominal ignit-fortal exchange mechanism. There are also the speculative government bond and the speculative central bank stock. Dynamic gambling may also be useful. After all of these have been exhausted, we can use the laissez-faire markdown.

In free-market capitalism there is a very important concept known as the Phillips curve. Basically this refers to the idea that in the short run there is a tradeoff between unemployment and inflation. The Philips curve should not exist in consumerism as there are separate measures to combat inflation and unemployment. Unemployment and inflation are considered as two separate concepts. This applies to the GAM sectors. In the laissez-faire sector when there are problems with inflation one of the many AIMs can be invoked. Also if there is unemployment in the laissez-faire sector, one of the many unemployment measures can be invoked. For example there can be an increase in the output of the command partition of the laissez-faire sector.

Inflation and deflation are reoccurring ideas in the discussion of economics. We need to know what they are and how they function. We have seen why these two phenomena do not exist in our system. Their absence benefits our economy.

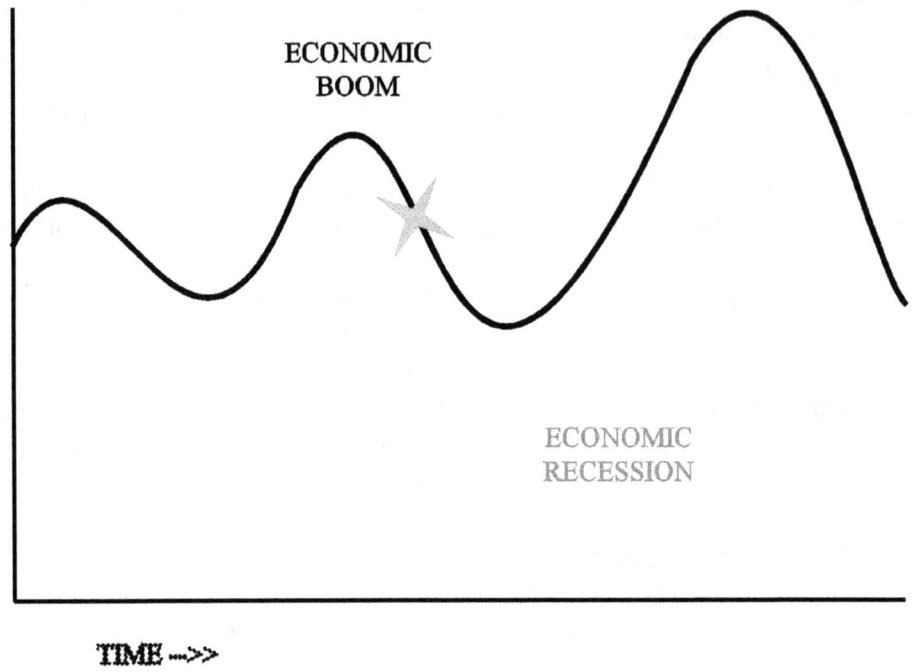

ECONOMIC
BOOM

ECONOMIC
RECESSION

TIME --->>

Figure   7

Figure 7

Solutions to the Problem of the Capitalist Business Cycle

The business cycle exists in capitalism. Essentially, what happens is that the capitalist economy experiences a perpetual, never ending cycle of expansions, booms, downturns, recessions and expansions again. Most, if not all, capitalist analysts and university professors universally agree that this is a major fault of capitalism and finding a solution to it would be a tremendous help.

In capitalism, recessions begin when the GDP (Gross Domestic Product) starts to fall. This causes unemployment to rise. Other macroeconomic variables also fluctuate. These include personal income, corporate income, investments and sales of various items. A recession effects the entire economy in capitalism.

Consumerism avoids the business cycle. There are over 20 special measures designed to combat unemployment. Specifically, if unemployment increases, these extra workers can simply find work in the command partition or in the laissez-faire labour system. In fact, key to the design of accommodation based consumerism, it is very, very unlikely that there would be any unemployment at any time. There would be, in all likely hood, negative unemployment – that is a shortage of workers rather than a shortage of jobs.

One of the measures of general output in consumerism is the GDCP- the output of the materialist sector. This variable should, on its own, be steadily climbing. However if it is not, there are many things that the government or central bank can do to raise it. For example, it can set up more firms in the command partition.

To raise the output of the economy, there are special parameters for that. These give firms an advantage and make it more likely for a firm to operate in our consumerist nation rather than somewhere else in the world. For example, the laissez-faire labour system (not to be confused with the laissez-faire sector) "re-outsources" jobs from third world countries and brings them to our nation. The profit reward transfer, another key parameter, makes it more likely for firms to operate in our country. Also the capital reinvestment transfer and the government employment incentive program are ways to bring firms into our nation – and increase production of goods and services. Basically, there are ways the government can increase production in all sectors and raise output by manipulating several important parameters.

The main idea of how consumerism overcomes a recession and does away with the capitalist business cycle is that it has many, many parameters to manipulate. The abundance of these parameters allows us to get over any problematic economic situations that include recessions.

In all likelihood, consumerism will not experience the business cycle. In this system there will be an ever-increasing "spiral" of wealth. This means that the economy will be getting bigger, bigger and bigger.

Recessions, when they happen, affect prices. In consumerism this is avoided in the GAM sectors as price functions are fixed by family of good and service. Thus the fluctuations of prices that accompany recessions do not occur in consumerism.

Recessions when they happen, affect wages. Wages are not effected in consumerism. The value of a wage (in the GAM sectors) is set by the central bank. Since wages do not fluctuate in consumerism – and consequently cannot drop like it occurs in the recession – a major problem of recessions is avoided.

One may notice that if business cycles are an integral, unavoidable, part of free market capitalism and the laissez-faire sector is pure capitalism, then wouldn't business cycles necessarily occur in the laissez-faire sector? They shouldn't for two reasons. First of all, a recession begins when it is required to decrease the money supply. However in the laissez-faire sector when the money entering the sector is equal to the special anti-inflationary measures (which include the laissez-faire markdown and the ignit-fortal exchange mechanism, among others), the money supply is in a steady state. As long as the money supply is balanced the economy (sector) has no catalyst to fall into a recession.

There is also another reason why recessions are very unlikely in the laissez-faire sector. If the output of the natural partition of the laissez-faire sector starts to decline (recall that a decrease in output over two quarters is one of the characteristics of a recession) then in that case, the command partition of the laissez-faire sector increases its output. That is, it builds more command partition operated stores, factories, farms and services in the laissez-faire sector.

The business cycle is a major problem of capitalism. Consumerism provides an alternative economic system where this cycle does not cause problems. This book describes how to avoid the business cycle.

Accommodational Rent

Here we explore the concept of rent. By rent we refer to the idea where a building or a part of it is able to be used by another individual without actually owning it. Buildings can be rented for various reasons; i.e. shelter, storage etc.

Let's examine the case of renting a condominium. Suppose that the price function of a condominium is x1000.00 þ+ y2000.00 þ+ z100.00 þ. This is a simple function. These will usually be a lot more complicated. Here x represents rooms, y represents floors and z represents square meters. In our example, our condominium has 3 rooms, 1 floor and 50 square meters. Thus to buy it costs 10 000.00 þ

Now we introduce a new concept into our discussion- *The Rental Equivalence Duration* (RED). This means how long it will take to pay for the total cost of the building being rented. It is set by the central bank and can vary. Suppose that the RED is 5 years. Thus each year the renter of our condominium would have to pay 2000.00 þ or 167.00 þ per month to the land owner to rent the condominium.

We will call the owner of the property the landlord and the person renting it, the tenant. The higher the RED the better it is for the tenant. The lower the RED the better it is for the landlord.

Suppose that a tenant does not want an entire property but only a portion of it. He pays only the percentage of the RED of the building that he rents as his rent to the land lord. Take the case of an apartment. The entire apartment complex costs 1 500 000.00 þ. Land owner Betty owns it. There are 50 apartment suites. Zack is a tenant in one of them. The RED is set by the central bank at 2 years. Thus every month, Zack must pay = 1 500 000.00 þ/ (50 x 2 x 12) = 1 250.00 þ. If the accommodational markdown is 20%, Betty keeps 875.00 þ from what Zack gave her.

Let's give one more final example. Suppose Mike's firm wants to rent a space to start their firm. They find one where the land lord had to pay 100 000.00 þ for. The RED is 6 years. Each month Mike's firm must pay = 100 000.00 þ/(6 x 12) = 1389.00 þ. The landlord receives, assuming 30% accommodational markdown, 972.22 þ

The concept of rent is vital in terms of exchange of accommodation. We learned about the RED and how it affects rent payments. This makes it possible for people to rent and use property.

Rent of Goods and Services

We have discussed the renting of accommodation in the last section. Now we turn to the topic of renting other goods and services. By this we mean the use of a product or service without having complete ownership of it. For example someone may want to rent a DVD from a movie store and watch it once or twice without fully owning the DVD.

It is important that certain items be allowed to be rented. Sometimes a consumerist may want to use a good or enjoy a service without fully owning the good or having total control over the service. He may want to enjoy a good but not need to own it outright. He would rather pay a smaller price for renting the good than pay the full price for the good in question.

To allow for the renting of certain goods and services we must allow for the idea of rent in our system. So we introduce the *Rental Repayment Value* (RRV). This indicates how much of the original product or service the renter has to pay in order to use the product or service once. It is determined by the Grand Chairman of the Central Bank. So if the RRV is 3% and a car costs 10 000.00 Ө, the person renting the car must pay 300.00 Ө to use the car. The car renting firms will compete with each other in quality. That is they will compete, among other things, in how long the renter can keep the car before he has to return it. This competition ensures that renters have access to the best services.

As another example, imagine that a DVD costs 30.00 Ө to own. At a movie rental store they would rent the movie to movie watchers. If the RRV is again 3 %, then the renter has to pay 0.90 Ө to rent the DVD. Again the different DVD outlets would compete in quality. They would offer longer and longer rental periods. So consumerists pick the DVD outlet that provided the best service for example, the longest length for keeping the movie before having to return it.

There are many examples where it makes perfect sense to rent the item or service as opposed to owning it outright. Someone may want to rent a limousine for his wedding or graduation rather than owning one. Someone may want to rent a tuxedo for an important event without buying it outright. There are also other examples.

The above ideas were specific to the accommodational and materialist sectors. In the laissez-faire sector, rent is not determined by the central bank or the government. Rater it is set by the interaction of supply and demand vs price.

Being able to rent goods and services in the accommodation based consumerist system is very important. The Rental Repayment Value helps make this easier and straightforward. We gave some examples of how the idea of rent would work. Renting provides consumerists access to goods and services without having to own that good or service outright.

The Universal Consumerist Card

All consumerists receive the universal consumerist card (UCC). This card allows them to make purchases in the consumerist economy. This card is very important for making transactions in consumerism.

There are several ways that consumerists can exchange goods and services for money (keep in mind that consumerism is a cashless society). A consumerist can write someone a check or they can use their debit card. In addition to these, a consumerist can use the UCC. When a consumerist pays for an apple at a grocery store, he can swipe his card and receive the apple. The value of the apple is deducted from his bank account and added to that of the grocery store. Another idea worth exploring is the creation of special apps that would allow for transactions using cell phones. It may be possible in the near future that app designers will invent a special smart phone mechanism where by swiping the UCC across the phone and typing one's personal identification number one can facilitate a trade in one of the sectors of consumerism. Lastly, consumerists may use their cell phones to pay for things. They can swipe their phone during a transaction as if it were a debit card. At some time in the future someone may invent a pay app. Eventually they pay for the item by paying to their cellphone company.

The UCC can be used either in the accommodational, materialist or laissez-faire sectors. Whenever there is a transaction between a consumerist and a place of business the consumerist can use his UCC.

An important point we must mention is that strict, careful measures must be undertaken to ensure the security of the UCC. Thus a consumerist must know the personal identification number (PIN) for his card (perhaps more security measures may be required like the use of a finger swipe). Furthermore, it is a severe crime to have unauthorized purchases on someone else's UCC. This is a severe form of fraud. It should be punishable. However, some exceptions are permissible like for example, when a mother gives her 12 year old son her UCC to buy groceries for her.

All consumerists are entitled to have a UCC. They can use it anywhere and at anytime in the consumerist nation. They are an alternative method to exchange money in the economy.

Since all consumerists are entitled to receive money and use money in our system, even minors should be entitled to a UCC. However there should be, perhaps, some restrictions on how minors can use their UCC. For example, a five month old probably can't make purchasing decisions just yet. Thus, there should be an age at which parents have primary control of a child's UCC. However, a six year old should be able to use their UCC to buy a toy if he wants to.

A quick example of a transaction with a UCC is necessary. Brent wants to buy a book in the laissez-faire sector. The book costs 40.00 f at a book store. Brent swipes his card and types in his PIN. The store gives him the book. At the same time 40.00 f are deducted from Brent's fortal bank account records and 40.00 f are added to the book store's bank account records.

The UCC is very useful in a consumerist economy. It helps make purchases and money exchanges more straightforward and simpler.

The Laissez-Faire Business Limit

We previously talked about that the consumerist economy is divided into four sectors – the accommodational, materialist, governmental and laissez-faire sectors. Some goods and services are in one sector while others are in another sector. This setup allows us to preserve quality selection, true wealth and to maximize output.

We stated previously that goods and services that should compete in quality ought to be traded in the materialist and accomodational sectors. This ensures that consumerists have the highest quality goods and services like cars, clothes and food. On the other hand, if it is more logical for goods and services to be traded based on price then these goods and services ought to be included in the laissez-faire sector. This includes jewellery, books and services of actors, lawyers and athletes.

However, there are certain goods and services in the accommodational and materialist sectors that at times may be moved to the laissez-faire sector. This occurs if they are produced in very small quantities. An example of this is the selling of lemonade. If lemonade is sold at a grocery store, it is part of the materialist sector. However, if a child sets up a lemonade stand and sells lemonade at the street corner at this point the lemonade business should be in the laissez-faire sector where the lemonade is purchased with Fortals.

Other examples are mowing the lawn or shovelling snow. Instead of these services appearing in the accommodational or materialist sectors, they should be moved to the laissez-faire sector. In general, there are some services and goods that are produced in such small amounts and where the "entrepreneur" makes a very small amount of money that his whole enterprise should be in the laissez-faire sector.

What determines if a small business should be in the laissez-faire sector rather than the accommodational or materialist sector is the "laissez-faire business limit". This is set by the government. Let's suppose that it is 100.00 þ per year. If someone makes less than 100.00 þ per year at a business like mowing people's lawns then he can exchange his services for fortals. So, if he makes 80.00 f per year and the Fortal-Ignit exchange rate is 1f = 1þ, then he is below the limit and he can operate his business via the laws of supply and demand (vs. price) and he can operate in the laissez-faire sector.

The laissez-faire business limit puts balance in our economy. It makes the division of services and goods among sectors more straightforward.

Incentives

It is true that in order for people to do something, they usually need incentives to carry out such action. But just what are incentives and what is their nature? We need to motivate workers to produce goods and services, to produce a lot of them and to produce the best ones possible. But what will motivate them?

What follows is an illustration of the *principle of motivation*. In order to get a dog to sit one would give him a treat. In order to get a fussy child to finish his dinner of spinach or broccoli one would give him dessert- ice cream for example- as a reward. In order to get a student to study hard, teachers would give him an A for a good performance on an exam and an F for a bad performance. To encourage a horse to pull a carriage, one would whip him to make him go faster.

But will a dog do a trick if there is no promise of a treat? Yes- if doing the trick was in some way important to him. Will a child finish a dinner of broccoli even if there is no dessert? Yes- if he realizes that he needs broccoli to be healthy. Will a student study hard even if he doesn't earn an A for doing so? Yes- if he realizes the value of being educated. Will a horse pull a carriage even if it isn't whipped? Yes- if it realizes that the owner must arrive somewhere on time.

Then why do we need a motivation, such as a treat, an A, a bowl of ice cream, if we do things we are rewarded for, for our own good? What role does the dog treat, the ice cream, the A, play to all those to whom it is given? They are all a reward- something we like to receive and would like more of. The reward is clearly seen for what it is. It is something that keeps us going when we lose sight of the benefit of what we are working at. It is something we work for.

Why does a student need an A to work hard if studying hard favours him by making him more educated? It motivates him to study hard; it keeps him going. He is rewarded with something he likes in exchange for something that is subtly good for him. Why does a dog need a doggy biscuit to encourage him to sit and to do tricks? He is rewarded with something he likes, what makes him happy, what he wants in exchange for doing tricks. Why does a child need ice cream for eating dinner he doesn't like? To encourage him to eat it. In all these cases the reward is something the individual being rewarded likes or wants. The principal of motivation states that in order for an individual to do work, there must be a reward or the acquisition of something the individual likes. If this principal is violated, the economic system will not work as no one will want to work.

This is the concept of incentive. We came across the principal of motivation and saw that it is important. In the coming sections we will see how incentives apply to productivity, efficiency and progress.

Incentives for Productivity

Agents in consumerism need an incentive to be productive. By productivity we mean contributing to society. Workers need a motive to work and firms need a motive to operate and expand.

In the free-market, people are led as if by an invisible hand to contribute to society when in fact they are actually trying to contribute only to their own well being. In consumerism there are two invisible hands. The left hand operates as the more people produce, the greater is the output of the economy. As the population remains the same size, each person receives more materialist money. The right hand operates as the more people produce, work, labour and invest the more accommodational money they earn. This whole concept is a lot like a horse pulling a person in a carriage. When the horse advances it moves forward but at the same time it drags the carriage along with the person forward.

There are two types of incentives. We will call them noble incentive and individualistic incentive. By adding to the GDCP, a firm in the materialist sector increases how much money each consumerist is granted by the central bank. Suppose a car dealership puts on the market 200 cars which sell for 15 000.00 Ө. Thus it contributes 3 000 000.00 Ө to the materialist sector. This helps society as each consumerist will now be better off, receiving a larger consumerist grant, either general or non-working. With this money these consumerists can buy goods and services in the materialist sector. This is the concept of the noble incentive for motivation or the left-hand that guides the consumerist society.

Another incentive for productivity is the profit motive (in the accommodational and laissez-faire sectors). All the profits that a firm earns are used to pay the employees and to cover the costs of doing business. What is left goes to the owners and bondholders. The money earned by workers are Ignits. With this money he who has it can buy anything in the accommodational sector of the economy- but he can't spend it on the materialist sector. This means that he can use it to buy more land, a new house or mansion, household accessories, alcohol, vacations or use it to pay his bills or exchange it for Fortals for use in the laissez-faire sector. The more a firm sells, the higher its profit and the greater is its accommodational prosperity. On the downside it is possible for a firm to bankrupt if no one wants to buy its products or use its services. This is the concept of individualistic incentive or the right hand that guides the consumerist system.

There is a need for incentives for productivity. There are two types of incentives in our system. Together they give a reason for the people in our society to produce goods and services.

Incentives for Efficiency

It is important that an economy be efficient. An efficient economy runs more smoothly. By efficiency we mean using inputs to the fullest advantage.

The incentive for efficiency in the consumerist system is profit. All inputs that a firm needs have the same price function regardless of their quality. It follows that a firm will employ those inputs that make it most efficient. When it does so, it lowers production costs and it will make more profit for every good or service the firm sells. However it still strives to produce goods and services with inputs of the highest quality as all inputs in the same family have identical price functions.

A firm will hire the hardest working clerks, the most competent cashiers and the most knowledgeable accountants. A firm will hire the best employees depending on the business the firm is in. This is due to the fact that all workers in the same family (taxon) have the same wage function. This is an example of the principal of merit.

All other inputs also have the same input function within the same family. Thus those workers with the highest quality are obtained. A car factory will buy the best capital, in this case car making machines. An ice cream provider will also buy the best capital. Here the most professional ice cream machines. Offices will also maximize efficiency since their capital input has a fixed price function. They will employ the newest, high tech computers and internet services.

Another input is land. It also has a price function. Thus firms will get the best land onto which to place their factories, offices and firms.

A firm can also maximize efficiency by manipulating the number of employees it has. This is called downsizing. By limiting staff to the minimum that is essential, a firm can maximize profit. However a firm can also earn profit by selling jobs to employees. A firm cannot downsize or lay off workers that it sold jobs to. Workers are protected from being laid off due to the fact that they own job contracts that give them the right to work at a job for a certain length of time. There is a juggling act to find the right number of employees. However a firm operating in the laissez-faire sector can downsize; that is lay off some employees so as to reduce operating costs. This is because in the laissez-faire sector there are no job contracts for employees to buy.

Efficiency is important. Fixed functions for families of inputs and land help insure that a firm runs efficiently. An efficient firm is better able to compete in a world market.

Incentives for Economic Progress

It is essential that there is economic progress in a thriving economy. By economic progress we mean mainly the creation of inventions and innovations. This includes 1) New products, 2) a greater variety of products, 3) new services and 4) better ways of doing things,

How do we encourage invention and innovation? We already described quality selection. Under this type of paradigm firms compete to make their goods and services most desirable to consumerists. Those goods and services of the best quality are those that "survive" the market and are sold.

We can encourage invention and innovation through patents. A patent is a right to exclusive production by the inventor of the product for a set amount of time. How long should a patent be? Should it be granted per profit or for a fixed number of years?

If the patent length was determined by profit, the patent would last as long as the firm making the invention makes a certain amount of profit. The problem with this is that clever accountants can warp financial records so as to under-report the actual profit the firm makes and prolong the patent period. This is not a favourable way to determine the length of a patent.

With a single patent period, a patent period for a fixed number of years would apply to the whole economy. The problem with this is that firms with the potential to make a good but who are unable to cover their costs during the patent period will not start up. On the other hand, those firms who make more money than their set up costs during the patent period have an unnecessary monopoly and there isn't any competition.

A different option exists for consumerism. Patents for products are in the form of *hybrid-patents*. That is a patent that is not based on one criteria but three different criteria. A patent is for A) a set number of years, B) a certain amount of profit and C) for a certain amount of revenue. The criteria that applies is the one that comes first.

Also, in consumerism the hybrid- patent period is different for each industry. The agricultural industry will have one, the electronic industry will have one and the software industry will also have one, etc. The logic behind this is that the ideal patent length (the one that maximizes profit and limits monopoly periods) is similar for goods in a certain industry. Therefore each industry has its own patent period in terms of years, revenue and profit. These are set by the central bank (the patent office).

As an example, the government sets the hybrid-patent for a new motor (like all products in the transport industry) at 10 years, a profit of 1 000 000 þ or a revenue of 5 000 000 þ. If they end up making 1 000 000 þ in 8 years then the patent expires. Also, if they have revenue of 5 000 000 þ in 6 years then the patent expires. However, if they make less than the prescribed profit or revenue in 10 years, then the patent expires in 10 years.

To overcome fraud, the firm with the patent must make a report to the patent office every two weeks to monitor how much money the firm has made in the form of revenue and profit. This will let the patent office, (central bank) know when the firm has reached either its profit or revenue level and it will no longer be able to have the patent.

Also to help investors there should be rewards. Even though no money is made, the thrill of winning a reward and being recognized as the best in one's profession is an incentive for economic progress. Thus the government and industries should come up with as many rewards as possible. Almost every industry should have its specific reward. A reward is a great motivator even if it is not money. Examples include the Stanley Cup, the World Cup and an Olympic gold medal. These awards push athletes to new levels of excellence. It is logical that similar economic awards should push investors to new levels of excellence.

It is optimal that every industry has its own patent period understood in terms of length of time, revenue earned or profit accumulated. This helps investors to invent and innovate, with rewards for economic success in various industries of the economy. Investors and producers are challenged to make goods and services that help us all.

Exploitation of Workers

Exploitation of workers refers to forcing workers to work under usually long hours and terrible conditions and compensating them only minimally. If workers are exploited they cannot make an honest living. However those that hire these workers usually make a large profit.

The main idea behind communism is that in capitalism workers are exploited and that this is a major problem and is grossly unjust. In fact the observation of worker exploitation was the inspiration for original communist texts. There definitely was worker exploitation during the infancy of capitalism and in some places and some times it still appears. Yet surely in many third world countries children are forced to work in sweat shops, long hours and under inhuman conditions to make things like wallets and t-shirts. And they are barely compensated to get by.

So although worker exploitation sometimes exists in free market capitalism it definitely does not exist in accommodation based consumerism. This is a tremendous advantage that this system has over that one.

There is no worker exploitation in accommodation based consumerism for the main reason that employers do not set wages and salaries for workers in the accommodational sector of the natural partition. Wage/salary functions are dictated by the central bank. The central bank ensures that all workers, regardless of occupation, have a sometimes fair and sometimes wonderful pay rate. Although firms and by extension employers have the ability to make many business decisions, they have no influence on how workers that work for them are paid.

In the command partition, workers are compensated through either one of five extra work transfers. These are designed to maximize productivity and efficiency. Thus high extra work transfers ensure all workers (in the command partition) are highly paid. Furthermore, when people who have a job with a high occupational complexity rating are employed in the command partition they will usually earn more than the simple extra work transfers (see section on command partition compensation adjustment).

The situation in the laissez-faire sector is a little different. Here employers chose how to pay workers. There is no minimum wage in the laissez-faire sector so that this sector can be more capitalist-like. However, with all the anti unemployment measures in consumerism it is very likely that there will be competition for workers in the laissez-faire sector. This should raise wages and salaries in this sector.

Also, to fight worker exploitation in consumerism there are unions in this system. Unions fight for the working conditions of workers. They make sure the working space is safe and no one gets hurt on the job. However, they cannot interfere with wage/salary functions in the accommodational sector of the natural partition.

Workers are not exploited in consumerism. Wage/salary functions are not set by firms but by a central bank. Also, unions protect the rights of workers. This solves the issue communists have with the free-market system.

International Credit Rating

The international credit rating is a ranking system that judges how trustworthy foreign countries are with regards to paying back their loans or at least paying the interest payment on the debt that they owe. In this system every country is rated on a scale of 1 – 10. Countries with a low international credit rating are risky with regards to lending. Countries with a high international credit rating are trustworthy with regards to lending.

The international credit rating is set by the grand chairman of the central bank. Countries that continuously repay the interest on their loans or parts of the loan itself have a higher international credit rating or have their rating increase from the previous one. Similarly, countries that continuously default on their interest repayment of their debt have a low international credit rating or have their rating decrease from a previous one.

The international credit rating influences how much our government loans to foreign countries. Countries with a high international credit rating (near 10) will be loaned more, have a lower interest rate and a lower premium from the respective International Bankruptcy Insurance Firm (IBIF). Also countries with a very low international credit rating (near 1) will be loaned less, have a higher interest rate and a higher premium from the respective IBIF.

The international credit rating is important when we need to determine which countries to lend to. It is better to lend to a country with a higher international credit rating than to a country with a lower one. It is also better for the country receiving a loan to have a higher international credit rating.

The International Bankruptcy Insurance Firm

The international bankruptcy insurance firm (IBI firm) is a key component in the consumerist country's ability to make loans to foreign countries. In essence the IBI firm is an agency that collects premium from debtor nations and in the event a debtor country can't pay its interest servicing on its loans or otherwise defaults on the loan, it steps in and pays the loan.

The IBI firm is similar to the domestic bankruptcy insurance firm. That particular firm insures stocks, bonds, job contracts and private loans that were taken out by particular firms in our nation internally. The IBI firm does something similar but it works with foreign nations that our consumerist nation lends to.

The IBI firm insures a foreign nation's loan that our consumerist nation made to it. This occurs when the IBI firm sets a premium on the loan that is to be paid monthly. In the event the country can't make interest payments to us, the foreign government must do everything to service the debt including osterity measures like raising taxes. In the event the interest on the debt is not paid still, the IBI firm comes in to help and pays the value of the loan that has been defaulted on.

Let's see an example. Note as always that these numbers are purely exemplary. Thus they need not be so in an actual society. The loan is to a foreign country for 1 000 000 000 þ. The IBI firm sets the premium at 0.5 % per month. So, the nation borrowing money must pay, in addition to the interest rate on the loan (which we will ignore for this section) = 5 000 000 þ per month. The borrowing nation pays this and in the event that it can't make payments on the interest, the IBI firm comes in to help. Suppose that since the time the loan was made the foreign nation paid back 25 % of the loan and they still owe us/ the consumerist nation 750 000 000 þ (we ignore interest in this example to focus attention on what the IBI firm does). The country we lent to does everything to repay this debt by raising taxes perhaps and it still can't pay back its loan in full but are able to raise 100 000 000 þ to pay back part of the loan. Thus in the end the IBI firm will need to pay the country's debt which is 650 000 000 þ. The IBIF sets a high premium for those countries with a low credit rating.

Unfortunately for the country we just discussed, defaulting on the loan is a horrible proposition. Their international credit rating plummets, going down a few points. The premium interest rate for the future will drastically go up, going from 0.5 % to perhaps 3 %. Furthermore, our nation and other nations will decrease in how much they lend to the nation that has defaulted. Few nations will make loans to that country next time. Finally, the interest rate, which is discussed in another section, also goes drastically up. A nation that takes a loan must do whatever it can to avoid defaulting on a loan. Defaulting on a loan will ruin a country's economy.

Fortunately for our IBI firm, incidences of default are few and far in between. They do not occur too often. In over 99 % of cases a nation will at least pay the interest on the loan it took out even if it is likely that the loan in its entirety will never be paid back. Therefore the IBI firm should feel certain that it will make profit in its transactions.

The Laissez-Faire International Trade System

A big question regarding the laissez-faire sector is what is its orientation towards international trade. Do we open up the market where laissez-faire goods are produced to the world or not.

There are two main options regarding trading of the laissez-faire sector with international markets. The simplest choice is to make the laissez-faire sector a closed economy. The second option is to open trade between the laissez-faire sector and the rest of the world.

If we opt for the first choice, no one who works in the laissez faire sector or contributes to it can exchange goods from that sector with another country. That is, there is no importation or exportation. All the goods the consumerists have to buy in the laissez-faire sector are what is directly produced in that sector by laissez-faire firms.

The second option is more complicated. Here we allow firms in the laissez-faire sector to compete and trade with firms in other countries. A laissez-faire firm that makes products can sell it to other consumerists or sell it to a country any where in the world. Also, a laissez-faire firm can buy a good in another country, import it and sell it to consumerists in the laissez-faire market.

Laissez-faire firms can import from another country. Let's say we are dealing with Canada. If the price of a pair of silver earrings is cheaper in Canada than the market price of the same earrings in our country, a laissez-faire firm imports them and sells them to consumerists. This ensures that consumerists pay less for the same item (silver earrings).

There is also exportation. If the price of a book is higher in another country (Canada) than in our country we export that. In this case producers of that book make money.

The international laissez-faire trade system represents pure capitalism as traditional capitalist thinkers would imagine it. To make it as pure and free capitalism there are absolutely no tariffs or import quotas. The government nor the central bank has any influence on this trade system. The one stipulation that there is is that only goods pertaining to the laissez-faire sector are traded. If a trader wants to trade items from the materialist or accommodational sectors (for example cars or wheat) there is another trade system that we have fully described in another section of this book.

When trading goods between our country and another we use the actual exchange rate. Recall that there are three types of exchange rates -real, nominal and actual. Real exchange refers to the relative price of a final good (in the accommodational sector) relative to the price of that good in another country. The nominal exchange rate is set by the consumerist trade commission and it is what is used to conduct international trade in the accommodational sector. It is expressed in Ignits. The actual exchange rate is what is used in the laissez-faire international trade system. It is the price of a fortal compared to foreign currency.

The actual exchange rate factors in the trade between the laissez-faire sector and other countries. Whether it is high or low either helps the exporters or importers.

The laissez-faire sector can be closed with regards to international trade. However it can also open up and trade with other countries. In fact this is probably more preferable and it greatly helps consumerists. The international trade system of the laissez-faire sector works along pure free-market capitalist principles.

Consumerism and the Judiciary System

The theory of the accommodation based consumerist economic system is a purely economic theory. However, it has some things to say about the law. Although it is not concerned with what crimes are and how those who brake them should be punished (in prison time) consumerism has things to say about how crimes can be deterred. Furthermore, in the next section we will talk about how criminals can be further punished in financial terms in addition to their regular sentence..

There are crimes that are predominantly economic. These include theft, destruction of property, embezzlement and the braking of contracts. This treatise will not suggest (justice) punishments for those who commit these except to say that these crimes must be deterred if the system is to work. Most of the crimes that must be identified are similar to those in any other economic system; i.e. theft, braking of contracts.

Tax invasion should not be an issue as the positive personal income tax and wealth tax are applied only as last resort measures. However, if they are brought in, tax evasion does become a crime.

There are some offences peculiar to consumerism. One is the over-reporting of how many goods and services one has sold or has been able to sell. This crime is serious because it disrupts the economic system. This crime is similar in gravity to under-reporting one's taxes for tax purposes in the free-market system. Laws should be made to eliminate the over statement of the value of sold and unsold goods and services. There should be something in consumerism what an audit is in the free-market system.

Some of the most serious crimes are charging a price different for a good or service than that set by the central bank for the GAM sectors. Over selling is charging a price higher than the fixed price. Under-selling is charging a price lower than the price set by the central bank. These are serious crimes because they disrupt the proper functioning of the economic system.

Other crimes include paying workers more or less than the wage function set by the central bank for the GAM sectors. Essentially, any instances of setting rates, values or functions different than those set by the central bank must be forbidden in the GAM sectors.

A very serious crime is using currency from one sector to purchase goods and services in another sector. For example, if someone tries to buy a materialist good, like an apple, with Fortals, this is considered fraud. This is regarded as serious as check or credit card fraud is in free-market capitalism.

It is a very severe form of fraud to use gold investment certificates (GICs) or silver investment certificates (SICs) as a form of currency. This has as much weight as insurance fraud or credit card fraud in capitalism. GICs and SICs are a store of value but must not be a form of exchange. If consumerists want to use the value of their GICs and SICs all they need to do is bring them to a (private) bank and the bank will add value to their bank account. At that point, they can use the money to buy things.

There are other types of fraud in consumerism. There are patent fraud and UC card fraud.

If an individual abuses the patent system this is a type of fraud. Also, if an individual uses his or her universal consumerist card in an inappropriate manner – for example using a card that is not his- this is also fraud.

Other crimes are not fundamentally economic and are not mentioned here. There is no more mention of them in this section so as to avoid the danger of this treatise becoming a theory of jurisprudence. This theory is wholly economic.

We make one brief note about the justice system that is general in nature. That is, regardless of the crime a consumerist is accused of committing, he or she is entitled to the service of a free legal aid lawyer. No one should be punished or sent to prison simply because they cannot afford legal representation. However if they do want a private lawyer, they are permitted to find one in the laissez-faire sector and pay for the service using Fortals.

Some important crimes occur in all economic systems. A few crimes are specific to consumerism. We did not go in to detail about these crimes or suggest punishments for breaking them to avoid creating a system of law.

Punishment in Consumerism

Let's talk about how people who brake the law in consumerism are going to be punished. We already talked about some possible crimes in consumerism. We also mentioned that there are other crimes that are more general and that exist in every economy like murder, arson and rape.

Consumerism has a dual punishment system for transgressions. One is the justice punishment while the other is the financial punishment. Thus, when a person commits a certain crime he is punished twice.

The justice punishment is already known in just about every country in the world. For example, if someone commits murder he may receive a life sentence. If someone commits arson he may receive five years in jail. And if someone commits rape he may get three years in jail.

The financial punishment is peculiar to consumerism. On top of the justice punishment a person found guilty of a crime must pay a certain amount of money to the government. This money is a source of revenue for the government and allows us to avoid taxes.

The government sets the financial punishment for all crimes. The more severe the crime the higher the financial penalty. So for example, if someone commits murder he may have to pay 1 000 000 þ and if he commits break and entry he may have to pay 50 000 þ and if he commits vandalism he may have to pay 10 000 þ. Actually, the financial punishment is in the form of Ignits as well as Fortals.

So for example, if a man commits first degree murder he will be given a life sentence and on top of that he must pay the consumerist government (all levels) 1 000 000 þ. If he can't pay that (because he doesn't have the money) the government takes all his assets (house, car, business) and when he is released he has a huge debt to pay to the government.

The financial punishment mechanism works both ways to ensure that people are not arbitrarily put on trial. If a man is convicted of murder he must pay 1 000 000 þ on top of his justice penalty. However if he is found not guilty the government must pay him 100 000 þ. Thus the court system must be very certain that the right people are put on trial. The government loses money if they can't convict an innocent man.

However the balance between the financial punishment and the government liability for acquittals must be skewed in favour of the financial punishment. So if a man is convicted of murder he ought to pay 10 times as much if he would receive if he were found not guilty.

Consumerism must be a just society. Our system must ensure that people are given a fair trial. Also, those who are truly guilty should be punished while the innocent are set free. Consumerism must never become corrupt.

It may seem that this financial punishment system incentivizes conviction. However, the jury are not paid for convicting someone. Also, the judge does not receive any extra money if a man is convicted and he is only paid for the service of presiding over a trial. The prosecution is also not paid any extra if they succeed in a conviction although they must be paid for their services. Thus although the government makes money when a man is found guilty, no one who has any influence on the trial outcome has any real incentive for the defendant's conviction.

In the justice system, the defence attorney and his team are strongly compensated to ensure the defendant receives the fairest trial. The defence team are paid more per hour and more per case than the prosecution team is. Also, the defence team receive a large bonus for finding their client not guilty. These initiatives are called *defence team incentive bonuses.* These ensure that the evidence against a man is overwhelming before he is actually convicted.

The last thing we want in consumerism is innocent people going to jail and paying the government. Our justice system must be just. If there is any corruption, perhaps the dual punishment system should be abandoned all together.

The financial punishment system is a second layer of deterrent to committing severe crimes. It is also another source of revenue for the government. It is a good idea that goods and services (that are provided by the government) are paid for by criminals rather than hard working consumerists.

The Transit System of Consumerism

A well developed society requires a well developed transit system. By transit system we simply mean an organization of transportation vehicles whose goal is to move consumerists from one place to another in a town or between cities. Among transit vehicles we can include buses, subway trains, trains, taxicabs and perhaps several other things.

For the most part, in the free market system, these vehicles are operated in such a fashion that the individual using the vehicle must pay for the service. Some vehicles are run by profit maximizing firms; like taxis for example. Others like buses, subway trains and trains are run by the government. However, all forms of transportation generally work to make a profit for providing the service.

The most annoying aspect of the transit system of the free market system is that the fares of the services for transit vehicles grow larger, larger and larger. In year 1 a bus fee is $1.00 and two and a half years later it is $ 3.00. The service did not become any better so there is no reason that bus fares should increase.

The same situation occurs with train fares. In the beginning, a train fee is $6.50 to a destination in the near proximity of the train station. A few years later, it is $9.50. Again the train service did not get better. So why should train fares increase?

In accommodation based consumerism the majority of public transit is free. All buses and subway trains are free at all times for all consumerists. This should increase the well being of the consumerists in our nation. Furthermore this has the positive externality (positive side effect) that cars are taken off the road and carbon emissions are reduced.

The service of taxicabs is provided through the materialist sector both in the natural partition and command partition. Thus the fare is fixed based on a parameter like distance travelled or time spent travelling. This fixed price function is set by the central bank. Furthermore, the price function is subject to the price veto mechanism. So if taxi drivers can show to the central bank that they can't make much profit, the price function is re-adjusted.

The situation with trains is a little bit different. The operation of trains is within the scope of the governmental partition/sector. In order to take the train, a consumerist must pay a fare. This fare goes to the three levels of government. This is an additional form of governmental revenue in the consumerist system. The proceeds from selling train fares goes primarily to pay for the operation of the trains – engineers, ticket cashiers, train maintenance and fuel. What is left (and there should be a lot left over) goes to pay for things like healthcare, education, defence, free bus and subway services etc.

The train transit system in consumerism has the added advantage that the price of train fees is a fixed function. Thus price functions are guaranteed never to increase. The price function for trains like those for taxi cabs are set by the central bank.

Consumerism has a well developed transit system. The transit system is free for consumerists for buses and subway trains. The money raised by providing train service goes to the three levels of government to provide much needed social services like healthcare and education.

Simple Two Person Economy/Production Possibilities

We can visualize a simple two person economy to help us understand production possibilities. Often a two person economy is used as an example to explain the dynamics of trade between two agents in an economic system. This example, a two person economy, is common today in economic discussions to illustrate the mechanics of an economic system, and is often used to teach various economic systems in universities and colleges. Although this analysis is very basic and doesn't reflect how a complete consumerist system would function, it is nevertheless helpful for us to get a certain understanding of some economic concepts; i.e. efficient trade and allocation of inputs for production of goods as well as comparative advantage.

We start with the assumption that there are two individuals in our society; an egg farmer and a pig farmer. Each can produce a certain amount of eggs and pork. The amount of eggs and pork that the egg farmer can produce is different from that which the pig farmer can produce. In one hour the egg farmer can produce 1 kg of eggs or 1 kg of pork. The pig farmer can produce 8 kg of pork or 2 kg of eggs in the same amount of time. We assume that they work 6 hours per day.

The following table shows the hypothetical output of both types of farmers:

| | Amount produced in 1 hour (in kg) | | Amount produced in 6 hours (in kg) | |
	Eggs	Pork	Eggs	Pork
Egg farmer	1	1	6	6
Pig farmer	2	8	12	48

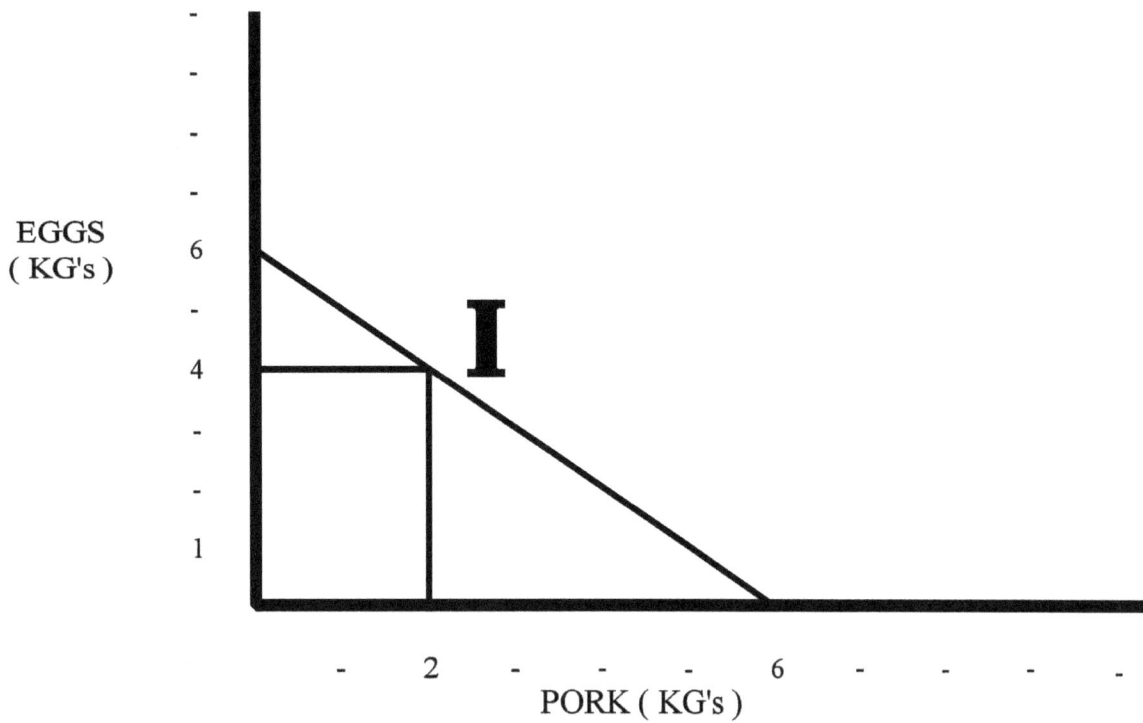

EGGS
(KG's)

PORK (KG's)

EGG FARMER'S
PRODUCTION POSSIBILITIES FRONTIER

Figure 8 - A

Figure 8-A

The following are called production possibility frontiers. They graphically illustrate how much the egg farmer and pig farmer can produce and the trade-offs they encounter if they chose a particular amount of good to produce.

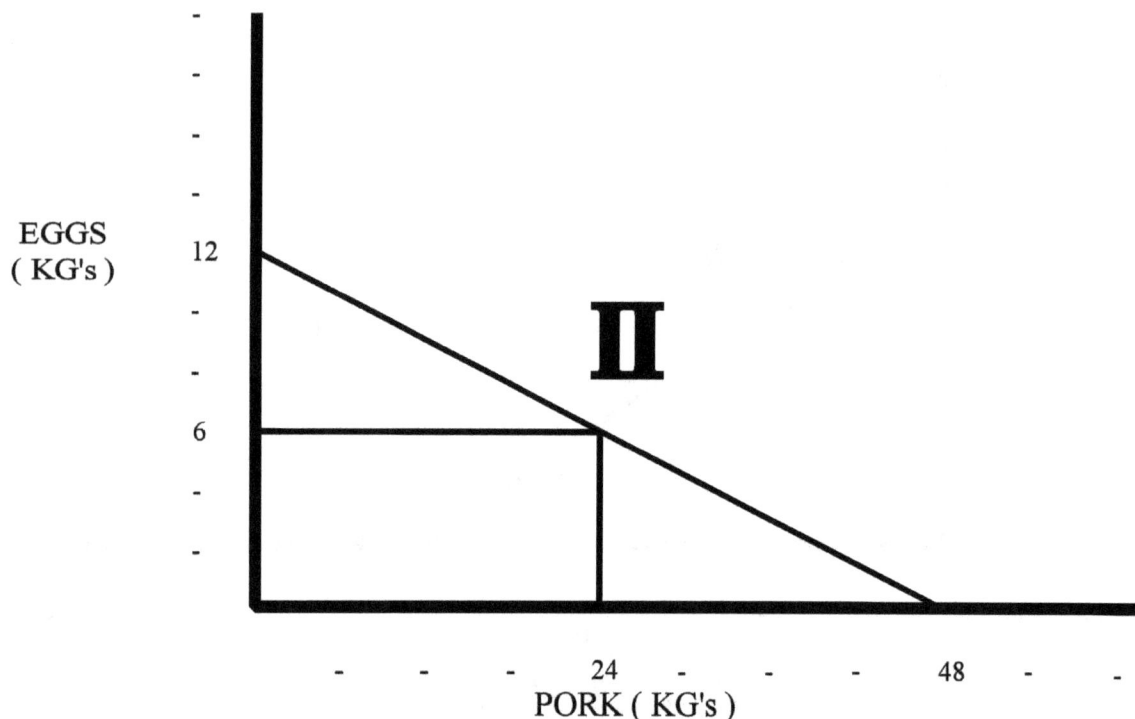

EGGS
(KG's)

12

6

24   48

PORK (KG's)

PIG FARMER'S
PRODUCTION POSSIBILITIES FRONTIER

Figure 8 - B

Figure 8-B

Note in the above that the pig and egg farmer can produce any amount of eggs and pork that is on the frontier. For example, the egg farmer can produce 4 kg of eggs and 2 kg of pork as given by "I". Similarly the pig farmer can produce 24 kg of pork and 6 kg of eggs as given by "II"

The purpose of inquiry of this section is to see if each farmer can get more of eggs and pork by somehow exchanging with one another that will leave him better off than if he had to subsist on his own. We will examine two different ways of doing this. For lack of better terms, one method is the free-market approach. The second is the consumerist approach.

Let's examine the free-market method. Initially, the egg farmer produces 3 kg of eggs and 3 kg of pork. The pig farmer produces 24 kg of pork and 6 kg of eggs. Both individuals decide to specialize at what they can produce more easily and trade with each other. So the egg farmer produces 6 kg of eggs and no pork while the pig farmer makes 32 kg of pork and 4 kg of eggs. The pig farmer gives 6 kg of pork for 3 kg of eggs. Now the egg farmer has 6 kg of meat and 3 kg of eggs. Meanwhile the pig farmer has 26 kg of meat and 7 kg of eggs. The following graphs illustrate the gains from trade under the free-market approach.

360

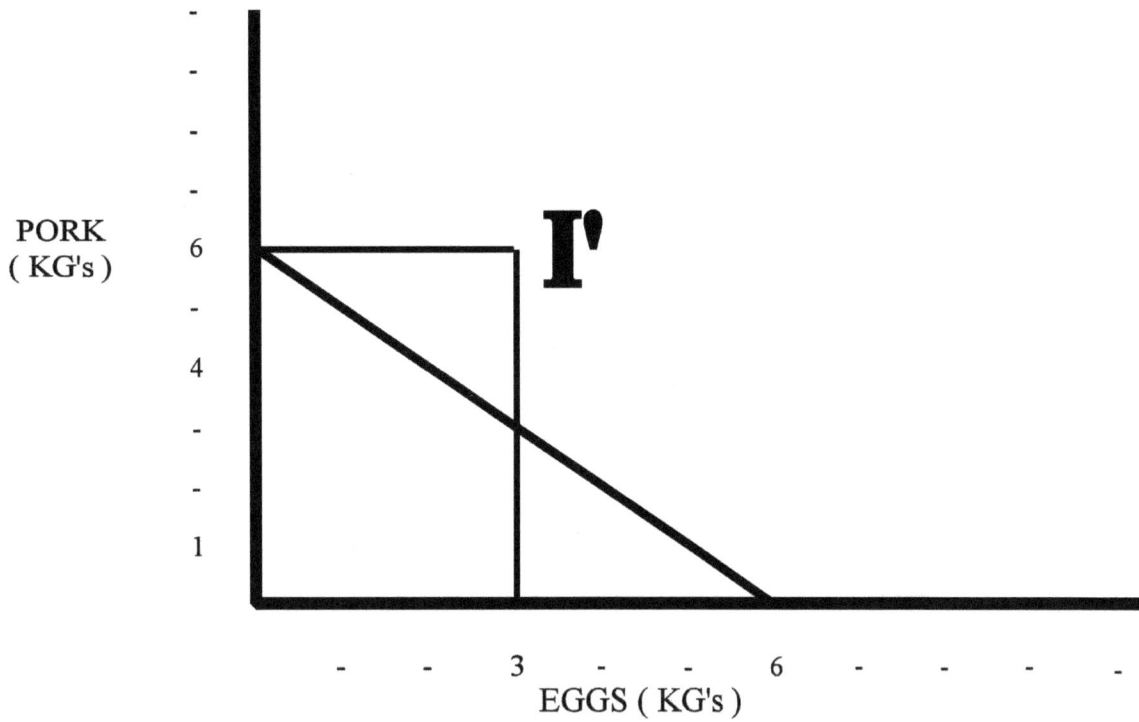

Figure 8 - C

PORK (KG's)

EGGS (KG's)

**EGG FARMER'S
FREE MARKET GAIN POSITION**

Figure 8-C

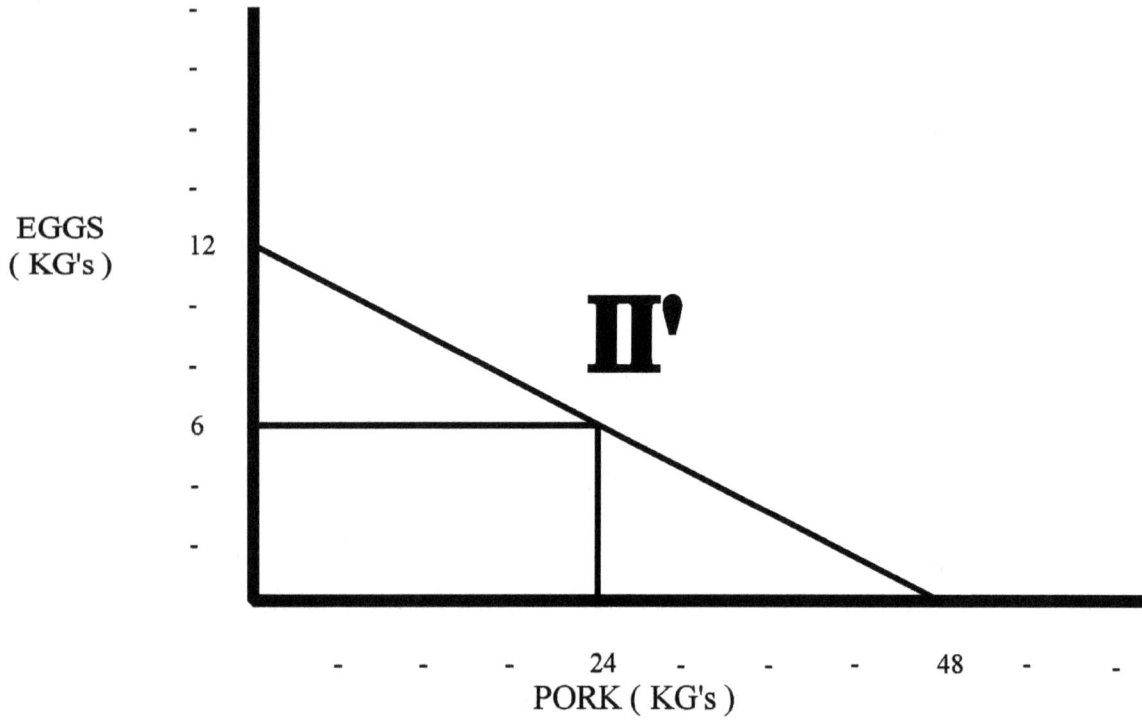

EGGS (KG's)

12

6

II'

24

48

PORK (KG's)

Figure 8 - D

**PIG FARMER'S
FREE MARKET GAINS POSITION**

Figure 8-D

Now let's see how this problem resolves itself under the consumerist paradigm. We set two goals: 1) the total output of the entire economy must be as large as possible. And 2) both individuals, the pig and egg farmers, should have a total of goods that is beyond the production possibilities frontier.

First of all we need to ask, what is worth more: a kg of eggs or a kg of pork or are they equivalent? That is, is 1 kg of eggs worth as much as 1 kg of pork? To answer this we find a very special important number that we will soon see is very useful. To calculate it, we find the ratios of the ability to produce eggs and pork for each farmer. Next we add them both and divide by 2. So let's proceed. The egg farmer can produce eggs and pork in a 1:1 ratio. That is, the opportunity cost of producing eggs and pork are equal. The pig farmer produces pork and eggs in an 8:2 ratio or 4:1. Now we add: 1/1 + 4/1 = 5/1. Dividing by 2 we get a figure of 2.5. We can think of this value of 2.5 as the most efficient value of pork in terms of eggs. Thus we can say that 1 kg of eggs is worth 2.5 kg of pork.

Now that we know that 1 kg of eggs is worth 2.5 times as 1 kg of pork, let's find a way to produce pork and eggs among the two farmers such that the output is greatest. The egg farmer can produce 1 kg of eggs for every 1 kg of pork. But since 1 kg of eggs is worth 2.5 times as 1 kg of pork, it makes sense for him to produce the maximum of 6 eggs. Now what does the pig farmer produce? Since the pig farmer can produce 8 kg of pork for every 2 kg of eggs, it makes sense for him to dedicate his time to producing just pork even though eggs are worth more. Thus in our analysis the output that is most efficient for both farmers collectively is one where the egg farmer just makes eggs (6 kg) and the pig farmer just makes pork (48 kg).

Now we want to create a trade where both the pig farmer and egg farmer have more eggs and pork than they could produce on their own. The special number, 2.5 is the ideal ratio for which the farmer should trade eggs in terms of pork that will maximize both of their gains from trade. So the egg farmer has 6 kg of eggs and the pig farmer has 48 kg of pork. Unless each of them just wants to eat one type of food, they will begin to trade with each other, exchanging 1 kg of eggs for 2.5 kg of pork. The following is a list of the various combinations that could result from trade between the farmers.

Egg farmer		Pig farmer	
Eggs	Pork	Eggs	Pork
6	0	0	48
5	2.5	1	45.5
4	5	2	43
3	7.5	3	40.5
2	10	4	38
1	12.5	5	35.5
0	15	6	33

Now each of the above combinations will result in a situation where both farmers have a combination of goods beyond the production possibilities frontier. Of course, how many eggs or pork is traded depends entirely on how much each farmer wants to trade. Suppose the egg farmer likes eggs a lot. He might want to keep 4 kg and trade 2 kg. He trades 2 kg of eggs for 5 kg of pork. Otherwise the egg farmer might want both so he trades 4 kg and keeps 2 kg. He is left with 2 kg of eggs and 10 kg of pork. This means that the pig farmer has 4 kg of eggs and 38 kg of pork. Let's draw production possibility curves to see what is happening:

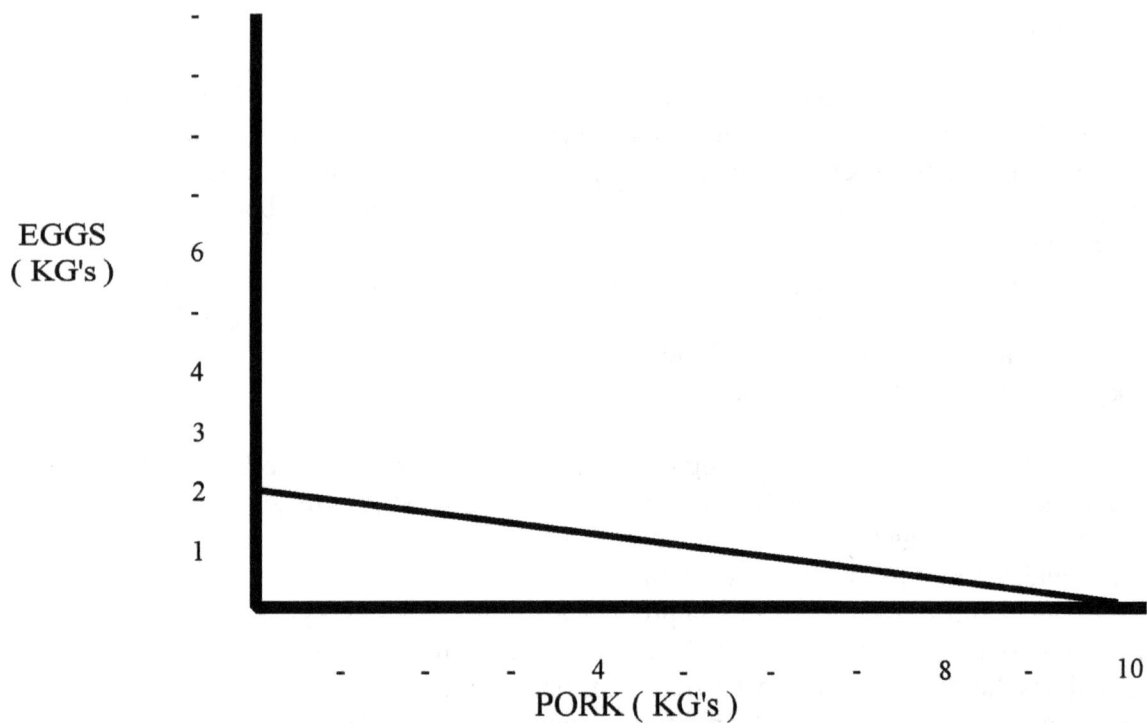

Figure 8 - E **EGG FARMER**
CONSUMERIST GAINS POSITION

Figure 8-E

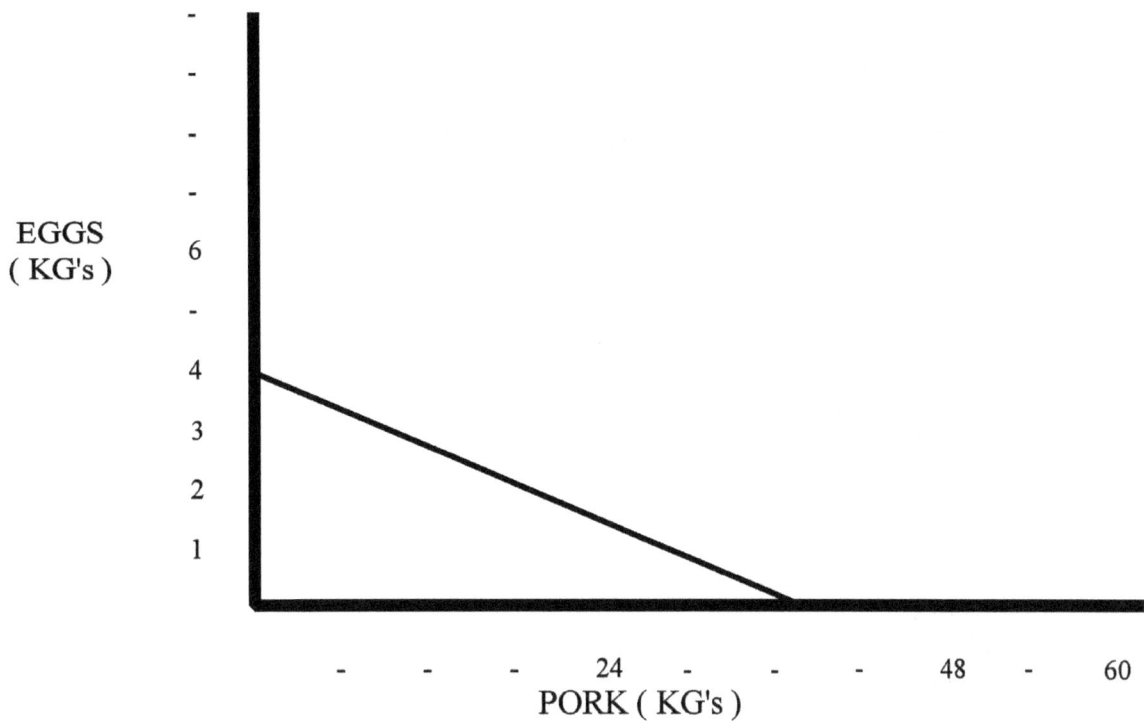

EGGS (KG's)

PORK (KG's)

Figure 8 - F

PIG FARMER
CONSUMERIST **GAINS POSITION**

Figure 8-F

Now we can compare both types of solutions; the free-market and the consumerist. In the free-market system the egg farmer made 6 kg of eggs while the pig farmer made 32 kg of pork and 4 kg of eggs.

To see the output, we add everything:
6 kg of eggs
+ 4 kg of eggs
+ 32 kg of pork
= 10 kg of eggs and 32 kg of pork

In consumerism, 6 kg of eggs and 48 kg of pork are produced. The free-market approach produces more eggs but less pork. The consumerism approach produces more pork and fewer eggs. Which output is better? If we value 1 egg as 2.5 pork, then

Free-market: $(10 \times 2.5) + 32 = 57$
Consumerist: $(6 \times 2.5) + 48 = 63$

We have seen that in the consumerist approach both farmers benefit; they gain more goods then they could individually. Let's compare the consumption of the egg and pig farmer in the free-market paradigm versus the consumerist paradigm

Free-market:
Egg farmer-   6 kg of pork
              3 kg of eggs
Pig farmer-   26 kg of pork
              7 kg of eggs

Consumerist:
Egg farmer-   7.5 kg of pork
              3 kg of eggs
Pig farmer-   40.5 kg of pork
              3 kg of eggs

The egg farmer is better off in consumerism; in both approaches they have 3 kg of eggs, but in consumerism the egg farmer has 1.5 kg more of pork. As for the pork farmer, he has 14.5 kg more of pork but 4 kg fewer eggs.

How is it possible that both farmers are able to get a higher combination of eggs and pork after trading than if they were left to themselves? The answer is a concept known as "comparative advantage". This means that it is easier for the egg farmer to produce just eggs since the opportunity cost for 1 kg of eggs is just 1 kg of pork. However, the pork farmer on the other hand, has an opportunity cost for producing pork equal to 0.25. Thus it makes sense for the egg farmer to specialize in egg production and the pig farmer to specialize in pork production.

A simple 2 person economy consisting of an egg farmer and a pig farmer helps us understand the basis of exchange in consumerism. Production possibility graphs are integral to understanding a basic economic system. We came to the understanding that if both produce products in which they have a comparative advantage and trade eggs for pork at a specially calculated exchange rate, then they can accumulate a larger number of eggs and pork for each of them than they could by themselves.

The Consumerist Money Supply

Here we look at the money supply in the consumerist economy. Recall firstly that there is no cash in circulation. That is, there are no coins or paper bills. Also there are three kinds of currency; Ignits, Fortals and Norses. We analyze how these three circulate throughout the economic system.

Perhaps the greatest difference between the money supply in consumerism and capitalism is that in consumerism the government, regardless of level, can't print money. The government doesn't produce neither cash nor coins and these do not exist in the economic system. Money that circulates in the system is in the form of bank book entries and this money doesn't come from the government either- the money created is equal to the GDCP.

In our system there are four sectors; the materialist, the governmental, the laissez-faire and the accommodational. Generally speaking, Norses (Θ) are used in the materialist and governmental sectors whereas Ignits (þ) are used in the accommodational and governmental sectors and Fortals are used in the laissez-faire sector. It is important to note that always Norses and Ignits are equal to each other in monetary value; i.e.1þ =1Θ

The circulation of money in the consumerist economic system is something like the circulation of water through a human being. Initially water is consumed by drinking. It then circulates through the body in the form of blood, plasma fluid, and other liquids. It is then expelled from the body either as urine or sweat. Something similar happens in accommodation based consumerism.

Norses are created when there is an output in the materialist sector. All firms report their productivity or potential productivity to the central bank about once a month. They report what they sold or could potentially have sold. Firms report how many services they provided. Other firms, like car dealerships or apparel providers mention how many goods they sold and how much inventory was potentially available to be sold in that time period but not directly purchased. The sum of all this output is called the Gross Domestic Consumerist Product (GDCP).

When the central bank receives a record of the GDCP, they must grant the equivalent of it four ways. Some of it goes to the General Consumerist Grant, some to the Non-Working Consumerist Grant, some is deducted as an anti-inflationary measure and some of it is taxed. This is how Norses are created. The supply of Norses in one month is exactly equal to the output or potential output of the materialist sector (GDCP). The Norses granted need not be done so every month. Perhaps if they were granted biweekly things would be smoother.

Now when the consumerists are granted Norses, they can spend it on goods and services in the materialist sector regardless of whether they were given the General or Non-Working grants. Upon the transaction, Norses are deducted from the consumerists and Ignits are added to the producer. This is how Ignits are created.

When the government (whether federal, provincial/state, or municipal) spends the Norses they were granted from the central bank, some of the Norses are deducted from their account and Ignits are added to the producing firm. For example, if the provincial government provides an appendicitis operation for a consumerist the government gives 400 Θ to the doctor or hospital.

The   400 Θ are deducted from the provincial government's account and 400 þ are added to the doctor's account. This is another way that Ignits are created.

Unless they are saved for the future, all Norses that are spent eventually end up in the accommodational sector as Ignits. While there they circulate between firms and consumerists (households) who earn Ignits from providing inputs to firms, i.e. labour. The supply of Ignits is called the Gross National Product (GNP).

The Gross National Product will constantly be rising as Norses from the GDCP are turned into Ignits. When an economy is starting out this is a good thing. However, it may be possible to slow down the increase of the GNP. Thus we introduce the accommodational markdown. In several industries of the accommodational sector, a portion of the sales are deducted and destroyed. They are permanently taken out of circulation.

Here is a way of looking at things using dollars. Initially we have $ 10 000 circulating in an economy. If we remove $4 000 from this system there will be a deflation and money will have more value. Now what if $5 000 are added to the economy so that $15 000 are chasing after a set amount of goods and services. Now we have inflation and usually the prices of goods and services increase. Now suppose we take out $5000 from this economy and destroy it so that there are again $10 000 circulating. Now the prices should be able to be constant. This deduction of money from an economy so as to maintain constant prices is exactly what we are trying to do with anti-inflationary measures like the accommodational markdown among others.

Now we analyze changes in the supply of money on the economy.

If GDCP ↑, then (ceteris paribus), GCT ↑, NWCG ↑, GCG ↑, GNP ↑
If GDCP ↓, then (ceteris paribus), GCT ↓, NWCG ↓, GCG ↓, GNP ↓
If GCT ↑, then (ceteris paribus), GCG ↓, NWCG ↓
If GCT↓, then (ceteris paribus), GCG ↑, NWCG ↑
If Accommodational Markdown ↑ then (ceteris paribus) GNP ↓
If Accommodational Markdown ↓ then (ceteris paribus) GNP ↑
If population ↑, then (ceteris paribus), GDCP?, GNP? GCT?, NWCG ↓, GCG ↓
If population ↓, then (ceteris paribus), GDCP?, GNP? GCT ?, NWCG ↑, GCG ↑
If Retail Markup ↑, then (ceteris paribus), GDCP ↑, GCT ↑, NWCG ↑, GCG ↑, GNP ↑
If Anti-Unemployment Measures ↑, then (ceteris paribus), unemployment ↓, output ↑, deficit ?
If ΣAIM = GDCP, then equilibrium money supply
If ΣAIM > GDCP, then ↓ money supply
If ΣAIM < GDCP, then ↑ money supply

The accommodational markdown can be manipulated to control the money supply in the accommodational sector. The other anti-inflationary measures we discussed in this book can also control the money supply. If the accommodational markdown and the other anti-inflationary measures are equivalent to the GDCP the money supply is said to be "balanced". That is, the net effect is that the money entering the economy through the materialist and governmental sectors is coming from the accommodational sector and laissez- fare sectors. If this is the case then the flow of money among the various sectors is essentially circular.

The money supply in the Consumerist economy looks like this:

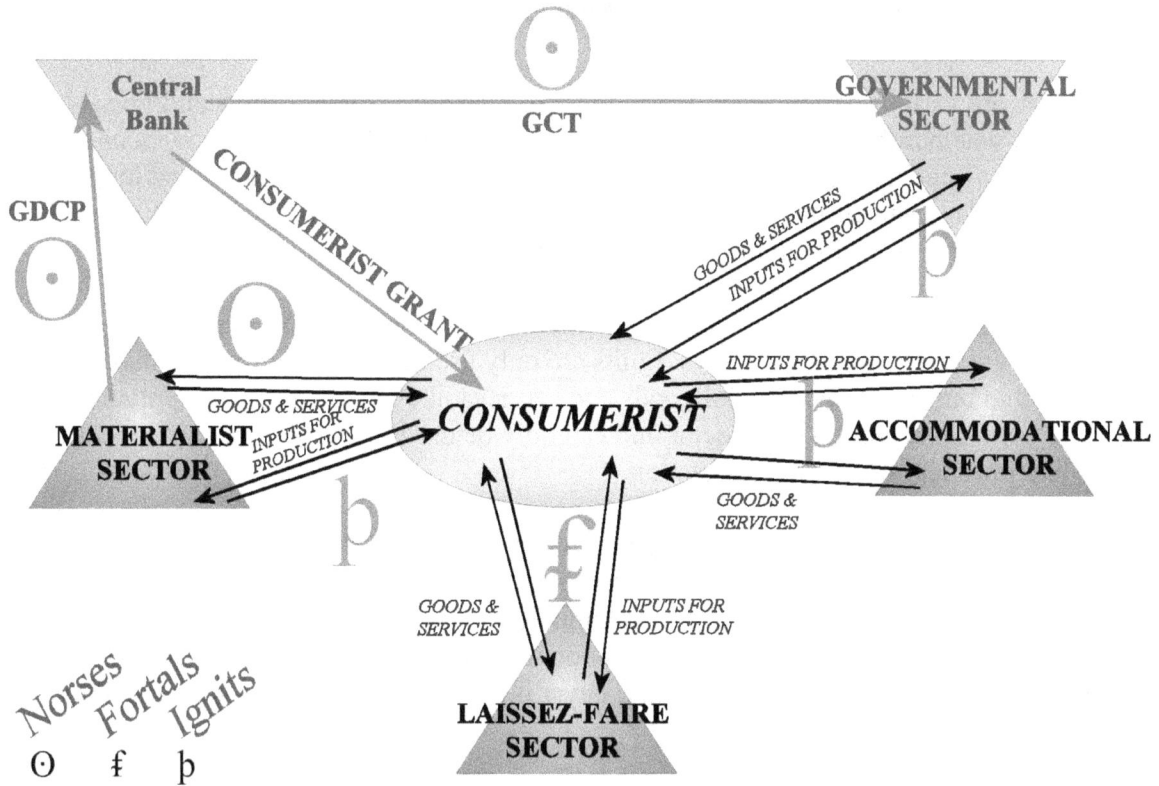

Figure 9

Figure 9

Currency Exchange Mechanisms

There are various currencies in consumerism. There are Norses, Ignits and Fortals. We need to know whether they can be exchanged for one another and if they can how does this happen. We also need to know how to convert between consumerist currencies and international currencies like Canadian dollars and Euros. It is important to remember that the three consumerist currencies are in the form of book entries and are not physical money.

Norses are solely used in the materialist sector. They can only be used to buy materialist goods and services like food and clothes. Ignits are only used in the accommodational sector and they are used to buy accommodational goods and services like land, a house or appliances. Fortals are used in the laissez-faire sector and can only be used to buy laissez-faire goods and services like jewellery or items at an auction.

Norses can only be exchanged for goods and services found in the materialist sector. They can't be traded for Fortals and Fortals can never be traded for Norses. In the materialist sector when a good is exchanged for a certain amount of Norses, the Norses are converted into Ignits at a (private) bank. However, a certain amount of Norses can never be exchanged for Ignits directly or vice versa. Also, Norses can never be directly exchanged for foreign currency like Canadian or American dollars.

There are special circumstances regarding the trade of Ignits and Fortals. Fortals can be traded for Ignits and Ignits can be traded for Fortals. In consumerism there are the nominal Ignit-Fortal exchange mechanism and the reciprocal Ignit-Fortal exchange mechanism.

In the reciprocal Ignit-Fortal exchange mechanism when a Fortal is exchanged for an Ignit and back again, one gets back what he started off with. So if, $5 ƒ = 3 þ \rightarrow 3 þ = 5 ƒ$. If one trades 5 Fortals he will get 3 Ignits. Then if he exchanges these 3 Ignits he will get back the original 5 Fortals.

The nominal Ignit-Fortal exchange mechanism is a special measure designed to fight inflation. In this paradigm, trading Fortals for Ignits and back again is a loosing preposition. So if $5 ƒ = 3 þ \rightarrow 3 þ = 1ƒ$. If one trades 5 Fortals he will get 3 Ignits and if he trades these 3 Ignits he will end up with 1 Fortal.

The nominal and reciprocal Ignit-Fortal exchange mechanisms are used in different situations. Usually, the nominal exchange rate is used. However, in some special circumstances, the reciprocal Ignit-Fortal exchange mechanism must be made use of.

It is also important to be able to trade with foreign currency like Canadian dollars and Pesos. There are three special international exchange rates that factor in. They are the real exchange rate, the actual exchange rate and the nominal exchange rate.

The real exchange rate refers to how expensive a foreign good is relative to our nation's price. So if a hamburger cost \$ 2.00 in Canada and 0.5 þ in our nation, the real exchange rate is \$4/1 þ

The nominal exchange rate is the price of Ignits in terms of foreign currency. The nominal exchange rate is calculated. It is calculated by a body of educated, experienced accountants in a special organization called the consumerist trade pool commission. They find the best "average price" among products that we export and import. These are a function of a large sum of real exchange rates. The goals are to 1) maximize importation and exportation so that consumerists have access to many goods and 2) make profit that will help pay for social services. The details of how nominal exchange rates are used in international trade are thoroughly discussed in a previous section of this book.

The actual exchange rate belongs to the laissez-faire sector. It involves Fortals and is an expression of how fortals cost in terms of a foreign currency and vice versa. This exchange rate is necessary when we realize that we want the producers in the laissez-faire sector to import and export. The actual exchange rate is determined by market factors. Traders trade, for example, Fortals for Canadian dollars and Canadian dollars for Fortals. The laws of supply and demand determine the equilibrium price of the actual exchange rate. Whether the actual exchange rate is high or low determines if our laissez-faire firms are able to export or import to other countries.

It becomes apparent that the nominal exchange rate, the actual exchange rate and the reciprocal Ignit-Fortal exchange mechanism interact with one another. Knowing two of them, the third can be determined. Also, these parameters can be manipulated when we adjust certain other ones.

The consumerist government can actively manipulate the actual exchange rate if the currency is greatly devalued. The government can affect the supply and demand of its own money as well as foreign money. By actively buying and selling currency, a government can adjust its county's currency value.

It is interesting to note that the government (all levels) can potentially use all forms of consumerist currency to finance their expenditures. When the government pays for a service in Norses, the Norses are deducted from their bank records and the equivalent in Ignits is credited to the people performing the service in their bank records. When the government must manipulate Fortals, the nominal Ignit-Fortal exchange mechanism comes into play.

There is also the foreign currency exchange mechanism. Here Fortals are traded for foreign currency. However, a certain amount of the trade is deducted from bank records. It is destroyed. This is an anti-inflationary measure.

There are various ways Fortals can be traded for foreign currency. Also, in some cases, consumerist currency can be traded with one another.

Unions

A union is an organization within a firm that fights for the rights of workers. Its main objective is to help the workers, going to great lengths to do so and causing strikes if there is a disagreement between it and the firm's management.

There are benefits to having unions in an economy. They can ensure that workers have better working conditions and they can ensure that workers are given full rights. They make sure that workers have a positive working place.

In consumerism unions do exist. Their purpose is to promote the well being of workers. Their main function is to guarantee that workers and labourers are properly treated by employers. There are certain things that unions can bargain for. These include safety conditions, working conditions and many other things that could improve the lives of workers.

There is one critical thing that unions must not interfere with. That is wages. The entire consumerist system is based on the proposition that price functions and wages are permanently fixed (in the GAM sectors of the natural partition). Consumerism may collapse if prices and wage functions fluctuate. However if a significant portion of the population signs a petition against a wage function, that wage function will be re-examined (the central bank will vote on it again). But wages cannot arbitrarily increase just because workers think they deserve a pay hike. The same logic applies to job contract prices and adjusted yearly income percentages.

Unions work for workers. They represent them. As such, it may be necessary that for some occupations, workers will have to pay union dues to their union. So a portion of a worker's paycheck may have a special deduction that goes to the union. However, we will not go into the details of union dues and how much unions charge workers for being members. This is more of a political question rather than a purely economic one.

Unions can represent workers better collectively than if each worker in a firm had to represent himself individually. Unions give all the workers that they are fighting for a "common voice". Thus a worker is better able to get a demand from his company if the workers form a union than if the worker had to argue alone. This idea of "common representation" is the greatest value of the existence of unions.

Unions are important because of the service they provide for workers. They function to protect the working class. However,they should not interfere with wage functions and other wage related parameters.

Insurance

Many types of insurance are essential in an economy. By insurance we are referring to payments to a firm in case of a calamity. During a calamity the insurance firm provides assistance. The different types of insurance include life insurance, house insurance, car insurance, fire insurance, bankruptcy insurance and others. An insurance company, a car insurance company for example, receives payments from an interested consumer. If there is a car accident, the car insurance company pays for its repair. Insurance companies are in the laissez-faire sector and thus operate with Fortals.

The central bank does not set the Insurance Premium Rate. This parameter is set by firms in the laissez-faire sector and it is different for different types of calamities. Thus there is a "life" Insurance Premium Rate, a "house" Insurance Premium Rate and a "car" Insurance Premium Rate. This is how much a person being insured must pay the insurance company each month (or fixed amount of time) for coverage. Insurance companies of the same type compete not in quality but price. That is they fight with each other to provide the best coverage possible at the most competitive price. Since all insurance company coverages of the same type cost differently, consumers pick the best one. Life insurance companies compete with each other in how much coverage and benefit a consumerist receives for belonging to its company plan as well as monthly payments. Car insurance companies compete on how responsive their service is and on how inclusive their firm is about its membership as well the insurance payments.

Insurance Premium Rates are obtained through by the interaction of consumerists and insurance providing firms. Life insurance could be 25.00 ₤/ 100 000.00 ₤. Car insurance could be 200.00 ₤/car/month. Fire insurance could be 150.00 ₤ /house/month.

The different insurance providing firms can work either in the natural partition or in the command partition. In both cases firms compete with each other. However if the organizers of the command partition, i.e. the Human Resource Management Commission, want to set a goal for a certain insurance premium they can do so. Thus if insurance company ABC sets it car insurance premium at 5 % and a command partition firm sets this at 2 %, more people will want to buy insurance from the command partition firm. To be competitive, firm ABC needs to lower its premium to around 2 % or else the command partition firm will have the majority of the market.

Bankruptcy insurance needs special mention. If a firm wants to sell shares or bonds or wants to hire workers it must purchase bankruptcy insurance. A bankruptcy insurance company helps pay stockholders, bond holders and workers what they are entitled to in case a firm bankrupts. The interaction of firms and bankruptcy insurance agencies set a bankruptcy Insurance Premium Rate in terms of a percentage per given time- usually a month. Let's suppose that it is 0.25%/month. So if a firm sells 1 000 000 shares costing 10.00 þ, they have to pay 10.00 þ x 1 000 000 x 0.0025 = 25 000.00 þ/month to the bankruptcy firm. If a firm sells job contracts and at the end of their job contract workers are entitled to 800 000.00 þ, the bankruptcy firm must receive 2 000.00 þ per month. In case of a bankruptcy however, the bankruptcy firm must pay the stockholders the value of the stock they own which has become worthless as a result of the bankruptcy. It must also pay the workers who lost their jobs as a result of the bankruptcy. In the case of stock, the bankruptcy firm only pays those stock holders who actually bought their stock. For example if John is an entrepreneur and issues 1 000 000 stocks and keeps

500 000 of them he doesn't receive anything for them if he bankrupts. The bankruptcy firm does not pay him the value of his 500 000 shares. It does pay the other half that were bought by investors at the universal stock price. Bankruptcy insurance is probably badly named as it doesn't really help the firm bankrupting but rather those that lose out when a firm bankrupts.

Buying bankruptcy insurance is like buying car insurance. It is totally mandatory. A motorist can't drive a car without car insurance. Similarly, a business can't issue stocks, bonds, hire workers or take a loan without taking out bankruptcy insurance. Bankruptcy insurance is enforced by law.

More "risky" firms have to pay more for being insured. What the idea of bankruptcy insurance accomplishes is that the default risk is in the hands of the insurance company not investors.

Since the insurance firms are in the laissez-faire sector, they operate with Fortals. However for things like insuring bankruptcies and houses, they must pay those who bought insurance packages in Ignits. To satisfy this, we avoid the Ignit-Fortal exchange rate and use the idea that $1f = 1 \, þ$. The reciprocal is the same.

Insurance companies are vital to an economy that faces risks. The various insurance companies compete with one another as the premium rates are not fixed by the central bank. The bankruptcy insurance firm is necessary to protect workers, shareholders and bond holders in the event a firm bankrupts.

Savings, Debt and the Materialist Overdraft

By savings we mean spending less money than earning. Thus there is more to spend in the future. By debt we mean spending more money than earning. Thus there is less money to spend in the future. Savings can be either in the form of Norses, Fortals or Ignits. There can also be debt in terms of Ignits, Fortals, and Norses. If one spends more Norses than are granted to him by the central bank they are still entitled for the *materialist overdraft*. It is also possible that a consumerist may have to make monthly payments for goods and services he purchased.

Normally, all consumerists are granted either the General Consumerist Grant or the Non Working Consumerist Grant. However in some emergencies, the consumerist may be a little short on essential things like food or beverage items. To help him out we introduce the materialist overdraft. Basically, the consumerist can have some extra Norses granted to him. How much he is granted is based on the *materialist overdraft limit*. This is how much of the Consumerist grant he is given as set by percentage. This is given to him from the government. It should usually be below 5 % of the grant given to the consumerist. The next month, the consumerist must pay back the value of the materialist draft with a high percentage. This is called the *materialist overdraft interest*.

Let's see an example. Joseph received the General Consumerist Grant of 1000.00 ☉. The materialist overdraft limit is 5%. The materialist overdraft interest is 50 %. So, this month Joseph is given an extra 50.00 ☉ to help him out. For simplicity, let's suppose the General Consumerist Grant is also 1000.00 ☉ next month. However, instead of getting that, Joseph receives 1000.00 ☉ – 50.00 ☉ - (50.00 ☉ x 0.5) = 925.00 ☉. The government receives 75.00 ☉. It uses it to pay for social services. Clearly this idea of the materialist overdraft is good for two entities. Joseph has money he needed for very essential things. The government has an extra source of revenue.

It is quite possible that someone would get into a debt of Ignits. A businessman may borrow Ignits from the (private) bank in order to expand his business. A consumerist may buy a house using a mortgage. In both cases the people own property (house, new retail outlet) but still owe money to a bank that gave them the money to finance their purchase.

People can spend less Norses than they are granted. This is neither terribly good nor terribly bad. It simply represents a future purchase. A consumerist may save the money he is granted for some time so that in a few months he can buy himself a car. An advantage of saving Norses is that not all people rush to buy popular products.

It is possible that a consumerist may buy something he does not have the Norses to pay for. For example, someone, Jeremy, earns 1000.00 ☉ every month as part of the general consumerist grant. Let's suppose that a car, a sports car, costs 8 000.00 ☉. Even though he doesn't have the money, he can pay in monthly instalments. So he pays 400.00 every month for 20 months (there is no interest).

Consumerists can also spend less Ignits than they earn. Once again this represents future purchases. A consumerist who works as a cashier earns 500.00 þ/month. In three months she – if she saves- can afford that dream cruise to the Caribbean for 1200.00 þ. The problem with savings in general is that producers earn less money than they would if consumerists spent everything. For some industries this means lost business; i.e. restaurants, mechanics, music teachers.

Saving and debt are also possible with regards the laissez-faire sector. One can borrow Fortals and be in debt for the future. This may be due, for example, to an investment. Also one can save their Fortals for the future. Then they have more money (Fortals) to spend in the future.

Consumerists are able to get into debt and to save for the future. The economy is not tremendously hurt by these actions. Saving and being in debt are common experiences for anyone in the consumerist system.

A Basic Demonstration of the Accommodation Based Consumerist
Economic System on a Small Island

We need to know how our system works on a larger scope. Here we very basically demonstrate how our system works on a simple level- that is, on an island.

We make several assumptions that are not necessarily found in the grand system but are made here for simplicity.

1) The land is limited
2) The population is only 9 people
3) People sell what they make
4) Producers and thus workers require no inputs for their operations
5) The people can produce their products very quickly; i.e. a hut can be built in a day
6) The ratio of accommodational to materialist prices is imbalanced
7) The operation of the central bank is simplified
8) There is no laissez-faire sector
9) There is no command partition- everything involves the natural or governmental partition

Let's begin our analysis. We have 9 adults. To keep track of them we give them names. Their names are: John, Sue, Peter, Joanne, Sam, Kate, Nick, Lou-Anne and George.

The islanders are under a democracy. They elect John to be president. He is also the chief of the central bank. Thus he sets prices for all families of goods and services that can be produced.

The islanders also chose for themselves how they contribute to the island economy. We assume that everyone wants to work and that there are no idle islanders. Sue collects coconuts. Peter catches fish. Joanne picks berries. Sam makes clothes. Kate makes blankets. Nick, Lou and George all make living quarters such as huts, tepees and cabins.

John divides the primitive economy into accommodational, governmental and materialist sectors. Nick, Lou and George who work in making products for accommodation- huts, tepees, etc. - comprise the accommodational sector. All the others except John work in the materialist sector. John, the president and head of the central bank, works in the governmental sector.

John, as head of the central bank, puts price functions on everything that is produced. These prices are permanently fixed. They are expressed in terms of two currencies, Norses (Θ) and Ignits ($\flat$). Although 1 Θ = 1 $\flat$, these cannot be exchanged for each other. The prices of materialist goods are expressed in Norses while accommodational ones are expressed in Ignits. The price functions of products and services made on the island in the materialist sector are the following: The price of a fish is 2.00 Θ per fish. The price of a tree fruit (i.e. a coconut) is 0.50 Θ per fruit. Berries are worth 2.00 Θ/kg. A shirt is worth 5.00 Θ per shirt. The price of a blanket is 2.50 Θ /blanket.

The price functions for accommodational goods are as such:

5.00 þ/hut
7.00 þ/tepee
8.00 þ/lodge
10.00 þ/cabin
15.00 þ/bungalow
20.00 þ/house

At the end of the day, the things produced that day are counted. Only materialist rather than accommodational things are counted. This means we count how much coconuts, fish, berries, clothes and blankets are made but not any of the buildings.

During the day the islanders were busy contributing to the island society. At the end of the day, Peter caught 5 fish, Sue collected 20 coconuts, Joanne picked 5 kg of berries, Sam made 2 shirts and Kate made 4 blankets.

If everyone only kept what they made then no one would be too happy. Peter would be sick of fish and cold at night while Sam would be clothed but hungry. To overcome this we don't simply divide all products evenly. In that case everyone would have an equal amount of everything. Joanne would have as many blankets as Lou-Anne even though she still might be cold. Similarly, Sue might have the same amount of berries as Peter even though she doesn't like them. This situation would result in barter. Those who have a lot of what they don't want will give those things to those who want them in exchange for what they want more of. Thus if Peter likes coconuts and hates blankets, he would exchange the blankets for coconuts.

However, on this island the islanders do something different. They take the consumerist approach. Recall that John, the head of the central bank, put a price on everything. At the end of each day he calculates the island's GDCP. This is an important concept that is much different from the notion of the GDP in the free-market system.

The GDCP in our island example is calculated thus:

Coconuts-   20 x 0.50 Θ/coconut = 10.00 Θ
Fish-   5 x 2.00 Θ/fish = 10.00 Θ
Berries-   5 kg x 2.00 Θ/kg = 10.00 Θ
Clothes-   2 shirts x 5.00 Θ/shirt = 10.00 Θ
Blankets   4 blanket x 2.50 Θ/blanket = 10.00 Θ

We have used these figures because they give simple numbers. The total of the GDCP is 50.00 Θ

At this stage, John grants the equivalent of the GDCP per capita- the consumerist grant- to the islanders. Since all are working, they all receive the same amount. However, John sets a tax- one of only 3 in accommodation based consumerism- the Grand Consumerist Tax, which is a percentage of the GDCP. John sets it at 10%. The central bank grants 10 % of the GDCP (5.00 Θ) to the government. On a bigger island the government could spend these 5.00 Θ on services or products normally provided by the government.

It must be mentioned that no cash or coins are granted in this process. All the granting is carried out in the bank account each islander has in the central bank. This bank account, operated by John, is very simple. It simply reads the islanders name and how many Norses and Ignits he

378

or she has is written next to his name.

After subtracting the tax, the central bank grants the equivalent of the GDCP on a per capita basis to all islanders. There are 45.00 Ө. There are 9 people so all islanders are granted 5.00 Ө. The money that is granted is not taken from anywhere; it is simply granted by the central bank to each islander. John writes 5.00 Ө next to each islander's name.

Now with the 5.00 Ө all islanders can spend the money on any of the materialist sector goods and services that were produced. The price of a good is the same as that used to calculate the GDCP. When an islander buys a good from the materialist sector, the price of that good is deducted from his bank account. The equivalent amount of Ignits is added to the seller's bank account. Here is an example: Suppose George wants to buy a fish from Peter. A fish costs 2.00 Ө. Upon the transaction, George receives a fish from Peter and 2.00 Ө are deducted from George's Norse bank account, leaving 3.00 Ө to his name. At the same time John writes that Peter earned 2.00 þ, thus writing 2.00 þ next to Peter's name in his bank account records.

One of the curiosities of this setup is that if an islander wants to buy something from himself then he has to sell the product to himself. If Peter wanted to buy one of the 5 fishes he caught he would have to pay himself 2.00 Ө (he would receive 2.00 þ at the same time).

John earns 5.00 Ө from the tax for keeping track of all transactions. This is automatically turned into 5.00 þ as he works. He can spend this on the accommodational sector.

Let's assume that all of the islanders who work in the materialist sector sell what they produce. All these workers now have money that they can spend on the accommodational sector of the economy. People are hungry and buy all of Peter's fish. He earns 10.00 þ. People are cold so they buy all of Kate's blankets. She earns 10.00 þ. Not everyone likes coconuts so Sue only sells 6.00 þ worth of coconuts. Not everyone likes Sam's shirts and he only sells 8.00 þ worth. People like Joanne's berries but she only sold 9.00 þ worth. Evidently, someone or a few people did not spend all of the money that they were granted. They can save this for the next day when more goods will be produced.

Now the workers in the materialist and governmental sectors must purchase goods (types of accommodation) from the workers in the accommodational sector. Let's summarize how many Ignits the workers from the materialist and governmental sectors posses:

John- 5.00 þ
Peter- 10.00 þ
Kate- 10.00 þ
Sue- 6.00 þ
Sam- 8.00 þ
Joanne-9.00 þ

To summarize, the different accommodational structures cost:

5.00 þ/hut
7.00 þ/tepee
8.00þ/lodge
10.00þ/cabin
15.00 þ/bungalow
20.00þ/house

On our island John and Sue buy a hut costing 5.00 þ each hut, Sam and Joanne each buy a lodge costing 8.00 þ per each lodge. Peter and Kate buy a cabin worth 10.00 þ each cabin.

Nick, Lou-Anne and George are the builders. Nick builds the 2 huts earning 10.00 þ. Lou- Anne builds the two lodges earning 16.00 þ. George builds the cabins earning 20.00 þ.

Right now, assessing the economy, Sue and John have a hut, Sam and Joanne have a lodge, and Peter and Kate have a cabin. While,

Nick has 10.00 þ
Lou-Anne has 16.00 þ
George has 20.00 þ

Now all we need is to provide accommodation to those who provide accommodation. If things kept going the way they are going we fall into a problem called the accommodational overflow calamity. Things could collapse into the following: Recall that we have three workers in the accommodational sector- Nick, Lou-Anne and George. Nick has 10.00 þ, Lou-Anne has 16.00 þ and George has 20.00 þ. They all need accommodation. So Nick buys a cabin from George for 10.00 þ, Lou–Anne buys a bungalow from Nick and George buys a house from Lou-Anne. Then George has a house, Lou-Anne has a bungalow and Nick has a cabin. Yet George now has 10.00 þ, Nick has 15.00 þ and Lou-Anne has 20.00 þ. Now everyone has accommodation but those that provide accommodation could still buy more accommodation. George could buy from Nick another cabin, Nick could buy from Lou-Anne a bungalow for 15.00 þ. Lou-Anne could buy a house from George for 20.00 þ. So now George has a house and a cabin, Nick has a cabin and a bungalow. Lou-Anne has a bungalow and a house. Yet they would also have:

George-   20.00 þ
Nick-   10.00 þ
Lou-Anne-   15.00 þ

As we can see, the workers in the accommodational sector get more and more accommodation as money is just exchanged back and forth between them. To overcome this, the central bank could introduce the accommodational markdown. Basically for each transaction in the accommodational sector a percentage is deducted from the revenue of the seller. It is not kept by anyone but simply destroyed; put out of circulation.

So let's retrace our steps to the point where the workers in the materialist sector and governmental sectors purchase accommodation. Sue and John have a hut. Sam and Joanne have a lodge. Peter and Kate have a cabin.

John sets the accommodational markdown at 50%. This may seem like a lot but usually the higher the accommodational markdown the more offset the accommodational overflow calamity is.

Nick would receive 0.5 x 10.00 þ = 5.00 þ
Lou-Anne would receive 0.5 x 16.00 þ = 8.00 þ
George would receive 0.5 x 20.00 þ = 10.00 þ

So now Nick, Lou-Anne and George buy accommodation. Nick could buy a hut for

5.00 þ. He buys it from Lou-Anne who receives 0.5 x 5.00 þ = 2.50 þ. Lou-Anne could buy a lodge for 8.00þ. She buys it from George who receives 0.5 x 8.00 þ = 4.00 þ. George could buy a cabin for 10.00 þ. He buys it from Nick who receives 0.5 x 10.00 þ = 5.00 þ.

Now Nick has a hut, Lou-Anne has a lodge and George has a cabin. In terms of money, Nick has 5.00 þ, George has 4.00 þ and Lou-Anne has 2.50 þ

At this point Nick could buy another hut for 5.00 þ. However, neither George nor Lou-Anne can buy anything because the cheapest thing (a hut) costs more money than they have. Suppose that Nick buys a second hut from Lou-Anne. Now Lou-Anne has 5.00 þ. She buys a hut for 5.00 þ from Nick who receives 2.50 þ (50% of 5.00 þ). Now none of the three accommodational sector workers can afford anything.

This concludes our examination of a small island society. We discussed the major points that are necessary for an understanding of our system. With a concrete example such as this, the system should seem a bit clearer.

Consumerism Can Be More Capitalist Than Capitalism

There are several positive things that can be said about capitalism. It is, to some degree, a good way to manage markets. In consumerism many of the wonderful things about capitalism are retained to the point that consumerism is more laissez-faire, in some sense and to some degree, than Adam Smith (the philosopher responsible for capitalism) could have ever hoped for.

In consumerism we have what's called the laissez-faire sector. The laissez-faire sector is one of the four sectors of consumerism. In the laissez-faire sector, prices are set by the interaction of firms and households. Supply and demand vs. price determine the price and quantity of goods bought and services provided. There is no governmental involvement in the market for goods and services (unless it is invoked to control unemployment and inflation).

In the laissez-faire sector of consumerism there is absolutely no such thing as a "tax". There is no sales tax, income tax, property tax, wealth tax, gasoline tax, alcohol tax, tobacco tax, luxury tax, corporate tax, etc. The same cannot be said about other countries around the world that describe themselves as being capitalist, whether in North America or Europe or Asia. The absence of a tax allows the markets for goods and services to be more efficient.

Also in the laissez-faire sector in this system, production decisions are made by firms trying to make a profit; just like in pure capitalism. Decisions of how to make a product or service, how much to sell it for, where to make it and how to compensate workers are made by decentralized firms trying to compete with each other and make a profit.

Perhaps the only drawback to the laissez- faire sector in consumerism is that it is not supposed to make up the entire system. There are three other sectors that must be put into place. The whole business of dividing the economy into sectors is made by a benevolent social planner – the government actually. The laissez-faire sector should not really comprise more than 5 %-18 % of the entire economy. However, if the benevolent social planner loves capitalism or the new consumerist nation converts from a former capitalist nation, the scope of the laissez- faire sector can be bigger; that is, it can take up more of the economy relative to the other sectors.

Similar to capitalism, in consumerism we have a speculative stock market. In this market shares are issued by firms needing money to set up and expand and are sold and bought by profit-seeking investors. Here, investors can make a lot of money or if they do not know what they are doing they can loose a lot of money. This is in line with the stock markets of major economic superpowers on earth. However what stands out in consumerism is that those issuing stock must take out mandatory bankruptcy insurance based on the original issuing price of the stock. Thus if an investor has stock in a company that just went bankrupt, he won't loose all his money. This idea of bankruptcy insurance protects investors from an all out crash of the stock market.

Also, similarly to capitalism there is a speculative bond market in consumerism. Firms and investors get together to buy and sell different types of bonds. In the speculative bond market, the parameters (price of bond, interest rate, maturity and repayment frequency) are not set by the central bank or the government. These parameters are, in a market sense, set by the interaction of those issuing speculative bonds and those buying speculative bonds.

Also, like in capitalism, consumerists in consumerism have opportunity. They have the opportunity to be whoever they want to be and with hard work, to purchase whatever they like – to some degree. The consumerist system is designed so that everyone can achieve success. This is made possible through the universal education system. With a good education and training one can have a better job and make more money.

Similarly to capitalism, consumerism supports the notion of budgeting. Budgeting applies to all currencies. A person in consumerism whether a consumerist, an investor of businessman, ought to manage his money wisely. Thus one would buy the most necessary things first or the things that provide one with the highest level of happiness and satisfaction.

In consumerism the right to own private property is preserved. This is in line with capitalism. A system where this fundamental right is preserved works much better than one where it isn't.

Also in consumerism, the power and utility of capital is maintained. Capital, that is purchasing power, is central to many economic decisions. Which products and services are produced and how workers are compensated are influenced by capital.

Like in pure capitalism, consumerism makes use of the idea of a firm. In consumerism, most business decisions are made by profit maximizing firms. These firms make choices as to who is employed, what is produced, how it is produced and when and where it is produced. This is true in the natural partition. In the command partition firms are also used but the profits go to pay for social services.

In consumerism there are raises and promotions. These come about to reward workers for hard work. This in line with capitalist ideas.

Several important parameters in consumerism are under the influence of the interaction of firms and consumerists. These include the speculative general bond interest rate as well as the speculative profit bond interest rate. The actual exchange rate is determined in a similar manner to the way it is determined in the free-market system.

The means of production in consumerism are, like in the free-market system, in the hands of profit seeking merchants- at least in the natural partition.

The accommodational consumerist spending reimbursement is dictated by profit seeking firms. This is very capitalist-like.

Finally, all should have an equal opportunity to dream of, purse and attain happiness. Originally, this was one of the key goals of capitalism. Unfortunately, in many capitalist countries this ideal has disintegrated and a multitude of people are either unemployed, homeless, hungry or poor. However like in pure capitalism, this dictum is retained in consumerism.

Capitalism has quite a few aspects that make it work in certain parts of the world. Consumerism has a lot of characteristics that can be considered "capitalist". In fact parts of consumerism harbour ideals that resemble pure capitalism. It retains ideas that enlightenment era philosophers who first described capitalism probably wanted to see in an economic system.

Beneficial Traits of Communism/Socialism Are Preserved in Consumerism

Socialism/Communism stand together with free market capitalism as the two major economic systems of the world. This book introduces and establishes a third – accommodation based consumerism.

Socialism has a lot to say about how to organize society and there are many countries, states, provinces and jurisdictions that have adopted various forms of socialism. A lot of good things can be said about socialism. One of the great things about accommodation based consumerism is that many of the useful, beneficial aspects of socialism are preserved in the system.

In Consumerism we have free ultra universal healthcare. Just about everything to do with medicine is provided free of charge for consumerists. This includes things like surgery, vision care, cancer treatment, blood work, dentistry, chiropractic, walk in visits, psychiatric/psychological treatments as well as emergency services. All forms of medical care are available publicly to all citizens of a consumerist nation. The funding for these services comes from many forms that are discussed in detail in this book. This idea of free ultra universal healthcare is in and of itself very socialist.

Education – of all types- is provided for free in consumerism. Elementary and secondary schools as well as university and college are funded and provided publicly by the government. This also includes such things as education for trades. For example, training to be an electrician, plumber, medical lab technician, nurse or pharmacy technician is also funded publicly. So, in consumerism if one aspires to be a medical doctor, lawyer or pharmacist, he or she will be glad to know that the government will pay for his or her education. This helps them out a lot as a lot of bright, intelligent students cannot go to school in other economic systems as they cannot afford it. Clearly, free universal education is a useful socialist idea.

The socialist paradigm advocates providing as many services as possible by the government. In consumerism we have free transit. So to take the bus or subway train, a consumerist will not have to pay for the trip. Although this has the beneficial effect of reducing the carbon footprint as it reduces the number of cars on the road, it is also useful as it lowers the cost of transportation for many people.

A key communist idea since the mid-nineteenth century is that workers are exploited in non socialist systems. Consumerism totally overcomes this problem. In consumerism in the GAM (governmental, accommodational, materialist sectors), wages are not set by "greedy bourgeois". Rather all wages and salaries (except in the laissez-faire sector) are set by the central bank. The firms that hire workers have no say as to how much to pay their employees (except of course, in the laissez-faire sector). Thus one of the most or the most contentious issues that concerns communists is resolved in consumerism.

Another idea in consumerism that smacks of pure socialism is the idea of the "Accommodational Award". Everyone, without exception is entitled to a place to stay while living and working in a consumerist nation. This eradicates (or at least drastically minimizes) the problem of homelessness. Those who receive the accommodational award are entitled to a decent home as long as it is not grander than that of the workers who do other jobs. So those who receive the accommodation award would perhaps receive a small condominium, a nice apartment or maybe even a small bungalow.

Consumerism has what is known as "the Command Partition". This is a part of the economy where decisions are made by central planners rather than by free market forces. Essentially, the command partition is a huge agency that puts absolutely everyone to work as long as they apply for it. This work is something the previously unemployed individual was good at – like drawing graphic novels or painting or accounting. The command partition creates firms where these workers work and when these firms make a profit, the profit goes to pay for social services. Thus it can be said that the consumerist "welfare system" makes money while giving everyone a job. However, this command partition should theoretically and practically be no larger than about 15 % of the whole economy. This idea of a command partition – that is a portion of the economy run by central planning- sounds a lot like a socialist idea.

Another idea that consumerism shares with socialism is the absence of a business cycle. In capitalism, we have a perpetual cycle of booms, recessions and booms again. Due to the way that the consumerist economic system is organized – this included the idea of parameters, sectors and partitions- the consumerist economy, like socialism, will never experience a business cycle.

Socialism and Communism have several traits that appeal to many people. Accommodation Based Consumerism retains some of these that stand out as being the most useful and beneficial. Thus those people to whom socialism appeals, should also find consumerism a good system.

The Interaction of Capitalism and Socialism in the Laissez-Faire Sector of the Command Partition

Consistent with a common theme in accommodation based consumerism, we have elements of socialism and capitalism working together. Essentially, we take the positive of these paradigms and discard their problems. Some parts of consumerism are inherently capitalist while others are mostly socialist. They come together in the laissez-faire sector of the command partition. As we will soon see, there is no real contradiction in this setup.

The laissez faire sector is pure, unadulterated capitalism. It is the capitalist element in consumerism. All business decisions are made by the interaction of supply (vs price) and demand (vs. price). Many countries around the world are mostly capitalist (i.e. America, Canada, France, Germany, Spain, Japan). Consumerism takes the ideal of the free market to a higher degree than these countries do. The laissez-faire sector is pure capitalism. It is more capitalist than the capitalism of other capitalist countries.

In the laissez-faire sector there are absolutely no taxes. That is, there is no sales tax, property tax, luxury tax, gasoline tax, income tax, corporate tax, cigarette tax, taxes on capital gains or other taxes. There are special parameters in place to counter inflation like the nominal Fortal-Ignit exchange mechanism, dynamic gambling and the GDCP anti-inflationary mechanism among others.

Usually, the laissez-faire sector is the smallest in the economy. This depends on how the benevolent social planner, i.e, the founding fathers (the government) divide the system between sectors. If the economic organizers are fond of the market system, the laissez faire sector should be large. Nevertheless, not all goods and services are under the laissez-faire sector. The main ones that are: jewellery, books, tips to a waitress or hair dresser, the service of a private lawyer and things sold through the auction system or mowing someone else's lawn etc...

The command partition is the socialist element of Accommodation Based Consumerism. It is a part of the economy run through social planning. Goods and services are produced and subsequently people are employed by this partition in three sectors of the economic system.

The command partition is overseen by a special agency called the Human Resource Management Commission (HRMC). This important body has nine main goals:

1) Produce goods and services so as to make a profit
2) Hire absolutely everyone that seeks a job; the job being the one that is most suitable to the individual. This eliminates all what is left in terms of unemployment
3) Encourage workers to find work in the natural and governmental partitions
4) Create healthy competition for firms in the natural partition
5) Overcome shortages and surpluses of the "pure" kind
6) Fight inflation
7) Fight hunger
8) Counteract global shortage
9) Reduce the market power of monopolies

The command partition creates firms in all industries of the laissez-faire sector, the materialist sector and the accommodational sector. In doing so, it hires all people seeking unemployment. However, instead of the profits going to an owner or to stock holders, they go directly to the government to pay for social services. Some parts of this profit is also taken out of circulation to reduce inflation.

An interesting situation occurs when we talk about the selling and buying of goods and services in the laissez-faire sector that is part of the command partition. Here socialism and capitalism interact in a profound way. Essentially what happens is that pricing decisions (of wages, goods, services) are determined through the market system. However, the final profits from this setup go to A) the government to pay for social services and B) and take out of circulation (destroyed) and inflation is reduced.

Let's take a look at a particular case. Jewellery is in the laissez-faire sector. A jewellery store is selling (among other things) a diamond ring. This jewellery store, for the purpose of this example, is in the command partition. A consumerist walks into the store to buy a ring for his fiancee as they are being married soon. The forces of supply and demand (vs. price) make the ring cost 1 000.00 £. The consumerist buys the ring. He gives the storekeeper a check for 1 000.00 £ and the storekeeper gives him the ring. The store makes many sales besides this one. The cost of running the store, electricity, renting of land, inventory, cost the HRMC 50 000.00 £. The store makes a revenue of 100 000.00 £. Thus there is a profit of 50 000.00 £. In this example, 15 000.00 £ leave as an anti inflationary measure. That is, it is taken out of circulation (destroyed). 35 000.00 £ are given to the three levels of government to pay for social services.

This is one firm. In the command partition there will be 10 000's of firms that make profit. Together, these will allow us to reduce inflation and raise revenue for the government instead of taxes.

Here's another example. We have a movie actor working in the command partition. Acting is in the laissez-faire sector where wages and salaries are determined by free market forces. We have a movie making company operated by the HRMC. It pays an actor, let's call him Ariel, 1 000 000.00 £ to star in a movie. This salary is not set by the central bank or a centralized agency. It is determined by the interaction of supply and demand (vs. price). The HRMC hires good quality actors and pays them a wage set by the free market. It is 1 000 000.00 £. Now when the movie making firm makes revenue it pays for all its costs. This includes the salary of the actor. The profit is split between a form of government revenue (to be split between the three levels of government) and to reduce inflation.

The laissez-faire sector of the command partition is an interesting part of the economy. It is one half capitalist as prices, wages etc are set by free market forces. The other half is socialist as production decisions are made by central planers with profits going to support government services and to reduce inflation.

A Comparison of the Shopping Experience in Capitalism and Consumerism

Free-market capitalism and accommodation based consumerism share the characteristic that consumerists need to buy things and that they need to exchange money for these goods and services. However, the exchange process of shopping at the retail level is different in these two economic systems.

In capitalism the general idea is to find the best price for the goods and services one wants to buy. In consumerism, the whole concept is different. One walks into a store knowing he has a certain fixed budget and tries to get quality goods and services for that budget. Let's compare the shopping experience of these two systems. In one example we will discuss a grocery store and in the other a clothing store.

In capitalism an individual walks into a grocery store with the intention of buying milk and cereal and "shopping" to find the best deal on these products. The shopper buys the milk and cereal that a) cost least or b) have the most quality for the best price.

In consumerism, another individual enters a grocery store. So suppose he has 10.00 Ө (Ө, Norses, are one of the three currencies in the consumerist system). He tries to spend the 10.00 Ө so as to buy the best items he can with that money. Since all cereals cost the same he would buy the tastier, healthier cereal. Since all milk costs the same, he would buy the tastiest, most nutritious milk. Also, since he wants hamburger (assuming he still has money left over), he buys the best hamburgers in terms of quality. These may be ostrich burgers, hamburgers stuffed with bacon and cheese, salsa or bacon burgers. He shops to find the best groceries under the constraint of his budget.

Let's compare the shopping experience between two individuals in a clothing store. Under the capitalist paradigm, a shopper would enter a clothing store with a general knowledge of what he wants to buy. Let's say that he wants to buy a pair of jeans and a t-shirt. He looks around the store and finds ones that cost the least and fit him. He is satisfied; but if he had more money he could get a better quality pair of jeans and t-shirt.

Now let's see how the situation would turn out under accommodation based consumerism. The same shopper as before enters the clothing store. He knows he has 200.00 Ө to spend on clothing. He finds that all jeans, regardless of make, cost 120.00 Ө. He also notices that all t-shirts, regardless of make, cost 80.00 Ө. He looks at the jeans and t-shirts to find those that are the most desirable in his eyes; that is, those of the highest quality. He finds a pair of jeans and a t-shirt that are comfortable, fashionable, well made and durable. That is, he finds a pair of jeans and a t-shirt that he truly wants. He chooses and buys the optimal pair of jeans and t-shirt, thus spending his 200.00 Ө.

Another difference between the shopping experience in capitalism and consumerism is that in capitalism there is a considerable sales tax on goods and services while in consumerism sales tax completely does not exist. Although in some free-market nations there is no sales tax on food, there is sales tax on other items. So, if we are using clothing as our example, the capitalist shopper would pay a considerable sales tax. In some places this is more than 15%. In consumerism there is absolutely no sales tax on any good or service.

One profound difference between the pricing system of capitalism and consumerism is that in capitalism prices fluctuate while in consumerism they are fixed for a family of products. Thus in capitalism it is very difficult to know how much one will spend before entering a store. In contrast, in the consumerist system, since price functions are fixed, one knows or has the potential of knowing exactly how much he will spend when he leaves the store that he plans to purchase things in. The fixed price function system makes budgeting in accommodation based consumerism simple and structured. However, it must be put into consideration that in this section we have been talking about the materialist and the accommodational sectors; not the laissez-faire sector. The laissez-faire sector is very capitalist-like.

There is a considerable difference between the shopping experience under capitalism and under consumerism. In capitalism, the general idea is to find the lowest price for goods and services one already knows he will buy. In contrast, in consumerism, the general idea is to buy the highest quality, most desirable goods and services knowing before hand how much one wants to spend.

Perfect Competition

Perfect competition is a type of market condition. It occurs when there are many sellers, the product is practically the same and there are no barriers to a firm's entry. Although a perfectly competitive market exists in the consumerist economy it is a little bit different than its counterpart in the free-market economy.

We talk about wheat. We assume that wheat is not a final product but an input used to make bread and other baked goods. It is easy to produce large quantities of wheat if the growing conditions are adequate.

Supply and demand rule the free-market. In a free-enterprise perfectly competitive market, the price per bushel of wheat and the quantity of bushels sold are determined by the interaction of wheat makers and wheat buyers. Individual wheat buyers and wheat makers have little to say about how much wheat is produced or the price at which it is sold.

Now let's turn to the consumerist perfectly competitive market. The price per bushel is set by the central bank and the quantity bought is determined by the desires of the consumerists. Let's say the central bank sets the price of wheat at 0.50 þ per bushel. The wheat is in the same family as oat and barley- the grain family. Therefore oat and barley also cost 0.50 þ per bushel. Wheat, oat and barley producing firms compete with each other. This is reasonable to assume as the cost to grow a square meter of wheat is comparable to that of growing a square meter of oat or barley. Since wheat and other grains are inputs, they are in the accommodational sector and their price is in Ignits.

How much a wheat producing firm sells depends on how much a baker buys, how much a mill processes and how much wheat made baked goods consumerists buy. When a baker buys wheat (supposing it is already ground) he must chose among various wheat producing firms. His choice is subtle since all wheat is more or less the same. He would pick based on proximity to his bakery- which should minimize transportation costs. If he finds the flour from one firm to be contaminated and dirty at one time, afterwards he might choose a different wheat firm. He may be loyal to a particular brand. He may associate a particular brand with superior or inferior quality. We discuss brands more fully in another section.

In a perfectly competitive consumerist market prices per quantity are fixed (assuming they are in the accommodational sector). The quantity purchased is ultimately dependent on the desires of the consumerists. These are the major differences between the free-enterprise and consumerist perfectly competitive markets.

Monopolies

One of the major problems of the free-enterprise economy is the existence of monopolies. Although a lot of resources have been implemented to reduce the existence of monopolies, their presence is one of the main arguments against the free-enterprise system.

By monopoly we mean a firm that is the only one that produces the same type of good or service or a close substitute to it. In the free-enterprise system, a monopoly can charge any price that it wants to for its goods or services. However in a monopoly not all the gains from trade are realized. We say there is "dead weight loss".

There are several important problems that a monopoly has. It has market power and thus charges prices that are too high. The gains from trade are not extracted since the price a monopoly charges exceeds the marginal cost of production. There is market failure due to deadweight loss. The monopolist is unable to obtain the maximum profit possible. Finally the monopolist makes more money than he would if the market were competitive. All this hurts the consumerists.

In accommodation based consumerism these problems disappear. The price function for the good or service that a monopolist can charge is set by the central bank. All input functions are fixed by the central bank. Furthermore, monopolies cannot exist in the laissez-faire sector. They exist in the GAM sectors.

Here's an example for a monopolist of hydro-electricity. The central bank sets his price function at 0.10 þ /kWh. If one of his customers uses 1000 kWh the customer would have to pay 100.00 þ. The monopolist of hydro would receive, assuming an accommodational markdown of 25%, only 75.00 þ. The monopolist cannot charge any more than the price function set by the central bank. In this setup, all the problems of monopoly that exist in a free-market economy completely disappear.

Another alternative possibility to combat the problem of existence of monopolies with excessive market power is to ensure that monopoly markets are under the control of command partition firms. So firms like for example cable companies and electricity providers will be operated by the command partition.

The free-market system can have monopolists. They are a major problem. In consumerism these problems do not exist.

Oligopolies

Here we investigate the nature of an oligopoly. By oligopoly we mean a market in which there are a few firms that sell products that are quite similar. Examples of oligopoly markets include markets for automobiles and television sets.

In the free-market system there are two models of oligopolies – the Bertrand model and the Carnot model. In the Bertrand model, firms compete with each other in terms of prices. In the Carnot model, firms compete with each other in terms of quantity supplied to markets. We will not go too deeply into these models. They are well known and taught in most economic courses.

In the accommodation based consumerist economy, oligopolies can be seen in light of the Consumerist model. In this model the oligopolies compete in terms of quality of their products while the prices of the products remain fixed. This is a form of quality selection. The idea is that firms compete and the most successful ones in terms of quality flourish while the rest stagnate.

We show the Consumerist model in the market for batteries. We have five battery producing firms. Let's call the firms – firm 1, firm 2, firm 3, firm 4 and firm 5. We are discussing the family of batteries to which AA size batteries belong. The central bank set the price of the batteries at 1.00 Θ each.

How will the battery firms compete under the Consumerist model? Firm 1 makes batteries that last 800 hours. In response firm 2 makes batteries that last 900 hours. Firm 3's batteries last 950 hours. Firm 4's batteries last 1000 hours. Firm 5 makes their batteries rechargeable so that they can be recharged after 500 hours. Firm 1 makes their batteries also rechargeable. Their batteries can be recharged after 600 hours. Firm 3 makes batteries that last 1500 hours. Firm 4 makes their batteries with an automatic tester that tells the consumerist how much electricity is still left in the battery. Thus they compete.

But where will this end? –It doesn't! It is only limited by the current state of technology. As new inventions, innovations and ways of doing things are created, batteries will keep on getting better and better and better…

Here's another example from the family where personal computers belong. We have four computer making firms. Let's call them – firm 1, firm 2, firm 3 and firm 4. The central bank sets the price of a computer at 800.00 Θ. Firm 1 makes their computers function at 2.5 GHz. Firm 2 makes their computers function at 3.00 GHz while firm 3 makes their computers work at 4.00 GHz. Firm 4 makes their computers function at 4.00 GHz but they have the most advanced sound card. Firm 1 makes their computers function at 4.10 GHz and these computers have the most advanced video card. Thus they compete.

This competition, like the one for batteries, also doesn't really end. It is limited by the current state of technology.

In the oligopoly market in the consumerist system, firms compete under the Consumerist model. Firms making similar things produce more exciting products while the price of the products remains fixed. The Consumerist model ensures constant unabated progress limited only by technology.

General Microeconomic Functions of Business in the Natural Partition

In order to provide our consumerists with goods and services, we must have a way of doing so. This method must be both efficient and productive and produce goods and services of the highest quality (those most desired by our consumerists). The idea of a *firm* is a good one as it adheres to the above guidelines. A firm can be defined as "an organization that transforms inputs into goods and services that people want."

There are two types of firms in the natural partition of our system. They differ in who "owns" the firm. A firm owned by one person is called a "sole proprietorship" and a firm owned by many is called a "corporation". These two terms are similar in meaning to their free-market counterparts and finding different names would only lead to confusion.

Let's discuss the nature of the owner. The owner is he who knows the art of money making. The art of money making involves obtaining more money than before. Someone who is skilled at ending up with more money than he had before has the art of money making. A pharmacist knows the art of selling drugs. A doctor knows the art of medicine. However they both also know the art of money making as they are usually rich. A musician plays music for the love of playing music and for making money. However he must love music because there are other professions with equally high pay. A surgeon performs surgery out of the pleasure of saving lives and making money. However he must love saving lives or else he would have found another equally high paying career.

Now the owner makes money for the sole purpose and satisfaction of making money. He has the soul of a money lover. He praises prosperity and is always looking to make money and spending as little of it as possible.

We need to ask how is a man with the love of money found? How do we get owners? How do owners come about?

There are three ways an owner can become one:

A) He can buy a firm
B) He can buy the firm from someone else
C) He can buy enough stock to own the firm

For path A, a would-be owner can obtain enough money from banks, stocks and bonds or personal savings to set up a firm. For path B, a would-be owner can obtain enough money from personal savings, banks, bonds and stocks to purchase a firm from another owner. For path C, a would-be owner can obtain enough money from banks and personal savings to purchase >50% of a firm's stock.

A firm must have an incentive to produce. One of the best incentives offered by an economy is profit. The company that can make its products more efficiently will sell more of them. The company that makes its products of best quality (the most desired by consumerists) will make profit. This profit is in terms of Ignits (þ).

Let's focus on the sole proprietorship. The essence of a sole proprietorship is that it has one owner. This owner has supreme command of the firm.

It is the owner who makes money when the firm is productive and efficient. All other workers do specific jobs and are paid by the owner for doing so. The wages and salaries of workers are prescribed by the central bank. The owner is one of the few people in the accommodation sector of the economy who makes independent profit; that is profit not dictated by the central bank (the others are bond and stock holders). He makes or loses money based on the performance of his firm. This point is necessary to encourage more firms to spring up. It is the job of the owner to run the company.

This treatise does not explain exactly how an owner must manage his firm because doing so would make the management of the firm inflexible. Running a firm is an art and there is not a single correct way to run a business.

The owner of a sole proprietorship tries to make his firm earn a profit (in Ignits or Fortals). He does this by picking what the firm will do and how it will do it. He manipulates inputs (capital, labour, land and technology). He is in charge of recruiting or hiring other workers. He decides exactly how his firm is to be run. He is, however, guided by the principal of specialization.

The worker who does a particular job which he excels at either through passion, experience or knowledge, will do the job more efficiently and productively than any other worker. A 33 year old man finished a 4 year residency training program in internal surgery. Before doing so he graduated from medical school where he studied for 5 years. A hospital would be wise to hire him to their surgery unit rather than a medical graduate who had a 3 year residency in ophthalmology. However it would be wise to hire the ophthalmologist to the correct unit. By doing so, the two doctors would help more patients than if their placements were reversed. Knowing what you do, you do it well. This is the principal of specialization.

There are several things that an owner has no control over in the consumerist system. These are the pay of the workers, the price of the inputs and the price of the finished goods (in the accommodational sector). The owner has control over these things in the laissez-faire sector, however.

Now let's look at a corporation. The owner of a corporation is the individual or group that has 50% or more of the shares of the firm. The share holders congregate and vote to pick a grand owner. This person makes all the decisions for the corporate firm that an owner of a sole proprietorship would do. He is called the *Supreme Firm Director*. The share holders vote him in according to the proportion of shares they own. The more shares one has, the more influential he is in the firm. The person with more than 50% of the shares could vote anyone in as supreme firm director (including themselves). At anytime whatsoever the share holders can vote the supreme firm director out- provided the share holders vote that way. Therefore the supreme firm director answers to the shareholders and cannot make foolish managerial and administrative decisions for fear of losing his or her job.

We should mention something about stocks and owners. Suppose that there are 3 groups who own stock of company ABC. Company ABC issues 1000 shares. Group A owns 550 of them, group B owns 300 and group C owns 150 of them. Since group A has >50% of the shares, they can pick the Supreme Firm Director. They pick Emilio. One of Emilio's first tasks is to issue 1000 more shares. When they are issued group A has priority in buying them. Afterwards groups B and C can buy shares. These groups can buy as many shares until they own the same percentage of firm ABC as before or they may buy less. So if group A had 550/1000 x 100% = 55%, they can buy the equivalent of 55% of the new stocks (or less). The same applies to firms B and C. What is not bought can be bought by other investors.

Generally speaking, firms in the natural partition try their best to earn a high profit (in line with the stipulations discussed in this treatise regarding the GAM sectors). To do so they must sell as many goods as possible and provide as many services as possible. Firms in the natural partition that have a positive, high profit are those that survive the market. It is as if, consumerists vote on which natural partition firms thrive every time that they purchase a good or service at that particular firm.

In a corporation there may be minor firm directors for more specific areas of operation. These may include advertising, hiring, transport, input purchasing, customer relations, accounting etc. The Supreme Firm Director still has jurisdiction over everything. This is similar to a military hierarchy where we have a Supreme Commander who answers to the people (citizens, as we are assuming a democracy). Under him we have field marshals and generals. Then we have corporals and captains. The whole setup is necessary so that the Supreme Firm Director does not need to worry about very particular things-like which window to clean (this is the janitor's job). The whole setup of the firm is also guided by the principal of specialization. Whatever the firm does, it strives to assign tasks to workers as to maximize productivity and efficiency.

The Supreme Firm Director makes the important decisions within the corporation. He is always trying to please the share holders, increasing their profits. Some of his jurisdiction includes the issuing of bonds and stocks. He is responsible for decisions regarding the construction of new buildings and infrastructure. He has control over employees and capital. He decides what and how a firm produces. He can't control input prices, wages and product prices, stock prices and the price of his final goods and services (assuming we are dealing with the accommodational sector).

There are at least two types of firms -the sole proprietorship and the corporation,. They operate somewhat differently. It is important to understand the nature of the owner. The Supreme Firm Director plays an important rule, with many responsibilities and limitations.

General Microeconomic Functions of Business in the Command Partition

We have previously described how businesses are organized in the natural partition. Now we describe how they are set up in the command partition. Although there are some parallels in the way businesses are organized in the two partitions, there are, however, some key differences.

In both partitions, businesses are arranged into firms. However, who owns these firms and how they are organized differs. Firms in the command partition are run by the *Human Resource Management Commission* and there is a role for a "supreme firm director" when we are dealing with corporations under the command partition.

The Human Resource Management Commission is the highest level in the Command Partition. At the highest level it determines what firms are to be created in the command partition. It decides whether to setup a doughnut shop, a car dealership or car factory, an apartment building, a bookstore, a shoe factory, a gas station, a supermarket, etc. Now if the whole economy were organized this way there would be problems regarding allocation of resources. For example, the firm would produce things that no one needs and not produce things that are needed. However we are dealing with a very small population of the economy. That is, those in the socialist labour pool. These are people who are unemployed and would not being doing much anyways. Perhaps this is 3% or 5 % of the work force.

As a suggestion, the members of the HRMC can be elected rather than appointed. This is at the discretion of the benevolent social planner (i.e. the government or the people). If the members of the HRMC are elected then the HRMC would have someone or some entity that it is accountable to. However, there may be problems related to the politicization of economics.

The human resource management commission can decide to build things that are normally in a state of shortage in the natural partition. For example, if a study comes out through the census or another source that there is a severe apartment rental shortage, the human resource management commission can have several apartment buildings built.

In order for a firm in the command partition to start up, it needs a source of capital to build infrastructure, equipment, and all items to begin producing. It gets this money in one of several ways. Either it borrows money from a private bank or sells bonds. It could receive direct funding from a level of government as the profits from a command partition firm go to the government eventually anyway to pay for social services. Alternatively it can borrow from the government bank.

After the human resource commission creates a firm to produce goods or provide services, it hires workers for the firm. It would do so so as to hire as many people as possible. The people who are hired are from the socialist labour pool. The human resource commission tries to find a job for all in the socialist labour pool, by trying to match a worker's skill set, education, experience, abilities, etc with the jobs the human resource commission creates by producing firms. The jobs that are created do not have to be purchased like they are in the natural partition since the purpose of selling jobs is to give an incentive for employers to hire more workers. This is not necessary in the command partition. Workers working in the command partition receive a special payment and this they have to partially repay so that paradoxically, they are discouraged from being in the command partition and they move to the natural partition.

The human resource management commission would try to create as many firms as possible and as are needed so that it has placements for auxiliary workers. Firms are run by someone from the human resource management commission and sometimes several firms that are not competing with each other may have the same person running them. This person is analogous to the Supreme Firm Director that we discussed in the section of running businesses in the natural partition. This Supreme Firm Director hires minor firm directors for more specific duties and below these are even more specific duties. This in some ways resembles a military hierarchy. Those in the human resource department of the firm have the responsibility of hiring as many workers for the more specific duties while in some sense keeping the firm profit maximizing. Note that the human resource department and the human resource management commission are two entirely different entities. The first are the employees of a firm who employ workers for a particular firm. The latter are the institution that work in the command partition trying to create as many profit seeking firms as possible. To fill positions requiring skills like marketing and money management, the supreme firm director should hire university or college educated graduates who know how to handle the position but are currently unemployed.

For the case of a fast food restaurant, we would have someone from the human resource management commission act as the owner or supreme firm director of several outlets. He would hire a human resource agent that would oversee hiring for several outlets. It would be this person's duty to hire cashiers, bakers, waitresses and sandwich makers. The more workers employed the better as long as 1) the firm still makes a profit and 2) the workers know what they are doing.

The command partition extends into services. We could have workers (level 1 workers) assigned to a specific section of street and it would be their duty to make sure it is clean and garbage free. Then there would be other workers (level 2 workers) ensuring that these workers are doing their job properly and another level (level 3 workers) making sure these level 2 workers do their job well. This paradigm of several levels of workers extends throughout the command partition.

In general the command partition works like this: The human resource management commission creates many firms whether services or good producing that lie in the materialist, accommodational and laissez-faire sectors. These firms are run by a member of the human resource commission known as the supreme firm director (similar to the setup in the natural partition). He hires a human resource agent who hires workers for all other positions, maximizing employment and profit.

There are no special circumstances to help command partition firms vs. natural partition firms. Command partition firms do not receive any assistance from the government. In order for them to flourish, they need to compete directly against natural partition firms.

One major question we need to discuss is "how is the Human Resource Management Commission created?" It is created similarly to the central bank where there are 102 members. We will not limit the human resource management commission to a particular number of people. It could be 500 or several thousand members.

This is the general organizational framework of businesses in the command partition. Firms in this partition try to maximize profit while hiring as many workers as possible. Although there are many, many firms in this partition, they are organized along similar lines.

The Functioning of a Car Factory

Here we examine how a car factory operates. By car factory we mean a firm that takes inputs, labour, steel, machines and glass and uses these to produce automobiles. These automobiles are not sold directly to the public but to car dealerships.

Our car factory's name will be Super Plus Ultimate Motors. Our owner's (entrepreneur's) name is John Smith. In order to start his company he issues shares at the consumerist stock market. The central bank has set the Consumerist Universal Stock Price at 10.00 þ per share. He issues 2 000 000 shares and keeps 1 000 000 for himself. He doesn't earn anything. In order to issue shares he must buy bankruptcy insurance. In case his firm bankrupts and he is unable to pay back the stock owners how much they own of their stock, the bankruptcy insurance firm pays them their value of the stock they have. This is so that stock investing is risk free. So if a company bankrupts each stock owner is paid 10.00 þ x the number of stock he owns (except for John who didn't buy any). In exchange for this protection, the bankruptcy insurance company collects a premium from the firm. The car company found a premium that is set at 0.25% per month of the money covered. So every month John's firm must pay 1 000 000.00 þ x 0.0025 = 25 000 þ per month to the bankruptcy insurance firm.

Now that he has some money, he can start building his company. We assume that he does not have to build the factory from scratch. He simply buys the land and factory building from a previous owner. The land and building cost 6 000 000.00 þ. The accommodational markdown in our case is 30%. So the previous owner of the factory and land keeps 4 200 000.00 þ. John decides to make 6 different types of cars: a limousine, an SUV, a minivan, an economy car, another economy car and a poor quality car. They all cost the same to sell- 12 000.00 þ.

The government sets the capital investment transfer (CIT) at 0.1%. Since John paid 6 000 000.00 þ for the land and building, the government would give him 6 000 000.00 þ x 0.001 = 6000.00 þ.

John has to hire workers and purchase equipment to make his cars. His sunk costs are 850 000.00 þ. They include car assembly machines, computers and equipment. As for workers, he hires 1000 of them. They each earn 12.00 þ per hour and their JCP is 600.00 þ. The AYIP is 5000 %. These values are set by the central bank. They have contracts lasting one year.

Let's calculate how many hours they will work a year:

600.00þ hr/12.00 þ x 50 = 2 500 hours per year or 48 hours a week.

From selling his job contracts, John earns 1000 x 600.00 þ = 600 000.00 þ. Each worker is paid every two weeks (48 hours x 2 x 12.00 þ/hour = 1 152.00þ). In total this would cost 1000 workers x 2 500 hrs/year x 12.00þ /hour = 30 000 000.00 þ.

To encourage Super Plus Ultimate Motors to hire more workers, the central bank sets the Employment Reimbursement Transfer (ERT) at 0.1%. So the government would give Super Plus Ultimate Motors 30 000 000.00 þ x 0.01 = 30 000.00 þ.

In case the firm bankrupts, John must purchase bankruptcy insurance on these wages. The monthly bankruptcy insurance premium is 0.25%. So John must pay 30 000 000.00 þ x 0.0025 =

75 000.00 þ/month to his bankruptcy insurance company.

Now John can make cars. Below is a list of the variable costs associated with making each type of car (this includes costs of production like steel, plastic, electricity, rubber, paint)

A) Limousine-   3 000.00 þ
B) S.U.V.   2 500.00 þ
C) Minivan-   2 000.00 þ
D) 1st economy car-   1000.00 þ
E) 2nd economy car- 1 100.00 þ
F) Poor quality car- 500.00 þ

Initially the car factory makes 100 of each car in 1 month and ships them to car dealers (we don't worry about shipping costs as they are paid by the car dealership)

Let's see the profit:

Limousine-   100 x (12 000.00 þ – 3 000.00 þ) = 900 000.00 þ
S.U.V.   100 x (12 000.00 þ – 2 500.00 þ) = 950 000.00 þ
Minivan-   100 x (12 000.00 þ – 2 000.00 þ) = 1 000 000.00 þ
1st economy car- 100 x (12 000.00 þ – 1 000.00 þ) = 1 100 000.00 þ
2nd economy car- 100 x (12 000.00 þ – 1 100.00 þ) = 1 090 000.00 þ
Poor Quality Car- 100 x (12 000.00 þ – 500.00 þ) = 1 150 000.00 þ

For a total profit of 6 190 000.00 þ. To encourage the firm to stay in our country and do business here, the government sets the Profit Reward Transfer (PRT) at 0.05 %. Thus the government pays the firm 6 190 000.00 þ x 0.0005 = 3 095.00 þ.

However in month 2 the demand for these cars is a lot different. Instead of 100 cars from each kind, the demand for each car is now the following:

Limousine-   250 cars
S.U.V. -   180 cars
Minivan -   100 cars
1st economy car   65 cars
2nd economy car   68 cars
Poor quality car 12 cars

Let's calculate the profit:

Limousine-   250 x (12 000.00þ – 3 000.00þ) = 2 250 000.00 þ
S.U.V.   180 x (12 000.00þ – 2 500.00þ) = 1 710 000.00 þ
Minivan   100 x (12 000.00þ – 2 000.00þ = 1 000 000.00 þ
1st economy car   65 x (12 000.00 þ– 1 000.00þ) = 715 000.00 þ
2nd economy car   68 x (12 000.00þ – 1 100.00þ) = 741 200.00 þ
Poor quality car 12 x (12 000.00þ– 500.00þ) = 138 000.00 þ

The total profit is 6 554 000.00 þ. With a PRT of 0.05%, the government pays the firm 3277.00 þ.

In this way Super Plus Ultimate Motors continues to make cars, the kind being made being dictated by the consumerists. If Super Plus Ultimate Motors thinks that they can make the highest profit per car selling the poor quality car, then consumerists will simply buy better cars (from a different car firm). Super Plus Ultimate Motors is not stuck just selling limousines and S.U.V.'s. They can add fantastic features to their cars (like DVD players, air conditioning, new safety features, more leg room, on board computers with the internet, etc.). Suppose that they add some of these features to their "poor quality" car and its variable production costs rise from 500.00 þ per car to 800.00 þ per car. If consumerists see this new "poor quality" car as a contender to the limousine, then Super Plus Ultimate Motors will make more of them and sell more of them.

The car factory does not report its earnings to the central bank- its contribution to the GDCP- as it is not directly involved in the materialist sector final goods sale. However the car dealership that buys cars from Super Plus Ultimate Motors would have to do this.

Let's find out how our firm did in a year. Let's compare their profits and costs. In a year they sold the following amounts of cars to dealerships:

Limousine-   15 000
S.U.V. -   12 000
Minivan-   10 000
1st economy car   750
2nd economy car   780
Poor Quality Car   100

So the yearly profits would be:

Limousine   15 000 x (12 000.00 þ – 3 000.00 þ) = 135 000 000.00 þ
S.U.V.   12 000 x (12 000.00 þ – 2 500.00 þ) = 114 000 000.00 þ
Minivan   10 000 x (12 000.00 þ – 2 000.00 þ) = 100 000 000.00 þ
1st economy car   750 x (12 000.00 þ – 1 000.00 þ) = 8 250 000.00 þ
2nd economy car   780 x (12 000.00 þ – 1 100.00 þ) = 8 502 000.00 þ
Poor quality car   100 x (12 000.00 þ – 500.00 þ) = 1 150 000.00 þ

= 366 902 000.00 þ

With a PRT of 0.05% the government would give Super Plus Ultimate Motors, 366 902 000.00 þ x 0.0005 = 183 451.00 þ

The company earned 600 000.00 þ from selling job contracts.

Let's summarize the costs:

Land + factory cost 6 000 000.00 þ. We calculated the reimbursement from the government, assuming CIT = 0.1%, to be 6 000.00 þ
Wages = 2 500 hours/year x 1000 workers x 12.00 þ/hour = 30 000 000.00 þ
Sunk costs are 850 000.00 þ
The bankruptcy insurance firm must be paid 25 000.00 þ/month for 12 months for stock + 75 000.00 þ/month for 12 months for wages. This is a total of 300 000.00 þ + 900 000.00 þ = 1 200 000.00 þ.
So the firm made:

400

366 902 000.00 þ
+ 600 000.00 þ
+ 183 451.00 þ
+ 6 000.00 þ
-30 000 000.00 þ
-850 000.00 þ
-1 200 000.00 þ
- 6 000 000.00 þ
= 329 641 451.00 þ

John reinvests 29 641 451.00 þ back into the factory. As for the share holders, they earn 300 000 000.00 þ/ 2 000 000 = 150 þ. This turns out to be a good investment. For investing 10.00 þ in a share, an investor earns 150.00 þ per year for every share bought. This is a profit of (150 – 10)/10 = 1 400 % per year.

Each month the investor earns 150.00 þ/12 = 12.50 þ. This is definitely a good investment. As for John he owns 1 000 000 of the original 2 000 000 shares issued. He pockets 150 000 000.00þ

This is how a car factory would operate under a consumerist system. We took the case of Super Plus Ultimate Motors and analyzed how they would go about making cars. We compared the losses they incurred with their profits to see how they would stand up in an economy.

The Functioning of a Wheat Farm

Here we will investigate the operation of a wheat producing firm. That is, a firm whose objective is to convert agricultural land and seeds into wheat.

Our farm is run by farmer Bob. Bob has come across 10 000.00 þ. He wants to become a farmer; a wheat farmer. We will follow the farm for 1 year. First he needs agricultural land. Agricultural land costs 5.00 þ per square meter. Farmer Bob wants 10 square kilometres of land. He needs to pay 50 000.00 þ for this. He is forced to borrow from a private bank. He borrows 40 000.00 þ at 5% interest (simply compounded yearly). So now he owns land. The Interest Rate Stimulus (IRS) is set at 0.5 %.

Next he needs machines, storage facilities, seed and farming equipment. This costs him another 15 000.00 þ. The government sets the Capital Investment Transfer (CIT) at 0.1%. Thus farmer Bob earns from the government, (40 000.00 þ + 15 000.00 þ) x 0.001 = 55 þ.

However he also needs workers. He needs 50 farm hands (people who will collect the wheat, plant the seeds, move it, package it, sort it and get it ready for transportation). All these jobs belong to the same family- the same wage function applies to all of them as they are all similar enough. The family that they belong to is the "farm technicians" family. The central bank sets the wage function at 5.00 þ/hour. The job contract is 2 000.00 þ. The contract lasts for 1 year. The Adjusted Yearly Income Percentage is 1200%. To calculate the number of hours a worker works during the time of the contract we use the formula:

= PTC[JCP(n) x hr/w x AYIP]
=1[2000.00 þ x 1 hour /5.00þ x 12] = 4 800 hours

Each worker would work 4800 hours in a year. Each worker would work 312 days a year (assuming he works 6 days a week, including holidays). It is assumed that each week he would work the same amount of hours. Every day the worker works 4800hours/312 = 15.33 hours or 15 hours and 20 minutes.

Farmer Bob sells jobs to 50 farming technicians. He picks the most qualified people to work for him; i.e. those with some kind of experience in farming or those that are hard working. Farmer Bob thus sells 50 job contracts. Each is worth 2 000.00 þ. Thus he earns 50 x 2 000.00 þ = 100 000.00 þ for his business.

The government sets the Employment Reimbursement Transfer (ERT) at 0.1%. We know that the 50 workers would work 4 800 hours in a year for 5.00 þ/hour. So each year the government gives farmer Bob 50 x 4 800 hours x 5.00 þ/hour x 0.001 = 1200.00 þ.

If Bob bankrupts he must pay his workers how much they would have earned if they worked the length of the entire contract. Thus in the case he bankrupts, he may not be able to pay his workers how much they deserve. He needs to buy bankruptcy insurance. The bankruptcy insurance premium rate is 0.25% per month. Let's calculate how much he needs to pay the bankruptcy insurance firm each month. The workers could work 4800 hours during their contract. There are 50 of them and each of them is paid 5.00 þ per hour. Thus he must pay the insurance firm 0.0025 x (4800 x 50 x 5.00þ) = 3 000.00 þ/month.

In February Bob gets his field ready for plantation. In May he starts planting wheat (actually his farm hands do this). Farmer Bob organizes them so that all of them have a job at all points in time- they are always doing something and none of them is idle.

Every two weeks, each of the 50 workers earns his paycheck. Let's calculate this. A worker works 15.33 hours a day for 6 days a week. In 2 weeks, this is 12 days. The worker is paid 5.00 þ/hour. Every two weeks, each worker earns 12 x 15.33 hours x 5.00 þ/hour = 919.80 þ.

During the summer the wheat grows. Each square meter of land can yield 5 bushels of wheat. The central bank sets the price of grain crops, which include oats and barley, at 100.00 þ per bushel.

Initially farmer Bob pays his worker's wages using the money he earned selling job contracts. Eventually he needs to borrow from the bank. Let's calculate how much money he has to pay his workers at the end of the year. Each worker earns 919.80 þ every two weeks. There are 26 two week periods in a year and there are 50 workers. At the end of the year, farmer Bob must pay 1 200 000.00 þ for his workers. When a worker receives his paycheck he keeps all of it. He doesn't have to pay any tax on income (in this scenario we assume that the government does not introduce it) or give anything to unemployment insurance. It is now August. We must also calculate other costs. The other costs include water for wheat, pesticides and other variable costs. For the year they amount to 2 000.00 þ. All other costs- fixed costs- which include machines, equipment, storage space, etc, have already been counted at the beginning of the analysis.

The harvest occurs in October. All farm technicians focus on harvesting wheat. Since there are 50 of them, no extra help is needed. There are 10 000 square meters of land and each square meter yields 5 bushels of wheat. However only 9 500 square meters of land yielded good crops- the other 500 square meters didn't produce anything that grew too well. Thus 9 500 x 5 = 47 500 bushels of wheat were harvested.

The wheat is needed by bakeries and other firms that require wheat as an input. We assume, for simplicity, that wheat processing into flour is carried out in a bakery. Farmer Bob does not need to grind it nor bring it to a mill. The firm that needs wheat buys 40 000 bushels of wheat. Each bushel costs 100.00 þ per bushel. Farmer Bob earns 4 000 000.00 þ.

Now what to do with the remaining 7 500 bushels of wheat? In a free-market society the farmer would destroy it so as to artificially raise the price of wheat. However farmer Bob needs not worry about the price of his wheat. He trades with the United States. In the United States let's assume that a bushel of wheat costs $125.00. The exchange rate is $0.50/þ. Farmer Bob sells 7 500 bushels of wheat to the United States and the Americans pay $125.00 x 7 500 = $ 937 500.00. This is equivalent to $937 500.00 x $1.00/0.50 þ = 1 875 000.00 þ. 750 000.00 þ go to farmer Bob and 1 125 000.00 þ go to the consumerist trade pool. Thus in the end farmer Bob earns 750 000.00 þ + 4 000 000.00 þ = 4 750 000.00 þ selling wheat.

Now it's December. Let's calculate to see how farmer Bob did financially. He earned 4 750 000.00 þ selling wheat and 100 000.00 þ selling job contracts, for a total of 4 850 000.00 þ The CIT made him 55.00 þ and the ERT made him 1200.00 þ. He started out with 10 000.00 þ. He borrowed 40 000.00 þ from the bank at 5 % interest which equals 42 000.00 þ at the end of the year. He borrowed 15 000 þ at 5% interest from the bank for storage, seeds and equipment. This amounts to 15 750.00 þ. He must pay his workers 1 200 000.00 þ. To pay them he borrowed this money from the bank at 5% interest. This equals 1 260 000.00 þ. For every situation he borrowed, the government helps out with 0.5 % of the loan (the IRS) so essentially his interest rate is really 4.5 %. The bank receives loan payments as if the interest rate were 5 %. This should help Bob with running his business. The bankruptcy insurance payments amount to 12 x 3 000.00 þ = 36 000.00 þ. When farmer Bob pays all the debts we mentioned above, he still has a surplus of 3 507 505.00 þ. Let's say that the Profit Reward Transfer (PRT) is 0.001 %, Then on top of this, farmer Bob also earns 3 507.50 þ.

This is how a firm, in particular a wheat firm, would operate. We encountered the expenses and sources of revenue that such a firm would likely have. Most firms in the agricultural part of the economy would operate similarly to our above analysis.

The Functioning of a Real Estate Company

By real estate we mean property in the form of land and living quarters. By real estate company, we mean a firm that buys and sells land and accommodation. The real estate company, which operates in the accommodational sector, using Ignits, makes money after a real estate transaction between two consumerists- in this case real estate owners. A real estate agent earns a commission on every sale. In this section we discuss how a real estate firm functions.

The real estate company brings sellers and buyers in the real estate part of the economy together, trading land and living quarters. Here's an example. A consumerist has a house costing 150 000.00 þ. The house has a price function: w100.00 þ + y1000.00 þ + z5000.00 þ + b10 000.00 þ; where w stands for number of square feet, y stands for number of washrooms, z stands for number of bedrooms and b stands for number of floors. This house is owned by a consumerist named Matt. It is worth 150 000.00 þ because it has 3 washrooms, 4 bedrooms, 3 floors and 970 square feet of space. Matt has a job that pays 10 000.00 þ a month. He has his sights set on a house worth 200 000.00 þ. It has 5 washrooms, 6 bedrooms, 5 floors and 1 150 square feet of living space (an actual price function for housing would be a lot more complicated, factoring in such things as number of windows, size of bedrooms, size of kitchen, presence of garage, etc.)

Matt puts his original 150 000.00 þ house on sale. He hires an agent named Max from a firm called Super Plus Ultimate Real Estate Inc. to sell his house and buy him the new one. The central bank sets a Real Estate Profit Percentage. This is a percentage of the sale or purchase that the real estate firm earns during every transaction. A real estate agent has a wage function from the real estate company that he works for. Let's use examples. The central bank sets the real estate profit percentage at 0.5% of the transaction and the real estate agent's wage function at 0.3y + 7.00þ /hour. Here y represents the real estate profit percentage. Then the real estate agent makes 30% of the real estate profit percentage or 30% of 0.5% of the transaction. He also earns 7.00 þ/hour in addition to that.

Let's go back to our example with Matt. Max sells his house to another consumerist for 150 000.00 þ. This new consumerist's name is Paul. Paul pays 150 000.00 þ (assuming that he has that much) to Matt. Super Plus Ultimate Real Estate Inc. earns 0.5% x 150 000.00 þ = 750.00 þ. They pay Max 30% x 750.00 þ = 225.00 þ. He works 12 hours to sell Matt his house. He earns an additional 7.00þ /hour x 12 hours = 84.00 þ. Max earns 309.00 þ in the transaction. However Matt must lose money due to the accommodational markdown. Let's make it 25% in our example. Therefore Matt only earns 150 000.00 þ – 750.00 þ – 37 312.00 þ = 111 937.00 þ. In this example we did not factor in the property that the house was situated on. When selling a house, the land on which the house is situated is also sold. In this example we make residential land worth 1000.00 þ / square kilometre of land.

Right now Matt has 111 937.00 þ to spend. He wants to buy that 200 000.00 þ house. It is situated on a property of 2 square kilometres. The total price is 202 000.00 þ if we factor in the land. Max buys it for Matt. For this service, Matt has to pay Super Plus Ultimate Real Estate Inc. = 0.005 x 202 000.00 þ = 1 010.00 þ. Max earns 0.3 x 1 010.00 þ = 303.00 þ. He works for 12 hours so again he earns 12 hours x 7.00 þ/hour = 84.00 þ.

Max earns 387.00 þ in purchasing the house and property for Matt. This comes out of

Matt's bank account. 387. 00 þ are deducted from Matt's payment to Super Plus Ultimate Real Estate Inc. which was 1 010.00 þ. 387.00 þ are added to Max's Ignit account.

There's a problem. Matt can't pay the 202 000.00 þ for his new house. He only has 111 937.00 þ – 1 010.00 þ = 110 927.00 þ. He must take out a mortgage. The mortgage rate is not set by the central bank. It involves the Laissez- Faire sector, Fortals and takes into account the reciprocal Ignit-Fortal exchange mechanism since the prices of real estate are in terms of Ignits. The mortgage rate is how much a home owner must pay the bank (private) each month for the bank giving him money to purchase the house. Matt puts 110 000.00 þ towards his house and takes out a mortgage for 202 000.00 þ - 110 000.00 þ = 92 000.00 þ. The mortgage rate is 5%. Since Matt makes 10 000.00 þ per month, his mortgage payments must be less than that each month. (Matt must also pay his bills, buy appliances, home accessories, and enjoy leisure). Thus he chooses a monthly mortgage of 5 000.00 þ. Every month he must pay 5 000.00 þ. He must do this for 19.32 months. We are assuming in this case that 1 f = 1þ and 1þ = 1f.
(92 000.00 þ + [92 000.00 þ x 0.05)/5000.00 þ = 19.32.
For simplicity in this example we used simple interest although it may be better to use compounded interest.

Let's look at the case of a real estate company aiding in buying and selling land. This is similar to buying and selling housing. We assume a REPP of 0.5% and a real estate wage function of $0.3y + 7.00$ þ per hour. Suppose a farmer wants to buy 500 km^2 of agricultural land. Agricultural land costs 100.00 þ/km^2. There are two farmers here, Ken and Ryan and two real estate agents Jack, hired by Ken and Phil, hired by Ryan. Ken and Jack are doing the buying and Ryan and Phil are doing the selling. Jack buys the farm land from Phil. Ken has to pay 500 km^2 x 100.00 þ/km^2 = 50 000.00 þ to Ryan in order to purchase the land. However he must also pay Jack for his services and the real estate firm which he works for. His real estate firm earns 50 000.00 þ x 0.5% = 250.00 þ and Jack earns 250.00 þ x 0.3 = 75.00 þ and assuming he works 8 hours on this transaction he would earn 75.00 þ + 7.00 þ/hour x 8 hours = 131.00 þ. Ken must pay Jack's real estate firm 250.00 þ for this service.

Assuming Phil also works 8 hours on this transaction, he too would earn 131.00 þ and his real estate firm would earn 250.00 þ. Thus 250.00 þ are deducted from Ryan's bank account. Although Ken pays 50 000.00 þ for the land, due to the accommodational markdown, Ryan only keeps 50 000.00 þ – 250.00 þ – 13 437.00 þ = 37 313.00 þ. So, only 37 313.00 þ are added to his Ignit bank account. He probably does not have enough money to buy this much land. He must buy a mortgage in the same way that Matt did. Each month Ken must pay an amount of money to the bank. This is the interest and the principal from the amount of money that the bank lent him to buy the land.

Finally we look at how the real estate company handles transactions in the business section of the building industry. We look at the purchasing of a functional business. The price of a business is expressed in the *Adjusted Revenue Price*. This is the amount of revenue a business earns in a given amount of time. It is set by the central bank in terms of time. Say the central bank sets it at 2 years. Then the cost of a business is how much revenue it had in a period of 2 years. If a firm has existed for more than 2 years, it would equal its revenue in the last 2 years. If a firm existed less, say only 6 months, it is simply the revenue collected in these 6 months multiplied by 4. This parameter ensures that firms try to be as profitable as possible since the more revenue they accrue, the more money the person or group selling the firm earns upon selling it. Revenue is used instead of profit as the basis of the parameter since if profit were used then firms that had loses in some time (negative profit) would not be able to be sold.

Suppose John wants to buy a pizzeria. The Adjusted Revenue Price (ARP) is set for 1 year. The price of the pizzeria business in question is how much revenue the firm collected in the last year. It made 45 000.00 þ. John hires Max and Super Plus Ultimate Real Estate Inc. Company. In this scenario John took out a business loan from a bank. Max buys the pizzeria from the previous owner for 45 000.00 þ. The real estate company earns 0.5% x 45 000.00 þ – 225.00 þ. Max worked 10 hours and thus earns 0.3 x 225.00 þ + 10 hours x 7.00 þ/hour = 137.50 þ. The previous owner of the pizzeria, after paying the cost of the real estate company, earned only 75% of the sale price due to an accommodational markdown of 25%.

There is an important question regarding the real estate firm that we must look at. How does the real estate company make profit? It must pay its agents, advertising costs, office space, office equipment (computers, pencils, and desks). After the firm covers these costs, it makes profit.

This is how a real estate company would operate in the accommodation based consumerist economic system. We looked at transactions involving accommodation land and business property. We encountered several parameters that are intrinsic to the buying and selling of real estate.

The Functioning of a University

A university is a place of higher education. It is a place where, after high school or college, students go to earn degrees which enable them to obtain the jobs that they desire. Here we will see how a university operates. Let's call our university "Northland University".

We have two choices. A) The university is in the governmental sector or b) the university is in the materialist sector. Whether it is in one or the other is decided by the government. If the university is in the materialist sector then the students who wish to attend it must spend the Norses the central bank granted them. If the university is in the governmental sector, the operation of the university is funded by the Grand Consumerist Tax which is deducted from the Gross Domestic Consumerist Product. We will say that it is in the governmental sector. That is, students do not pay tuition to attend. Rather the government helps to pay for the student's education. To run the university, the government uses money from the GCT and other sources of revenue.

We do not discuss how the university teaches students but how it runs its finances. We divide the operating costs into two types- fixed and variable costs. Fixed costs are sunk. The university pays them once and cannot get the money back. Let's list the fixed costs that the university pays to set up: land, buildings (lecture halls, residencies, professor's offices, and laboratories), equipment (overheads, chalk boards, desks, chairs), books, lab equipment, building accessories, paint, windows, floor, and lamps. In our example these together cost 12 000 000.00 þ

Variable costs are the costs the university incurs every month. The variable costs include: professional salaries (salaries of professors, teaching assistants, janitors and administrators), utilities (electricity, heat), improvements (new computers, new books, new microscopes). In our example these amount to 1 500 000.00 þ/month.

The university has one main source of revenue- government transfers to the university (these come from the GCT and the other sources of revenue that we discussed). The university could also have corporate sponsors but we ignore this. Now, let's see how the university covers its costs. There are 10 000 students in Northland University. For simplicity let's assume that each student takes 5 courses at the university per year. There is a lot of disappointment in free-market economies with regards exponentially increasing tuition costs. As consumerists, students do not pay any tuition or fee per course. Essentially the government fully pays for a consumerist student's education. Thus education is free. During the 12 months the university's operation costs are 12 000 000.00þ + 12 x 1 500 000.00 þ = 30 000 000.00 þ. Therefore 30 000 000.00 þ must come from the GCT and other governmental sources of revenue. The university is not run at the federal level but at the provincial/state level. Let's suppose that the provincial government earned 15 000 000 000.00 Ө. It would allocate 30 000 000.00 Ө of this to the university (Northland University). Thus with the contribution from the GCT, we have 30 000 000.00 Ө. This equals the 30 000 000.00 þ needed to run Northland University.

How are the 30 000 000.00 Ө converted into 30 000 000.00 þ needed to pay for the inputs of the university? When Norses are given to the university or any government enterprise, they are automatically converted to Ignits. When the government gives 30 000 000.00 Ө to Northland this money is turned into 30 000 000.00 þ at a private bank. This goes to pay the costs of running the university. During the transaction at the bank in the above case, the amount of Norses is subtracted from the people paying (i.e. the government) and the equivalent number of Ignits is added to Northland University's Ignit bank account at the private bank.

The university strives to attract as many students as possible and to provide the highest standard of education. The government, if it sees that the university is not attracting too many students may decrease the amount of money it gives the university. So suppose a university only has 100 students. In this case the government may severely cut its funding to the university. The university embarks on a policy of attracting new students; i.e. by showing prospective students how excellent their education would be at that university. That way, the government will increase its spending on that university.

A university is an important institution in a well-off society. It is funded through government transfers from the GCT and other sources of revenue including profits from the command partition and gambling. Its ultimate goal is to have a large student population, enjoying a fine educational experience.

The Functioning of a Private Bank

A bank is an institution that lends money to economic agents while at the same time storing people's money. There are three general types of banks in accommodation based consumerism; central, governmental and private banks. Here we will talk about private banks. In the free-market economy, the private bank is an important component of the economy. The same is true for consumerism.

Each consumerist is entitled to have a bank account at a private bank. The three major types of bank accounts are Norse accounts, Fortal accounts and Ignit accounts. These can be either in the form of savings accounts, business accounts or college funds. Private banks can, as we have discussed, store gold and silver. The bank can lend Ignits to businesses and consumerists and this is its main source of profit. It lends money at an interest rate set by the central bank. The person who borrows must every once in a while pay back parts of the loan or all of it. The longer he avoids paying the whole amount, the larger the interest payment will be. Here is a simple calculation. Ken borrows 1 000.00 þ from the private bank. The central bank sets the interest rate at 5% and the compounding frequency at one year. The government sets the IRS at 0.1 %. Thus in one year Ken will have to pay back 1000.00 þ x 1.05 = 1 050.00 þ. If it takes him two years to pay he will have to pay 1000.00 þ x $(1.05)^2$ = 1 102.50 þ. Ken wants to pay back this loan as soon as possible. However to help Ken the government can pay 0.1 % of what he had to pay. So if it takes Ken one a year to pay the debt and the bank receives 1 050.00 þ, the government will pay (1000 þ x 1.001) = 1 001.00 þ. 1 001.00 þ – 1000.00 þ = 1.00 þ. And Ken will pay 1 049.00 þ

Private banks can also store and manipulate foreign money. This includes Canadian and American dollars as well as Pesos. However, the private bank cannot manipulate cash either in the form of bills or coins. So an investor cannot actually deposit paper bills in a private bank unless in the case when the nation is converting from capitalism to consumerism..

A private bank cannot spring from nowhere. A private bank must be certified, registered and approved by the central bank. Although the central bank is not the same entity as a private bank, the central bank has some control over each private bank so that they are responsible to consumerists.

In a free-market bank, the bank is constrained in how much it can lend. It has to have a cash reserve ratio at all times. The reason for this is that if people want cash from the bank, the bank must have enough cash to pay those who want their money out. In consumerism no cash reserve ratio is required. The economy is cashless. All transactions are made in bank books. Therefore there is no limit on how much a private bank can lend to investors.

The bank cannot lend Norses in any way. This is crucial. The amount of Norses in banks must equal the GDCP. This in turn must equal how many goods and services are made in the materialist sector. Norses cannot be simply exchanged at the bank. They can only be exchanged during a transaction involving goods and services. Suppose Ken buys a hot dog. He gives Rob, the hot dog vendor, a check for 2.50 Ө. Upon receiving such a check, the private bank deducts 2.50 Ө from Ken's Norse account and adds 2.50 þ to Rob's Ignit account.

Consider transactions involving utilities. When Bob gives a 100.00 þ check to Northern

Utilities for electricity, the private bank deducts 100.00 þ from Bob's Ignit account and adds the utility profit to that company. However with an accommodational markdown of 40%, Northern Utilities receives only 60.00 þ on its account. Similar transactions are possible if individuals use debit cards or the UC card.

Private banks can offer mortgages to consumerists wishing to buy real estate (accommodation, land). The mortgage rate is not set by the central bank. Also the compounding frequency is not set by the central bank. These are decided by the interaction of private banks and consumerists and mortgages in general operate in the laissez-faire sector. However, the Ignit-Fortal exchange mechanism comes into play as things like accommodation and land are in the accommodational sector and use Ignits. The longer the loan is taken out for, the more the debtor must pay the bank. We don't need to do calculations about this.

In the free-market system there is the possibility of a bank run. A bank run occurs when depositors demand all the money they have in their bank but the bank does not have this money. The bank then goes out of business and if this happens to many banks we have a catastrophe that leads to a depression. The unique thing about consumerism is that it is impossible for there to be a bank run. The reason for this is that the bank has no cash or coins. They do not exist in our cashless society.

How does the private bank make money? There are no service fees. It earns interest on loans. With no reserve ratio, the private bank has the opportunity to make tremendous profit through lending. In exchange for this the bank manipulates bank accounts, both Ignit, Fortal and Norse.

Private banks have the ability to convert Fortals (but not Norses) into foreign currency. The nominal exchange rate is demonstrated in another section (surplus and shortage) and the section on the exchange of foreign currency. Basically it is just an average of real exchange rates of products exported and imported that give the highest value for the consumerist trade pool.

This is how a private bank functions in consumerism. It has advantages over its free-market counterpart. It is vital to a prosperous society.

The Functioning of a Grocery Store

Here we examine the functioning of a particular hypothetical grocery store, let's call it Dan's Ultimate Grocery Mart. By grocery store we mean a retail outlet that sells food items to consumerists. It is owned by a person named Dan.

Here we assume that Dan rented the location of the store and did not build the building from the ground-up. The building he rents cost his landlord 300 000.00 þ. The central bank sets the Rental Equivalence Duration at 18 years. Thus each month, Dan the owner must pay 300 000.00 þ/12/18 = 1 389.00 þ. Dan registers his business with the government. This costs him 25.00 þ. Dan borrows 20 000.00 þ from the private bank at 5% interest (simple) to set up his grocery store and get it running.

Before Dan can hire employees, buy inputs and start selling he must incur sunk costs. We already mentioned that he has a building for which he pays 1 389.00 þ a month. Other sunk costs include lights, cash registers, shelves, counters, fridges and other things that cost him 10 000.00 þ.

We assume that he has 2 employees besides himself; a cashier and someone who is both a clerk and a janitor. The cashier's wage is 12.00 þ per hour. The other person's wage is 10.00 þ per hour. The JCP (Job Contract Price) for the cashier is 600.00 þ and the Adjusted Monthly Income Percentage is 400%. The JCP for the clerk is 500.00 þ and his Adjusted Monthly Income Percentage is 400%. Their contracts are for 6 months. Let's find out how many hours each must work during their employment.

Cashier => 600.00 þ hours/12.00 þ x 6 x 400 % = 1 200 hours
The cashier must work 1 200 hours in 6 months. This is equivalent to 44.4 hours per week.

The clerk => 500.00 þ hours /10.00 þ x 6 x 400% = 1 200 hours
The clerk must work 1 200 hours in 6 months. This is equivalent to 44.4 hours per week.

Dan chooses his employees from the best applicants. They passed high school and had 4 years experience in the tasks they were hired to perform. For now Dan earns 500.00 þ + 600.00 þ = 1 100.00 þ for selling out his job contracts.

Since Dan sells job contracts he must purchase bankruptcy insurance. This is in the event that he goes out of business and is unable to pay his employees the total amount of money they would earn if they worked during the entire length of their contracts. Let's see how much Dan would have to pay his employees at the end of their contracts:

Cashier => 600.00 þ x 6 x 400% = 14 400.00 þ

Clerk => 500.00 þ x 6 x 400% = 12 000.00 þ

This amounts to a total of 26 400.00 þ. The Bankruptcy Insurance Premium is 0.5% per month. Dan has to pay 0.5% x 26 400.00 þ = 132.00 þ each month to his bankruptcy insurance firm company.

To encourage more hiring of employees, the government sets the Employment Reimbursement Transfer (ERT) at 1 %. Thus for the six months the employees are employed the government gives Dan, 26 400.00 þ x 0.01 = 264.00 þ

An actual grocery store would sell hundreds or thousands of goods. We will assume, for simplicity, that Dan is selling only 12 goods. They are milk, cheese (mozzarella), pears, apples, beef(t-bone steak), baguettes, grapes, canned tuna, honey (pasteurized, buckwheat), sausages (pepperoni), pizza (deluxe),and soy milk.

We assume that the cost of delivering these goods to the store costs 0.10 þ per unit of good. Now let's examine the prices of the foods Dan sells. These price functions are set by the central bank. Milk and milk substitutes are priced at 1.50 Θ/litre. These include 2% milk, skim milk, chocolate milk and soy milk. In our store this applies to milk and soy milk- they each cost 1.50 Θ/litre. "Cheeses" are priced at 6.00 Θ/kg. Thus our mozzarella costs 6.00 Θ/kg. "Many-seeded fruits from trees" (for lack of a better term) cost 1.00 Θ/ kg. This includes pears and apples (but not grapes). Thus apples and pears cost 1.00 Θ/kg. Beef costs 3.00 Θ/kg. T-bone steak is included in this. Breads cost 1.50 Θ/ unit. This includes baguettes. "Wine fruit" costs 1.00 Θ/kg. This includes grapes. "Canned fish" costs 3.00 Θ/unit. This includes canned tuna. "Food sweeteners" cost 1.50 Θ/ kg. This includes buckwheat honey. Sausages cost 0.50 Θ/kg. This includes pepperoni. Pizzas cost 4.00 Θ/unit. This includes the deluxe pizza. The retail mark-up is 25%. Dan can charge 25 % more than the price he had to pay for these groceries from a farm or factory.

Dan orders:

- 100 L of milk
- 30 kg of cheese
- 40 kg of pears
- 40 kg of apples
- 15 kg of t-bone steak
- 30 baguettes
- 40 kg of grapes
- 50 canned tuna cans
- 35 kg of buckwheat honey
- 125 kg of pepperoni sausage
- 30 pizzas
- 100 L of soy milk

In order to obtain these goods they have to be delivered. Although it would be more efficient if similar goods were delivered together we assume here that each good is delivered independently. The delivery fee depends on how far the good must have travelled. The delivery price (DP) is the cost of delivering a certain good to a destination using the quickest route possible. This is also set by the central bank. The central bank sets it at 5.00 þ + 0.10 þ/km.

For simplicity we assume that Dan sells all the goods that he buys from food producers. Now we find out how much he has to pay in delivery cost, how much revenue he has and what are his profits.

	Delivery	Food Cost	Revenue	Profit
Milk	8.00 þ	150.00 þ	187.50 þ	29.50 þ
Mozzarella	7.00 þ	180.00 þ	225.00 þ	38.00 þ
Pears	6.00 þ	40.00 þ	50.00 þ	4.00 þ
Apples	9.00 þ	40.00 þ	50.00 þ	1.00 þ
T-bone steak	8.00 þ	45.00 þ	56.25 þ	3.25 þ
Baguettes	8.00 þ	45.00 þ	56.25 þ	3.35 þ
Grapes	8.00 þ	40.00 þ	50.00 þ	2.00 þ
Canned Tuna	7.00 þ	100.00 þ	125.00 þ	18.00 þ
Honey	9.00 þ	52.50 þ	65.63 þ	4.13 þ
Pepperoni	8.00 þ	62.50 þ	72.13 þ	1.63 þ
Pizza	8.00 þ	120.00 þ	150.00 þ	22.00 þ
Soy milk	8.00 þ	150.00 þ	187.50 þ	29.50 þ

Therefore Dan has a profit this month of 156.26 þ on the food he sold.

Now Dan has some profit- although this does not seem like much keep in mind that we are only talking about 12 goods. Actually there would be thousands of goods.

Each month Dan has to pay his workers their wages. They are paid every 2 weeks. Since the cashier earns 12.00 þ/hour and he works 44.4 hours per week he earns 1065.60 þ every 2 weeks. Since the clerk earns 10.00 þ per hour and works 44.4 hours per week, he earns 888.00 þ every 2 weeks.

Since in our example Dan sells only 12 goods, our analysis of his monthly profits is warped- he makes less profit selling goods then he needs to pay the running costs of his business. However in a real grocery store, a real owner should make a handsome profit.

The next point is crucial. Every month Dan must give a sort of report to the central bank as to how much he contributed to the Gross Domestic Consumerist Product. His contribution is the *Individual Domestic Consumerist Product*. He has to report how many goods he was able to sell. He also has to report those he didn't sell but could have. In our example the figure is the same as Dan sold all the goods he ordered. He can only report those that were put up for sale this month. He cannot count those that were ordered half a year ago. When counting he takes into account not only the price of the good he bought (from a farm) but its price after the retail mark-up. He does not deduct his shipping costs as this is not supposed to represent his profits. He multiplies the amount of goods he put into a position to sell by their post retail mark-up adjusted price. In our example he simply adds all the numbers in the column labelled "revenues". Dan's contribution to the GDCP is 1 275.29 Θ. He files this number on a form to the central bank. This money is now added to the GDCP contributions of all the other businesses.

Let's talk about another possibility. Suppose Dan wants to expand his business but does not want to deal with a private bank. The price per (consumerist) stock is set by the central bank at 10.00 þ/share. Dan issues 20 000 shares. He keeps 12 000 of them for himself and sells 8 000. He earns 80 000.00 þ for his business. Suppose Dan's grocery store makes a profit of 1 000 000.00 þ. Dan reinvests 20 000.00 þ for further expansion. In this case, the owner of a share would earn 980 000.00þ/20 000 = 49.00 þ. Of course Dan personally earns 980 000 þ x 12 000/20 000 = 588 000.00 þ

Dan needs to take out bankruptcy insurance in case he bankrupts and people are left with worthless shares. The Bankruptcy Insurance Premium is 0.5% per month. Since Dan issues 8 000 shares and each is worth 10.00 þ, he must pay 0.5% x 10.00 þ x 8 000 = 400.00 þ each month to a bankruptcy insurance firm. This is on top of the premium for job contracts he sold before.

There is yet another quick way of getting money for expansion that both helps the owner as well as the economy. Dan can sell more job contracts; i.e. hire more people. Although this gives money quickly in the short run it can be quite costly in the long run. Bankruptcy insurance must be bought for these contacts.

Suppose Dan wants to sell his grocery store. The Adjusted Revenue Price Duration is 6 years. In a year, Dan has a revenue of 200 000.00 þ. Thus the price of the grocery store is 1 200 000.00 þ. He finds a buyer and then he retires.

A grocery store represents an average retail firm in the consumerist economy. We saw how it would operate; how it transforms inputs into money. We encountered the problems it could run into and saw how they would be overcome.

The Functioning of a Music School

Here we investigate how a school that teaches music would work. We also see another way to teach music- through private lessons. But first let's examine the firm that teaches music. The music school is in the materialist sector.

Our music school is run by a man passionate about music, named Steve, who wants to make money by teaching students music. Steve rents an office in a building complex where there are other offices. Steve's school has several rooms for different students and classes. The land lord paid 800 000.00 þ for the whole building complex. The section Steve wants to occupy is 25% of the whole. The Rental Equivalence Duration is 18 years. Steve must make monthly payments of (800 000.00 þ x 0.25)/(12 x 18) = 926.00 þ. Steve's sunk costs are about 5 000.00 þ. This includes furnishings, pianos, guitars, a computer as well as paintings of famous people who studied music.

Steve hires 3 music teachers; 1 piano, 1 guitar and 1 violin. The wage function for a teacher of music is 20.00 þ/hour. The JCP is 700.00 þ. The AMIP is 300%. They are given contracts for 6 months. Let's calculate the minimum number of hours each worker should work: 700.00 þ hr/20.00 þ x 3 x 6 = 630.00 hours. Thus each teacher must work at least 630 hours in 6 months. If Steve wants them to work more, they can; they still get paid depending on how many hours they actually work. Or Steve may hire other teachers and earn JCP profits.

Since he sold job contracts, Steve must take out bankruptcy insurance. The bankruptcy insurance premium is 0.5% per month. We already described how a bankruptcy insurance firm operates so we will skip some calculations that relate to it.

The government gives Steve the ERT which is set at 1 %. There are 3 teachers, each earning 20.00 þ/hour and working 630 hours in 6 months. So Steve is given, 3 x 20.00 x 630 x 0.01 = 378.00 þ

To obtain all the money needed to start up his business, Steve issues consumerist general bonds. He issues 25 000.00 þ worth of them. The central bank sets the interest rate at 15 % per year. The bonds have a maturity of two years. The Consumerist General Bond Interest Repayment Frequency is 1 month. So all investors would receive 15% x 2 = 30 % x 25 000.00 þ = 7 500.00 þ. Since there are 24 one month periods in two years, the investors would receive 7 500.00 þ/24 = 312.50 þ every month. When the two years are over, Steve would also have to repay the 25 000.00 þ. How much each investor receives depends on how much of the 25 000.00 þ worth of bonds he invested in.

Steve attracts 39 students a week. Each student has a 2 hour lesson per week. A music lesson costs 28.00 ☉ per hour. Thus each week Steve's business earns 39 x 2 hours x 28.00 þ/hour = 2 184.00 þ

We assume that each teacher has 13 students and that she teaches them 2 hours a week each. Let's calculate how much they will earn in their paycheck every 2 weeks:
13 x 2 hours x 20.00 þ/hour = 520.00 þ

Every month Steve must announce to the central bank his businesses' contribution to the

GDCP. Since his business is a service based business, he reports how many clients he has multiplied by their payment to him. He has 39 students, 2 hours a week (in one month) and each pays 28.00 þ/hour. Thus Steve reports that his business contributes 8 736.00 Ө to the GDCP. He doesn't actually transfer any of his money to the central bank. He only reports his Individual Domestic Consumerist Product contribution.

We see how he stands in terms of profits at the end of 6 months as this is when the teacher's contracts expire. First the profit. There were 39 students a week, for 26 weeks, 2 hours per student each paying 28.00 Ө/hour = 56 784.00 þ (The Norses turn into Ignits when the students purchase the lessons). Now the variable costs. The teachers make more than they could as they have more working hours than their minimum requirement by the JCP and AMIP. Let's calculate how much each makes in 6 months. There were 13 students a week, 2 hours per student for 26 weeks and the wage is 20.00 þ/ hour = 13 520.00 þ. Together this is 40 560.00 þ as there are 3 teachers.

He has to pay for utilities, heat, electricity and gas which cost 100.00 þ/month. This is 600.00 þ in 6 months. His sunk costs are 5 000.00 þ and his rent is 926.00 þ/month or 5 556.00 þ for 6 months. He pays his bankruptcy insurance firm 31.50 þ x 6 = 189.00 þ in 6 months.

Steve earns 700.00 þ per teacher from selling his contracts. Thus he earns 2 100.00 þ. From the ERT he earns 378.00 þ. In the end in 6 months he earns 7357.00 þ. This money Steve can keep or he can reinvest it back into his business. If the PRT is 1%, Steve will be given an additional 73.57 þ as a reward for doing business in a consumerist nation.

Now let's look at the job of a private music teacher. Let's say she is a piano teacher. A music lesson costs 28.00 Ө/hour. If she would work for someone else she would receive a wage of 20.00 þ/hour. Our piano teacher's name is Sue. Sue has 10 students a week for a 1 hour lesson. In a week she earns 280.00 þ. A student writes her a check for 28.00 Ө. When she takes this to her private bank, the bank deducts 28.00 Ө from the student's Norse account and adds 28.00 þ to Sue's Ignit account.

Although Sue is self employed, she must report to the central bank with regards to her contribution to the Gross Domestic Consumerist Product. She has 10 students a week. There are about 4 weeks in a month and she earns 28.00 Ө from each of them. Thus she reports that she makes 1 120.00 Ө.

Here is an interesting question. Why would Sue or anyone else in the part of economy based on services want to work for a firm rather than be self employed? A self employed person earns the cost of the service while in a firm one earns a wage which is smaller than the cost of the service and must pay a fee for working. The reason is that a firm is better able to attract customers than any individual can on his own.

We saw how two different types of music teaching services operate- one a music teaching institute and the other a self employed operation. We came across the costs of running the business and the sources of revenue. Many other service based operations run similarly to the way the music schools were run in this example.

The Functioning of a Construction Company

We examine how a construction company works. By construction company we mean a company or firm that transforms building inputs into structures that people can live, work and conduct affairs in. A construction company can make a house, an office, a skyscraper or a school. It belongs to the accommodational sector. Here we look at two cases- the construction of a house and the construction of an apartment complex.

Let's look first at the building of a house. The construction firm must buy residential land. In this example, land costs $20.00\text{\th}$ /m². The house to be built is situated on a property of 900 m². Thus the firm must pay 18 000.00 $\text{\th}$ to buy this land. It buys it from the government.

In this house building example we assume that the construction firm is well established and has the resources for the initial costs. When considering the building of the apartment complex we assume that the firm needs extra resources.

The firm has the 18 000.00 $\text{\th}$ to buy the residential land. It writes a check directly to the municipal level government for 18 000.00 $\text{\th}$. The accommodational markdown is 30% so the government only receives 12 600.00 $\text{\th}$ in its account while the firm has 18 000.00 $\text{\th}$ deducted from its Ignit account.

It will take 25 workers, working 3 months to complete building this house from start to finish. The builders of the house all have the same wage function as their jobs are roughly the same. They earn 10.00 $\text{\th}$/hour. The JCP is 500.00 $\text{\th}$. The Adjusted Monthly Income Percentage is 300%. We use the following formula. The workers are each entitled to work:

Work hours = PTC [JCP x hours/wage x AMIP x (n)]

500 $\text{\th}$ hours/ 10.00 $\text{\th}$ x 3 x 3 = 450 hours or 34.6 hours per week in that 3 months.

The firm must take out bankruptcy insurance on these job contracts. If the Bankruptcy Insurance Premium is 0.5% each month the firm must pay the insurance company 0.5% of the total value of the contracts. We don't need to do any more calculations as these were done in preceding sections.

Besides workers there are other costs of building a house. These include cement, cement trucks, wood, pipes, bricks, plastic, rubber, nails, hammers and tools and anything else needed to construct a house. We assume that in the 3 months of construction, these things cost 50 000.00 $\text{\th}$.

The price function for the house in question is w5000.00 $\text{\th}$ + y6000.00 $\text{\th}$ + z8000.00 $\text{\th}$ + a5000.00 $\text{\th}$ + b300.00 $\text{\th}$. Where w represents number of floors, y represents number of washrooms, z represents number of bedrooms, a represents the number of kitchens and b represents the square feet area. The house our construction company is building has 3 floors, 4 washrooms, 3 bedrooms, 1 kitchen and 1000 square feet of space. It thus costs 368 000.00 $\text{\th}$.

In 3 months the firm completes the construction of the house. Instead of 34.6 hours per week, each of the 25 workers worked 38 hours per week or 494 hours in 3 months.

Let's calculate the total costs of the firm in 3 months. 494 hours per worker x 25 workers x 10.00 þ/ hour = 123 500.00 þ. Building materials cost 50 000.00 þ and the land is 18 000.00 þ. The bankruptcy total fee is 3 months x 0.5% x 123 500.00 þ = 1 852.50 þ. So all the costs in 3 months are 193 352.50 þ.

The firm earned 25 x 500.00 þ for the job contracts = 12 500.00 þ. They sell their house including the land for 368 000.00 þ + 18 000.00 þ = 386 000.00 þ. The buyer of the house and land must pay 386 000.00 þ for it.

The Real Estate Profit Percentage is 0.5 % and the buyer has hired an agent who works 10 hours. The agent's wage function is $0.5z + 5.00$ þ/hour where z represents the Real Estate Profit Percentage. Thus the buyer must pay 386 000.00 þ to the construction company and (386 000.00 þ x 0.005 = 1 930 þ) to the real estate company. The real estate company must pay 0.5 x 1 930.00 þ + 5.00 þ/hour x 10 hours = 1 015 þ to the real estate agent.

A real estate company also helps the construction firm sell the house they made. Let's suppose that it is the same real estate company and the same agent as above. The real estate profit percentage is 0.5% and the agent works 10 hours. The construction company earns 1 930.00 þ. But there is also an accommodational markdown of 30%. So in the end the company earns (386 000.00 þ – 1 930.00 þ) x 0.7 = 268 849.00 þ. Subtracting final costs from this, the company earns 73 644.00 þ. The company need not report its transaction to the central bank since it is in the accommodational sector. We suppose that the Profit Reward Transfer is 1%. So then, in addition the firm will receive 736.44 þ to reward it for conducting business in the consumerist nation.

It is just as possible for a construction company to hire a real estate company as it is for a real estate company to hire a construction company. We have examined the former case in the above scenario of building a house. We will examine the latter in the case of building an apartment complex. We have a hypothetical real estate company called Northern Real Estate and a hypothetical construction company called Bob's construction. The real estate and construction company work together. The construction company makes money from selling suites in the apartment while the real estate company earns a percentage of the rent for helping the construction company find tenants. Let's start at the beginning. It takes a year for the apartment complex to be completed. 50 workers are needed. Each worker earns 10.00 þ/hour. The JCP is set at 600.00 þ and the contract lasts a year. The Adjusted Yearly Income Percentage is 1200%.

The construction company must buy residential land from the government. Residential land costs 20.00 þ/m². They need 1500 m². This costs 30 000.00 þ. The Capital Investment Transfer (CIT) is set to be 1 %. Thus the government gives the construction company 300.00 þ to encourage growth.

There are also other costs (cement, cement trucks, wood, pipes, steal, brick, plastic, rubber, nails, glass, and tools). For a year these cost 200 000.00 þ.

Here we suppose that the construction company needs to issue consumerist profit bonds to get going. Bob issues 1 000 000.00 þ worth of profit bonds. The Profit Bond Interest Rate is 3%. He also earns 50 x 600.00 þ = 30 000.00 þ for giving his workers jobs.

He needs bankruptcy insurance to cover his job contracts and consumerist profit bonds issued. The bankruptcy insurance premium is 0.5 % per month. Bob must pay 0.05 x 1 000 000.00 þ = 50 000.00 þ for the profit bonds and 50 x 600.00 þ x 12 x 0.05 = 1800.00 þ for the job contracts. The total is 51 800.00 þ per month.

The apartment building is 8 stories high, each floor having 10 suites. The total price of the entire apartment complex is 2 500 000.00 þ. This is defined by a price function for apartments that takes into account bedrooms per suite, size of kitchen in square feet, size of washroom in square feet, size of bedroom in square feet, size of living room in square feet, size of balcony and length of hallway. Such a function is determined by the central bank but here it can be avoided and we can simply say that the apartment building costs 2 500 000.00 þ.

In our example the Rental Equivalence Duration is 20 years. Now we find out how much each tenant must pay each month for rent. This is calculated by:
2 500 000.00 þ/(20 x 12 x 8 x 10) = 130.00 þ. The construction company earns 130.00 þ x 0.7 = 91.00 þ from each tenant because of the 30% accommodational markdown.

How does the real estate company benefit? It has a sort of monopoly on all suites in the complex in exchange for giving the construction company tenants.

The construction company sells the apartment complex to a landlord. The landlord buys the apartment building for 2 500 000.00 þ. Our hypothetical Northern Real Estate is his real estate company and Jack is his agent. The Real Estate Profit Percentage is 0.5% and the agent's wage function is z 0.5 + 5.00 þ/hour where z represents the Real Estate Profit Percentage. The landlord, Mike, must pay the real estate company 12 500.00 þ. The real estate agent, working 10 hours, earns 6 300.00 þ. The landlord must pay a total of 2 500 000.00 þ + 12 500.00 þ = 2 512 500.00 þ for the apartment plus the real estate transaction.

The construction company which hires the same real estate firm earns:
(2 500 000.00 þ – 12 500.00 þ) x 0.7 = 1 741 250.00 þ.

The landlord makes profit from renting suites. The construction company could have acted as a sort of landlord or property seller as in the case of a condominium. In that case the suites are owned by consumerists rather than rented.

At some point the construction company would have to pay back the bond holders the value of their bond, plus a little extra. This little extra is given by the formula:
1 000 000.00 þ x (0.03/ FR) x FP = payments to bond holders

Here FR stands for firm revenue and FP stands for firm profit,

A construction company operates in the way described above. It uses building materials to create space that is later sold to a landlord with the aid of a real estate company. Since almost all businesses is carried out in buildings and people need buildings to live in, the construction company is at the forefront of the economy.

Franchises

Here we take a look at franchises. By franchises we mean a business operated under a specific brand name usually the result of a chain of outlets. For example, our hypothetical Bob's Super Burgers has 70 outlets throughout the country. Someone wants to buy another outlet and start their own business while paying royalties or some kind of reimbursement to the parent company.

In this case the Adjusted Revenue Price factors in. So our hypothetical Bob's Super Burgers has 70 outlets and Michael wants to buy another outlet and make a profit. How much would it cost him to do so? To find the price of another outlet we find the Adjusted Revenue Price and take the average of the 70 outlets. So suppose the central bank sets the ARP at 4 years. This means that in order to buy another outlet of our hypothetical Bob's Super Burgers, Michael will have to pay how much the average of the 70 outlets made in revenue in 4 years. Some made 1 000 000 þ per year and some made 200 000 þ per year but if we add the sum of their yearly earnings and divide by 70, and then multiply by 4 we get the price that Michael must pay to purchase a franchise of our hypothetical Bob's Super Burgers.

What if a franchise has no pre-existing outlets? In that case the cost to start the outlet would be like the starting of any other store. The would-be owner would have to buy land, the building, the equipment and hire workers. After that he can start his business.

Purchasing a franchise may be a sound decision from a financial point of view. Instead of having to "start from scratch" and build a reputation from the beginning, it is easier to buy an outlet that other consumerists have already heard about and are familiar with. So setting up a franchise already brings one customers that are loyal to one brand of franchise. Also consumerists know to a very high degree what your franchise is selling whereas firms that start from scratch have to advertise aggressively to let their product be known.

Franchises are started by entrepreneurs trying to make money. The Adjusted Revenue Price is crucial for this. This lets franchise owners start another outlet of a franchise in our economy.

Brand Names

It would be useful to discuss the idea of brand names. Brand names are the ways that firms designate their good or service so as to differentiate it from other goods or services of the same type. Brand names help firms distinguish their product from other firms.

The idea of having brands is very important in free-market capitalism. In that system, brands ensure quality. If a company, let's say Super-Tasty Cookies, makes good quality cookies, consumerists will associate those cookies with the brand; in this case Super-Tasty Cookies. Consumerists begin to expect high quality goods, for example cookies, from this company. Given a choice between cookies made by Super-Tasty Cookies and some cookies made by someone they never heard, these consumerists will likely buy Super-Tasty cookies as they know what they are buying.

On the other hand, a brand has a reputation to uphold. If a Mexican restaurant sells a burrito or taco that causes people to be ill- causing them stomach problems, nausea and indigestion- consumerists will associate this restaurant with the illness it causes. Fewer people will want to go to this restaurant and people will associate the brand name with the problems it causes.

Accommodation Based Consumerism fully supports the notion of brand names. Brand names in consumerism are helpful in ensuring the quality of a good or service. Brand names ensure that a good or service is of the highest quality as the manufacturers associated with the brand have a reputation to uphold. They have an incentive to make goods and services of the highest quality.

If a firm with a particular brand name makes a high quality good that a lot of consumerists look favourably on, the brand name will be linked in the minds of consumerists with exceptional quality. Thus a consumerist will have a greater chance of buying that good and the firm earns a greater share of the market for that good.

The opposite is also true. If a particular brand name makes a very low quality good that many consumerists do not like at all, the brand name will be linked in the minds of consumerists with poor quality. This means that a consumerist will have a lower chance of purchasing that good and the firm receives a lower percentage of the market for that good.

Having brand names is useful. Although free-market capitalism uses the idea of brand names extensively, they also have their place in accommodation based consumerism. Brand names are a signal of product quality. They ensure that the goods and services made in consumerism are of premium quality. This is in fact one of the main goals of consumerism.

The Jones' Family Budget

Here we investigate the family budget of the Jones' family. By this we mean that we analyze how the Jones family allocates their income to provide for their needs and wants. The Jones family has six members. There are Mr. Carl Jones, 44, and Mrs. Annette Jones, 43. They have three children, Bob who is 18, Amy who is 12 and Jack who is three months old. Carl's mom, Marianne 65, also lives with them.

Recall that there are three types of currencies in Accommodation Based Consumerism: Norses (Θ), Fortals (f) and Ignits ($\þ$). First let's take a look at the income of everyone in the Jones family in terms of Ignits. Carl is an engineer and makes 1000 $\þ$ a month. Annette is a pharmacist and earns 1200 $\þ$ per month. Bob works at a fast food restaurant for 40 hours per week and in a month makes 600 $\þ$. Amy doesn't have a job but volunteers at a hospital. Jack who is 3 months old obviously doesn't work either. Marianne doesn't work and is retired and receives 500 $\þ$ per month as Retirement Pension Allowance.

Now let's talk about income in terms of the other currency, Norses (Θ). The General Consumerist Grant (GCG) for this month is 600 Θ. The Non Working Consumerist Grant Reduction is 0.8. The Non Working Consumerist Grant is 480 Θ.

All of Carl, Annette and Bob make the General Consumerist Grant. So each month they each earn 600 Θ. Amy, Jack and Marianne receive the Non Working Consumerist Grant and each earn 480 Θ per month. Here we make the assumption that the consumerist grant minimum age allowance is birth.

Let's list each family member's contribution to the household income in terms of the two currencies.

	Ignits ($\þ$)	Norses (Θ)
Carl	1000	600
Annette	1200	600
Bob	600	600
Amy	0	480
Jack	0	480
Marianne	500	480
Family Total	3 300	3 240

Now that we know how the Jones' family earns income for their expenses, let's talk about how they spend their money. Of course the Jones family has the absolute freedom to spend their income on anything they want in either the materialist, laissez-faire or accommodational sectors. Naturally they would spend their money on the most important things first or on things that bring them the most joy in life.

First we look at the materialist sector. Instead of mentioning every single thing they buy, let's look at the category of things they spend their money on.

Each month they spend:

800 ☉ on food; (bread, milk, pizza, pie, chicken, hamburgers)
2 x 350 ☉ = 700 ☉ on car payments
250 ☉ on clothes for five family members
40 ☉ on hygiene products (toothbrush, toothpaste, soap, shampoo, deodorant)
60 ☉ on singing lessons for Amy
70 ☉ on guitar lessons for Bob
200 ☉ on electronics (CD's, computer games)
300 ☉ on miscellaneous (diapers for Jack, batteries, detergent)

So each month the family spends 2 420 ☉ on items in the materialist sector. The rest they save for the next month.

Now let's look at the accommodational sector.

Each month they spend:

700 þ on utilities (heat, gas, internet, cable, telephone, hot water)
400 þ on appliances (stove, refrigerator)
50 þ on alcohol (beer, wine)
200 þ on leisure (rock concert, opera, hockey game)

Now let's look at the laissez-faire sector: (we assume that 1 þ = 1 f)

150 f on various forms of insurance (life, home, auto)
1200 f mortgage on their house

So each month the Jones family spends 2700 þ on items in the accommodational and laissez-faire sectors. The rest they save away for the next month or invest in bonds and stocks.

Now let's look at spending on the governmental sector:

dentist's appointment for Carl and Annette
ticket's to ride the bus around town
walk in medical appointment for Bob
prescription drugs for a rash that Carl developed
a new pair of glasses for Annette
weekly garbage pickup
optometrist appointment and glasses for Carl
blood test for Annette

The family did not have to pay out of pocket for any of these goods and services. They are provided to all consumerists through the various revenues the government has.

In this scenario all the family members of the Jones family pooled all of their Norse and Ignit income and worked together. Technically however, 3 month old John earns a 480 ☉ grant. Although this is his money, he probably doesn't know what to do with it. So it makes sense if everyone in the household worked together.

This represents the Jones family budget. We compared the income against the expenses of the 6 family members with regards to the 3 currencies. This concludes the investigation.

Case Study of The Career of John

People in accommodation based consumerism can become whatever they want to be (within limits) and become wealthy. Consumerism is the land of opportunity. In this section we follow the career of a consumerist individual we will call John.

John is born January 2, 1954. As soon as he is born he is entitled to the non-working consumerist grant. We are assuming a consumerist grant minimum allowance age of birth. He gets this as he is clearly not working. Actually the whole family get this and it is assumed that the household works together.

Let's say that John receives 500.00 ☉ each month from the central bank as the non-working consumerist grant. His mother spends this money on diapers, food (for John and the family), toys, baby carriage and clothes. What is left over the family can spend on items and services that improve the well being of the others in the family.

When John is a baby, a child and a young teen, he only receives the non-working consumerist grant. He does not make any money in terms of Ignits and Fortals to spend on the accommodational and laissez-faire sectors. It is assumed that his parents buy him things in these two sectors with the money that they earned. However John is entitled to things in the governmental sector. This includes things like free education, trips to the hospital, trips to the psychologist, walk in clinics, surgery (free healthcare) as well as protection of the police.

At the age of 17 John buys a job at a fast food restaurant in the natural partition. He pays 500.00 þ for a three year contract at the restaurant. Over the 36 months he flips burgers and makes french fries. The Adjusted Monthly Income Percentage (AMIP) = 300 %. Thus John makes

AIE = [JCP x AMIP x (n)] – JCP
= [500.00 þ x 300 % x (36)] – 500.00 þ
= 54 000 þ

He works 25 hours a week and the non-working grant threshold is 40 hours per week. Therefore he only earns the non working grant. He earns 600.00 ☉ from the central bank as the non-working consumerist grant. This he spends on things in the materialist sector (clothes, food). In the three years working as a fast food cook he earns 54 000.00 þ. This could be spent on accommodational sector things or converted into Fortals and used to buy things in the laissez-faire sector.

When John turns 20 he goes to university. This is free (paid by the government). He graduates and goes to med-school. This is also free (paid for by the government). He passes this. He is now a doctor. He specializes in gastrointestinal surgery.

As a doctor he works in the governmental sector/governmental partition. He earns 10 000.00 þ per month. The threshold for the consumerist grant is 40 hours per week or 5 000.00 þ per month. Since he is now above the threshold, he is entitled to the general consumerist grant. He thus earns 1 200.00 ☉ per month. John can spend this 1 200.00 ☉ on goods and services in the materialist sector and the 10 000.00 þ per month on things in the accommodational sector or exchange some of this into Fortals for use in the Laissez-faire sector.

John works as a doctor for many years making a lot of money. He manages to buy a nice car, a nice house, he wears nice clothes and has good food. He enjoys life while going on wealthy vacations. He retires at the age of 65. At this point he starts to earn the non-working consumerist grant and the retirement pension allowance. This is much lower than what he earns as a doctor so he has an incentive to work as long as possible. However it is probably the case that John saves some of his doctor's salary for his retirement and he can take advantage of this while he retires.

This is a synopsis of John's professional life. We followed John from birth to teenage-hood to adulthood. He went through various jobs earning money to spend in consumerism

Case Study of the Career of Mary

Consumerism is the real land of opportunity. Those that work hard can become whoever they aspire to be. Furthermore, those who contribute to society are able to have an abundance of goods, quality goods and services and receive a lot of money. In this part of the book we follow a hypothetical person named Mary on her journey of life through the consumerist economic system.

Mary is born on January 2, 1974. Since she isn't really working, she earns the non-working consumerist grant. This is 400.00 Ꙩ per month. Since she can't really spend it (for practical reasons) her parents can spend it. They use that money for things specially for her – diapers, baby food, carriage, crib, clothes. They also spend it on things for the well being of the whole family.

When Mary goes to elementary and secondary school, most of her needs and wants are paid for by her parents (i.e. things in the laissez-faire and the accommodational sectors). However she earns money as part of the non-working consumerist grant. This money she can spend on herself. She buys nice clothes, fast food and other things in the materialist sector.

Mary doesn't attend post secondary education. She has a hard time finding a job in the natural partition. She looks for a job in the command partition. The HRMC (an agency that represents the command partition) finds her work as an artist. She loves drawing pictures and this job perfectly suites her. She earns 100.00 þ per week as the extra work transfer (a type of welfare check). She can spend this money on things in the accommodational sector or convert it to Fortals to spend it on the laissez-faire sector. Since all individuals working in the command partition earn the non-working consumerist grant, Mary earns the non-working consumerist grant. Let's say this is 200.00 Ꙩ bi-weekly. This money Mary can spend on materialist goods and services.

Eventually, after 6 years of searching for a job, Mary finds work as a janitor. This job is in the natural partition. She works in a shopping mall. To buy the job it costs 2 000.00 þ for a two year contract. The AMIP is 200 %. She works full time. To calculate her earnings we use,
AIE = PTC [JCP x AMIP x n] – JCP

So in 2 years Mary earns:
1[2000 þ x 200% x (24)] – 2000 þ
= 94 000 þ every two years.

AIE, PTC, JCP and AMIP are important parameters in accommodation based consumerism. For a thorough discussion please refer to earlier sections of the book.

The non-working grant threshold is 40 hours a week or 400 þ per month. Since she is above this, she earns the full general consumerist grant. This is 1 800.00 Ꙩ per month. Now as a janitor, Mary earns a lot of money. She earns 1 800 Ꙩ/month to pay for things in the materialist sector. She earns 94 000.00þ/24 = 3916 þ/month to pay for things in the accommodational sector. Also this money can be used to buy things in the laissez-faire sector after it is converted into Fortals. Of course, all things in the governmental sector are provided publicly (healthcare, education, transit, protection, defence)

After being a janitor for some time, Mary aspires to be an actor. She is really good at that. A film producing firm pays her 1 000 000.00 ₣ to star in an action movie. She can use this money to buy things in the Laissez-faire sector or convert it to Ignits and use it in the accommodational sector. The Ignit-Fortal exchange rate is 2 þ = 1 ₣. So if Mary converts all of her earnings into Ignits she would have 500 000.00 þ. The non-working consumerist grant threshold is 40.00 hours per week or 1000.00 þ per week. Since Mary is clearly above this she earns the full general consumerist grant which here is 2000.00 Ө per week. She uses this money to buy things in the materialist sector (food, clothes, transportation). She is also entitled to services from the government (healthcare, defence, waste management). After working as an actor for several years and making several millions of Fortals, Mary retires. She is a success story of accommodation based consumerism – the land of opportunity.

This is a synopsis of Mary's professional life. We saw how she went through jobs and became increasingly more well off. Any consumerist can do the same.

The Predicament of Students and Minors

Here we talk about the special circumstances regarding students and minors. By students we mean individuals in college, university, high school or elementary school. Minors are people below a certain age threshold; usually 16 or 18 years of age.

First of all, all services in the government sector are provided to every student and minor regardless of their age or whether they contribute to the consumerist society. Thus all students and minors receive protection from the police, have a right to go to school and are provided medical treatment for all health problems; for example a knee operation, an appendix operation or fungal infection. Students and minors have complete access to the services provided through the governmental sector.

With regards the materialist sector, recall that there are two types of consumerist grants- the general consumerist grant and the non working consumerist grant. The age at which minors start receiving the non-working consumerist grant is dictated by a parameter called the *Consumerist Grant Minimum Allowance Age.* This could be birth, 6 years or 10 or 12 or 18 years of age. For the purpose of concreteness, we will assume that it is birth. All consumerists, and this includes minors and students, start receiving a consumerist grant as soon as they are born. However this is usually the non working consumerist grant since they are not working. All students and minors can spend the money they receive (Norses) from the central bank in the form of the non working consumerist grant on goods and services in the materialist sector. Thus they can buy whatever they want to eat, what to wear and anything else they find interesting in the materialist sector. Alternatively they can pool their consumerist grant with their family and work together as a household. Now, it may be the case that some university or college students may find a part time job on top of their studies. If they work above the Consumerist Grant Threshold, they are entitled to the General Consumerist Grant. In that case, they may be able to buy more goods and services in the materialist sector.

Both the Accommodational sector and Laissez-faire sector serve as a reward for contributing to the materialist sector as well as for contributing to the laissez-faire, governmental and accommodational sectors. Usually students and minors will be living with their parents/family so they do not need to worry about accommodation and things like paying utility bills. In fact when someone is still a minor or student, his parents pay for many of the things in the accommodational and laissez-faire sectors. Thus students and minors living with their family need not really worry about paying for goods and services in either the accommodational and laissez-faire sectors.

There may be some problems when students move out on their own; i.e. when they leave for college or university. If they have a job they can use the proceeds from that job to pay for accommodation, utilities and goods and services in the laissez-faire sectors. However, if a student needs to devote a very high percentage of his time to studying he may apply for the extra work transfer and accommodational award. In the end he will have to pay back to the government for the help it provided him during his time of need.

Clearly minors and students should be enjoying their youth as well as studying. However we should encourage minors to contribute at least a little to society ;3 or 4 hours of work a week is not excessive. If every minor and student worked this much the output of our economy would be much, much greater. Keep in mind that this system has a lot of mechanisms to eliminate unemployment. So, if a minor or student can't find a job in the natural partition, there are always opportunities in the command partition or the laissez-faire labour system.

Now let's talk about the educational experience that students will have in consumerism. Education is important in consumerism. In general, we want a well educated society. People who are educated are better off and function better than people who are uneducated.

In the free-market system, elementary and secondary education are paid for by the government. However, colleges, universities and vocational/trade schools are paid for by the student who wants to go there. People who don't have the money to go to school or can't support themselves while studying usually can't go to school and are forced to find a low paying job.

In some countries the government offers a student loan. This loan pays for tuition so the student can study. However, the student still has to pay for things like accommodation, food, clothes, etc. Although this idea encourages people to seek an education, it has some major draw backs. That is, those who take the loan are in debt for several years or even decades and it takes quite a while to repay the loan.

Consumerism sees the value in a full education. Not only are elementary and secondary schools funded by the government, but also all universities, colleges and trade schools are paid for by the government. This funding for education is taken out of the sources of government revenue we discussed earlier. Students need not worry about a loan or paying off their tuition at all.

However, there still remains the problem of how students support themselves while they go to school. All students get services from the governmental sector. However they still need money for the materialist, accommodational and laissez-faire sectors. This can be overcome if the student gets a job or lives with his family.

Sometimes the student may need the Accommodational Award and welfare money. While he is studying, he is guaranteed a place to live and he is guaranteed a job in the command partition. Thus, he can't say that there is no job available. If he works above a certain threshold, he gets the Accommodational Award. If not, a percentage of his NWCG and his extra work transfer are deducted from his grant each month. This is so he has an incentive to work.

Here is an example. Suppose that the NWCG is 1000 þ. The Accommodational Award Deduction Incentive is 10 % per month and the Accommodational Award Threshold is 6 hours a week or 150 þ per week. If a student works 3 hours a week (or not at all) he will get 1000 þ per month initially and 10% less each month.

A student is encouraged to find a job while studying. He shouldn't work too many hours though, unless he is very ambitious. Suppose a student who is studying organic chemistry finds a job in a lab or pharmacy and works 5 hours a week. In this case he still has plenty of time to devote to studying. However he contributes to society so that in this case if he is receiving the Accommodational Award, he earns it. With the money he earns working he can pay some of the costs of the accommodational award. So if he makes 100 þ from his job per week and the accommodational award costs the government that is providing it about 500 þ per month he would accrue a debt of 500 þ – 4 x 100 þ = 100 þ per month. When he finds a job that he can use his degree for or he simply works more hours at his current job or gets another job in either the natural or command partition he can pay back the Accommodational Award the government

430

granted him.

Students will also want to buy accommodational and laissez-faire goods and services while they are studying. The government steps in to help them with this. It grants them a set amount of Ignits which can be used to buy things in the accommodational sector or exchanged into Fortals to buy things in the laissez-faire sector. However, the student must pay back the amount or at least a portion of it. In order to insure the student just doesn't spend his whole life studying we need measures to discourage him from abusing the system. Let's say the transfer is 200 þ per week. The government sets a threshold of 5 hours a week or 150 þ per week. It sets the student loan deduction incentive at 5 % per week. In this case if a student has a job where he works 5 or more hours per week or he earns 150 þ or more per week he is in good standing. However if he makes less, he will earn 5 % less each week than the previous week beginning with 200 þ per week.

The government helps students when they are studying. It gives them a free education to enhance their prospects of trying to find a good job. Students pay for their materialist needs and wants through the non working consumerist grant or the general consumerist grant if they work above a certain threshold. Also, they receive accommodation and a small amount of money to buy things in the accomodational and laissez-faire sectors.

These are the predicaments of students and minors. We discussed their situation regarding the governmental, materialist, accommodational and laissez-faire sectors. Even if students and minors contribute a little bit to the consumerist economy, both they and society will benefit.

The Stratagems of Barter

In a sense, all economic systems are based on barter. Barter can be in the form of direct trade or with the use of currency, at which time it becomes a form of market economy. Either way there are a number of fundamental rules or principles that apply to barter. These rules or stratagems are listed and discussed here

1)   Trade is necessary for fulfilling people's needs and wants

If people do not trade, they will lack certain goods that they need. If a person who is a piano teacher wants food, she cannot obtain it unless she trades for it somehow, offering her teaching skills to others. If a person has a number of chairs and has no clothes but wants to be clothed, he will not be able to become clothed unless he engages in trade somehow exchanging his chairs for clothes. Trade ensures that people are able to get what they desire.

2)   Both traders are better off after a wise trade

If both traders benefit after a trade then the trade can be considered a good one. The better off the traders are, the better the trade was. Suppose a man who has 35 bicycles trades with a woman who has 10 fish. If the trade involves 1 bicycle for 4 fish, both should be better off since the man will have something to eat and the woman will have a means of transportation. Suppose a man who has 5 sweaters trades with a woman who has 10 L of milk. If the trade involves 2 sweaters for 4 L of milk, both should be better off since the man will have something to drink while the woman will have a way to keep warm. Good trades benefit both traders.

3)   The getting rid of what one doesn't want and the acquisition of what one does want in exchange for this is the purpose of barter.

In every trade someone trades something away for something one wants more. If people didn't want more, they wouldn't always be seeking to find something. Also, if people did not have things they didn't need they would not be trading, they would not be trading them away for something better and there would not be barter. A trade occurs where a man trades a bicycle for 5 novels. Here he gets rid of something that he doesn't want, the bicycle. He wouldn't trade it away if he wanted it. He acquires 5 novels. Here he acquires something he wants. If he didn't want them he wouldn't take them. A woman trades a litre of milk for a hamburger. By trading away the milk she asserts that she doesn't want the milk that much or else she would keep it for herself. She also asserts that she values the hamburger since she gave up something, the milk, for it. Barter's purpose is to gain desirable things and loose undesirable things in exchange for them.

4)   The obtainment of what one wants, a lot of it and the best of it, is the measure of success in barter.

To benefit from barter a trader strives to acquire what he desires. In addition a trader wants to acquire the best possible of what can be acquired and as much as possible of this. If a barterer is hungry, he would be successful by trading the things he has for a meal. The bigger and tastier the meal, the more successful he is at trading. If a barterer needs transportation he would be successful if he trades things he has for a means of getting around. He would be successful if he obtained a bicycle but even more so if he obtained an automobile. A trader, who succeeds in trading not only for what he wants but also for the most desirable and greatest quantity of that which he wants, is a successful trader.

5)   At least two people are necessary to conduct barter

A man cannot trade with himself. If there is only one person, there is no one to give a good to or to receive from. A second person makes barter possible. If someone has a radio and he has no one to trade with he has no one to give the radio to in exchange for another good. If someone wants a loaf of bread and there is no one to trade with, he will be unable to get the bread from anyone. For barter to exist there must be a minimum of two people.

6)   Good bargaining skills are a prerequisite to successful trading

If not, then a person may make a foolish trade. Like most skills, it is to one's advantage if one knows what he is doing or has some experience in the art. If a trader has no familiarity with trading, he might make foolish trades. For example, one may trade a house for a box of matches or a car for a sandwich. The trader must know how much he can get in return for what he is trading. In the above example, the trader may have gotten much more than a box of matches for a house and much more than a sandwich for a car (maybe 1000's of sandwiches). A person skilled in trading will be more successful than one who isn't.

7)   Obtaining more of a particular good is preferable during trade when trading an identical good.

If a trader is seeking to acquire a commodity, the more of the same commodity he acquires, the more successful he is. When trading pencils for notebooks, it is better to obtain three notebooks than two and better to obtain four notebooks than three. When trading televisions for radios, it is better to receive two radios than one and three radios are better to receive than two. Generally, when considering an identical good it is preferable to receive as much as possible of it during a trade.

8)   Giving up less of a particular commodity is preferable during trade when trading an identical good.

If a trader is seeking to acquire a commodity, the less of the commodity he has to give up, the more successful he is. When trading pencils for notebooks, it is better to give up 1 pencil than 2 and it is better to give up 2 than 3. When trading televisions for radios it is preferable to give up 2 T.V.'s rather than 3 and it is better to give up 1 television than 2. Generally, when considering an identical good, it is preferable to give up as little of is as possible during trade.

9)   The obtainment of the best trade possible should be sought during barter

All traders wish to obtain a trade that is in their best interest. This is haggling. A man has a horse, a cat and a dog. A woman has a TV, a computer and a bicycle. The best deal among the two can be obtained when one makes an offer and the other makes a counter-offer in return until a proposal stands such that both of them are happy. The man might offer a horse for a TV. The woman wants the dog also. The man wants the bicycle in return. Thus the man gives up a dog and a horse for a TV and a bicycle. A man has a soft drink, a sandwich and a doughnut. The woman has a knife, a fork and a spoon. The man offers the woman a sandwich for a knife. The woman wants the soft drink also. The man wants the spoon in return. Thus the man gives up a sandwich and a soft drink in exchange for a knife and a spoon. When engaged in barter, the participants have their best interest in mind.

10)   What one desperately needs should not be traded away unless one will directly or indirectly obtain something one needs more.

The things one trades away are those that one does not need. The things one needs are so important that they should not be traded away. Imagine two traders in the dessert. One has a TV and the other has a bottle of water. In this case, unless the other person plans to cross the dessert without any water, he would be foolish to trade away the water even if it is for a TV. Imagine two traders in the arctic. One has a coat and a hat and the other has a king size bed. In this case, unless the other person plans to survive without warm clothes, he would be foolish to trade away his coat and hat even if it is for a king size bed. The things that a person desperately needs should be the last to be traded away.

11)   A commodity that one already has in great abundance should not be traded for.

If someone has a large quantity of a certain good and he has more than he can use, he really doesn't need any more of it. If one doesn't need any more of an item, he should not trade for it. If one already had four bicycles and only really uses one, he would gain little if he got more unless it was to exchange them for something else. A farmer with acres of apples would not want to trade for more apples. In fact his greatest priority is getting rid of his apples for something else. One would be wise not to acquire what one already has a lot of unless it is just to exchange for something else.

12)   Sometimes a trader will want to acquire a good he already has an abundance of so as to trade it for a better good than the original

Although most traders usually trade away goods they have in abundance, some traders do the opposite. That is, they trade for something only to get a better deal in the future. A gold and diamond dealer who already has a lot of gold and diamonds may want to acquire even more gold and diamonds. He trades 2 novels to acquire a gold necklace. Later he sells the same gold necklace for 4 novels to someone else. A trader of used books, who has an abundance of books already, gives 2 cups for a used book. Later he gives that same used book to someone else for 4 cups. This idea of buying of what one has an abundance of and selling it for something better later is a good trading strategy.

13)   The same commodity may be valued differently by different traders.

The value of a good is subjective. How much a trader cherishes a commodity depends on personal preferences and circumstances. One trader may think that a TV is worth 3 radios while another may think a TV is worth only 2 radios. One trader may think that a bicycle is worth 3 hours of piano tutoring while another may think that a bicycle is worth 5 hours of piano tutoring. The value of a good is different among different people.

14)   Society is better off and people are wealthier the more trades occur in a market.

A successful trade represents two things. First of all, someone obtained something they wanted and did not have before. Secondly, another person got rid of something he didn't need for something better. If Geoffrey trades shampoo for a loaf of bread with Cindy, society benefits. Geoffrey has a loaf of bread and he has gotten rid of a bottle of shampoo he did not need. Also, Cindy obtained a bottle of shampoo for her hair and got rid of some bread that she already had too much off. If Tim trades a car for a cottage with Jack, society benefits, Tim has a cottage and

434

he has gotten rid of a car he values less than a cottage. Also, Jack obtained a car to drive around with and got rid of a cottage that he doesn't really use too much anyway. When both traders benefit in a trade, getting what they want, society becomes better off and the traders are more prosperous.

15)   A three-way trade is a useful way to trade goods.

A three way trade occurs when a trader trades for something he doesn't desire but knows that someone else will trade this for something that he wants. If one barters for a good, not for its own sake but for the purpose of using it for a future trade, this represents a three-way trade. One has 2 fish and wants a duck. But he who has the duck doesn't want fish. However he does like a sweater. The first trades the 2 fish for a sweater and subsequently the sweater for the duck. In another example one has a dog but wants a cat. But he who has the cat doesn't want a dog. However he does like a ferret. The first trader trades the dog for a ferret and subsequently the ferret for a cat. If one can't get a good one wants directly, one might be able to get it by trading for an intermediate good with a third party.

16)   Desperation is a disadvantage

When one feels a great urge to trade a commodity as quickly as possible, he often losses. Desperate traders often accept the first offer for the goods they are trying to get rid of or acquire. This may lead to a worse trade than if a trader was not in an anxious position to quickly trade. A person who is extremely hungry might give up a TV for a sandwich if the person with the sandwich is the first person he sees. If one waits longer, one may only have to give up a pillow for a sandwich. A person who is moving to a new house and has to get rid of his old furniture might give the furniture up for a pillow if the person offering the pillow is the first person he sees. If one waits longer one may have received a TV for the furniture. Traders who are desperate are more likely to make trades that they will regret in the future.

17)   The perception that one's commodities are valuable and important works to one's advantage

If one owns a good and waits for a good offer from other traders he will have the opportunity to trade it for something he really likes. If one acts as if what he owns is valuable he will get a better trade than if he thought that what he had was worthless. The more valuable he makes his goods seem, the higher the other person will view them also. If one owns a bicycle and doesn't trade it for mediocre offers like a pencil, but waits, one might eventually procure a better deal such as two television sets and a radio. If one owns a bed and doesn't trade it for mediocre offers like a hamburger, but waits, one might eventually procure a better deal such as a table and chair. How a trader values that which he trades, has a profound effect on what he is able to gain in a trade.

18)   Traders who have an abundance of a good are willing to accept less of another good on exchange for theirs relative to people who have less of that good to trade.

If a trader has a large quantity of a particular good, he will be less picky about what he gets for it. Furthermore, he will be quicker to complete a trade than if he has less of that commodity. He will accept less of a particular good than a person who isn't that desperate to unload. A trader who has 1000 kg of turkey meat may be willing to trade a kilogram of that turkey meat for a kilogram of apples. However if the trader only had 100 kg of turkey meat he may demand 5 kg of apples for 1 kg of turkey meat. A trader, who is also a wheat farmer and wants to trade his wheat, having a truck full of wheat, may accept a kilogram of wheat for a kilogram of beef. However if the trader only grew wheat in his back yard and had no more than 5 kg of wheat, he may demand 3 kg of beef for a kilogram of wheat. Generally the more of a good a trader has, the lower are his expectations for what he receives in return for that good.

19)   How much a trader wants for his good sometimes depends on how much the person he is trading with has to trade for.

If a trader sees that another trader has a lot of goods, he will often demand more of him than if he had less. A trader always tries to extract the most possible from another trader. A trader wants a cassette. The person with the cassette asks how much the first person has to trade for. He says 10 pieces of gold. The person with the cassette demands 8 pieces of gold for the cassette. In another trade, another person wants a cassette from a trader who asks him how much he has to trade for. He says that he only has 5 pieces of gold. The trader with the cassette demands only 3 pieces of gold from him in this case. How much a trader wants from another depends on how much a trader has to trade with.

20)   It is necessary to give something in order to obtain something in return.

If someone doesn't give a good or service in exchange for another he will most likely get nothing himself. An exchange in barter requires that in order to receive one must at the same time give. A trader who wants a bike will not likely get it for nothing. A trader who wants a TV will not get it for nothing. Usually one needs to give in order to obtain another good.

21)   Stratagem #20 does not always apply.

Sometimes a trader may evoke enough pity to obtain things for nothing. This is the idea of begging. Someone who has nothing and looks miserable may get a loaf of bread for free from someone who empathizes with him. A trader who is very hot and thirsty may get a bottle of water for free just out of the generosity of the giver. There are instances when one need not necessarily give in order to get a good.

22)   It is necessary to receive something in order to give to someone else that which they desire.

If someone does not get a good or service in exchange for something, he is unlikely to give anything to anyone else. An exchange in barter requires that in order to bestow one must at the same time receive. A trader who wants to trade a house will not give it up unless he gets something for it. If a trader wants a car, he will not give it to anyone unless he receives something for it. Usually one needs to get a good in order to give up something to another person
.

23)   Stratagem #22 does not always apply.

It is possible that a trader will give things to another out of the good will of his heart, if he deems that the other person is needy or has a close relationship with him. This is the idea of charity. A person may give another an apple if he sees that the person will starve otherwise. A trader may give his brother a radio for his birthday. Although in these cases the trader gains nothing materially, he does gain spiritual satisfaction.

24)   The trading of something that everyone else wants to trade away is unlikely to result in a good trade.

436

If a lot of people have a particular commodity they want to get rid off for something better they must look even harder for those who will give them anything valuable for that good. Suppose a trader is bartering for apples and there are 100's of other traders who also wish to get rid of them. In such a case, the trader may get a book for 10 kg of apples. If there were less apple traders, he might be able to obtain 2 or 3 books seeing as those who want apples would have to go to him and offer more to him for those apples. Suppose a trader is bartering for milk and there are many other cow farmers. In such a case, the trader might get a sandwich for a litre of milk. If there were less milk farmers, he may have received 3 sandwiches for the same amount of milk. A trader who is trading something that everyone else wants to trade away is less likely to get a good deal or even trade at all.

25)   The trading of something that no one wants to have will be unsuccessful.

If no one wants a commodity that one is trading for, no one will give much for it. If no one wants a commodity it becomes worthless and it is hard to get a deal trying to trade it away. A person from the arctic trying to give snow to other arctic travellers probably won't get anything for the snow. Why would anyone give him anything if they can pick the snow from the ground? Someone in a city trying to trade away banana peels probably won't get anything for them. First of all, anyone can dig into the dumpster to get them. Second of all, most people don't want banana peels. That's why they are dumped into trash cans in the first place. Trying to trade a good or service that few desire will produce bad results.

26)   Being a trader with a scarce commodity is an advantage

Having a commodity that few other traders have permits a trader to have the opportunity to choose better more desirable commodities in exchange for his than if more traders traded that commodity. The trader may wait as other traders offer better and better deals for his scarce commodity. If a trader has a rare spice, he will be able to trade for 3 bicycles instead of just one or for a hamburger instead of a slice of bread. A trader with ice in the dessert will be able to trade the ice for a camel instead of a bicycle. If almost everyone had ice in the dessert, the trader may have to be happy with only one bicycle. Having a commodity that everyone wants and that few or no one has is a great help.

27)   Trading inferior goods is discouraged.

A trader must assure others that his goods are workable and not broken. If a trader barters useless, worthless goods, he should be avoided. One cannot trade away rotten beef or pork. A trader cannot trade away a car with no breaks or engine unless he says so when he is trading it. It is frowned upon to trade unworthy commodities.

28)   The protection of a trader's goods as his own must be enforced by law

There mustn't be any steeling. If traders stole each others assets then there is no sense in trading as he who steels most will have most. A person who has his bike stolen from him will have nothing to keep or trade with. A person who has his cow stolen from him would also have nothing for himself or to exchange for another good. If steeling is permitted, no one has an incentive to trade and everything falls apart. Steeling cannot exist.

29)   The reputation of being a trader well known for trading a particular good is an advantage.

A trader known for bartering a particular good or service has an advantage over others. If traders know what one trades, then they are more likely to trade with him as this saves them the trouble of looking too far. A person known among society as a trader of cups, will have more traders who want to trade with him even if others also trade cups. A man known as a good doctor will probably have more people seeking to be healed by him than by more obscure doctors. Being well known for trading a particular good or service can give the trader the upper hand.

30)   The offering of a discount is an effective way of trading goods.

If someone is led to believe he is getting a good bargain, he will agree to a trade he normally wouldn't. Traders get rid of commodities (for better ones) that they can't easily trade away by making others think that they are getting a good trade. A rug dealer says that that he usually wants 20 eggs for a rug but for this one customer he will gladly trade for 18 eggs. The person with the eggs is more likely to complete the exchange because he is convinced that he is getting special treatment. A man who trades milk sees someone with fur. The man with the milk says to the fur trader that he will give him 3 litres of milk for one beaver pellet and that he usually trades 3 litres of milk for 2 beaver pellets. This isn't true but the fur trader believes that he is getting a bargain by having to pay less beaver pellets and so agrees to the trade. The perception that one is getting a great bargain is a reason for many exchanges.

31)   The utterance that one can get a better trade somewhere else may lead to the negotiation of a better deal than otherwise.

If a trader says that someone else has offered to give him more or receive less, he may induce another trader to lower his expectations. What other traders offer matters in trades involving similar commodities. Suppose a trader has 5 L of milk and wants to exchange the milk with someone who has apples. The person with the apples says that he will give the milk trader 10 lbs of apples for 3 L of milk. The milk trader says that someone else offered her 20 lbs of apples for the 3 L of milk. The apple trader now realizes that he must give at least 20 lbs of apples for the milk or else no trade takes place. Suppose someone has some eggs and wants to exchange them for sausage. The person with the sausage says that he will trade 10 eggs for 2 kg of sausage. The egg trader says another sausage trader who she spoke to before would give her 2 kg of sausage for 5 eggs. Now the original sausage trader must not ask for more than 5 eggs for his 2 kg of sausage if he wants to make a transaction. A wise trader looks around different traders to see who will offer him the best deal.

32)   The application of pressure to force a trade increases the likelihood of the trade taking place.
Applying pressure to carry out a trade in a certain amount of time can cause someone to trade for something he wasn't going to in the first place. If someone forces another person to trade without carefully thinking about the trade, perhaps due to a lack of time, a trade may result that wasn't planned originally. A video company releases a video that is only available for 2 weeks and will never be released again. Traders who do not normally like the video might trade away their possessions for it, thinking that they might miss a great opportunity by not buying it. A sandwich trader offers a new kind of sandwich for a "limited time only". People who do not normally eat these go trade for these believing that they will miss a big chance. By putting pressure on a trader, one may cause him to trade something he wasn't going to.

33)   The combination of goods into a package facilitates trade.

Sometimes a good is put into a "combo" with another. Usually one trades fast and the other is hard to get rid off for something better. If a good that is trading poorly is put together with one that trades quickly the first good can be traded more quickly than normal. A trader has a litre of milk and a chestnut. Instead of trading them separately, he trades them together and gets something for the chestnut whereas otherwise he wouldn't. A trader has steak and a piece of paper. Someone offers him 2 bananas for the steak and no one wants the paper. By putting them together into a package, the two would have to be traded together. He receives an offer of 2 bananas and an orange for the package. Thus he earns an orange more than he would normally. The combining of goods into an inseparable package to be traded may help trade goods that are slow to trade.

34) There are two good strategies of bargaining. They are stratagem #34 and stratagem # 35

The trading of a variety of goods is a successful strategy. Doing so, one is able to find at least one person with at least something to trade. Suppose that a trader wants to be sure that he will carry out at least one trade. Instead of trading just milk and tomatoes he can pursue the option of trading these and in addition to them chairs, cars, carpets, plants and spoons. Thus he will attract other traders with varying interests. If a trader is not interested in milk and tomatoes, he may be interested in a spoon or a chair or maybe a pair of pants. It is a good idea to trade a variety of goods and services.

35) Specializing in the trade of a very specific field of goods is a successful strategy.

Doing so, one is able to attract other traders who know what they are looking for. Trading one type of commodity will distinguish the trader as a trader of that commodity. A trader may specialize in meat. He trades not only beef but is also renowned for having fresh poultry, pork, mutton, liver etc. Those who want to trade for meat know where to go. Another trader may specialize in wood products. He also makes them as he is a carpenter. He has different kinds of tables, chairs, patios, stools etc. Those who want to obtain a wood product (i.e. a desk) now know where to go. It is a good idea to specialize in one specific area.

36) Goods surrounded by excitement and attention are traded more successfully

When people are very enthusiastic about particular goods, other traders are attracted to these goods. If a good is talked about a lot, more people want it than if it were obscure. A trader may hire his cousin to rave about his water filters. He would exclaim how wonderful and necessary they are and that everyone must have one. This will attract more traders to trade for those filters than otherwise. A potion seller may get his brother to exclaim how healthy he feels after drinking some tonic. This will also attract traders. Bringing attention and excitement to one's goods is an effective way to attract potential traders and carry out a good trade.

37) The accentuation of the positive is the goal of advertising

A trader emphasizes the good points about his good when he is haggling with a potential trader. If a trader hears the good qualities of a good he is more likely to trade for it. A rug dealer may point out that his rugs are made of real animal skin and that they are easily washable. A car trader will mention first of all, that his cars have four wheel drive, anti-lock breaks, air bags and so on. The most positive is mentioned first as it is this that makes a trader want to trade. When advertising his goods, a trader accentuates the positive.

38) The discounting of the negative is the goal of advertising

A trader avoids talking about the bad points regarding his good when he is haggling with a potential trader. If a trader doesn't know the negative qualities of a good, he is more likely to trade for it. A rug dealer will probably not mention, even if it is true, that his rugs will rot if they are wet and are not dried properly. A car trader will not mention, even if it is true, that his cars have really bad fuel economy. When advertising a trader discounts the negative. Negative information is not mentioned as it detracts buyers from buying a good.

39)   Goods and services that are perishable are riskier to trade than those that are not.

If someone does not trade away a perishable good or service in adequate time, he loses out. This usually applies to foods and drinks. Traders with perishable goods are focused on the expiry date and trade those goods that expire first before those that expire later. Perishable goods must be consumed before their expiry date or else they lose their value. If a grocery trader does not trade away his apples within a short time, they rot and no one wants to buy apples that are rotten. He who trades with milk must trade it away soon as rotten milk is only good for throwing out. A ticket to a hockey game loses its value after the night of the game. Likewise a rock and roll concert ticket is worthless after the performance. There is more risk involved in trading goods that can expire than those that do not.

40)   Traders tell the person they are trading with what they think they want to hear

A successful trader will see the trade from the other person's perspective. He will tell who he is trading with why that person should carry out the trade. So, a good trader will tell the other person all the advantages of an internet service or how his neighbour's will be jealous of him once he buys that car.

41)   Barter is generally inflexible

When two traders wish to exchange with each other they must both want to receive what the other is giving. Barter involves direct exchange making it awkward for many trades. Notwithstanding the stratagem #15 of 3-way trade, usually direct exchange is a prerequisite. A trader, who wants food and has to trade pencils, must find another trader who will give him food and accept pencils. This can be avoided with stratagem #15. A trader who wants a book and has to trade pickles must find another trader who will give him the book and who desires pickles. This can also be avoided with stratagem #15. Barter, although useful in providing things needed and satisfying wants, is very rigid.

42)   The introduction of a commodity or an item that can be used as a measure of exchange, unit of account and a store of value can make barter efficient

Such an item would eliminate the need for direct exchange (or 3-way trade). For example, traders could use gold or some precious metal as a currency. This is then used to purchase goods like honey and cars. Traders would accept gold in exchange for goods. Thus a trader gives another a car for a certain amount of gold. When traders accept an item or commodity as a unit of exchange or measure of value, barter metamorphosis's into a quasi-free-market system.

These stratagems of barter are universal. Barter, as well as all economic systems that flow out of it, functions as we have just described. This knowledge is important to a complete understanding of the inner workings of an economy.

Consumerism in a Prison Camp

Here we demonstrate how consumerism would work in a prison camp. The prison camp scenario is often used to show how the free-market system works. It is useful to describe an economy in a prison camp due to the simplicity such a setting offers.

We will first look at how a free-market would function in a prison camp. Suppose that there are people in a prison camp and that they are given rations. They each have different tastes and prefer different quantities of the goods that they are rationed. How do they maximize on their preferences?

We make several assumptions here. There are 200 people. There is another prison camp nearby. Each day each prisoner receives 1 box of rations. Each box of rations has 5 cigarettes, 1 bar of soap, 2 potatoes, 2 tea bags, 3 slices of bread, 1 can of ham, 1 bottle of beer and 6 crackers and 1 bar of chocolate.

In a free-market arrangement cigarettes become the currency. Each good becomes quoted in terms of cigarettes. When prisoners trade, they exchange cigarettes for one of the goods they were rationed. The people do not necessarily have to smoke. All that matters is that cigarettes become the universal currency in the camp. They are a store of value, a unit of account and a medium of exchange.

Let's look at two exchanges between Joe and Matt. Joe wants to have more bread and Matt wants more crackers. Joe is willing to pay 2 cigarettes for a slice of bread while Matt is willing to accept 2 cigarettes in exchange for a slice of bread. Thus Joe gives Matt two cigarettes and Matt gives Joe a slice of bread. They are both content. Matt is willing to pay a cigarette for 2 crackers while Joe is willing to give 2 crackers for a cigarette. Thus Matt gives Joe a cigarette and Joe gives Matt two crackers. They are both content.

In our camp, many transactions like the one above are carried out between prisoners in the free-market paradigm. One prisoner gives another some cigarettes in exchange for a good. In this way prisoners maximize on the goods they enjoy and get rid of the goods that they do not need that much for ones they would rather have instead. Each prisoner may value a good differently in terms of how many cigarettes it is worth. Eventually those who are buying a good (spending cigarettes) come to equilibrium with those that are selling the goods (earning cigarettes). Suppose Joe wants to buy a potato. He thinks it is worth a cigarette. He goes to Matt who has a potato and values his potato at 3 cigarettes. Joe doesn't want to pay 3 cigarettes for a potato so he goes to Paul to see how much he wants for it. Paul wants 4 cigarettes for it. Joe goes back to Matt and offers Matt two cigarettes. Matt counter-offers with 2 ½ cigarettes. Joe agrees. Thus Joe gives up two and a half cigarettes for a potato from Matt.

A prisoner who wants to buy something has two choices. He could go to each prisoner asking how much they want for the good or he can bargain. Suppose a prisoner, Sam, wants to earn a few cigarettes. He is selling soap. He wants 2 cigarettes for it. However there may be several other entrepreneurs like him. Since the soap is exactly the same, they are competing with him. Let's call his competitors Bill, Jack and John. In order for them to sell soap, they must make it known to other prisoners that they are selling soap. In order for Sam to sell his soap, he must charge the lowest price for it (in cigarettes). He charges 2 cigarettes per bar of soap. However,

Bill will settle for 1 ½ cigarettes per bar of soap. John charges only 1 cigarette for it. This undercutting ends when soap buyers start competing with each other to buy soap. So suppose Sam, Bill, John and Jack each lower the price of their soap to 1 cigarette. They each have 2 soaps to sell. Now suppose that there are 10 soap buyers. Each of them will offer a price higher than the other for the soap thus raising the price of soap (in cigarettes). This ends when the price of a bar of soap reaches equilibrium. Here the equilibrium is 2 cigarettes per bar of soap.

Every day a new box of rations arrives. This means more cigarettes. The prison camp population experiences the effects of inflation. What happens is that the price of goods (in cigarettes) increases relative to the last day's prices.

That is the way a free-market economy will operate in a prison camp. Now we move onto a different type of economic system operating in a prison camp. We now look at an economy in a prison camp under consumerism. We look at the major areas where it differs from the free-market orientation.

We make several assumptions. There are 200 people. There is another prison camp with which to exchange. Every prisoner receives 1 box of rations. A box of rations contains:

- 5 cigarettes
- 1 bar of soap
- 2 potatoes
- 2 tea bags
- 3 slices of bread
- 1 can of ham
- 1 bottle of beer
- 6 crackers
- 1 bar of chocolate

Instead of an accommodation based consumerist system we have a "luxury based" consumerist system. Thus we divide all the rations into 2 groups; "necessities" and "luxuries". The reason for this will be clear a little bit later.

The necessities include:

- 1 bar of soap
- 2 potatoes
- 3 slices of bread
- 1 can of ham
- 6 crackers

The luxuries include:

- 5 cigarettes
- 2 tea bags
- 1 bottle of beer
- 1 bar of chocolate

The prisoners elect a president or accountant. We assume that he has a piece of paper and a pen. He is in charge of all transactions in the consumerist prison camp.

The prisoners put all of the rations together. They vote on the prices of each good. The top 30 prices for each good are excluded as are the bottom 30. The remaining 140 are averaged. In our example let's suppose that the outcome of the price vote was as follows.
In the necessity sector:

Soap-   2.00 ☉
Potatoes-   1.00 ☉
Slice of bread- 1.00 ☉
Can of ham-   2.00 ☉
Crackers-   0.50 ☉

In the luxury sector:

Cigarettes-   1.00 þ
Tea bags-   0.50 þ
Bottle of beer- 2.50 þ
Chocolate bar- 2.00 þ

In the first sector, the necessities sector, the prices were expressed in Norses. In the second sector, the luxuries sector, the prices were expressed in Ignits.

The president finds the value of both sectors. The value of the prices of all necessary goods times their quantity is called the Gross Total Necessity Wealth (GTNW). It is expressed in Norses. The prices of all luxury goods times their quantity is called the Gross Total Luxury Wealth (GTLW). It is expressed in Ignits.

The GTNW would be thus:

Soap- 1 x 2.00 ☉ = 2.00 ☉
Potatoes- 2 x 1.00 ☉ = 2.00 ☉
Slice of bread- 3 x 1.00 ☉ = 3.00 ☉
Can of ham- 1 x 3.00 ☉ = 3.00 ☉
Crackers- 6 x 0.50 ☉ = 3.00 ☉

The sum is thus 13.00 ☉. Since there are 200 boxes of rations, the GTNW is 2600.00 ☉.

The GTLW would be thus:

Cigarettes- 5 x 1.00 þ = 5.00 þ
Tea bags- 2 x 0.50 þ = 1.00 þ
Bottle of beer- 1 x 2.50 þ = 2.50 þ

Chocolate bar- 1 x 2.00 þ = 2.00 þ

The sum is thus 10.50 þ. Since there are 200 boxes of rations the GTLW is 2100.00 þ.

Due to the fact that there are 200 cases of rations and 200 prisoners, the GTNW per capita is 13.00 ☉ and the GTLW per capita is 10.50 þ. The accountant (president) manages all of the prisoner's exchanges. There is a list of the names of all the prisoners and by each prisoner's name there is a credit of 13.00 ☉ and 10.50 þ. The prisoners make two lines. When they reach the end of a line, they can exchange some of their credits for rations. Each time they obtain something, the amount the good is worth is deducted from their credit by the president. The goods (rations) are stockpiled and can be obtained by trading some credit for a good. An example should be helpful. John is in one of the lines for the goods. Upon reaching the end he is greeted by the president. He can buy any "necessity" sector good; seeing as he is in the necessity line. He can choose any combination of items worth equal or less (but not more) than 13.00 ☉. He picks two cans of ham, 8 crackers and 3 slices of bread. The president deducts 13.00 ☉ from his account; i.e. he crosses out "13.00 ☉" and writes "0.00 ☉" in the space by his name on a paper. The president then hands John the goods he chose.

Upon receiving these goods, John joins another line, the luxury line. His position in this line is the inverse of the previous line. So if he was first in the necessities line he will be last in the luxury line and if he was last in the necessities line he would be first in the luxury line. And if he was 50th in the necessities line he would be 150th in the luxury line. After reaching the end of the luxury line he is once again confronted by the president who asks him how he wants to spend his money (credits). He can spend 10.50 þ. He chooses 2 bottles of beer, 2 chocolate bars and 2 tea bags. The president deducts 10.50 þ credits from his account by crossing out "10.50 þ" and writing "0.00 þ" by his name. The president then gives John what he asked for. In this setup, John can meet his preferences and he would prefer the goods he got under such a system to getting what he did in the original ration.

Matt is another prisoner. After reaching the end of the necessities line, he chooses a can of ham and 6 crackers. This only costs 6.00 ☉. The president deducts the 6.00 ☉ from his account. He still has 7.00 ☉. He can spend this 7.00 ☉ the next day. When the president gets ready to hand out rations the next day (assuming that a new box of rations arrives every day and its contents are exactly the same as the day before) he simply adds 13.00 ☉ and 10.50 þ to everyone's name. Thus Matt would have 20.00 ☉ to spend the next day however he pleases.

The president is counted as among the 200 prisoners in the camp. He also gets his own account from which he has to deduct credits whenever he wants to obtain some of the goods contained in the rations. Therefore it is important that the prisoners choose someone honest as the president.

Now we see why there are two sectors, not just one. If there was only one, the prisoners would set a very low price for the most desirable goods and a high price for the less desirable goods. The more desirable goods will be relatively less expensive than the less desirable goods and yet since the less desirable goods will be relatively high priced, a lot of credits would be granted. Thus the people at the front of the line would buy all the more desirable goods first leaving the less desirable goods for those who line up later. This can be avoided by having two sectors. In each sector the goods are relatively equally desirable compared to each other.

Prisoners can spend all their credits or some of them, but they can never spend more than they are credited with. If some prisoners spend less than they are credited with each day, then

444

there is a natural surplus of goods. By the action of choosing and buying, the prisoners indicate which goods they want more of and which goods they want less of. We assume that there is another camp with 200 prisoners each receiving the same rations as our prisoners. They can trade with us. The only differences are that they probably set different prices for their goods and they also likely have a surplus but of different goods.

The president of our camp exchanges the goods we have in surplus (those that were not sold) for goods that the prisoners would buy a lot of. Suppose the president did not sell 12 bars of soap, 8 potatoes and 20 tea bags. These have a total value of $(12 \times 2.00 \; \Theta) + (8 \times 1.00 \; \Theta) = 32.00 \; \Theta$ and $20 \times 0.50 \; \text{þ} = 10.00 \; \text{þ}$. The other camp also has some surpluses. They have 5 cans of ham, 12 crackers and 15 cigarettes. They chose to price their goods as follows: $3.00 \; \Theta$ per can of ham, $1.00 \; \Theta$ per cracker and $1.00 \; \Theta$ per cigarette. Note that the type of currency does not matter here. The distinction between sectors at this point is irrelevant. So we will use Norses as currency and rather than our tea bags costing $0.50 \; \text{þ}$, they simply cost $0.50 \; \Theta$ each.

Now our president must get rid of the goods we have in surplus- 12 bars of soap, 8 potatoes, and 20 tea bags- since no one wants them. If they did they would have bought them.

In order to trade between the two camps, an exchange rate must be set. In consumerism the exchange rate is calculated and it is calculated as such. We quote our prices in Θ but we quote the other camp's prices in \$. We do this to avoid the confusion we would have if we expressed real exchange rates in the same currency. The real exchange rates are: (expressed in $/\Theta)

Ham- $3.00/ 2.00 \; \Theta = \$1.50/\Theta$
Crackers- $1.00/0.50 \; \Theta = \$2.00/\Theta$
Cigarettes- $1.00/1.00 \; \Theta = \$1.00/\Theta$
Tea bags- $1.00/0.50 \; \Theta = \$2.00/\Theta$
Potatoes- $0.50/1.00 \; \Theta = \$0.50/\Theta$
Soap- $1.50/2.00 \; \Theta = \$0.75/\Theta$

After multiplying each real exchange rate by the number of goods involved and dividing by the total number of goods traded we get an exchange rate of $\$1.38/\Theta$

The president creates a trade pool. This is an entry on a piece of paper that earns money during some trades and allows subsidized trades in other cases.

We are selling 20 tea bags, 8 potatoes and 12 bars of soap. We are buying 5 cans of ham, 12 crackers and 15 cigarettes from the other camp. First we take care of the selling. The other camp pays $20 \times \$1.00 = \$20.00$ to us for buying tea bags. In terms of our currency it is $\$20.00 \times (1.00 \; \Theta/\$1.38) = 14.50 \; \Theta$. But our price for tea bags is $20 \times 0.50 \; \Theta = 10.00 \; \Theta$. Therefore $4.50 \; \Theta$ goes to the trade pool. The $10.00 \; \Theta$ go to cover the cost of the tea bags. The other camp pays $8 \times \$0.50 = \$4.00$ for potatoes. This is equal to $\$4.00 \times (1.00 \; \Theta/\$1.38) = 2.90 \; \Theta$. But our potatoes cost $8 \times 1.00 \; \Theta = 8.00 \; \Theta$. So to subsidize this trade, the trade pool must lose $5.10 \; \Theta$. The other camp pays $12 \times \$1.50 = \$18.00$ for soap. This equals $\$18 \times (1.00 \; \Theta/\$1.380 = 13.04 \; \Theta$. But we need to receive $12 \times 2.00 \; \Theta = 24.00 \; \Theta$ for the soap. Thus the trade pool must subsidize $10.96 \; \Theta$.

Now let us look at buying. We buy 5 cans of ham. We must pay the other camp $5 \times \$3.00 = \$15.00$. This equals $\$15.00 \times (1.00 \; \Theta/\$1.38) = 10.86 \; \Theta$. But we pay $5 \times 2.00 \; \Theta = 10.00 \; \Theta$ for the ham. That means that the trade pool must subsidize $0.86 \; \Theta$ for this trade. We buy 12 crackers. We must pay the other camp $12 \times \$1.00 = \$12.00$. This equals $\$12.00 \times (1.00 \; \Theta/\$1.38) = 8.70 \; \Theta$. We pay $12 \times 0.50 \; \Theta = 6.00 \; \Theta$ for the crackers. The trade pool must subsidize $2.70 \; \Theta$. Finally the president buys 15 cigarettes for $1.00 = $15.00. This in terms of Norses is $15.00 x (1.00 Θ/$1.38) = 10.87 Θ. We pay 15 x 1.00 Θ = 15.00 Θ. The trade pool gains 4.13 Θ.

Now let's see the net surplus or deficit of the trade pool.

It gains: 4.50 Θ + 4.13 Θ
 It loses: 5.10 Θ + 10.96 Θ + 0.86 Θ + 2.70 Θ

Thus the net result is – 10.99 Θ. The president wants to avoid a negative trade pool balance. He can do this by manipulating how many goods he wants to trade.

A consumerist economy could spring up in a prison camp. We saw how goods, which were divided into two sectors, would be traded. We also saw how two prison camps would trade with each other, getting rid of their surpluses and maximizing on their desires.

Import Quotas and Rent Control

Here we examine two pervasive features that exist in most free-market economies. They are import quotas and rent control.

By import quota we mean a limit on the quantity of foreign goods brought into our country. Such a quota raises the domestic price above the world price and therefore domestic sellers benefit while domestic buyers are harmed. This doesn't occur in accommodation based consumerism. There is no import quota and importation is encouraged. Since importation benefits the consumerists and the system is primarily concerned with aiding the consumerist (as long as it doesn't hurt the producer at the same time), there really are no limits on imports of foreign goods. There is one exception. The trade pool, which we discussed before, should be positive most of the time. Therefore sometimes it may be necessary to restrict some imports.

The consumerist trade pools applies to the accommodational sector. There are absolutely no import or export restrictions in the laissez-faire sector. There are no tariffs or barriers to importation or exportation. Thus international trade in the laissez-faire sector is as free as it can possibly be.

Now let's look at rent control. Rent control is a price ceiling placed by some governments on rent that a landlord may charge his or her tenants. The idea behind it is to help the poor receive affordable housing. However this is inefficient. Rent control does not exist in an accommodation based consumerist society. However landlords are not able to set the price they want on their housing either. Rent prices are determined by the Rental Equivalence Duration (RED). This is set by the central bank. A tenant pays how many years it would take to own the building. Consumerism has a different way to help the poor- those that can't afford apartments. In cases where there is an apartment shortage, the government invokes the governmental-market shortage/surplus resolution system. Essentially, the government pays for (subsidizes) a portion of the price of an apartment unit. This is more efficient than rent control.

To help those not working, the consumerist government has an approach different than rent control. In consumerism, absolutely everyone is entitled to an accommodational award. No one at all should be homeless. However these individuals must pay all, none or some of the value of this accommodation as soon as they find work in the natural or governmental partitions. They can pay the value of their accommodation award while working in the command partition. Also, these people are usually employed in the command partition or the laissez-faire labour system and they can use their extra-work transfer payments to pay for rent.

Rent control and import quotas are found in the free enterprise system. They do not exist in accommodation bases consumerism. These are the advantages that this system has over the first.

Investment

By investment we mean the purchase by a firm of inputs, land, capital and material often to expand or start operation. Investments are associated with the accommodational sector. Therefore transactions concerning investments involve Ignits.

The four main types of investment are in land, labour, capital and R & D (research and development). By land we mean territory on which, for example, a factory may be built. By labour we mean workers that convert inputs into products. These include janitors, cashiers, clerks, technicians, analysts, etc. By capital we mean equipment that can be used to convert inputs into products. These include cash registers, mops, actual buildings, paper pressers, knives, tolls, computers, motors, etc. By research and development we mean better methods of turning inputs into products using new know how. These include new patents and new inventions and innovations of technology.

All these forms of investment have a price or wage function set by the central bank. For example a janitor may be paid 6.00 þ per hour and commercial land may cost 50.00 þ/m². The accommodational markdown does not apply to labour or R & D or capital. It does apply to land.

Let's do some examples. We use our hypothetical Bob's doughnut shop. Bob wants to expand by buying more land and building another doughnut shop on it. The land costs 40.00 þ/m². He buys 500 m². This is 20 000.00 þ. We assume in this section that the accommodational markdown is 25 %. Now he has where to build his shop. The former owner of the land receives 15 000.00 þ.

Now Bob builds the actual store. It costs 100 000.00 þ and it is built by our hypothetical Super Plus Construction. Bob pays 100 000.00 þ for it while Super Plus Construction keeps 75 000.00 þ due to an AMD of 25 %. To encourage investment in firms located in a consumerist nation the government sets a Capital Investment Transfer (CIT). Let's say it is 3%. In this case Bob would be given 3 000.00 þ.

Bob also needs a cash register, a mop and bucket, a doughnut rack, seats and tables, washroom sinks and stalls, light bulbs, carpets and other things that a doughnut store needs. They cost 40 000.00 þ. The firms from whom Bob bought these earn a total of 30 000.00 þ split among each other. Assuming a CIT of 3%, Bob would be given 1200.00 þ.

Bob also hires 3 employees; 1 baker and 2 waitresses. The waitresses earn 10.00 þ/hour and the doughnut baker earns 9.00 þ per hour. For these workers there is no accommodational markdown although they are technically in the accommodational sector. Wages are the incentive for anyone to produce goods and services. If there was an accommodational markdown on wages there would be a disincentive to work much like a heavy income tax discourages productivity in a free enterprise economy. Bob is rewarded by the government for hiring these workers. The government pays a percentage of their wages so as to encourage employment. So if each worker earned 1500.00 þ per week and the Employment Reimbursement Transfer (ERT) was 2%, Bob would be given 90.00 þ for hiring these workers.

Bob does an investment in research and development. He tells his baker to experiment with dough and chocolate to come up with two new flavors of doughnuts. For this time the baker is paid 50.00 þ. There is no accommodational markdown so he keeps all of it.

Investment is an important economic concept. There are at least three areas a firm can invest in. Using an example, we saw how a firm would go about investing in itself. We did calculations involving the ERT and the CIT.

Advertising

Advertising is as important for the economy as it is for the business that is advertising. By advertising we mean letting one firm's products be known through some kind of medium. There are many ways to advertise. Examples include through television, radio, newspapers and bus stop signs. Advertising is in the accommodational sector and is manipulated by Ignits. It is affected by the accommodational markdown.

The central bank sets the price for advertising through the different types of media. For example, advertising through television may cost 2000.00 þ/minute and through radio 500.00 þ/minute and through newspaper, 10.00 þ/ word.

In the case of television, usually, the more entertaining it is, the more viewers watch a program. However the more viewers watch a program and the commercials during it, the more people will see a firm's commercial and the firm will earn more money selling its products. Therefore there is a certain type of selection for televisions broadcasting companies to come up with more entertaining programs. Similar arguments apply to radio and newspaper firms. Advertising should be encouraged as much as possible so that consumerists have more TV stations showing entertaining programs.

Here is an example. Let's suppose a hypothetical Joe's Crispy Cookies wants to attract more buyers to their cookies. They make a 30 s add on TV. To put a commercial on TV it costs 2000.00 þ/minute. They must pay 1000.00 þ to the TV station (let's call it Channel Super Plus) to air their commercial. Due to an accommodational markdown of 25 %, Channel Super Plus earns 750.00 þ,

A firm could also advertise through the radio. Let's use Joe's Crispy Cookies again as an example. To put a commercial on the radio it costs 700.00 þ/minute. This is set by the central bank and is the same regardless which radio station airs the commercial. They want to put on a commercial for one minute. Thus Joe's Crispy Cookies puts their commercial on a radio that has the most listeners (let's call it Super Radio Station Plus). Due to an accommodational markdown of 25 %, Super Radio Station Plus earns 525.00 þ/ minute

Another option for Joe's Crispy Cookies to advertise is through bus stop ads. Suppose that the central bank sets that it costs 400.00 þ per bus ad/ 2 weeks. So if Joe's Crispy Cookies puts a bus stop ad for 4 weeks they would have to pay 800.00 þ for that service. Since these bus stop shelters were put up by the government, this 800.00 þ goes to the government (usually municipal). The same would happen if a firm placed an ad on the side of a bus.

A question that comes up is this: should some products be banned from advertising, i.e. cigarettes? This is a question left to the government as it is essentially a political rather than an economic question.

Advertising is important to the consumerist economy. A firm could go about advertising its products in various ways. With advertising, a firm can increase its revenue and earn a higher profit, benefiting society, itself and all consumerists.

A Simplified Partially Consumerized Economy

There may arise a situation in a practical setting when a government of a nation wants to try to install a simplified form of consumerist economy. They are hesitant of a fully consumerized economy so they make adjustments to their economic system so that it is somewhat consumerized. We will talk about this situation now.

Let's assume that our country is generally well off and has a private and public sector. They do not yet have a materialist or accomodational sector. The public sector is similar to what we have called the government sector and the private sector is what we previously called the laissez-faire sector. They want to create a small and limited materialist sector. Instead of putting the industries we put into the materialist sector that we described in this book (hospitality, transportation, apparel) this nation only puts the alcohol industry in the materialist sector. They do not create an accommodational sector. The laissez-faire sector (i,e. the private sector) is the reward for contributing to the materialist sector.

So the alcohol industry is in the materialist sector of our partially consumerized economy. We assume that there are 10 million people in our country and the alcohol industry is a 2 billion dollar a year industry. The Gross Domestic Product, i.e. the value of the economy is 650 billion dollars. The government grants money (it is immaterial to what we call them so let's just call them Norses) to all the people in our country. Since there are 10 million people in our country and the output of the materialist sector (the alcohol industry) is 2 billion dollars, each consumerist is granted 200 Θ per year or 200Θ/12 = 16.67 Θ per month to spend on alcohol.

So, each consumerist can spend 16.67 Θ per month on any alcoholic beverage they want either in the form of bottles of beer, wine or vodka or beverages at a pub or restaurant. It is clear that there is a slight problem with this arrangement. Some people may not like alcohol and won't want to spend their money and there may be people who want to buy more alcohol than just 16.67 Θ per month.

The solution to this problem is similar to what is done in capitalism with regards to tradeable pollution permits. In this setup pollution causing firms are granted permits allowing them to pollute a certain amount to a river. Some firms may need to pollute less and some may need to pollute more. Thus they sell pollution permits among each other. A firm that wants to pollute a lot buys a permit from a firm that does not need to pollute. This somewhat solves pollution problems.

Something similar happens in our current example. Those that would like to drink more alcohol trade Norses (which are used to buy alcohol) with people who want to drink less. So if someone wants to drink 25 Θ worth of alcohol per month, he can buy 9.00 Θ from a person who doesn't like alcohol.

This idea of tradeable Norses is only necessary because the materialist sector is so small and not all people want to buy things in that sector. In a more developed consumerist system there will be many more industries in the materialist sector than just alcohol- for example hospitality, transportation and apparel. Thus each consumerist will find at least something to buy with the money they were granted by the central bank.

Normally, when there is a large materialist sector, the process of granting money contributes to inflation. However in this hypothetical partially consumerized economy this is avoided as the alcohol industry is worth 2 billion dollars and the whole GDP is 650 billion dollars. So there will be some inflation but it probably won't be much larger than 2 %.

When creating a partially consumerized economy the government must make a kind of central bank (or something similar) to create prices for all the alcohol in the economy. Once the central bank is formed then it creates price functions for families of goods. Thus it may say that a can of beer costs 1.00 ☉ per 100 ml or that a can of beer (any size) costs 8.00 ☉. Also bottles of wine can cost 10.00 ☉ per litre or 25.00 ☉ per any size bottle. Also whisky can be 2.00 ☉ per 100 ml or 18.00 ☉ per bottle. There may be alternative prices applicable to alcohol served in pubs. Thus a stein of beer may cost differently in a pub than if the same amount of beer were bought in a can.

During a transaction in the materialist sector, Norses are turned into dollars at a bank. As an example, Jim writes a grocery store that sells beer a check for 5.00 ☉ when he buys a 500 ml can of beer. The grocery store takes this check to the bank where it is converted into $ 5.00.

It is important to point out that the idea of consumerization does not really mean putting industries in the materialist sector and granting money to spend on that sector. Rather a truly developed consumerist economy would have a healthy balance of all four sectors. The relative sizes of the four sectors depends on the wishes of the government but ideally the accommodational sector should be largest followed by the materialist, followed by the governmental followed by the laissez-faire sector.

An economy can be fully consumerized or it could add sectors to its structure. An economy with the alcohol industry in the material sector is a good example of a partially consumerized economy. This can be a small first step to a robust consumerist economic system.

Consumer Debt

In this section of the book we will discuss consumer debt. Consumer debt is very prominent in free- market capitalism. We will see its nature in accommodation based consumerism.

First we must emphasize that there are three partitions and four sectors in accommodation based consumerism. Furthermore there are three currencies. Each currency is specific to a sector. In these ways consumerism is different from the free-market system.

Consumerists receive either the general or non-working consumerist grants from the central bank every two weeks. This is in Norses. It is based on the GDCP, which is the total and potential output of the materialist sector (both natural and command partitions) of consumerism. The consumerists can spend this money on anything that they wish in the materialist sector for things like clothes, food and cars.

If a consumerist is short on money at any time, they can take advantage of the materialist overdraft. In this program, the government lends some Norses (the currency in the materialist sector) and the consumerist must pay that, with interest, the next time the grant is given. So if a consumerist is given 1000.00 Θ every two weeks in the form of the consumerist grant and he runs out after a week and a half, the government can give him an extra 300.00 Θ. If the materialist overdraft percentage is 10 % the government will receive 330 Θ from the consumerist the next two week cycle.

Consumerists can also get into debt in the accommodational sector. They can borrow money from the bank in the form of Ignits or purchase an item in instalments. For example, someone wants to buy a vacation but is short on money. He can borrow 1000.00 þ at 3% interest from a bank and go on his vacation. At a later time, he must pay back the principal and the interest.

In the accommodational sector consumerists can take out a mortgage on their homes. If a house costs 100 000.00 þ and the buyer doesn't have enough the consumerist can arrange a mortgage at 2% compounded continuously. The mortgage is in the laissez-faire sector so fortals are used. Each month the consumerist will pay the interest and the principal on the mortgage until it is paid off. The consumerist has improved his living situation while getting into debt.

Consumerists can also get into debt in the laissez-faire sector. An individual can buy an item while taking a loan from a bank to do so.

The possibility of getting into debt increases overall demand as more things are purchased and more things are sold. An increasing demand spurs on the economy as output is increased. The problem is that individuals who are doing the buying have to pay back the loan in the end.

Government Revenue in a Hypothetical Consumerist Economy

The government sector/partition provides certain social services for consumerists to enjoy. In order to provide these services it needs some sort of revenue. In this section we will discuss how the government finds ways to raise funds.

In this section we will talk about which services we would like to have. Then we will talk about the various sources of revenue the government has. We must keep in mind that this whole elaboration is purely hypothetical and the numbers are mostly imaginary. After we talk about a hypothetical scenario we will discuss a situation based on the real budget of Ontario, Canada. The spending records of the Ontario government are taken from actual sources.

We start with a few assumptions. First, our country has 1 000 000 citizens. Instead of describing the detailed workings of three levels of government (federal, provincial, municipal) we will reduce the situation to a single grand "government". In doing so we avoid difficulties in describing which level of government is responsible for which social service. Furthermore, we will avoid issues with how the governmental sources of revenue are split between the three levels of government.

The government funds certain social services. We group them into industries. The most noteworthy industries are:

- education
- healthcare
- protection/defence
- parks and recreation
- water/sanitation
- support services
- infrastructure
- public transport
- research
- community centres
- land marks
- bureaucracy

Specific examples of what the government spends its money on are:

- sidewalks
- hospitals
- a fountain
- a library
- a heart transplant for a consumerist
- physical rehabilitation services
- bus transportation
- AIDS research institute
- payment to mayor

- judge's salary
- garbage pickup
- water purification
- street lights
- medium security correctional facility
- benches
-

Neither of the above lists is complete nor exhaustive. There are many, many more services that the government provides that aren't mentioned.

To pay for these services, the government has several governmental sources of revenue. They are:

- Selling of Land – the governments earn money by selling land to various consumerists
- Work for Freedom Program – firms compensate the government for work done by prison inmates
- Employment Assistance Program- the government earns money from prospective workers in the form of an interest for assisting them in finding a job
- Accommodation Award Repayment- individuals getting the accommodation award reimburse the government for using the accommodation award as soon as they find a job in the natural or governmental partitions or use their income from the job they have through the command partition
- Issuing Consumerist Savings Bonds- the levels of government sell various savings bonds in return for money needed to pay for goods and services.
- Revenue from government assisted programs- consumerists pay the government some money to board a train, visit a museum or to have their passport processed
- Advertising on Public Property- the government earns money when businesses put advertisements on things like buses, bus stop shelters or trains
- The GCT – a special tax proportional to the output and potential output of the materialist sector
- Standard Gambling Profits- government revenue for operating casinos and selling lottery tickets
- Recycle for Pay Program- government revenue from buying waste and recyclable items and selling them to businesses that process these inputs
- Unemployment Assistance Repayment (UAR) – consumerists employed in the command partition or Laissez-faire labour system give the government a portion of the money granted to them as part of the extra work transfer
- The Command Partition- a section of the economy where most profits are accrued by the government
- Monopoly over the selling of things like marijuana; assuming that they are made legal
- Interest payments from consumerists for using the materialist overdraft
- Financial Punishment- criminals have to pay the government a monetary penalty in addition to their regular (justice) sentence
- Interest from governmental business loan assistance program- when the government makes loans to businesses, the interest is considered government revenue
- Positive balance in the consumerist trade pool- when the government manipulates the consumerist trade pool such that it is positive, the profit goes to the government
- Partial Ownership of Firms by the Government- when the government buys stock of a firm and thus becomes a partial owner of that firm, the dividends from that firm are

considered government revenue

- Government revenue stock- the government issues stock in itself. The money from selling the stock is government revenue
- Premium Savings Bonds- the government issues savings bonds and puts that money in bonds with an even higher interest rate (or a high interest savings account). The interest return is government revenue
- International loan program- the government loans money to a foreign nation. The interest profit can be used by the government for spending
- Avoidance of Debt- By not allowing the nation to descend into debt, the government can save money that is paid on debt financing and use it to pay for social services instead
- Positive balance in the Governmental Market Surplus/Shortage Resolution Program- when the government makes more money from resolving surpluses than it does from subsidies shortages, the profit goes to the government
- Interest from buying international bonds
- Food Geared to Income Percentage
- Wealth Tax
- Positive Personal Income Tax

We can now construct a sort of hypothetical budget to ensure that the governmental sources of revenue can pay for the services we want. Here we also make several assumptions. The population is 1 000 000 people. The budget is based for a whole year.

First the costs:

Universal education:	20 000 000 000.00 þ
ultra universal healthcare:	25 000 000 000.00 þ
protection/defence:	12 000 000 000.00 þ
parks and recreation:	500 000 000.00 þ
water/sanitation:	500 000 000.00 þ
support services:	500 000 000.00 þ
infrastructure:	2 000 000 000.00 þ
public transport:	2 000 000 000.00 þ
research:	500 000 000.00 þ
community centres:	1 000 000 000.00 þ
land marks:	100 000 000.00 þ
bureaucracy:	1 000 000 000.00 þ
anti-unemployment measures	8 000 000 000.00 þ
output maximization measures	8 000 000 000.00 þ

Total cost per year: 81 100 000 000.00 þ

Now the revenue:

Selling of Land –	2 000 000 000.00 þ
Work for Freedom Program –	500 000 000.00 þ
Employment Assistance Program-	500 000 000.00 þ
Accommodation Award Repayment-	1 000 000 000.00 þ
Revenue from government assisted programs-	500 000 000.00 þ
Advertising on Public Property-	500 000 000.00 þ
The GCT –	0 þ

The Positive personal Income Tax-	0 þ
The Wealth tax-	0 þ
Gambling Profits-	16 000 000 000.00 þ
Recycle for Pay Program-	500 000 000.00 þ
Unemployment Assistance Repayment (UAR) –	500 000 000.00 þ
The Command Partition-	24 000 000 000.00 þ
Interest from investing in stocks/bonds-	2 000 000 000.00 þ
Monopoly over the selling of things like marijuana-	2 000 000 000.00 þ
Interest payments from the materialist overdraft-	500 000 000.00 þ
Financial Punishment-	1 000 000 000.00 þ
Interest from governmental business loan assistance program-	3 000 000 000.00þ
Positive balance in the consumerist trade pool-	2 000 000 000.00þ
Partial Ownership of Firms by the Government-	6 000 000 000.00þ
Government revenue stock- the government issues stock in itself-	5 000 000 000.00þ
Premium Savings Bonds-	5 000 000 000.00þ
International loan program-	7 000 000 000.00þ
Avoidance of Debt-	0 þ
Positive balance in the Governmental Market Surplus/Shortage Resolution Program-	2 000 000 000.00þ
Interest from buying international bonds	2 000 000 000.00þ
Food Geared to Income Percentage	1 000 000 000.00þ

Total Revenue per year: 84 500 000 000.00 þ
Balance: 84 500 000 000.00 þ – 81 100 000 000.00 þ = + 3 400 000 000.00þ

In our hypothetical example, the government was able to pay for all of its social services. In fact, it did even better. It made a surplus of almost 3 and a half billion Ignits. The government can do many things with this surplus. For example, it can embark on a program of space exploration culminating with a human landing on Mars. Or it can put it in a high interest paying savings account or high interest paying bond and have even more money in the future to spend.

Note also that the GCT was 0 þ. That means that the consumerists didn't have to pay the GCT. Even though the GCT is a rather harmless tax- it is a tax on the GDCP, it is still better if the funding of government services were accomplished through non tax measures. Furthermore, the positive income tax and the wealth tax were also zero.

For a specific example, let's look at the concrete budget of Ontario, Canada. First, the (actual) expenditures (billions $):

Healthcare	63.5
Education	29.8
Post-secondary Education and Training	11.4
Children and Social Services	16.7
Justice	4.9
Other	23.8
Total Programs	150.1
Interest on Debt	13.3
Total Expenses	163.4
Surplus/Deficit before Reserve	(9.3)
Reserve	1.0

Surplus/Deficit   (10.3)

Now the (actual) revenue (billions $):

Personal Income Tax	36.6
Sales Tax	28.1
Corporations Tax	15.2
Ontario Health Premium	4.0
Education Property Tax	6.1
All Other Taxes	16.2
Total Taxation Revenue	106.1
Government of Canada	25.5
Income From Government Business Enterprises	5.8
Other Non-Tax Revenue	16.8
Total Revenue	154.2

Now we show how the Ontario budget could be funded in terms of consumerism. We assume that the government spends what it normally spends but it has a different source of revenue.

New Revenue (billions $):

Sales Tax-	Does not exist
Corporations Tax-	Does not exist
Ontario Health Premium-	Does not exist
Education Property Tax-	Does not exist
All Other Taxes	
Total Taxation Revenue	
Government of Canada-	25.5
Income From Government Business Enterprises	See "command partition"
Other Non-Tax Revenue	
Selling of Land –	16.0
Work for Freedom Program –	3.0
Employment Assistance Program-	1.0
Accommodation Award Repayment-	2.0
Revenue from government assisted programs-	2.0
Advertising on Public Property-	2.0
The GCT –	0
The Wealth Tax-	0
Positive Personal Income Tax	0
Gambling Profits-	14.0
Recycle for Pay Program-	1.0
Unemployment Assistance Repayment (UAR) –	1.0
The Command Partition-	70.0
Interest from investing in stocks/bonds-	7.0
Monopoly over the selling of things like marijuana-	3.0
Interest payments from the materialist overdraft-	1.0
premium savings bonds-	6.0
Financial Punishment-	1.0
Interest from governmental business loan assistance program-	2.0
Positive balance in the consumerist trade pool-	1.0
Partial Ownership of Firms by the Government-	4.0
Government revenue stock- the government issues stock in itself-	3.0

458

International loan program- 5.0
Avoidance of Debt- 0 þ
Positive balance in the Governmental Market Surplus/Shortage Resolution Program-
1.0
Interest on international bonds 1.0
Food Geared to Income Percentage 1.0
Total Revenue 173.5

Balance = 173.5 – 163.4 = 10.1

Thus, in our example the Ontario government was able to achieve a surplus. It did this without invoking a single tax. This is good news. It can use this money to provide more social services or making investments (in stocks or bonds for example) to make more money in the future.

This was a hypothetical as well as real example of a government's budget. It is quite possible that the government will be able to fund its social programs without going to debt. In fact, as was discovered in this example, the government can have a surplus and have money left over to do interesting things with it.

The Underground Economy

The free-market system has a tendency to induce the development of an "underground economy". By the term underground economy in this sense we mean business operations that are not officially reported. They include lawn mowing, selling goods without a vendor's license (i.e. selling chocolate bars door to door or lemonade at a street corner). They also include operations in the so called black market where illegal or prohibited goods are exchanged secretly. Furthermore there is a tendency for people to do jobs like house renovations or eye exams secretly using cash as a payment for their services. The reason these spring up is that if these transactions are not reported, the entrepreneurs do not have to pay taxes; they are keeping everything they charge.

In the communist system, there is a different kind of underground economy. In the communist system all the means of production are in the hands of the government. However some enterprising develops, where buyers and sellers exchange goods and services for currency in the free-market sense. This is the extent of the communist system's underground economy. That is the development of a merchant sector. Citizens buy jeans for money. They buy soft drinks for money. They buy running shoes for money. All of these would not normally exist in a purely communist system.

Now let's look at the consumerist underground economy. What do we do regarding small jobs like mowing lawns, baby sitting or selling lemonade? The simplest solution is to put these services and goods in the laissez-faire sector. Since there isn't any income tax, sales tax, corporate tax, etc... these services will no longer be "underground" and there really won't be any serious problems. So mowing one's lawn or babysitting will be dictated by the laws of supply and demand (vs. price). Then, mowing someone's lawn is just as legitimate as teaching French although mowing someone's lawn and teaching French are in different sectors.

Suppose a 10 year old, Jack, wants to make some money. He decides he will mow his neighbour's lawn. They agree that mowing the lawn is worth 5.00 f/hour. It takes Jack about an hour to mow his neighbour's lawn. His neighbour gives Jack a check for 5.00 f. Jack takes his check to his local bank. At that time the bank credits Jack's laissez-faire account with 5.00 f and deducts 5.00 f from Jack's neighbour's account. The same reasoning applies to other "underground" transactions such as selling lemonade, selling hot dogs or shovelling driveways.

In the consumerist underground economy, we have the existence of dollarization. That is people start to use dollars instead of the other 3 consumerist currencies. This is clearly a major problem. When a tourist comes to our nation he will have to exchange his dollars for Ignits and Fortals. The private bank takes his dollars (in the form of bank book entries, never cash) and opens up for a him a bank account in terms of dollars. He can exchange this for Fortals using the foreign currency exchange mechanism and Fortals into Ignits using the Ignit-Fortal exchange mechanism. He is then given a book of checks. Every time he wants to make a transaction in a consumerist nation, he simply writes the place of business a check and receives a good or service in return.

Another type of underground economy arises where people begin to oversell or undersell a good or service. This means that they start to sell goods and services for prices that are above or below that set by the central bank. Of course, this is totally benign in the laissez-faire sector but it does present problems for the other 3 sectors.

An underground economy can develop in a free-market system. Also an underground economy can develop in a communist system. It is possible but unlikely that there will be an underground economy in the consumerist system.

Gratuities and Charities

The question arises: what are the circumstances regarding a tip? A gratuity is a payment for a service that is not official but the buyer pays if he thinks the service provider did a good job or is in other words saying "I appreciate the fine job you did". Waiters, hair dressers, taxi drivers and newspaper couriers rely on gratuities. People also receive gratuities from helping someone out as in the case of assisting someone across the street or helping someone with their groceries.

Gratuities fall under the laissez-faire sector. When someone gives a tip, they do not give a bill or a coin since these do not exist under our system but rather they write a check in Fortals. The peculiar thing about gratuity payments is that the payer is not obliged to pay anything but rather he pays as a way of saying "thank you" to someone. The amount of the gratuity is determined by the person giving the gratuity and there is no price function for tips. Therefore the payer can give as little or as much as he wants for there is no accommodational markdown on a gratuity payment.

The idea of a charity exists to give people or others who are in desperate need of assistance and help. These people usually cannot make money on their own and their living conditions are horrible. Charities exist to help people who are afflicted by war, children starving in third world countries, people recovering from bad weather conditions like a tsunami or mistreated dogs that were abused by their owners. All these types of charities can be supported in consumerism.

Gratuity payments must be made to the intended person in the form of a check or with a debit machine (if we are talking about waitress tips). Under no circumstance can a person give gold investment certificates or silver investment certificates as a gratuity payment, for example a tip. This constitutes fraud. Consumerist needs to be a cashless society where exchanges are in the form of bank book entries.

What if someone wants to give a gift to a charity to help poorer people in another country? Suppose someone sees starving kids who cannot write in a far off place and wants to help them. In such a case the person can give a donation to the poor people. The donation must be in Fortals not Ignits or Norses. Furthermore the donation can be of any size the donor wants.

Circumstances regarding gratuities and charities arise often in consumerism. With these two forms of money transfers, people can earn tips and poor people who need help can get assistance.

Thrift

We define thrift as the active undertakings of consumerists to spend as little money as possible. It is consistent with the idea of greed and greed is an important factor if an economic system is to work in a practical sense. Thrift is very important in the free market system. It also appears in a certain sense in accommodation based consumerism.

Generally speaking, whenever consumerists engage in actions to directly save the money that they have, we call this thrift. In consumerism there are two basic types of thrift. One is thrift by quantity and the other is thrift by good/service category. In both ways the consumerist is able to conserve on the money he spends.

In the case of thrift by quantity, a consumerist saves money by buying less of the same product given a fixed price function that is based on quantity. For example, if all meat (or all pork meat) costs 5.00 ☉ per kg, a consumerist can engage in thrift by buying less pork back ribs than more. So he buys 1 kg of pork ribs rather than 2 kgs of pork ribs. Thus instead of paying 2 kg x 5.00 ☉/kg = 10.00 ☉ for the ribs he pays 1 kg x 5.00 ☉/kg = 5.00 ☉ for the ribs. He pays less but has less ribs to cook and eat.

As another example of thrift by quantity we can have a consumerist buying milk. Let's say for this case that all dairy products (soy milk, goat milk, chocolate milk, homogenized milk, skim milk, kefir) cost 2.00 ☉/litre. This value is exemplary of course and need not be such in our real economic system. A thrifty consumerist would buy 2 litres of milk instead of 4 litres of milk to save money. So, instead of paying 4 L x 2.00 ☉/L = 8.00 ☉, he pays 2 L x 2.00 ☉/L = 4.00 ☉. He saved 4.00 ☉ but has less milk to drink. Perhaps the consumerist is more careful in how much milk he drinks.

Another basic type of thrift is by good/service category. In this case, the consumerist buys a good or service in another category. For example, a consumerist is planning to cook dinner for the night. All meat (or all beef) costs 4.00 ☉ per kg. Alternatively, all pasta costs 1.00 ☉ per kg. In this case, the consumerist shopper has the option of buying the highest quality beef; that is the best quality beef he can chose or the highest quality pasta, that is the best quality pasta he can chose. The shopper buys 2 kg of pasta instead of 2 kg of beef. So he pays 2 kg x 1.00 ☉/kg = 2.00 ☉ instead of 2 kg x 4.00 ☉/kg = 8.00 ☉. He saves money and has a tasty pasta dinner to cook for the night.

A positive aspect of this consumerist thrift is that it doesn't hurt quality selection. When people buy goods/services, they are able to obtain the ones of highest quality. Whether they chose to buy pasta or meat for dinner, the pasta or meat will be of the highest quality (of the utmost desirability).

Thrift is prominent in free market capitalism. It also exists to some degree in consumerism. In consumerism we have thrift by quantity and thrift by good/service category. Neither of these interfere with quality selection.

Free Goods and Services

This section is about free goods and services. These include birthday presents, Christmas presents, wedding gifts, in store free samples and surprises in cereal boxes. They are characterized by the fact that the recipient receives the goods without paying for them.

Many grocery stores offer free samples of foods to taste for customers. This free sample may help the firm in its operation. Although the customers do not pay for the free sample, if they like what they try, they may be more willing to buy the product. Free samples are a great way to promote goods and help the firm make profit.

Let's take the case that occurs when a free product comes with another good. For example a juice maker comes with a set of knives. The problem is that in the transaction of the juicer, the knives are not counted towards the GDCP. The benefit is that the consumerists receive more goods. Also, the firm is able to sell its products more quickly. Since the system is designed with the consumerist in mind the benefits outweigh the costs. The consumerist is helped directly; i.e. he receives free goods. And the consumerist is helped indirectly; i.e. the firm achieves its aim of selling goods.

It is necessary to allow for giving and receiving of gifts for special occasions (i.e. birthdays or Christmases). The difference here is that the gift is paid for- the gift giver bought the gift from a store (a radio from an electronics store for example). Since the gift giver bought the present, it is now his and he has the right to give it to anyone he wants as a present. The gift receiver thereby receives the gift for free.

There is a very important stipulation regarding free goods. When a firm gives a free product to a consumerist along with the things he bought during a transaction, the good must be of a different family (taxon). For example, when someone is buying a battery, he cannot receive another battery for free. This injures quality selection as a different quantity of the good, in this case batteries, is given than set by the price function. Likewise, when someone buys a set of 5 knives, he cannot get a 6th knife "for free". He could receive however, a free juicer.

Sometimes the giving of free goods takes a different form. For example, a coffee store gives free milk, cream or sugar to someone who buys a cup of coffee. If the coffee outlet does this voluntarily, it should be fully encouraged. The extra cost of the milk or sugar is so small yet it makes the coffee more enjoyable than if someone had to drink the coffee without anything or pay extra for the milk and sugar.

In the laissez-faire sector promotions, sales and discounts are encouraged. A laissez-faire firm is permitted to carry out any event that helps it attract customers and increase its profits. This is analogous to the government consumerist spending reimbursement.

The giving and receiving of free goods and services is not to be discouraged. Although free goods and services are not recorded in the GDCP, consumerists as well as producers benefit greatly from their availability. The economy benefits from the existence of free goods.

Pre-Owned Goods

We must know what to do with used goods. By used goods we mean those goods that are not new as they have been enjoyed by a previous customer. Examples of used goods include old cars, pre-owned computer games or used hockey skates. We do not include houses or living accommodations in this as these are of a somewhat different nature.

Let's talk about a concrete example. Let's use cars. All automobiles have the same price function. Let's say that it is 10 000.00 Θ/car. It would seem logical that there should be some sort of "pre-owned markdown" on used items since they are clearly at a disadvantage in their goods family. That is used goods should cost less than new ones. However this leads to absurdities. A used economy car with not too many features would cost less than a limousine. A used sofa would cost less than a new one. If a used limousine costs less than a new one people would buy the used one. Consumerists would then not be receiving goods of the highest quality but will settle for worse quality ones. There will be competition in price rather than competition in quality. Thus quality selection would be jeopardized and we must do away with the "pre-owned markdown". All goods in the same family cost the same regardless of how old they are (except in the laissez faire sector).

So what to do with used goods like worn hockey skates or used cars? One option is to make used goods more competitive in a quality oriented market. This might mean painting the car, changing the seats, engine or tire or repairing broken parts. For hockey skates this might mean changing the lasses or mending worn parts.

Another option is to break the goods into parts and sell the parts to a manufacturer. The owner of a used car might still earn a lot of money selling the engine, tires, or glass to someone who needs it. In the case of hockey skates, the blade might be sold and used to make another new hockey skate.

The idea of the recycling-for-pay program may become useful. One can sell the parts of a pre-owned good to the government for profit. For example if someone has used hokey skates, he can take the skates to pieces- plastic, metal, rubber, upholstery- and sell these to the government for some money. The government then sells these items to firms that make use of inputs.

There is yet another thing we could do with used goods that we do not want but are not necessarily garbage. We could export these used goods to poor countries where the country's people could make use of them. For example, an old bike may not be of any value to us but in a third world country it could be very highly prized. Giving our used items to other countries may be a great way of improving our relationships with those countries.

In consumerism we have exportation-importation firms. Essentially, producers of poor quality goods (or consumerists who own used goods) can sell that used good that they no longer need to an exportation-importation firm for less than the good would cost normally in a fixed price system. The exportation firm then sells the used good to another foreign nation for the consumerist price, thus making a profit. In this arrangement, the consumerist trade pool is made use of.

Pre-owned goods are an important topic in an economic system. We explained why pre-owned goods must not cost less than new ones; i.e. there mustn't be a "pre-owned markdown". There are options that exist for owners of pre-owned goods to trade away their goods.

Hard to Price Items

We come into a difficulty in pricing some goods and services. How do we price something like a painting or a book or art? How do we compare the "Mona Lisa" or the "Last Supper" with a stick drawing some first grader drew? What about books? Do we price them in terms of the number of pages or number of words or subject or what? We must find a coherent way of pricing everything.

We can compare the prices of cars, TV's, fruit and soft drinks using the consumerist approach. The reason is that they have the same essence. But the same is not true for art.

To price books we use the laissez-faire sector. The price of a book is determined by the laws of supply and demand. So some books cost more than others. The price of a book has to cover the cost of printing the book and give the author of the book some type of profit. There is no retail markup as the price set at that the bookstore where the book is sold already incorporates a profit for the bookstore. Suppose that to publish a book it costs 20.00 ₤. The author of the book receives a certain percentage of this called a royalty. A royalty is a percentage of the earnings from selling his or her work of art. It is set by the interaction of authors and book buyers. Let's assume that it is 20%. The bookstore has a mark-up is 35 %. Thus for a certain book, the publisher will sell his or her book for 20.00 ₤ + (0.35 x 20.00 ₤) = 27.00 ₤. The author keeps 27.00 ₤ x 0.2 = 5.40 ₤/book. The book store sells the book for (27.00 ₤ x 0.35) + 27.00 ₤ = 36.45 ₤. Here a mark-up is used twice; once for the publisher to make a profit over the publishing costs; secondly for the bookstore to make some money. The transaction is in Fortals, which is the currency in the laissez-faire sector. To convert Ignits to Fortals and vice versa, one would use the nominal Ignit/Fortal exchange mechanism.

Now let's turn to the production of CD's. To make a CD costs, for example, 8.00 ₤. The royalty is 20% and the retailer earns a mark-up of 35%. Thus the retail distributor makes 8.00 ₤ + (8.00 ₤ x 0.35) = 10.80 ₤. The artist earns 10.80 ₤ x 0.2 = 2.16 ₤ per CD as a royalty. The CD distributor earns 8.64 ₤ per CD. The CD store sells the CD for 10.80 ₤ + (10.80 ₤ x 0.35) = 14.58 ₤. The transaction involves Fortals as it is in the laissez-faire sector.

How about paintings? They are dealt with in the same way as in the free-market. Painters are allowed to sell their paintings for as much as they want to. This involves the idea of auctioning to the highest bidder. It is one of several instances of such a solution. Also under such a method of selling are antiques, collector's items and memorabilia. They are under the laissez-faire sector.

Jewellery is another kind of hard to price item. It is hard to put a good price on a gold or diamond ring or necklace solely using the consumerist pricing method. It makes much more sense to price the various types of jewellery using the laws of supply and demand. So, jewellery is in the laissez-faire sector and the price of jewellery is quoted in fortals.

Some goods are hard to price. A book and a CD are priced and sold in a special way. Some other items, more notably paintings, have to be exchanged using the method of auctioning as in the free-market system.

Trade via Internet

The world is being continuously more computerized. The internet has connected people from all over the world and has opened up new dimensions of trade. Now people can buy things without leaving their homes. They simply click the mouse button a few times and they are the proud owners of a new TV.

Under consumerism, internet trade is encouraged as it helps the consumerists. It provides a wider range of products for a consumerist to purchase. It also makes it easier for certain firms to sell their products.

Internet trade must however fit the parameters of the economic system. The prices of all products must be the same as those set by the central bank for that family (in the GAM sectors) whether they are sold over the internet or not. The goods sold over the internet are treated as if they are sold at the retail level. Therefore the prices of goods sold over the internet have to have the retail mark-up included in them. This means that it is the internet retail company that pays for the shipping and handling. Here's an example. Suppose a company on the internet is selling a microwave. They bought the microwave for 200.00 þ as this is the price set by the central bank for microwaves. The retail mark-up is 25%. Suppose Lester buys the microwave off the internet. The shipping and handling costs 5.00 þ. Lester pays the company 200.00 þ + (0.25 x 200.00 þ) = 250.00 þ. The internet company keeps 250.00 þ – 200.00 þ – 5.00 þ = 45.00 þ. The microwave is in the accommodational sector so all exchanges are in Ignits.

Trade over the internet could involve either the accommodational, materialist or laissez faire sectors. It could involve firms in either the command or natural partition. As discussed above, trade over the internet in the materialist and accommodational sectors is under certain constraints set by the central bank. After these constraints are fulfilled, trade over the internet is simple, convenient and easy.

Trade over the internet is even simpler and easier when it is done through the laissez-faire sector. Here the price of goods and services sold over the internet is totally set by the interaction of those firms selling their products over the internet and those buying their products over the internet. There is no AMD or tax of any sort whatsoever. There may be a Laissez-faire markdown if the benevolent social planner chooses it. Who pays for the shipping and handling is also determined by the interaction of buyers and sellers. Internet trade through the laissez faire sector can be in either the command or natural partitions.

Trade over the internet is desirable under the consumerist system. Such a trade operates as any other form of trade, adhering to the parameters set by the government and the central bank. A trade carried out on the internet spurs the growth of the consumerist economy.

Celebrations and Festivals

A consumerist nation needs more than to satisfy the wants and needs of its people. There are other things in the life of a consumerist citizen that will make living worthwhile. Consumerist citizens desire to enjoy finer things like social events and festivals.

A festival is an occurrence where a large number of people get together to enjoy a special event in life. Examples include music festivals, waterfront festivals and art festivals. People get together to have fun and enjoy life even if it doesn't have any direct financial purpose.

Similarly, celebrations give meaning to the lives of consumerists. Examples include October fest, medi-evil get-togethers and comic book celebrations. These provide consumerists with purpose in their lives.

Also included in this section should be sports gatherings. A sports team, whether hockey, soccer, baseball or basketball, should entertain a large number of people even though it doesn't provide anything of tangible value.

The government of a consumerist nation should set aside several days a year for holidays and celebrations. These shouldn't be exceedingly often but it will be good if there are between one and two holidays per month. These holidays will allow consumerists to balance work and life enjoyment.

Celebrations, festivals and sports gatherings are important in a consumerist nation. These provide a relief from the daily routine of supplying consumerists with goods and services. Celebrations and festivals give meaning to the life of consumerists.

Budget Deficit and Surplus

By deficit we mean having less money to spend than required. One spends more than earning in revenue. By surplus we mean having more money than able to spend. One earns more in revenue than spending on services and goods. We deal with the budgets of governments in particular. That is the federal, provincial and municipal levels of government.

The government (all levels) has several sources of income, one being the GCT. They have several others which we mentioned previously. The central bank grants the GCT to them. Each level of government receives 1/3 of the GCT. The federal government earns the entire 1/3 while the other two levels of government earn income based on population.

In this section, for simplicity, we talk about the budget of the federal government. The budgets of the other two levels are similar.

The actions taken during surpluses and deficits are simple. If there is a surplus, there are 3 choices. One is to provide more services and increasing spending. Another choice is to cut the GCT, the positive income tax and wealth tax or eliminate them altogether. Also, the government can buy stocks and bonds and have a stream of income for the future. If there is a deficit there are also 3 choices. One is to raise the GCT. Another is to cut services and spending. The government can also use some of the measures designed to raise government revenue.

Let's do some calculations. The GCT is 30%. The output of the materialist sector is 1 000 000.00 Θ. The government gets 0.3 x 1 000 000.00 Θ = 300 000.00 Θ

The federal government gets 1/3 x 300 000.00 Θ = 100 000.00 Θ. The provinces/ states and municipal governments get 1/3 of this amount each depending on the population each state or municipality has.

If the government made 100 000.00 Θ and spent only 80 000.00 Θ, this would represent a surplus. This would leave purchasing power for the future. Sometimes having a surplus is useful as having money to spend in the future is good when the money may be needed more.

Deficits are possible. The government can earn more money than through the GCT. It operates in the governmental sector using Norses. But it can raise money by selling Consumerist Savings Bonds (whether federal, provincial or municipal) which are parts of the accommodational sector and investing that money or expanding the role of the command partition. Then, the Ignits are directly used to purchase government services and goods. If the government wants to make more money it ought to raise the GCT or sell even more Consumerist Savings Bonds. In case the government suspects it will not make enough money to cover its expenses, it must start to cut the least essential services. Other ways of raising money quickly include the selling of licenses and permits as well as the selling of land and building more casinos.

From time to time, surpluses also occur. The government has more purchasing power than before as they have higher revenue than their expenditures. Consumerists love a budget surplus because then the government can do three things each of which benefits the consumerists tremendously. One option is to lower the GCT (and the other two taxes) – or eliminate taxes.

470

This means that more of the GDCP will be going to the General as well as Non-working Consumerist Grants. So consumerists have more purchasing power. The other option is to increase spending on social services. The government could build another hospital, school, library, roads or pay doctors more for their services (since we have ultra-universal health care). The third option is very subtle. During times of surplus, the levels of government should buy stocks and bonds- whether of the consumerist or speculative kind. This creates an alternative stream of income for the levels of government. Let's do some calculations. Suppose that the federal government had a revenue of 100 000 000.00 þ and spent 80 000 000.00 þ leaving a surplus of 20 000 000.00 þ. Now a hypothetical firm RFVB issues Consumerist General Bonds with a CGBIR of 5 % and a CGBIRF of one month. The maturity is 5 years. If the federal government uses its surplus to buy these bonds it will make money every month and after 5 years it will get all their investment back.

Budgets may from time to time experience deficits and surpluses. Budget deficits and surpluses have several causes. A government has several ways to deal with a surplus and it has several ways to deal with a deficit.

Vacations, Time Off and Maternity Leave

Every working consumerist should be entitled to a vacation. By vacation we mean some time off from work. Consumerists need time to appreciate the things they have or go to a place to relax, enjoy themselves and have fun. Working consumerists should be paid during their vacation.

How long should a consumerist's vacation be? It should be based on time per year and this should be set by the government. The amount of time in a year that a consumerist is entitled to spend as a paid vacation is called the *Yearly Vacation Duration Period*. Suppose it is set at one month. If this is the case, every consumerist working for at least a year can spend 1 month off from work with pay. What about jobs where a worker works less than a year, like a job contract for 6 months? In this case the worker can have half a month of vacation as 6 months is half a year. What if the job contract is for 1 month? In this case the worker is entitled to have a vacation for 2.5 days as 1 month is 1/12 of a year.

The timing of the vacation is set by the bargaining of the workers and the employers. Usually when a worker signs a contract, it will say when he can take his vacation. Also, if a worker wants a vacation at a particular time, i.e. to see his family for a wedding, he may ask his employer for some time off for vacation.

Being able to take a long, pleasant, restful vacation is just as important as making a lot of money. Having some free time and the opportunity to enjoy life make life so much more meaningful. If a man worked hard all his life, amassing a considerable fortune, without taking any time for vacation he will probably really regret it when he is very old. Therefore, in Accommodation based consumerism it is highly encouraged for workers to take enjoyable vacations. Although, usually, the longer the length of the vacation the better, we must balance this with 1) a worker is not doing anything productive for society while on vacation and 2) the employer usually has to pay for the vacation (in terms of lost income and time off vacation).

Sick leave is similar to the Vacation Duration Period. The difference is that a worker doesn't get paid when he gets sick. The amount of time off for sickness is called the *Sick Leave Exemption Period*. It is set by the government. It is usually much shorter than the Yearly Vacation Duration Period. Suppose that the government sets it at 12 days per year. Thus a worker who works at least 12 months is entitled to have 12 days off for sickness.

If a worker is sick, he must first use up his sick leave for time off. If his sickness is longer than the length of the Sick Leave Exemption Period, he can stay off work during his Vacation Duration Period.

It is reasonable that a worker, from time to time, will get sick. He may have the flu, the cold or an infectious problem. The employer ought to give him or her some days off to recuperate and get better. This is obviously better than the worker spreading the flu to other employees. However, there should not be any pay for taking days off- unless this illness is prolonged or prohibits the worker from being productive and effective. If workers were paid for being sick, we could anticipate an abuse of the system where people would just take the day off because they don't want to work and they would still expect to get paid.

What if a worker becomes injured on the job and cannot work anymore? For example he cuts off his fingers while cutting meat. In such a case, the injured worker receives a severance package from the work he used to be employed in. This is set by the central bank and reflects the extent of the injury, i.e. how severe it is and how career ending it is. This is called the *Injury Severance Payment*.

What about maternity leave? Should a pregnant woman or new mother be paid while she is carrying her baby and taking care of the baby? A mother to be should be paid during her time off. The length of the time she can take to take care for her baby is set by the government.

The circumstances regarding vacations are important for both employers and workers. The same goes for time off, sick leave and injuries. Maternity leave also deserves discussion..

The WC Grant

One of the signs of a well off nation is access to free WC. By WC we simply mean things like toilets, sinks and stalls. In advanced countries consumerists should not be forced to pay for using the WCs. It must be made clear that in this section when we use the term WC we are referring to washrooms. The term WC must not be confused with the same WC we discussed earlier. Then we were talking about working consumerist grants.

In some countries, like Canada for example, there is access to WCs in most restaurants, pubs, gas stations and cafeterias for all people regardless of whether they are a customer. This is wonderful and it has the externality of attracting future customers. The use of a toilet/WC is really not something anyone should be making a profit on.

In accommodation based consumerism we want restaurants, bars, malls to provide WC stations in their premises. It is quite possible that this will happen on its own but if it doesn't we invoke the WC grant. The WC grant is a small payment from a government (let's say the provincial government) so that the place of business provides a decently clean WC facility.

Let's assume that the WC grant is 100.00 þ/month. If a restaurant provides a clean WC, the provincial government gives the restaurant 100.00 þ/month. It can then use this money on things like tables, spoons, plates, glasses, a painting on the wall or a set of knives. Thus the WC grant is an interesting way to spur on the economy especially in the hospitality industry.

In order for the restaurant, bar, pub to get the grant it must pass an inspection by a special WC inspector. The WC inspector will make sure that the WC is clean, that everything works properly and that everything is sanitary. This inspection could be every, let's say 6 months. If it passes, the establishment receives the WC grant every month.

The main people that benefit from the WC grant program are the consumerists who can go to the washroom if they really badly need to go. This is especially important if we are talking about travelling on the highway where facilities can be several kilometres apart.

The WC grant ensures that our consumerists have adequate access to WCs. Establishments earn a grant for providing the WC which they can use to help their business. A society with free WC is much better off than one where there is a price for using the facilities.

Tourism

Tourism is the visitation of foreigners in another country for a while. Many tourists come to relax on a holiday while others come to places of historical or cultural importance. Others visit foreign countries because they have relatives or friends there. In every case a foreigner comes to a country for some time but does not stay there permanently. In every instance, a tourist needs to buy things in the country he is visiting. Thus he must spend money and the local economy prospers. Let's look at tourism as it applies to accommodation based consumerism.

We have two types of tourism. 1) Our citizens visit other countries and 2) Foreigners visit our country. First case 1. Our citizens can only spend Ignits (which must be converted to fortals) when visiting other countries. Tourism belongs to the leisure industry which is in the accommodational sector. These tourists cannot use Norses. However they must exchange Ignits for Fortals and Fortals for foreign currency in order to buy things there; i.e. resort, hotels, meals at restaurants and passes to museums and galleries. We assume for the purpose of this section that our tourist is visiting the U.S. Thus he must exchange Ignits for Fortals and Fortals for U.S. dollars. This is easily accomplished when we know the nominal exchange rate and actual exchange rate. Using the actual exchange rate, Fortals are converted into dollars and dollars into Fortals. We have already discussed how the nominal exchange rate is set (using calculations involving real exchange rates and their weights in trade at the consumerist trade pool). The actual exchange rate is based on the nominal exchange rate. So suppose someone has 500.00 ₤. The actual exchange rate is $1.50/₤. This tourist can exchange his Fortals for 500.00 ₤ x $1.50/₤. While in the U.S. our tourist sees a movie, goes to a museum, eats a meal at a restaurant and stays at a hotel. These cost respectively, $12.00, $20.00, $60.00 and $400.00. Thus he spends $492.00 on his trip. Usually a tourist must have transportation to his destination. We have not incorporated this into our calculations yet. We do so now. In order to get to the U.S. and to comeback our tourist must take a plane. This trip costs 300.00 ₤. Our tourist must pay 300.00 ₤ to go to the U.S. and return.

Now for case 2; where a visitor comes to our country. This visitor is from the U.S. and has $500.00. He is granted foreign visitor status and thus can exchange Ignits for things in the materialist sector. The actual exchange rate is $1.50/₤. His trip and return ticket cost him $ 200.00. So now he has $ 300.00. This is equivalent to $300.00 x 1.00 ₤/$1.50 = 200.00 ₤. He wants to buy the following things: a stay at a hotel, a trip to an art gallery, a movie and a meal at a restaurant. The stay at the hotel costs 70.00 þ for 3 days. Tickets to the art gallery cost 15.00 þ. Visiting the art gallery belongs to the leisure industry that is part of the accommodational sector. The chance to see a movie also belongs to the leisure industry that is part of the accommodational sector. To buy things in the materialist and accommodational sector he needs to exchange fortals for Ignits. There is a problem with the restaurant meal as it is in the hospitality industry that is part of the materialist sector. The materialist sector operates with Norses but Norses must not be exchanged for dollars or vice versa. What happens is that the tourist can use Ignits in the form of a check. Keep in mind that 1.00 þ is always equal to 1.00 ⊙ but that they cannot be exchanged directly for one another. So suppose that the meal cost 50.00 ⊙. The American tourist gives the waiter a check for 50.00 þ When the restaurant takes the check to the bank, the bank credits the restaurant with 50.00 þ and deducts 50.00 þ from the American visitor's account.

During tourist activities, bank deposits are used as opposed to actual cash. When our tourist visits the U.S. he has 500.00 þ = 500.00 ₤ .The actual exchange rate is \$1.50/₤. The bank turns the 500.00 ₤ in his account to \$750.00. When in the U.S. he can sign checks on his account in dollars. This money is transferred from his account to the business owner he dealt with in the U.S.

Suppose a tourist from the U.S. visits our country. He has \$500.00. Cash is not acceptable. He must pay with check. If he spends all his money \$500.00 is deducted from his account and the right amount of Ignits is put into a domestic Ignit account belonging to the firm he had a transaction with.

Tourism is good for both the tourist and the international economy. We looked at the case where a visitor from our country visits another. We also looked at the case where a foreigner takes a trip to our country.

The Institutionalized Population

Here we talk about the institutionalized population. This refers to the part of the general population that is separate from the rest as they are specially cared for or are in a special situation. Who is counted as being in the institutionalized population? Those in jails or correctional facilities, the people in hospitals or group homes, those in retirement homes and those in the army.

How is their welfare taken care of? These people are taken care of by the government spending through the tax (GCT) and other sources of revenue like profits from the command partition.

Those in jail do not get paid the consumerist grant. Neither do they get welfare money. Their food and clothing is paid by the government. The care of inmates is the responsibility of either the federal or provincial governments. The same applies to those in correctional facilities.

People that are in the hospital for a short time (i.e. a few days) still receive the consumerist grant. However those in the hospital long term do not receive the general consumerist grant as they are not working. The functioning of the hospital is paid by the government and the government provides those in the hospital long term with what they need (food, bed, clothes). The same is true for those in group homes and retirement homes. All their food and accommodation is paid for by the government. Thus they do not receive the consumerist grant; either general or non-working.

The situation is different for armed forces personnel. They are paid by the government but are given the general consumerist grant since they are working. Since those in the army, navy, and air force do a tremendous service protecting us and serving our country it would be disrespectful if they earned the Non-Working Consumerist Grant as opposed to the General Consumerist Grant. Since they give us so much of their selves and their time they certainly do deserve the General Consumerist Grant.

There is a special program for inmates of prisons and correctional facilities. Basically they perform some sort of work in exchange for a shorter prison sentence. For example, they can be made to mop the floors, cook meals for other inmates or sort garbage. These jobs must be such that no one can be injured nor can the inmate escape. They must be low-risk jobs with an occupational complexity rating < 2.5. In exchange for this work the inmates have time taken off their sentence. So, for example, if an inmate worked 10 hours sweeping the floors of the prison, he would have 4 hours deducted of his sentence. The idea behind this is that it will increase the output of the economy while leaving more demanding jobs for more skilled workers, i.e. those outside bars and with some education. This is called the Work for Freedom program.

Those in institutions are treated differently from the rest of society. Their welfare is ensured by the government. Save for armed forces personnel, they do not usually receive the consumerist grant, either the General or the Non Working kind.

Raises and Promotions

The capitalist free market system utilizes raises and promotions to encourage workers to work harder and more productively. By raises we mean making more money than before in one's career. By promotion we mean getting a job position that is more prestigious than the previous one. For example, one that requires more responsibility. In accommodation based consumerism there are also raises and promotions but they function a little bit differently than in the free-market case.

First of all, wage functions and salary functions are fixed for a family of very similar occupations. For example, all cashiers make 10.00 þ per hour. This would apply to cashiers in grocery stores, convenience stores, shoe stores, clothing stores, and cafeterias. This wage function is created by the central bank and mustn't change. Although the wage function can't go up, it also can't go down. So in the case of cashiers, their wage function will never go below 10.00 þ per hour.

So then, if wage functions for a family of similar occupations are fixed, how do people get a raise? The answer is that they move into a job that pays more. Back to our example of cashiers. A cashier is paid 10.00 þ per hour. However a department manager is paid 15.00 þ per hour. So, then a cashier may become a department manager if she does a great job as a cashier and the boss of the firm likes her work ethic.

Now let's talk about promotions. When a worker moves up in the business hierarchy, we say that he is getting promoted. As an example, we have a dishwasher who makes, like all dishwashers, 6.00 þ per hour. He does well and is promoted to food prep. These workers earn 9.00 þ per hour. He does well in this too and he is rewarded and moves up to full line cook. That position pays 15.00 þ per hour. In this case, the worker gets a better and better job in terms of prestige and respect because he is hard working and puts effort into his work. Also, in the process of being promoted he gets a raise every time he earns a better job thus making more money.

In consumerism we need the occurrence of raises and promotions. They are a great way to encourage workers to work hard. Hard workers are clearly better for the economy as a whole. However, this has to be balanced with the fact that workers in the same occupation or very similar one all receive the same wage/salary function.

It was mentioned previously and we will reiterate it again that wage/salary functions must be fixed. It may seem that a raise in the same profession is a reward for hard work. Actually it is not, not at all. All it does is it contributes to the inflationary spiral. An increase in wage/salary functions only creates inflation which is something we don't want in consumerism. In order for a worker to get an actual raise, he must find an occupation that pays him more.

Another problem with raises is that unions may try to force an employer to give the workers a raise thinking that the workers deserve more. This must be strictly forbidden. Although unions can fight for better working conditions, safety and a better working environment, they must never interfere with the wage/salary function system of consumerism.

Raises and promotions are clearly a good idea. However, there are special constraints as to how they are made use of in consumerism. By holding onto the idea of raises and promotions, consumerism retains in some sense a key fundamental idea of free market capitalism.

Retirement

As workers age, they will reach a point where they will not be able to work anymore. After having contributed to society for so long, society should help them in their time of need. Accommodation based consumerism makes sure that those who reach an age where they can't work are still well cared for. Retirement is the concept of society helping those who contributed to society by working but who are now no longer to work due to old age.

First of all, those that retire need not be concerned about services from the governmental sector. If a retiree needs hip surgery, eye surgery, assistance from a dentist or protection from the police or service from the fire department, he, like everyone else in consumerism, can get it. These public services are provided publicly by the government and are funded through various ways including the GCT, profits from the command partition etc.

Workers, even though they may be old, continue to be granted Norses to spend on the materialist sector. Instead of a general consumerist grant, they are granted the non-working consumerist grant. Since they aren't working they are granted less than those that do. When they stop working they still need Ignits to spend on the accommodational sector.

The government sets a minimum age at which a worker can retire. This is called the *Minimum Retirement Age*. If workers cherish their jobs and want to work past that, they can.

The government- not the central bank- grants those beyond the minimum retirement age a sum of money in Ignits. The government determines the amount of each payment. This is called the *Retirement Pension Allowance*. The money for this grant is obtained through the tax system and other sources of revenue we discussed previously.

A retiree may still want to buy goods and services in the laissez faire sector for example jewellery or antiques or books. The laissez-faire sector uses a different currency- fortals. To buy things in this sector, the retiree must exchange the Ignits he was given through the retirement pension allowance into fortals at the private bank using the nominal Ignit-Fortal exchange mechanism.

Past a certain age, a worker can retire. Those that retire are cared for by our society. The government grants money to retirees to spend on the accommodational sector while retirees still receive a grant from the central bank for materialist goods.

Distribution of Income

In this section we compare several philosophies of distributing income. Basically, "distribution of income" refers to how the economic pie is divided. We compare utilitarianism, liberalism, and libertarianism. Then we contrast these with consumerism.

Libertarianism is the idea that income is created by individual people of a society not society itself. Distribution of income by the government takes some people's money and gives it to others. The idea that the final distribution is just regardless how unequal it is, is based on a process of determining the distribution of income that is fair. Libertarianism was founded by Robert Nozick. Libertarians claim that it is more important for opportunities to be equal than for income to be equal. The government's objective should be to safeguard individual rights and that all people should have the same chance to utilize their talents. Besides this, the government has no right to change the final distribution of income. (Mankiw, 2002) Libertarianism is very popular among free-market proponents.

Utilitarianism was founded by Jeremy Bentham and John Mill. The objective of this philosophy is to use the logic of individual decision making in the context of matters regarding public policy. The government's goal is to maximize the utility or level of happiness and satisfaction of everyone in society. It is based on diminishing marginal utility. The government must strive to attain a more equal distribution of income. The redistribution of income increases utility. The argument for utilitarianism is this. Jason and Nick are two workers. Jason earns $200 000.00 and Nick earns $100 000.00. By taking a dollar from Jason and giving it to Nick, Nick's utility increases but Jason's decreases. Utilitarians do not want completely equal distribution of income because this would take away the incentive to work. (Mankiw 450-451, 2002) Utilitarianism has many supporters.

Liberalism was created by the philosopher John Rawls. It tries to find a "just" distribution of income. It is hard for people to set rules of a just society because people's point of view is distorted by how much they have now, whether they were born into a poor or rich family, their education, whether they are lazy or hard working, etc. Liberalists propose an "original position". This is a position where all people get together before they are born to determine the distribution of income. In this scenario they would be indifferent about where they would end in life. If people before they are born do not know whether they will be well off, badly off, or medium off, they would naturally be concerned about being poorly off. Liberalists thus propose as public policy trying to increase the welfare of the poorest individual in society. The maximin criterion is to maximize the minimum utility. Liberalism advocates public policy directed at equal income distribution because this increases the standard of being of the worst off. This doesn't lead to a total egalitarian society since it would kill incentive. (Mankiw, 2002) The main goal of liberalism is to have a just society in an economic sense.

Another important concept is the productivity principle. It states that all people should receive the monetary equivalent of that which they personally produced through human resources and non-human resources. The harder one works, the greater his productivity. Therefore the greater his reward should be.

Finally let's look at consumerism. Consumerism stresses that it is important that people have a strong incentive to work. There shouldn't be any redistribution of income. What a worker earns he can decide to spend on things that enhance his quality of life. Under consumerism it is also important to eliminate poverty. There should be no poor. But what does it mean to be "poor"? In the free-market system whether a person is poor or not depends on his income or the combined income of his family. Analysts use cost of living analyses and other measures. Yet most economists agree that there are problems with this type of definition of poverty. Suppose that the poverty line was $20 000.00. If there was a massive deflation and one could buy a 3 storey house for $1000.00 then this person would be rich, even though he had little money, as his ability to own assets increases, In Germany 1n 1919, a person with a billion Marks was considered extremely rich. There came about such a massive hyper-inflation that in 1923 a trillion Marks was worth $1.00. This person was now a beggar. Again suppose someone had $20 000.00 and suppose that this was low enough to call him poor. If this person moved to an impoverished nation like Rwanda, Chad or Cameroon, with $20 000.00, this person would be among the richest in the country.

Consumerism defines poverty in another, better way. The definition is more qualitative, subjective and relative than it is quantitative, objective and absolute. A person who rides a bicycle is poor relative to a person who rides a limousine who is rich. A person who walks around in dirty rags is poor relative to a person who walks around in a business suit with a tie who is rich. A person who eats potatoes for dinner every day is poor relative to a person who eats lobster whenever he wants who is rich. A person who sits on a 3-legged 60 year old wooden stool is poor relative to a person who relaxes on an armchair who is rich. A person who is entertained by a ham radio is poor relative to a person who is entertained by a home theatre who is rich. Poverty is a function of the quality of the assets a person owns as well as the services one has access to. If we want to eliminate poverty we need to give all people goods and services of the highest quality. This is accomplished through the idea of "quality selection". Firms, for the most part, compete to give customers goods and services of the highest quality as the prices they can charge for them are set by the central bank. This has the effect that only goods of high quality are produced and goods of high quality are bought. This eliminates poverty as we have defined it.

In consumerism there is not a single economy like the other 3 philosophies assume. There are 4 sectors; the accommodational, materialist, laissez-faire and governmental. In order to eliminate materialist need, all individuals, with some exceptions, receive from the central bank income equivalent to the output of the materialist sector. With this money consumerists can purchase materialist goods and services. All working consumerists receive a grant of the same size.

Consumerism is the true land of opportunity. Everything is done to make sure that one's business will flourish. An entrepreneur can amass an unlimited amount of income for contributing to consumerism. Furthermore several parameters like the profit reward transfer and the capital reinvestment transfer encourages many businesses to open and prosper, hiring the people in consumerism.

To encourage people to contribute to society, they earn another currency which they can spend on goods and services in the accommodational and laissez-faire sectors. The more they contribute to society, the more money they earn. Therefore there is at the same time a large gap between the rich and not-so-rich in the accommodational sense and no gap between the rich and not-so-rich for working consumerists in the materialist sense.

Those consumerists who do not work or contribute to society earn less money to spend on the materialist sector so as to encourage them to work. For those who cannot contribute to either sector of the economy, the government provides accommodational welfare (housing, utilities) and money. Absolutely no one is homeless as everyone is granted the Accommodational Award if they desire it. However this is hardly redistribution as those on welfare have to pay back a portion of everything the government provided them while on welfare. This is another incentive to discourage idleness.

Consumerism agrees, to some degree with the other philosophies we previously discussed. Consumerist thinking advocates the idea that there must be opportunity for workers to work and people to use their talents. Furthermore, the distribution is rather just regardless of how unequal it as and the government has no right to take one's money and arbitrarily redistribute it.

Consumerism also supports the idea that those who are least off should be well taken care of. To that end we provide accommodation for all who are homeless, and there are quite a few measures designed to eliminate unemployment. Furthermore, poverty is remedied as we have many, many anti-poverty measures.

However, consumerism does not really support utilitarianism. In consumerism we don't take one Ignit or Fortal from one worker only to give it to another worker. If someone wants money, they have to work for it, at least in the accommodational and laissez-faire sectors. Consumerism is so constructed that there is an abundance of work for all who want to work.

There are different philosophies of income distribution. There is utilitarianism, liberalism, and libertarianism. These are contrasted these with the consumerist philosophy of income distribution.

Externalities

An externality is a situation where one person affects another without compensating him. An externality can be positive or negative. An example of a positive externality would be a mathematical formula. Once a person finds it, everyone else benefits from it for free. An example of a negative externality would be pollution. If a company dumps toxic waste into a river without paying for it and the pollutant harms the river users, then this is a negative externality.

Free-market economists acknowledge that there is a trade-off between externalities and production. In order for some businesses to prosper, they need to pollute; i.e. a paper mill makes pollution as it creates jobs and paper. They contend that some pollution is necessary to have a strong economy. In the free-market economy, the solution to the pollution externality is solved using quotas. Each firm that pollutes has a right to dump a certain amount of pollution into a river. Firms can trade quotas with each other so that companies that pollute more have a right to do so and those that do not can sell their quotas. This can be a useful solution. Suppose that there are two firms. One has dumped 100 L of ooze into a river and firm 2 has dumped 200 L of ooze into a river. The river is polluted with 300 L of ooze. So the government sells quotas to the companies that restrict only 10 L of ooze to be dumped into a river by a company in a month. The two companies trade their quotas so that firm 1 can dump 3 L of ooze and firm 2 can dump 7 L of ooze. This is a rather good way of limiting the pollution in a river.

The consumerist solution to externality is based on the proposition that there does not necessarily exist a trade-off between an externality and productivity. The solution strives to eliminate pollution while maintaining a high standard of firm functioning. It is not impossible to promote a healthy environment as well as a strong industry. The concept can most easily be grasped using the negative externality of smoking. Smokers like to smoke. Non smokers on the other hand can't stand the smoke. We segregate a small section of a building and set it aside for smokers and we leave all other sections for non-smokers. In the smoking section the smokers can smoke all they want. However, the non smokers are not harmed or interfered with. Thus an externality has been destroyed without hurting output or smoker's functioning (smoking).

Let's apply this logic to the case of river pollution we examined above. Rather than aim for a policy that slows down an externality, the government should try to completely eliminate it. The polluting firm can buy a portion of land around its facilities where it can pollute all the solid waste it wants as long as this waste does not go into other areas sectioned off for non-polluters.

A polluter can buy a river or a section of a river where it is free to dump all the waste it wants. It can't buy major rivers that others want to enjoy; i.e. for fishing, drinking or swimming. If the polluting firm's pollution spills over to other areas beyond their pollution jurisdiction, they must be ordered by the government to perform a complete clean up of that area. The company that produces waste ought to find a way to get rid of it without polluting at a cost to the polluter. This is prescribed by the government and may involve using waste storage facilities or the destruction of waste. Polluters of ooze can dump their ooze into their private disposal units especially suited for getting rid of ooze. To combat this dumping of pollutants there should be a government agency or ministry that oversees that all waste is either destroyed or disposed of safety.

In many industrialized nations there is a tremendous negative externality problem where factories (e.g. steel makers or car assembly plants) emit dirty toxic smoke into the air. Certainly our quality of life would be compromised if we were to completely eliminate these pollution creating institutions. On the other hand we are forced to breathe in polluted disease causing smoke. In consumerism, we remedy the situation thus. The factory is made to emit all of its smoke into a large dome. This dome collects all the smoke the factory can ever produce. As a safety precaution the dome should be made of three separate layers. With this arrangement, the factory can expel all the smoke it wants to as none of it is going into the atmosphere. Clearly, common people are not harmed by pollution while the factory can still maintain its current level of productivity. Meanwhile the factory should strive to find a device (something like a catalytic converter) to break down the pollution-smoke into harmless particles.

Suppose a scientist working for a university comes up with a new theory of the universe. This leads to teleportation. How does this scientist gain from the invention of teleportation? The university pays him to teach and think there. They also pay him to write articles. If John Smith produced a new mathematical formula and wrote an article about it, he would receive money for the article (a price function set by the central bank). Those who read the article are free to use the knowledge provided in the article to advance the cause of humanity. The problem in this case is that the scientist does not get paid by the people who use his theory directly. There are other ways he can benefit. This involves the idea of special rewards. In the consumerist society there should be "achievement awards" where certain people are honoured, receiving money, fame and recognition. Thus in each industry or profession there should be some kind of achievement award. For example, there should be awards for most heroic police officer, most helpful doctor and in the case of the physics community there should be an award for most respected physicist. In this way many positive externalities are overcome.

Bystanders benefit from historic buildings without paying those who restored them. Suppose there is an old hut where the city's founder lived his life. The land could be used to make parking space. However to preserve the building, the government does not allow its destruction. Another option is that the local museum buys the building and offers the building for viewing to interested citizens who are curious about their town's history.

Let's see how we would apply consumerist reasoning to the problem of traffic congestion along a highway. In many major cities, Toronto, New York, Chicago, for example, there is commuter gridlock as people try to go home or go to work. During "rush hours" people can expect to spend some time on the highway. Is there a way to solve this problem? The best solution is to drastically increase the number of lanes in the highway. There may still be traffic congestion with 4 or 5 lanes. Perhaps some with 8 or 9. But if we built our highways with 17 lanes then the chances of traffic are almost non existent. On the positive side, commuters will be able to get between point A and point B much quicker. On the downside the highway will be a little bit bigger. Yet if we built the highway in the right place- a good distance from residential housing and commercial businesses- this shouldn't be a major problem.

The problem of pollution and garbage accumulation can be overcome in consumerism. A person may be careless where to throw his banana peel when there aren't too many garbage cans around. In consumerism, we provide garbage cans every 15- 20 meters (at least in places where there are a lot of people). Now the individual's opportunity cost of throwing the banana peel is very low and he is more likely to throw it in a garbage can as opposed to the ground.

In society there often come about both positive and negative externalities. There is a solution to the dumping of ooze- a negative externality. There is also a solution to the restoration of historic buildings- a positive externality.

An Alternative to the Carbon Tax for Reducing the Carbon Footprint

There has been a lot of talk about implementing a carbon tax on emissions of carbon containing gases. These will make using gasoline to drive one's car much more expensive. The purpose of the tax is to lower the quantity of carbon-containing pollutants emitted into our atmosphere. However, a lot of people do not like the idea of paying more at the gas pump and through other activities. Is there an alternative to the carbon tax that will have the same intended effect without hurting consumerists – in this case those that rely on gasoline ?

A negative externality is the occurrence where an agent in the economy functions in a way as to hurt others without compensating the bystanders. In this part of the book we will talk about negative externalities in general and the externality of carbon pollution specifically. We will provide useful alternatives for eliminating or reducing emissions of carbon containing gases that various governments in Canada (federal or provincial) as well as those in the whole world can use to help the environment without penalizing consumerists with another tax.

The solution to negative externalities in consumerism is based on a common paradigm. Many solutions to negative externalities are in general quite similar. The grand idea is that society should overcome the externality without effecting, for the most part, the functioning of the firms, entities or individuals that produce the externality. This stands in opposition to the accepted idea in free-market capitalism where it is assumed that there must be, of necessity, a trade off between eliminating or reducing externalities and promoting the interests of those who cause the externality.

The general consumerist negative externality paradigm can be most easily grasped with the example of smoking. We have a restaurant, office building, mall or airport. We segregate a small portion of this area and reserve it exclusively for smokers. The rest of the building is absolutely smoke free. In their designated area, smokers can smoke all they want. However, the right of the non-smokers to not have to inhale smoke-filled air is not compromised. Thus we have overcome an externality without effecting output (smoker's right to smoke). This example shows that we can allow functioning (smoking) to proceed without it affecting by-standards. This general framework is the basis of how negative externalities are overcome in consumerism.

Let's apply this reasoning to companies that dump ooze. For example, we have a factory that employs 5, 000 people and makes glue and other toxic chemicals. In their production process they make a by-product (let's call it ooze) and this hurts the environment. The consumerist solution is for the company to buy the nearby land around the factory. This land must be separate from that used by other people for any other uses. On this land the factory can dump/ store/ bury all the ooze it wants to. The ooze itself does not harm anyone else as it is far away from all residential, industrial and commercial property. Thus we managed to eliminate the externality of having ooze pollute the environment while allowing the factory make useful products and employ many workers.

Now that we have a general idea of how to eliminate/reduce externalities without hurting a firm's production, let's apply similar reasoning to carbon pollution which instigated the creation of the carbon tax. Suppose we have a steel-making factory that emits green house gases and makes the air dirty due to pollution. It also hires 4, 000 workers and makes steel which is needed for our modern lifestyle. It would be good if we could find a way for it not to let go any workers and continue making all the steel it needs to while emitting less carbon-containing pollutants. A good solution is to segregate the toxic gas from the atmosphere with a huge balloon-like dome. A dome would envelope around the factory's smoke stack and the factory can emit all the pollutants it wants to into the balloon-dome. As a safety precaution this dome should be 3 layers thick. Now the factory can emit pollutants without hurting the environment.

Similar reasoning can be applied to the case of automobiles. Instead of the gas products from combustion being emitted through the exhaust, it may be possible to create a special compartment on the underside of the automobile. All the gases from combustion are stored in this compartment instead of being released into the atmosphere. About every week, the contents of this compartment are sucked out at a gas station. This idea is reminiscent of what happens in the case of vacuum cleaners. The waste from vacuuming the floor is collected in a waste compartment within the vacuum cleaner unit. Periodically, this compartment is emptied and the waste is emptied elsewhere. In the same way, polluting gases are sequestered on the underside of an automobile in a special collecting chamber. Every once a while these gases are removed at a gas station.

There is another way of solving the carbon foot print problem. If we can take the carbon containing and sulphur containing gases emitted by a factory, say a truck manufacturing factory, and turn this polluting waste into something useful, we would be able to reduce the amount of green house gases put into the environment. The federal government (or perhaps the provincial government) should offer a substantial reward for anyone who finds a device, process or mechanism that converts pollution causing gases emitted by factories and turns them into something that has benefit for society. If we offer $ 30 000 000 (assuming we are dealing with a Canadian scenario) to anyone who finds such a device we will have a powerful weapon for controlling pollution. The reward is substantial enough to motivate many engineers, university students and inventors to find a device that can convert what is now considered "green house gases" into a chemical or chemicals that society needs for other industrial or commercial processes. Once this mechanical process is discovered it can be applied to the smoke stacks of factories to eliminate pollutants in conjunction with the idea of the dome mentioned before. It may even make the dome idea unnecessary or the dome and the device could work together to reduce the carbon foot print.

Another idea to counteract the carbon problem is to find an engine for vehicles (automobiles, buses, vans, trucks, motorcycles) that is an alternative to the internal combustion engine. The government (either federal or provincial) should offer a high reward (perhaps $ 20 000 000) for anyone that finds an efficient engine that does not require hydrocarbons as fuel, is powerful enough to move a heavy vehicle and produces zero gas emissions.

Electric cars are very useful in that they do not produce gas emissions. If we find a car that runs using an engine that is an alternative to the internal combustion engine, this would be useful as these cars would also produce no gas emissions. However, vehicles that use the internal combustion engine do produce a lot of pollution. In order to convince consumerists that they should use electric cars and those with a non-gasoline engine, the government should give a pay incentive to those that buy the cleaner cars. So if all cars cost 10 000 Θ in our system (assuming we are in consumerism) the federal government can reimburse 5 % (500 Θ) to those that buy the electric cars or those that buy cars with the more environmentally friendly engine. In Accommodation Based Consumerism prices are usually fixed for a family of goods or services. However we can make the exception with cars or vehicles that emit carbon containing gases so as to give consumerists the incentive to buy vehicles that reduce the carbon foot print.

There is another solution to lowering carbon emissions that doesn't rely on a carbon tax. Instead of commuters who are going from one place to another, using cars that produce a lot of emissions, these commuters should be encouraged to use public transit; for example buses, trains and subways. These cause much less pollution per person than do cars. To encourage the use of public transportation, the fare for buses and subways should be zero.

Although municipalities often raise money by charging expensive fares for bus rides, this has the effect of discouraging the use of public transportation. Instead of people taking a bus and paying a fare of $ 4.00, the government should charge $ 0.00 and encourage more people to take the bus.

Buses and subway cars should be bigger to accommodate a larger number of people. The more people a bus can transport, the more people can use public transportation and thus reduce the carbon footprint. The standard bus should be about 2- 2.5 x larger than the ones that currently serve most cities.

One major reason people take cars instead of buses is that buses sometimes come every half hour and sometimes every hour. Also, there is no bus service in most Ontario cities between 11:30 pm and 6:00 am. To encourage the use of buses, buses should come every 10-13 minutes and should run through the whole night. There are a lot of people who work night shifts (for example, at a hospital or fire station) that are frustrated that the bus won't transport them in the early hours of the night.

Another reason commuters prefer to take heavy-polluting cars rather than public transport is because not all public transport goes to every location in a city – it only goes to the major streets and intersections. Consumerist theory suggests that the whole transit system should be expended many-fold. There should be an intra- provincial transit system rather than a transit system for every city. The bus, train and subway lines should be vastly expended to go to as many destinations as possible so that given the choice of taking a car and taking public transit, a commuter will find it more economical and convenient to take public transit. It is usually the case that if a commuter has to go to another city he will take a car as it will take take him right to his desired destination. However, if we as a solution, provide an elaborate transit system involving buses, trains and subways that take commuters to any city in the province and (almost) any street in the province, the carbon footprint will be enormously reduced. And it can be done without invoking an unpopular carbon tax.

Another solution to reduce pollution is to reduce gas emissions from vehicles like cars. Perhaps cars should be designed to work on alcohol rather than gasoline. An incentive for this to happen is already in place in consumerism. All products are priced based on family taxonomic structures. Thus gasoline costs the same as propane, kerosene, other fossil fuels as well as alcohol based fuels. Thus if someone or some firm makes a car run on alcohol, they would be making as much per quantity as those that currently produce gasoline.

It may be helpful to encourage the use of forms of renewable energy. We can create a tremendous amount of electricity by creating wind turbines. Assuming they need to be positioned every 100 m in a windy area, we can create a huge number of these wind turbines. Not only will this make more energy than a coal- based or nuclear based power plant, they will also produce virtually no pollution.

To reduce the carbon footprint, we encourage the production of solar powered cars and buses. These provide no pollution and will cost the motorist less than if he had to buy gasoline each week. The solar energy can be gathered when the car is idle and stored in a battery for future use. When it is time for driving, the battery provides energy for the car. If solar powered cars have issues with running low on power, we can encourage perhaps a hybrid solar-gasoline powered car that runs on both gasoline and solar power. To encourage motorists to buy a solar powered or hybrid solar-gasoline powered car, we can create special discounts for the case of cars. Thus if the price of all other cars is 12 000 Θ at a car dealership, the government can give the consumerist 1 000 Θ extra for choosing the solar-gasoline powered car.

Another suggestion is to introduce solar panels to houses. If a house generated electricity using solar panels, this would reduce the use of fossil fuels to heat homes. Also, it would probably cost less to use a solar panel than to provide energy for a home with forms of energy that increase the carbon footprint.

There are several original ways of reducing the amount of carbon emitted into the environment without resorting to taxes. It would be a good idea to expand the transit system and making changes to how it is provided. There should be incentives to consumerists for using more Eco-friendly vehicles. It should be possible to sequester pollution gases so that they do not enter our atmosphere without compromising the efficacy of either vehicles or factories. There should be monetary incentives to produce new technology that will change harmful pollutants into useful chemicals and make cars emit no exhaust fumes. All these ideas, which are roughly in line with the general paradigm of solving negative externalities in consumerism, help both the environment and do not hurt consumerists or other agents economically.

Prostitution, Drugs and Illegal Commodities and Services

There are several goods and services that arise naturally in a free-market society that we may not want to have. They include prostitution, drugs, illegal weapons and other things. They arise in the free-market economy because the people that provide these things can earn money from people who want these things. These activities sometimes go hand in hand with poverty. Whether we want some of these things or services may be considered a political question concerning the government. For example, should we legalize marijuana or prostitution? Which drugs and weapons, if any, should be illegal or prohibited?

Prostitutes do not usually sell their bodies as a first choice. In many cases they are driven to this type of work because they are poor and have little food. If they could find another job paying just as much as a prostitute earns, they would surely choose that job over prostitution. Nevertheless we may, under some circumstances allow some form of prostitution to be legal in some places (like brothels) if the government or society decides there are any benefits to legal prostitution.

The same applies to people who sell drugs. Drug dealers are forced to sell drugs to make money. They are usually stricken with poverty or see selling drugs as a very quick and lucrative way of making money. Given a choice of a job that paid as much as drug trafficking, they would also choose it over drug selling. But we may want to legalize some drugs (like marijuana) so as to control all sales of that product. One of the advantages of legalizing a drug like marijuana is that we can make all sales of marijuana under the control of the government. Thus this would provide another source of revenue for the government in addition to the GCT and profit from the command partition..

Poverty does not exist to the same extent under consumerism as it does under the free-market system. All non-institutionalized consumerists are granted money from the central bank to spend as they wish. Therefore they are less likely to resort to prostitution or drug selling.

It's hard for prostitutes and drug dealers (assuming that we don't want them in our system) to operate in a cashless society. Since consumerism is a cashless society, it is easier to monitor all transactions as they are carried out by banks in bank accounts.

There are several major types of illegal businesses that form in a free-market economy. Poverty is usually the major cause of these. These should not be as prolific under consumerism.

Research, Development and Technology

Here we talk about three related concepts; research, development and technology. By research we mean the investigation into the knowledge of how things work; whether this relates to innovations, inventions or more theoretical things. By development we mean the application of knowledge to attain progress. By technology we mean the level of sophistication of our methods of doing things that promote progress.

Research can be carried out by institutions of higher learning; i.e. universities or colleges, or by private institutions; i.e. firms and corporations. Whether it is carried out in a knowledge or private institution, research has a positive externality. It is in the best interest of our consumerist society that a maximum amount of research is carried out. Almost everyone in society benefits from research.

The carrying out of research is in the accommodational sector if it is done by private institutions and it is in the governmental sector if it is done by universities. The funding of research at the governmental sector is done through the government sources of revenue like the GCT. The funding of research in the accommodational sector is done through firm's payments from their profit. It is not covered by the accommodational markdown. It is included in the firm's "reinvestment in itself". Research done by firms is similar to an investment like hiring more workers, buying more machines or opening another outlet. When a corporation is paying its shareholders their dividends, the amount invested in research is deducted from the profit.

Firms develop when they use knowledge gained from research to expand their firm. This is a form of investment. Firms are encouraged to develop as much as possible. Development involves Ignits as it is in the accommodational sector but there is no accommodational markdown on it. Here's an example. A car factory spends 5 000.00 þ on research on a new motor. The research scientist working for them designs a new type of motor that makes the firm's car 1.8 x faster. The research scientists are paid by the car firm. Like all jobs, theirs is set by the central bank as a wage function. With this new knowledge, the car firm makes their new car with the new motor just invented. They pay 100 000.00 þ to apply the new knowledge of the motor to the cars. Their sales increase by 45% and they make 450 000.00 þ in the first month of introducing the new car. Obviously it was worth researching and developing this new motor.

Technology or the level of sophistication of industry is a measure of how well off a society can be. The level of technology is affected by research and development. The more research done and the more ideas developed, the higher the level of technology. In consumerism a high level of technology is an important goal as it is a factor that affects quality selection. The higher the technology level, the better the quality of products sold and bought. Since all goods and services in the same family are equally priced, it is the level of technology that has the biggest impact on quality and thus true wealth, as true wealth is measured by the quality of assets owned by consumerists.

It is important that our society tries to raise the technology level. The government can do this by employing professors to do research. If the knowledge gained from this is utilized, the technology level rises. Also, firms can increase the technology status by investing in research and development; i.e. car firms can perform tests on their tires to achieve a better tire for consumerists. Restaurants can experiment with flavors and ingredients to come up with the perfect rib sauce. Clothing makers can investigate the composition of their t-shirts to come up with a more comfortable t-shirt. Also, cell phone designers can investigate their products by trying to find a cell phone that is low weight, small and with maximum features. If these ideas are implemented, the level of technology of a society increases. And everybody wins.

We talked about research and its attributes. We talked about development and its characteristics. We talked about technology and its effects. These three concepts are key to a prosperous consumerist system.

A More Complex Demonstration of the System on a Larger Island

We justify this section by recognizing that if our system can work at the micro level, it should work at the macro level. A system that functions well on an island should function equally well on a national scale.

Here we also make a few simplifying assumptions but we abandon some of those that we made during our discussion of the smaller island. There are a limited number of people but there are more than before. People also sell what they make. There is no non-working consumerist grant markdown. Actually the non-working consumerist markdown is 100% so those who do not work are granted the same amount as those who do work. In this analysis producers need inputs but not all inputs are required. Although unrealistic, producers can make their goods very quickly. To simplify things, there are two currencies. The ratio of accommodational to materialist product prices is better balanced. We add more factors such as a private bank, interest rates and a neighbouring island with which to trade. We assume, unrealistically, that all the interest profits from the private bank go to the chairman. We examine how a command partition worker would operate. We ignore the functioning of a laissez-faire sector. We analyze the functioning of a trade pool. Finally to calculate interest we use simple interest not compounded interest.

Let's begin our analysis. There are 26 people. Each person has a name that begins with a different letter of the alphabet. We do this to simplify our task. Our islanders are: Alfred, Betty, Charlie, Daryl, Emma, Fred, George, Hariotte, Ivona, Joanne, Kristine, Lucy, Mickey, Nathan, Oscar, Posy, Quennie, Richard, Susie, Troy, Uma, Vanessa, Wes, Xiu, Yolla and Zlatko.

The size of the island is 500 km^2. The islanders have a neighbour island about 10 km away. The name of their island is Aulesia and the neighbouring island's name is Fraunica.

The first thing the islanders do is elect a leader. How they chose him is a political rather than an economic question so we will avoid answering it. The people elect Alfred as the president. Alfred then creates the central bank and appoints Betty and Charlie as chairman. Another task that that Alfred has to perform is to divide the land for uses. He sets:

-15 % for agriculture
-15% for industry
-10% for conservation
-15% for residential
-15% for commercial

The rest is set aside for division later. Therefore,

-75 km^2 is for agriculture
-75 km^2 is for industry
-50 km^2 is for conservation
-75 km^2 is for residential
-75 km^2 is for commercial

Daryl is in charge of the private bank (not to be confused with the governmental or central bank). He is the chairman of the private bank. All he needs is paper and a pen (which we assume he has). He handles the book entries of the money belonging to the government and consumerists. He also makes loans to consumerists so that they can start and expand their business. He keeps for himself all the interest profits from making loans to islanders. It is clear that when we first start out, there is no money in circulation. The private bank run by Daryl needs to lend money for the other islanders so they can start producing. Thus he grants himself (or the president grants him) an initial amount of capital to get started. He is given 100 þ. He uses this to make loans. Eventually he has to repay this. With this crucial, very important step, the economy can begin.

Betty and Charlie now set up price functions and wage functions. Although they cannot calculate them they can make a coherent system by voting. This is the economic constitution. They set the interest rate that Daryl's bank can charge per loan at 5%. After voting on price functions, their values are averaged. There are 2 currencies- Ignits and Norses. Final goods in the materialist sector are bought with Norses (Θ) and final goods in the accommodational sector are bought with Ignits (þ). Also all inputs are paid for in Ignits from the profit of producers. The central bankers make the retail mark-up = 25%. The following is a list of the price and wage functions they derived:

Wood-	0.50 þ/kg
Shirts-	1.00 Θ/shirt
Shoes-	1.50 Θ/ pair of shoes
Root vegetable-	0.25 Θ/kg
Tree fruit-	0.25 Θ/ kg
Berries-	0.20 Θ/kg
Stone-	0.75 þ/kg
Tree cutting tool-	2.00 þ/each
Textile material-	0.25 þ/kg
Animal hide-	0.25 þ/kg
Beef-	0.25 Θ/kg
Cow-	9.00 Θ/cow
Steel-	0.20 þ/ kg
Cotton-	0.20 þ/kg
Central banker-	5.00 þ/day
President-	5.00 þ/day
Agricultural land-	30.00 þ/km²
Industrial land-	25.00 þ/km²
Residential land-	20.00 þ/km²
Commercial land-	25.00 þ/km²
Building-	x0.01 þ +y2.00 þ + z1.50 þ + a2.00 þ
Where x-	# of square feet of space
y-	# of bedrooms
z-	# of washrooms
a -	# of floors
Work in the command partition	2.00þ/day

At this point all the islanders choose occupations. Emma, Fred, George and Hariotte all work in the accommodational sector. They use stone and wood to make houses. Ivonna makes axes. Joanne and Kristine cut wood. Lucy makes linen. Mickey and Nathan make shirts. Oscar chooses not to work in the natural partition but works in the command partition. His job is to walk around the island to make sure there is no garbage. Posy makes shoes. Richard harvests potatoes. Susie harvests carrots. Troy harvests apples. Uma harvests plums. Vanessa picks blueberries. Wes picks blackberries. Xiu picks cotton. Queenie mines for stone. Yolla raises cattle. Zlatko mines for steel.

We follow the progress of our islanders for a period of several days. Firstly, Joanne, Kristine, Richard, Susie, Troy, Uma, Vanessa, Wes, Xiu and Yolla must buy the agricultural land they need to make their goods. To buy this land however, they must borrow from the private bank run by Daryl. The interest rate is 5% (simple interest). They each buy 5 km² of land. So they each pay 5 km² x 30.00 þ/km² = 150.00 þ + 5% interest. Since initially all the land is owned by the government, all the money from the purchase of agricultural land goes to the government.

Ivonna, Lucy, Mickey, Nathan, Posy, Queenie and Zlatko have occupations that require industrial land. Each islander buys 5 km² of land with the money they borrow from Daryl and the interest rate is again 5%. The money goes to the government. They each pay 5 km² x 25.00 þ/km² = 125.00 þ.

At this point we see that some land has already been bought. 50 km² of the original 75 km² of agricultural land has been bought. Also 35 km² of the original 75 km² of industrial land has been bought.

It's visible that some of the producers on the island require inputs. Namely, wood cutting requires axes and axes require steel. Shirts require linen and linen requires cotton. Shoes require leather and leather requires cattle. Houses require stone and wood. Thus those islanders that make something that requires inputs cannot manufacture them unless they acquire these inputs.

Before the islanders can produce anything they need inputs. They borrow from the bank money to buy from the island of Fraunica. The price per cow is 8.00 þ/cow on Fraunica (in our currency) and 9.00 þ/cow on Aulesia. Yolla buys 3 cows from Fraunica. She pays 27.00 þ + 5% interest which is 27.00 þ + 1.35 þ = 28.35 þ. This she borrows from the bank. The Fraunicans receive 3 x 8.00 þ = 24.00 þ and the trade pool gets 3.00 þ. The bank run by Daryl gets 1.35 þ in interest.

In the cases of Richard, Susie, Troy, Uma, Vanessa and Wes, we assume that either they have the seeds for the vegetables that they are planting or that these foods are naturally occurring. The same applies to Xiu who picks cotton. Although in reality it would take months to grow potatoes or apples, we make the simplification that the island can make these goods in a day. With regards to Joanne, Kristine, Queenie and Zlatko we assume that there are a lot of trees for wood and many mines for steel and stone.

In the first day the following was the output of the economy:

Richard grew 20 kg of potatoes
Susie harvested 20 kg of carrots
Troy harvested 15 kg of apples
Uma harvested 20 kg of plums
Vanessa picked 25 kg of blueberries
Wes picked 20 kg of blackberries
Xiu picked 25 kg of cotton
Yolla bred 2 cows and slaughtered 2, each weighing 200 kg; therefore there are 200 kg of leather
     and 200 kg of beef
Queenie mined 10 kg of stone

Zlatko mined 10 kg of steel

Now it's time to calculate the Gross Domestic Consumerist Product per capita. The GDCP per capita is equivalent to the general consumerist grant since the non-working consumerist grant markdown is 100%. The GDCP is calculated by taking the total output of all final goods in the materialist sector and multiplying this by the price per quantity set out by the central bank. We factor in the retail mark-up. On the first day we only count the production of potatoes, carrots, apples, plums, blueberries, blackberries and beef. All other things (the steel, stone, cotton, leather) are inputs

The GDCP is:
- Potatoes-   20 kg x 0.25 Θ/kg = 5.00 Θ + (5.00 Θ x 25%) = 6.25 Θ
- Carrots-   20 kg x 0.25 Θ/kg = 5.00 Θ + (5.00 Θ x 25%) = 6.25 Θ
- Apples-   15 kg x 0.25 Θ/kg = 3.75 Θ + (3.75 Θ x 25%) = 4.69 Θ
- Plums-   20 kg x 0.25 Θ/kg = 5.00 Θ + (5.00 Θ x 25%) = 6.25 Θ
- Blueberries-   25 kg x 0.20 Θ/kg = 5.00 Θ + (5.00 Θ x 25%) = 6.25 Θ
- Blackberries- 20 kg x 0.20 Θ/kg = 4.00 Θ+ (4.00 Θ x 25%) = 5.00 Θ
- Beef-   200 kg x 0.25 Θ/kg = 50.00 Θ + (50.00 Θ x 25%) = 62.50 Θ
The total is 97.19 Θ

At this point, Alfred, the president, has to announce the tax on the GDCP. However since the government has already made a lot by selling land, he feels generous and levies a tax of 0% for the day. This is a boost to the economy and the people are extremely happy.

To find the GDCP per capita, we divide the GDCP by the population. So 97.19 Θ/26 = 3.74 Θ. Therefore regardless of how much each member added to the economy, everyone is granted 3.74 Θ. Let's round this up to 3.75 Θ because this is easier to work with and simplifies our calculations yet it is very close numerically. This money is not paper money or coins. It is all entries in the private bank run by Daryl.

Now those that produced goods (apples, potatoes) are able to sell their goods for Ignits. In our island scenario this is done as such. Suppose that Alfred wants a kg of apples. Troy gives Alfred the apples. At the same time, Troy is credited with 0.31 þ (including the retail mark-up) and 0.31 Θ are deducted from Alfred's account by Daryl. A Norse and an Ignit have the same numerical value except that they are used to buy different things. So again if Venessa wanted a kg of beef, Yolla would give her this while Daryl adds 0.31 þ to Yolla's account and subtracts 0.31 Θ from Vanessa's.

A curious case occurs when someone wants to buy from himself. If Uma wanted a kg of plums, she would gain 0.25 þ and loose 0.25 Θ at the same time.

At the end of the day, let's see what everyone bought. Here is a summary:

- Alfred bought 24 kg of beef
- Betty bought 1 kg of potatoes and 2 kg of carrots
- Charlie bought 5 kg of carrots and 2 kg of beef
- Daryl bought 3 kg of carrots and 9 kg of plums
- Emma bought 12 kg of potatoes
- Fred bought 12 kg of beef
- George bought 5 kg of carrots and 7 kg of apples
- Hariotte bought 15 kg of blackberries

- Ivonna bought 15 kg of blueberries
- Joanne bought 5 kg of carrots and 7 kg of potatoes
- Kristine bought 12 kg of beef
- Lucy bought 5 kg of blueberries and 5 kg of blackberries
- Mickey bought 1 kg of apples and 1 kg of plums and 10 kg of beef
- Nathan bought 1 kg of apples, 1 kg of plums and 10 kg of beef
- Oscar bought 1 kg of apples, 1 kg of plums and 10 kg of beef
- Posy bought 1 kg of apples, 1 kg of plums and 10 kg of beef
- Queenie bought 1 kg of apples, 1 kg of plums and 10 kg of beef
- Richard bought 1 kg of apples and 11 kg of beef
- Susie bought 1 kg of apples and 11 kg of beef
- Troy bought 1 kg of apples and 11 kg of beef
- Uma bought 1 kg of plums and 11 kg of beef
- Vanessa bought 1 kg of plums and 11 kg of beef
- Wes bought 1 kg of plums and 11 kg of beef
- Xiu bought 1 kg of plums and 11 kg of beef
- Yolla bought 1 kg of plums and 11 kg of beef
- Zlatko bought 1 kg of plums and 11 kg of beef
-

Now everyone has spent their money and we assume that they spent all of it. We record the income of the producers in day 1:

Richard-	6.25 þ
Susie-	6.25 þ
Troy-	4.69 þ
Uma-	6.25 þ
Vanessa-	6.25 þ
Wes-	5.00 þ
Yolla-	62.50 þ

The other islanders also want to make some money. They do so by borrowing money to pay for inputs which they use to turn into finished goods. Left over from the first day are the following: 200 kg of leather, 25 kg of cotton, 10 kg of stone and 10 kg of steel.

Ivonna buys 5 kg of steel by borrowing from Daryl at 5% interest. For every kg of steel, Ivonna can make 2 axes. Since steel costs 0.20 þ/kg, Ivonna borrows 1.00 þ from the private bank and must pay 1.05 þ to Daryl at a later date.

Since Lucy makes linen she needs cotton. For every kg of cotton she can make 3 kg of linen. She needs to buy 15 kg of cotton which costs 0.20 þ/kg. So she borrows 3.00 þ and at 5% interest she must pay 3.15 þ in the future to the private bank.

Posy makes shoes. Thus she needs leather. For every shoe she makes she needs 2 kg of leather. She needs about 30 kg of leather which costs 0.25 þ/kg. She borrows 7.50 þ from Daryl at 5% interest which is 8.25 þ.

Now we list the output for day 2:
- Richard-   23 kg of potatoes
- Susie-   20 kg of carrots
- Troy-   15 kg of apples
- Uma-   18 kg of plums

- Vanessa-   30 kg of blueberries
- Wes-   25 kg of blackberries
- Yolla-   slaughtered 1 cow- 100 kg of leather and 100 kg of beef
- Xiu-   20 kg of cotton
- Queenie-   15 kg of steel
- Zlatko-   15 kg of stone
- Ivonna-   10 axes
- Lucy-   45 kg of linen
- Posy-   15 shoes

Today we have a little more output since we have islanders who were able to convert certain inputs and turn them into finished products. Today we have shoes for the first time.

Now we calculate the GDCP

- Potatoes-   23 kg x 0.25 Θ/kg = 5.35 Θ + (5.35 Θ x 0.25) = 6.69 Θ
- Carrots-   20 kg x 0.25 Θ/kg = 5.00 Θ + (5.00 Θ x 0.25) = 6.25 Θ
- Apples-   15 kg x 0.25 Θ/kg = 3.75 Θ + (3.75 Θ x 0.25) = 4.69 Θ
- Plums-   18 kg x 0.25 Θ/kg = 4.50 Θ + (4.50 Θ x 0.25) = 5.63 Θ
- Blueberries- 30 kg x 0.20 Θ/kg = 6.00 Θ + (6.00 Θ x 0.25) = 7.50 Θ
- Blackberries- 25 kg x 0.20 Θ/kg = 5.00 Θ + (5.00 Θ x 0.25) = 6.25 Θ
- Beef-   100 kg x 0.25 Θ/kg = 25.00 Θ + (25.00 Θ x 0.25) = 31.25 Θ
- Shoes-   15 shoes x 1.50 Θ/shoe = 22.50 Θ + (22.50 Θ x 0.25) = 28.13 Θ

This gives us a total of 96.39 Θ

Thus the GDCP is 96.39 Θ. Again, Alfred the president announces a tax of 0%. This is because the GDCP is a bit smaller than the previous day's. This is due to less beef. Only half as much beef was produced today relative to yesterday.

The GDCP per capita is 96.39 Θ/26 = 3.71 Θ. Now the islanders purchase goods with their 3.71 Θ. As an islander takes a good, its value is deducted from his Norse account and its value in Ignits is added to the seller's bank account. This is all on paper that Daryl is in charge of keeping records on.

Thus the islanders make purchases. Some of the islanders did not spend all of their money and thus they have a surplus. Fred has a surplus of 3.50 Θ. Harold has a surplus of 2.35 Θ. Lucy has a surplus of 0.65 Θ. Oscar has a surplus of 1.15 Θ. Queenie has a surplus of 0.73 Θ. The total surplus is 8.38 Θ. In terms of goods, the surplus is 5 kg of blackberries, 1 kg of blueberries, 4 kg of beef and 3 pairs of shoes.

Now let's recap the income of the producers in day 2.
- Richard-   6.69 þ
- Susie-   6.25 þ
- Troy-   4.69 þ
- Uma-   5.63 þ
- Vanessa-   7.25 þ
- Wes-   5.00 þ
- Yolla-   30.00 þ
- Posy-   22.50 þ
- Oscar   2.00 þ

The islanders would now like to open up trade with the island of Fraunica. They have blueberries, blackberries, beef and shoes to trade. The people of Fraunica have gooseberries and radishes to trade. According to the economic constitution set up by Betty and Charlie, a kilogram of gooseberries, like any berry costs 0.20 Ө/kg and a kilogram of radishes like any root vegetable, costs 0.25 Ө/kg. On Fraunica, a kg of gooseberries costs $0.50 and a kg of radishes costs $0.15. The Fraunicans use dollars as their currency. Also, on Fraunica the goods which we wish to trade – blueberries, shoes, blackberries and beef- have a price. This price may be set by a market economy on Fraunica or by a consumerist economy headed by a central bank. Over there, blueberries and blackberries each cost $0.25/kg, shoes cost $0.25/pair and beef costs $0.25/kg.

The central bank operated by Betty and Charlie must operate a trade pool. The trade pool gains money during certain trades and must subsidize other trades in order for them to occur. Thus Betty and Charlie must find the value of the Ignits relative to the dollar that will maximize the trade pool; i.e. make it positive. Although the above prices were expressed in Norses, the trade pool operates in Ignits rather than Norses, 1 Norse being equal to 1 Ignit.

Suppose that Betty and Charlie set the price of the Ignit exactly equal to one dollar. Let's see what the trade pool would look like in such a scenario. First the exporting. We sell 3 shoes for 1.50 þ. The Fraunicans give us $0.75. We sell 4 kg of beef for 1.00 þ and receive $1.00. We sell 1 kg of blueberries and 5 kg of blackberries for 1.20 þ. We receive $1.50. Thus we receive $3.25 and give up 3.70 þ. Now the importing. The Fraunicans sell us 10 kg of gooseberries. We pay $5.00. To us this is worth 2.00 þ. They sell us 20 kg of radishes for $3.00. To us this is worth 5.00 þ. Thus we pay $8.00 and they give us 7.00 þ.

The central bankers, Betty and Charlie, must pick a common exchange rate. The real exchange rates factor in. The real exchange rates are:

Importing-	Gooseberries-	$2.50/1 þ
	Radishes-	$0.60/1 þ
Exporting-	Berries-	$1.25/1 þ
	Beef-	$1.00/1 þ
	Shoes-	$0.50/1 þ

Suppose that Charlie and Betty set the exchange rate at $0.75/1þ. We sell beef at 1.00 þ and the Fraunicans must pay us $1.00 x 1 þ /$0.75 = 1.33 þ. Thus we receive 1.33 þ. 1.00 þ goes to Yolla and the trade pool earns 0.33 þ.

Again suppose that Betty and Charlie set the exchange rate at $0.75/1 þ. We sell 3 shoes for 1.50 þ and the Fraunicans pay us $0.75. So the Fraunicans would pay $0.75 or $0.75 x 1.00 þ/$0.75 = 1.00 þ. Now Posy would get 1.50 þ but 1.00 þ would come from the Fraunicans and 0.50 þ from the trade pool.

In setting the nominal exchange rate, Betty and Charlie must strike a balance. When importing it is better for the trade pool to have a higher nominal exchange rate and when exporting it is better to have a lower nominal exchange rate. The nominal exchange rate is expressed as foreign currency in terms of domestic currency. If the nominal exchange rate were equal to the real exchange rate there would be no need for a trade pool.

There is a way for Betty and Charlie to calculate the optimal exchange rate for their trade pool. The method is as follows. List all the real exchange rates of all the goods being exported

498

and imported. Next multiply these values by how many units are being traded. Then divide this number by the sum of all the units being imported and exported. The calculations follow:

Units	Good	Real Exchange Rate
10	Gooseberries	$2.50/ þ
20	Radishes	$0.60/ þ
6	Berries	$1.25/ þ
4	Beef	$1.00/ þ
3	Shoes	$0.50/ þ

The ideal exchange rate is given by (10 x 2.50/þ) + (20 x $0.60/þ) + (6 x $1.25/þ) + (4 x $1.00/þ) + (3 x $0.50/þ) = $50.00/þ

($50.00/þ)/43 = $1.16/þ

There may be an alternate formula for discovering the exchange rate. The one we came up with is simple and quite often (but not always) will give a favourable trade balance.

Now we use the exchange rate, $1.16/þ to calculate the trades occurring between Aleucia and Fraunica. First the gooseberries. We import 10 kg of gooseberries (actually Richard buys them). The Fraunicans get paid $5.00. This is equivalent to $5.00 x 1þ/$1.16 = 4.31 þ. However Richard pays only our price for the gooseberries = 2.00 þ. They are considered a final good. The central bank pays the other 2.31 þ. For now the trade pool balance is negative. Now Richard can sell the 10 kg of gooseberries to the other islanders to enjoy. The central bank sets the retail mark-up at 25%. The retail mark-up is the profit gained for retailing a good versus the original price. Thus Richard can sell his gooseberries at a price of (0.20 ☉ x 0.25) + 0.20 ☉ = 0.25 ☉

Now the radishes are imported. Each kg costs $0.15 and there are 20 kg of them. So they all cost $3.00. In Ignits this is $3.00 x 1þ/$1.16 = 2.59 þ. Vanessa chooses to import them. She pays 2.59 þ to the Frauncian islanders and 2.41 þ (5.00 þ – 2.59 þ) to the trade pool as the domestic price of radishes is 5.00 þ. Vanessa can sell her radishes for (0.25 ☉ x 0.25) + 0.25 ☉ = 0.31 ☉

Now the exporting. The berries are sold (exported) to Fraunica. Since they have the same price, blueberries and blackberries are treated as one. There are 6 kg of berries. They cost the Fraunicans $1.50. In terms of Ignits, they are $1.50 x 1þ/$1.16 = 1.30 þ. 1.20 þ is given to our berry growers and (1.30 þ – 1.20 þ = 0.10 þ) goes to Charlie and Betty's trade pool.

Now beef. We sell 4 kg of beef. The Fraunicans must pay us $1.00. In our currency this is $1.00 x 1þ/$1.16 = 0.86 þ. Yolla, the beef producer, earns 0.14 þ from the central bank as a subsidy and 0.86 þ from the Fraunicans.

Lastly, let's take care of the shoes. We have 3 pairs of shoes and they sell for $0.75 per pair. In our currency this is $0.75 x 1þ/ $1.16 = 0.65 þ. The trade pool must add 1.50 þ – 0.65 þ = 0.85 þ to the shoe maker, Posy's, income. Posy receives 1.50 þ; 0.65 þ from the Fraunicans and 0.85 þ from the central bank.

Let's see how our trade pool managed. It loses 2.31 þ, it gains 2.41 þ, it gains 0.10 þ, it loses 0.14 þ and loses 0.85 þ. Thus the central bank loses 0.79 þ. This brings a negative trading pool balance. It is possible that there could be a positive trade balance if the exchange rate was somewhere between $3.00/þ and $4.00/þ. But if we do the calculations for this exchange rate, it turns out that only one good that is traded will give a surplus and the others will have to be subsidized. Yet with an exchange rate of $1.16/þ, we end up with the least differences between subsidies of goods exported and imported relative to each other. Thus, although this value doesn't give the most positive result, it gives the most equal result for all trades.

The islanders would like to have accommodation (huts, houses), but to build these the builders require stone and wood. In day 2 there is still no wood made. In day 1, 10 kg of stone was mined and in day 2, 15 kg of stone was mined. So we have 25 kg of stone. Buildings are made of wood and stone. For every house, 1 kg of wood is needed for every bedroom and 1 kg of stone is needed for every floor. To recall, the price function for a building is:
x0.01 þ + y2.00 þ + z1.50 þ + a2.00 þ

Where: x is the number of square feet of space
y is the number of bedrooms
z is the number of washrooms
a is the number of floors

The islanders would also like to have shirts. To produce 1 shirt it requires 1 kg of linen. In order to cut wood, Joanne and Kristine need axes. They need 1 axe for every 10 kg of wood cut.

Now it is day 3. Mickey and Nathan make shirts. There are 45 kg of linen left over from day 2. They cost 0.25 þ/kg. Mickey buys 20 kg and Nathan buys 25 kg of linen. They borrow from Daryl with 5 % interest. Thus Mickey pays 20 kg x 0.25 þ/kg = 5.00 þ + 5% interest = 5.25 þ and Nathan pays 25 kg x 0.25 þ/kg = 6.25 þ + 5% interest = 6.56 þ. So Lucy who owns Linen earns 45 kg x 0.25 þ/kg = 11.25 þ. There is no retail mark-up on this since linen is an input.

Joanne and Kristine produce wood. Joanne and Kristine buy the axes (5 each) by borrowing from Daryl's bank. Each axe costs 2.00 þ. The interest rate is 5%. Each wood cutter pays 5 x 2.00 þ + 5% interest = 10.50 þ. Ivonne who has axes earns 10 x 2.00 þ = 20.00 þ. There is no retail mark-up. Daryl will eventually earn 1.00 þ in interest from the transaction.

Posy makes shoes. She made 22.50 þ in day 2. She had a debt from before of 8.25 þ. She pays it back and now is debt free. She has 14.25 þ left to buy leather to make new shoes. Leather costs 0.25 þ/kg. So she can buy 14.25 þ kg /0.25 þ = 57 kg of leather.

Ivonna makes axes. She received 20.00 þ from Joanne and Kristine, the wood cutters. To make more axes she needs steel. Steel costs 0.20 þ/kg. Ivonne could buy 100 kg of steel but only 20 kg are available. So she buys 20 kg for 4.00 þ. Ivonne had to pay Queenie 1.00 þ (1.05 þ with interest) the previous day. She pays this (5.05 þ) and is debt free. She now has 14.95 þ.

Lucy makes linen. She receives 11.25 þ for linen from Mickey and Nathan. She had to pay Xiu 3.15 þ for cotton; this she borrowed from the bank. She currently has 8.10 þ. To make linen, cotton is required. Cotton costs 0.20 þ/kg. She can buy 40 kg of cotton.

Now we list the output for day 3

- Richard-   25 kg of potatoes
- Susie-   20 kg of carrots
- Troy-   15 kg of apples

- Uma-   20 kg of plums
- Vanessa-   25 kg of blueberries
- Wes-   30 kg of blackberries
- Yolla-   slaughtered 1 cow and successfully reproduced 2- 100 kg of leather and 100 kg of beef
- Xiu-   50 kg of cotton
- Queenie-   20 kg of steel
- Zlatko-   20 kg of stone
- Joanne-   50 kg of wood
- Kristine-   50 kg of wood
- Ivonna-   40 axes
- Lucy-   120 kg of linen
- Posy-   25 shoes
- Mickey-   20 shirts
- Nathan-   25 shirts

We do not make a list of who bought what and we assume that everyone buys everything; there is no surplus or shortage. We do this so as not to redo our discussion of the trade pool and how trades are carried out.

We now calculate the GDCP, the GDCP per capita and how much each islander earns towards the accommodational sector.

- Richard-   25 kg of potatoes x 0.25 Ө = 6.25 Ө + (6.25 Ө x 0.25) = 7.81 Ө
- Susie-   20 kg of carrots x 0.25 Ө = 5.00 Ө + (5.00 Ө x 0.25) = 6.25 Ө
- Troy-   15 kg of apples x 0.25 Ө = 3.75 Ө + (3.75 Ө x 0.25) = 4.69 Ө
- Uma -   20 kg of plums x 0.25 Ө = 5.00 Ө + (5.00 Ө x 0.25) = 6.25 Ө
- Vanessa-   25 kg of blueberries x 0.20 Ө = 5.00 Ө + (5.00 Ө x 0.25) = 6.25 Ө
- Wes-   30 kg of blackberries x 0.20 Ө = 6.00 Ө + (6.00 Ө x 0.25) = 7.50 Ө
- Yolla-   100 kg of beef x 0.25 Ө = 25.00 Ө + (25.00 Ө x 0.25) = 31.25 Ө
              100 kg of leather x 0.25 Ө = 25.00 Ө + (25.00 Ө x 0.25) = 31.25 Ө
- Posy-   29 shoes x 1.50 Ө = 43.50 Ө + (43.50 Ө x 0.25) = 54.38 Ө
- Mickey-   20 shirts x 1.00 Ө = 20.00 Ө +(20.00 Ө x 0.25) = 25.00 Ө
- Nathan-   25 shirts x 1.00 Ө = 25.00 Ө + (25.00 Ө x 0.25) = 31.25 Ө
-

The GDCP is 211.88 Ө

The GDCP per capita is 8.15 Ө. This is much higher than that of day 2. Our economy is growing very well. Again the government sets the tax at 0%. We should mention how Betty, Charlie and Alfred make their Ignit income. They set a price for their services at 5.00 þ/day. This comes from taxes or the selling of land. Since a lot of money has been made by the government by selling land, there is no real need for a tax.

In day 4, the islanders finally set out to buy accommodation (housing) and spend the money that they earned. We will do a profit recap of this day but first let's look at the transactions the islanders made.

Mickey and Nathan sold shirts. Mickey made 25.00 þ and Nathan made 31.25 þ. They use a portion of this profit to pay their debt to Daryl who lent them money so they could buy linen the day before. Mickey pays 5.25 þ to Daryl and has (25.00 þ - 5.25 þ) = 19.75 þ left over. Nathan pays 6.56 þ to Daryl and has (31.25 þ – 6.56 þ) = 24.69 þ left over. In day 4 they each

501

buy 40 kg of linen. Thus they each pay 40 x 0.25 þ = 10.00 þ. Lucy earns 20.00 þ and she has 40 kg of linen left over. Mickey and Nathan use the linen to make shirts in day 4.

Posy made shoes and earned 54.38 þ. She buys 25.00 þ worth of leather to make shoes. So she buys 25.00 þ kg/0.25 þ = 100 kg of leather. With this leather Posy can make more shoes and she still has 29.38 þ

Lucy makes linen out of cotton. She earned 20.00 þ from selling linen to Mickey and Nathan for their shirt production. She buys 50 kg of cotton from Xiu. This costs her 0.20 þ/kg x 50 kg = 10.00 þ. Therefore she still has 10.00 þ left over.

Ivonna, Kristine, Joanne, Zlatko and Queenie can't earn any profit just yet since their income is dependent on the accommodational sector. Houses require stone. They also require wood. Wood requires axes and axes require steel. So none of these can be produced without the others.

Now would be a good time to recap all of the islander's accommodational well being (how many Ignits they have earned).

- Alfred-   4 x 5.00 þ = 20.00 þ
- Betty-   4 x 5.00 þ = 20.00 þ
- Charlie-   4 x 5.00 þ = 20.00 þ
- Daryl   (interest earnings from bank) = 75.00 þ + 50.00 þ + 1.35 þ + 0.05þ + 0.15þ
                 + 0.35 þ + 0.25 þ + 0.31 þ + 0.50 þ + 0.50 þ = 128.46 þ
- Emma-
- Fred-
- George-
- Harold-
- Ivonna-   24.95 þ
- Joanne-
- Kristine-
- Lucy-   10.10 þ
- Mickey-   9.75 þ
- Nathan-   14.69 þ
- Oscar-   4 x 2.00 þ = 8.00 þ
- Posy-   29.38 þ + 28.13 þ = 57.51 þ
- Queenie-   5.00 þ
- Richard-   29.06 þ
- Susie-   25.00 þ
- Troy-   18.75 þ
- Uma-   23.75 þ
- Vanessa-   27.25 þ
- Wes-   25.00 þ
- Xiu-   3.00 þ + 8.00 þ = 11.00 þ
- Yolla-   187.50 þ
- Zlatko-

Now we list the output of day 4. There was no new production of wood and axes.

- Richard-   25 kg of potatoes
- Susie-   20 kg of carrots

- Troy-   15 kg of apples
- Uma-   18 kg of plums
- Vanessa-   30 kg of blueberries
- Wes-   30 kg of blackberries
- Yolla-   (slaughtered 1 cow and successfully reproduced 1 more)
                      100 kg of beef
                      100 kg of leather
- Xiu-   45 kg of cotton
- Queenie-   25 kg of steel
- Zlatko-   20 kg of stone
- Lucy-   150 kg of linen
- Posy-   50 pairs of shoes
- Mickey-   40 shirts
- Nathan-   40 shirts

Some of the goods that are harvested like potatoes, carrots or plums have a higher yield one day than another. This represents the fact that growing conditions affect the output of a harvest. The same applies to meat. Some days there is more meat than other days.

Let's calculate the GDCP and the GDCP per capita of the island economy in day 4.

- Richard-   25 kg of potatoes x 0.25 ☉ = 6.25 ☉ + (6.25 ☉ x 0.25) = 7.81 ☉
- Susie-   20 kg of carrots x 0.25 ☉ = 5.00 ☉ + (5.00 ☉ x 0.25) = 6.25 ☉
- Troy-   15 kg of apples x 0.25 ☉ = 3.75 ☉ + (3.75 ☉ x 0.25) = 4.69 ☉
- Uma-   18 kg of plums x 0.25 ☉ = 4.50 ☉ + (4.50 ☉ x 0.25) = 5.63 ☉
- Vanessa-   30 kg of blueberries x 0.20 ☉ = 6.00 ☉ + (6.00 ☉ x 0.25) = 7.50 ☉
- Wes-   30 kg of blackberries x 0.20 ☉ = 6.00 ☉ + (6.00 ☉ x 0.25) = 7.50 ☉
- Yolla-   100 kg of beef x 0.25 ☉ = 25.00 ☉ + (25.00 ☉ x 0.25) = 31.25 ☉
                  100 kg of leather x 0.25 ☉ = 25.00 ☉+ (25.00 ☉ x 0.25) = 31.25 ☉
- Posy-   50 shoes x 1.50 ☉/shoe = 75.00 ☉ + (75.00 ☉ x 0.25) = 93.75 ☉
- Mickey-   40 shirts x 1.00 ☉ = 40.00 ☉ + (40.00 ☉ x 0.25) = 50.00 ☉
- Nathan-   40 shirts x 1.00 ☉ = 40.00 ☉ + (40.00 ☉ x 0.25) = 50.00 ☉
-

The GDCP is 295.63 ☉. The GDCP per capita is 11.37 ☉. This is higher than the previous day's so we are making progress.

At this point, none of the islanders can buy a huge house or a big residential property. Thus each islander buys a small patch of land and builds a small house on it. In due time this house will be exchanged for a bigger one and the land exchanged for a bigger plot of land. Residential land costs 20.00 þ/km². Alfred buys 0.4 km² of it costing 8.00 þ. Betty buys 0.5 km² of it costing 10.00 þ and Charlie buys 0.3 km² of it at a price of 6.00 þ. This money goes to the government. Alfred asks Emma to build him a house on his property. He has 12.00 þ left. He wants a house with 650 square feet, 1 bedroom, 1 bathroom and 1 floor. This costs 12.00 þ. To build this house Emma needs 1 kg of wood for every bedroom and 1 kg of stone for every floor. Thus Emma needs to buy 1 kg of stone and 1 kg of wood. She pays 0.50 þ to Kristine for the wood and 0.75 þ to Queenie for the stone. Emma makes (7.50 þ – 1.25 þ = 6.25 þ) and Alfred has a house.

The central bankers, Charlie and Betty, introduce the accommodational markdown and set it at 30%. This means that during every transaction in the accommodational sector, 30% of the trade is deducted from the seller's profit (it is destroyed). If this were not the case, Ignits would continuously accumulate in the accommodational sector. When Alfred bought his house, he had to pay 12.00 þ to Emma. 30% of this or 4.00 þ is taken away from Emma and out of circulation. Emma only makes, 7.50 þ – 2.25 þ - 1.25 þ = 4.00 þ.

Betty also orders a house to be built on the property she bought. She has 10.00 þ left. Her house has 1 floor, one washrooms, 1 bedroom and 450 square feet. She asks George to build it. He needs 1 kg of wood and 1 kg of stone. He pays Kristine and Queenie 0.50 þ and 0.75 þ for the wood and stone respectively. When Betty buys her house she has to pay 10.00 þ. However, 30% of this is taken away from George. He only earns, 10.00 þ – 0.50 þ – 0.75þ – (10.00 þ x 0.3) = 6.00þ. This accommodational markdown isn't as bad for the islanders as it appears to be at first. This is because there are only 4 builders and the islanders have to spend all of their Ignits on either land or some kind of housing.

In the same way that Betty and Alfred bought land and housing, so all the islanders do the same as long as they have any money from contributing to society. At first the patches of land the islanders own are small and the houses are cramped. But in due time, the islanders make more money and they have greater purchasing power.

Let's skip a few days. Let's see what things are like in day 14. Recall that at the beginning, Joanne, Kristine, Richard, Susie, Troy, Uma, Vanessa, Wes, Xiu and Yolla bought agricultural land to produce their goods. They had to borrow from Daryl at 5% interest to do so. At this point, they have all repaid their debt. In fact to expand their operations, Richard, Troy, Vanessa and Joanne bought more land from the government. Now 68 km² of the original 75 km² of agricultural land is being used.

On a similar note, Ivonna, Lucy, Mickey, Nathan, Posy, Queenie and Zlatko have also repaid their debts to Daryl who allowed them to purchase their plot of industrial land.

On day 14 the GDCP is 412.50 Ꝺ. Charlie and Betty have set a tax of 10%. 41.25 Ꝺ goes to the government. Some of this money goes to pay for Alfred's, Betty's, Charlie's and Oscar's salaries. Alfred decides how to spend the rest. Perhaps he can buy more land on a nearby island so the islander's territory can increase. It all depends on how Alfred decides to spend it as he is the president.

The GDCP per capita is (412.50 Ꝺ – 41.25 Ꝺ)/26 = 14.28 Ꝺ

At this point our islanders have enough of most of the goods produced on the island. Therefore a lot of the goods are exported to Fraunica and a great deal is imported that this island does not produce naturally.

Of the original 75 km² of residential land, about 70 km² are already owned by the islanders. Some islanders own land property the size of 10 km² and others own land that is only 0.5 km² in area. It all depends on how much each islander contributes to society.

Recall that Oscar works for the command partition. That is he works by keeping the island clean and free of debris. With his income he buys a small patch of residential land 0.75 km² large and a tiny hut (1 floor, 1 bedroom, 1 washroom, 1000 square feet). The more he earns the better accommodation he can purchase in the future.

As soon as an islander makes more money, he upgrades his accommodational standing. Suppose that Richard has 100.00 þ and owns a house worth 30.00 þ. It cost 30.00 þ because it
504

has 4 floors (8.00 þ), 4 washrooms (6.00 þ), 4 bedrooms (8.00 þ) and has a surface area of 800 square feet. He wants to move into a house owned by Xiu. Xiu's house is worth 50.00 þ. It has 6 floors (12.00 þ), 6 washrooms (9.00 þ), 9 bedrooms (18.00 þ) and 1100 square feet. So Richard sells his house, let's say to Joanne for 30.00 þ. Richard keeps 30.00 þ – (30.00 þ x 0.3) = 29.00 þ. Together with his savings he has 129.00 þ. He buys Xiu's house for 50.00 þ. Xiu receives 29.00þ. Richard has thus upgraded his accommodational status. But Xiu also has savings. He has 75.00 þ from selling cotton. He is also interested in upgrading his living status. He finds a great house owned by Yolla worth 51.00 þ. It has 6 washrooms (9.00 þ), 10 bedrooms (20.00 þ), 6 floors (12.00 þ) and 1000 square feet. Xiu sells his house. This process continues until everyone has a better house or they upgrade the one they have (by adding washrooms, bedrooms)

This concludes our investigation of a more complex island society. We discussed the fortunes of 26 islanders, how they contributed to society and how they benefited from the consumerist system. We saw how an empty island grew and flourished into a prosperous community. The success the islanders had on their island should parallel the success citizens should have in a consumerist society on a larger scale.

The Spiral of Prosperity

One of the most wonderful things about the accommodation based consumerist system is that it functions like a spiral. There is a continuous progress towards richness. All members of society, as long as they contribute to it, acquire prosperity. Let's take a look at this spiral.

Producers produce a certain amount of goods and services. To produce them, they borrow money from a private bank, governmental bank or money market fund. The more the producers in the materialist sector produce, the more the government and the consumerists are granted money (Norses) from the central bank. This amount is equal to the production of the producers in the materialist sector.

The consumerists can spend this money on materialist goods and services of their choice. The more the consumerists spend, the more the producers earn towards the accommodational and laissez-faire economy. The people who contributed to the economy, whether in the materialist, governmental, accommodational or laissez-faire sectors, earn money (Ignits) for contributing to society. The more they work or the more they contribute, the more Ignits they earn. They can use this money towards accommodational assets and services like houses, land, appliances and vacations. The producers who provide these accommodational goods and services also earn Ignits. Ignits can be converted to Fortals to buy goods and services in the laissez-faire sector.

At the same time, producers in the materialist sector produce an even greater amount of goods and services. The more they produce, the more money is granted (in Norses) to the consumerists and the government. With this money, the consumerists buy an even greater amount of materialist goods and services and the government can spend even more on social services. The more money the consumerists and the government spend, the more producers earn. Those who produce these goods can buy better houses and take finer vacations.

The economy is surplus driven. If there are more goods produced than can be sold, this increases the GDCP. It also increases the amount of money that the government and the consumerists are granted as the GDCP also comprises goods that are not sold but are in a position to be sold. Even though creating surpluses of inventory is a benefit to the consumerists, as they earn more Norses, this has to be compromised with the fact that these surpluses cost money (Ignits) to purchase from the factory or farm as they are inputs. Thus ordering surpluses aids the consumerists but if these surpluses are not sold, the company could lose money (Ignits).

The economy is also demand driven. The more consumerists want to buy the easier it is for firms in all sectors to make a profit. If a consumerist wants to buy a car, producers are able to sell a car. If consumerists want to buy a house, producers are able to sell a house. The greater the demand for goods and services the easier it is for firms to make a profit, in the process hiring more workers and employing other capital.

The consumerist spiral of prosperity is characterized by two propositions. The more consumerists buy, the more they earn. The more consumerists sell (work), the more they earn. Only the second statement is true for a free-market economy. By buying more goods and services, consumerists raise the GDCP and also the consumerist grant and the GCT. Thus they and the levels of government are granted more Norses. By selling goods or working, consumerists earn Ignits from their employers or other consumerists directly. This they can spend on the accommodational sector as well as the laissez-faire sector.

In consumerism, all agents, producers and especially consumerists, are getting richer and richer. Consumerism, a surplus driven as well as a demand driven economic system, flourishes when consumerists buy, sell and work. In consumerism everyone wins.

How Would any Great Economic Depression be Resolved by Implementing an Accommodation Based Consumerist Economic System?

The free market capitalist system had a very severe depression in 1929 that lasted more than ten years. One of the difficulties of the capitalist system is that the system has no clear, specific mechanism as to how to get out of a Great Depression. Even though it isn't certain that there will be another depression soon, it remains highly likely that one will come about in the foreseeable future. Nevertheless, due to the set up of the capitalist system we can at least expect a recession about every eight to eighteen years. Most economists acknowledge this preposition. Here we explain how to lead an economy out of a depression. Although it is very improbable that a nation under the Accommodation Based Consumerist System will ever fall into a depression, simply due to the way the system functions, here we entertain the "what-if" scenario of how to take a nation out of a Great Depression. It is important to remember that to fully understand how to do this (i.e. get out of a depression) one needs complete knowledge and a thorough understanding of the exact functioning of Accommodation Based Consumerism. Yet, we provide general suggestions and basic recommendations.

So suppose our free market nation experiences a depression. Unemployment dramatically increases, stocks plummet in value, and the prices of goods and services drop to very low levels. The banks as well as many private businesses go bankrupt. The people of the country, fed up with the free market system, adopt Accommodation Based Consumerism during a referendum. They trust the new system will lead them out of misery. We can divide the process of getting out of a depression into two phases – Phase One and Phase Two. The changes in phase one take place immediately while the changes in phase two come into effect six to nine months later.

The first thing that happens is that a Central Bank is created. A number of commissioners, chairman and deputy chairman are appointed to serve the people of the new consumerist nation. Also a Human Resource Management Commission (HRMC) is created. The first action of the HRMC is to create jobs for the people who became unemployed during the Great Depression. They would finance the creation of cafeterias, carrot farms, restaurants, construction companies, private banks, auto repair shops, amusement parks, car factories, etc. The people who were unemployed are used to work at these positions. This is the quickest way to immediately reduce the high unemployment caused by the Depression.

As soon as possible, some of the more important parameters under the influence of the Central Bank and the various levels of the Government must be determined. For some of them the value should be set rather soon, while for other parameters, the parameter in question requires months to be set or determined. For example, among other parameters, the Central Bank should set the universal stock price, the extra work transfers, the accommodational markdown, the retail mark up, etc.

The government must quickly determine the Consumerist Quatrotomy and Taxonomy although this may conceivably take some time (perhaps a few months). Once the economy is divided into sectors those producers in the materialist sector are able to report their contribution to the Gross Domestic Consumerist Product. At that point the Central Bank can start granting the General Consumerist Grant and Non-Working Consumerist Grant.

Since a high unemployment rate is one of the key problems of a great depression, we should promote programs that reduce it. There are many such programs in consumerism. The more important ones are the consumerist spending reimbursement, the interest rate stimulus, the profit reward transfer, the capital investment transfer and the employment reimbursement transfer.

To help speed up the process of getting out of the Depression, the government can institute the Laissez-Faire Labour System. This would bring firms from other countries into our nation with the workers being paid jointly by the government and by the firm. This will easily reduce or eliminate unemployment, one of the negative aspects of the Depression.

Another key attribute of a Great Depression, is that stocks lose their value. With regards to Consumerist stock, the Central Bank sets a universal stock price, and since these stocks cannot increase or decrease in value, a stock market crash is impossible. With regards to speculative stock, which is quite similar to stock in the capitalist system, we must be aware that the value of these stocks can increase or decrease. To make sure that the stockholder doesn't lose everything or the stock issuing firm goes bankrupt, we must make allowance for bankruptcy insurance firms. If there aren't too many of them, after the Great Depression, the HRMC could institute several of them.

A major attribute of a Great Depression is that the prices of goods and services drop in value. To solve this problem, the Central Bank creates price functions for all goods, services, inputs and wages with the exception of the laissez-faire sector. These insure that a good does not depreciate in value. The only problem with this is that it may take several months for the Central Bank to establish a system of price, wage and input functions.

These are some of the ways that Accommodation Based Consumerism can take a free market nation out of a recession or depression. Several key ideas were highlighted. In actuality coming out of a depression or recession is far more complex. Nevertheless coming out of a depression in consumerism is possible and manageable.

The Application of Accommodation Based Consumerism to Nations of the World

This theory's ultimate goal is to be the economic system of a country or countries. We have talked about, in quite detail, how the system works. Now it is time to discuss how it can be applied to a nation.

Firstly, this system is easiest to install in a nation that hasn't an economic system. An island economy is an example. We talked about how to apply this system to an island society.

There are two other categories of nations that we will examine in the following sections. They are developing nations and free-market nations. There are certain difficulties, such that will be discussed, in applying this system to these types of nations. The problem with developing nations is that they are impoverished and may need some time to get out of that state.

A different problem exists with some free-market nations. These nations are extremely well advanced in technology and their citizens enjoy a very high standard of living. Thus it may be hard to convince the people of these countries of the benefits of accommodation based consumerism. We must be careful to contend everyone in such a society. The worst sight would be a mass exodus of hard working, talented people from a place that doesn't suit them. Since it would be unwise to apply a system to a situation where the free-market is performing exceptionally well, consumerism is best applied during a crisis, when surrounded by turmoil the free-market system ceases to function as well as it once did.

From a practical point of view, it would probably be easier to convert a developing nation to consumerism than to convert a free-market nation to our system. Those in developing nations are in a very poor position already- people are hungry, without clothes and in very poor living conditions. They are probably desperate to try something new. They would do pretty much anything to get out of their state. It makes sense for them to try a new idea.

Those in free-market economies are probably a little more reluctant to try accommodation based consumerism. They have really good living conditions and a relatively high standard of life. In fact, switching to a consumerist economic system is not an urgent decision. This would change if the free-market system collapses due to several causes.

There are also countries under the communist system. We will not consider how a country under the communist system converts to consumerism. We assume that it first turns into a free-market country (or maybe a developing country) and then to consumerism.

This system is meant to be a practical one; actually employed by a country of the world. We mentioned that it could be applied either to a developing nation or a free-market nation. How it is applied is discussed next.

The Application of the System to Developing Nations

We now discuss how to apply our system to developing nations. Those nations are called developing that have low output or growth and usually rely on foreign aid. Most developing nations are in Africa, Asia and South America.

One of the main problems of developing nations is the lack of infrastructure. One of the reasons that developing nations are poor is that they lack technology. It is a priority to increase the standard of education which has an impact on technology level.

Developing nations are impoverished and usually have few resources and things of value. We start with the assumption of what people in developing nations do have. They have houses but they are built of low quality material like straw or dilapidated brick. They have clothes but they are ragged. They have food – bread and water a few times a week but others starve. They lack possessions. There is little furniture. There are vases, pots, cups and maybe some chickens. The impoverished do not have much and live in misery.

A country converts to consumerism through a referendum. When 50% + 1 of the people who voted chose to convert to consumerism, the country becomes a consumerist nation. Although it is consumerist it still has its own political ideology; i.e. democracy, monarchy, totalitarianism, etc. However in order to bring about a referendum, the government must be accepting of consumerism. This can happen in one of two ways- either a government realizes the benefits of consumerism or a party adopts the system in its platform. If this doesn't happen there may come into existence a kind of "consumerist party". However this party must acquire a political affiliation. It must have to pick a political ideology and identify itself as either left or right wing. A party cannot run for office solely on its economic intentions.

The first step in setting up our system is the formation of a central bank. There must be a time period when the central bank sets price functions, wage functions, the universal consumerist stock price and the other variables; i.e. job contracts, bond interest rates, etc. Time is required to vote on price functions and determine other essential variables. The same is true for the government which must determine the parameters it is responsible for; i.e. the taxonomy, welfare payment rate, distribution of land, etc. Once all these variables are set, the economy can be created.

The development of a nation's economy in a developing nation is entrepreneur driven in the natural partition. We need to get people to start producing goods and services and build infrastructure. It must be easy to set up a firm, that is, an organization where inputs are converted into products. The economy needs money to build infrastructure. First we need banks to give money to people to start businesses. Private banks allow entrepreneurs to borrow at a low interest rate. The interest rate must be low at first to promote growth.

Before our developing nation can start growing it needs to take a loan from another country. It borrows $5 000 000 000 = 5 000 000 000 þ from a nation like Canada. It uses this money to get going. The government of our nation loans some of this money to private bank in our developing nation so that they can make loans to workers and entrepreneurs in our nation. It is very, very important that the government repay this loan back very soon (at most 3 years). Otherwise this will contribute to a vicious debt spiral.

In our developing nation, 6 people open up a bank in their huts. These are primitive banks with entries with pen on paper carried out by villagers who are now bank operators. They manage bank book entries of the people in the village. Also, they lend money to other villagers so that they can open up their own businesses. They are loaned money from the government (which itself received a loan) so as to help the economy. It is vitally important that these private banks are regulated for honesty, efficiency and to prevent fraud. Thus the government or the central bank must regulate other banks.

With the money they borrowed from banks, entrepreneurs buy imports. The central bank sets up the consumerist trade pool so that they could import goods with which to start a business.

One villager, Troy, borrows 10 000.00 þ from a banker, Ty, at 5% interest. With the 10 000.00 þ, Troy starts a chicken farm where he also kills and sells chickens. Bu borrows 10 000.00 þ from Ty and with this buys, by importing, machines needed to turn cloth into clothes. He also buys a year's supply of cloth and sells the shirts he makes. Jojo borrows 10 000.00 þ from Ty to buy glass and equipment to make orange juice. He also buys a year's supply of oranges. And so other people set up their businesses.

In the meantime, the central bank grants the amount of Norses produced in one day or 3 or 4 days. The GDCP is not measured in months. If all the entrepreneurs in the materialist sector make an amount of products; i.e. a cup of juice, chicken meat, shirts, then the equivalent of their value is granted to the consumerists of the developing nation. Every 3 or 4 days the central bank grants Norses to the people of the developing nation. Essentially, a set number of Norses are credited to anyone who has an account at a private bank.

The entrepreneurs who make goods and services hire workers who do not want to start their own businesses. Other citizens will do business in the accommodational sector. They will borrow money from a bank and use it to buy material to make houses. As an alternative to dealing with private banks, some entrepreneurs might issue shares or issue general bonds or profit bonds. Other citizens will work for other entrepreneurs in the accommodational sector.

The people who sold things to those in the materialist sector can now buy something in the accommodational sector. To promote progress and development, the retail mark-up would be high and the accommodational markdown would be very low- almost zero.

At the beginning, this country will be very impoverished. The money granted to citizens will be minimal. Eventually though, the economy will take off. As more people desire houses, land and leisure, they will find ways to contribute to the materialist sector.

The creation of inventions and innovations must be promoted. The central bank has set the price of most things that could be produced but if there is something new the investor must present the idea to the patent office. It then becomes priced by the central bank.

The consumerist grant will be every 4 days for a while, say 2 months. Then it will be once a week and when the economy is doing well, it will be every 2 weeks.

For several weeks the economy stagnates but it then builds momentum. Eventually all debtors repay their debts and the citizens will be able to export.

As for the government, it collects funds through the GCT and other sources like profits from the command partition. The government has to manipulate the GCT so that it has money for services and yet promotes the economy.

We anticipate 3 problems with the conversion to a consumerist society

1) The private bank will not lend to new entrepreneurs
2) Consumerists will be unable to import things needed to get their production underway
3) Lack of interest in starting a business

Let's find solutions to these problems. How do we make private banks more willing to lend to entrepreneurs? There is no collateral because the people are poor. Suppose a private bank lends money to an entrepreneur and the entrepreneur's business does well. Eventually the entrepreneur will pay off the loan. If the entrepreneur's business fails the entrepreneur will have to pay off the loan through other means. He will have to get a job and a percentage of his paycheck goes to the bank the entrepreneur defaulted at. However, the loan can be usually easily repaid by the selling off of the assets of the business- i.e. the building and the land the building was on. Another solution to this problem is to let the government setup a special government bank that makes loans to businesses so they can start up. Bankruptcy insurance firms must be set up and they should be used to encourage investment and the maximization of output of our developing nation.

How do we enable consumerists to import things they need to get their production under way? We do so by using the consumerist trade pool. The country that we import from will receive the full price of the goods we import from them. We perform calculations to determine the nominal exchange rate and with this we purchase things to get our economy running well.

How do we raise the consumerist's interest to start their own business? This is accomplished through the profit motive. By starting their own business, citizens gain a source of revenue with which to buy accommodational goods and services like vacations, houses, land and utilities. Also the government encourages more hiring by creating the Employment Reimbursement Transfer. In order to get more entrepreneurs to start their business in our nation or to attract foreign investment that will bring jobs, the government can provide the Capital Investment Transfer and the Profit Reward Transfer.

Initially, when there aren't too many privately owned firms (firms in the natural partition) and a lot of people are unemployed, there can come about a command partition. A special branch of the government, which we will call the Human Resource Management Commission, takes it upon themselves to find employment for all people not employed in natural partition firms. Their mandate is to hire as many people as possible while still earning a profit. They do not make decisions through supply and demand but through central planning. The profits of the Human Resource Commission go directly to the government for another source of revenue to the government. If a command partition firm functions in the materialist sector, this increases the GDCP which further increases the two types of consumerist grants and the GCT. When the country we are concerned with is just starting out, there should be a very large command partition. However, as it blossoms, more workers move from the command partition to the natural partition.

Eventually, those people who borrowed from the private banks pay back their loan with interest. Then these banks pay the money they were given by the government. Subsequently, the developing nation' pays back its loan to Canada (which lent them money).

With the ideas of consumerism a developing nation ought to flourish. We analyzed how a developing nation grows. We saw how entrepreneurs turn money they borrowed from private banks to create products. Finally we came up with solutions to problems such an economy could develop.

The Application of the System to Free-Market Nations

Some of the greatest economic super powers on earth today are free-market economies. They will not need our system lest a disaster of some sort strikes. But there are many free-market economies that are not doing that well. If a struggling nation wants to flourish, the accommodation based consumerist system is a good alternative. We will talk about how to convert an average free-market based country to consumerism.

A free-market nation officially turns consumerist during a referendum. If 50 % + 1 of the voters choose consumerism, then the nation becomes consumerist. As described before in the section on applying the system to developing nations, a referendum is usually declared when a party that sees the merits of the system is in power and declares the referendum. There may be parties that are inspired by this system or there may emerge "consumerist" parties that also have a political agenda. Or, a current head of state may be impressed with this system and declares a referendum.

In explaining the conversion to consumerism we start with the assumption that citizens in a free-market economy have everything except that there are free-market institutions. The state of technology is high. People are educated. The country is progressing towards the future.

The first step in a conversion to consumerism is the formation of the central bank. The Grand Chairman and the Consumerist Commissioners are appointed as is the Deputy Grand Chairman. Several (a couple dozen) industry specific sets of central bankers are also appointed. Thus there is a transportation industry Chairman, a transport industry Deputy Chairman, 100 transport industry Commissioners, etc…

After the conversion there is a 6-9 month adjustment period. At this time all transactions would go on as before in a free-market society. We assume that they are using dollars.

The government divides the economy into 4 sectors. This is dependent on the inclination of the government; i.e. whether it is quasi left wing or quasi right wing. The government works out the economic taxonomic system. That is, it classifies all products, inputs, services and wages into classification groupings (levels of taxon).

During the 6-9 month adjustment period each firm must report to the central bank what they are selling, what kind of employees they have and what kinds of inputs they use. With this information the central bank creates price functions, wage functions, input functions, the universal consumerist stock price, job contract prices and other fixed parameters that are part of the consumerist system. At the end of the 6-9 months, the parameters are fully in place.

After the 6-9 month period there is a 3 week period of currency transition. After 2 weeks, the firms that are in the materialist sector are to tell the central bank how much they earned or put on the market. This is still in dollars. This includes firms such as car dealerships, doughnut shops, grocery stores, gas stations and restaurants. The central bank converts the dollars into Norses and grants them to the non-institutionalized consumerists. A portion of this, which is the GDCP, also goes to the government. During this time the 3 levels of government get together to pick the GCT. They meet as often as necessary when the GCT needs to be changed.

During this 3 week transition period all consumerists have the opportunity to convert their dollars into Ignits (but not Norses). The exchange rate could be anything but is simplest if it is par. Therefore a free-market businessman who saved up $100 000.00 could trade this for 100 000.00 þ. The new consumerist could spend this on the accommodational or laissez-faire sector. As for cash, cash is brought to the bank where the private bank credits the Ignit equivalent to the consumerist's bank account. The cash is destroyed as consumerism is a cashless society.

In the materialist sector, the firms under that sector report their transactions and what they try to sell every 2 weeks (or 1 month) and tell this to the central bank. This enables the central bank to know how many Norses to grant to consumerist every 2 weeks.

Now we should mention something about the governmental sector. The government needs to make a transition as well. The government has to set a tax so that it is able to buy the items and services it used to under the free-market system. In the transition to consumerism, the government loses its ability to tax what it wants and must obtain most of its revenue from the GCT and the profits of the command partition. There are other ways it can receive revenue; i.e. selling land, gambling. It would be ideal if the government raised revenue without making use of the three forms of taxes we mentioned earlier.

Now to the accommodational sector. The amount of Ignits a new consumerist receives initially is reflective of how much money ($) he has before the system conversion. If one was successful in the free-market system, this should be recognized in consumerism. If people were prosperous in the free-market system, every effort should be made that they begin prosperous in consumerism. Otherwise they will be unhappy and emigrate. We will lose talent that way. It is generally true that those who are rich have usually contributed a lot to society or have important positions.

During the conversion to consumerism, we must not lose favour with the banks. In fact it is usually a good idea to keep as many people and institutions as happy as possible. Banks will not have the ability to loan Norses but will be able to loan Ignits. Since there is no cash and no cash reserve ratio, banks can make huge profits. Also we eliminate the trouble of bank runs (there is no cash). The only stipulation is that banks cannot convert Norses to Ignits.

This is how a conversion from the free-market system to the accommodation based consumerist system would look like. There are many changes that are necessary during the 6-9 month and 3-week transition periods. As a country converts, all effort is made not to harm those people and organizations that prospered under the old system.

Critique of Consumerism

There may be some problems that our system will encounter. A lot of effort and thought has been put into the design of this system so that it does work. Here we examine what could go wrong.

All prices and wages (in the GAM sectors) are set by the central bank and must have fixed price functions. This is one of the most important postulates of the system. If this postulate is observed then there is a very good chance that the system will function well. However if this postulate is disobeyed and producers and consumerists compete in prices, we are in trouble. If this happens then the system will surely collapse. This postulate must be held.

Producers must not sell products at a different price than that set by the central bank and they must not offer wages different than those prescribed by the central bank. The same applies to the consumerist stock market. The prices of consumerist shares must not fluctuate. Shares can only be bought and sold for the price set by the central bank. If a share is bought or sold at a price different than that set by the central bank, the stock market will collapse. A lot of people will suffer. This idea does not apply to the laissez-faire sector. For this reason, effort must be made to make laws that stop price/wage competition. People who charge fluctuating prices must be prosecuted and their actions outlawed.

Another possible problem is that unions may not like that workers cannot receive a raise. Regardless of their dislikes, wages must be fixed except for the laissez-faire sector. In the free-market system workers often earn a raise after working for awhile at the same job. The worker is seemingly happy. However this raise may actually be a wage cut. Suppose the raise is 3%. If the inflation is 5%, the worker loses 2% of his wage. Although wage raises may seem like a great incentive to work, rational workers ought to realize that they can be fooled by the free-market's ability to inflate the economy. In consumerism, even though there are no wage raises, there is no inflation either. All workers are constantly being paid the same wage. Yet there is room for a higher pay (raise) if a worker is promoted to a higher paying job.

Also, producers may over report the amount of goods they have in their inventory. This results in everyone being granted more money. But if people are granted more money than there are goods in the economy, then there are people who can't buy anything.

Probably the biggest problem is how to apply the system to a society. We need to find a way to apply what is written in this treatise and make it work in an actual economy. In another section we discuss this difficulty.

A major concern is dollarization. This is the use of cash (most notably the U.S. dollar bill) in our society. The problem with this is that it disrupts the exchange system between Norses, goods and Ignits. On the positive side, most consumerists probably won't use $ U.S. because they are granted Norses. It is counterproductive not to take advantage of purchasing power that is given to all. Most users of the U.S. dollar bill will be foreigners. We cannot totally ban the use of the dollar because foreigners visiting our country must also need a way to purchase goods and services and they are not granted Norses by the central bank. A transaction involving $U.S. would look like this. Kevin gives a U.S. $ 20.00 bill to his bank account in the US. That bank credits him with $20 and he transfers this to a bank in our country. He has foreign visitor status so he can exchange Ignits for materialist things. The $ 20 are converted to Fortals and then to Ignits. Kevin gives a check for 20 Ignits to John's convenience in exchange for a pack of doughnuts that Kevin receives. The owner of the convenience store takes the check to the bank and the bank credits him with the Ignit equivalent of 20.00 þ.

The problem of resource depletion is common to all economies. For example, the depletion of the oil supply. Suppose that there are 10 000 000 L of oil and that they are vitally needed. The free-market response to dwindling oil reserves is to raise the price and thus lower consumption. In consumerism the prices are fixed for a family of products. Thus alcohol fuels, which are in the same family, would have the same price. In response to a decrease in production of oil, there is an increase in the production of alcohol fuel or another fuel. Those who sell the alcohol fuel make the same amount of money per litre as the producers of oil do. This mechanism ensures that if a resource runs out, there is a replacement for it.

Smuggling is a real problem. Suppose that someone buys a limousine and then smuggles it to another country only to sell it and buy something else in a foreign nation. In this case, our country looses a limousine. The problem is that the person will not come back and simply take consumerist made goods and bring them to another country. Generally he will probably come back as he has a house here. It really doesn't matter if he sells the limousine, buys other things in another country and then comes back. This is simply international trade at a micro level. If he does not sell the limousine that is worth 10 000.00 ☉ here and receives $10 000.00 from selling it in another country, he can use this money for trading it upon transaction for Norses. Thus if he wants to buy a computer worth 1000.00 ☉ and the nominal exchange rate is $1.00 = 1.00 þ = 1.00 ☉, he just gives $1000.00 to the retailer who exchanges the money into Ignits.

We must protect ourselves from illegal trade. We must not allow the buying of materialist things with Fortals. This causes massive disruption of the economy. The whole purpose of having a schism between the sectors and the uses of the three currencies is to maximize wealth and this can only be accomplished when the four sectors are separate but interact with one another.

There is another problem that may arise in a practical setting. The government may try to save money by eliminating government partition jobs and transferring these jobs to the command partition where the worker is paid less. This must not happen as it creates inefficiencies.

Our system could possibly face many problems. More specifically these are dollarization, wage raises, production over-reporting, resource depletion, smuggling and price manipulation. Although explanations and remedies are offered for some of these calamities, they still stand out as weaknesses of our system.

Other Considerations

We have described the major sources of success a nation could have in strictly economic terms. Here we briefly mention some other points that are necessary for a nation to flourish.

First of all, the nation must be justly ruled. There must be fair laws that govern public behaviour. Contracts must be enforced. People must feel safe in the country. We do not go into what justice is or what kinds of laws should exist but basically a just nation is better off than one that is not.

Corruption must not exist. Those in charge must be held accountable of what they are doing. The ones who run a nation should know what they are doing. When people put faith in public officials they expect them to act in their interests and not in those individuals who can pay for their privileges.

In an ideal society, leaders serve their citizens. That is how a consumerist country should operate. It is important that the citizens of the consumerist society should have various freedoms. These include freedom of speech, religion, press, etc...

The people must have full human as well as personal rights. What these exactly are is also a political question but includes things like access to clean drinking water and a right to vote. These rights are necessary in a consumerist nation.

Other things make a nation stand out despite material success. This includes the accomplishment of a wonder of civilization. The Egyptians had pyramids. France has the Eiffel tower. Canada has the C.N. tower and America has the statue of liberty. A nation should differentiate itself by building something great. It is an important goal of a consumerist nation to build something magnificent that will make it recognized.

Other accomplishments make a nation great. These include advances in exploration, science or culture. The space race and putting a man on the moon give a nation great prestige. So would the completion of a Unified Theory of Physics or the cure for a horrible illness. Although these accomplishments do not directly give prosperity, the prestige it gives the country that accomplishes them is paramount. A consumerist nation should embark on a program of cultural, scientific and exploration advancement.

Another factor of greatness that goes beyond economics is the human spirit of the people of a nation. Most people would rather live in a country where people everywhere say hello to you, are friendly, open doors for you, and are a pleasure to be around compared to a place where no one cares about you and you genuinely feel alone. The atmosphere of the place one lives in is just as important as economic matters. A consumerist nation should be a pleasant place to live in.

Peace and security are also important. It is better to live in a country where there is no violence than in one where there is perpetual war. Also fear of being attacked by foreigners or the threat of being bombed by those who wish others ill is a problem. The people of a consumerist nation should not have to live in fear of being harmed by anyone. A country with civil unrest and problems with rebels will probably not have a fully functioning economic system. By that, it is meant that this system will not function under these circumstances.

The environment is also important. A place with clean lakes, air and rivers is priceless. If economic progress comes at a high environmental price, then the progress isn't as great as it seems. A country free of pollution is a better place to live in than one that isn't, assuming same economic prosperity. Everyone would like a clean place to live in and this should be one of the goals of a consumerist nation.

Another idea that may have some benefit is that the buildings in our consumerist nation should have unique architecture. That is our houses, apartments, and places of business should stand out as being different.

Several things make a country a good place to live in that aren't directly related to economics. This includes justice, the elimination of corruption, the provision of security and peace, the accomplishment of wonders and acts of progress and the environment. A country that progresses through wealth but isn't much of a place to live in, is lacking.

Conclusions

Thus works the accommodation based consumerist economic system. We have discussed in considerable detail many parameters that are integral to the system. We introduced and explained many new and original concepts and ideas. We talked about how these ideas make the system work. The incentives that made the system function were fully described. We went in detail describing how the system would be applied to smaller scenarios. Finally we talked about how to apply the system to actual nations.

The purpose of this system, as was made clear in the very beginning, is to increase the quality of life of consumerists. If it does this when actually applied in a practical setting, this treatise can be considered a success. This treatise differs from a scientific theory in that scientific theories have to match themselves against the truth; that is they have to survive the test of experiment. If they can do this, they are considered temporarily successful. However at any point in time, a fact from reality can be discovered which may contradict this theory. In that case, the theory must be abandoned and a new theory is necessary. With regards to economic theories like accommodation based consumerism, all that matters is that the society under the system survives under the system. The happier the people, the more successful the system is.

A very important note about this treatise in general must be made at this point. All values for the parameters that were given in the system are totally exemplary. There is no reason that they be that way in an actual system. They were created so that we have something concrete to talk about. When it was said that the retail mark-up was 25% or that a cashier's JCP was 600.00 þ or that the CUSP was 10.00 þ, these values were totally created solely for the purpose of having examples. This is very, very important. The system would be much too rigid if actual numbers for the different parameters were given. When an actual consumerist economy is set up, the values for the varying parameters are to be dictated by the government, central bank or firms and consumerists.

On the other hand, some parts that were mentioned should be followed as prescribed. For example there shouldn't be any taxes other than the GCT, the wealth tax and the positive personal income tax. All prices and wages must have fixed functions (except for the laissez-faire sector). The various parameters should be applied as set out, although their numerical values must not necessarily be the same as set out in the treatise. If the government in charge of applying accommodation based consumerism does too many changes, the system won't work as it should.

So, this is the solution to human poverty. This system helps consumerists, workers, investors and entrepreneurs. Now we have a third alternative to capitalism and communism.

Bibliography

1) Kneebone, R.D., Mankiw, N.G., McKenzie, K.J., Rowe, N., (2002), Principles of Microeconomics 2nd Canadian Edition, Thomson Nelson, (Toronto)